The Reformation

Old Western Culture Reader

Volume 12

The Reformation

Post Tenebras Lux

Old Western Culture Reader
Volume 12

Companion to *Christendom: The Reformation*,
a great books curriculum by Roman Roads Media

The Reformation, Post Tenebras Lux: Old Western Culture Reader, Volume 12

Published by Roman Roads Media, LLC
Moscow, Idaho 83843
romanroadsmedia.com

General Editor and Introductions: W. Bradford Littlejohn
Series Editor and Preface: Daniel Foucachon
Assistant Editors: George Callihan, Brian Marr, Andrea Pliego
Cover Design: Valerie Anne Bost, Daniel Foucachon, and Rachel Rosales
Interior Layout: Valerie Anne Bost

Modernization of *The Book of Common Prayer* 1559 by Brian Marr and Daniel Foucachon
Modernization of *The Laws of Ecclesiastical Polity* by Davenant Institute

Printed in the United States of America

The Reformation, Post Tenebras Lux: Old Western Culture Reader, Volume 12
Roman Roads Media, LLC
ISBN: 978-1-944482-22-0 (hardback clothbound), 978-1-944482-23-7 (paperback)

Version 1.0.3 2017

This is a companion reader for the *Old Western Culture* curriculum by Roman Roads Media. To find out more about this course, visit www.romanroadsmedia.com.

Old Western Culture

Great Books Reader Series

THE GREEKS

VOLUME 1	*The Epics*
VOLUME 2	*Drama & Lyric*
VOLUME 3	*The Histories*
VOLUME 4	*The Philosophers*

THE ROMANS

VOLUME 5	*The Aeneid*
VOLUME 6	*The Historians*
VOLUME 7	*Early Christianity*
VOLUME 8	*Nicene Christianity*

CHRISTENDOM

VOLUME 9	*Early Medievals*
VOLUME 10	*Defense of the Faith*
VOLUME 11	*The Medieval Mind*
VOLUME 12	*The Reformation*

EARLY MODERNS

VOLUME 13	*Rise of England*
VOLUME 14	*The Victorian Poets*
VOLUME 15	*The Enlightenment*
VOLUME 16	*The Novels*

CONTENTS

PREFACE

> From this buoyant humility, this farewell to the self with all its good resolutions, anxiety, scruples, and motive scratchings, all the Protestant doctrines originally sprang. For it must be clearly understood that they were at first doctrines not of terror but of joy and hope: indeed, more than hope, fruition, for as Tyndale says, the converted man is already tasting eternal life. The doctrine of predestination, says the Seventeenth Article, is "full of sweet, pleasant and unspeakable comfort to godly persons." . . . Relief and buoyancy are the characteristic notes.
>
> —C.S. Lewis, *English Literature in the Sixteenth Century*

"What is your only comfort in life and in death?" So begins the Heidelberg Catechism, representing the important pastoral legacy of the Reformation. "That I, with body and soul, both in life and in death, am not my own, but belong to my faithful Savior Jesus Christ" answers the catechism. Following a century of ecclesiastical upheaval, Medieval Christians throughout Europe eagerly grasped the simple truths emphasized by the Reformers. But the Reformation was not a tidy, easy, or monolithic event. It was also a time of much anguish, debate, and fighting, both on paper and on the battlefield. Anathemas were issued, kings and princes took sides, kingdoms quarreled, men and women and children were killed or imprisoned for their faith. And all of this was done within the bounds of Christendom, by people who bear the name of Christ. The Reformation is a difficult period of history to study.

The purpose of this reader is to give students of *Old Western Culture* a broad view of the Reformation, starting with its early events and documents. In keeping with the primary-source approach of the *Old Western Culture* curriculum, students will read source documents. All sides of the Reformation debate are included. Read the actual words from Popes Boniface the VIII and Leo X, the response from Luther, the decrees of the Council of Constance, the Council of Trent, Calvin's words to King Francis I, Ursinus on the *Heidelberg Catechism*, Field and Wilcox's *Admonition to Parliament*, and more, bookended on either side by the Renaissance era poetry of Chaucer and Spenser. The theological texts are introduced by Dr. W. Bradford Littlejohn, situating the documents in history and explaining their significance.

Whether you are coming to this Reader as a Protestant or not, I hope you will first and foremost come to this Reader as a historic *Christian*, rooted in your own tradition. The short introductions to each text are included to give some historical context, but the primary documents are the centerpiece of this Reader. The introductions are from a Protestant perspective, but also from an irenic Reformed view; that is, rooted in the historic Christian faith while being appreciative of the width and breadth of Christian tradition and shared Creeds of the church.

In many ways this is a history of division in the church. But in the midst of a world filled with man's fallen nature, Christ is purifying his bride. As my pastor often says, "God draws straight with crooked lines." There is vice in every human heart, and yet God raises up heroes of the faith, with virtue worthy of emulation in our midst. Lewis expressed this sentiment well in a letter to an old Catholic priest, "But what would I think of your Thomas More or of our William Tyndale? Both of them seem to me most saintly men and to have loved God with their whole heart...Nevertheless they disagree and (what racks and astounds me) their disagreement seems to me to spring not from their vices nor from their ignorance but rather from their virtue and the depths of their faith, so that the more they were at their best the more they were at variance, I believe the judgment of God on their dissension is more profoundly hidden than it appears to you to be: for his judgements are indeed an abyss."[1]

As Christians we should all pray for the unity of the Church, and eagerly look to that day when Christ's Bride will be perfected (Eph. 5:27). Part of working towards that day is understanding the history of God's people.

The name of this reader series and of its accompanying curriculum, *Old Western Culture*, is a term coined by C.S. Lewis, taken from his essay *On the Description of Times*. A student who has been with us from the first year of this curriculum knows that "Old Western Culture" refers to that body of knowledge that until recent times was the common possession of every educated person. One of the objections that I sometimes encounter from Christians is to question whether this "old Western culture" is truly our possession. They repeat the question of Tertullian, "what hath Athens to do with Jerusalem?" Part of the answer to that question has been to show that the early church and early Christians fully embraced this possession, "plundering the Egyptians" (as Augustine of Hippo said), and used these tools of learning for the kingdom of God, finding truth wherever it may be found. When it comes to church history leading up to and during the Reformation, some Christians become even less certain about what is their possession. The result is often skipping over periods of history. They are too messy, too controversial, too unknown. But I don't believe we are doing ourselves a favor. The Protestant who skips pre-Reformation history is behaving in a decidedly un-Protestant way, and puts himself at a disadvantage by not understanding an essential part of the Reformation. To Protestants, the Reformation was not the formation of a new church, but a purification of the church; a return to apostolic teaching. You will find among the writings of Reformers like John Calvin constant reference to the church fathers before him, as well as the pre-Christian authors.

1 Letters: C. S. Lewis/Don Giovanni Calabria (25 November 1947).

The non-Protestant who skips the study of the Reformation is behaving in an un-catholic (or universal Christian) way, and also at a disadvantage, failing to see how much the Reformation affected all of Christendom, including his own tradition. Skipping the Reformation also means skipping his own tradition's history during this period.

The Reformation, like the rest of *Old Western Culture*, should be the common possession of all those educated in the Western tradition, and specifically of all "mere Christians" (to borrow Lewis' term). The divisions which accompany this period should not make us shy away. On the contrary, we should rejoice in all the history of God's people!

Sola Deo Gloria.

DANIEL FOUCACHON,
Founder, Roman Roads Media

> We are all rightly distressed, and ashamed also, at the divisions of Christendom. But those who have always lived within the Christian fold may be too easily dispirited by them. They are bad, but such people do not know what it looks like from without. Seen from there, what is left intact despite all the divisions, still appears (as it truly is) an immensely formidable unity. I know, for I saw it; and well our enemies know it.
>
> —C.S. Lewis, Introduction to Athanasius' *On the Incarnation*

CANTERBURY TALES

Geoffrey Chaucer

TRANSLATED BY RONALD L. ECKER AND EUGENE J. CROOK

GENERAL PROLOGUE

When April's gentle rains have pierced the drought
Of March right to the root, and bathed each sprout
Through every vein with liquid of such power
It brings forth the engendering of the flower;
When Zephyrus too with his sweet breath has blown
Through every field and forest, urging on
The tender shoots, and there's a youthful sun,
His second half course through the Ram now run,
And little birds are making melody
And sleep all night, eyes open as can be
(So Nature pricks them in each little heart),
On pilgrimage then folks desire to start.
The palmers long to travel foreign strands
To distant shrines renowned in sundry lands;
And specially, from every shire's end
In England, folks to Canterbury wend:
To seek the blissful martyr is their will,
The one who gave such help when they were ill.

Now in that season it befell one day
In Southwark at the Tabard where I lay,
As I was all prepared for setting out
To Canterbury with a heart devout,
That there had come into that hostelry
At night some twenty-nine, a company
Of sundry folk whom chance had brought to fall
In fellowship, for pilgrims were they all
And onward to Canterbury would ride.
The chambers and the stables there were wide,
We had it easy, served with all the best;
And by the time the sun had gone to rest
I'd spoken with each one about the trip
And was a member of the fellowship.
We made agreement, early to arise
To take our way, of which I shall advise.
But nonetheless, while I have time and space,
Before proceeding further here's the place
Where I believe it reasonable to state
Something about these pilgrims—to relate
Their circumstances as they seemed to me,
Just who they were and each of what degree
And also what array they all were in.
And with a Knight I therefore will begin.
There with us was a KNIGHT, a worthy man
Who, from the very first time he began
To ride about, loved honor, chivalry,
The spirit of giving, truth and courtesy.
He was a valiant warrior for his lord;
No man had ridden farther with the sword
Through Christendom and lands of heathen creeds,
And always he was praised for worthy deeds.
He helped win Alexandria in the East,
And often sat at table's head to feast
With knights of all the nations when in Prussia.
In Lithuania as well as Russia

No other noble Christian fought so well.
When Algaciras in Granada fell,
When Ayas and Attalia were won,
This Knight was there. Hard riding he had done
At Benmarin. Along the Great Sea coast
He'd made his strikes with many a noble host.
His mortal battles numbered then fifteen,
And for our faith he'd fought at Tramissene
Three tournaments and always killed his foe.
This worthy Knight was ally, briefly so,
Of the lord of Palathia (in work
Performed against a fellow heathen Turk).
He found the highest favor in all eyes,
A valiant warrior who was also wise
And in deportment meek as any maid.
He never spoke unkindly, never played
The villain's part, but always did the right.
He truly was a perfect, gentle knight.
But now to tell of his array, he had
Good horses but he wasn't richly clad;
His fustian tunic was a rusty sight
Where he had worn his hauberk, for the Knight
Was just back from an expedition when
His pilgrimage he hastened to begin.

There with him was his son, a youthful SQUIRE,
A lover and knight bachelor to admire.
His locks were curled as if set by a press.
His age was twenty years or so, I guess.
In stature he was of an average height
And blest with great agility and might.
He'd ridden for a time with cavalry
In Flanders and Artois and Picardy,
Performing well in such a little space
In hopes of standing in his lady's grace.
He was embroidered like a flower bed

Or meadow, full of flowers white and red.
He sang or else he fluted all the day;
He was as fresh as is the month of May.
His gown was short, his sleeves were long and wide.
And well upon a horse the lad could ride;
Good verse and songs he had composed, and he
Could joust and dance, drew well, wrote gracefully.
At night he'd love so hotly, without fail,
He slept no more than does a nightingale.
He was a courteous, humble lad and able,
And carved meat for his father at the table.

Now he had brought one servant by his side,
A YEOMAN—with no more he chose to ride.
This Yeoman wore a coat and hood of green.
He had a sheaf of arrows, bright and keen,
Beneath his belt positioned handily—
He tended to his gear most yeomanly,
His arrow feathers never drooped too low—
And in his hand he bore a mighty bow.
His head was closely cropped, his face was brown.
The fellow knew his woodcraft up and down.
He wore a bracer on his arm to wield
His bolts. By one side were his sword and shield,
And on the other, mounted at the hip,
A dagger sharply pointed at the tip.
A Christopher of silver sheen was worn
Upon his breast; a green strap held his horn.
He must have been a forester, I guess.

There also was a Nun, a PRIORESS,
Her smile a very simple one and coy.
Her greatest oath was only "By Saint Loy!"
Called Madam Eglantine, this Nun excelled
At singing when church services were held,
Intoning through her nose melodiously.
And she could speak in French quite fluently,

After the school of Stratford at the Bow
(The French of Paris wasn't hers to know).
Of table manners she had learnt it all,
For from her lips she'd let no morsel fall
Nor deeply in her sauce her fingers wet;
She'd lift her food so well she'd never get
A single drop or crumb upon her breast.
At courtesy she really did her best.
Her upper lip she wiped so very clean
That not one bit of grease was ever seen
Upon her drinking cup. She was discreet
And never reached unseemly for the meat.
And certainly she was good company,
So pleasant and so amiable, while she
Would in her mien take pains to imitate
The ways of court, the dignity of state,
That all might praise her for her worthiness.
To tell you of her moral consciousness,
Her charity was so great that to see
A little mouse caught in a trap would be
Enough to make her cry, if dead or bleeding.
She had some little dogs that she was feeding
With roasted meat or milk and fine white bread;
And sorely she would weep if one were dead
Or if someone should smite it with a stick.
She was all tender heart right to the quick.
Her pleated wimple was of seemly class,
She had a well formed nose, eyes gray as glass,
A little mouth, one that was soft and red.
And it's for sure she had a fair forehead—
It must have been a handbreadth wide, I own,
For hardly was the lady undergrown.
The beauty of her cloak I hadn't missed.
She wore a rosary around her wrist
Made out of coral beads all colored green,
And from it hung a brooch of golden sheen

On which there was an A crowned with a wreath,
With *Amor vincit omnia* beneath.
She brought along another NUN, to be
Her chaplain, and her PRIEST, who made it three.
A MONK there was, a fine outrider of
Monastic lands, with venery his love;
A manly man, to be an abbot able.
He had some dainty horses in the stable,
And when he rode, his bridle might you hear
Go jingling in the whistling wind as clear
And loud as might you hear the chapel bell
Where this lord not too often kept his cell.
Because Saint Maurus and Saint Benedict
Had rules he thought were old and rather strict,
This mounted Monk let old things pass away
So that the modern world might have its day.
That text he valued less than a plucked hen
Which says that hunters are not holy men,
Or that a monk ignoring rules and order
Is like a flapping fish out of the water
(That is to say, a monk out of his cloister).
He held that text not worth a single oyster,
And his opinion, I declared, was good.
Why should he study till he's mad? Why should
He pore through books day after day indoors,
Or labor with his hands at all the chores
That Austin bids? How shall the world be served?
Let such works be to Austin then reserved!
And so he was a pricker and aright;
Greyhounds he had as swift as birds in flight,
For tracking and the hunting of the hare
Were all his pleasure, no cost would he spare.
His sleeves, I saw, were fur-lined at the hand
With gray fur of the finest in the land,
And fastening his hood beneath his chin
There was a golden, finely crafted pin,

A love knot in the greater end for class.
His head was bald and shinier than glass.
His face was shiny, too, as if anointed.
He was a husky lord, one well appointed.
His eyes were bright, rolled in his head and glowed
Just like the coals beneath a pot. He rode
In supple boots, his horse in great estate.
Now certainly he was a fine prelate,
He wasn't pale like some poor wasted ghost.
Fat swan he loved the best of any roast.
His palfrey was as brown as is a berry.

A FRIAR there was, a wanton one and merry,
Who begged within a certain limit. None
In all four orders was a better one
At idle talk, or speaking with a flair.
And many a marriage he'd arranged for fair
And youthful women, paying all he could.
He was a pillar of his brotherhood.
Well loved he was, a most familiar Friar
To many franklins living in his shire
And to the worthy women of the town;
For he could hear confessions and played down
The parish priest. To shrive in every quarter
He had been given license by his order.
He'd sweetly listen to confession, then
As pleasantly absolve one of his sin.
He easily gave penance when he knew
Some nice gift he'd receive when he was through.
For when to a poor order something's given,
It is a sign the man is truly shriven.
If someone gave, the Friar made it clear,
He knew the man's repentance was sincere.
For many men are so hard of the heart
They cannot weep, though grievous be the smart;
Instead of tears and prayers, they might therefore

Give silver to the friars who are poor.
He kept his cape all packed with pins and knives
That he would give away to pretty wives.
At merriment he surely wasn't middling;
He sang quite well and also did some fiddling,
And took the prize with all his balladry.
His neck was white as any fleur-de-lis,
His strength like any wrestler's of renown.
He knew the taverns well in every town,
Each hosteler and barmaid, moreso than
He knew the leper and the beggarman.
For anyone as worthy as the Friar
Had faculties that called for something higher
Than dealing with those sick with leprosy.
It wasn't dignified, nor could it be
Of profit, to be dealing with the poor,
What with the rich and merchants at the store.
Above all where some profit might arise
Was where he'd be, in courteous, humble guise.
No man had greater virtue than did he,
The finest beggar in the friary.
(He paid a fee for his exclusive right:
No brethren might invade his begging site.)
And though a widow shoeless had to go,
So pleasant was his "*In principio*"
He'd have a farthing when he went away.
He gained much more than what he had to pay,
And he could be as wanton as a pup.
He'd arbitrate on days to settle up
In law disputes, not like a cloisterer
Dressed in a threadbare cope as students were,
But rather like a master or a pope.
He wore a double-worsted semicope
As rounded as a church bell newly pressed.
He lisped somewhat when he was at his best,
To make his English sweet upon his tongue.

And when he fiddled and his songs were sung,
His eyes would twinkle in his head as might
The stars themselves on any frosty night.
Now Hubert was this worthy Friar's name.

A MERCHANT with a forked beard also came,
Dressed in a motley. Tall and proud he sat
Upon his horse. A Flemish beaver hat
He wore, and boots most elegantly wrought.
He spoke with pomp on everything he thought,
And boasted of the earnings he'd collected.
He felt the trade route had to be protected
Twixt Middleburgh and Orwell by the sea.
He speculated in French currency.
He used his wits so well, with such finesse,
That no one guessed the man's indebtedness,
So dignified he was at managing
All of his bargains and his borrowing.
He was a worthy fellow all the same;
To tell the truth, I do not know his name.
There also was an Oxford STUDENT, one
Whose logic studies long since had begun.
The horse he rode was leaner than a rake,
And he was hardly fat, I undertake,
But looked quite hollow, far from debonair.
And threadbare was the cloak he had to wear;
He had no benefice as yet and, most
Unworldly, wouldn't take a secular post.
For he would rather have at his bed's head
Some twenty books, all bound in black or red,
Of Aristotle and his philosophy
Than finest robes, fiddle or psaltery.
Philosopher he was, and yet his coffer
Had little of the gold that it should offer.
But all that from his friends he could acquire
He spent on books and learning, didn't tire

Of praying for the souls of all those who
Would give to help him see his schooling through,
For study was the foremost thing he heeded.
He never spoke one word more than was needed,
And then he spoke with formal reverence;
He'd make it short but make a lot of sense.
Of highest moral virtue was his speech,
And gladly he would learn and gladly teach.

A wise and prudent SERGEANT OF THE LAW,
One who at Saint Paul's porch one often saw,
Was with us too, a man of excellence.
Discreet he was, deserving reverence
(Or so it seemed, his sayings were so wise).
He often was a judge in the assize
By virtue of his patent and commission.
He had with his renown and erudition
Gained many fees and robes in his career.
A purchaser of land without a peer,
His holdings were fee simple in effect;
No one could prove one purchase incorrect.
Nowhere was there a busier man, yet he
Seemed busier than even he could be.
He knew each court decision, every crime
Adjudicated from King William's time.
He'd execute a deed with such perfection
No man could call its writing into question,
And every statute he could state by rote.
He wore a simple multicolored coat
Girt by a striped silk belt. Enough to tell,
On what he wore I will no longer dwell.
There was a FRANKLIN in his company
Whose beard was lily-white as it could be,
Though his complexion was a healthy red.
In wine he loved to sop his morning bread;
A devotee of all delights that lure us,

He truly was a son of Epicurus
(Who thought the life that's pleasure-filled to be
The only one of true felicity).
He was a great householder, and his bounty
Made him Saint Julian to those in his county.
His bread and ale were always fresh and fine,
And no one had a better stock of wine.
Baked meat was always in his house, the best
Of fish and flesh, so much that to each guest
It almost seemed to snow with meat and drink
And all the dainties of which one could think.
His meals would always vary, to adhere
To all the changing seasons of the year.
The coop was partridge-filled, birds fat as any,
And in the pond the breams and pikes were many.
Woe to the cook unless his sauce was tart
And he had all utensils set to start!
His table would stay mounted in the hall
All set and ready at a moment's call.
In county sessions he was lord and sire,
And often he had been Knight of the Shire.
A dagger and a purse made out of silk
Hung from his belt, as white as morning milk.
A sheriff he'd been, and county auditor.
There wasn't a more worthy vavasor.

A HABERDASHER, DYER, CARPENTER,
TAPESTRY MAKER, and a WEAVER were
All there as well, clothed in the livery
Of guildsmen, of one great fraternity.
Their gear was polished up till it would pass
For new. Their knives were mounted not with brass
But all with silver. Finely wrought array
Their belts and pouches were in every way.
Each one looked like a burgess, one whose place
Would be before the whole guild on a dais.

They had the means and wits, were it their plan,
Each of them to have been an alderman;
They had enough income and property
And wives who would to such a plan agree,
Or else they'd have to blame themselves alone.
It's very nice as "Madam" to be known,
And lead processions on a holy day
And have one's train borne in a royal way.

They brought along a COOK with them to fix
Their meals. He boiled their chicken in a mix
Of marrowbones, tart herbs and galingale.
He knew right off a draught of London ale,
Knew how to boil and roast and broil and fry,
Whip up a stew as well as bake a pie.
It seemed a shame, and caused me some chagrin,
To see he had an ulcer on his shin.
He made blancmange that I'd rank with the best.

There was a SKIPPER hailing from the west,
As far away as Dartmouth, I'd allow.
He rode a nag as best as he knew how.
A woolen gown down to his knees he wore,
And round his neck and neath his arm he bore
A strap from which a dagger dangled down.
The summer sun had turned his color brown.
He surely was a festive sort of fellow;
Many a pilfered wine draught made him mellow
While sailing from Bordeaux, the merchant snoring.
He had no use for conscience, thought it boring.
In battle, when he gained the upper hand,
By plank he'd send them home to every land.
As for his skill in reckoning the tides
And all the dangers of the sea besides,
By zodiac and moon to navigate,
From Hull to Carthage there was none as great.
Hardy and shrewd in all he'd undertaken,

His beard by many tempests had been shaken;
And he knew well the havens everywhere
From Gotland to the Cape of Finisterre,
And every creek in Brittany and Spain.
The Skipper's ship was called the Maudelayne.

There also was among us a PHYSICIAN,
None like him in this world, no competition,
To speak of medicine and surgery.
He was well grounded in astrology:
He tended patients specially in hours
When natural magic had its greatest powers,
For he could tell by which stars would ascend
What talisman would help his patient mend.
He knew the cause of every malady
Whether from hot, cold, wet, or dry it be,
And of each humor what the symptoms were.
He truly was a fine practitioner.
And once he knew a malady's root cause
He'd give the cure without a further pause,
For readily apothecaries heeded
When there were drugs or medicines he needed,
That profit might be shared by everyone
(Their fellowship not recently begun).
The ancient Aesculapius he knew,
And Dioscorides and Rufus too,
Hali and Galen, old Hippocrates,
Serapion, Avicenna, Rhazes,
Gaddesden, Damascenus, Constantine,
Bernard and Averroes and Gilbertine.
His diet was as measured as could be,
Being not one of superfluity
But greatly nourishing as well as prudent.
He hardly could be called a Bible student.
He decked himself in scarlet and in azure,
With taffeta and silk. Yet he'd demure

If something might necessitate expense;
He saved his gains from times of pestilence,
For gold's a cordial, so the doctors say.
That's why he loved gold in a special way.
From near the town of BATH a good WIFE came;
She was a little deaf, which was a shame.
She was a clothier, so excellent
Her work surpassed that of Ypres and Ghent.
When parish wives their gifts would forward bring,
None dared precede her to the offering—
And if they did, her wrath would surely be
So mighty she'd lose all her charity.
The kerchiefs all were of the finest texture
(And must have weighed ten pounds, that's no conjecture)
That every Sunday she had on her head.
The fine hose that she wore were scarlet red
And tightly laced, she had a nice new pair
Of shoes. Her face was ruddy, bold and fair.
She was a worthy woman all her life:
At church door with five men she'd been a wife,
Not counting all the company of her youth.
(No need to treat that now, but it's the truth.)
She'd journeyed to Jerusalem three times;
Strange rivers she had crossed in foreign climes;
She'd been to Rome and also to Boulogne,
To Galicia for Saint James and to Cologne,
And she knew much of wandering by the way.
She had the lover's gap teeth, I must say.
With ease upon an ambling horse she sat,
Well wimpled, while upon her head her hat
Was broad as any buckler to be found.
About her ample hips a mantle wound,
And on her feet the spurs she wore were sharp.
In fellowship she well could laugh and carp.
Of remedies of love she had good notions,
For of that art's old dance she knew the motions.

There was a good man of religion, too,
A PARSON of a certain township who
Was poor, but rich in holy thought and work.
He also was a learned man, a clerk;
The Christian gospel he would truly preach,
Devoutly his parishioners to teach.
Benign he was, in diligence a wonder,
And patient in adversity, as under
Such he'd proven many times. And loath
He was to get his tithes by threatening oath;
For he would rather give, without a doubt,
To all the poor parishioners about
From his own substance and the offerings.
Sufficiency he found in little things.
His parish wide, with houses wide asunder,
He'd never fail in either rain or thunder,
Though sick or vexed, to make his visitations
With those remote, regardless of their stations.
On foot he traveled, in his hand a stave.
This fine example to his sheep he gave:
He always did good works before he taught them.
His words were from the gospel as he caught them,
And this good saying he would add thereto:
"If gold should rust, then what will iron do?"
For if a priest be foul in whom we trust,
No wonder that the ignorant goes to rust.
And it's a shame (as every priest should keep
In mind), a dirty shepherd and clean sheep.
For every priest should an example give,
By his own cleanness, how his sheep should live.
He never set his benefice for hire,
To leave his sheep encumbered in the mire
While he ran off to London and Saint Paul's
To seek a chantry, singing in the stalls,
Or be supported by a guild. Instead
He dwelt at home, and he securely led

His fold, so that the wolf might never harry.
He was a shepherd and no mercenary.
A holy, virtuous man he was, and right
In showing to the sinner no despite.
His speech was never haughty or indignant,
He was a teacher modest and benignant;
To draw folks heavenward to life forever,
By good example, was his great endeavor.
But if some person were too obstinate,
Whether he be of high or low estate,
He would be sharply chided on the spot.
A better priest, I wager, there is not.
He didn't look for pomp or reverence
Nor feign a too self-righteous moral sense;
What Christ and his apostles had to tell
He taught, and he would follow it as well.

With him his brother came, a PLOWMAN who
Had carted many a load of dung. A true
And well-intentioned laborer was he,
Who lived in peace and perfect charity.
The Lord his God with whole heart he loved best,
When times were good as well as when distressed,
And loved his neighbor as himself, for which
He'd gladly thresh, or dig to make a ditch,
For love of Christ, to help the poor in plight
Without a wage, if it lay in his might.
He paid his proper tithes religiously,
Both of his labor and his property.
He wore a tunic and he rode a mare.

A MILLER and a REEVE also were there,
A SUMMONER, also a PARDONER,
A MANCIPLE and me, no more there were.
The MILLER was as stout as any known,
A fellow big in brawn as well as bone.
It served him well, for everywhere he'd go

He'd win the ram at every wrestling show.
Short-shouldered, broad he was, a husky knave;
No door could keep its hinges once he gave
A heave or ran and broke it with his head.
His beard like any sow or fox was red,
And broad as any spade it was, at that.
He had a wart upon his nose, right at
The tip, from which a tuft of hairs was spread
Like bristles on a sow's ears, just as red;
The nostrils on the man were black and wide.
He had a sword and buckler at his side.
Great as a furnace was his mouth. And he
Could tell some jokes and stories, though they'd be
Mostly of sin and lechery. He stole
Much corn, charged three times over for a toll;
Yet he'd a golden thumb, I do declare.
A white coat and a blue hood were his wear.
He blew the bagpipe, knew it up and down,
And played it as he brought us out of town.
From an Inn of Court a gentle MANCIPLE
Was with us, one who set a fine example
In buying victuals wisely. Whether he
Would buy with credit or with currency,
He took such care in purchases he made
He'd come out well ahead for what he paid.
Now is that not a sign of God's fair grace,
That such a simple man's wit can displace
The wisdom of a heap of learned men?
His masters numbered more than three times ten,
All lawyers of a very skillful sort;
A dozen of them in that Inn of Court
Were worthy to be stewards of the treasure
Of any lord in England, that in pleasure
He might live, enjoying all that he had
Without a debt (unless he had gone mad),
Or live as simply as he might desire;

If need be, they could help an entire shire
Through any circumstance that might befall.
And yet this Manciple could shame them all.

The REEVE was a slender, choleric man.
He shaved his beard as closely as one can;
His hair was shortly clipped around the ears
And cropped in front just like a priest's appears.
The fellow's legs were very long and lean,
Each like a staff, no calf was to be seen.
Well could he keep a granary and bin
(No auditor could challenge that and win),
And he could augur by the drought and rain
The true yield of his seed and of his grain.
His master's sheep, his cattle, milk cows, horses,
His poultry, swine, and all his stored resources
Were wholly left to this Reeve's governing,
For by contract his was the reckoning
Since first his lord had grown to twenty years.
No man could ever put him in arrears;
There was no bailiff, herdsman, not one servant
With sleight unknown—the Reeve was too observant,
And feared like death itself by all beneath.
He had a lovely dwelling on a heath
Where green trees stood to shade it from the sun.
In gaining goods his lord he had outdone,
He stored up many riches privately.
To please his lord, he'd give him subtly
A gift or loan out of the lord's own goods,
Receiving thanks and things like coats and hoods.
He'd learnt a good trade as a youth, for he
Was quite a gifted man at carpentry.
He rode a steed with quite a sturdy frame,
A dapple gray (the horse was Scot by name).
He wore a long surcoat of bluish shade,
And at his side he had a rusty blade.

From Norfolk was this Reeve of whom I tell,
Nearby a town that's known as Bawdeswell.
His coat was tucked up like a friar's. He
Rode always last among our company.

A SUMMONER was with us in the place
Who like a cherub had a fire-red face,
So pimply was the skin, eyes puffed and narrow.
He was as hot and lecherous as a sparrow.
With black and scabby brows and scanty beard,
He had a face that all the children feared;
There's no quicksilver, litharge or brimstone,
Borax, ceruse, no tartar oil that's known—
No ointment that could cleanse, to keep it simple,
And rid his face of even one white pimple
Among the whelks that sat upon his cheeks.
He loved his garlic, onions and his leeks,
And strong wine red as blood once he had eaten.
Then he would speak and cry out like a cretin,
And when with wine he was quite well infused,
Some Latin words were all the words he used.
He knew a few good phrases, two or three,
Which he had learnt to say from some decree.
(No wonder, what with hearing it all day;
And after all, as you well know, a jay
Can call out "Walt!" as well as any pope.)
But once a question came to test his scope,
He had no learning left to make reply,
So "*Questio quid juris*!" was his cry.
He was a gentle, kindly rascal, though;
A better fellow men may never know.
Why, he'd be willing, for a quart of wine,
To let some rascal have his concubine
For one whole year, excusing him completely.
He well could "pluck a bird" (always discreetly),
And if he found a fellow rogue wherever

He'd teach him that he should in his endeavor
Not be afraid of the archdeacon's curse—
Unless the fellow's soul was in his purse,
For that is where his punishment would be.
"The purse is the archdeacon's hell," said he.
(I know that was a lie; a guilty man
Should be in dread of Holy Church's ban,
It slays as absolution saves. He best
Beware also a writ for his arrest.)
The Summoner controlled, himself to please,
All of the young girls of the diocese;
He knew their secrets, counseled them and led.
A garland he had set upon his head
As great as any ale sign on a stake.
He'd made himself a buckler out of cake.

With him there rode a gentle PARDONER
Of Rouncivalle (comrades and friends they were),
Who'd come straight from the court of Rome. And he
Would loudly sing "Come hither, love, to me!"
The Summoner bore him a stiff bass staff;
No trumpet ever sounded so by half.
The Pardoner's hair was as yellow as wax,
But hung as smoothly as a hank of flax;
In little strands the locks ran from his head
Till over both his shoulders they were spread
And thinly lay, one here, another there.
In jolly spirit, he chose not to wear
His hood but kept it packed away. He rode
(Or so he thought) all in the latest mode;
But for a cap his long loose hair was bare.
Such glaring eyes he had, just like a hare!
A veronica was sewn upon his cap.
He had his bag before him in his lap,
Brimming with pardons hot from Rome. He'd speak
In voice as dainty as a goat's. From cheek

To cheek he had no beard and never would,
So smooth his face you'd think he'd shaved it good.
I think he was a gelding or a mare.
But speaking of his craft, Berwick to Ware
There was no pardoner could take his place.
For in his bag he had a pillowcase
That used to be, he said, Our Lady's veil;
He claimed he had a fragment of the sail
That took Saint Peter out upon the sea
Before Christ called him to his ministry;
He had a cross of latten set with stones,
And in a glass he had some old pig's bones;
And with these relics, when he saw at hand
A simple parson from the hinterland,
He'd make more money in one day alone
Than would the parson two months come and gone.
So he made apes, with all the tricks he'd do,
Of parson and of congregation too.
And yet I should conclude, for all his tactic,
In church he was a fine ecclesiastic,
So well he read a lesson or a story,
And best of all intoned the offertory.
For well he knew that when the song was sung,
He then must preach, and not with awkward tongue.
He knew how one gets silver from the crowd;
That's why he sang so merrily and loud.
As briefly as I could I've told you now
Degree, array, and number, and of how
This company of pilgrims came to be
In Southwark at that pleasant hostelry
Known as the Tabard, which is near the Bell.
And so with that, it's time for me to tell
Exactly what we did that very night
When at this inn we'd all come to alight;
And after that I'll tell you of our trip,
Of all that's left about our fellowship.

But first I pray that by your courtesy
You will not judge it my vulgarity
If I should plainly speak of this assortment,
To tell you all their words and their deportment,
Though not a word of theirs I modify.
For this I'm sure you know as well as I:
Who tells the tale of any other man
Should render it as nearly as he can,
If it be in his power, word for word,
Though from him such rude speech was never heard.
If he does not, his tale will be untrue,
The words will be invented, they'll be new.
One shouldn't spare the words of his own brother,
He ought to say one word just like another.
Christ spoke broad words himself in Holy Writ,
And you know well no villainy's in it.
And Plato says, to all those who can read
Him, that words must be cousin to the deed.
I also pray that you'll forgive the fact
That in my tale I haven't been exact
To set folks in their order of degree;
My wit is short, as clearly you may see.

Our HOST made welcome each and every one,
And right away our supper was begun.
He served us with the finest in good food;
The wine was strong to fit our festive mood.
Our Host performed, so it seemed to us all,
As well as any marshal in a hall.
A robust man he was, and twinkle-eyed,
As fine as any burgess in Cheapside,
Bold in his speech, one wise and educated,
A man whose manhood could not be debated.
He also was a merry sort of bloke,
As after supper he began to joke
And spoke to us of mirth and other things

When we had finished with our reckonings.
"My lords," he then addressed us, "from the start
You've been most welcome here, that's from the heart.
In faith, this year I've truly yet to see
Here at this inn another company
As merry as the one that's gathered now.
I'd entertain you more if I knew how.
Say, here's a thought that just occurred to me,
A way to entertain you, and it's free.
"You go to Canterbury—may God speed,
The blissful martyr bless you for the deed!
And well I know as you go on your way,
You plan to tell some tales, to have some play.
There won't be much amusement going on
If everybody rides dumb as a stone.
So as I said, I would propose a game
To give you some diversion, that's the aim.
If it's agreed, by everyone's assent,
That you'll stand by the judgment I present,
And strive to do exactly as I say
Tomorrow when you're riding on your way,
Then by my father's soul, who now is dead,
You'll have some fun or you can have my head!
Let's have a show of hands, no more to say."

We let our will be known then right away;
We didn't think it worth deliberation
And gave him leave without a hesitation
To tell us what his verdict was to be.
"My lords," he said, "then listen well to me,
And may this not, I pray, meet your disdain.
Now here's the point, speaking short and plain:
Each one of you, to pass the time of day,
Shall tell two tales while you are on the way
To Canterbury; then each one of you
On the return shall tell another two,

About adventures said once to befall.
And he who bears himself the best of all—
That is to say, the one who's judged to tell
The tales that in both aim and wit excel—
Shall win a supper paid for by the lot,
Here in this place, right at this very spot,
When we return again from Canterbury.
For in my wish to make your journey merry,
I will myself most gladly with you ride—
And at my own expense—to be your guide;
And if my judgment one disputes, he'll pay
For all that we shall spend along the way.
If you will grant me that it's to be so,
Then tell me in a word that I may know
To make my preparations for the start."
It was so granted, each with happy heart
Gave him his oath. We therefore asked our Host
To vouchsafe that indeed he'd take the post
And function as our governor, to hear
Our tales and judge, and make his judgment clear,
And set the supper at a certain price;
Then we would all be ruled by his device,
Come high or low. And so it was agreed
By one assent, his judgment we would heed.
With that, more wine was fetched for every guest.
We drank it, then were ready for some rest
And went to bed with no more tarrying.

Next morning, when the day began to spring,
Up rose our Host and roused us like a cock.
He gathered us together in a flock,
Then forth we rode at but a walking pace
Out to Saint Thomas's watering place.
Our Host there checked his horse and said to all:
"My lords, now listen, if you will. Recall
The pact, as I remind you, made with me.

If evensong and matins both agree,
Let's see now who shall tell us the first tale.
And if I've ever drunk of wine or ale,
Whoso resists the judgment I present
Shall pay along the way all that is spent.
Draw lots before we travel farther, then,
And he who draws the shortest shall begin.
Sir Knight," he said, "my master and my lord,
Now draw a lot, to keep with our accord.
Come here," said he, "my Lady Prioress,
And you, Sir Student—quit your bashfulness
And studies too. Lay hand to, everyone!"
And so the drawing was at once begun.
I'll keep it short and tell you how it went:
Whether by chance or fate or accident,
The truth is that the lot fell to the Knight—
A fact in which the rest all took delight.
As was required, then tell his tale he must,
By the agreement that was made in trust
As you have heard. What more is there to know?
And when this good man saw that it was so,
As one with wisdom and obedient
To that to which he'd given free assent,
He said, "Since I'm the one to start the game,
The lot I drew is welcome, in God's name!
Now let us ride, and hear what I've to say."
And with that word we rode forth on our way,
As he began at once with merry cheer
To tell his tale, and spoke as you may hear.

THE KNIGHT'S TALE

Part I

Once upon a time, old stories tell us,
There was a duke whose name was Theseus.
Of Athens he was lord and governor,
And in his time was such a conqueror

That none was greater underneath the sun,
So many wealthy countries he had won.
What with his wisdom and his chivalry,
He conquered all the realm of Femeny,
Which then was known as Scythia, and married
The queen named Hippolyta, whom he carried
Back home with him amid much pageantry
And glorious ceremony. Emily,
Her younger sister, also went along.
And so in victory and glorious song
I leave this noble duke as he is bound
For Athens, with his warriors all around.
And if there weren't so much to hear, I now
Would fully have related for you how
That land was won, the realm of Femeny,
By Theseus and by his chivalry;
I'd tell you of the battle that was waged
As Athens and the Amazons engaged,
And of the siege in which was finally seen
Defeat for Scythia's fair and hardy queen,
And of the feast upon their wedding day
And the rousing welcome home. But as I say,
I must forbear describing all that now.
I have, God knows, a lot of field to plow,
The oxen in my yoke have got it rough.
And since the rest of my tale's long enough,
Not holding back the group is my concern;
Let every fellow tell his tale in turn
And let us see who shall the supper win.
Where I left off, then, I'll once more begin.

This duke of whom I spoke, when he almost
Had reached the gates of town with all his host,
In such high spirits and so full of pride,
Became aware, as he looked to the side,
That kneeling by the road there was in rue

A company of ladies, two by two,
One pair behind another, in black dress.
So woeful were the cries of their distress
No living creature ever heard before
Such lamentation uttered. Furthermore
They did not cease until his horse was idle,
For they had grabbed the reins upon its bridle.
"What folk are you, against our joy vying,
Disturbing our homecoming with your crying?"
Said Theseus. "So envious can you be
That you protest the honor given me?
Or who mistreated you, who has offended?
And tell me if the damage can be mended,
And why it is in black you are arrayed."

The eldest lady answered, though she swayed
Half in a swoon of such deathlike degree
It was a pity both to hear and see.
"My lord," she said, "whom Fortune chose to give
The victory, as conqueror to live,
Your glory and honor are not our grief,
It's mercy that we're seeking and relief.
Have mercy on our woe and our distress!
Some drop of pity, through your gentleness,
Upon us wretched women please let fall.
In truth, my lord, there's none among us all
Who hasn't been a duchess or a queen;
Now we are wretches. As may well be seen,
Thanks be to Fortune's faithless wheel, there's no
One whose well-being is assured. And so,
My lord, that in your presence we might be,
The temple of the goddess Clemency
Is where we've waited for a whole fortnight.
Help us, my lord, if it be in your might.

"The wretch I am, now weeping, wailing thus,
Was once the wife of King Capaneus,

Who died at Thebes—and curséd be that day!
And all of us you see in this array
Are crying so, our spirits beaten down,
Because we lost our husbands in that town
During the time that under siege it lay.
And yet this old Creon—ah, wellaway!—
Who is in Thebes, now lord of all the city,
Iniquitous and ireful, without pity,
Has for despite and by his tyranny
Inflicted on their bodies villainy:
The corpses of our lords, all of them slain,
He threw into a heap where they have lain,
For he gives no assent, will not allow
That they be burnt or buried, rather now
He makes hounds eat them, such is his despite."

And with that word, they cried without respite
And then they groveled, weeping piteously.
"Have mercy for us wretched," was their plea,
"Your heart be open to our grief today."

This gentle duke dismounted right away
With pitying heart when hearing these words spoken.
He felt as if his heart were nearly broken,
To see so pitiful, in such a strait,
Those who had once been of such great estate.
He took them in his arms then and consoled them;
He comforted as best he could, and told them
That by his oath, that of a faithful knight,
He would do all that lay within his might
Upon this tyrant vengefulness to wreak,
That afterwards all those in Greece might speak
Of how Creon by Theseus was served
His just deserts, the death he so deserved.
Immediately, without the least delay,
His banner he displayed and rode away
For Thebes, with all his host on every side;

No nearer Athens did he choose to ride
Nor take his ease for even half a day,
But slept that night somewhere along the way.
The queen was not among his company,
But with her fair young sister Emily
Was sent forth into Athens, there to dwell
While he rode on his way. No more to tell.

The red image of Mars with spear and targe
So shone upon his banner white and large
That up and down the meadows seemed to glitter;
A pennon by his banner was aflitter
In richest gold, upon it, as was meet,
The Minotaur that he had slain in Crete.
Thus rode this duke, this conqueror, in power,
The men with him of chivalry the flower,
Until he came to Thebes, there to alight
Upon a field where he was set to fight.
But only speaking briefly of this thing,
He fought and slew Creon, the Theban king,
In open battle, as befits a knight
So manly. Creon's men he put to flight.
The city by assault he won thereafter
And tore it down, each wall and beam and rafter;
And to the ladies he restored again
The bones of all their kinsmen who'd been slain,
For obsequies then custom of the day.
But it would take too long here to delay
By telling of the din, the lamentation
Made by these ladies during the cremation,
And honor paid, all that one could confer,
By Theseus, the noble conqueror,
To the ladies when on their way they went.
To speak with brevity is my intent.

This worthy Theseus, when he had slain
Creon and captured Thebes, chose to remain

Upon the field that night to take his rest,
With all that country under his behest.
To rummage through the heap of Theban slain,
The corpses' clothes and armor to retain,
The pillagers worked hard and carefully
After the battle and the victory.
It so befell that in the heap they found,
With grievous wounds there lying on the ground,
Two youthful knights who side by side had fought,
Identical their arms and richly wrought.
As for their names, Arcite was that of one,
The other knight was known as Palamon;
Not yet alive nor dead did they appear,
But by their coat of arms and by their gear
The heralds knew that these two specially
Were members of the royal family
Of Thebes, two sisters' sons. Their finders then
Removed them from the heap where they had been,
And had them carried gently to the tent
Of Theseus, who promptly had them sent
To Athens, there to dwell perpetually
In prison—to no ransom he'd agree.
And when this worthy duke thus held his sway,
He took his host and rode home straightaway.
As conqueror with laurel he was crowned,
And lived in joy and honor, much renowned
Throughout his life. What more is there to know?
And in a tower, in anguish and woe,
Are Palamon and his good friend Arcite
Forevermore. No gold could end their plight.

So year by year it went, and day by day,
Until one morning it befell in May
That Emily, a fairer sight to see
Than lilies on a stalk of green could be,
And fresher than the flowers May discloses—

Her hue strove with the color of the roses
Till I know not the fairer of the two—
Before daylight, as she was wont to do,
Had roused herself and was already dressed.
For May will leave no sluggard nightly rest;
The season seems to prick each gentle heart,
It causes one out of his sleep to start
And says, "Arise, it's time to pay respect!"
And this caused Emily to recollect
The honor due to May and to arise.
She brightly dressed, a pleasure to the eyes.
Her hair was braided in one yellow tress
A good yard down her back, so I would guess.
And in the garden, as the sun arose,
She wandered up and down, and, as she chose,
She gathered flowers, white as well as red,
To make a dainty garland for her head;
And like that of an angel was her song.

The tower, of great size and thick and strong,
Which was the castle's major dungeon—there
The knights were held in prison and despair,
As I have said, though more will soon befall—
Was built adjacent to the garden wall
Where Emily was then about her play.
The sun was bright, and clear the early day,
As Palamon, in woe with no reprieve,
As was his wont—the jailer gave him leave—
Was roaming in a chamber of great height
From which all of the city was in sight,
As was the green-branched garden near the tower
Where Emily, as radiant as a flower,
Was in her walk and roaming here and there.
So Palamon, this captive in despair,
Was pacing in this chamber to and fro,
And to himself complaining of his woe.
That he was born he often said "Alas!"

And then by chance or fate it came to pass
That through the window (thick with many a bar
Of iron, as great and squared as girders are)
He cast his eyes upon fair Emily.
He blanched and cried an "Ah!" of such degree
It was as if he'd been pierced through the heart.
And at this cry Arcite rose with a start
And said, "My cousin, what is ailing you
That you're so pale, a deathlike thing to view?
Why did you cry? Has someone done you wrong?
For God's love, it's the patient gets along
In prison, that's the way it has to be.
We owe to Fortune this adversity.
Some wicked aspect or configuration
Of Saturn with some certain constellation
Gave this to us, for all we might have sworn.
So stood the heavens when we two were born;
We must endure it, to be short and plain."
But Palamon replied, "You have a vain
Imagination, cousin, truthfully,
To be expressing such a thought to me.
It wasn't prison that caused me to cry.
I just received a shot, struck through my eye
Right to my heart, and it will finish me.
The fairness of that lady that I see
In yonder garden, roaming to and fro,
Is cause of all my crying and my woe.
I don't know if she's woman or a goddess,
But truly it is Venus, I would guess."
Then Palamon fell down upon his knees
And said this prayer: "Dear Venus, if you please
To be transfigured so, to be seen by
A woeful, wretched creature such as I,
Out of this prison help us to escape.
But if it is my fate, one taken shape
By eternal word, to die in this fashion,

Upon our royal house have some compassion,
For we are brought so low by tyranny."

And with that word, Arcite then chanced to see
This lady who was roaming to and fro;
And at the sight, her beauty hurt him so
That if the wound to Palamon was sore,
Arcite himself was hurt as much or more.
And with a sigh he then said piteously,
"By such fresh beauty I'm slain suddenly,
The beauty of her roaming in that place!
Unless I have her mercy by her grace
That I at least may see her in some way,
I am but dead, there is no more to say."

When Palamon heard this, with angry eye
He turned to look at Arcite and reply,
"You speak such words in earnest or in play?"

"In earnest," Arcite said, "is what I say!
God help me, I've no mind for joking now."

And Palamon at this then knit his brow.
"It does you little honor," he replied,
"To be a traitor to me, to have lied
To me, as I'm your cousin and your brother;
For we have sworn, each of us to the other,
That never we, on pain of death—until
Death do us part—would do each other ill,
In love one to be hindrance to the other
Or in whatever case, beloved brother;
That you would further me in what I do
In every case, and I would further you;
This was your oath, as well as mine. I know
That you would never dare deny it's so.
You then are in my counsel, there's no doubt,
And yet now falsely you would go about

To love my lady, whom I love and serve
And always will until I die. What nerve!
False Arcite, you would surely not do so;
I loved her first, and told you of my woe
As to my counsel, to the one who swore
To further me, as I have said before.
And so, my cousin, you're bound as a knight
To help me, if it lies within your might,
Or else be false, and such I dare to say."
But Arcite proudly answered in this way:
"It's you instead who would be false to me,
And false you are, I tell you utterly.
For par amour, I loved her first, not you.
What can you say? You don't know which is true,
She's 'woman or a goddess'! You profess
Affection felt in terms of holiness,
But I feel love that's for a creature, such
That I've already said to you as much,
As to my brother, one who to me swore.
But let's suppose you did love her before:
Have you not heard the learned man's old saw
That 'Who shall give a lover any law'?
Love, by my crown, is law that's greater than
All law that Nature gives to earthly man;
That's why, for love, decrees or laws men pass
Are broken every day in every class.
A man must love despite himself; albeit
His death may be the cost, he cannot flee it,
Be she a maiden, widow, or a wife.
But it's not likely that in all your life
You'll stand once in her grace, nor myself either;
You know as well as I it shall be neither,
For you and I have been forever damned
To prison without ransom. We have shammed,
We strive just as the hounds did for the bone:
They fought all day to find the prize was gone,

For while they fought a kite came winging through
And bore away the bone from twixt the two.
And therefore at the royal court, my brother,
It's each man for himself and not another.
Love if you like, I love and always will,
And truly, brother, that is that. Be still;
Here in this prison we must not succumb
But each take his own chances as they come."

The strife between the two was long and great;
Had I the time, more of it I'd relate.
But to the point. It happened that one day
(To tell it all as briefly as I may)
Perotheus, a worthy duke who'd been
A friend of Theseus since way back when
The two of them were children, came to pay
His friend a visit and to have some play
In Athens, as he'd often done before.
In all this world he loved no fellow more
Than Theseus, who cherished him the same;
They loved so greatly, so the old books claim,
That when one died, as truthfully they tell,
The other went to look for him in hell—
But that's a tale I don't wish to recite.
Duke Perotheus also loved Arcite,
Whom he'd known in Thebes for many a year.
At last, when Perotheus had bent his ear
With the request, Duke Theseus agreed
To free Arcite from prison; he was freed
Without a ransom and allowed to go
Where he desired—on one condition, though.

The understanding, plainly to relate,
With Theseus regarding Arcite's fate
Was that if Arcite ever should be found,
By day or night or any time, on ground
Of any country ruled by Theseus,

And he were caught, it was accorded thus:
He was to lose his head then by the sword.
There was no action Arcite could afford
Except to make for home a speedy trek;
One must beware when he must pledge his neck.

How great a sorrow Arcite had to bear!
His heart was smitten with deathlike despair;
He wept and wailed, and pitifully he cried,
And even contemplated suicide.
He said, "Alas, the day that I was born!
Worse than before in prison I'm forlorn.
It's now my fate eternally to dwell
Not as in purgatory but in hell.
I wish I'd never known Perotheus!
I'd still be dwelling with Duke Theseus,
Be fettered in his prison—not like this,
Not in this woe. Then I would be in bliss;
The sight of her, the lady whom I serve,
Although her grace I never may deserve,
Would have sufficed and been enough for me.
O my dear cousin Palamon," said he,
"You've won in this adventure, that's for sure.
In prison blissfully you may endure—
In prison? Surely not! In paradise!
Fate's passed to you the dice to seek the prize,
You have her sight, which I no more shall see.
Since you're so near her presence, it may be,
As you're a knight, a worthy one and able,
That by some chance—as Fortune's so unstable—
You may attain your great desire in time.
But I, who am exiled to other clime
And barren of all grace, in such despair
That neither earth nor water, fire nor air,
Nor any creature that is made of these,
Can ever give me any help or ease—

Well should I die without a hope, in sadness.
Farewell my life, my pleasure, and my gladness!

"Alas, why do folks so complain about
The providence of God or feel put out
By Fortune, when they're often given more
In many ways than they could bargain for
Themselves? A man's desire for wealth may well
Leave that man sick or murdered. From his cell
A prisoner may long for freedom, then
At home have his own servants do him in.
So many ills befall us in this way,
We don't know really that for which we pray.
We fare as one who's drunken as a mouse:
Although a drunkard knows he has a house,
He doesn't know the right way there. The road
Is slippery for a man who drinks his load.
So fare we in this world, most certainly;
We search with vigor for felicity,
But it's so true we often go awry.
We all can vouch for that, and namely I,
Who had this great opinion overall
That if I could escape that prison wall
I then could live in perfect health and bliss—
From which I have been exiled now for this.
Since I may never see you, Emily,
I'm good as dead, there is no remedy."

Now Palamon, meanwhile, was still confined,
And when he learnt Arcite was gone, he whined
And wailed with so much sorrow it resounded
Throughout the tower. Utterly confounded,
He wet the mighty fetters round each shin
With bitter, salty tears in his chagrin.
"Alas," said he, "my cousin, dear Arcite,
The fruit is yours, God knows, you've won the fight!
To walk at large in Thebes now you may go

And give but little thought to all my woe;
And you may, in your wise and knightly manner,
Assemble all your kinsmen to your banner
And on this city make a sharp attack,
By treaty or by Fortune to go back
To Thebes with her, your lady and your wife,
For whom I now must forfeit here my life.
When one weighs every possibility—
Since you are now at large, from prison free,
And are a lord—you have a great advantage.
I'm dying in a cage, what can I manage?
Here I must weep and wail long as I live
With all the woe that prison has to give,
And with the heartache love has given me
That doubles my torment and misery."
The fire of jealousy with sudden start
Was raging in his breast, and caught his heart
So madly he was whiter to behold
Than box-tree or the ashes dead and cold.

He said then, "O cruel gods, eternal tribe
Who rule us by your word, and who inscribe
Upon a tablet made of adamant
Your every judgment and eternal grant!
Why is it mankind in esteem you hold
More than the sheep that cowers in the fold?
For man is slain like any other beast,
Or dwells in prison, not to be released,
Confronted with adversity and illness—
And often, by my faith, when he is guiltless.

"What is the reason in your prescience
That torment's the reward for innocence?
And only adding more to all my strife
Is that a man must live a moral life
In God's name, and keep rein upon his will,
While every beast may all his lust fulfill.

And when a beast is dead, he has no pain,
While man in death must still weep and complain
Though in this world he had his share of woe.
Without a doubt that's how it stands, although
I'll leave it to the clergy to explain.
How well I know this world is full of pain.
Alas, I see a serpent or a thief,
From whose deceit the righteous seek relief,
Go freely as he pleases on his way;
Yet I'm a captive, under Saturn's sway
And that of Juno, who in jealousy
And wrath has well nigh cut off totally
The blood of Thebes, laid waste the walls once grand.
And Venus slays me, on the other hand,
With jealousy and fear of this Arcite."

On Palamon I'll cease now if I might
And leave him in his prison still to dwell,
That further word on Arcite I may tell.

The summer passed. The winter nights so long
Increased twofold the pains that were so strong
In both lover and prisoner. I know
Not which one had to bear the greater woe:
For Palamon, with brevity to tell,
Was damned to life inside a prison cell,
In iron fetters until he be dead;
Yet banishment had fallen on the head
Of Arcite, from that land he had to flee
And nevermore might he his lady see.

I now will ask you lovers, who's the one
Who has it worse, Arcite or Palamon?
For one may see his lady day by day
But must in prison waste his life away;
The other may go riding where he please,
But now his lady nevermore he sees.

Make your own judgment on it, if you can.
I will go on, meanwhile, as I began.

Part II

When back to Thebes Arcite had made his way,
With many an "Alas!" he pined each day,
For nevermore his lady might he see.
To summarize his woe with brevity,
No creature's had such sorrow, to be sure,
Nor will as long as this world may endure.
Of sleep and meat and drink he had so little
That lean and dry he grew, shaftlike and brittle;
His eyes were hollow, ghastly to behold,
His sallow skin like ashes pale and cold.
And he kept to himself, always alone,
And all through every night he'd wail and moan.
And when he heard a song or instrument,
He wept, shed tears that nothing could prevent.
So feeble were his spirits and so low
That, if he spoke, no man would ever know
Him by his speech or voice, he had so changed.
He moodily behaved, as if deranged
Not only by lovesickness (*hereos*
Is what it's called) but mania that grows
From melancholic humor that arises
From that front brain cell where one fantasizes.
In short, all was in overturned position
In both the habit and the disposition
Of this despairing lover, Sir Arcite.
Should I go on all day about his plight?
Now when he had endured a year or so
This cruel torment, all this pain and woe
At home in Thebes (as you have heard me say),
One night he dreamt while in the bed he lay
That winged Mercury came to appear
Before him, bidding him to be of cheer.

His sleep inducing wand he held upright,
A hat was on his head, his hair was bright;
As Arcite noticed, Mercury was dressed
Just as when Argus he induced to rest.
The god said this: "To Athens you shall go,
Where destined is an end to all your woe."
With that, Arcite woke with a start and said,
"No matter what sore pain may lie ahead,
Right now to Athens truly I must fare;
Though death be dreaded, I'll be seeing there
My lady whom I love and serve, and I
Shall not, in her dear presence, fear to die."

He picked up a large mirror then to see
The great change in his color, the degree
To which his face looked like another kind.
Immediately the thought ran through his mind
That since his face had been disfigured so
By all that he had suffered, he could go
And live in Athens, in some lowly guise,
And who he was no one would realize;
Then he could see his lady every day.

And so at once he changed his knight's array
For that of a poor laborer for hire;
Then all alone (save only for a squire
Who knew his secret, all there was to know,
And was disguised in poverty also),
He went to Athens by the shortest way.
Then to the royal court he went one day
And offered at the gate his worker's hands,
To drag and draw, to follow all commands.

To tell you what occurred without ado,
He got a job with an attendant who
Was dwelling in the house of Emily;
For he was shrewd and very quick to see

Which of them served his lady there. Well could
He bear the water and he hewed as well the wood,
For he was young and equal to the task,
Big-boned and strong. What any man might ask,
Whatever one devised, Arcite could do.

He served in this way for a year or two,
The chamber-page of lovely Emily,
And said his name was Philostrate. And he
Was twice as loved as any other man
Of equal rank at court, for in this span
His character was of such noble sort
That he won quite a name throughout the court.
As charity, they said, it would be noted
If Theseus would have the man promoted
To higher station, so that servicewise
His virtue he might fully exercise.
And so it was in time his fame had sprung
Out of his gentle deeds and pleasant tongue
Until the duke took him and set him higher,
To serve him in his chamber as a squire,
And gave him gold to keep himself in style.
From his own country, too, from while to while
Men brought to him a secret increment
That honestly and slyly would be spent,
That none might wonder how he had so much.
He lived this way three years, his bearing such,
In time of peace as well as time of war,
That there was none whom Theseus loved more.
I now leave Arcite in this blissful state
That more on Palamon I may relate.

In dark and solid prison, horrid, drear,
Now Palamon endures a seventh year
And pines away in sorrow and distress.
Who feels such double wounds, such heaviness,
As Palamon whom love destroys so,

Almost out of his wits through all his woe?
And Palamon's a captive, be it clear,
Perpetually, not only for a year.

O who could rhyme in English properly
His martyrdom? It's not I truthfully,
So I'll pass on as briefly as I may.

Now in the seventh year (the old books say,
With more detail, it was the third night in
The month of May), the time came finally when,
Whether it was by chance or destiny—
As when a thing's determined, it shall be-—
With a friend's help, soon after midnight fell,
Palamon escaped from his prison cell
And fled the town as fast as he could go.
He'd given his jailer drink, and it was so
Well mixed—a honeyed wine, along with some
Narcotics, like fine Theban opium—
That all that night, as hard as men could shake him,
The jailer slept and no one could awake him,
While Palamon fled swiftly as he may.
The night was short, and fast would come the day,
When at all costs he knew he'd have to hide.
And so a grove that stood off to the side
He fearfully approached. It was his plan,
Which I will tell as briefly as I can,
Inside that grove to hide himself all day,
Then at the fall of night to make his way
To Thebes. There all his friends he would implore
To help him march on Theseus in war,
And, to be brief, unless he lose his life,
To win the lovely Emily as wife.
That was his whole intention, short and plain.

And now to Arcite I'll return again,
Who little knew how nigh had grown his care
Till Fortune was to catch him in her snare.

The busy lark, the messenger of day,
Salutes now with her song the morning gray,
And fiery Phoebus rises up so bright
Till all the east is laughing in his light,
The beams of which dry every bush where cleaves
The silver droplets, hanging on the leaves.
And Arcite, who is in the royal court
As Theseus's squire of good report,
Has risen and looks on the merry day.
To give the honor that was due to May
(Recalling, too, his object of desire),
He set out on a courser quick as fire
Into the fields to have a little play.
A mile or two from court he rode his way
Till he came to the grove of which I spoke.
By chance along that grove his course he broke
To make himself a garland from the growth,
With woodbine or with hawthorn leaf or both,
While in the sunshine singing heartily:
"O May, with flowers and with greenery,
You are so welcome, fresh and fairest May!
I hope that I may get some green today!"
Down from his courser, with a lusty heart
Into the grove he promptly made his start
And roamed a path wherever it would chance.
Now Palamon, as was the happenstance,
Was hidden in a bush where none could see,
As fearful for his life as he could be.
He'd no idea that this could be Arcite;
God knows, he had no cause to think it might,
But it's been truly said down through the years,
"The field is blest with eyes, the wood has ears."
It's best a fellow always be discreet,
For when they least expect men often meet.
Little did Arcite know that near him there
Was his old friend to hear him sing his air,
For he sat in the bush completely still.

When of his roaming Arcite had his fill
And he had sung his rondel lustily,
Into a muse he fell then suddenly
As lovers do, so variable their mood—
First treetop high, then in the briers they brood,
Now up, now down, like buckets in a well;
Like on a Friday, truly I can tell,
At first it shines, then rains start coming fast.
Just so can fickle Venus overcast
The hearts of lovers; Friday is her day,
And just as she keeps changing her array
Few Fridays are like other days, for sure.

When he had sung, Arcite became demure,
He sighed and sat down without further song.
"Alas," said he, "the day I came along!
O Juno, how much longer will it be
That you wage war on Thebes with cruelty?
Alas! so much confusion is brought on
The royal blood of Cadmus, Amphion—
Of Cadmus, who's the one who first began
To build the town of Thebes, and he's the man
Who was the first the city crowned as king;
I'm one of his descendants, his offspring,
By true descent I'm of the royal stock;
Yet I'm just like a slave sold on the block,
For he who is my mortal enemy
Is whom I serve as squire so wretchedly.
And evermore does Juno cause me shame,
For I dare not to tell them my own name;
For whereas I was once known as Arcite,
I now am Philostrate, not worth a mite.
Alas, you evil Mars! Juno, alas!
Your wrath has caused our house to all but pass,
There's left but me and Palamon (in woe,
As in the dungeon he's still martyred so).

And more than that, to slay me utterly,
Love with his fiery dart so burningly
Has struck my loving heart with such a hurt,
My death was knit before this very shirt.
You've slain me with your eyes, fair Emily,
You are the cause I die, that's all there be.
And for the rest of all my earthly care
I wouldn't give one weed the field may bear
If but to please you I could have a chance."
And with that word he fell down in a trance
Where long he lay, till rising with a start.

This Palamon, who felt that through his heart
A cold sword suddenly had glided, shook
With anger, not much time at all he took,
For when he finished hearing Arcite's tale,
He leapt as if gone mad, face deathly pale,
Out of the thicket not one second later,
And said, "Arcite, you false and wicked traitor!
Now you are caught who loves my lady so,
She for whom I have had such pain and woe;
You're of my blood, and to my counsel swore,
As I have often said to you before.
So you have fooled Duke Theseus, you claim,
And also you have falsely changed your name,
But you shall die, or else it shall be me:
You shall not love my lady Emily.
For I and I alone shall love her so;
I'm Palamon himself, your mortal foe.
And though I have no weapon in this place
(I just escaped from prison, by God's grace),
You'll either die—of that there's no mistake—
Or else not love my Emily. So make
The choice you will, you'll not escape from me."

Now when Arcite had heard and turned to see
That it was Palamon, as spite coursed through

His heart he fiercely as a lion drew
His sword and said, "By God who sits above,
If you were not so sick and crazed with love,
And if you had a weapon at your side,
You'd not walk from this grove a single stride,
For by my hand you would be lying dead.
The pledge, the guarantee that you have said
I gave you, I renounce. Why, you must be
A perfect fool, I tell you love is free,
And I will love her, try all that you might!
But inasmuch as you're a worthy knight
Who'd wager her to see who should prevail,
Here is my oath: tomorrow without fail,
In secret, known to no one else around,
It's right here as a knight that I'll be found,
With arms for you as well—and you be first
To choose the best ones, leave for me the worst.
Some meat and drink tonight I'll bring to you,
All that you need; I'll bring some bedding too.
And if it be my lady you shall win
And slay me in this wood that we are in,
You well may have her, nothing more from me."

And Palamon then answered, "I agree."
And so till then they parted, when they both
Had pledged in all good faith with solemn oath.

O Cupid, so devoid of charity!
O rule where no compeer's allowed to be!
It truly has been said that love or power
Won't willingly give fellowship an hour;
So Palamon has found, as has Arcite.
The latter rode at once to town that night,
Then in the morning, just before the sun,
Sneaked out the armor he and Palamon
Would need; he brought enough to more than do
For battle in the field between the two.

So as alone as he was born he rode
His horse, with all this armor as his load,
And at the time and place that had seen set,
There in the grove, the two of them were met.
The hue began to change in each's face,
Like in the hunter's who in distant Thrace
Stands in the gap with spear in hand, as there
He's hunting for the lion and the bear;
He hears it coming, rushing through the branches
And breaking boughs asunder; then he blanches:
"Here comes," he thinks, "my mortal enemy!
Without fail one must die, it's him or me,
For either I will slay him at the gap
Or he slay me, if that be my mishap."
That's how they were in changing of their hue
As soon as each one had his foe in view.

There was no "Good day," not one salutation.
Without a word before the confrontation
Each of the two first helped to arm the other
As courteously as if he were his brother.
And then, with sharpened spears of sturdy strength,
They plunged into a fight of wondrous length.
To watch this Palamon you might have thought
He was a maddened lion, the way he fought,
And like a cruel tiger was Arcite.
They smote each other as wild boars would fight
When frothing white with foam, so mad each one.
They fought till ankle deep the blood had run.
I'll leave them, on their fight no more to dwell,
Now something more of Theseus to tell.

That minister general, Destiny,
Who executes all that must come to be
(The providence foreseen by God on high),
Is so strong that although the world deny
A thing shall be, by vow, by "yea" or "nay,"

It still will come to pass upon its day,
Though not again till pass a thousand years;
Each appetite that in this world appears,
Be it for war or peace or hate or love,
Is governed by this providence above.

Of mighty Theseus I say the same,
For he had such desire for hunting game,
Especially the great hart, all that May
There didn't dawn on him a single day
That didn't find him clad and set to ride
With hunters, horns, hounds running at his side;
For in his hunting he took such delight
That it was all his joy and appetite
To be the great hart's mighty bane and dread;
He served Diana after Mars the Red.

Clear was the day, as I've said prior to this,
As Theseus—all joyful, full of bliss,
Along with Hippolyta, his fair queen,
And Emily, clothed all in lovely green—
Was out upon a royal hunting ride;
And to the grove that stood so near beside,
In which there was a hart (so men had said),
Duke Theseus directly turned and sped.
He rode straight for the glade, which was the place
To which the hart was wont to go, to race
Across the brook and flee as harts will do;
The duke would have a run at him or two
With hounds such as it pleased him to command.

But when the duke had reached this open land,
There in the glaring sun he caught the sight
At once of Palamon and of Arcite,
Still fighting like two boars. It seemed as though
The two bright swords, there flashing to and fro
So hideously, could with the lightest stroke

Be either one enough to fell an oak.
Now who these people were he didn't know;
The duke at once then spurred his courser, though,
And in a trice he was between the two,
Pulled out his sword, and said, "Halt! That will do!
No more, on pain of parting with your head!
By mighty Mars, he'll be as good as dead
Who strikes another blow that I may see.
Tell me what sort of men you two must be,
In such a hardy fight here as you were
Without a judge or other officer
Though as if in a tournament today."

Then Palamon responded right away:
"Sire, there are no more words that need be said,
We both are quite deserving to be dead.
Two woeful wretches, prisoners are we,
Both weary of our lives, that's him and me.
And as you are a righteous judge and lord,
No mercy nor refuge for us afford,
But slay me first, in saintly charity.
But slay this fellow here as well as me—
Or slay him first, when you have seen him right:
This is your mortal foe, this is Arcite,
Whom you have banished or would have his head,
For which he's now deserving to be dead.
This is the one who came up to your gate
And told them that his name was Philostrate,
The one who's made a fool of you for years—
You made him your chief squire, from all his peers.
And he's in love with Emily. And I,
Since now has come the day that I shall die,
Shall plainly here confess and have it done
That I am that same woeful Palamon
Who broke out of your prison wickedly;
I am your mortal foe, and I am he

Who loves so hotly Emily the Bright
I'd die for it here in my lady's sight.
I therefore ask for death, for it is just.
But you will slay this fellow too, I trust,
For both of us deserve to die, not one."

This worthy duke then answered Palamon
At once. He said, "Then here's the long and short:
The confession from your mouth, your own report
Has damned you, so I'll thereby note the fact
That there's no need to flog or have you racked.
By mighty Mars the Red, you'll die and should!"

But then the queen, in all her womanhood,
Began to weep, and so did Emily
And all the ladies in their company.
They thought it such a pity, one and all,
That ever such misfortune should befall;
For gentlemen these were, of great estate,
And nothing but of love was their debate.
To see the two men's bloody wounds so wide,
Both young and old among the women cried,
"Have mercy, lord, upon us women all!"
And on their bare knees they began to fall,
And would have kissed his feet there as he stood.
At last, as pity rises in a good
And gentle heart, his anger finally slaked;
For though the duke at first with ire quaked,
He gave consideration with a pause
To what had been their trespass and the cause.
Though, to his mind, of guilt they stood accused,
His reason said that they should be excused;
He settled on the thought that every man
Will help himself in love all that he can,
And free himself from jail in any fashion.
And also in his heart he had compassion
For all these women who were still in tears.

He gently took to heart the women's fears,
Then softly told himself, "Fie on a lord
Who has no whit of mercy to afford,
Who's lionlike in all that's done and said
To those who are repentant and in dread,
As well as to a proud, defiant man
Who aims to finish that which he began.
That lord has no discriminating vision
Who can't in such a case make some division
But weighs pride and humility as one."
So when its course his wrath had shortly run,
Duke Theseus looked up toward the skies
And spoke aloud, a sparkling in his eyes:

"The god of love! Ah, *benedicite*!
How great a lord, how mighty is his sway!
Against his might there are no obstacles;
Call him a god for all his miracles.
For he can mold according to his muse
All of our hearts however he may choose.
This Palamon, this Arcite whom you see,
Were from my prison both completely free;
They might have lived in Thebes and royally so,
For they both know I am their mortal foe
And death for both within my power lies;
Yet love, in spite of all before their eyes,
Brought them back here to die, back to the brink.
Now this is some high folly, don't you think?
Who else may be a fool but one in love!
Look, for the sake of God who sits above,
See how they bleed! Are they not well arrayed?
Thus by their lord, the god of love, they're paid
For serving him, they have their fee and wage.
Yet they think they are wise who so engage
In serving love, whatever may befall.
But this is yet the biggest joke of all,

That she for whom they passionately vie
Can give them thanks about as much as I—
She knew no more about this whole affair
Than knew, by God, a cuckoo or a hare!
But all must be assayed, both hot and cold,
A man must be a fool, though young or old.
From long ago I know myself it's true,
For in my time I was love's servant too.
And therefore, since I recognize love's pain
And know full well love's power to constrain
(As one so often captured in his net),
This trespass I'll forgive and I'll forget,
As my queen has requested, kneeling here
Along with Emily, my sister dear.
But both of you shall swear to me: my land
Shall nevermore be threatened by your hand,
You shan't make war against me day or night;
You'll be my friends in every way you might,
Then I'll forgive this trespass as I may."
And they swore as he asked in every way,
And for his lordship's mercy then they prayed.
He granted grace, and then this speech he made:
"Regarding royal blood and riches too,
Were she a queen or princess, each of you,
I have no doubt at all, has worthiness
To marry her in time; but nonetheless
I speak now for my sister Emily
For whom you've had this strife and jealousy.
You know that two at once she cannot marry
No matter how this fight you choose to carry.
No, one of you, no matter what the grief,
Must go and 'whistle with an ivy leaf';
She cannot have you both, that is to say,
Be you as mad and jealous as you may.
This proposition, then, I put to you:
Each one shall have his destiny, his due,

However it's been shaped—and listen how,
For here's your end as I devise it now.

"My will is this (this matter to conclude
Once and for all, no protest to intrude,
So if you like it, make of it the best):
Where you may wish to go, by me you're blest,
Go freely, there's no danger in your way;
But after fifty weeks right to the day,
Each of you shall bring back one hundred knights,
Armed for the lists to represent your rights,
All set to fight for her. For here's an oath
That this is what shall be, I tell you both
Upon my word and as I am a knight:
When we have seen which has the greater might—
That is to say, whichever of the two
With his one hundred (as I've said to you)
Shall slay or from the lists the other drive—
To him I shall give Emily to wive,
To him who Fortune gives so fair a grace.
I'll have the lists built in this very place,
And—God bestow my soul with wisdom's order—
I'll be a true judge on the battle's border.
With me you have no other way to go,
One of you shall be killed or taken. So
If you believe this judgment is well said,
Advise me now and count yourselves ahead.
That is your end, that's how it shall be done."

Who looks as happy now as Palamon?
And who but Arcite springs with such delight?
Who could explain, who has the skill to write
About the joy witnessed in the place
That Theseus has granted such a grace?
Then everyone went down on bended knee
And gave him thanks in most heartfelt degree—
Especially the Thebans, more than once.

And so, with high hopes and ebullience,
The two then took their leave, they were to ride
Back home to Thebes, to walls so old and wide.

Part III

I know that men would deem it negligence
If I forgot to tell of the expense
To which Duke Theseus went busily
To build the lists. He built them royally,
A theatre so noble standing there
I daresay none was finer anywhere.
Its circuit measured one full mile about,
Its wall of stone, a circling moat without.
As surely as a compass it was round,
And sixty rows it stood above the ground,
So that a man on one row wouldn't be
The reason that another couldn't see.

On the east stood a great, white marble gate,
Another on the west. I'll briefly state,
Concluding, there was no such other place
In all the earth that took so little space.
For there was not one craftsman in the land
With math and his geometry in hand,
No single sculptor or one painter, who
Duke Theseus did not hire for the crew
That worked on this theatre. So that he
Might sacrifice, do all rites properly,
At the eastern gate he had built above,
In honor of Venus, goddess of love,
An altar and an oratory. Then,
Above the west gate, he constructed in
The memory of Mars the very same;
A cart of gold was spent in Mars's name.
In a turret, built on the northern wall
In coral and white alabaster all,

The duke had nobly wrought an oratory
Magnificent see, built for the glory
Of Diana, most chaste of deities.

Yet I've forgotten to describe with these
The sculptures, paintings, noble works of art,
The shapes and figures that were all a part
Of the work in these oratories three.

In the temple of Venus you could see
(Wrought on the wall, and piteous to behold)
The broken sleep, the lonely sighs, the cold
And sacred tears, the sad laments; the burning,
The fiery strokes of all desire and yearning
That servants of love in this life endure;
The oaths by which covenants they assure;
Pleasure and Hope, Desire, Foolhardiness,
Beauty and Youth and Riches, Bawdiness,
Seduction, Force, Falsehood and Flattery,
Extravagance, Ado and Jealousy
(Who wears a garland, yellow marigolds,
And in her hand a bird, the cuckoo, holds);
The banquets, instruments, the carols, dances,
Lust and array. All of the circumstances
Of love that I'm recounting here were all
In proper order painted on the wall—
And more than I'd be able to recount,
For truly all the Cytherean mount,
The place where Venus has her major dwelling,
Was in the scenes on that wall for the telling
With all its gardens and its lustfulness.
Nor was forgotten the porter Idleness,
Nor Narcissus, that ancient, fairest one,
Nor all the folly of King Solomon,
Nor yet the mighty strength of Hercules,
Medea's enchanting power nor Circe's,
Nor Turnus with a heart so fierce and bold,

Nor Croesus, rich but captive with his gold.
So you can see that neither wisdom, wealth,
Nor beauty, sleight, nor strength nor hardy health
Can hold with Venus an equality,
For as she wills she guides the world to be.
Look how these people, caught up in her snare,
So often cried "Alas!" in their despair.
Suffice here these examples one or two,
Though I could tell a thousand more to you.

Venus's statue, glorious to behold,
Was naked, and the sea about her rolled,
As from her navel down were shown to pass
Green waves that were as bright as any glass.
She had a harp in her right hand, and she
Had on her head, a seemly sight to see,
A fresh rose garland, fragrant as the spring.
Above her head her doves were flickering.
Before her Cupid stood, who is her son;
He had two wings and was superbly done,
And blind he was, as is so often seen.
He held a bow, and arrows bright and keen.

Why should I not as well tell you of all
The paintings that appeared upon the wall
In the temple of mighty Mars the Red?
From roof to floor the wall was overspread
With painted scenes like in that grisly place
That's known as his great temple back in Thrace—
That cold and frosty region where, I'm told,
He has his sovereign mansion from of old.

A forest, first, was painted on the wall
In which there dwelt no man nor beast at all.
Its knotty, gnarled trees were bare and old,
The stubs were sharp and hideous to behold;
And through it ran a rumble and a sough

As if a storm would break off every bough.
And downward from a hill, below the bent,
Stood the temple of Mars of Armament,
Made all of burnished steel. The entrance there
Was long and straight, indeed a sight to scare,
And out of it came such a raging wind
The very gate was made to shake and bend.

In through the doors there shone the northern light
(No window being in that temple's height
Through which to see a single light). Each door
Was of eternal adamant and, more,
Was reinforced as wide as well as long
With toughest iron. To make the temple strong,
Each pillar had the girth of any cask,
Each of bright shiny iron fit for the task.
There I first saw the dark imagination
Of Felony, the scheme of its creation;
Cruel Ire that burns till like a coal it's red;
The pickpurse and the pallidness of Dread;
The smiler with the knife beneath his cloak;
The stable burning up with blackest smoke;
The treachery of murder in the bed;
The wounds of open Warfare as they bled;
Strife with its threats and with its bloody knife.
With frightful sounds that sorry place was rife.
The suicide I saw, too, lying there,
The blood of his own heart had bathed his hair;
The driven nail in someone's head by night;
Cold Death laid out, his mouth a gaping sight;
Right in the temple's center sat Mischance,
Uncomforted, and sad his countenance;
There I saw Madness laughing in his rage,
And armed Complaint, Outcry and fierce Outrage;
The carrion found in the bush (throat slit),
A thousand slain, no plague the cause of it;

The tyrant with his booty, battle's gains;
The town laid waste till nothing now remains.
I saw the burning ships dance on the tide;
The hunter strangled by wild bears; I spied
The sow devour the child right in the cradle;
The scalded cook despite his lengthy ladle.
Not one misfortune that Mars could impart
Was overlooked; the carter by his cart
Run over, underneath the wheel laid low.
Of those who follow Mars, there were also
The barber and the butcher, and the smith
Who forges at the anvil, busy with
Sharp swords. Above, where seated in his tower,
I saw Conquest depicted in his power;
There was a sharpened sword above his head
That hung there by the thinnest simple thread.
The killing, too, was shown of Julius,
Of mighty Nero, of Antonius—
Though at that time they all were still unborn,
Their deaths appeared upon that wall forlorn
By threat of Mars and by prefiguration.
So it was shown in that wall's illustration
As is depicted in the stars above:
Who shall be slain and who shall die for love.
(Old stories tell it; one example's good,
I can't recount them all, although I would.)

His statue on its chariot, lifelike
In arms and grim, looked mad enough to strike.
Two starry figures shone above his head,
Puella one (as in the old books read),
The other one as Rubeus was known.
That's how this god of armament was shown.
There was a wolf before him at his feet
With red eyes, as a man he set to eat.
With subtle brush depicted was the story
Of Mars, redoubtable in all his glory.

Now to the temple of Diana chaste
As briefly as I can I'll turn with haste
To give you a description that's complete.
The walls all up and down were made replete
With scenes of hunting and of chastity.
I saw how sad Callisto came to be
(When she had caused Diana some despair)
Changed from a woman first into a bear
And then into the lodestar. (That's the way
That it was painted, what more can I say?)
Her son's also a star, as men may see.
There I saw Daphne turned into a tree.
(Diana I don't mean, she's not the same;
Peneus's daughter, Daphne her name.)
I saw Actaeon turned into a hart
(He saw Diana nude, which wasn't smart),
And then I saw his hounds run and surprise him
And eat him up (they didn't recognize him).
And painted on the wall was furthermore
How Atalanta hunted after boar,
As did Meleager and some others (though
For this Diana brought Meleager woe).
I also saw there many a wondrous tale
On which I'd rather let my memory fail.

This goddess on a hart had taken seat,
And there were slender hounds about her feet,
And underneath her feet there was a moon
(One that was waxing, to be waning soon).
Her statue was arrayed in green; she wore
A quiver filled, her bow in hand she bore.
Her eyes were looking down, extremely so,
Toward Pluto's dark region far below.
Before her was a woman in travail,
Trying to have her child to no avail
As to Lucina she began to call,

"Please help me, for your help's the best of all!"
How lifelike were these scenes the artist wrought!
The paint cost many a florin that he bought.

Now when these lists were finished, Theseus,
Who'd gone to great expense in building thus
The theatre and temples, was elated
With all of it as finally consummated.
On Theseus I'll cease now if I might,
Of Palamon to speak and of Arcite.

The day of their return was drawing nigh,
When each should bring one hundred knights to vie
For Emily in battle, as I've told.
To Athens, their covenants to uphold,
Each one of them thus brought one hundred knights,
Well armed and set for battle by all rights.
And certainly, as thought then many a man,
Not once before since this world first began
(Regarding knighthood, deeds of gallant hand),
As surely as God made the sea and land,
Had there been such a noble company.
For every man with love of chivalry
And who desired to make himself a name
Had prayed that he might take part in the game.
The chosen surely had no cause for sorrow;
If such a thing were taking place tomorrow,
You know right well that every lusty knight
Who loves his paramours and has some might,
Whether it were in England or elsewhere,
Would thankfully and willingly be there.
To fight for a lady, benedicite!
It was a lusty sight, this whole array.

The many knights who rode with Palamon
Were of that lusty spirit, every one.
Now some of these had chosen to be dressed

In hauberk, breastplate, and a simple vest;
Some wore two plates (both front and black, and large),
While some preferred a Prussian shield or targe;
Some liked to arm their legs against attacks
And have a mace of steel or else an ax.
There's no new armored style that isn't old,
They all were armed, as I have briefly told,
According to the liking of each one.

There you may see approach with Palamon
Lycurgus, who's the mighty king of Thrace.
His beard was black, and manly was his face.
The fellow's eyes were glowing in his head
With light that was half yellow and half red,
And like a griffin he would look about
From neath two shaggy brows. The man was stout;
He had great limbs, with muscles hard and strong,
His shoulders broad, arms barrel like and long.
As was the custom in his land, he rolled
Along upon a chariot of gold,
Four white bulls in the traces at the fore.
Instead of coat of arms Lycurgus wore
A bearskin that was coal black, very old,
Its yellow claws as bright as any gold.
His hair shone, long and combed behind his back,
Bright as a raven's feather, and as black.
His strong and shaggy head was underneath
A mighty weight, an arm-sized golden wreath,
Inlaid with bright and precious stones in plenty.
White wolfhounds were around him, more than twenty,
Each one of them as big as any steer,
That he would use to hunt for lion or deer.
They followed him with muzzles tightly bound,
Their collars gold with collar rings filed round.
He had a hundred lords there in his rout,
All fully armed. Their hearts were stern and stout.

With Arcite, as we find old tales relate,
The Indian king, Emetrius the Great—
His bay steed with steel trappings, covered by
A motley cloth of gold—came riding. Why,
The god of arms, new Mars he looked to be.
His surcoat was of cloth from Tartary,
With all the large white pearls that it could hold.
His saddle, newly forged, was burnished gold.
A mantle from his shoulders hung, attire
Brimful of rubies sparkling red as fire.
His crisp hair into ringlets seemed to run,
So yellow it would glitter like the sun.
His nose was high, his eyes bright and citrine;
He had full lips, and skin that had a fine
Sanguinity, with freckles on his face
From black to yellow and from place to place.
And like that of a lion was his gaze.
His age was twenty-five, I would appraise.
His beard had very well begun to grow;
His voice thundered like a trumpet's blow.
He wore a garland made of laurel, green
And freshly picked and pleasant to be seen.
Upon his hand he bore, to his delight,
An eagle that was tame and lily white.
He had a hundred nobles with him there,
Armed to the teeth with all a warrior's wear,
Fully equipped with all that battle brings.
For take my word that earls, dukes, and kings
Were gathered in this noble company
For love of and the growth of chivalry.
Around this king, among this noble tide,
Tame lions and leopards ran on every side.
And in this manner nobles all and some
Had on that Sunday to the city come,
There in the early morning to alight.
Now Theseus, this duke and worthy knight,

When he had brought them all into the town
To inns where they would all be bedded down
According to their rank, gave them a feast.
He honored all, ignoring not the least.
It still is said that none, however great,
Could have done better. Here I could relate
The music and the service at the feast,
The gifts both to the highest and the least;
The rich array with which he decked the place,
And who sat first and last upon the dais;
Which ladies were the fairest, danced the best,
Or which of them sang better than the rest;
Or who could speak most feelingly of love;
What hawks were sitting on the perch above,
What hounds were lying on the floor below—
Of all this I will make no mention, though.
To tell what followed seems the best to me,
So let's get to the point, if you agree.

That Sunday night, before day came along,
When Palamon had heard the lark in song—
It was two hours till day would begin,
And yet the lark sang—Palamon right then
In hopeful spirit and with holy heart
Arose, then as a pilgrim to depart
To Cytherea, blissful and benign
(That is, to Venus, honored and divine);
For in her hour he walked out to where
Her temple stood in the theatre. There
He knelt down with a humble, aching heart
And prayed, as you shall hear me now impart.

"O lady Venus, fairest of the fair,
Jove's daughter, wife of Vulcan, hear my prayer!
O gladness of the Cytherean mount!
By your love for Adonis—such amount!—

Have pity on my tears, their bitter smart,
And take my humble prayer into your heart.
Alas! I have no language that can tell
The ravages and torments of my hell,
The many ills my heart cannot convey;
I'm so confused there's nothing I can say
But 'Mercy, lady bright, who, as I kneel,
Knows all my thought and sees what woe I feel!'
Consider all and rue me, I implore,
As surely as I shall forevermore
(Give me the might!) your truest servant be
And always be at war with chastity.
I give to you my vow, give me your aid.
For I don't care to boast of arms displayed
Nor ask that mine shall be the victory
And fame; I do not seek the vanity
Of warriors' glory, praised both far and wide;
I wish but full possession as my bride
Of Emily, and death in serving you.
Determine now the way, what's best to do.
I do not care, whichever's best to be—
To vanquish them or have them vanquish me—
That I might hold my lady safe from harms.
For though it's true that Mars is god of arms,
Your virtue, Venus, is so great above,
If you but will it I shall have my love.
I'll worship at your temple ever biding;
At every altar where I may go riding
My sacrifice will be with fiery heat.
But if you will it not, my lady sweet,
I pray tomorrow, when we're fighting here,
Arcite will run my heart through with a spear;
Then I won't care, when I have lost my life,
Though he indeed should win her as his wife.
This is my prayer, it all concludes in this:
Give me my love, dear lady of all bliss."

When the prayer of Palamon was done,
He gave a sacrifice, and it was one
Of all good form and fullest piety.
(I won't go into all the liturgy.)
Then at the last the Venus statue shook
And made a sign to him, which he then took
To mean acceptance of his prayer that day;
For though the sign had come with some delay,
He well knew she had granted his request.
He hurried home with gladness in his breast.

Three hours after he had made his way
Out to the temple of Venus to pray,
The sun arose and so did Emily.
She started for Diana's temple, she
And all the maidens in her following
Who brought the fire to burn the offering,
The incense, clothes, all the accoutrements
Required for sacrificial sacraments;
As was the custom, horns were full of mead;
They brought all things that sacrificers need.
The temple smoked, the vestments all were fair,
As Emily, with heart so debonair,
Her body washed with water from a well.
How she performed the rite I dare not tell
Unless it's in a very general way.
(A pleasure it would be were I to say,
And, meaning well, there's nothing I could lose,
But it's good for a man to pick and choose.)
She combed her loose bright hair, smooth to the stroke.
A crown of green leaves taken from the oak
Was on her head, the arrangement meet and fair.
Two fires she kindled at the altar there
And then performed the rites (as men may note
In old books like the Theban Statius wrote).
The fire once lit, she in a piteous way

Addressed Diana, as you'll hear me say.
"O most chaste goddess of the woods so green,
By whom all heaven, earth, and sea are seen!
Queen of the realm of Pluto dark below!
Goddess of maidens! My heart you well know
And have for years, you've known what I desire.
O keep me from your vengeance and your ire,
For which Actaeon paid so brutally!
You've seen, chaste goddess, one desire in me:
I long to be a maiden all my life,
Not ever to be lover or a wife.
You know that I'm yet of your company,
A maiden who's in love with venery,
One who desires to walk the woods so wild
And not be someone's wife and be with child
Or have to know the company of man.
Now help me, lady, since you may and can,
By these three forms that you possess. I see
That Palamon has such a love for me,
And Arcite too, and for them I implore,
One grace I ask, and pray for nothing more:
That love and peace between the two you'll send
And turn their hearts from me, to such an end
That all their burning love and their desire,
That all their busy torment and their fire
Be quenched, or else turned to another place.
But if you will not grant me such a grace,
Or destiny is shaped in such a way
That I must have one of the two, I pray
You'll send me him with most desire for me.
Behold, O goddess of pure chastity,
Upon my cheeks the bitter tears that fall.
You are a maiden, keeper of us all;
My maidenhood now keep and well conserve,
And you, while I'm a maiden, I will serve."

The fires burnt clearly on the altar there
While Emily was kneeling in her prayer.
Then suddenly so strange a sight she flinched,
For all at once one of the fires was quenched,
Then lit again; and after that the other
Was gone as quickly, as if in a smother—
And as it went, it made a whistling noise
Like firebrands when they're wet. She lost all poise
When from the firebrand's end began to run
What looked like drops of blood, and many a one.
Poor Emily, aghast at such a sight,
Began to cry, half maddened in her fright,
Not knowing what this all might signify;
It was pure fear alone that made her cry,
And cry she did, a woeful sound to hear.
Just then Diana seemed there to appear,
Like any huntress, in her hand a bow.
"Daughter," she said, "put off your heavy woe.
Among the gods on high it is affirmed
By word eternal, written and confirmed:
You shall be wedded to one of the two
Who have endured such care and woe for you.
But as to which of them, I may not tell.
No longer may I tarry, so farewell.
The fires that here upon my altar burn
Shall say to you, before away you turn,
What in this case shall be your fate in love."
With that, the arrows in the quiver of
The goddess rang with noisy clattering,
Then she was gone. Upon this vanishing,
Astonished by the things that she had seen,
Emily said, "Alas, what can it mean?
I put myself now under your protection,
Diana, I shall follow your direction."
She then at once went home the nearest way,
And that was that, there is no more to say.

The next hour of Mars to follow this,
Arcite went to the temple in the lists
To offer fiery Mars his sacrifice
With all the rites that such a god suffice.
With piteous heart and very high devotion
He said to Mars the following orison.
"O god of strength, who in cold Thracian regions
Is honored as a lord by all your legions;
Who has in every realm and every land
All arms as but a bridle in your hand,
Whose fortunes are your pleasure, your device;
Accept, I pray, my humble sacrifice.
If it be by my youth I might deserve,
And by my strength have worthiness, to serve
Your godhead and to be among your train,
I pray that you'll have pity on my pain.
By that same pain, that same hot, blazing fire
In which you too were burning with desire,
When you once had the fair, the fresh young beauty
Of Venus—when you had her in your duty,
When in your arms you had her at your will
(Although there was a time it brought you ill,
The time when Vulcan caught you in his net
And found you with his wife, to your regret)—
By that same sorrow that was in your heart,
Now rue my pains as well, for how they smart!
I'm young, unknowing, as you are aware;
By love I'm hurt, and have much more despair
Than any creature ever drawing breath.
For she, for whom I must endure to death
This woe, cares not if I should sink or swim—
No mercy from her, not a trace or whim,
Unless by strength I win her in this place.
And well I know, without your help or grace,
My strength will not avail me in my plight.
So help me, lord, tomorrow in my fight.

By that same fire that once caused you to burn
(Those flames that now cause me as well to yearn),
Let victory tomorrow be my story;
Let mine be all the trial, yours the glory.
Your temple I will honor without measure,
Above all places; always at your leisure
And in your crafts I'll work in mighty manner.
And in your temple I will hang my banner,
And all the arms of all my company,
And henceforth, till the day I die, I'll see
That there's eternal fire before you found.
And also to this oath I will be bound:
My beard and hair, that now hang down so long
And never yet have suffered any wrong
From razor or from shear, I'll give to you,
And be long as I live your servant true.
Now, lord, look on my sorrow ruefully;
I ask for nothing more than victory."

Now when this prayer of strong Arcite was ended,
The rings that on the doors had hung suspended,
And then the doors themselves, began to clatter
(With Arcite somewhat frightened by the matter).
The altar fires began to burn so bright
That Mars's temple soon was all alight.
The floor gave up an odor sweet and grand.
Immediately Arcite raised up his hand,
As more incense into the fire he cast,
With other rites as well, when at the last
The statue's hauberk then began to ring,
And with the sound was heard a murmuring:
Though low and dim, and word was "Victory!"
Then Mars he praised and honored joyfully;
His hopes were high as to how well he'd fare
As to his inn he then went to repair,
As happy as a bird to see the sun.

And right away such strife was then begun,
By these accords, in the heavens above
Between fair Venus, goddess of all love,
And Mars, stern god of every sword and plate,
That Jupiter could hardly arbitrate—
Until his father Saturn, pale and cold,
Well taught by many fortunes from of old,
Recalled from his experience an art
By which they were appeased for each's part.
It's truly said the elder has advantage,
On wisdom and on life he has the vantage;
Men may outrun but not outsmart the old.
At once to end this strife he'd seen unfold,
Old Saturn (though it wasn't like himself)
Sought ways to put this quarrel on the shelf.

"Dear daughter Venus," Saturn said, "my course
Must take a lengthy turn, yet it's a force
And power like no man can bring to be.
Mine is the drowning in the pallid sea;
Mine is the prison cell where shines no speck
Of light; the strangling, hanging by the neck,
The murmur and rebellion of the throng,
The secret poison, and complaints of wrong;
I take revenge, complete correction's mine,
While I am dwelling in the Lion's sign.
Mine's the ruin of many high built halls,
The falling of the towers and the walls
On carpenter and miner. I'm the killer
Of Samson as he shook the mighty pillar;
And mine are all the maladies so cold,
The plans of all dark treasons from of old;
My glance is father of all pestilence.
Now weep no more, for by my diligence
This Palamon, who is your worthy knight,
Shall have her as you promised him tonight.

Though Mars shall help his knight, this has to cease,
Between you once again must be some peace,
Although you're not the same in temperament
(Which causes all the day such argument).
I'm your grandfather, ready at your will;
No longer weep, your wish I shall fulfill."

Now I will cease to speak of gods above,
Of Mars and Venus, gods of war and love,
And tell you now, as plainly as I can,
The end result for which I first began.

Part IV

Great was the feast in Athens on that day,
And such a lusty season was that May
That everyone took pleasure at the chance
To joust all of that Monday and to dance
And serve fair Venus as he might devise.
But by the fact that they would have to rise
Up early if they were to see the fight,
They finally went to bed that Monday night.

Next morning, when the day began to spring,
Of horse and harness, noise and clattering,
The sounds were heard in all the inns about.
Then to the palace rode a mighty rout
Of lords upon their steeds and palfreys. There
One might see many styles of knightly wear,
Exotic, rich, all wrought with great appeal,
Combining gold, embroidery, and steel;
Bright shields, headpieces, gear for all alarms,
Gold-tinted helmets, hauberks, coats of arms;
Lords robed on mounts, with knights in retinue
Attending to their needs; and squires too
Were in attendance, buckling up headgear
And strapping shields and nailing every spear
(The needs were such these squires were never idle).

The foaming steeds gnawed at the golden bridle,
While through the throng ran armorers also,
With file and hammer, pricking to and fro;
Yeomen on foot, and many commoners too,
With short staves, were as thick as could get through;
The pipe, the trumpet, clarion, kettledrum,
From which in battle bloody sounds would come;
The palace full of people wall to wall,
Three here, ten there, discussing one and all
The question of these two young Theban knights,
Some saying this, some that; as for the fights,
Some favored yon black-headed, some the bald,
While triumph for that thick-haired others called;
Some said, "He has a grim look, he can fight;
His ax weighs twenty pounds, that isn't light."
And so the hall was filled with such divining,
The sun long since arisen, brightly shining.

Great Theseus, now from his sleep awaking
To minstrelsy and noise they were making,
Within his splendid palace chamber stayed
Until the Theban knights, who both were paid
The honor due, were fetched. The duke with that
Made his appearance, at a window sat,
And like a god enthroned the duke was dressed.
At once all of the people forward pressed
To see him and to pay high reverence
And hear what judgments he might then dispense.

A herald on a scaffold bellowed "Hear ye!"
Until the noise quieted down; then he,
On seeing that the crowd below was still,
Disclosed to them Duke Theseus's will:

"Our lord discreet, upon deliberation,
Considers it would be a desolation
Of gentle blood here in this enterprise

To fight a mortal battle for the prize.
Wherefore, to see that no one here should die,
His former purpose he will modify.
No man, on pain of forfeiture of life,
Shall send a missile, poleax, or a knife
Into the lists, nor bring such weapons there;
No short, well-sharpened sword shall anywhere
Be drawn, nor shall one bear it by his side;
And no man shall against his fellow ride
With finely sharpened spear more than a course
(But may defend with it if off his horse).
And anyone in trouble they shall take—
That there should be no slaying—to a stake
That shall be ordered, one on either side,
Where he'll be put by force and there abide.
And if one of the chieftains, once we start,
Is taken, or has slain his counterpart,
The tournament is over, come and gone.
And so Godspeed! Go forward and lay on!
With long sword and with maces fight your fill.
Go on your way now, this is our lord's will."

High as the heavens rose the people's voice,
So merrily and loud did they rejoice.
"God save a lord so noble!" was the cry.
"He wills no blood be shed, that none should die!"
The trumpets blew, then with much melody
Toward the lists rode all this company
In order down the city's thoroughfare,
Where cloth of gold, no serge, hung everywhere.
This noble duke was lordlike on the ride,
With these two Theban knights on either side;
And after rode the queen and Emily,
And after that a mighty company
In groups that were arranged by social order.
They passed through all the city to its border,

Out to the lists, with none arriving late.
The hour of day was sometime after eight
When Theseus sat high and regally,
And Hippolyta and fair Emily,
With other ladies of degree about.
Then to the seats went pressing all the rout.
Then through the west gates under Mars the Red
Arcite immediately his hundred led,
His banner bright and red beneath the sun.
In that same moment entered Palamon
Under Venus on the east. His banner
Was white, and there was boldness in his manner.
In all the world, were you to seek throughout,
You'd find no other two such groups without
A difference, well matched in every way
Till there was no one wise enough to say
If either of the two had any edge
In worthiness or age or heritage,
So evenly, it seemed, the Thebans chose.
They lined up fairly, two opposing rows.
And when the name of everyone was read,
That in their numbers no one be misled,
The gates were shut, and this cry rang aloud:
"Now do your duty, knights so young and proud!"

The heralds cease their pricking to and fro;
Now trumpets and the clarion loudly blow;
There is no more to say but east and west
The spear now steady goes into its rest,
And sharpened spur into the courser's side.
They see now who can joust and who can ride:
Shafts splinter on the stout shields tough and thick;
Right through the breastbone one now feels the prick;
Up spring the spears some twenty feet in height,
Out come the swords all sharp and silver bright;
The helmets they begin to hew and shred,

Out bursts the blood in sternest streams of red;
With mighty maces bones they break and bust;
Right through the thickest throng one rides to thrust;
Strong steeds begin to stumble, there's a fall,
The rider underfoot rolls like a ball;
He parries with his shaft against a thrust,
Another with his horse now hits the dust—
He's wounded, so here's one whom they must take,
Despite his protests, over to the stake
Where by the ruling he will have to stay;
Another knight is led across the way.

At times Duke Theseus will have them rest,
Refresh themselves, and drink if they request.
And these two Theban knights time and again
Have clashed together, brought each other pain,
Each twice unhorsed now in their rivalry.
No tiger in the vale of Gargaphy
Whose young whelp has been stolen in the night
Is so cruel to the hunter as Arcite,
So jealous, is to Palamon; and there
Is not a hunted lion anywhere
In Benmarin, though crazed with hunger, so
Intent to slay, to spill blood of its foe,
As is fierce Palamon against Arcite.
The jealous strokes into their helmets bite,
Out runs the blood, down both their sides they bleed.

In time there comes an end to every deed,
As when that day, before the sun had set,
Strong King Emetrius charged forth to get
At Palamon as he fought with Arcite;
His sword out of his flesh took quite a bite,
Then twenty men grabbed Palamon, to take
Him, though he struggled, over to the stake.
Strong King Lycurgus moved with the intent
To rescue him, but down Lycurgus went,

While King Emetrius, for all his strength,
Got knocked from his saddle by a sword's length,
From Palamon receiving such a blow.
But to the stake now Palamon must go;
His hardiness of heart went all for naught,
He had to stay right there once he was caught,
By force and rules by which the jousts were run.
Who sorrows now but woeful Palamon,
Unable to return again to fight?
When Theseus had witnessed such a sight,
To those who fought, to each and every one,
He cried, "Hear ye! No more, for it is done!
As true impartial judge I now decree
Arcite the Theban shall have Emily,
For by his fortune he has fairly won."
Such noise by the crowd was then begun
In joy at this, so loud and high the sound,
It seemed the lists would fall right to the ground.

And what now can fair Venus do above?
What can she say or do, this queen of love?
She weeps at this denial of her will
Till with her tears the lists begin to fill.
"Without a doubt I'm put to shame," she cried.

"Be still, my daughter!" Saturn then replied.
"Mars has his will, his knight has all his boon,
But, by my head, you'll have your pleasure soon."

The trumpeteers, musicians playing loud,
And heralds loudly crying to the crowd
Were all in utter joy for Sir Arcite.
But stop and hear me now as I recite
A miracle that suddenly took place.

Fierce Arcite, to reveal his joyous face,
Had taken off his helmet. On his horse

He then set out across the lengthy course
While gazing up at Emily on high;
And she in turn cast him a friendly eye—
For womenfolk in general, I must say,
Will follow Fortune's favor all the way—
And she was all his joy, his heart's delight.

A Fury sent from Pluto bounded right
Out of the ground (sent by request, of course,
Of Saturn), which so frightened Arcite's horse
It turned and reared, and foundered in the act,
So quickly that before he could react
Arcite was thrown and landed on his head,
And lay there as if likely he were dead;
His breast was shattered by his saddlebow.
He lay as black as any coal or crow,
The blood rushed so profusely to his face.
Arcite at once was borne out of the place,
With aching heart, back to the palace. There
They cut him out of all his armored wear,
Then quickly but with care put him to bed;
For he was still alive and in his head
And crying evermore for Emily.
Duke Theseus, with all his company,
As he returned to Athens, made his way
With all the usual pageant and display;
For though mischance had surely cast a pall,
He didn't want to disconcert them all.
And men were saying, "Arcite shall not die,
His wounds shall all be healed." And they could sigh
As well in the relief that, though it thrilled,
The tourney ended up with no one killed—
Though some were badly hurt, and namely one
Who'd caught a spear, which through his heart had run.
For other wounds and for the broken arms,
Some had some salves and some had magic charms;

They drank of sage, all herbal remedies
Designed to save them their extremities.
This noble duke, as such a noble can,
Both comforted and honored every man,
And gave a revel lasting all the night
For all these foreign nobles, as was right.
For there was held to have been no defeat
Save what in jousts and tourneys one may meet;
Defeat was truly no one's circumstance.
To take a fall is nothing more than chance,
As to be led by force out to the stake,
With protest it takes twenty knights to break—
One man all by himself with twenty foes
And carried by his arms and feet and toes,
His courser being driven forth with staves
By footmen (some were yeomen, some were knaves).
No man could be maligned because of this;
There is no man could call it cowardice.

So Theseus at once gave the decree,
To stop all rancor and all enmity,
That one side's strength did not exceed the other's,
That both sides were alike, as if all brothers.
By rank he gave them gifts as well as praise,
Gave them a feast that lasted three whole days;
Then all the kings who had been at the tourney
He rode with from his town a lengthy journey,
And every man went home his proper way,
And that was that, with "Farewell!" and "Good day!"
So of this battle no more I'll recite,
But speak of Palamon and of Arcite.

The breast of Arcite swelled, the pain and sore
About his heart increasing more and more.
The clotting blood, despite physicians' art,
Corrupted as it spread out from his heart,

So that no bleedings nor the cuppings made,
Nor drinking herbal mixtures, were of aid.
The expulsive power (being the "animal")
From that one that is known as "natural"
Could not void all the venom nor expel.
The pipes within his lungs began to swell,
And every muscle that was in his chest
With venom and corruption filled his breast.
And there was nothing gained, that he might live,
By upward vomit, downward laxative,
For all had been so shattered in his breast
That Nature had no power to arrest.
And certainly if Nature won't work, tote
The man to church, farewell to antidote.
Arcite would die and that's the summary.
And so he sent for lovely Emily
And Palamon, his cousin once so dear,
And then he spoke as you will promptly hear.
"The woeful spirit that is in my heart
Cannot describe my sorrows, all the smart,
O lady whom I love, that you might hear it.
But I bequeath the service of my spirit
To you above all creatures on the earth,
Since now my life must end, for what it's worth.
Alas, the woe, alas, the pain so strong
That for you I have suffered for so long!
Alas, now death! Alas, my Emily,
Alas, bereft of your sweet company!
Alas, queen of my heart! Alas, my wife,
My heart's own lady, ender of my life!
What is this world? What is it men so crave?
Now with his love, now in his frigid grave
Where he's alone with none for company.
Farewell, my sweetest foe, my Emily!
Now softly take me in your arms, I pray,
For love of God, and hear what I must say.

"I have here with my cousin Palamon
Had strife and rancor many days, not one,
For love of you and in my jealousy.
O Jupiter so wise, be guide to me
To speak now of a servant as I should—
That is to say, of virtues like knighthood,
Like wisdom, honor, truth, humility,
High birth and rank, like generosity,
And all the things that are to these akin.
As Jupiter may take my spirit in,
In all this world right now I know of none
So worthy to be loved as Palamon,
Who serves you and will do so all his life.
And if you ever would become a wife,
Forget not Palamon, this gentle man."
And with those words, failing of speech began,
As from his feet up to his breast had come
The cold of death, which had him overcome;
In his once mighty arms the vital strength
Began to wane, till finally lost at length;
And then the intellect, all that remained
And dwelt within his heart so sick and pained,
Began to fail. The heart was feeling death;
His eyes were glazed, and failing was his breath.
His lady was the last thing he could see,
And his last words were, "Mercy, Emily!"
His spirit left its house and went to where
I cannot say, I've never journeyed there—
I'll stop, for I'm no good at divination;
This tale is not of souls for registration
Nor do I wish opinions here to tell
Of those who write of where a soul may dwell.
Arcite is cold, Mars guide his spirit free!
Now I will speak again of Emily.

She shrieked; Palamon howled, such was his plaint;
So Theseus then took his sister, faint,

And from the corpse at once bore her away.
But would it help were I to take all day
To tell how she wept day and night? For in
Such cases women have such sorrow (when,
That is to say, their husbands from them go)
They usually will grieve exactly so,
Or else fall sick with such a malady
That death comes to them too with certainty.

Unending were the sorrow and the tears
Of elders and of those of tender years
In all the town because of his demise;
For him both child and man had tearful eyes.
So great a weeping surely wasn't heard
When they brought Hector, slain, to be interred
At Troy. Alas, the mourning that was there,
Gashing of cheeks and pulling out of hair.
"Why dead?" the women cry. "Why should you be,
Who had both gold enough and Emily?"
No man could bring some cheer to Theseus
Except for his old father Aegeus,
Who knew this world with all its transmutation
As he had seen it change with alternation,
Joy after woe, and more woe after joy.
Then cases and examples he'd employ:

"Just as there's never died a man," said he,
"Who didn't live on earth to some degree,
So there's no man who's ever drawn a breath
In all this world whose time won't come for death.
This world is but a thoroughfare of woe
And we are pilgrims passing to and fro.
Death is an end to every worldly care."
And he had many other words to share
In this regard, that people might be taught
To take more comfort, not be so distraught.

Duke Theseus then took the greatest care
In looking for a proper setting where
They'd build for good Arcite a sepulchre
That most deserving honor would confer.
At last the duke decided on the one
Where at the first Arcite and Palamon
For love in battle with each other strove;
There in that very same green, fragrant grove
Where Arcite spoke his amorous desires,
Where he complained of love's hot burning fires,
For services a fire the duke would light
And at the pyre perform the funeral rite.
He gave command at once for them to mow
The ancient oaks and lay them in a row
Of fagots set for burning. Rapidly
His officers would run, immediately
To mount and ride away at his command.
And after this, the duke dispatched a band
To go and bring a bier, one fully clad
With cloth of gold, the richest that he had,
And with a matching suit he clad Arcite.
On Arcite's hands were fitted gloves of white,
Upon his head a laurel crown of green,
And in his hand a sword both bright and keen.
The duke then laid him barefaced on the bier
And wept till it was pitiful to hear;
And so that Arcite might be seen by all,
When it was day he brought him to the hall,
Which roared with all the crying and the din.

The woeful Theban Palamon came in
With frowsy beard and rough ash-covered hair,
His clothing black and stained with tears. And there,
Surpassing all who wept, came Emily,
The one most grieved of all the company.
Because he thought the services should be

Noble and rich for one of such degree,
Three steeds Duke Theseus then had them bring,
With trappings made of steel, all glittering,
And covered with the arms of Sir Arcite.
Upon these steeds, which all were large and white,
Were mounted men—one Arcite's shield to bear,
Another with his spear high in the air,
His Turkish bow the third one proud to hold,
With quiver and with trim of burnished gold.
And forth they sadly rode at mourners' gait
Toward the grove as you'll hear me relate.
The noblest of the Greeks from far and near
Upon their shoulders carried Arcite's bier
At slackened pace, their eyes a tearful red,
Along the city's main street. They had spread
Black cloth along the street, and from great height
The same hung on each side. Upon the right
Hand there came next the old man Aegeus
And on the other side Duke Theseus,
In hand fine golden vessels, which had in
Them milk and honey, blood and wine; and then
Came Palamon with a great company,
And after that came woeful Emily
With fire in hand (the custom of the day,
That all the rites be done the proper way).

Much labor and the greatest preparation
Were spent upon the pyre and ministration—
A pyre so high its top the heavens fetched,
And in its breadth some twenty fathoms stretched
(So broad were all the boughs, that is to say).
First there was many a load of straw to lay.
But how the pyre was made so high to reach,
And names of trees like alder, maple, beech,
Fir, laurel, plane, birch, poplar, aspen too,
Elm, willow, hazel, chestnut, aspen, yew,

Box, dogwood, ash, and oak, as well as how
They felled them all, I won't go telling now;
Nor how the deities ran to and fro
(The dryads, nymphs, and fauns), all forced to go,
Abandoning the habitations where
They'd known such rest and peace without a care;
Nor how the beasts and birds in those woods all
Began to flee as trees began to fall;
Nor how the ground was fearful of the light,
Not ever having seen the sun so bright;
Nor how with straw they first began the fire,
Then dry sticks split in threes to build it higher;
Then spices, then wood hewn from greenest limbs,
Then cloth of gold, along with precious gems
And many flowered garlands, myrrh, incense,
With odor great and pleasant to the sense;
Nor how among all this Arcite lay there
With riches all about him; nor how fair
And mournful Emily went to the pyre,
As was the custom, with the funeral fire;
Nor how she swooned as flames began to start,
Nor what she spoke, nor what was in her heart;
Nor what jewels into the fire were cast
When it was leaping high and burning fast;
Nor how one cast a shield, and one a spear,
And some parts of their clothes, about the bier;
Nor how the wine and milk and blood were poured
Into the fire, nor how it wildly soared;
Nor how the Greeks in one huge mounted rout
Three times from left to right then rode about
The fire with mighty shouts, and three times more
Gave out a clatter with their lances; nor
How thrice the ladies cried out piteously,
Nor how led home at last was Emily;
Nor how to ashes cold had burnt Arcite,
Nor how for him a wake was held that night,

Nor how the Greeks performed each funeral game—
To speak of such as that is not my aim
(Who wrestled best while nude and well anointed
And never got in trouble or disjointed);
I also shall not tell how everyone
Went home to Athens when the games were done.
To get right to the point I intend,
To bring my lengthy story to an end.

In course of time, the length of certain years,
There ended all the mourning and the tears
Among the Greeks by popular assent.
I think that there was then a parliament
In Athens to discuss affairs of state.
Among the things decided in debate
Was to ally themselves with certain lands
And also govern Thebes with firmer hands.
And so this noble Theseus decreed
That Palamon appear, as was agreed—
The reason why unknown to Palamon,
Who still in black, still as a mourning one,
Came at the duke's commandment hastily.
And Theseus then sent for Emily.
When they had sat, and hushed was all the place,
Duke Theseus was silent for a space;
Before a word came from the wise duke's breast,
He looked about, then his eyes came to rest.
His face was sad, he sighed as all was still,
Then he began to speak to them his will:

"When the Prime Mover, that First Cause above,
First made the chain so fair that's known as love,
The effect was great, and high was his intent—
He knew the *whys* and *wherefores*, what he meant.
For with that chain of love the Mover bound
The fire, the air, the water, and the ground

To certain bounds from which they may not flee.
And that same Prince and Mover," then said he,
"Established in this wretched world below
The days of the duration they may know,
All those who are engendered in this place,
Beyond which days they cannot take a pace
But which may well be shortened. Here we see
There is no need for an authority,
For it is proven by experience.
I want you to be clear as to my sense:
By this Prime Mover's order men are able
To see that he's eternal, always stable;
For every man should know, unless a fool,
Each part comes from the whole (a simple rule),
For Nature has not taken its beginning
From any part or portion of a thing
But from a thing that's perfect, without change,
Corrupted only in this lower range.
And so he has, in his wise providence,
Established without flaw his ordinance
That kinds of things in all of their progressions
Shall have endurance only by successions
And shall not be eternal. This is seen
With but a glance, you follow what I mean.

"Look at the oak, how long its flourishing
Since way back when it first began to spring;
It has so long a life, as men may see,
Yet wasted at the last is every tree.

"Consider, too, the hardness of each stone
Beneath our feet: each one we're treading on
Will finally waste away where it may lie.
The broadest river someday will be dry,
We see great cities wane till they have passed.
And so we see that nothing's born to last.

"Of men and women, we can also see
That in whichever term of life we be
(That is to say, in youth or else in age),
We all must die, the king just like the page,
Some in the sea, some in the bed serene,
Some on the battlefield, as men have seen.
There is no help, we all wind up one way.
So everything must die, well I can say.

"And who does this but Jupiter the king
Who is the prince and cause of everything,
Converting all that is back to the well
From which it sprung, as truly we can tell?
And here again no creature that's alive
Will find avail, however one may strive.

"Then it is wisdom, it appears to me,
To make a virtue of necessity
And take well that which we cannot eschew,
Especially that which is all our due.
Complaint is folly, whoso has decried
Resists the very one who is our guide.
And surely one's most honored if his time
Has come while in his excellence and prime,
When he can die still sure of his good name.
He's done to friend and to himself no shame;
Then should his friend be gladder at his death,
When it's with honor he yields up his breath,
Than when his name is faded later on
And he's forgotten, youth and glory gone.
So it is best, in terms of lasting fame,
To die while at the height of one's acclaim.

"To be opposed to this is willfulness.
Why do we groan, or let it so depress,
That Arcite in the flower of chivalry

Has passed away, with honor, dutifully,
Departing the foul prison of this life?
Why grieving are his cousin and his wife—
Whom Arcite loved so much—for his well being?
Can Arcite thank them? No, God knows, when seeing
How they offend themselves, not just his soul.
Yet these are feelings they cannot control.

"How shall I end this lengthy argument
Save after woe let there be merriment,
With thanks to Jupiter for all his grace?
And I advise before we leave this place
We take two sorrows and with them endeavor
To make one perfect joy to last forever.
Let's look to where most sorrow lies herein,
Where we can help amend and so begin."
He said, "My sister, this is my intent,
With the advice here of my parliament:
This gentle Palamon who is your knight,
Who serves you with his will and heart and might
(And always has since you first saw his face),
You shall have pity on, and by your grace
Shall take him as your husband and your lord.
Lend me your hand, for this is our accord,
And, as a woman should, show sympathy.
He's nephew of a king, and yet if he
Were nothing but a poor knight bachelor,
So many years he's served you, as it were,
And has for you known such adversity,
I'd still consider him most favorably,
For mercy should transcend one's social station."

To Palamon he said then in summation:
"I don't think there's a sermon I need bring
To get you to assent to such a thing;
Come here and take your lady by the hand."

The two at once were joined in the grand
And holy union that is known as marriage
Before the council and the baronage.
And so amid much bliss and melody
Has Palamon been wed to Emily;
So God on high, who all this world has wrought,
Has sent to him his love so dearly bought.
Now Palamon had all that's known as wealth,
To live in bliss, in richness and in health;
And Emily loved him so tenderly,
And he served her with such nobility,
That not one word between this man and wife
Would ever be of jealousy or strife.
So ended Palamon and Emily,
And God save all this lovely company! Amen.

THE PRIORESS'S TALE

Prologue

"O Lord our Lord, how marvelous thy name,
Spread so afar through this wide world," said she.
"Thy precious praise not only they proclaim
Who are among good men of dignity,
But from the mouths of babes thy charity
Is praised as well. Babes sucking at the breast
May often show their praises like the rest.
"Wherefore as best I can or may, in praise
Of thee and of that whitest lily flower
Who gave thee birth and is a maiden always,
To tell a tale I'll labor in this hour—
Increasing not her honor by my power,
For she herself is honor, root and palm
Of bounty (next to Christ), and our souls' balm.
"O mother Maiden, maiden Mother free!
O bush unburnt, burning in Moses' sight,
Thou who drew down, through thy humility,
The Spirit from the Godhead, to alight

In thee, conceiving, as thy heart grew bright,
The Wisdom of the Father—now this story
Help me to tell, related for thy glory!
"Lady, thy goodness, thy magnificence,
Thy power, and thy great humility
No tongue may yet express with competence;
For sometimes, Lady, ere men pray to thee,
Thou goest before in thy benignity,
Securing for us through thy orison
The light to guide us to thy precious Son.
"O blissful Queen, my learning is too weak
To be declaring thy great worthiness;
I cannot bear such burden, I would speak
As does a child who's twelve months old or less,
One who can scarcely any word express.
That's how I fare, and therefore hear my plea
To guide my song that I shall sing of thee."

The Prioress's Tale

A great city of Asia once contained,
Amid the Christians in majority,
A Jewry that a local lord maintained
For venal lucre, foulest usury,
Hateful to Christ and to his company;
And through its street all men might ride or wend,
For open was this Jewry's either end.
A little Christian school stood by this place
Down at the farther end, to which would go
Many a child of Christian blood and grace.
There they would learn, as yearly they would grow,
Such things as in that land were good to know—
That is, they learnt to sing and read, as all
Such children learn to do when they are small.
Among these children was a widow's son,
A little scholar seven years of age,
Whose daily wont was to this school to run;

And if he chanced to see at any stage
An image of Christ's mother, he'd engage
In that which he was taught: he'd kneel and say
His Ave Maria ere he went his way.
Thus was the youngster by this widow taught
Our dear and blissful Lady to revere;
And so he kept her near to him in thought—
A guiltless child learns quickly, seeing clear.
(Always when I recall this matter, dear
Saint Nicholas stands ever in my presence,
So young he was to do Christ reverence.)
And while his book this child was studying
As he sat with his primer in the hall,
Alma redemptoris he heard them sing,
As children learn from the antiphonal;
Nearer and nearer he would draw, that all
The words he might then hear, and every note,
Until the first verse he had learnt by rote.
He didn't know what all this Latin meant,
For in his tender years he was too young;
One day he begged a friend there to consent
To tell to him this song in his own tongue,
Or tell him why this song so much was sung;
That he might so instruct him was his plea
Many a time on bare and bended knee.
His friend (older than he) said to him thus:
"This song was written, so I've heard them say,
For our dear Lady, blissful, generous,
To praise her, and that she be (as we pray)
Our help and succor when we pass away.
I can no more expound, I'd only stammer;
I've learnt the song but still know little grammar."
"Then is this song composed in reverence
For our Lord's mother?" asked this innocent.
"Now certainly I'll learn with diligence
The entirety ere Christmastide is spent.

Though from my primer I shall thus relent
And get three beatings in one hour, I
Shall learn it all, to honor her on high!"
His friend taught him in secret after school
From day to day till he knew it by rote;
He boldly sang, and well by any rule,
He knew it word for word and note for note;
And twice a day it wafted from his throat
When off to school and homeward he would start.
On Christ's dear mother he had set his heart.
This little child, as you have heard me say,
As through the Jewry he went to and fro,
Would merrily be singing every day
O Alma redemptoris as he'd go,
The sweetness of Christ's mother piercing so
His heart that, praying to her his intent,
He couldn't keep from singing as he went.
That serpent known as Satan, our first foe,
Who has his wasp's nest in the Jewish heart,
Swelled up and said, "O Hebrew people! Woe!
Is this a thing of honor for your part,
That such a boy should walk at will, and start
To sing out as he's walking such offense
To spite you, for your laws no reverence?"
Thenceforth the Jews proceeded to conspire,
Out of this world this innocent to chase;
They found themselves a murderer for hire,
Who in an alley took his hidden place;
And as the child passed at his daily pace,
This curséd Jew grabbed hold of him and slit
His throat, and cast him down into a pit.
Into a privy place, I say, they threw
Him, where these Jews would purge their bowels. Wail,
O curséd Herod's followers anew!
Your ill intent shall be of what avail?
Murder will out, for sure, it will not fail;

That God's honor increase, and men may heed,
The blood cries out upon your curséd deed.
"O martyr, ever in virginity,
Now may you sing and follow ever on
The Lamb white and celestial," said she,
"Of whom the great evangelist Saint John
In Patmos wrote. He said that those who've gone
Before this Lamb and sing a song that's new
Are those who never carnally women knew."
This poor widow awaited all that night
Her little child, but waited all for naught;
When morning came, as soon as it was light,
Her face grown pale with dread and worried thought,
At school and elsewhere then her child she sought;
She'd finally learn, when she'd gone far and wide,
That in the Jewry he'd last been espied.
With mother's pity in her breast enclosed,
She went as if halfway out of her mind
To every single place where she supposed
It likely that her child there she might find;
And ever to Christ's mother meek and kind
She cried. At last, completely overwrought,
Among the curséd Jews her child she sought.
She piteously inquired, she prayerfully
Asked every Jew who dwelt within the place
To tell her if her child they'd chanced to see.
They answered, "Nay." But Jesus by his grace
Put in her mind, after a little space,
To cry out for her son, and where she cried
The pit wherein he lay was near beside.
O God so great, so praised in many a hymn
By mouths of innocents, behold thy might!
This emerald, of chastity the gem,
Of martyrdom as well the ruby bright,
With throat cut, facing up toward the light,
The *Alma redemptoris* began to sing

So loudly that the place began to ring.
The Christian folk who through that Jewry went
Came by and stopped to wonder at this thing,
And for the provost hastily they sent.
He came without the slightest tarrying,
With praise for Christ who is of heaven King,
And for his mother, honor of mankind;
And after that the Jews he had them bind.
This little child with piteous lamentation
Was taken up while still he sang. They had
A great procession then, its destination
The nearest abbey. By his bier his sad
And swooning mother lay to mourn the lad,
And scarcely when they had to interfere
Could they move this new Rachel from his bier.
To pain and shameful death this provost sent
Each of the Jews known to participate
In knowledge of the crime. They early went,
For no such cursedness he'd tolerate;
What evil shall deserve is evil's fate.
He had them drawn by horses, then he saw
That they be hanged according to the law.
Upon his bier still lay this innocent
Before the altar while the mass progressed.
After that, the abbot with his convent
Made haste that they might lay the child to rest;
With holy water by them he was blest—
Yet spoke the child, when sprayed with holy water,
And sang *O Alma redemptoris* mater.
This abbot, who was such a holy man
As all monks are (or so they ought to be),
To conjure this young innocent began:
"Dear child, I'm now entreating you," said he,
"By power of the holy Trinity,
To tell me by what cause you sing, for it
Would surely seem to me your throat is slit."

"My throat's cut to my neckbone," then replied
The child, "a wound that is of such a kind
That long ago indeed I should have died.
But Jesus Christ, as in books you will find,
Wills that his glory last and be in mind;
And for the worship of his mother dear,
Yet may I sing O Alma loud and clear.
"This well of mercy, Christ's sweet mother, I
Have always loved as best as I know how;
And when I was to forfeit life and die,
She came to me and bade me give a vow
To sing this anthem when I die (as now
You have already heard). When I had sung,
I thought she laid a grain upon my tongue.
"Wherefore I sing, and sing I shall again,
In honor of that blissful maiden free,
Till from my tongue they take away the grain.
For afterwards here's what she said to me:
'My little child, I'll fetch you, as you'll see,
When that same grain has from your tongue been taken.
Be not afraid, you will not be forsaken.'"
This holy monk (the abbot's whom I mean)
Pulled out the tongue and took away the grain:
The child gave up the ghost, soft and serene.
And when he saw this wonder so obtain,
With salty tears that trickled down like rain
He, groveling, fell flat upon the ground
And stilly lay there, as if he were bound.
Upon the pavement, too, the whole convent
Lay weeping, and they praised Christ's mother dear;
And afterwards they rose and forth they went
And took away this martyr from his bier;
Inside a tomb of stone, of marble clear,
They put away his body small and sweet.
There he remains. God grant we all shall meet!
O youthful Hugh of Lincoln, slain also

By curséd Jews, as is so widely known
(As it was but a little while ago),
Pray for us too (in sin we've wayward grown),
That gracious God, in mercy from his throne,
Increase his grace upon us as we tarry,
For reverence of his sweet mother Mary. Amen.

THE TALE OF SIR TOPAZ

Prologue

This miracle, when told, made every man
So sober that it was a sight to see—
Until our Host to joke with us began,
Then for the first time took a look at me.
"And may I ask, what man are you?" said he.
"You look as if you think to find a hare,
For always at the ground I see you stare.
"Come closer now, and look up merrily—
Attention, sirs, and let this man have place!
About the waist he's shaped as well as me.
Now he'd be quite a doll for the embrace
Of any woman small and fair of face.
He seems so baffling by his countenance,
Disporting with no one in any sense.
"Say something now, as other folks have done;
Tell us a mirthful tale, and promptly so."
"Sir Host," said I, "don't let me spoil your fun,
For now of other tales naught do I know
But for a rhyme that I learnt long ago."
"That's good enough," said he, "now shall we glean
Some worthy thing, if I judge by his mien."

The First Fit

Listen, lords, with good intent,
I'll truly tell of merriment,
A pleasant story, as
It's of a knight, a worthy gent

In battle and in tournament,
His name was Sir Topaz.
Where he was born lies distantly
In Flanders far beyond the sea,
Poperinghe was the place;
So noble was his father, free,
And lord of all that land was he,
As it was God's good grace.
Sir Topaz grew, a doughty swain;
His face was bread white, yet again
His lips red as a rose;
His hue was scarlet dyed in grain,
And I can say as sure as rain
He had a seemly nose.
Like saffron were his beard and crown
With hair that to his belt hung down,
His shoes were hide of Spain;
His hose of Bruges were colored brown,
He wore a thinnish silken gown
That cost him many a jane.
He'd hunt wild game such as the deer,
Along the river he'd appear
With gray goshawk for hawking;
A perfect archer (pretty near),
At wrestling he had not a peer,
Each ram he took a-walking.
And many a maiden, bright in bower,
Desired him—each impassioned hour
She'd best have slept instead;
For he was chaste, for all his power,
And sweet as is the bramble flower
That bears the hip so red.
It so befell upon a day,
To tell you truly as I may,
Sir Topaz wished to ride;
He got upon his steed of gray

With lance in hand and rode away,
A long sword by his side.
He'd pricked his way before he ceased
Into a forest—many a beast
Was there, both buck and hare;
And as he pricked both north and east,
He almost had, to say the least,
A sorry bit of care.
There herbs of various sizes grew,
It had setwall and licorice too,
And many a clove to offer,
And nutmeg like we put into
Our ale (whether it's old or new)
Or lay up in the coffer.
The birds sang, I can truly say,
The sparrow-hawk and popinjay,
A joy it was to hear;
The thrush as well sang out his lay,
The wood-pigeon upon the spray
Was singing loud and clear.
Such lust in Sir Topaz had sprung
When he heard how the thrush had sung,
He pricked as if insane;
His fair steed sweat, so sharply stung,
Till like a wet rag to be wrung,
His sides one bloody stain.
Sir Topaz, too, tired from the chase,
From pricking round at such a pace
With fierce heart so amazing;
So in the soft grass of the place
He lay, and gave his steed a space
To rest and do his grazing.
"Saint Mary, bless me!" then said he.
"What ails this love that's binding me
With head and heart so sore?
I dreamt through all the night, pardie,

An elf-queen would my lover be
And sleep beneath my gore.
"An elf-queen surely I will love,
For in this world none's worthy of
My love—no woman will I take
In town;
All other women I forsake,
For to an elf queen I'll betake,
In dale and over down!"
His saddle he was quickly on,
Went pricking over stile and stone,
An elf-queen for to see,
Till so far riding had he gone
That he found, in a land alone,
The Fairyland, country
so wild;
For in that land none of their own
Dared to go near this knight unknown,
Neither wife nor child.
But then a giant came to vaunt,
One who was named Sir Elephant,
A perilous man indeed;
He told him, "Child, by Termagaunt,
If you don't prick out of my haunt,
At once I'll slay your steed
With mace.
For here the queen of Fairyland,
With harp and pipe and all her band,
Is dwelling in this place."
The child replied, "As I may thrive,
Tomorrow with you I will strive
When I have all my gear,
And I am hoping, par ma fay,
That by this lance that I display
You'll sorely suffer here;
Your maw

I'll pierce in two, if that I may,
Before it's fully prime of day,
You shall not win or draw."
Sir Topaz drew back quick and fast
As stones at him this giant cast
With slingshot worth bewaring;
The child Sir Topaz from the scrape
Through grace of God made his escape,
And through his own good bearing.
Now listen, lords, yet to my tale
That's merrier than a nightingale,
I'll whisper up and down
How Sir Topaz, so trim and hale,
Now pricking over hill and dale
Has come again to town.
His merry men commanded he
To make both game and melody,
For he would have to fight
A giant whose heads numbered three,
All for the love and jollity
Of one who shone so bright.
"Have come," he said, "the minstrelsy,
And jesters telling tales for me,
While I arm as I must;
Romances that are royal,
Of pope as well as cardinal,
Of love as well as lust."
They fetched him sweet fruit of the vine,
A bowl of mead came with the wine,
And spicery for zest
Like gingerbread and cumin fine
And licorice, all to combine
With sugar of the best.
He dressed as white as any seen
In linen that was fine and clean,
Then breeches and a shirt;

A tunic next was his avail,
And over that a coat of mail
To shield himself from hurt;
And over that a fine hauberk
That was all wrought of Jewish work,
Strong-plated, too, at that;
And over that his coat of arms
So lily-white, against the harms
That he must then combat.
The shield he bore was gold and red,
Emblazoned on it a boar's head,
A carbuncle beside;
And then he swore on ale and bread
How "that great giant shall be dead,
Betide what shall betide!"
His jambeaux tough and leathery,
His sword's sheath was of ivory,
His helmet brassy bright;
His saddle was made of whalebone,
His bridle like the sun that shone
Or moon at brightest light.
Of finest cypress was his spear
(That bode of war, no peace was here),
The head was sharply ground;
The steed he rode was dappled gray,
And it would amble on its way
So gently all around
        The land.
Listen, my lords, for here's a fit,
And if you would have more of it
I'll take it right in hand.

The Second Fit

Now shut your mouth, for charity,
Sir knight as well as lady free,
And listen to my spell;
Of battle and of chivalry

And lady's love, as you will see,
At once to you I'll tell.
Men tell romances, strong and mild,
Both of Ypotis and Horn Child,
Of Bevis and Sir Guy,
Of Lybeaus and Playndamour,
But Sir Topaz the flower wore
Of royal chivalry.
His valiant steed he was astride,
Upon his way he seemed to glide
Like sparks out of the flame;
As for his crest, it was a tower
In which was stuck a lily flower—
God shield him, none to maim!
And so adventurous in his powers,
He slept in no house after hours
But slept out in his hood;
His pillow was his helmet bright,
And his horse fed nearby at night
On herbs both fine and good.
He drank spring water as withal
That knight did named Sir Perceval,
So worthy in his wear,
Till on a day—

THE TALE OF MELIBEE

Prologue

"No more of this, for our Lord's dignity,"
Then said our Host, "for you are making me
So weary with your utter foolishness
That, as all-knowing God my soul may bless,
My ears are aching from your cruddy speech.
The devil take such rhyming, I beseech!
At best this is rhymed doggerel," said he.

"Why so?" said I. "Why do you hinder me
More than you do another man although

I'm telling you the best rhyme that I know?"
"By God," he said, "I'll tell you in a word:
Your wretched rhyming isn't worth a turd!
The only thing you're doing's wasting time.
Sir, in a word, no longer shall you rhyme;
Let's hear you tell us in another style
Of verse, or else in prose, something worthwhile,
In which there's mirth or doctrine anyhow."
"Gladly," said I, "by God's sweet pain! I now
Will tell to you a little thing in prose—
One that you ought to like, as I suppose
(Or else you're very hard to please for sure),
A moral tale of virtue, one that's pure.
As it's been told at times in sundry wise
By sundry folks, allow me to advise
You first. You know that each Evangelist,
For all Christ's pains that for us he may list,
Won't tell each thing the way his fellow might;
But nonetheless their meaning's true and right
And all agree as to their stories' sense
Though in their telling there is difference;
Like some of them say more and some say less
When Jesus's sad passion they express
(I speak of Mark and Matthew, Luke and John),
Yet there's no doubt of what they're preaching on.
Therefore, my lords, you all I do beseech:
If you think that I vary in my speech
That way, and tell you proverbs that are more
Than any others you have heard before
(Compressed in this small treatise I select,
To give my subject matter more effect),
And find the same exact words I don't say
That you have heard some other time, I pray
Don't blame me. For in meaning you will find
That there's no difference of any kind
Between this merry tale I write and this

Small treatise on which it is based. Don't miss
One part, therefore, of what I have to say,
And let me tell you my whole tale, I pray."

THE NUN'S PRIEST'S TALE

Prologue

"Whoa!" said the Knight, "good sir, that's quite enough!
You've said what there's to say about such stuff
And even more—a little of distress
Is quite enough for most folks, I would guess.
As for myself, it's worse than a disease
To speak of those who had great wealth and ease,
Then hear about their sudden fall and grief.
The opposite is joy and great relief,
As when a man who is in poorest state
Climbs upward, Fortune lessening the weight,
Till he's abiding in prosperity—
A thing for gladness, so it seems to me,
And of such things it would be good to tell."

"Aye," said our Host, "by Saint Paul and his bell,
You speak the truth. This Monk, he chatters loud.
He tells how Fortune covered with a cloud
I know not what, and, too, of tragedy,
As you have heard. It is no remedy
For one to be bewailing, to complain
That such and such is done. It's all a pain,
Just as you say, to hear of such distress.

"Sir Monk, no more of this, God may you bless;
Your tale's a nuisance, you annoy us by
Such talk, it isn't worth a butterfly,
For in it we can find no sport or game.
And so, Sir Monk—or Sir Piers by your name—
I pray that something else you might expound.
But for your bells with all their clanging sound
(Those bells hung on your bridle), I confide,

By heaven's King who for all of us died,
I would have fallen long ago asleep
Although the mire might be so ever deep;
Then would your tale have all been told in vain.
For certainly, as clerks can well explain,
If there's a man who has no audience,
It doesn't help if he makes any sense—
Yet I know well there's sense enough in me
If anything's reported sensibly.
Say something of your hunting, sir, I pray."

"No," said the Monk, "I've no desire to play.
Let's have another tale, as I have told."
Then spoke our Host, his speech both rude and bold,
Without delay to the Nun's Priest. He said,

"Come forth, you priest—Sir John, now come ahead!
Tell something that will gladden us inside,
Be blissful, though a nag you have to ride.
So what if you've a horse both foul and lean?
If he will serve you, should you care a bean?
Be merry in your heart and always so."
"Yes, sir," said he, "yes, Host, so may I go,
If I'm not merry I know I'll be blamed."
To tell his tale at once the fellow aimed,
And here is what he said as he went on,
This gentle priest, this kindly man Sir John.

A widow who was rather old and poor
In a small cottage dwelt in days of yore,
Beside a grove that stood within a dale.
This widow whom I tell of in my tale
Had from the day that she was last a wife
In patience led a very simple life,
So little were her gain and property.
With what God gave her, though, she thriftily
Cared for her daughters and herself. Three cows

She had, no more, along with three big sows,
And but one sheep named Molly—that was all.
And sooty were the bedroom and the hall
In which she'd eaten many a scanty meal.
With pungent sauce she never had to deal.
No dainty morsel passed her throat, it's not
A fancy diet found in such a cot,
So overeating never caused her qualm.
A temperate diet was her only balm,
With exercise and a contented heart;
The gout did not stop dancing on her part,
And apoplexy never hurt her head.
She had no wine to drink, nor white nor red,
Her board was mostly served with white and black
(Milk and brown bread, of which she found no lack),
Broiled bacon, and sometimes an egg or two.
Her work was much like dairywomen do.

She had a yard that was enclosed about
By paling and a dried up ditch without,
In which she had a cock named Chanticleer,
In all the realm of crowing without peer.
His voice was merrier than the play
Of the church's organ each holy day.
And surer was his crowing than a clock
(Even that of the abbey), for this cock
By instinct knew each move of the equator
As it progressed, that none too soon nor later
But on the dot, fifteen degrees ascended,
He crowed the hour no clock so well attended.
His comb was finest coral red and tall,
And battlemented like a castle wall.
His bill was black and like the jet it glowed,
His legs and toes like azure when he strode.
His nails were whiter than the lilies bloom,
Like burnished gold the color of his plume.

This gentle cock commanded at his leisure
A flock of seven hens to do his pleasure,
His paramours and sisters, each of whom
Like him had wondrous coloring in her plume.
But she with fairest coloring on her throat
Was that one called fair damsel Pertelote;
Discreet and gentle, showing courtesy,
She was so gracious, such nice company,
Right from the day she was seven nights old,
That she had Chanticleer's heart in her hold
Completely, as if under lock and key.
He loved her, that was his felicity.
And such a joy it was to hear them sing,
At morning when the sun would brightly spring,
In sweet accord, "My Love's Gone Far Away."
(For in those days, so I have heard men say,
The beasts and birds alike could speak and sing.)

It so befell, as day began to spring,
That Chanticleer was on his perch, with all
His seven wives there with him in the hall,
Beside him being fairest Pertelote,
When he began to groan down in his throat
As men in troubled dreams have done before.
And when fair Pertelote thus heard him roar,
She was aghast and said to him, "Dear heart,
What's ailing you that makes this groaning start?
For shame, so sound a sleeper to complain!"

"My lady," Chanticleer sought to explain,
"I pray, don't take me wrong in my distress.
By God, I dreamt I was in such a mess
That even now my heart is full of fright.
May God," he said, "help me divine it right
Lest into foul captivity I go.
I dreamt that I was roaming to and fro
Here in our yard when I espied a beast

Much like a hound, who would have at the least
Laid hold of me and left me cold and dead.
His color was betwixt yellow and red;
His tail as well as both his ears had hair
With tips of black, unlike his coat elsewhere.
His snout was small, a glow was in each eye.
Still of that look I fear that I could die,
And this has caused my groaning, there's no doubt."

"Oh fie," she said, "faint-hearted you've turned out!
Alas," said she, "for by the Lord above,
Now you have lost my heart and all my love.
I cannot love a coward, there's no way!
For certainly, whatever women say,
We all desire, if heaven let it be,
Wise, hardy men of generosity,
Husbands discreet—not niggards, fools aghast,
Afraid of every weapon that comes past,
Nor haughty boasters. By that God above,
How dare you say, for shame, to your true love
That anything can make you so afeard!
Have you no manly heart to match your beard?
Alas! can you be so afraid of dreams?
Illusion's all it is, not what it seems.
Such dreams from overeating come to pass,
Or else from humors (if not simply gas)
When they get too abundant as they might.
For sure this dream that you have had tonight
Resulted from there being great excess
In your red bile—the very thing, God bless,
That makes folks when they're dreaming have such dread
Of arrows or of fire that's flaming red,
Of red beasts that pursue to bite and maul,
Of strife and of fierce dogs both great and small;
Like melancholy's humor comes about
To make so many sleeping men cry out

For fear of big black bears, and bulls to boot,
Or else black devils that are in pursuit.
Of other humors I could tell also
That torture many a sleeping man with woe,
But I will pass as lightly as I can.

"Look at Cato, who was so wise a man:
Did he not say to 'pay no mind to dreams'?
Now, sire," she said, "when we fly from the beams,
For love of God please take a laxative.
On peril of my soul, as I may live,
This counsel is the best, I will not lie:
Of choler and of melancholy hie
To purge yourself. And there's no need to tarry
Though in this town there's no apothecary,
For I myself will teach you of the herbs
That aid your health when choler so disturbs;
And in our yard these very herbs I'll find,
And these will by their property and kind
Purge you beneath as well as purge above.
For this do not forget, for God's own love:
You have a very choleric temperament.
Beware unless the sun in its ascent
Should find you with hot humors so intense;
For if it does, then I would bet a fourpence
You'll have a tertian fever or an ague,
And either one could be a bane to you.
A day or two you'll have some worm digestives,
Then after that you'll take your laxatives—
Some laurel, fumitory, centaury,
Or hellebore, that grows here as you see;
Or else the caper and the dogwood berry,
Or ivy growing in our yard so merry.
Go pick them where they grow and take them in.
Be merry, husband, by your father's kin,
And do not dread a dream. I say no more."

"Madam," said he, "I thank you for your lore.
But nonetheless, concerning Master Cato
(So much renowned for all his wisdom, though
He said that dreams are not a thing to dread),
By God, in many old books it is read
That many a man of more authority
Than ever Cato was—or woe is me—
Says the exact reverse of Cato's sentence,
And has discovered by experience
That dreams have often been significations
Of joy as well as tribulations
That folks endure as this life may present.
Of this there is no need for argument,
Experience is proof enough indeed.

"One of the greatest authors men may read
Says once upon a time two fellows went
Upon a pilgrimage with good intent,
And came upon a town wherein they found
Such people congregated all around
That there was lack of lodging. Up and down
They couldn't find one cottage in the town
In which they both might be accommodated.
And so it was, as circumstance dictated,
That for the night they parted company
And each of them sought his own hostelry
And took his lodging as it might befall.
So one of them was lodged inside a stall
In a barnyard with oxen of the plow;
The other one lodged well enough somehow,
Whether it was by fate or by the fortune
That governs each of us in equal portion.

"It so befell that long before the day,
This man dreamt in his bed there as he lay
That he could hear his friend begin to call,
Saying, 'Alas! for in an ox's stall

Tonight I will be murdered where I lie.
Dear brother, come and help me or I die.
Come here,' said he, 'as quickly as you can!'
Out of his sleep with fright uprose the man;
But once awake, he was not overwrought
And lay back down without a further thought—
He felt such dreams were only fantasy.
Twice in his sleep this vision came to be,
And then he thought his friend had come again
For yet a third time, saying, 'I am slain!
Behold my bloody wounds so wide and deep!
Rise early in the morning from your sleep
And at the west gate of the town,' said he,
'A cart that's full of dung there you shall see,
In which my hidden body is contained.
Now boldly see that this cart be detained.
They murdered me, in truth, to get my gold.'
Then each detail of how he died he told
With such a piteous face, so pale of hue.
And you can trust he found the dream was true;
For in the morning, at the break of day,
To his friend's lodging place he took his way;
And when he came upon the ox's stall
For his companion he began to call.

"Here's what at once he heard the hosteler
Reply: 'Your friend is gone. The fellow, sir,
Went out of town as soon as it was day.'
The man became suspicious right away,
Recalling what he dreamt. He didn't wait
A minute more, but to the western gate
Out of the town he went, and saw at hand
A dung cart headed out to dung some land
(At least it so appeared), and its array
Was just as you have heard the dead man say.
Then he began to cry out heartily

For justice to avenge this felony:
'My friend last night was murdered, here to lie
Flat on his back inside this cart! I cry
Out to you ministries, all you,' said he,
'Who in this town are in authority,
For help! Alas, my friend is lying slain!'
What more about the tale need I explain?
The people cast the cart then to the ground,
And in the midst of all the dung they found
The dead man who so lately had been slain.

"O blessed God, so just and true, again
As always murder is revealed by thee!
Murder will out, as day by day we see;
It's loathsome and abominable to God,
Who, just and reasonable, spares not the rod,
Will not allow that murder hidden be.
Though it abide a year, or two or three,
Murder will out, that's all I have to say.
The officials of the town without delay
Commanded that the carter then be racked;
The hosteler was tortured, too, in fact,
And soon they both confessed to their misdeed,
And hanging by the neck was then decreed.

"Here men may see that dreams are things to dread.
And truthfully in that same book I read,
In the very next chapter after this
(I speak the truth, or banish me from bliss),
Of two who would have sailed the ocean for
A certain cause upon some foreign shore,
Had not the wind developed so contrary
That in a city they were forced to tarry—
A merry city on the harborside.
But then one day, when it was eventide,
The wind began to change to suit them best;

Jolly and glad the two went to their rest,
That early they might sail when day began.
But then great marvel fell upon one man;
It happened as he slept, for as he lay
He dreamt a wondrous thing toward the day.
He thought a man was standing at his side,
One who commanded that he should abide.
'Tomorrow if you sail as you intend,
You shall be drowned. My tale is at an end.'
He woke and told his friend the dream and prayed
That he'd agree his voyage be delayed.
One day, at least, he begged him to abide.
His friend, though, from his bed nearby his side
Began to laugh, and scorn upon him cast.
'No dream,' said he, 'makes my heart so aghast
That I'll delay to do as best it seems.
I do not give a straw for all your dreams.
For dreams are just illusions, only japes.
Men always dream of owls or else of apes,
Of things amazing to absurd degree,
Things that have not, and will not, come to be.
But as I see that here you will abide,
Thereby forsaking willfully the tide,
God knows I'm sorry and I say "Good day."'
And so he took his leave and went his way.
But half his course the fellow hadn't sailed
When—I don't know by what mischance it failed—
Quite suddenly the vessel's bottom rent
And ship and man beneath the waters went,
In sight of other ships that were beside,
That sailed with him upon that very tide.
And so, my dear and fairest Pertelote,
Of old examples such as this take note.
No man should act so carelessly about
His dreams. I say to you without a doubt
That many a dream is one to sorely dread.

"Look, in the life of Saint Kenelm I've read
(His father was Kenulphus, noble king
Of Mercia) how he dreamt a dreadful thing
A little before his death. Upon that day
He dreamt about his murder. Right away
His nurse explained it in detail, and she
Then bade him guard himself from treachery.
But as he was but seven years of age,
He put too little stock in dreams to gauge
One of them right, so holy was his heart.
By God, I'd give my shirt if, for your part,
You would have read this legend as have I!
"Dame Pertelote, I'm telling you no lie.
Macrobius says a dream came long ago
In Africa to worthy Scipio
That was affirmed, and says that dreams can mean
A warning of things men have later seen.
And furthermore, I pray you take a look
In the Old Testament. Look in the Book
Of Daniel—were his dreams all vanity?
Or read of Joseph and there you will see
That dreams are sometimes (I don't say they're all)
A warning of things that later befall.
Look at the king of Egypt, mighty Pharaoh,
His baker and his butler—did they know
Nothing of dreams' effects? Whoever traces
Through history the events of sundry places
May read of visions many a wondrous thing.
Did Croesus, when he was the Lydian king,
Not dream that he was sitting on a tree,
Which signified that hanged he was to be?
Look at Andromache, young Hector's wife:
The day that Hector was to lose his life,
She had a dream that day before the dawn
Of how his life was to be lost if on
That morning he should go into the fray.
She warned him but to no avail; that day

He still went forth to fight the foe again,
And promptly by Achilles he was slain.
But that's a story much too long to tell;
It's almost day, on such I cannot dwell.
For my conclusion I will simply say
That from this vision I shall have someway
Adversity. And I say furthermore
That in these laxatives I put no store—
They're venomous, I'm well aware of it.
Fie on them, for I like them not a bit!

"Now let us speak of mirth, no more of this.
Dame Pertelote, if ever I have bliss,
One thing God's given me with special grace;
For when I see the beauty of your face,
The scarlet red you have about your eyes,
It makes my dread all wither and it dies,
As certainly as *In principio,*
Mulier est hominis confusio—
Madam, the meaning of this Latin is
'A woman is man's joy and all his bliss.'
For when I feel at nighttime your soft side
(Although, alas, upon you I can't ride,
Because our perch is built so narrowly),
Such joy and comfort swell inside of me
That I defy nightmare as well as dream."
And with that word he flew down from the beam,
For it was day. His hens flew to the ground,
And with a "chuck" he called them, for he found
That in the yard a bit of kernel lay.
Royal he was, his fear had gone away.
Dame Pertelote was feathered by this cock
And trodden twenty times ere nine o'clock.
Then, with a grim look like a lion's frown,
Upon his toes he wandered up and down,
Not deigning to set foot upon the ground.

He chucked each time another corn he found,
And all his wives came running to his call.
Thus royal as a prince within his hall
I leave this Chanticleer there in his yard.
To his adventure next I'll give regard.

Now when the month in which the world began
(The month of March, when God created man)
Was over and indeed had been exceeded
(The days were thirty-two that were completed),
It happened that this cock in all his pride,
His seven wives all walking by his side,
Cast eyes up to the brightly shining sun
That in the sign of Taurus then had run
Some twenty-one degrees and even more.
He knew by nature and no other lore
That it was nine, and blissfully he crew.
"The sun," he said, "has climbed the heavens through
More than forty and one degrees, no less.
Now Madam Pertelote, my happiness
On earth, hear how these blissful birds all sing,
And see the newborn flowers, how they spring;
My heart is full of solace, revelry!"
But sad fate then befell him suddenly;
The latter end of joy is always woe.
God knows how worldly joy will quickly go;
A rhetorician who can well indite
Might safely in his chronicle so write,
For it's a royal notability.
Let every wise man listen now to me—
This story is as true, I undertake,
As the book of Lancelot of the Lake
That women hold so much in great esteem.
And so I'll turn again now to my theme.

A black-marked fox, iniquitous and sly,
Who'd lived for three years in the grove nearby

(By heaven's high design right from the first),
That very night had through the hedges burst
Into the yard where Chanticleer the Fair
And all his wives were accustomed to repair.
There in a bed of cabbages he lay
Completely still till well into the day,
Waiting his time on Chanticleer to fall,
As gladly do homicides one and all
Who wait to ambush and to murder men.
O false murderer, lurking in your den!
O new Iscariot, new Ganelon!
O false dissembler, like the Greek Sinon
Who brought the Trojans sorrow so severe!
A curse upon that day, O Chanticleer,
When to that yard you flew down from the beams!
Full warning you were given by your dreams,
That very day would bring adversity.
But that which God foreknows is what must be,
Or so, at least, some learned men contest.
As any worthy scholar will attest,
In schools there is a lot of altercation
About the matter, mighty disputation
(A hundred thousand men are in the rift).
In this the grain from chaff I cannot sift
As can the holy doctor Augustine,
Boethius, or Bishop Bradwardine,
Whether God's knowing what our futures bring
Constrains me so that I must do a thing
(By which I mean simple necessity),
Or whether there's free choice granted me
To do the thing or not (though there is naught
That God does not foreknow before it's wrought),
Or if his knowing constrains not one degree
Beyond conditional necessity.
But I will have no part of such debate;
My tale is of a cock, as I'll relate,

Who took his wife's advice, to his dismay,
And walked within the yard that very day
Despite what he had dreamt, as I have told.
How often women's counsels prove so cold;
A woman's counsel brought us first to woe,
From Paradise poor Adam had to go,
From where he'd been so merry and at ease.
But as I don't know whom it might displease
If I should give to women's counsel blame,
Please let it pass, I'm only making game.
Read authors where such stuff is their concern,
And what they say of women you may learn.
These words have been a cock's, they are not mine;
No harm in any woman I divine.

Sunbathing in the sand, fair Pertelote
Lay blithely by her sisters, while the throat
Of Chanticleer made song as merrily
As that of any mermaid in the sea.
(The Physiologus, with truth to tell,
Says mermaids sing both merrily and well.)
It so befell that as he cast his eye
On the cabbage bed, to catch a butterfly,
He caught sight of the fox there lying low.
He didn't have the least desire to crow—
He cried at once "Cock, cock!" with quite a start,
As any man fear-stricken in his heart.
By instinct every beast desires to flee
When he has seen his natural enemy,
Though never laying eyes on him before.

This Chanticleer would not have tarried more
Once he espied the fox, had not the latter
Said, "Gentle sir, alas! what is the matter?
I am your friend—are you afraid of me?
I'd be worse than a fiend, most certainly,

To do you harm. And please don't think that I
Come here upon your privacy to spy;
The reason that I've come is not a thing
Except that I might listen to you sing.
For truly you've a voice as merry, sire,
As any angel's up in heaven's choir.
Because of this, in music you've more feeling
Than had Boethius, or all who sing.
My lord, your father (his soul blessed be)
And mother (she of such gentility)
Have both been in my house, to my great pleasure.
To have you, sir, I'd love in equal measure.
For when men speak of singing, I must say—
As may my eyes see well the light of day—
Till you, I never heard a mortal sing
As did your father when the day would spring.
And all he sang was surely from the heart;
That more strength to his voice he might impart,
He used to strain himself until his eyes
He'd have to blink, so loud were all his cries;
And he would have to stand up straight on tiptoe
And stretch his neck as far as it would go.
And he was one of such discretion, sire,
No man was to be found in any shire
Who could in song and wisdom him surpass.
I've read the story Sir Burnel the Ass,
Wherein it's said that there was once a cock
Who from a priest's son suffered quite a knock
Upon his leg (a foolish lad's caprice),
For which he made him lose his benefice.
But there is no comparing to be based
Upon your father's wisdom, his good taste,
And a wounded cock's avenging subtlety.
Now, sir, please sing, for holy charity;
Let's see how well your father you repeat."
Then Chanticleer his wings began to beat,

As one who'd been betrayed but couldn't see,
So ravished was he by such flattery.

Alas! my lords, there are within your courts
False flatterers and other lying sorts
Who please you, by my faith, more than the man
Who speaks to you the truth as best he can.
In Ecclesiastes read of flattery;
Beware, my lords, of all their treachery.

This Chanticleer stood high upon his toes;
Stretching his neck, he let his two eyes close
And loudly he began to crow. Apace
The fox Sir Russell sprang out from his place
And by the throat grabbed Chanticleer. He bore
Him on his back toward the woodland, for
The fox as yet by no one was pursued.

O Destiny, you cannot be eschewed!
Alas, that Chanticleer flew from the beams!
Alas, his wife did not believe in dreams!
And on a Friday fell all this distress.

O Venus, goddess of all pleasantness,
Since servant you have had in Chanticleer,
Who used his powers in your service here
More for delight than world to multiply,
Why would you suffer him this day to die?
O Geoffrey, sovereign master, when was shot
And slain your worthy Richard, did you not
Complain so sorely of his death? O would
I had your gift and lore, so that I could
Chide Friday as you did! (For it was on
A Friday Richard died, as is well known.)
Then I would show you how I could complain
For Chanticleer, for all his fear and pain.

Surely not such a cry or lamentation
Did ladies make at Troy's devastation—
When Pyrrhus seized King Priam by the beard
And with his straight, unsparing sword then speared
And slew him (so relates the Aeneid's bard)—
As made all of the hens there in the yard
When they had seen the plight of Chanticleer.
Shrieked Pertelote so loudly all could hear,
More loudly than did King Hasdrubal's wife
When her husband at Carthage lost his life
And Romans made the town a conflagration.
(So filled with torment and with indignation,
The queen jumped willfully into the fire
And burnt to death, as death was her desire.)
O woeful hens, your crying is the same
As when by Nero Rome was set aflame
And tears were shed by senators' wives
Because their husbands all then lost their lives.
(They had no guilt but Nero had them slain.)
Now to my tale I will return again.

This simple widow and her daughters heard
The woeful crying of the hens. They stirred
Themselves at once, leapt up and ran outside;
The fox toward the grove they then espied,
Bearing away the cock upon his back.
They cried out "Help!" and "Mercy!" and "Alack!
Hey, hey, the fox!" And after him they ran,
And joining in with staves came many a man,
And our dog Collie, Talbot too, and Garland,
And Malkin with a distaff in her hand.
Ran cow and calf and even all the hogs,
So frightened by the barking of the dogs
And shouting of each woman, every man.
They thought their hearts would burst, so hard they ran.
They yelled like fiends in hell, such was the cry;

The ducks all quacked as if about to die;
The geese in fear flew up above the trees;
Out of the hive there came a swarm of bees.
God knows, the noise was hideous and loud!
I'm certain that Jack Straw and all his crowd
Did not produce a shouting half as shrill
(When they had found a Fleming they could kill)
As all the noise directed at the fox.
They brought out trumpets made of brass and box,
Of horns and bone, on which they blew and tooted;
They also shrieked, they whooped as well as hooted,
Until it seemed that heaven itself would fall.

Good men, I pray, please listen one and all,
For see how Fortune upsets suddenly
The hope and pride now of her enemy!
This cock, who on the fox's back still lay,
Despite his fear said to the fox, "I say,
What I would do, my lord, if I were you,
So help me God, is tell those who pursue,
'Turn back, you fools, you haughty churls all,
And may a pestilence upon you fall!
For now that I have reached the woodland's side,
In spite of you this cock shall here abide—
I'll eat him up right now in front of you!'"

The fox replied, "In faith, that's what I'll do."
But as he spoke those words, without a pause
The cock broke nimbly from the fox's jaws
And immediately flew high up in a tree.
And when the fox had seen his captive flee,
"Alas," he said, "O Chanticleer, alas!
Against you I am guilty of trespass.
I made you fear what it was all about,
To grab you in the yard and bring you out.
But, sir, I did it with no ill intent.

Come down, and I will tell you what I meant—
The truth, so help me God! You have my oath."

"Nay," said the cock, "a curse upon us both.
And first I curse myself, by blood and bone,
If more than once I let you lead me on.
You shall no more, with words so flattering,
Inveigle me to close my eyes and sing.
For him who wills to blink when he should see,
God never let there be prosperity!"

"No," said the fox, "but God bring to defeat
One whose demeanor is so indiscreet
That when he ought to hold his peace he chatters."

Lo, such it is to trust in one who flatters,
Be negligent, and act so carelessly.

But you who judge this tale frivolity
(As it's about a fox, or cock and hen),
Take seriously the moral, gentlemen.
For all that has been written, says Saint Paul,
Is written so that we might learn it all.
So take the fruit and let the chaff be still.

Now, gracious God, if it should be thy will,
As says my lord, make all of us good men
And bring us to high heaven's bliss! Amen.

INTRODUCTION TO
Boniface VIII
CLERICIS LAICOS & UNAM SANCTAM

The tragicomic saga of conflicts between princes and popes that dominated the later Middle Ages reached its climax—and its low point—the ugly high-stakes brawl between Pope Boniface VIII and King Philip IV of France from 1296–1303. The episode reflected badly on all parties, and ended ignominiously for Boniface himself, but not before producing an enduring statement of some of the most extreme pretensions of the medieval Catholic church.

There was, of course, no neat distinction of church and state in the Middle Ages in the modern sense—after all, every member of Western European society was in theory a Christian. But there was a sharp distinction of clergy and laity, and with it, a series of escalating conflicts about just how much power each party had. On the one hand, the Church had succeeded in establishing the clergy as a virtually autonomous state-within-a-state in each of Western Europe's kingdoms: they were immune from taxes, from civil courts, and from many laws, ultimately answerable to the pope alone. As rising royal powers sought to contest this autonomy (after all, the Church's estates were often fabulously rich, and their tax immunity took a huge bite out of royal revenues), the popes for their part often went even further, claiming not merely sole authority over the clergy, but an indirect authority over lay rulers as well. Christ had given Peter "two swords" (Luke 22:38) which referred to the sword of spiritual authority and that of temporal authority. To be sure, the pope normally delegated the latter to kings and princes, but he could in principle intervene directly in civil affairs or even depose rulers when he saw fit. If he had seen fit only for holy and spiritual reasons, things might not have been so bad, but many popes of this period were as worldly and ambitious as their royal rivals.

Boniface VIII, although apparently sincere in his commitment to the theological principles which undergirded his sometimes extraordinary claims, was not a particularly likable character. Scholar Brian Tierney describes him as "an arrogant, very able ruler, impatient of opposition, given to hot outbursts of rage" and his rival, Philip IV, as "a man of cold ambition."[1] Their particular dispute, though rooted in the long-simmering conflicts described above, emerged out of one of France's regular wars with England. Both parties, desperate to fund their "just war" against one another, resorted to taxing the clergy within their realms, in violation of papal decrees. Although neither party responded particularly well when Boniface tried to bring them to heel, Philip proved more brazenly defiant than his English counterpart, Edward Longshanks.

When Boniface issued the bull *Clericis Laicos* in 1296, threatening Philip and his courtiers with excommunication if they continued to tax the Church, Philip duly forbade the export of any currency from France. Since the Papacy itself had no compunction about levying a heavy tax on French churchmen to finance its own expenditures, Philip had deftly succeeded in driving Boniface to the brink of bankruptcy. Boniface soon capitulated, issuing another bull which, while not retracting *Clericis Laicos* directly, sullenly conceded that if a king deemed there to be a national emergency, he could tax the clergy without consulting the pope.

Gaining confidence after this easy victory, Philip provoked another round of conflict in 1301 by arresting and trying a French bishop for heresy and blasphemy. Clergy, of course, were only supposed to be tried by other clergy, so Boniface summoned his advisors and released another bull, *Ausculta Fili*, which

1 *Crisis of Church and State*, 172.

condescendingly reprimanded Philip and reminded him that he was subject to Boniface's authority. Boniface did not say in exactly what sense he meant this, but Philip and his advisors took it as the pope's claim to be feudal overlord over the kingdom of France. They had little difficulty in rallying most of the nation, including even many French clergy, against the pope.

In response, Boniface issued the justly famous bull *Unam Sanctam*, which is widely considered the starkest and strongest official statement of papal authority ever produced. In it, Boniface put forth two sets of claims, insisting on a plenitude of power in all spiritual matters, and in temporal matters as well. Under the former heading, he declared that "it is absolutely necessary for salvation that every human creature be subject to the Roman Pontiff." Under the latter, he confidently asserted the "two swords" theory in which the material sword was administered "by the hands of kings and soldiers, but at the will and sufferance of the priest," so that "temporal authority [is] subjected to spiritual power." None of the arguments that he cobbled together for the purpose were new as such, but nowhere else had they all been brought together in one place for the purpose of making such sweeping claims (nowhere, at least, except in the treatise On Ecclesiastical Power penned a few months earlier by *Unam Sanctam*'s ghost-writer, Giles of Rome).[2]

Although the full temporal claims of the document were soon rendered a dead letter (Philip responded by raiding the papal palace, having Boniface beaten by thugs, and then, when he died soon afterward, posthumously condemned in a mock trial convened by a puppet pope, his successor, Clement V), they have never been retracted by the Catholic Church, and the spiritual claims continued to be broadly accepted in the centuries that follow. The document thus remains an eloquent statement of the highly institutional and authoritarian ecclesiology that the Protestant Reformers set out to replace.

2 See an introduction to and translated excerpts from this text in O'Donovan and O'Donovan, *From Irenaeus to Grotius*, 362–78).

CLERICIS LAICOS

Boniface VIII

TRANSLATED BY ERNEST F. HENDERSON

Bishop Boniface, servant of the servants of God , in perpetual memory of this matter. Antiquity teaches us that laymen are in a high degree hostile to the clergy, a fact which is also made clear by the experiences of the present times; in as much as, not content within their own bounds, they strive after what is forbidden and loose the reins in pursuit of what is unlawful. Nor have they the prudence to consider that all jurisdiction is denied to them over the clergy—over both the persons and goods of ecclesiastics. On the prelates of the churches and on ecclesiastical persons, monastic and secular, they impose heavy burdens, tax them and declare levies upon them. They exact and extort from them the half, the tenth or twentieth or some other portion or quota of their revenues or of their goods; and they attempt in many ways to subject them to slavery and reduce them to their goods; and they attempt in many ways to subject them to slavery and reduce them to their sway. And with grief do we mention it, some prelates of the churches and ecclesiastical persons, fearing where they ought not to fear, seeking a transitory peace, dreading more to offend the temporal than the eternal majesty, without obtaining the authority or permission the Apostolic chair, do acquiesce, not so much rashly as improvidently, in the abuses of such persons. We, therefore, wishing to put a stop to such iniquitous acts, by the counsel of our brothers, of the apostolic authority, have decreed: that whatever prelates, or ecclesiastical persons, monastic or secular, of whatever grade, condition or standing, shall pay, or promise, or agree to pay as levies or talliages to laymen the tenth, twentieth or hundredth part of their own and their churches' revenues or goods—or any other quantity, portion or quota of those same revenues or goods, of their estimated or of their real value-under the name of an aid, loan, subvention, subsidy or gift, or under any other name, manner or clever pretense, without the authority of that same chair.

Likewise emperors, kings, or princes, dukes, counts or barons, podestas, captains or officials or rectors—by whatever name they are called, whether of cities, castles, or any places whatever, wherever situated; and any other persons, of whatever pre-eminence, condition or standing who shall impose, exact or receive such payments, or shall any where arrest, seize or presume to take possession of the belongings of churches or ecclesiastical persons which are deposited in the sacred buildings, or shall order them to be arrested, seized or taken possession of, or shall receive them when taken possession of, seized or arrested—also all who shall knowingly give aid, counsel or favour in the aforesaid things, whether publicly or secretly—shall incur, by the act itself the sentence of excommunication. Corporations, moreover, which shall be guilty in these matters, we place under the ecclesiastical interdict.

The prelates and above-mentioned ecclesiastical persons we strictly command, by virtue of their obedience and under penalty of deposition, that they by no means acquiesce in such demands, with. out express permission of the aforesaid chair; and that they pay nothing under pretext of any obligation, promise and confession made hitherto, or to be made hereafter before such constitution, notice or decree shall come to their notice; nor shall the aforesaid secular persons in any way receive anything. And if they shall-pay, or if the aforesaid persons shall receive, they shall be, by the act itself, under sentence of excommunication. From the aforesaid sentences of excommunication and interdict. Moreover, no one shall be able to be absolved, except in the throes of death, without the authority and special permission of the apostolic chair; since it is our intention by no means to pass over with dissimulation so horrid an abuse of the secular powers. Notwithstanding any privileges whatever—under whatever tenor, form, or manner or conception of words that have been granted to emperors, kings, and other persons mentioned above; as to which privileges we will that, against what we have here laid down, they in no wise avail any person or persons. Let no man at all, then, infringe this page of our constitution, prohibition or decree, or, with rash daring, act counter to it; but if any one shall presume to act shall know that he is about to incur the indignation of Almighty God and of His blessed apostles Peter and Paul.

Given at Rome at St. Peter's on the sixth day before the Calends of March (Feb 25), in the second year of our pontificate.

UNAM SANCTAM

Boniface VIII

TRANSCRIBED BY BOB VAN CLEER

FROM A DOCTORAL DISSERTATION PUBLISHED BY

CATHOLIC UNIVERSITY OF AMERICA PRESS, 1927

Urged by faith, we are obliged to believe and to maintain that the Church is one, holy, catholic, and also apostolic. We believe in her firmly and we confess with simplicity that outside of her there is neither salvation nor the remission of sins, as the Spouse in the Canticles [Sgs 6:8] proclaims: "One is my dove, my perfect one. She is the only one, the chosen of her who bore her," and she represents one sole mystical body whose Head is Christ and the head of Christ is God [1 Cor 11:3]. In her then is one Lord, one faith, one baptism [Eph 4:5]. There had been at the time of the deluge only one ark of Noah, prefiguring the one Church, which ark, having been finished to a single cubit, had only one pilot and guide, i.e., Noah, and we read that, outside of this ark, all that subsisted on the earth was destroyed.

We venerate this Church as one, the Lord having said by the mouth of the prophet: "Deliver, O God, my soul from the sword and my only one from the hand of the dog." [Ps 21:20] He has prayed for his soul, that is for himself, heart and body; and this body, that is to say, the Church, He has called one because of the unity of the Spouse, of the faith, of the sacraments, and of the charity of the Church. This is the tunic of the Lord, the seamless tunic, which was not rent but which was cast by lot [Jn 19:23–24]. Therefore, of the one and only Church there is one body and one head, not two heads like a monster; that is, Christ and the Vicar of Christ, Peter and the successor of Peter, since the Lord speaking to Peter Himself said: "Feed my sheep" [Jn 21:17], meaning, my sheep in general, not these, nor those in particular, whence we understand that He entrusted all to him [Peter]. Therefore, if the Greeks or others should say that they are not confided to Peter and to his successors, they must confess not being the sheep of Christ, since Our Lord says in John "there is one sheepfold and one shepherd." We are informed by the texts of the gospels that in this Church and in its power are two swords; namely, the spiritual and the temporal. For when the Apostles say: "Behold, here are two swords" [Lk 22:38] that is to say, in the Church, since the Apostles were speaking, the Lord did not reply that there were too many, but sufficient. Certainly the one who denies that the temporal sword is in the power of Peter ha s not listened well to the word of the Lord commanding: "Put up thy sword into thy scabbard" [Mt 26:52]. Both, therefore, are in the power of the Church, that is to say, the spiritual and the material sword, but the former is to be administered for the Church but the latter by the Church; the former in the hands of the priest; the latter by the hands of kings and soldiers, but at the will and sufferance of the priest.

However, one sword ought to be subordinated to the other and temporal authority, subjected to spiritual power. For since the Apostle said: "There is no power except from God and the things that are, are ordained of God" [Rom 13:1–2], but they would not be ordained if one sword were not subordinated to the other and if the inferior one, as it were, were not led upwards by the other.

For, according to the Blessed Dionysius, it is a law of the divinity that the lowest things reach the highest place by intermediaries. Then, according to the order of the universe, all things are not led back to order equally and immediately, but the lowest by the intermediary, and the inferior by the superior. Hence we must recognize the more clearly that spiritual power surpasses in dignity and in nobility any temporal power whatever, as spiritual things surpass the temporal. This we see very clearly also by the payment, benediction, and consecration of the tithes, but the acceptance of power itself and by the government even of things. For with truth as our witness, it belongs to spiritual power to establish the terrestrial power and to pass judgment if it has not been good. Thus is accomplished the prophecy of Jeremias concerning the Church and the ecclesiastical power: "Behold today I have placed you over nations, and over kingdoms" and the rest. Therefore, if the terrestrial power err, it will be judged by the spiritual power; but if a minor spiritual power err, it will be judged by a superior spiritual power; but if the highest power of all err, it can be judged only by God, and not by man, according to the testimony of the Apostle: "The spiritual man judgeth of all things and he himself is judged by no man" [1 Cor 2:15]. This authority, however, (though it has been given to man and is exercised by man), is not human but rather divine, granted to Peter by a divine word and reaffirmed to him (Peter) and his successors by the One Whom Peter confessed, the Lord saying to Peter himself, "Whatsoever you shall bind on earth, shall be bound also in Heaven" etc., [Mt 16:19]. Therefore whoever resists this power thus ordained by God, resists the ordinance of God [Rom 13:2], unless he invent like Manicheus two beginnings, which is false and judged by us heretical, since according to the testimony of Moses, it is not in the beginnings but in the beginning that God created heaven and earth [Gen 1:1]. Furthermore, we declare, we proclaim, we define that it is absolutely necessary for salvation that every human creature be subject to the Roman Pontiff.

INTRODUCTION TO
Marsilius of Padua
DEFENSOR PACIS

However much we may like to label great landmarks in the history of human thought as "revolutionary" and "ahead of their time," few books really deserve such clichéd epithets. Every writer is a product of his time and can hardly be expected to say something that is nowhere to be found in his contemporaries. One of the very rare exceptions to this rule is perhaps Marsilius of Padua's 1324 Defensor Pacis, a work so revolutionary and sweeping in its condemnation of the prevailing medieval Catholic understanding of the church and state that Marsilius was forced to flee even the anti-papal stronghold of Paris and take refuge with the German prince Ludwig of Bavaria. The book was anathematized in 1327 and a few years later Pope Clement VI was to write, "we are bold to say that we have almost never read a worse heretic than that Marsilius. For we have extracted from the mandate of Benedict our predecessor on a certain book of his [the Defensor] more than 240 heretical articles."[1]

Two hundred years later, many architects of the Protestant Reformation, especially in England, were to hail the Defensor as a great articulation of their own ecclesiological and political

1 Quoted in Carlo Pincin, Marsilio (Turin: Giappichelli, 1967), 233; translated in Annabel Brett, ed. and trans., Marsilius: Defender of the Peace, Cambridge Texts in the History of Political Thought (Cambridge: CUP, 2005)

principles, and to republish the text widely. Still later, historians and political theorists identified Marsilius's work as a truly startling anticipation of modern political ideas, with its focus on national sovereignty, representation as the foundation of legislative authority, and the thoroughly secular character of political life. Alexander Passerin d'Entreves says that, according to the "unanimous judgment of modern historians" the Defensor is "a landmark not only in the development of medieval political theory but in the history of political thought as a whole."[2]

And yet the context of Marsilius's great work was one we are already familiar with from the previous reading: the tussle between pope and prince over the rightful boundaries of ecclesiastical and civil authority within Western Christendom. Indeed, Marsilius's work can be considered in some ways the equal and opposite reaction to Boniface's extraordinary claims in Unam Sanctam. Rather than supreme earthly authority belonging to the pope, with the civil government little more than a department of the Church, Marsilius sketches a model in which supreme authority belongs to the civil magistrate, with the Church little more than a department of state. Indeed, beginning his treatise by sketching peace as the goal of every human society, Marsilius openly blames papal ambition and tyranny as the main cause for the war and discord in western Europe. In this, Marsilius draws extensively on the revival of Aristotle and his Politics that had fuelled many anti-papal political writings of previous decades, though he is much more thoroughgoing in his use of Aristotle to outline a basically self-sufficient civil order dedicated to the pursuit of earthly goods.

To understand what Marsilius is up to in the Defensor, however, one other key piece of context is necessary: the Franciscan poverty controversy. St. Francis of Assisi had a century before established a mendicant order of monks dedicated to the ideal of apostolic poverty—that is, the monks must claim no worldly possessions of their own, but only make use of the necessary goods made available to

2 Alexander Passerin d'Entreves, The Medieval Contribution to Political Thought: Thomas Aquinas, Marsilius of Padua, Richard Hooker (Oxford: OUP, 1939), 44.

them by Christian patrons. Although the Franciscans applied this principle only to their own order, not to the entire Church, the argument made the defenders of clerical wealth and power quite nervous. With good cause, as it turned out. Marsilius was to take up the arguments of the Franciscans and apply them to all clergy. The Church, he argued, was not to be in the business of piling up its own wealth; indeed, it could claim no earthly power over possessions at all, but must make humble use of what lay Christians provided.

Marsilius extended the argument further, however, to claim that properly speaking, the Church could not claim earthly power over people either—this was the fundamental confusion that had caused all the unnecessary conflicts. To be sure, the Church had the duty to preach the evangelical law of Christ, but this law did not, within history at least, function as law in the full and proper sense, which for Marsilius included coercive force. Christ himself would at the end of history act to enforce the consequences of his law, but until that time, ministers of his gospel proclaimed it only with a teaching authority. Accordingly, within history, the only properly political authority was the civil magistrate, who was responsible even for the external administration of the church (church buildings, tithes, and offices, the punishment of heresy, etc.).

The features of Marsilius's project that were to prove most attractive to later thinkers, though, were his emphasis on the people as the foundation of both church and state. The "authority of making laws belongs," he declares, "to the whole body of citizens, or its better part which represents the whole." The qualification at the end tells us that Marsilius does not envision pure democracy, but he did put great emphasis on the whole community as the basis and agent of political authority. Likewise, he was to define the church not as an institution or the body of the clergy, but as "the whole body of the faithful who believe in and invoke the name of Christ," and was to defend the authority of councils over against that of the pope. These ideas were shocking at the time but were to gain greater influence in the conciliar movement of the 15th century and even more so in the Protestant Reformation.

DEFENSOR PACIS

Marsilius of Padua

TRANSLATED BY OLIVER J. THATCHER & EDGAR HOLMES MCNEAL

Now we declare according to the truth and on the authority of Aristotle that the law-making power or the first and real effective source of law is the people or the body of citizens or the prevailing part of the people according to its election or its will expressed in general convention by vote, commanding or deciding that something be done or omitted in regard to human civil acts under penalty or temporal punishment; by the prevailing part of the people I mean that part of the community by whom the law is made, whether the whole body of citizens or the main part do this or commit it to some person or persons to be done; these last are not nor can be the real law-making power, but can only act according to instructions as to subject-matter and time, and by the authority of the primal law-making power.

On the authority of Aristotle by a citizen I mean him who has a part in the civil community, either in the government, or the council, or the judiciary, according to his position. By this definition boys, slaves, foreigners, and women are excluded, though according to different limitations. Having thus defined citizen and the prevailing section of the citizens, let us return to the object proposed, namely to demonstrate that the human authority of making laws belongs only to the whole body of citizens as the prevailing part of it. . . .

For the primal human authority of making laws belongs to that body by whom the best laws can be made. This, however, is the whole body of citizens or its better part which represents the whole. I now prove the second proposition, namely that the best law will result from the deliberation and decision of the whole body. . . . That this can be done best by the citizens as a whole or the better part of them, I demonstrate thus, since the truth of anything will be judged more accurately, and its common advantage be studied more diligently, if the whole body of citizens discuss it with intelligence and feeling. . . . So the reality of a general law will be best attended to by the whole people, because no one consciously injures himself.

On the other side we desire to adduce in witness the truths of the holy Scripture, teaching and counselling expressly, both in the literal sense and in the mystical according to the interpretation of the saints and the exposition of other authorized teachers of the Christian faith, that neither the Roman bishop, called the pope, nor any other bishop, presbyter, or deacon, ought to have the ruling or judgment or coercive jurisdiction of any priest, prince, community, society or single person of any rank whatsoever. . . .For the present purposes, it suffices to show, and I will first show, that Christ Himself did not come into the world to rule men, or to judge them by civil judgment, nor to govern in a temporal sense, but rather to subject Himself to the state and condition of this world; that indeed from such judgment and rule He wished to exclude and did exclude Himself and His apostles and disciples, and that He excluded their successors, the bishops and presbyters, by His example, and word and counsel and command from all governing and worldly, that is, coercive rule. I will also show that the apostles were true imitators of Christ in this, and that they taught their successors to be so. I will further demonstrate that Christ and His apostles desired to be subject and were subject continually to the coercive jurisdiction of the princes of the world in reality and in person, and that they taught and commanded all others to whom they gave the law of truth by word or letter, to do the same thing, under penalty of eternal condemnation. Then I will give a section to considering the power or authority of the keys, given by Christ to the apostles and to their successors in offices, the bishops and presbyters, in order that we may see the real character of that power, both of the Roman bishop and of the others. . . .

We wish, therefore, first to demonstrate that Christ wished to exclude and did exclude both Himself and His apostles from the office of ruler. This appears in John 18. For when Christ was accused before Pontius Pilate, vicar of the Roman emperor in Judea, for saying that he was king of the Jews, and Pilate asked Him if He had said that, or if He had called Himself a king, He replied to the question of Pilate: "My kingdom is not of this world"; that is, I am come not to reign by temporal rule and dominion, as the kings of the world reign. It remains to show that Christ not only refused the rule of this world and coercive jurisdiction on earth, whereby He gave an example for action to His apostles and disciples and their successors, but that He also taught by word and showed by example that all, whether priests or not, should be subject in reality and in person to the coercive judgment of the princes of this world. By His word and example Christ demonstrated this first in physical things, in the incident contained in Matthew 22, when to the Jews asking Him: "Tell us, therefore, what thinkest Thou; is it lawful to give tribute unto Caesar or not?" looking at the penny and its superscription, he replied: "Render, therefore, unto Caesar the things which are Caesar's, and unto God the things which are God's." . . . .

Further not only in physical things did Christ show that He was subject to the coercive jurisdiction of a prince of the world, but He showed it also in Himself . . . . for it plainly appears that He permitted Himself to be taken and led to the court of Pilate, vicar of the Roman emperor, and endured that He be condemned and handed over by the same judge to the extreme punishment.

Following upon this, it remains to demonstrate what power, authority and judgment Christ wished to give to the apostles and their successors, and did in fact give according to the words of the holy Scripture. Among other things which seem to have direct reference to this are the words which Christ spoke to Peter, Matthew 16: "I will give unto thee the keys of the kingdom of heaven"; also those spoken by Him to all the apostles, when He said: "Whatsoever ye shall bind on earth shall be bound in heaven, and whatsoever ye shall loose on earth shall be loosed in heaven." On these words especially is based the claim and title to the plenitude of power, which the Roman bishop ascribes to himself. . . .

By the sacrament of baptism, which Christ commanded to be administered by the apostles, He caused them to understand also the administration of the other sacraments instituted for the eternal salvation of mankind; one of these is the sacrament of repentance by which the actual guilt of the human soul, both mortal and venial, is destroyed, and the soul, corrupt in itself through guilt, is restored by the grace of God, without any human effort, God ordaining that meritorious works should not win eternal life. Hence it is written in Romans 6: "The gift of God is eternal life." The ministers of this sacrament, as of the others, are the priests and presbyters, as successors of the apostles of Christ, to all of whom it is shown by the aforesaid words of Scripture the power of the keys was given, that is, the power of conferring the sacrament of repentance, in other words, the power of loosing and binding men in regard to their sins. . . . It will appear later how it is possible for priests to receive into or exclude from the kingdom; and from this also the character and extent of the power of those keys, given by Christ to Peter and the other apostles. . . . By his guilt the sinner is under the bond of eternal condemnation for the future life, and if he persists in his guilt, he is cast off from the association of the faithful in this world, by a kind of punishment resting with the believers of Christ, called excommunication. . . .And on the other hand we should notice that the sinner receives a three-fold benefit through his sorrow for sin and open confession to the priests, to which acts, both singly and taken together, the name repentance is given. The first benefit is that he is cleansed from his inner guilt and restored to himself by the grace of God; the second, that he is freed from the bond of eternal damnation, to which he was bound by his guilt; and the third, that he is reconciled to the church, that is, he is reunited or ought to be reunited to the body of believers. . . .

From these words of the saints . . . it clearly appears that God alone remits to the truly penitent sinner his guilt and his debt of eternal condemnation, and that without any office of the priest preceding or intervening, as has been demonstrated above . . . . For it is God alone who cannot err as to whose sin should be remitted or retained. For He alone is not moved by unfair feeling nor judges unjustly. Not of such character is the church or the priest whoever he may be, even the Roman bishop . . . .The anathema of the church inflicts upon those who are justly expelled, this punishment: that the grace and protection of God is withdrawn from them and is abandoned by them themselves, so that they are free to rush into the destruction of sin, and greater power of destroying them is given to the devil. . . .

[St.] Ambrose says that "the word of God remits sins; the priest performs his service but has no right of authority. But we may say that the priest is as it were the turnkey of the heavenly judge, so that he frees the sinner in the same sense that the turnkey of an earthly judge frees a prisoner. For just as the guilty man is condemned to or released from guilt and civil penalty by the word or sentence of a judge of this world, so by the divine word anyone is either to be freed from or condemned to guilt and the debt of damnation and the punishment of the future life. And just as no one is freed from guilt and penalty or condemned by the action of the turnkey of a worldly judge, and yet by his action in closing or opening the prison the guilty one is shown to be freed or condemned, so no one is freed from or bound to guilt and the debt of eternal condemnation by the action of the priest, but it is demonstrated before the eyes of the church who is held bound or freed by God, when he receives the benediction of the priest, or is admitted to the communion of the sacraments." . . . . Therefore just as the turnkey of an earthly judge fulfills his office in opening and closing the prison, but exercises no right of judicial authority of condemning or pardoning, since even if he actually opened the prison for a criminal not pardoned by the judge and announced to the people with his own voice that the man was free, the guilty man would not on this account be freed from his guilt and the civil penalty, or on the other hand if he refused to open the prison and declared with his own words that he whom the judge had freed by his sentence was not pardoned but condemned, that man would not on this account be held subject to the guilt and penalty; so likewise the priest, the turnkey of the heavenly judge, performs his duty by the verbal pronunciation of the absolution or malediction. But if those who ought to be condemned by the divine judge or are already condemned, the priest should pronounce as not worthy to be condemned or as not condemned, or vice versa, through ignorance or deceit or both, not on this account would the former be dissolved or the latter damned, because the priest had not handled the key or keys with discretion according to the merits of the accused.

Proceeding from what has been demonstrated, we will show here first that no one of the apostles was given pre-eminence over the other in essential dignity by Christ. . . For Christ, giving to the apostles the authority over the sacrament of the eucharist, said to them: "This is My Body which is given for you, this do in remembrance of Me." . . . And he did not say these words more to Peter than to the others. For Christ did not say: "Do thou this, and give the right of doing it to the other apostles," but He said, "Do" in the plural, and to all without distinction. And later Christ said to the apostles: "As My Father has sent Me, even so send I you. He breathed on them and saith unto them, "Receive ye the Holy Ghost, whosoever sins ye remit, they are remitted unto them, and whosoever sins ye retain, they are retained." Now Christ said: "I send you as My Father sent Me"; He did not say to Peter or to any other apostle in the singular, "I send thee as the Father, etc., do thou send the others." Nor again did Christ breathe upon him, but upon them, not upon one through another. Nor did Christ say to Peter: 'Receive the Holy Ghost, and afterwards give it to the others," but he said, "Receive," in the plural and speaking to all indifferently. . . .

It likewise appears that neither St. Peter nor any one of the apostles had pre-eminence over the others in the right of distributing the temporal offerings of the primitive church; whence it is written in Acts 4: "For as many as were possessors of lands or houses sold them, and laid them at the apostles' feet, and distribution was made unto every man according as he had need." Behold, the distribution of the temporal offerings of the church was made by the apostles in general, not by Peter alone; for it is not said: they laid them at the feet of Peter, but of the apostles. Nor it is said that "Peter distributed them," but that "distribution was made." . . .

But if Peter has been called the prince of the apostles by some of the saints, the term is used broadly and by a misuse of the word prince, otherwise it would be plainly opposed to the opinion and oracle of Christ, where He said: "The princes of the Gentiles exercise dominion over them, but it shall not be so among you." And it must be said that the saints spoke thus not because of any power given to him by Christ over the other apostles, but because perchance he was older than the others: or because he was the first to confess that Christ was the true consubstantial Son of God, or perhaps because he was more fervent and constant in faith, or because he was intimate with Christ and was more frequently called by Him into His counsel and secrets. . . .

Moreover he did not have coercive jurisdiction over the rest of the apostles more than they over him, neither consequently have his successors. For Christ forbade this to them directly, as in Matthew 20, Luke 22: "And there was also a strife among them, which of them should be counted the greatest. And He said unto them: The kings and princes of the Gentiles exercise dominion over them, and they that are great exercise authority upon them, but it shall not be so among you"; Christ could not have denied this more plainly. Why then should anyone in regard to this believe more in human tradition, than in the most evident word of Christ? . . .

Further, the Roman bishop is not nor should he be called the successor of St. Peter by the laying on of hands, for there has been a Roman bishop upon whom St. Peter has not laid his hand either directly or indirectly; nor again because of the seat or the determination of the place, first because no one of the apostles was appointed to any people or any place by divine law; for he said to all:

"Go ye therefore and teach all nations"; and in the second place, St. Peter is said to have been at Antioch before he was at Rome.

The aforesaid plenitude of power the bishops of Rome have used continually up to the present and are now using for the worse, especially against the Roman prince and principality. For they are able to exercise against him this their wickedness, that is, the subjection of the empire to themselves, because of the division among the inhabitants of the empire, and are able by their so-called pastors and most holy fathers to stir up and nourish the discord already incited. For they further believe that, the empire once subdued, the way lies open for them to subject the rest of the kingdoms, although they are especially and peculiarly under obligation to the emperor and empire of the Romans, by reason of benefits received, as is known to all. But, to speak only of what is known to everyone and needs no word from us, smitten with cupidity and avarice, with pride and ambition, made even worse by ingratitude, they are seeking in every way to prevent the creation of a Roman emperor, and are striving either to break up the empire, or to transfer it in another form to their own control, lest the excesses which they have committed should be corrected by the power of the aforesaid princes and they should be subject to well-merited discipline. But although with the purpose which we have mentioned they are placing obstructions in the way of the prince on every side, yet craftily hiding their object they say they are doing this to defend the rights of the spouse of Christ, that is the church, though such pious sophistry is ridiculous. For temporal power and greed, and lust of authority and rule is not the spouse of Christ, nor has He wedded such a spirit, but has expressly repudiated it, as has been shown from the divine Scriptures. . . . Nor is this the heritage of the apostles which they left to their true, not fictitious, successors. . . .

And so by their striving for worldly things, the spouse of Christ is not truly defended. The recent Roman popes do not defend her who is the spouse of Christ, that is, the Catholic faith and the multitude of the believers, but offend her; they do not preserve her beauty, that is, the unity of the faith, but defile it. Since by sowing tares and schisms they are tearing her limb from limb, and since they do not receive the true companions of Christ, poverty and humility, but shut them out entirely, they show themselves not servants but enemies of the husband.

INTRODUCTION TO
Council of Constance
SACROSANCTA & FREQUENS

Pope Boniface VIII's ill-advised attempt in 1302 to assert the plenitude of papal authority over Christendom did not merely fail in the face of King Philip IV's determined opposition; it backfired rather spectacularly. Determined to prevent future popes from interfering in French affairs, Philip ensured that Boniface's successor, Clement V, was a Frenchman, and to make extra sure that he would not get too independent-minded, Philip pressured Clement to move the papal court to Avignon, in southeastern France, rather than Rome.

The notion of the Bishop of Rome ruling from somewhere that patently was not Rome certainly shocked many Christians of the time; however, such was the power and wealth of the French church that there was no successful opposition until 1378, when Pope Urban VI was consecrated in Rome. Thus ended what came to be called the Babylonian Captivity of the Church (since it lasted around seventy years), but the cure proved to be worse than the disease. The French cardinals disavowed Urban and elected an anti-pope, Clement VII, who maintained the papal court at Avignon. The two popes duly excommunicated one another, France and its political allies promptly lined up behind Clement, and its enemies promptly lined up behind Urban.

This unseemly spectacle, known as the Great Schism, did not merely diminish the authority of the papacy, but shook Western Christendom to its core. After all, for centuries the Church had elaborated a theory in which all power flowed downward from God through the pope and thence to kings, bishops, and the rest. If one could not even be sure who was rightfully pope, the whole legitimacy structure of European society was thrown into question.

Theologians from across Europe busied themselves with the question of how to make sense of the chaos and how to resolve it, foremost among them the great nominalist theologians at the University of Paris, Pierre d'Ailly and Jean Gerson. D'Ailly and Gerson laid the intellectual foundations of the movement known as conciliarism, which rethought the whole top-down conception of authority that had come to dominate the Church and proposed a more bottom-up approach. In this understanding, although the pope retained a preeminent role he was not above earthly accountability, for Christ had granted his authority to the whole body of the Church—although by this they meant the whole body of the clergy. This was by no means radical as the ideas of Marsilius, and indeed most of the conciliarists were relatively conservative thinkers. They admitted that normally, only the pope has authority to call a council, and has authority to preside over it, but insisted that this rule had not envisioned a crisis such as the Great Schism, when both popes were undermining rather than serving the good and health of the Church.

By 1409, the movement had gained enough traction to convene a Council at Pisa without papal support, but rather than ending the schism, it succeeded only in establishing a third rival pope, Alexander V. This new phase of crisis, along with the alarming support that the Czech reformer John Huss was gaining for his "heresies," was sufficient to goad leading churchmen, including two of the three rival popes, to convene a new council at Constance in 1414, with Gerson its lead theologian.

The 1415 decree *Sacrosancta* outlined the Council's self-understanding, asserting that it has its power immediately from Christ, and every one, whatever his state or position, even if it be the

Papal dignity itself, is bound to obey it in all those things which pertain to the faith and the healing of the said schism, and to the general reformation of the Church of God, in head and members.

This was not quite so radical a statement as it might first appear, since this conciliar authority was only envisioned as taking precedence in a time of great crisis and a vacuum of papal leadership. However, the conciliarists did envision church councils as playing an ongoing role in limiting papal authority, reforming abuses, and preventing any future schisms. Accordingly, in their 1417 decree *Frequens*, the Council provided for subsequent councils in 1423, 1431, and thereafter every ten years, and also issued several bold decrees restricting common abuses of papal power.

Although Constance did succeed in ending the Great Schism, with only one pope, Martin V, by the end of 1417, the larger success of the conciliar movement proved abortive. The Council of Basel which convened in 1431 became bolder in its assertion of conciliar authority, and clashed repeatedly with Pope Eugenius IV, who shrewdly outmaneuvered and undermined it until the movement petered out in 1450. However, with the shocking proliferation of papal abuses in the subsequent decades, the Protestant Reformers and their more conservative sympathizers were to appeal to the conciliarist legacy for a renewal of church councils that would reform abuses and restrain the authority of the pope.

SACROSANCTA

Council of Constance

TRANSLATED BY J. H. ROBINSON

In the name of the Holy and indivisible Trinity; of the Father, Son, and Holy Ghost. Amen. This holy synod of Constance, forming a general council for the extirpation of the present schism and the union and reformation, in head and members, of the Church of God, legitimately assembled in the Holy Ghost, to the praise of Omnipotent God, in order that it may the more easily, safely, effectively and freely bring about the union and reformation of the church of God, hereby determines, decrees, ordains and declares what follows: It first declares that this same council, legitimately assembled in the Holy Ghost, forming a general council and representing the Catholic Church militant, has its power immediately from Christ, and every one, whatever his state or position, even if it be the Papal dignity itself, is bound to obey it in all those things which pertain to the faith and the healing of the said schism, and to the general reformation of the Church of God, in head and members. It further declares that any one, whatever his condition, station or rank, even if it be the Papal, who shall contumaciously refuse to obey the mandates, decrees, ordinances or instructions which have been, or shall be issued by this holy council, or by any other general council, legitimately summoned, which concern, or in any way relate to the above mentioned objects, shall, unless he repudiate his conduct, be subject to condign penance and be suitably punished, having recourse, if necessary, to the other resources of the law.

FREQUENS

Council of Constance

TRANSLATED BY ERNEST F. HENDERSON (DECREES OF THE ECUMENICAL COUNCILS, EDITED BY NORMAN P. TANNER)

SESSION 39—9 OCTOBER 1417
ON GENERAL COUNCILS

The frequent holding of general councils is a pre-eminent means of cultivating the Lord's patrimony. It roots out the briars, thorns and thistles of heresies, errors and schisms, corrects deviations, reforms what is deformed and produces a richly fertile crop for the Lord's vineyard. Neglect of councils, on the other hand, spreads and fosters the aforesaid evils. This conclusion is brought before our eyes by the memory of past times and reflection on the present situation. For this reason we establish, enact, decree and ordain, by a perpetual edict, that general councils shall be held henceforth in the following way. The first shall follow in five years immediately after the end of this council, the second in seven years immediately after the end of the next council, and thereafter they are to be held every ten years for ever. They are to be held in places which the supreme pontiff is bound to nominate and assign within a month before the end of each preceding council, with the approval and consent of the council, or which, in his default, the council itself is bound to nominate. Thus, by a certain continuity, there will always be either a council in existence or one expected within a given time. If perchance emergencies arise, the time may be shortened by the supreme pontiff, acting on the advice of his brothers, the cardinals of the Roman church, but it may never be prolonged. Moreover, he may not change the place assigned for the next council without evident necessity. If an emergency arises whereby it seems necessary to change the place—for example in the case of a siege, war, disease or the like—then the supreme pontiff may, with the consent and written endorsement of his aforesaid brothers or of two-thirds of them, substitute another place which is suitable and fairly near to the place previously assigned. It must, however, be within the same nation unless the same or a similar impediment exists throughout the nation. In the latter case he may summon the council to another suitable place which is nearby but within another nation, and the prelates and other persons who are customarily summoned to a council will be obliged to come to it as if it had been the place originally assigned. The supreme pontiff is bound to announce and publish the change of place or the shortening of time in a legal and solemn form within a year before the date assigned, so that the aforesaid persons may be able to meet and hold the council at the appointed time.

PROVISION TO GUARD AGAINST FUTURE SCHISMS

If it happens—though may it not!—that a schism arises in the future in such a way that two or more persons claim to be supreme pontiffs, then the date of the council, if it is more than a year off, is to be brought forward to one year ahead; calculating this from the day on which two or more of them publicly assumed the insignia of their pontificates or on which they began to govern. All prelates and others who are bound to attend a council shall assemble at the council without the need for any summons, under pain of the law's sanctions and of other penalties which may be imposed by the council, and let the emperor and other kings and princes attend either in person or through official deputies, as if they had been besought, through the bowels of the mercy of our lord Jesus Christ, to put out a common fire. Each of those claiming to be the Roman pontiff is bound to announce and proclaim the council as taking place at the end of the year, as mentioned, in the previously assigned place; he is bound to do this within a month after the day on which he came to know that one or more other persons had assumed the insignia of the papacy or was administering the papacy; and this is under pain of eternal damnation, of the automatic loss of any rights that he had acquired in the papacy, and of being disqualified both actively and passively from all dignities. He is also bound to make the council known by letter to his rival claimant or claimants, challenging him or them to a judicial process, as well as to all prelates and princes, insofar as this is possible. He shall go in person to the place of the council at the appointed time, under pain of the aforesaid penalties, and shall not depart until the question of the schism has been fully settled by the council. None of the contenders for the papacy, moreover shall preside as pope at the council. Indeed, in order that the church may rejoice more freely and quickly in one undisputed pastor, all the contenders for the papacy are suspended by law as soon as the council has begun, on the authority of this holy synod, from all administration; and let not obedience be given in any way by anyone to them, or to any one of them until the question has been settled by the council.

If it happens in the future that the election of a Roman pontiff is brought about through fear, which would weigh upon even a steadfast man, or through pressure, then we declare that it is of no effect or moment and cannot be ratified or approved by subsequent consent even if the state of fear ceases. The cardinals, however, may not proceed to another election until a council has reached a decision about the election, unless the person elected resigns or dies. If they do proceed to this second election, then it is null by law and both those making the second election and the person elected, if he embarks upon his reign as pope, are deprived by law of every dignity, honour and rank—even cardinalatial or pontifical—and are thereafter ineligible for the same, even the papacy itself; and nobody may in any way obey as pope the second person elected, under pain of being a fosterer of schism. In such a case the council is to provide for the election of a pope. It is lawful, however, and indeed all the electors are bound, or at least the greater part of them, to move to a safe locality and to make a statement about the said fear. The statement is to be made in a prominent place before public notaries and important persons as well as before a multitude of the people. They are to do this as quickly as they can without danger to their persons, even if there is a threat of danger to all their goods. They shall state in their allegation the nature and extent of the fear and shall solemnly swear that the allegation is true that they believe they can prove it and that they are not making it out of malice or calumny. Such an allegation of fear cannot be delayed in any way until after the next council.

After they have moved and have alleged the fear in the above form, they are bound to summon the person elected to a council. If a council is not due for more than a year after their summons, then its date shall be brought forward by the law itself to only a year ahead, in the way explained above. The elected person is bound under pain of the aforesaid penalties, and the cardinals under pain of automatically losing the cardinalate and all their benefices, to announce and proclaim the council within a month after the summons, in the way mentioned above, and to make it known as soon as possible. The cardinals and other electors are bound to come in person to the place of the council, at a suitable time, and to remain there until the end of the affair.

The other prelates are bound to answer the cardinals' summons, as mentioned above, if the person elected fails to issue a summons. The latter will not preside at the council since he will have been suspended by law from all government of the papacy from the time the council begins, and he is not to be obeyed by anyone in any matter under pain of the offender becoming a promoter of schism. If the aforesaid emergencies arise within a year before the beginning of a council-namely that more than one person claim to be pope or that someone has been elected through fear or pressure—then those who claim to be pope, or the one elected through fear or pressure, as well as the cardinals, are deemed by law as having been summoned to the council. They are bound, moreover, to appear in person at the council, to explain their case and to await the council's judgment. But if some emergency happens during the above occurrences whereby it is necessary to change the place of the council—for example a siege or war or disease or some such—then nevertheless all the aforesaid persons, as well as all prelates and others who are obliged to attend a council, are bound to assemble at a neighbouring place suitable for the council, as has been said above. Moreover, the greater part of the prelates who have moved to a particular place within a month may specify it as the place of the council to which they and others are bound to come, just as if it had been the place first assigned. The council, after it has thus been summoned and has assembled and become acquainted with the cause of the schism, shall bring a suit of contumacy against the electors or those claiming to be pope or the cardinals, if perchance they fail to come. It shall then pronounce judgment and shall punish, even beyond the aforesaid penalties and in such a way that the fierceness of the punishment acts as an example to others, those who are to blame—no matter of what state or rank or pre-eminence, whether ecclesiastical or secular, they may be—in starting or fostering the schism, in their administering or obeying, in their supporting those who governed or in making an election against the aforesaid prohibition, or who lied in their allegations of fear.

The disturbance caused by fear or pressure at a papal election corrodes and divides, in a lamentable way, the whole of Christianity. In order that it may be assiduously avoided, we have decided to decree, in addition to what has been said above, that if anyone brings to bear or causes, or procures to be brought about, fear or pressure or violence of this kind upon the electors in a papal election, or upon any one of them, or has the matter ratified after it has been done, or advises or acts in support of it, or knowingly receives or defends someone who has done this, or is negligent in enforcing the penalties mentioned below—no matter of what state or rank or pre-eminence the offender may be, even if it be imperial or regal or pontifical, or any other ecclesiastical or secular dignity he may hold—then he automatically incurs the penalties contained in pope Boniface VIII's constitution which begins Felicis, and he shall be effectively punished by them.

Any city—even if it be Rome itself, though may it not be!—or any other corporation that gives aid, counsel or support to someone who does these things, or that does not have such an offender punished within a month, insofar as the enormity of the crime demands and there exists the possibility of inflicting the punishment, shall automatically be subject to ecclesiastical interdict. Furthermore the city, apart from the one mentioned above, shall be deprived of the episcopal dignity, notwithstanding any privileges to the contrary. We wish, moreover, that this decree be solemnly published at the end of every general council and that it be read out and publicly announced before the start of a conclave, wherever and whenever the election of a Roman pontiff is about to take place.

ON THE PROFESSION TO BE MADE BY THE POPE

Since the Roman pontiff exercises such great power among mortals, it is right that he be bound all the more by the incontrovertible bonds of the faith and by the rites that are to be observed regarding the church's sacraments. We therefore decree and ordain, in order that the fullness of the faith may shine in a future Roman pontiff with singular splendour from the earliest moments of his becoming pope, that henceforth whoever is to be elected Roman pontiff shall make the following confession and profession in public, in front of his electors, before his election is published.

In the name of the holy and undivided Trinity, Father and Son and holy Spirit. Amen. In the year of our Lord's nativity one thousand etc., I, N., elected pope, with both heart and mouth confess and profess to almighty God, whose church I undertake with his assistance to govern, and to blessed Peter, prince of the apostles, that as long as I am in this fragile life I will firmly believe and hold the catholic faith, according to the traditions of the apostles, of the general councils and of other holy fathers, especially of the eight holy universal councils-namely the first at Nicaea, the second at Constantinople, the third at Ephesus, the fourth at Chalcedon, the fifth and sixth at Constantinople, the seventh at Nicaea and the eighth at Constantinople—as well as of the general councils at the Lateran, Lyons and Vienne, and I will preserve this faith unchanged to the last dot and will confirm, defend and preach it to the point of death and the shedding of my blood, and likewise I will follow and observe in every way the rite handed down of the ecclesiastical sacraments of the Catholic church. This my profession and confession, written at my orders by a notary of the holy Roman church, I have signed below with my own hand. I sincerely offer it on this altar N. to you, almighty God, with a pure mind and a devout conscience, in the presence of the following. Made etc.

THAT PRELATES MAY NOT BE TRANSLATED WITHOUT THEIR CONSENT

When prelates are translated, there is commonly both spiritual and temporal loss and damage of a grave nature for the churches from which they are transferred. The prelates, moreover, sometimes do not maintain the rights and liberties of their churches as carefully as they otherwise might, out of fear of being translated. The importunity of certain people who seek their own good, not that of Jesus Christ, may mean that the Roman pontiff is deceived in such a matter, as one ignorant of the facts, and so is easily led astray. We therefore determine and ordain, by this present decree, that henceforth bishops and superiors ought not to be translated unwillingly without a grave and reasonable cause which, after the person in question has been summoned, is to be inquired into and decided upon with the advice of the cardinals of the holy Roman church, or the greater part of them, and with their written endorsement. Lesser prelates, such as abbots and others with perpetual benefices, ought not to be changed, moved or deposed without a just and reasonable cause that has been inquired into.

We add, moreover, that for abbots to be changed the written endorsement of the cardinals is necessary—just as it is necessary for bishops, as has been said—saving, however, the constitutions and privileges of any churches, monasteries and orders.

ON SPOILS AND PROCURATIONS

Papal reservations as well as the exacting and receiving of procurations which are due to ordinaries and other lesser prelates, by reason of a visitation, and of spoils on deceased prelates and other clerics, are seriously detrimental to churches, monasteries and other benefices and to churchmen. We therefore declare, by this present edict, that it is reasonable and in the public interest that reservations made by the pope, as well as exactions and collections of this kind made by collectors and others appointed or to be appointed by apostolic authority, are henceforth in no way to occur or to be attempted. Indeed, procurations of this kind, as well as spoils and the goods of any prelates found at their deaths, even if they are cardinals or members of the papal household or officials or any other clerics whatsoever, in the Roman curia or outside it, no matter where or when they die, are to belong to and to be received by, fully and freely, those persons to whom they would and ought to belong with the ending of the aforesaid reservations, mandates and exactions. We forbid the exaction of such spoils on prelates even inferior ones and others, which are outside and contrary to the form of common law. However, the constitution of pope Boniface VIII of happy memory, beginning Praesenti, which was published with this specially in mind, is to remain in force.

INTRODUCTION TO
Desiderius Erasmus
JULIUS EXCLUSUS

On the eve of the Reformation, the Papacy still faced significant rivals in both the vestiges of the conciliar movement and the ever-growing power and influence of the major monarchies of Europe, the Spanish now joining the French and the so-called Holy Roman Empire as a major European power. But rather than maintaining influence by exercising spiritual leadership, the popes of the later 15th and early 16th centuries were among the most wicked and corrupt ever to hold the office. Alexander VI (1492–1503) made no secret of his numerous mistresses and illegitimate children, some of whom he elevated to high church offices and showered with ecclesiastical wealth. His successor, Julius II, was less open about his own sexual scandals but more shameless in his Machiavellian connivings for political power.

In this period, then, the Papacy sustained its power by two related strategies. One was by centralizing more and more of the church's spiritual authority, so that the pope alone had the authority to forgive certain sins or grant exceptions from various church laws. This helped not merely in keeping many ordinary Chrisitans and churchmen dependent on the papacy, but also generated extraordinary wealth for the papal coffers. Of course, it was one of the most egregious instances of this profitable spiritual trade—the sale of indulgences (get out of purgatory free cards) by papal preacher Johann Tetzel in 1517—that prompted Luther's revolutionary protest against the Church. The Papacy's second strategy, though, was to become a political power player in its own right, both through the territory it controlled in central Italy (the Papal States) and through a cunning series of alliances between the rival powers that surrounded it. It was such brazen military campaigning and diplomatic scheming that Pope Julius II made the trademark of his tenure as pope, from 1503–13. However, whatever gains in worldly power he may have achieved for the papacy came at the cost of widespread disgust throughout Christendom, which helped lay the groundwork for the Protestant Reformation that was to burst forth soon after.

No one so fully represented the reforming ferment of the early 16th century as Dutch humanist Desiderius Erasmus. As the foremost scholar of the new classical learning that was sweeping Europe and also a peerless wordsmith able to make full use of the powerful new medium of the printing press, Erasmus was something of a rockstar during the decade leading up to the Reformation. He traveled throughout western Europe researching, writing, and publishing, while being wined and dined by scholars and noblemen. A master satirist, he often upset the church authorities with his witty and irreverent critiques of the Pharisaism and immorality that dominated the late medieval church, most notably in his 1511 *The Praise of Folly*. However, Kelley Sowards writes that for Erasmus, "however comic, its [his satire's] purpose was deadly serious: no less than the moral-religious reform of society."[1]

Indeed, Erasmus was an ardent and earnest advocate not merely of reforming the most obvious corruptions of the Church, but of restoring her to true simple Christian faith and discipleship, which was found in the heart, not in outward pomp and power. He was also a strong advocate of returning to the original text of the Scriptures, a project that he leant enormous momentum to through his 1516 publication of a critical Greek text and revised

1 J. Kelley Sowards, *"Introduction" to The Julius Exclusus of Erasmus*, trans. Paul Pascal (Bloomington, IN: Indiana University Press, 1968), 24.

Latin translation of the New Testament. This combination of biblical scholarship and commitment to a religion of simple personal faith made Erasmus a seemingly natural ally for the Protestant Reformation. Indeed, it was commonly said that "Erasmus laid the egg that Luther hatched." Still, Erasmus shrunk back from fully endorsing Luther's reforming project, making him despised by Protestants and conservative Catholics alike. Eramsus was better at pointing out the faults in the existing church than in proposing a comprehensive remedy for them.

Nowhere is he better at pointing out these faults with wit and rhetorical flair than in his 1517 satire *Julius Excluded from Heaven* (which Erasmus always studiously refused to admit writing), which narrates a conversation between the bombastic ghost of Pope Julius and the shocked St. Peter at the gates of heaven. In it, the full catalogue of Julius's vices is laid bare, with particular focus on the needless wars he started and his shameless maneuvering in ecclesiastical politics to prevent meaningful reform of the Church and protect his own wealth and position. Erasmus also shows his sympathy to the conciliar movement by chronicling at length Julius's successful efforts to thwart the work of the Council of Pisa and the absurdity of the pope's claims, articulated in conflict with the conciliarists over the preceding century, to be wholly above any earthly judge and council, whatever wickedness he be guilty of. However, Erasmus also displays a deeper theological concern about the meaning of the church, one that was to resonate deeply with the Protestant Reformers, in the following lines (not appearing in this excerpt):

> JULIUS: What is more apostolic than to enlarge the Church of Christ?
>
> PETER: But if the Church is the Christian people, bound together by the spirit of Christ, I would say that you have subverted the Church . . .
>
> JULIUS: What we mean by the Church is sacred buildings, priests, and especially the Roman Curia.[2]

2 Rummel 81.

This contest—between an essentially outward and institutional conception of the church, and the church as the whole body of believers united by the Spirit—was to erupt into a full-scale Reformation, beginning just a few months after the publication of the Julius Exclusus.

JULIUS EXCLUSUS

Desiderius Erasmus

TRANSLATED BY ROBERT M. ADAMS

JULIUS: What the devil is this? The doors don't open? Somebody must have changed the lock or broken it.

GENIUS: It seems more likely that you didn't bring the proper key; for this door doesn't open to the same key as a secret money-chest. Why didn't you bring both the keys you have? This is the key of power, not of wisdom.

JULIUS: I didn't have any other key but this; I don't see why we need a different one when we've got this.

GENIUS: I don't either; but the fact is, we're still on the outside.

JULIUS: Now I'm really getting mad; I'll knock the doors down. Ho! Ho! Somebody come and open this door right away! What's the hangup? nobody home? What's the matter with the doorman? He's asleep, I guess, or else drunk.

GENIUS: This fellow judges everyone else by himself.

PETER: A good thing our gates are of adamant, otherwise this one, whoever he is, would have kicked them in. He must be a giant of some sort, a general of the armies, a stormer of cities. But oh my God, what a sewer-stench is this! I certainly won't open the gates right away, but take a seat up here by a grated window where I can look out and keep an eye on the scene. Who are you and what do you want?

JULIUS: Open the door, will you? at least, if you can. And if you were really doing your job, it should have been open long ago, and decorated with all the heraldry of heaven.

PETER: Pretty lordly. But first tell me who you are.

JULIUS: As if you couldn't see for yourself.

PETER: See? What I see is new to me, like nothing I ever saw before, and I might say monstrous.

JULIUS: But if you're not stone-blind, you're bound to recognize this key, even if you aren't familiar with the golden oak tree. You can certainly see my triple crown, as well as my cloak all gleaming with gold and gems.

PETER: That silver key of yours I do recognize, though there's only one of them, and it's very different from those that were given to me long ago by the one true shepherd of the church, that is, Christ. But that glorious crown of yours, how could I possibly recognize it? No tyrant ruling over barbarian peoples ever ventured to wear one like it, much less anyone who came here asking for admission. Your cloak doesn't impress me either; for I always used to consider gold and jewels as trash to be despised. But what does this amount to really? In all this stuff-the key, the crown, the cloak-I recognize marks of that rascally cheat and impostor who shared a name with me but not a faith, that scoundrel Simon whom I once flung down with the aid of Christ.

JULIUS: Enough of these jokes, and watch yourself; for I, if you don't know, am Julius of Liguria, and I don't doubt you recognize these two letters P. M., unless you've forgotten how to read.

PETER: I expect they stand for "Pestiferous Maximus."

GENIUS: Ha ha ha! This porter is as good as a wizard; he's got the needle's touch.

JULIUS: What it means is "Pontifex Maximus."

PETER: If you were triply great, greater even than Hermes Trismegistus, you still wouldn't get in here unless you were supremely good, that is, holy.

JULIUS: Well, if it comes down to comparative holiness, you've got some nerve to keep me waiting outside here when for all these centuries you've only been called "holy," whereas nobody ever called me anything but "most holy." I have six thousand bulls to prove it.

GENIUS: That's what he said, bulls!

JULIUS: In which I am not only named "Lord most holy," but addressed as "your holiness," so that whatever I chose to do—

GENIUS: Even when he was drunk.

JULIUS: —people used to say that the holiness of the most holy lord Julius had done it.

PETER: Then you'd better ask those flatterers of yours to let you into heaven, because they're the ones who made you so holy. They provided the holiness, now let them provide the bliss. By the way, though I know you don't think it matters, do you actually imagine you were a holy man?

JULIUS: You really vex me. If I were only allowed to go on living, I wouldn't envy you your holiness or your bliss, either one.

PETER: The proper expression of a pious mind! But apart from that, when I look you over from head to foot, I see many a sign of impiety and none of holiness. What's the meaning of these many comrades of yours? They're certainly not a papal retinue. You have almost twenty thousand men at your back, and in this entire crowd I can't find one single individual who has so much as the face of a Christian. I see a horrifying mob of ruffians, reeking of nothing but brothels, booze shops, and gunpowder. They look to me like plain highway robbers or spooks stolen out of hell and now intent on stirring up wars in heaven. As for yourself, the more I look at you, the fewer traces do I see of any apostolic character. What sort of unnatural arrangement is it, that while you wear the robes of a priest of God, under them you are dressed in the bloody armor of a warrior? Besides that, what a savage pair of eyes, what baleful features, what a menacing brow, what a disdainful and arrogant expression! I'm ashamed to say, and even to see, that there's no part of your body not marked with traces of outrageous and abominable lust; in addition, you belch and stink like a man just come from a drunken debauch and fresh from a fit of vomiting. Judging from the appearance of your whole body, you seem to me, not worn out by age or disease, but broken down and shrivelled up by drunken excesses.

GENIUS: How vividly he portrays the man in his own colors!

PETER: I see you threatening me with your lofty expression; but my feelings won't be suppressed. I suspect you may be that most pestilent pagan of all, Julius the Roman, returned from hell to make mock of our system. Certainly everything about you agrees well with him.

JULIUS: Ma di si!

PETER: What did he say?

GENIUS: He's angry. At that expression, every one of the cardinals used to take flight, otherwise they'd feel the stick of his holiness on their backs, especially if he hadn't had his supper.

PETER: You seem to me to have some understanding of the man; tell me, who are you?

GENIUS: I am the particular Genius of Julius.

PETER: His bad Genius, no doubt.

GENIUS: Whatever I may be, I'm Julius's man.

JULIUS: Why don't you stop all this nonsense and open the doors? Perhaps you'd rather I broke them down. Why do we need all this palaver? You see the sort of troops I have at my command.

PETER: I do indeed see some highly practiced thieves. But you must be aware that these doors can only be opened in other ways.

JULIUS: Enough words, I say. If you don't hurry up and open the gates, I'll unleash my thunderbolt of excommunication with which I used to terrify great kings on earth and their kingdoms too. You see, I've , already got a bull prepared for the occasion.

PETER: Just tell me, please, what you mean by all this bombast about bulls, bolts of thunder, and maledictions. I never heard from Christ a single one of these words.

JULIUS: You'll feel their full force, if you don't watch out.

PETER: Perhaps you used to terrify people with that bluster, but it counts for nothing here. Here we deal only in the truth. This is a fortress to be captured with good deeds, not ugly words. But let me ask you, since you threaten men with the thunder of excommunication; what's your legal authority for that?

JULIUS: Very well: I take it you are now out of office and have no more standing than any other unbeneficed priest; indeed, you're not even a complete priest, since you lack the power to consecrate.

PETER: Doubtless because I happen to be dead.

JULIUS: Obviously.

PETER: But for the same reason, you have no more standing with me than any other dead man.

JULIUS: But as long as the cardinals are arguing over the election of a new pope, it counts as my administration.

GENIUS: He's still dreaming dreams about being alive!

JULIUS: But now, open the door, I tell you.

PETER: And I won't do a thing, I tell you, unless you give me a full account of your merits.

JULIUS: What merits?

PETER: Let me explain the idea. Did you distinguish yourself in theology?

JULIUS: Not at all. I had no time for it, being continually engaged in warfare. Besides, there are plenty of priests to do that sort of work.

PETER: Then by the holiness of your life you gained many souls for Christ?

GENIUS: Many more for hell, I'd say.

PETER: You performed miracles?

JULIUS: You're talking old-fashioned nonsense.

PETER: You prayed earnestly and constantly?

JULIUS: This is pure foolishness.

PETER: You subdued the lusts of the flesh with fasts and long vigils?

GENIUS: Enough of this, please; with this line of questioning, you're just wasting your time.

PETER: I never heard of any other gifts that an outstanding pope was supposed to possess. If he has some more apostolic talents, let him tell me about them himself.

JULIUS: Though it's a disgraceful thing for Julius who never lowered his crest before anyone else to yield to Peter—who was, to say nothing worse, a lowly fisherman and almost a beggar—still, just to let you know what sort of prince you're slighting in this way, now hear this. In the first place, I am from Liguria, not a Jew like you; but I'm afraid that like you I was once a boatman.

GENIUS: It's nothing to be ashamed of, for there's still this difference, that Peter fished for a living, while Julius plied the oar on a barge for minimum wages.

JULIUS: Then, as it happened that I was the nephew of Pope Sixtus the great.

GENIUS: Great in vices, he means.

JULIUS: -on his sister's side, his special favor combined with my industry first gave me access to ecclesiastical office; and so I gradually rose to the dignity of a cardinal's cap. Having undergone many reverses of fortune, and been tossed to and fro by various accidents-having suffered, among other diseases, from epilepsy and the pox they call French -I found myself quite overwhelmed; I was exiled, rejected, despised, despaired of, and almost given over as lost. Yet I never doubted that some day I would attain the papacy. That showed real strength of character, compared with you, who were terrified at the question of a serving girl, and gave up your faith on the spot. She weakened your courage, but I got new courage from a woman, a soothsayer and prophetess of sorts, who when she saw me overwhelmed with misfortunes secretly whispered in my ear, "Bear up, Julius! Don't be ashamed of anything you have to do or put up with. Some day you will attain the triple crown. You will be king of kings and ruler of all rulers." And in fact neither her prophecy nor my own instincts deceived me. Beyond all expectations I achieved my goal, partly with the help of the French who sheltered me in my hour of need, partly by the marvelous power of money in large quantities, which I increased by taking usurious rates of interest. And finally my own ready wit helped me—

PETER: What's this ready wit you're talking about?

JULIUS: —to coin money from the bare promise of ecclesiastical offices, making skillful use of brokers in the process, since the sums I demanded couldn't have been paid in cash by a man as rich as Crassus. But it's useless to describe the schemes to you, since not even all my bankers understood them. Anyhow, that's how I made my way. Now as for how I bore myself in the pontificate, I'll venture to say that none of the early popes (who seem to me to have been popes in name only), nor even of the later ones, deserve so well of the church and of Christ himself as I do.

GENIUS: Only listen to the bragging of the beast!

PETER: I'm waiting to hear how you got away with it all.

JULIUS: I discovered a great many new offices (that's what they're called) which in themselves brought goodly sums into the papal treasury. Then I found a brand-new way by which bishoprics could be bought without any taint of simony. For my predecessors had made a law that any man appointed bishop should lay down his previous office. I interpreted it this way; "You are ordered to lay down your previous office; but if you don't have one you can't lay it down, therefore you must buy it." By this means each individual bishopric brought in its six or seven thousand ducats over and above those that are traditionally extorted for bulls. Also the new money that I spread all over Italy brought in a very healthy sum. And I never let up on accumulating money, understanding as I did that without it nothing is managed properly, whether sacred or profane. Now, to come to my major achievements, I conquered Bologna, which had long been ruled by the Bentivogli, and restored it to the control of Rome. The previously undefeated Venetians I crushed with my army. For a long time I harassed the duke of Ferrara, and nearly caught him in a trap. I cleverly escaped from a schismatic council set up against me by convoking a fraudulent counter-council, and so, as they say, drove out one nail with another. Finally, I expelled from Italy the French, who at that time were the terrors of the whole world, and I would have driven out the Spanish too (for I had that project under way), if the fates had not suddenly removed me from the earth. And I ask you to admire my undaunted spirit throughout these trials. When the French looked like winners, I was already looking around for a good hiding place; when my position seemed almost desperate, I grew a long white beard as a disguise. But then the golden messenger of victory alighted unexpectedly on me at Ravenna, where a good many thousand Frenchmen were killed; and that was the resurrection of Julius. In fact, for three days I was believed to be at death's door; I thought so myself; and yet here again, against everyone's hopes and even my own expectations, I lived anew. In fact my power and my political shrewdness are so great to this day that there's none of the Christian kings whom I haven't brought to blows, breaking up the treaties by which they had painfully made peace with one another, ripping them to pieces, and trampling them underfoot. Indeed, I was so successful in abolishing the treaty of Cambrai, made between me, the king of France, the emperor Maximilian, and several other rulers, that nobody ever mentions it any more. Over and above all this, I raised several different armies, celebrated many grandiose triumphs, put on splendid shows, built numerous impressive structures, and then at my death left at least five million ducats, which I would have increased even further if that Jewish physician who saved my life on one occasion had been able to stretch it out a little longer. And I really wish now that some magician could be found to restore my earthly existence, so that I could put the finishing touches on the really marvelous projects that I had under way. Still, on my deathbed I tried to ensure that none of the wars I had stirred up throughout the world should be settled; I ordered that money set aside for those wars should not be diverted elsewhere; and that was my last wish as I breathed out my dying breath. Now do you hesitate to open the gates for a pontiff who has deserved so well of Christ and the church? And I expect you to be all the more impressed because all this was achieved by my individual constancy of mind alone. I had none of those helpers and favoring circumstances that others have enjoyed; I had no ancestors, for I didn't even know my own father (which indeed I say proudly); I had no personal attractions, since most people shuddered at my face as at an ogre; I had no education, since with me it never took; I had no physical strength, for reasons mentioned above; I was not possessed of youthful energy, for I did all these things as an old man; popularity played no part, for there was nobody who didn't hate me; and I got no credit for clergency because I punished savagely those whom other rulers commonly let off scot-free.

PETER: What's this all about?

GENIUS: He talks very tough, but there's something soft in it.

JULIUS: Thus, with everything against me—fortune, age, strength, briefly, without help from gods or men, by the unaided power of my spirit and my money, I accomplished in a few years so much, that my successors will be busy for at least a decade deciding what to do next. I've said all this about myself with the utmost truth and also, for that matter, with the utmost honesty. If one of those preachers who orate before me in Rome had been here to cover my account with his decorations, you'd have thought a god was being described, not a man.

PETER: Unconquerable warrior, since all these things you talk about are new to me and unheard-of, I beg your pardon for my amazement or inexperience; I hope it won't be too tiresome for you to answer a few clumsy questions about the details. Who, for example, are these little curly-headed striplings?

JULIUS: I brought them up for my diversion.

PETER: Who are these smoke-blackened and mutilated fellows?

JULIUS: They are soldiers and warriors who in behalf of me and the church bravely encountered death in battle. Some died in the siege of Bologna, many in the war against the Venetians, others still at Ravenna. They are all to be admitted to heaven by the terms of our contract, in which I promised, by promulgating some mighty bulls, to send anyone straight to heaven who died fighting for Julius, whatever his previous life had been like.

PETER: As far as I can see, these people must have been the very lot who before your coming were most hateful to me because they were always trying to break in by force, using leaden bulls to force their way.

JULIUS: Then, as I understand it, you didn't let any of them in?

PETER: Not a single one of that crowd did I admit. That's what Christ told me; he didn't say to admit those who came here lugging heavy leaden bulls, but only those who had clothed the naked, fed the hungry, given drink to the thirsty, visited the prisoners, aided the pilgrims. If he wanted me to keep out those who prophesied in his name, cast out devils, and did wonderful works, I do you suppose he would want people let in who just walk up with a bull in the name of Julius?

JULIUS: If I had only known!

PETER: I understand; if some demon out of hell had told you about it, you would have declared war on me.

JULIUS: I would have excommunicated you first.

PETER: But go on, why do you go about wearing armor?

JULIUS: As if you didn't know the holy pope wields two swords; you wouldn't want me to go into battle unarmed, would you?

PETER: When I held your position, I followed that rule in the word of God which says to use no sword save that of the Spirit.

JULIUS: That would surprise Malchus, whose ear you cut off—without a sword, no doubt.

PETER: I recall the event, and it's true; but at that time I was fighting for my master, Christ, not for myself; for the life of the Lord, not for loot or worldly booty; and I fought, not as pope, but as one to whom the keys had only been promised, not delivered, nor had I yet received the holy spirit. All the same, I was ordered to put up my sword as a clear warning that warfare of that sort was unbecoming to priests and even to Christians in general. But more of this elsewhere. Why are you so careful about calling yourself a Ligurian as if it mattered what part of the earth the vicar of Christ came from?

JULIUS: But I consider it an act of the highest piety to shed renown on my people; that's why I have this title inscribed on all my coins, statues, structures, and arches.

PETER: So a man can recognize his fatherland who doesn't know his father? At first I thought you had in mind that heavenly Jerusalem, the home of all true believers and of its unique prince in whose name those believers are eager to be sanctified and exalted. But why do you describe yourself as "nephew to Sixtus on his sister's side"? I'm surprised that this man Sixtus never showed up here, though he was pope and related to such a leader as yourself. Do tell me, if you will, what kind of man he was: was he a priest?

JULIUS: A might soldier he was, and a man of exemplary religion too; he was a Franciscan.

PETER: Indeed, I once knew a man named Francis, a layman distinguished among his fellows for virtue as well as his scorn for wealth, pleasure, and ambition. Does that poor man now have command of military commanders like this?

JULIUS: As far as I can see, you don't want anyone to better himself; even Benedict was a poor man once, but now his followers are so rich that even I am envious of them.

PETER: Fine! but let's go back a ways: you are the nephew of Sixtus.

JULIUS: Glad to confirm it; I'd like to stop the mouths of those who say I'm his son. That's slanderous.

PETER: Slanderous indeed—unless perhaps it's true.

JULIUS: It's an insult to papal dignity, which must always be protected.

PETER: But I think popes should protect their own dignity by not doing anything offensive to the moral law. Speaking of papal dignity, let me ask you, is that the common and accepted way of achieving the papacy that you were describing just now?

JULIUS: For some centuries now, that's been the way of it, unless my successor is created by some other procedure. For as soon as I achieved the papacy myself, I issued a formidable bull that no one else should seek the office by the means I had used; and I renewed that bull shortly before my death. How it will be observed is up to other people.

PETER: I don't see how anyone could describe a bad state of affairs any better. But this puzzles me, how anybody can be found to undertake the job, since so much hard work attaches to the office and so many difficulties must be overcome to acquire it. When I was pope, hardly anyone could be persuaded to accept the office of a presbyter or a deacon.

JULIUS: No wonder; for in those days the reward of bishops was nothing but hard work, sleepless nights, constant study, and very often death: now, it's a kingdom, with the privileges of a tyrant. And who, if he has a chance of a kingdom, won't grab at it?

PETER: Well, tell me now about Bologna. Had it departed from the faith that it had to be brought back to Rome?

JULIUS: Absurd! that wasn't the question at all.

PETER: Perhaps the Bentivogli were poor administrators and destroying the prosperity of the city.

JULIUS: Not a bit of it; the town was flourishing as never before, they had enlarged it and adorned it with many new buildings. That only made me more eager for it.

PETER: I understand; they had taken possession of it illegally.

JULIUS: No, again; the city was theirs by treaty.

PETER: Perhaps the citizens hated their ruler?

JULIUS: On the contrary; they clung to him tooth and nail, whereas they almost all loathed me.

PETER: What was the reason for it then?

JULIUS: Because, as the ruler arranged things, out of the immense sums that he collected from the citizens, only a few paltry thousands ever reached my treasury. Besides, its capture helped on some other plans that I had in mind. And so, with the French doing the work (mostly out of fear of my thunderbolt), I drove out the Bentivogli and put bishops and cardinals in charge of the town, so that all the money collected there, down to the last penny, came into the hands of the church of Rome. Besides, in the old days, all the titles and dignities of imperial rule seemed to belong to him. Now you see everywhere statues of me; my titles are inscribed everywhere, my trophies are admired; nothing to be seen but stone and bronze images of Julius. Finally, if you had seen the royal procession in which I entered Bologna, you would surely despise all the triumphs celebrated by the Octavii and Scipios; you would understand that there were good reasons why I fought so hard for Bologna; and you would see that at the same time the church was fighting and triumphing alongside me.

PETER: So when you were the monarch, as I understand it, that condition had come about for which Christ ordered us to pray: "Thy kingdom come." Now tell me what the Venetians did wrong.

JULIUS: First of all, they ran after Greek fashions, and they treated me almost as a joke, putting all sorts of obstacles in my way.

PETER: Were they right or wrong?

JULIUS: What does that matter? It's sacrilege even to mumble about the pope of Rome, except in the way of praise. Then they bestowed their priesthoods as they saw fit; they wouldn't allow lawsuits to be transferred to Rome; and they wouldn't allow the selling of dispensations. Do I have to go on? They inflicted unbearable damage on the authority of Rome, and took command of a significant part of your patrimony.

PETER: My patrimony? What patrimony are you talking about to me, who left all my possessions behind to follow, unclad, a barefoot Christ?

JULIUS: I say that various cities are the property of the Roman church, and it has pleased the most holy fathers to call by that name these their own special possessions.

PETER: Thus you use my shame to cover your own greed. And so this is what you call unbearable damage?

JULIUS: Why not?

PETER: Were their manners corrupted? Was piety growing cold?

JULIUS: Forget it! you're talking about trifles. We were being deprived of thousands upon thousands of ducats, enough to furnish out a legion of soldiers.

PETER: A terrible loss for a usurer, I'm sure. And now about the duke of Ferrara, what was the matter with him?

JULIUS: What did he do, that most ungrateful of men? Alexander the vicar of Christ did this miserable rogue the honor of bestowing on him, as a wife, his second daughter, and with her he gave an enormous dowry, more than a man so base of birth could have expected. Yet, indifferent to such humane treatment, he made nothing but trouble for me, accusing me of simony, pederasty, and mental instability. And besides, he held back some taxes, not the major ones, I concede, but still important enough not to be overlooked by a diligent shepherd.

GENIUS: Or a skinflint.

JULIUS: Besides, which is more to the point, Ferrara helped along the main project I had in mind to join this territory to my own because of its strategic location. At first I wanted to bestow the city on my kinsman, a man of energy who would have ventured anything in behalf of the dignity of the church. In fact, he recently killed the cardinal of Pavia with his own hands, in my behalf. As for my daughter's husband, he isn't the political sort.

PETER: What's this I hear? Do popes have wives and children nowadays?

JULIUS: Proper wives they don't have; but what's so strange about their having children, since they're men and not eunuchs?

PETER: But what sort of events led to the calling of that schismatic council?

JULIUS: It's a long story, but I'll cut it short. For a long time some people have been discontented with the Roman church. They complained of the shameful money-grubbing, of monstrous and abominable lusts, of poisonings, sacrilege, murders, public sales of simoniacal positions, pollution of every description. They called me a simonist, a drunkard, a low villain swollen with earthly lusts, and on every count the man least worthy of occupying the position that in fact I occupied; they called me the greatest of all perils to the Christian community. And in this troubled state of affairs they thought help was to be sought from a general council of the church. They added that I had sworn when I was created pope to call a general council within two years, asserting that I was created pope only on that condition.

PETER: Were they right about that?

JULIUS: Absolutely. But when it suited my convenience to do so, I absolved myself of my own oath. When a king wants to break his solemn oath, who has any doubt that he can do it? Keep your piety for another occasion, as the first Julius, my other self, used to say. But only note the audacity of these men, the schemes they devised. Nine cardinals made a separation, notified me of a council to be called, and invited me to attend, even to preside. When I declined, they announced the council to the whole world in the name of the emperor Maximilian (under the pretext that years ago councils used to be called by Roman emperors) and likewise Louis of France, the twelfth of that name. What they proposed-I shudder to say it-was to rip up the seamless garment of Christ, which even those who crucified the Savior left untorn.

PETER: But were you the sort of man they said?

JULIUS: What has that got to do with it? I was pope. Suppose I was a worse rascal than the Cercopes, stupider than a wooden statue or the log from which it was made, more foul than the swamp of Lerna; whoever holds this key of power must be revered as the vicar of Christ and reverenced as the holiest of men.

PETER: Even if he's openly evil?

JULIUS: As open as you like. It's just unthinkable that God's vicar on earth, who represents God himself before men, should be rebuked by any puny mortal or disturbed by any sort of popular outcry.

PETER: But common sense is outraged if we must feel warmly toward one whom we see to be evil, or speak well of one about whom we think ill.

JULIUS: Let every man think as he will, as long as he speaks well or at least holds his tongue. The pope of Rome cannot be censured by anyone, not by a general council.

PETER: This one thing I know, that Christ's vicar on earth should be as much like him as possible, and lead his life in such a way that nobody can blame any part of it, or justifiably speak evil of him. Things go badly with popes when, instead of earning men's commendations by good deeds, they extort praises with threats. Such popes cannot be praised without lying; indeed, they can't expect anything more than the sullen silence of those who hate them. Tell me now truly, is there no way at all to correct a criminal, infectious pope?

JULIUS: Absurd. Who is going to remove the highest authority of all?

PETER: That's exactly why he should be removed, because he's the highest figure; for the higher he is, the more pernicious his influence may be. If secular laws allow for a king who rules his land badly to be not only deposed but executed, why should the church be so helpless that it must put up with a pope who ruins everything, instead of expelling him as a public nuisance?

JULIUS: If the pope is to be corrected, it ought to be by a council; but against the will of the pope a council can't be called; otherwise it would be a mere convention, not a proper council. Even if it were called, it couldn't issue any decrees if the pope objected. And finally, my last defense is absolute power, of which the pope possesses more, all by himself, than an entire council. In short, the pope can't be removed from office for any crime whatever.

PETER: Not for homicide?

JULIUS: Not for parricide.

PETER: Not for fornication?

JULIUS: Ridiculous! not even for incest.

PETER: Not for the sin of simony?

JULIUS: Not for six hundred such sins.

PETER: Not for poisoning someone?

JULIUS: Not even for sacrilege.

PETER: Not for blasphemy?

JULIUS: No, I say.

PETER: Not for all these crimes poured together in a single sewer of a man?

JULIUS: Add if you like the names of six hundred other vices, each one worse than any of these, and still the pope cannot be removed from his throne for any such reasons.

PETER: This is a new doctrine about the dignity of the pope that I've picked up here; he alone, it seems, is entitled to be the worst of men. I've also learned about a new misery for the church, that she alone is unable to rid herself of such a monster, but is forced to adore a pope with a character that nobody would endure in a stable-boy.

JULIUS: Some say there is a single reason for which a pope can be removed.

PETER: What kind of good deed is that, please tell me—since he can't be removed for evil deeds, such as those I've mentioned.

JULIUS: For the crime of heresy; but only if he's been publicly convicted of it. In reality, this is just a flimsy thread of an exception, that doesn't limit papal authority by a single scintilla. The pope can always repeal the law, if it bothers him in the least. And then who would dare to accuse the pope himself, entrenched as he is behind so many lines of defense? Besides, if he were hard pressed by a council, it would be easy to save face with a recantation if a flat denial didn't dispose of the matter. Finally, there are a thousand different deceptions and evasions by which he could get away, unless he were a plain wooden stock instead of a man.

INTRODUCTION TO
Martin Luther
NINETY-FIVE THESES

Few documents in Christian history have become as iconic as Martin Luther's *Ninety-Five Theses*, the ringing denunciation of the corruptions of the late medieval church that was to spark the Protestant Reformation. Luther may or may not have posted them on the church door in Wittenberg (he almost certainly did not nail them, in any case, as later legend would have it), but his dissemination of them on October 31, 1517 marked a turning point not only in Luther's life but in the life of the whole Christian Church.

The *Theses* themselves, however, are an unlikely candidate for the role of revolutionary text or Protestant manifesto: composed chiefly for an academic disputation on a practice now long-forgotten and scarce understood, the theses are a bit bewildering to the modern reader looking for familiar Reformation slogans. Indeed, neither of Luther's two great principles—justification by faith alone or the authority of Scriptural alone—are to be found in these pages, even though the former had already begun to influence Luther's thinking and underlies several of his concerns in the *Theses*.

Judged by the standard of Luther's later work (even his writings from two or three years later), the *Theses* are a fairly conservative text, and Luther hardly expected them to unleash a full-scale reconception of Christian theology and division of the Church.

Luther here is not so much interested in overthrowing the whole penitential system of the Catholic Church as in purifying it from obvious abuses, and he continues to accept many of the pope's claims of authority. Indeed, in Theses 80–90 he says that one of his chief concerns is to defend the honor of the pope against the easy attacks that the careless teaching of the indulgence preachers has exposed him to.

On the other hand, it is easy to downplay too much the significance of the *Theses*. Luther was not, after all, just a random and inconsequential monk, as the pope and his advisors were to try and dismiss him; he was at this time one of the highest-ranking leaders of the Augustinian Order in Germany and an increasingly-renowned professor at one of its leading universities. Moreover, Luther did not compose the *Theses* on a whim; he had been long wrestling over the indulgences issue and was well aware that by attacking the practice, he would be likely earning himself some very powerful enemies. Finally, although theses were normally composed for academic disputations only, Luther seems to have from the first intended these for a wider audience. As scholar Timothy J. Wengert notes, the *Theses* are full of rhetorical flourishes that suggest Luther wanted to reach and persuade many educated readers,[1] and very unusually for such theses, Luther from the first invited scholars from around Germany to respond to the theses in writing. Indeed, there does not ever seem to have been an academic disputation in Wittenberg as would normally have followed such theses. Most striking of all, Luther took the extraordinary step of sending the *Theses* to Archbishop Albrecht of Mainz, the leading church authority in Germany, and exhorting him in no uncertain terms to restrain the indulgence preachers.

So who were these indulgence preachers and why was Luther so upset about them? The answer sheds light both on the astonishing depth of the corruption in the late medieval Church and on the often misunderstood heart of Luther's protest against it.

The theology and practice of indulgences had been around for centuries, although it had gotten increasingly out of hand in

1 Wengert, *Martin Luther's 95 Theses*, 5.

the decades leading up to 1517. At its root lay a long medieval distinction between guilt and punishment: although true repentance of sins and confession to a priest could give the believer absolution from *guilt* and therefore from hellfire, sin still demanded some kind of temporal punishment. Some of this punishment could be handled by taking penitential actions prescribed by the priest, but much of it would remain to be exacted after death. Accordingly, the medieval church came to increasingly teach the doctrine of purgatory, a place where the faithful must suffer long (perhaps even hundreds of thousands of years) of purifying suffering before they could enter heaven. But, there was some good news. By doing certain holy acts, like participating in or helping pay for a Crusade, Christians could receive an "indulgence" from the pope, shortening their time in purgatory or perhaps even skipping it altogether. Eventually, recognizing in indulgences a potentially immense source of revenue, later popes began offering them for money, rather than for good deeds, and needing to continue to expand the market to keep the revenues flowing, started allowing the faithful to buy indulgences for their dead relatives already in purgatory.

Johann Tetzel's indulgence campaign that prompted Luther's protest in 1517, though, was an extraordinary illustration of the corruption that came from mixing such absolute spiritual power with the wide-reaching worldly power of the late medieval church. Ostensibly ordered to help finance the construction of St. Peter's basilica in Rome, much of the money actually went into the coffers of Archbishop Albrecht of Mainz. Albrecht needed it in order to repay the Fugger banking family for the immense debts he had contracted from them in order to buy from the pope the most powerful church office in Germany at the age of 23. Since the most enthusiastic buyers of indulgences were the uneducated and gullible poor, Tetzel's indulgence campaign constituted an extraordinary redistribution of wealth upward from the poorest to the richest in Christendom.

Such exploitation of the poor infuriated Luther, and in thesis 45, he decries those who, instead of helping the needy, as Christ commanded for the truly penitent, spent all their spare money on indulgences. More fundamentally, though, Luther worried that indulgences were a form of cheap grace, a way for people to purchase false security for their souls without truly facing the depth of their sin and repenting from the heart. The earlier distinction between guilt and punishment had been thoroughly blurred so that indulgences had become a substitute for true repentance, purchasing freedom from guilt as well as punishment. This point is key to grasp, given how readily Luther's gospel of salvation by faith alone is often distorted. Luther's concern with the late medieval church was less that it had made salvation too hard (by endless works rather than simple faith) and more that it had made salvation too easy (by thoughtless outward works or transactions rather than heartfelt repentance, being crucified with Christ). The real gospel of Christ, charged Luther, was both much more serious, more frightening, and more liberating than the spiritual economy the popes had created to fill their own coffers.

NINETY-FIVE THESES

Martin Luther

TRANSLATOR UNKNOWN

Out of love for the truth and the desire to bring it to light, the following propositions will be discussed at Wittenberg, under the presidency of the Reverend Father Martin Luther, Master of Arts and of Sacred Theology, and Lecturer in Ordinary on the same at that place. Wherefore he requests that those who are unable to be present and debate orally with us, may do so by letter.

In the Name our Lord Jesus Christ. Amen.

1. Our Lord and Master Jesus Christ, when He said *Poenitentiam agite*, willed that the whole life of believers should be repentance.
2. This word cannot be understood to mean sacramental penance, i.e., confession and satisfaction, which is administered by the priests.
3. Yet it means not inward repentance only; nay, there is no inward repentance which does not outwardly work divers mortifications of the flesh.
4. The penalty [of sin], therefore, continues so long as hatred of self continues; for this is the true inward repentance, and continues until our entrance into the kingdom of heaven.

5. The pope does not intend to remit, and cannot remit any penalties other than those which he has imposed either by his own authority or by that of the Canons.

6. The pope cannot remit any guilt, except by declaring that it has been remitted by God and by assenting to God's remission; though, to be sure, he may grant remission in cases reserved to his judgment. If his right to grant remission in such cases were despised, the guilt would remain entirely unforgiven.

7. God remits guilt to no one whom He does not, at the same time, humble in all things and bring into subjection to His vicar, the priest.

8. The penitential canons are imposed only on the living, and, according to them, nothing should be imposed on the dying.

9. Therefore the Holy Spirit in the pope is kind to us, because in his decrees he always makes exception of the article of death and of necessity.

10. Ignorant and wicked are the doings of those priests who, in the case of the dying, reserve canonical penances for purgatory.

11. This changing of the canonical penalty to the penalty of purgatory is quite evidently one of the tares that were sown while the bishops slept.

12. In former times the canonical penalties were imposed not after, but before absolution, as tests of true contrition.

13. The dying are freed by death from all penalties; they are already dead to canonical rules, and have a right to be released from them.

14. The imperfect health [of soul], that is to say, the imperfect love, of the dying brings with it, of necessity, great fear; and the smaller the love, the greater is the fear.

15. This fear and horror is sufficient of itself alone (to say nothing of other things) to constitute the penalty of purgatory, since it is very near to the horror of despair.

16. Hell, purgatory, and heaven seem to differ as do despair, almost-despair, and the assurance of safety.
17. With souls in purgatory it seems necessary that horror should grow less and love increase.
18. It seems unproved, either by reason or Scripture, that they are outside the state of merit, that is to say, of increasing love.
19. Again, it seems unproved that they, or at least that all of them, are certain or assured of their own blessedness, though we may be quite certain of it.
20. Therefore by "full remission of all penalties" the pope means not actually "of all," but only of those imposed by himself.
21. Therefore those preachers of indulgences are in error, who say that by the pope's indulgences a man is freed from every penalty, and saved;
22. Whereas he remits to souls in purgatory no penalty which, according to the canons, they would have had to pay in this life.
23. If it is at all possible to grant to any one the remission of all penalties whatsoever, it is certain that this remission can be granted only to the most perfect, that is, to the very fewest.
24. It must needs be, therefore, that the greater part of the people are deceived by that indiscriminate and high sounding promise of release from penalty.
25. The power which the pope has, in a general way, over purgatory, is just like the power which any bishop or curate has, in a special way, within his own diocese or parish.
26. The pope does well when he grants remission to souls [in purgatory], not by the power of the keys (which he does not possess), but by way of intercession.
27. They preach man who say that so soon as the penny jingles into the money-box, the soul flies out [of purgatory].
28. It is certain that when the penny jingles into the money-box, gain and avarice can be increased, but the result of the intercession of the Church is in the power of God alone.

29. Who knows whether all the souls in purgatory wish to be bought out of it, as in the legend of Sts. Severinus and Paschal.

30. No one is sure that his own contrition is sincere; much less that he has attained full remission.

31. Rare as is the man that is truly penitent, so rare is also the man who truly buys indulgences, i.e., such men are most rare.

32. They will be condemned eternally, together with their teachers, who believe themselves sure of their salvation because they have letters of pardon.

33. Men must be on their guard against those who say that the pope's pardons are that inestimable gift of God by which man is reconciled to Him;

34. For these "graces of pardon" concern only the penalties of sacramental satisfaction, and these are appointed by man.

35. They preach no Christian doctrine who teach that contrition is not necessary in those who intend to buy souls out of purgatory or to buy confessionalia.

36. Every truly repentant Christian has a right to full remission of penalty and guilt, even without letters of pardon.

37. Every true Christian, whether living or dead, has part in all the blessings of Christ and the Church; and this is granted him by God, even without letters of pardon.

38. Nevertheless, the remission and participation [in the blessings of the Church] which are granted by the pope are in no way to be despised, for they are, as I have said, the declaration of divine remission.

39. It is most difficult, even for the very keenest theologians, at one and the same time to commend to the people the abundance of pardons and [the need of] true contrition.

40. True contrition seeks and loves penalties, but liberal pardons only relax penalties and cause them to be hated, or at least, furnish an occasion [for hating them].

41. Apostolic pardons are to be preached with caution, lest the people may falsely think them preferable to other good works of love.

42. Christians are to be taught that the pope does not intend the buying of pardons to be compared in any way to works of mercy.

43. Christians are to be taught that he who gives to the poor or lends to the needy does a better work than buying pardons;

44. Because love grows by works of love, and man becomes better; but by pardons man does not grow better, only more free from penalty.

45. Christians are to be taught that he who sees a man in need, and passes him by, and gives [his money] for pardons, purchases not the indulgences of the pope, but the indignation of God.

46. Christians are to be taught that unless they have more than they need, they are bound to keep back what is necessary for their own families, and by no means to squander it on pardons.

47. Christians are to be taught that the buying of pardons is a matter of free will, and not of commandment.

48. Christians are to be taught that the pope, in granting pardons, needs, and therefore desires, their devout prayer for him more than the money they bring.

49. Christians are to be taught that the pope's pardons are useful, if they do not put their trust in them; but altogether harmful, if through them they lose their fear of God.

50. Christians are to be taught that if the pope knew the exactions of the pardon-preachers, he would rather that St. Peter's church should go to ashes, than that it should be built up with the skin, flesh and bones of his sheep.

51. Christians are to be taught that it would be the pope's wish, as it is his duty, to give of his own money to very many of those from whom certain hawkers of pardons cajole money, even though the church of St. Peter might have to be sold.

52. The assurance of salvation by letters of pardon is vain, even though the commissary, nay, even though the pope himself, were to stake his soul upon it.

53. They are enemies of Christ and of the pope, who bid the Word of God be altogether silent in some Churches, in order that pardons may be preached in others.

54. Injury is done the Word of God when, in the same sermon, an equal or a longer time is spent on pardons than on this Word.

55. It must be the intention of the pope that if pardons, which are a very small thing, are celebrated with one bell, with single processions and ceremonies, then the Gospel, which is the very greatest thing, should be preached with a hundred bells, a hundred processions, a hundred ceremonies.

56. The "treasures of the Church," out of which the pope grants indulgences, are not sufficiently named or known among the people of Christ.

57. That they are not temporal treasures is certainly evident, for many of the vendors do not pour out such treasures so easily, but only gather them.

58. Nor are they the merits of Christ and the Saints, for even without the pope, these always work grace for the inner man, and the cross, death, and hell for the outward man.

59. St. Lawrence said that the treasures of the Church were the Church's poor, but he spoke according to the usage of the word in his own time.

60. Without rashness we say that the keys of the Church, given by Christ's merit, are that treasure;

61. For it is clear that for the remission of penalties and of reserved cases, the power of the pope is of itself sufficient.

62. The true treasure of the Church is the Most Holy Gospel of the glory and the grace of God.

63. But this treasure is naturally most odious, for it makes the first to be last.

64. On the other hand, the treasure of indulgences is naturally most acceptable, for it makes the last to be first.

65. Therefore the treasures of the Gospel are nets with which they formerly were wont to fish for men of riches.

66. The treasures of the indulgences are nets with which they now fish for the riches of men.

67. The indulgences which the preachers cry as the "greatest graces" are known to be truly such, in so far as they promote gain.

68. Yet they are in truth the very smallest graces compared with the grace of God and the piety of the Cross.

69. Bishops and curates are bound to admit the commissaries of apostolic pardons, with all reverence.

70. But still more are they bound to strain all their eyes and attend with all their ears, lest these men preach their own dreams instead of the commission of the pope.

71. He who speaks against the truth of apostolic pardons, let him be anathema and accursed!

72. But he who guards against the lust and license of the pardon-preachers, let him be blessed!

73. The pope justly thunders against those who, by any art, contrive the injury of the traffic in pardons.

74. But much more does he intend to thunder against those who use the pretext of pardons to contrive the injury of holy love and truth.

75. To think the papal pardons so great that they could absolve a man even if he had committed an impossible sin and violated the Mother of God—this is madness.

76. We say, on the contrary, that the papal pardons are not able to remove the very least of venial sins, so far as its guilt is concerned.

77. It is said that even St. Peter, if he were now pope, could not bestow greater graces; this is blasphemy against St. Peter and against the pope.

78. We say, on the contrary, that even the present pope, and any pope at all, has greater graces at his disposal; to wit, the Gospel, powers, gifts of healing, etc., as it is written in I Corinthians xii.

79. To say that the cross, emblazoned with the papal arms, which is set up [by the preachers of indulgences], is of equal worth with the Cross of Christ, is blasphemy.

80. The bishops, curates and theologians who allow such talk to be spread among the people, will have an account to render.

81. This unbridled preaching of pardons makes it no easy matter, even for learned men, to rescue the reverence due to the pope from slander, or even from the shrewd questionings of the laity.

82. To wit, "Why does not the pope empty purgatory, for the sake of holy love and of the dire need of the souls that are there, if he redeems an infinite number of souls for the sake of miserable money with which to build a Church? The former reasons would be most just; the latter is most trivial."

83. Again, "Why are mortuary and anniversary masses for the dead continued, and why does he not return or permit the withdrawal of the endowments founded on their behalf, since it is wrong to pray for the redeemed?"

84. Again, "What is this new piety of God and the pope, that for money they allow a man who is impious and their enemy to buy out of purgatory the pious soul of a friend of God, and do not rather, because of that pious and beloved soul's own need, free it for pure love's sake?"

85. Again, "Why are the penitential canons long since in actual fact and through disuse abrogated and dead, now satisfied by the granting of indulgences, as though they were still alive and in force?"

86. Again, "Why does not the pope, whose wealth is to-day greater than the riches of the richest, build just this one church of St. Peter with his own money, rather than with the money of poor believers?"

87. Again, "What is it that the pope remits, and what participation does he grant to those who, by perfect contrition, have a right to full remission and participation?"

88. Again, "What greater blessing could come to the Church than if the pope were to do a hundred times a day what he now does once, and bestow on every believer these remissions and participations?"

89. "Since the pope, by his pardons, seeks the salvation of souls rather than money, why does he suspend the indulgences and pardons granted heretofore, since these have equal efficacy?"

90. To repress these arguments and scruples of the laity by force alone, and not to resolve them by giving reasons, is to expose the Church and the pope to the ridicule of their enemies, and to make Christians unhappy.

91. If, therefore, pardons were preached according to the spirit and mind of the pope, all these doubts would be readily resolved; nay, they would not exist.

92. Away, then, with all those prophets who say to the people of Christ, "Peace, peace," and there is no peace!

93. Blessed be all those prophets who say to the people of Christ, "Cross, cross," and there is no cross!

94. Christians are to be exhorted that they be diligent in following Christ, their Head, through penalties, deaths, and hell;

95. And thus be confident of entering into heaven rather through many tribulations, than through the assurance of peace.

INTRODUCTION TO
Martin Luther
LETTER TO THE CHRISTIAN NOBILITY

The Reformation was almost from its very beginning entangled with politics; indeed, it could hardly be otherwise, given that the late medieval papacy had itself been profoundly entangled with politics, and many of its worst corruptions stemmed from its worldly ambitions. We have seen already in previous selections how there were no lack of voices to criticize the Church's overreaching temporal claims and contend for the right of civil authorities to govern their territories without papal intervention.

Indeed, it was Elector Frederick the Wise's jealous sense of his own authority within Saxony that helped protect Luther from the early counterattacks of the Roman authorities, after his attack on indulgences began to provoke serious concerns. In summer 1518 Luther was initially summoned to a hearing in Rome, but protests by Frederick led to the hearing, with leading Catholic theologian Cardinal Cajetan, being moved to Augsburg in southern Germany. Cajetan's insistence that Luther drop the theological debate and simply submit to papal authority hardened rather than weakened Luther's reforming resolve, and he began to reconsider many other elements of medieval theology that he had previously accepted. By his 1519 public debate with Jan Eck, the Leipzig Disputation, Luther had read and was willing to defend some of the writings of Jan Hus, the 15th-century Czech reformer burned for heresy. This scandalized Eck, who hastened to Rome to lobby for Luther's wholesale condemnation.

Meanwhile, however, a new Holy Roman Emperor had been crowned, Charles V, at the age of 19. Uniting for the first time the crowns of the Empire and Spain—including Spain's rapidly growing possessions in the New World—Charles was on paper the most powerful man ever to be crowned in Europe. In reality, though, he was to be faced with a hopeless task, pinned between the papacy, to which he was spiritually loyal even if something of a political rival, the growing power of the Ottoman Turks to the east, and the restive German nobility to the north, some of whom were ardent supporters of Luther's ideas and reforms, and others of whom simply smelled an opportunity to increase their power and autonomy. It was to these nobles of the myriad German principalities, as well as to the young emperor himself, that Luther addressed his appeal in the remarkable text *The Letter to the Christian Nobility of the German Nation*.

In many respects, with its emphasis on the authority of temporal rulers, and the superiority of councils to Popes, it can be seen as an extension of many late medieval arguments, and Erasmus's Julius Exclusus as well. But Luther, expecting an excommunication from Rome any day and increasingly convinced that a wholesale reconfiguration of the Western Church was in order, went considerably further than all his predecessors.

His key innovation is found in his attack on what he calls the "first wall of the Romanists"—the distinction of clergy and laity. This distinction, and the treatment of clergy as an entirely separate, "spiritual" body of Christians subject to the pope alone, had of course been a thorn in the side of lay rulers for centuries, unable as they were to tax the clergy or even prosecute them for crimes. Marsilius of Padua in particular had gone a long way towards erasing clerical autonomy, but even he did not question the fact of the distinction—indeed, in some ways he intensified it with his sharp dichotomy between spiritual and temporal affairs. Luther, however, made the revolutionary claim of what became known as the "priesthood of all believers," arguing that "all Christians are truly of the spiritual estate, and there is no difference among them, save of office alone," so much so that in a pinch, laymen could choose a priest from among themselves and ordain him, without needing the consecration of a bishop.

Luther's doctrine of the universal priesthood was not meant as a call for an "every man for himself" religion—the church still needed teachers and authorities—but ordained teaching authority emerged out of the whole community of believers, much as Marsilius had argued that political authority must be delegated upwards from the whole community. Moreover, as leading members of the church, placed by God in positions of power to care for their people, Christian rulers had a duty to take action for the reform of the church if the ordained clergy were not doing their jobs. This insistence on the legitimate role of lay authority in the Church was to be a consistent, and transformative, theme of the Reformation, though one that was to create many headaches for the Reformers as kings and princes sometimes tried to bend the church to worldly priorities and ambitions.

Having made his greatest argument in demolishing the "first wall of the Romanists," the latter two walls—that the pope alone has authority to declare the meaning of Scripture and to call councils—were easily dispensed of. Drawing on arguments of earlier conciliarists, direct appeals to Scripture, and his new conception of authority residing in the whole body of the Church, Luther argued that Scripture must take precedence over any papal claims, and if the pope was stubborn, councils or civil rulers should take steps to correct him.

In the remainder of the treatise, not included here, Luther goes on to offer a detailed indictment of the corruptions of wealth and power that had perverted the late medieval church, and detailed suggestions for how the papacy might be cut down to an appropriate size and properly spiritual function. He also offers extended advice for the reform of ecclesiastical and civil laws on such important matters as marriage, arguing above all that clergy should be allowed to marry. Many of his suggestions, and his expectation that godly rulers might actually implement them all, seem a bit idealistic. However, it should be recognized that the Reformation was not merely a church affair and it was not long before Protestant princes and city councils undertook thoroughgoing moral, civil, and educational reforms that were to have nearly as far-reaching a legacy as Luther's doctrinal reforms.

LETTER TO THE CHRISTIAN NOBILITY OF THE GERMAN NATION

Martin Luther

TRANSLATED BY C. A. BUCHHEIM

INTRODUCTION

TO HIS MOST SERENE AND MIGHTY IMPERIAL MAJESTY

AND TO THE CHRISTIAN NOBILITY OF THE GERMAN NATION.

DR. MARTINUS LUTHER.

The grace and might of God be with you, Most Serene Majesty, most gracious, well-beloved gentlemen!

It is not out of mere arrogance and perversity that I, an individual poor man, have taken upon me to address your lordships. The distress and misery that oppress all the Christian estates, more especially in Germany, have led not only myself, but everyone else, to cry aloud and to ask for help, and have now forced me too to cry out and to ask if God would give His Spirit to any one to reach a hand to His wretched people. Councils have often put forward some remedy, but it has adroitly been frustrated, and the evils have become worse, through the cunning of certain men. Their malice and wickedness I will now, by the help of God, expose, so that, being known, they may henceforth cease to be so obstructive and injurious. God has given us a young and noble sovereign,[1] and by this has roused great hopes in many hearts; now it is right that we too should do what we can, and make good use of time and grace.

The first thing that we must do is to consider the matter with great earnestness, and, whatever we attempt, not to trust in our own strength and wisdom alone, even if the power of all the world were ours; for God will not endure that a good work should be begun trusting to our own strength and wisdom. He destroys it; it is all useless, as we read in Psalm xxxiii., "There is no king saved by the multitude of a host; a mighty man is not delivered by much strength." And I fear it is for that reason that those beloved princes the Emperors Frederick, the First and the Second, and many other German emperors were, in former times, so piteously spurned and oppressed by the popes, though they were feared by all the world. Perchance they trusted rather in their own strength than in God; therefore they could not but fall; and how would the sanguinary tyrant Julius II. have risen so high in our own days but that, I fear, France, Germany, and Venice trusted to themselves? The children of Benjamin slew forty-two thousand Israelites, for this reason: that these trusted to their own strength (Judges xx., etc.).

That such a thing may not happen to us and to our noble Emperor Charles, we must remember that in this matter we wrestle not against flesh and blood, but against the rulers of the darkness of this world (Eph. vi. 12), who may fill the world with war and bloodshed, but cannot themselves be overcome thereby. We must renounce all confidence in our natural strength, and take the matter in hand with humble trust in God; we must seek God's help with earnest prayer, and have nothing before our eyes but the misery and wretchedness of Christendom, irrespective of what punishment the wicked may deserve. If we do not act thus, we may begin the game with great pomp; but when we are well in it, the spirits of evil will make such confusion that the whole world will be immersed

1 Charles V. was at that time not quite twenty years of age.

in blood, and yet nothing be done. Therefore let us act in the fear of God and prudently. The greater the might of the foe, the greater is the misfortune, if we do not act in the fear of God and with humility. If popes and Romanists have hitherto, with the devil's help, thrown kings into confusion, they may still do so, if we attempt things with our own strength and skill, without God's help.

THE THREE WALLS OF THE ROMANISTS

The Romanists have, with great adroitness, drawn three walls round themselves, with which they have hitherto protected themselves, so that no one could reform them, whereby all Christendom has fallen terribly.

Firstly, if pressed by the temporal power, they have affirmed and maintained that the temporal power has no jurisdiction over them, but, on the contrary, that the spiritual power is above the temporal.

Secondly, if it were proposed to admonish them with the Scriptures, they objected that no one may interpret the Scriptures but the pope.

Thirdly, if they are threatened with a council, they pretend that no one may call a council but the pope.

Thus they have secretly stolen our three rods, so that they may be unpunished, and entrenched themselves behind these three walls, to act with all the wickedness and malice, which we now witness. And whenever they have been compelled to call a council, they have made it of no avail by binding the princes beforehand with an oath to leave them as they were, and to give moreover to the pope full power over the procedure of the council, so that it is all one whether we have many councils or no councils, in addition to which they deceive us with false pretences and tricks. So grievously do they tremble for their skin before a true, free council; and thus they have overawed kings and princes, that these believe they would be offending God, if they were not to obey them in all such knavish, deceitful artifices.

Now may God help us, and give us one of those trumpets that overthrew the walls of Jericho, so that we may blow down these walls of straw and paper, and that we may set free our Christian rods for the chastisement of sin, and expose the craft and deceit of the devil, so that we may amend ourselves by punishment and again obtain God's favour.

(a) The First Wall: That the Temporal Power has no Jurisdiction over the Spirituality

Let us, in the first place, attack the first wall.

It has been devised that the pope, bishops, priests, and monks are called the spiritual estate, princes, lords, artificers, and peasants are the temporal estate. This is an artful lie and hypocritical device, but let no one be made afraid by it, and that for this reason: that all Christians are truly of the spiritual estate, and there is no difference among them, save of office alone. As St. Paul says (1 Cor. xii.), we are all one body, though each member does its own work, to serve the others. This is because we have one baptism, one Gospel, one faith, and are all Christians alike; for baptism, Gospel, and faith, these alone make spiritual and Christian people.

As for the unction by a pope or a bishop, tonsure, ordination, consecration, and clothes differing from those of laymen-all this may make a hypocrite or an anointed puppet, but never a Christian or a spiritual man. Thus we are all consecrated as priests by baptism, as St. Peter says: "Ye are a royal priesthood, a holy nation" (1 Peter ii. 9); and in the book of Revelations: "and hast made us unto our God (by Thy blood) kings and priests" (Rev. v. 10). For, if we had not a higher consecration in us than pope or bishop can give, no priest could ever be made by the consecration of pope or bishop, nor could he say the mass, or preach, or absolve. Therefore the bishop's consecration is just as if in the name of the whole congregation he took one person out of the community, each member of which has equal power, and commanded him to exercise this power for the rest; in the same way as if ten brothers, co-heirs as king's sons, were to choose one from among them to rule over their inheritance, they would all of them still remain kings and have equal power, although one is ordered to govern.

And to put the matter even more plainly, if a little company of pious Christian laymen were taken prisoners and carried away to a desert, and had not among them a priest consecrated by a bishop, and were there to agree to elect one of them, born in wedlock or not, and were to order him to baptise, to celebrate the mass, to absolve, and to preach, this man would as truly be a priest, as if all the bishops and all the popes had consecrated him. That is why in cases of necessity every man can baptise and absolve, which would not be possible if we were not all priests. This great grace and virtue of baptism and of the Christian estate they have quite destroyed and made us forget by their ecclesiastical law. In this way the Christians used to choose their bishops and priests out of the community; these being afterwards confirmed by other bishops, without the pomp that now prevails. So was it that St. Augustine, Ambrose, Cyprian, were bishops.

Since, then, the temporal power is baptised as we are, and has the same faith and Gospel, we must allow it to be priest and bishop, and account its office an office that is proper and useful to the Christian community. For whatever issues from baptism may boast that it has been consecrated priest, bishop, and pope, although it does not beseem everyone to exercise these offices. For, since we are all priests alike, no man may put himself forward or take upon himself, without our consent and election, to do that which we have all alike power to do. For, if a thing is common to all, no man may take it to himself without the wish and command of the community. And if it should happen that a man were appointed to one of these offices and deposed for abuses, he would be just what he was before. Therefore a priest should be nothing in Christendom but a functionary; as long as he holds his office, he has precedence of others; if he is deprived of it, he is a peasant or a citizen like the rest. Therefore a priest is verily no longer a priest after deposition. But now they have invented characteres indelebiles,[2] and pretend that a priest after deprivation still differs from a simple layman. They even imagine that a priest can never be anything but a priest—that is, that he can never become a layman. All this is nothing but mere talk and ordinance of human invention.

2 In accordance with a doctrine of the Roman Catholic Church, the act of ordination impresses upon the priest an indelible character; so that he immutably retains the sacred dignity of priesthood.

It follows, then, that between laymen and priests, princes and bishops, or, as they call it, between spiritual and temporal persons, the only real difference is one of office and function, and not of estate; for they are all of the same spiritual estate, true priests, bishops, and popes, though their functions are not the same—just as among priests and monks every man has not the same functions. And this, as I said above, St. Paul says (Rom. xii.; 1 Cor. xii.), and St. Peter (1 Peter ii.): "We, being many, are one body in Christ, and severally members one of another." Christ's body is not double or twofold, one temporal, the other spiritual. He is one Head, and He has one body.

We see, then, that just as those that we call spiritual, or priests, bishops, or popes, do not differ from other Christians in any other or higher degree but in that they are to be concerned with the word of God and the sacraments—that being their work and office—in the same way the temporal authorities hold the sword and the rod in their hands to punish the wicked and to protect the good. A cobbler, a smith, a peasant, every man, has the office and function of his calling, and yet all alike are consecrated priests and bishops, and every man should by his office or function be useful and beneficial to the rest, so that various kinds of work may all be united for the furtherance of body and soul, just as the members of the body all serve one another.

Now see what a Christian doctrine is this: that the temporal authority is not above the clergy, and may not punish it. This is as if one were to say the hand may not help, though the eye is in grievous suffering. Is it not unnatural, not to say unchristian, that one member may not help another, or guard it against harm? Nay, the nobler the member, the more the rest are bound to help it. Therefore I say, Forasmuch as the temporal power has been ordained by God for the punishment of the bad and the protection of the good, therefore we must let it do its duty throughout the whole Christian body, without respect of persons, whether it strikes popes, bishops, priests, monks, nuns, or whoever it may be. If it were sufficient reason for fettering the temporal power that it is inferior among the offices of Christianity to the offices of priest or confessor, or to the spiritual estate—if this were so, then we ought to restrain tailors, cobblers, masons, carpenters, cooks, cellarmen, peasants, and all secular workmen, from providing the pope or bishops, priests and monks, with shoes, clothes, houses or victuals, or from paying them tithes. But if these laymen are allowed to do their work without restraint, what do the Romanist scribes mean by their laws? They mean that they withdraw themselves from the operation of temporal Christian power, simply in order that they may be free to do evil, and thus fulfill what St. Peter said: "There shall be false teachers among you, . . . and in covetousness shall they with feigned words make merchandise of you" (2 Peter ii. 1, etc.).

Therefore the temporal Christian power must exercise its office without let or hindrance, without considering whom it may strike, whether pope, or bishop, or priest: whoever is guilty, let him suffer for it.

Whatever the ecclesiastical law has said in opposition to this is merely the invention of Romanist arrogance. For this is what St. Paul says to all Christians: "Let every soul" (I presume including the popes) "be subject unto the higher powers; for they bear not the sword in vain: they serve the Lord therewith, for vengeance on evildoers and for praise to them that do well" (Rom. xiii. 1–4). Also St. Peter: "Submit yourselves to every ordinance of man for the Lord's sake, . . . for so is the will of God" (1 Peter ii. 13, 15). He has also foretold that men would come who should despise government (2 Peter ii.), as has come to pass through ecclesiastical law.

Now, I imagine, the first paper wall is overthrown, inasmuch as the temporal power has become a member of the Christian body; although its work relates to the body, yet does it belong to the spiritual estate. Therefore, it must do its duty without let or hindrance upon all members of the whole body, to punish or urge, as guilt may deserve, or need may require, without respect of pope, bishops, or priests, let them threaten or excommunicate as they will. That is why a guilty priest is deprived of his priesthood before being given over to the secular arm; whereas this would not be right, if the secular sword had not authority over him already by Divine ordinance.

It is, indeed, past bearing that the spiritual law should esteem so highly the liberty, life, and property of the clergy, as if laymen were not as good spiritual Christians, or not equally members of the Church. Why should your body, life, goods, and honour be free, and not mine, seeing that we are equal as Christians, and have received alike baptism, faith, spirit, and all things? If a priest is killed, the country is laid under an interdict[3]: why not also if a peasant is killed? Whence comes this great difference among equal Christians? Simply from human laws and inventions.

It can have been no good spirit, either, that devised these evasions and made sin to go unpunished. For if, as Christ and the Apostles bid us, it is our duty to oppose the evil one and all his works and words, and to drive him away as well as may be, how then should we remain quiet and be silent when the pope and his followers are guilty of devilish works and words? Are we for the sake of men to allow the commandments and the truth of God to be defeated, which at our baptism we vowed to support with body and soul? Truly we should have to answer for all souls that would thus be abandoned and led astray.

Therefore it must have been the arch-devil himself who said, as we read in the ecclesiastical law, If the pope were so perniciously wicked, as to be dragging souls in crowds to the devil, yet he could not be deposed. This is the accursed and devilish foundation on which they build at Rome, and think that the whole world is to be allowed to go to the devil rather than they should be opposed in their knavery. If a man were to escape punishment simply because he is above the rest, then no Christian might punish another, since Christ has commanded each of us to esteem himself the lowest and the humblest (Matt. xviii. 4; Luke ix. 48).

Where there is sin, there remains no avoiding the punishment, as St. Gregory says, We are all equal, but guilt makes one subject

3 By the Interdict, or general excommunication, whole countries, districts, or towns, or their respective rulers, were deprived of all the spiritual benefits of the Church, such as Divine service, the administering of the sacraments, etc.

to another. Now let us see how they deal with Christendom. They arrogate to themselves immunities without any warrant from the Scriptures, out of their own wickedness, whereas God and the Apostles made them subject to the secular sword; so that we must fear that it is the work of antichrist, or a sign of his near approach.

(b) The Second Wall: That no one may interpret the Scriptures but the pope

The second wall is even more tottering and weak: that they alone pretend to be considered masters of the Scriptures; although they learn nothing of them all their life. They assume authority, and juggle before us with impudent words, saying that the pope cannot err in matters of faith, whether he be evil or good, albeit they cannot prove it by a single letter. That is why the canon law contains so many heretical and unchristian, nay unnatural, laws; but of these we need not speak now. For whereas they imagine the Holy Ghost never leaves them, however unlearned and wicked they may be, they grow bold enough to decree whatever they like. But were this true, where were the need and use of the Holy Scriptures? Let us burn them, and content ourselves with the unlearned gentlemen at Rome, in whom the Holy Ghost dwells, who, however, can dwell in pious souls only. If I had not read it, I could never have believed that the devil should have put forth such follies at Rome and find a following.

But not to fight them with our own words, we will quote the Scriptures. St. Paul says, "If anything be revealed to another that sitteth by, let the first hold his peace" (1 Cor. xiv. 30). What would be the use of this commandment, if we were to believe him alone that teaches or has the highest seat? Christ Himself says, "And they shall be all taught of God." (St. John vi. 45). Thus it may come to pass that the pope and his followers are wicked and not true Christians, and not being taught by God, have no true understanding, whereas a common man may have true understanding. Why should we then not follow him? Has not the pope often erred? Who could help Christianity, in case the pope errs, if we do not rather believe another who has the Scriptures for him?

Therefore it is a wickedly devised fable-and they cannot quote a single letter to confirm it-that it is for the pope alone to interpret the Scriptures or to confirm the interpretation of them. They have assumed the authority of their own selves. And though they say that this authority was given to St. Peter when the keys were given to him, it is plain enough that the keys were not given to St. Peter alone, but to the whole community. Besides, the keys were not ordained for doctrine or authority, but for sin, to bind or loose, and what they claim besides this from the keys is mere invention. But what Christ said to St. Peter: "I have prayed for thee that thy faith fail not" (St. Luke xxii. 32), cannot relate to the pope, inasmuch as the greater part of the Popes have been without faith, as they are themselves forced to acknowledge; nor did Christ pray for Peter alone, but for all the Apostles and all Christians, as He says, "Neither pray I for these alone, but for them also which shall believe on Me through their word" (St. John xvii.). Is not this plain enough?

Only consider the matter. They must needs acknowledge that there are pious Christians among us that have the true faith, spirit, understanding, word, and mind of Christ: why then should we reject their word and understanding, and follow a pope who has neither understanding nor spirit? Surely this were to deny our whole faith and the Christian Church. Moreover, if the article of our faith is right, "I believe in the holy Christian Church," the pope cannot alone be right; else we must say, "I believe in the pope of Rome," and reduce the Christian Church to one man, which is a devilish and damnable heresy. Besides that, we are all priests, as I have said, and have all one faith, one Gospel, one Sacrament; how then should we not have the power of discerning and judging what is right or wrong in matters of faith? What becomes of St. Paul's words, "But he that is spiritual judgeth all things, yet he himself is judged of no man" (1 Cor. ii. 15), and also, "we having the same spirit of faith"? (2 Cor. iv. 13). Why then should we not perceive as well as an unbelieving pope what agrees or disagrees with our faith?

By these and many other texts we should gain courage and freedom, and should not let the spirit of liberty (as St. Paul has it) be frightened away by the inventions of the popes; we should boldly judge what they do and what they leave undone by our own believing understanding of the Scriptures, and force them to follow the better understanding, and not their own. Did not Abraham in old days have to obey his Sarah, who was in stricter bondage to him than we are to anyone on earth? Thus, too, Balaam's ass was wiser than the prophet. If God spoke by an ass against a prophet, why should He not speak by a pious man against the pope? Besides, St. Paul withstood St. Peter as being in error (Gal. ii.). Therefore it behoves every Christian to aid the faith by understanding and defending it and by condemning all errors.

(c) The Third Wall: That no one may call a council but the pope

The third wall falls of itself, as soon as the first two have fallen; for if the pope acts contrary to the Scriptures, we are bound to stand by the Scriptures, to punish and to constrain him, according to Christ's commandment, "Moreover, if thy brother shall trespass against thee, go and tell him his fault between thee and him alone; if he shall hear thee, thou hast gained thy brother. But if he will not hear thee, then take with thee one or two more, that in the mouth of two or three witnesses every word may be established. And if he shall neglect to hear them, tell it unto the Church; but if he neglect to hear the Church, let him be unto thee as a heathen man and a publican" (St. Matt. xviii. 15–17). Here each member is commanded to take care for the other; much more then should we do this, if it is a ruling member of the community that does evil, which by its evil-doing causes great harm and offence to the others. If then I am to accuse him before the Church, I must collect the Church together. Moreover, they can show nothing in the Scriptures giving the pope sole power to call and confirm councils; they have nothing but their own laws; but these hold good only so long as they are not injurious to Christianity and the laws of God. Therefore, if the pope deserves punishment, these laws cease to bind us, since Christendom would suffer, if he were not punished by a council. Thus we read (Acts xv.) that the council of the Apostles was not called by St. Peter, but by all the Apostles and the elders. But if the right to call it had lain with St. Peter alone, it would not have been a Christian council, but a heretical conciliabulum. Moreover, the most celebrated council of all-that of Nicaea-was neither called nor confirmed by the Bishop of Rome, but by the Emperor Constantine; and after him many other emperors have done the same, and yet the councils called by them were accounted most Christian. But if the pope alone had the power, they must all have been heretical. Moreover, if I consider the councils that the pope has called, I do not find that they produced any notable results.

Therefore when need requires, and the pope is a cause of offence to Christendom, in these cases whoever can best do so, as a faithful member of the whole body, must do what he can to procure a true free council. This no one can do so well as the temporal authorities, especially since they are fellow-Christians, fellow-priests, sharing one spirit and one power in all things, and since they should exercise the office that they have received from God without hindrance, whenever it is necessary and useful that it should be exercised. Would it not be most unnatural, if a fire were to break out in a city, and every one were to keep still and let it burn on and on, whatever might be burnt, simply because they had not the mayor's authority, or because the fire perchance broke out at the mayor's house? Is not every citizen bound in this case to rouse and call in the rest? How much more should this be done in the spiritual city of Christ, if a fire of offence breaks out, either at the pope's government or wherever it may! The like happens if an enemy attacks a town. The first to rouse up the rest earns glory and thanks. Why then should not he earn glory that decries the coming of our enemies from hell and rouses and summons all Christians?

But as for their boasts of their authority, that no one must oppose it, this is idle talk. No one in Christendom has any authority to do harm, or to forbid others to prevent harm being done. There is no authority in the Church but for reformation. Therefore if the pope wished to use his power to prevent the calling of a free council, so as to prevent the reformation of the Church, we must not respect him or his power; and if he should begin to excommunicate and fulminate, we must despise this as the doings of a madman, and, trusting in God, excommunicate and repel him as best we may. For this his usurped power is nothing; he does not possess it, and he is at once overthrown by a text from the Scriptures. For St. Paul says to the Corinthians "that God has given us authority for edification, and not for destruction (2 Cor. x. 8). Who will set this text at nought? It is the power of the devil and of antichrist that prevents what would serve for the reformation of Christendom. Therefore we must not follow it, but oppose it with our body, our goods, and all that we have. And even if a miracle were to happen in favour of the pope against the temporal power, or if some were to be stricken by a plague, as they sometimes boast has happened, all this is to be held as having been done by the devil in order to injure our faith in God, as was foretold by Christ: "There shall arise false Christs and false prophets, and shall show great signs and wonders, insomuch that, if it were possible, they shall deceive the very elect" (Matt. xxiv. 23); and St. Paul tells the Thessalonians that the coming of antichrist shall be "after the working of Satan with all power and signs and lying wonders" (2 Thess. ii. 9).

Therefore let us hold fast to this: that Christian power can do nothing against Christ, as St. Paul says, "For we can do nothing against Christ, but for Christ" (2 Cor. xiii. 8). But, if it does anything against Christ, it is the power of antichrist and the devil, even if it rained and hailed wonders and plagues. Wonders and plagues prove nothing, especially in these latter evil days, of which false wonders are foretold in all the Scriptures. Therefore we must hold fast to the words of God with an assured faith; then the devil will soon cease his wonders.

And now I hope the false, lying spectre will be laid with which the Romanists have long terrified and stupefied our consciences. And it will be seen that, like all the rest of us, they are subject to the temporal sword; that they have no authority to interpret the Scriptures by force without skill; and that they have no power to prevent a council, or to pledge it in accordance with their pleasure, or to bind it beforehand, and deprive it of its freedom; and that if they do this, they are verily of the fellowship of antichrist and the devil, and having nothing of Christ but the name.

INTRODUCTION TO
Leo X
EXSURGE DOMINE

As Luther expected while he was writing his *Letter to the Christian Nobility*, his fate was already being sealed in Rome, where a bull of excommunication, *Exsurge Domine*, was being prepared by Pope Leo X and his advisors including Luther's earlier interlocutors Cardinal Cajetan and Johann Eck. There was indeed a sharp disagreement between Cajetan and Eck on the appropriate way to proceed, reflecting a deep-seated uncertainty within the Roman Church about how to handle calls for reform. It was clear to many, including Leo himself, that something had to change after the low point of worldliness reached by Popes Alexander VI and Julius II, and many of Leo's counselors were concerned to restore the church to its spiritual mission of serving the faithful.

Cajetan was among these, and argued that Luther's errors must be considered carefully one-by-one rather than condemned wholesale. But he was overruled by the uncompromising Eck, for whom Luther's defiance of papal authority and sympathy with the heretical Hussites could not be tolerated for a moment. The result was a somewhat curious document indeed, which lists off no less than forty-one statements supposedly extracted from Luther's writings that were "either heretical, false, scandalous, or offensive to pious ears, as seductive of simple minds." Of course, it made quite a difference to the assessment of Luther's theology which of these were to be considered *heretical* and which were merely "seductive of simple minds," but there was no attempt to rank the errors in the bull. What we find then is a list of forty-one disjointed statements, some fairly trivial and others momentous, with no context or elaboration to explain what Luther might have meant by them or why they were to be rejected.

Of course, this manner of proceeding was probably by design rather than carelessness (even if all did not agree in the design): after all, what better way to insist on the unquestionable authority of the pope than to simply declare by fiat, without any explanation, what was and was not to be permitted? In this, the pope and Eck misjudged the climate of the times and the power of the printing press: mere assertions of authority were no match for the eloquent but simple persuasive arguments that Luther was filling his pamphlets with.

To be sure, there was no lack of rhetorical crafting in *Exsurge Domine*'s opening and closing sections. Framed as an invocation to Christ, St. Peter, St. Paul, and all the saints to rise up and defend the church from the "wild boar" destroying the vineyard of the Church, the language of the opening paragraphs is a memorable cry of lamentation, positioning the papacy as the victim, rather than the oppressor. After the harsh words of condemnation that follow, the document resumes a gentler tone, flattering the German princes by saying that they have always been the most pious defenders of orthodoxy, and painting the pope as a gracious father trying to recall his wandering prodigal, Martin, to the fold. The first bit of rhetorical posturing was to prove effective in gaining the support of Charles V to prosecute Luther's heresy; the latter, needless to say, was laughed at in Wittenberg, where Luther was undaunted by the bull when it arrived late that year.

Just as the *Ninety-Five Theses* hardly make a very fitting manifesto for the Reformation which was to follow, so *Exsurge Domine* strikes the modern reader as something of a puzzling refutation. Leo and his advisors, after all, had no access to most of Luther's more revolutionary and memorable theological writings, which were indeed just beginning to appear that year. They had to make do with scattered treatises from 1518 and 1519, in which Luther was still feeling his way toward his final position. Moreover, the scholar Hans Hillerbrand concluded after a close review that "no less than twelve of the forty-one propositions did not accurately quote Luther or cannot be taken to express his sentiment."[1] It is also noteworthy that the pope and his theologians seem relatively uninterested in Luther's great doctrines of grace which were to be his greatest contribution, focusing instead on statements in which Luther emphasized the depth of sin and the hopelessness of human efforts to overcome it, especially the penitential system devised by the late medieval church for that purpose. Luther's insistence that Christ alone, by faith alone, could do far more than any rite of penance, went unmentioned in the bull, and was not tackled properly until the Council of Trent thirty years later.

1 Hans Hillerbrand, "Luther and *Exsurge Domine*," *Theological Studies* 30.1 (1969): 111.

EXSURGE DOMINE

Leo X

TRANSLATOR UNKNOWN

Arise, O Lord, and judge your own cause. Remember your reproaches to those who are filled with foolishness all through the day. Listen to our prayers, for foxes have arisen seeking to destroy the vineyard whose winepress you alone have trod. When you were about to ascend to your Father, you committed the care, rule, and administration of the vineyard, an image of the triumphant church, to Peter, as the head and your vicar and his successors. The wild boar from the forest seeks to destroy it and every wild beast feeds upon it.

Rise, Peter, and fulfill this pastoral office divinely entrusted to you as mentioned above. Give heed to the cause of the holy Roman Church, mother of all churches and teacher of the faith, whom you by the order of God, have consecrated by your blood. Against the Roman Church, you warned, lying teachers are rising, introducing ruinous sects, and drawing upon themselves speedy doom. Their tongues are fire, a restless evil, full of deadly poison. They have bitter zeal, contention in their hearts, and boast and lie against the truth.

We beseech you also, Paul, to arise. It was you that enlightened and illuminated the Church by your doctrine and by a martyrdom like Peter's. For now a new Porphyry rises who, as the old once wrongfully assailed the holy apostles, now assails the holy pontiffs, our predecessors.

Rebuking them, in violation of your teaching, instead of imploring them, he is not ashamed to assail them, to tear at them, and when he despairs of his cause, to stoop to insults. He is like the heretics "whose last defense," as Jerome says, "is to start spewing out a serpent's venom with their tongue when they see that their causes are about to be condemned, and spring to insults when they see they are vanquished." For although you have said that there must be heresies to test the faithful, still they must be destroyed at their very birth by your intercession and help, so they do not grow or wax strong like your wolves. Finally, let the whole church of the saints and the rest of the universal church arise. Some, putting aside her true interpretation of Sacred Scripture, are blinded in mind by the father of lies. Wise in their own eyes, according to the ancient practice of heretics, they interpret these same Scriptures otherwise than the Holy Spirit demands, inspired only by their own sense of ambition, and for the sake of popular acclaim, as the Apostle declares. In fact, they twist and adulterate the Scriptures. As a result, according to Jerome, "It is no longer the Gospel of Christ, but a man's, or what is worse, the devil's."

Let all this holy Church of God, I say, arise, and with the blessed apostles intercede with almighty God to purge the errors of His sheep, to banish all heresies from the lands of the faithful, and be pleased to maintain the peace and unity of His holy Church.

For we can scarcely express, from distress and grief of mind, what has reached our ears for some time by the report of reliable men and general rumor; alas, we have even seen with our eyes and read the many diverse errors. Some of these have already been condemned by councils and the constitutions of our predecessors, and expressly contain even the heresy of the Greeks and Bohemians. Other errors are either heretical, false, scandalous, or offensive to pious ears, as seductive of simple minds, originating with false exponents of the faith who in their proud curiosity yearn for the world's glory, and contrary to the Apostle's teaching, wish to be wiser than they should be. Their talkativeness, unsupported by the authority of the Scriptures, as Jerome says, would not win credence unless they appeared to support their perverse doctrine even with divine testimonies however badly interpreted. From their sight fear of God has now passed.

These errors have, at the suggestion of the human race, been revived and recently propagated among the more frivolous and the illustrious German nation. We grieve the more that this happened there because we and our predecessors have always held this nation in the bosom of our affection. For after the empire had been transferred by the Roman Church from the Greeks to these same Germans, our predecessors and we always took the Church's advocates and defenders from among them. Indeed it is certain that these Germans, truly germane to the Catholic faith, have always been the bitterest opponents of heresies, as witnessed by those commendable constitutions of the German emperors in behalf of the Church's independence, freedom, and the expulsion and extermination of all heretics from Germany. Those constitutions formerly issued, and then confirmed by our predecessors, were issued under the greatest penalties even of loss of lands and dominions against anyone sheltering or not expelling them. If they were observed today both we and they would obviously be free of this disturbance. Witness to this is the condemnation and punishment in the Council of Constance of the infidelity of the Hussites and Wyclifites as well as Jerome of Prague. Witness to this is the blood of Germans shed so often in wars against the Bohemians. A final witness is the refutation, rejection, and condemnation no less learned than true and holy of the above errors, or many of them, by the universities of Cologne and Louvain, most devoted and religious cultivators of the Lord's field. We could allege many other facts too, which we have decided to omit, lest we appear to be composing a history.

In virtue of our pastoral office committed to us by the divine favor we can under no circumstances tolerate or overlook any longer the pernicious poison of the above errors without disgrace to the Christian religion and injury to orthodox faith. Some of these errors we have decided to include in the present document; their substance is as follows:

1. It is a heretical opinion, but a common one, that the sacraments of the New Law give pardoning grace to those who do not set up an obstacle.

2. To deny that in a child after baptism sin remains is to treat with contempt both Paul and Christ.

3. The inflammable sources of sin, even if there be no actual sin, delay a soul departing from the body from entrance into heaven.

4. To one on the point of death imperfect charity necessarily brings with it great fear, which in itself alone is enough to produce the punishment of purgatory, and impedes entrance into the kingdom.

5. That there are three parts to penance: contrition, confession, and satisfaction, has no foundation in Sacred Scripture nor in the ancient sacred Christian doctors.

6. Contrition, which is acquired through discussion, collection, and detestation of sins, by which one reflects upon his years in the bitterness of his soul, by pondering over the gravity of sins, their number, their baseness, the loss of eternal beatitude, and the acquisition of eternal damnation, this contrition makes him a hypocrite, indeed more a sinner.

7. It is a most truthful proverb and the doctrine concerning the contritions given thus far is the more remarkable: "Not to do so in the future is the highest penance; the best penance, a new life."

8. By no means may you presume to confess venial sins, nor even all mortal sins, because it is impossible that you know all mortal sins. Hence in the primitive Church only manifest mortal sins were confessed.

9. As long as we wish to confess all sins without exception, we are doing nothing else than to wish to leave nothing to God's mercy for pardon.

10. Sins are not forgiven to anyone, unless when the priest forgives them he believes they are forgiven; on the contrary the sin would remain unless he believed it was forgiven; for indeed the remission of sin and the granting of grace does not suffice, but it is necessary also to believe that there has been forgiveness.

11. By no means can you have reassurance of being absolved because of your contrition, but because of the word of Christ: "Whatsoever you shall loose, etc." Hence, I say, trust confidently, if you have obtained the absolution of the priest, and firmly believe yourself to have been absolved, and you will truly be absolved, whatever there may be of contrition.

12. If through an impossibility he who confessed was not contrite, or the priest did not absolve seriously, but in a jocose manner, if nevertheless he believes that he has been absolved, he is most truly absolved.

13. In the sacrament of penance and the remission of sin the pope or the bishop does no more than the lowest priest; indeed, where there is no priest, any Christian, even if a woman or child, may equally do as much.

14. No one ought to answer a priest that he is contrite, nor should the priest inquire.

15. Great is the error of those who approach the sacrament of the Eucharist relying on this, that they have confessed, that they are not conscious of any mortal sin, that they have sent their prayers on ahead and made preparations; all these eat and drink judgment to themselves. But if they believe and trust that they will attain grace, then this faith alone makes them pure and worthy.

16. It seems to have been decided that the Church in common Council established that the laity should communicate under both species; the Bohemians who communicate under both species are not heretics, but schismatics.

17. The treasures of the Church, from which the pope grants indulgences, are not the merits of Christ and of the saints.

18. Indulgences are pious frauds of the faithful, and remissions of good works; and they are among the number of those things which are allowed, and not of the number of those which are advantageous.

19. Indulgences are of no avail to those who truly gain them, for the remission of the penalty due to actual sin in the sight of divine justice.

20. They are seduced who believe that indulgences are salutary and useful for the fruit of the spirit.

21. Indulgences are necessary only for public crimes, and are properly conceded only to the harsh and impatient.

22. For six kinds of men indulgences are neither necessary nor useful; namely, for the dead and those about to die, the infirm, those legitimately hindered, and those who have not committed crimes, and those who have committed crimes, but not public ones, and those who devote themselves to better things.

23. Excommunications are only external penalties and they do not deprive man of the common spiritual prayers of the Church.

24. Christians must be taught to cherish excommunications rather than to fear them.

25. The Roman Pontiff, the successor of Peter, is not the vicar of Christ over all the churches of the entire world, instituted by Christ Himself in blessed Peter.

26. The word of Christ to Peter: "Whatsoever you shall loose on earth," etc., is extended merely to those things bound by Peter himself.

27. It is certain that it is not in the power of the Church or the pope to decide upon the articles of faith, and much less concerning the laws for morals or for good works.

28. If the pope with a great part of the Church thought so and so, he would not err; still it is not a sin or heresy to think the contrary, especially in a matter not necessary for salvation,

until one alternative is condemned and another approved by a general Council.

29. A way has been made for us for weakening the authority of councils, and for freely contradicting their actions, and judging their decrees, and boldly confessing whatever seems true, whether it has been approved or disapproved by any council whatsoever.

30. Some articles of John Hus, condemned in the Council of Constance, are most Christian, wholly true and evangelical; these the universal Church could not condemn.

31. In every good work the just man sins.

32. A good work done very well is a venial sin.

33. That heretics be burned is against the will of the Spirit.

34. To go to war against the Turks is to resist God who punishes our iniquities through them.

35. No one is certain that he is not always sinning mortally, because of the most hidden vice of pride.

36. Free will after sin is a matter of title only; and as long as one does what is in him, one sins mortally.

37. Purgatory cannot be proved from Sacred Scripture which is in the canon.

38. The souls in purgatory are not sure of their salvation, at least not all; nor is it proved by any arguments or by the Scriptures that they are beyond the state of meriting or of increasing in charity.

39. The souls in purgatory sin without intermission, as long as they seek rest and abhor punishment.

40. The souls freed from purgatory by the suffrages of the living are less happy than if they had made satisfactions by themselves.

41. Ecclesiastical prelates and secular princes would not act badly if they destroyed all of the money bags of beggary.

No one of sound mind is ignorant how destructive, pernicious, scandalous, and seductive to pious and simple minds these various errors are, how opposed they are to all charity and reverence for the holy Roman Church who is the mother of all the faithful and teacher of the faith; how destructive they are of the vigor of ecclesiastical discipline, namely obedience. This virtue is the font and origin of all virtues and without it anyone is readily convicted of being unfaithful.

Therefore we, in this above enumeration, important as it is, wish to proceed with great care as is proper, and to cut off the advance of this plague and cancerous disease so it will not spread any further in the Lord's field as harmful thornbushes. We have therefore held a careful inquiry, scrutiny, discussion, strict examination, and mature deliberation with each of the brothers, the eminent cardinals of the holy Roman Church, as well as the priors and ministers general of the religious orders, besides many other professors and masters skilled in sacred theology and in civil and canon law. We have found that these errors or theses are not Catholic, as mentioned above, and are not to be taught, as such; but rather are against the doctrine and tradition of the Catholic Church, and against the true interpretation of the sacred Scriptures received from the Church. Now Augustine maintained that her authority had to be accepted so completely that he stated he would not have believed the Gospel unless the authority of the Catholic Church had vouched for it. For, according to these errors, or any one or several of them, it clearly follows that the Church which is guided by the Holy Spirit is in error and has always erred. This is against what Christ at his ascension promised to his disciples (as is read in the holy Gospel of Matthew): "I will be with you to the consummation of the world"; it is against the determinations of the holy Fathers, or the express ordinances and canons of the councils and the supreme pontiffs. Failure to comply with these canons, according to the testimony of Cyprian, will be the fuel and cause of all heresy and schism.

With the advice and consent of these our venerable brothers, with mature deliberation on each and every one of the above theses, and by the authority of almighty God, the blessed Apostles Peter and Paul, and our own authority, we condemn, reprobate, and reject completely each of these theses or errors as either heretical, scandalous, false, offensive to pious ears or seductive of simple minds, and against Catholic truth. By listing them, we decree and declare that all the faithful of both sexes must regard them as condemned, reprobated, and rejected . . . We restrain all in the virtue of holy obedience and under the penalty of an automatic major excommunication....

Moreover, because the preceding errors and many others are contained in the books or writings of Martin Luther, we likewise condemn, reprobate, and reject completely the books and all the writings and sermons of the said Martin, whether in Latin or any other language, containing the said errors or any one of them; and we wish them to be regarded as utterly condemned, reprobated, and rejected. We forbid each and every one of the faithful of either sex, in virtue of holy obedience and under the above penalties to be incurred automatically, to read, assert, preach, praise, print, publish, or defend them. They will incur these penalties if they presume to uphold them in any way, personally or through another or others, directly or indirectly, tacitly or explicitly, publicly or occultly, either in their own homes or in other public or private places. Indeed immediately after the publication of this letter these works, wherever they may be, shall be sought out carefully by the ordinaries and others [ecclesiastics and regulars], and under each and every one of the above penalties shall be burned publicly and solemnly in the presence of the clerics and people.

As far as Martin himself is concerned, O good God, what have we overlooked or not done? What fatherly charity have we omitted that we might call him back from such errors? For after we had cited him, wishing to deal more kindly with him, we urged him through various conferences with our legate and through our personal letters to abandon these errors. We have even offered him safe conduct and the money necessary for the journey urging him to come without fear or any misgivings, which perfect charity should cast out, and to talk not secretly but openly and face to face after the example of our Savior and the Apostle Paul. If he had done this, we are certain he would have changed in heart, and he would have recognized his errors. He would not have found all these errors in the Roman Curia which he attacks so viciously, ascribing to it more than he should because of the empty rumors of wicked men. We would have shown him clearer than the light of day that the Roman pontiffs, our predecessors, whom he injuriously attacks beyond all decency, never erred in their canons or constitutions which he tries to assail. For, according to the prophet, neither is healing oil nor the doctor lacking in Galaad.

But he always refused to listen and, despising the previous citation and each and every one of the above overtures, disdained to come. To the present day he has been contumacious. With a hardened spirit he has continued under censure over a year. What is worse, adding evil to evil, and on learning of the citation, he broke forth in a rash appeal to a future council. This to be sure was contrary to the constitution of Pius II and Julius II our predecessors that all appealing in this way are to be punished with the penalties of heretics. In vain does he implore the help of a council, since he openly admits that he does not believe in a council.

Therefore we can, without any further citation or delay, proceed against him to his condemnation and damnation as one whose faith is notoriously suspect and in fact a true heretic with the full severity of each and all of the above penalties and censures. Yet, with the advice of our brothers, imitating the mercy of almighty God who does not wish the death of a sinner but rather that he be converted and live, and forgetting all the injuries inflicted on us and the Apostolic See, we have decided to use all the compassion we are capable of. It is our hope, so far as in us lies, that he will experience a change of heart by taking the road of mildness we have proposed, return, and turn away from his errors. We will receive him kindly as the prodigal son returning to the embrace of the Church.

Therefore let Martin himself and all those adhering to him, and those who shelter and support him, through the merciful heart of our God and the sprinkling of the blood of our Lord Jesus Christ by which and through whom the redemption of the human race and the upbuilding of holy mother Church was accomplished, know that from our heart we exhort and beseech that he cease to disturb the peace, unity, and truth of the Church for which the Savior prayed so earnestly to the Father. Let him abstain from his pernicious errors that he may come back to us. If they really will obey, and certify to us by legal documents that they have obeyed, they will find in us the affection of a father's love, the opening of the font of the effects of paternal charity, and opening of the font of mercy and clemency.

We enjoin, however, on Martin that in the meantime he cease from all preaching or the office of preacher.

INTRODUCTION TO
Martin Luther
THE BABYLONIAN CAPTIVITY OF THE CHURCH

Having thrown down the gauntlet to the papal church in the *Letter to the Christian Nobility*, Luther knew an excommunication was probably not long in coming. Accordingly, he did not hesitate to mount a still bolder assault on the very foundations of the late medieval church—its sacramental system.

It is difficult for us today to imagine just how much of late medieval society revolved around the Church's seven sacraments, which covered every period of life: Baptism for the beginning of life, Confirmation for puberty, Marriage or Ordination for adulthood, Extreme Unction for the deathbed, and the Eucharist and Penance continually throughout. The Eucharist especially had morphed into something almost unrecognizable by comparison with early church practice. Celebrated nearly always in private by individual priests, it was no longer a fellowship meal, or even a distribution of the body and blood of Christ to the faithful (laity had, since the 13th century, only been allowed to receive the bread, not the wine), but a sacrificial offering performed by the priest to merit forgiveness of sins. Like the indulgence system, what had begun as a salve for the souls of the living was soon expanded to include the dead, with the wealthy leaving money in their estates to hire priests to say masses for their souls. (Recall the famous prayer on the eve of Agincourt in the play *Henry V*, where Shakespeare has Henry, worried that God might be punishing him for his father's treatment of King Richard II, say, "I have built two chantries, where the sad and solemn priests sing still for Richard's soul.") To say this was a lucrative business is an understatement; a large share of clergy were kept employed full-time doing little else. Once consecrated, the Eucharistic elements could then be reserved for adoration or paraded through the streets on festival days, opportunities for the common people to show devotion and seek forgiveness, and for the Church to bring in some cash. The immense power claimed by the Church for the sacraments, and the exclusive power over them reserved to the clergy, helped entrench the sharp divide between clergy and laity that Luther had attacked in the *Letter to the Christian Nobility*.

Accordingly, Luther dedicates *The Babylonian Captivity of the Church* to the task of rethinking the sacraments from the ground up. Borrowing the common term for the Papacy's 14th-century "captivity" at Avignon for his title, he argues that the sacramental system, far from being an economy of grace, had become a tool for holding believers captive to the power of the clergy. He argues for only three sacraments, rather than seven—the Eucharist, Baptism, and Penance—and strips down Penance to the point where it is not really a sacrament in the same sense as the others, and is not under the power of the priest. By far the largest section of the text (and the section we have chosen for this reader) is his discussion of the Eucharist, or "the Sacrament of the Altar."

Having the previous year declared his sympathy for the Hussites, whose greatest offense had been their insistence that the laity receive communion in both kinds—that is, the bread and the wine—he openly defends their position here, calling the restriction of wine to the priests "the first captivity of this sacrament." He spends several pages ridiculing the fanciful exegesis that the Romanists had developed to justify this restriction, and argues from both Scripture and church history that both bread and wine belong to the laity. The next section goes further, forcefully rejecting the scholastic doctrine of transubstantiation as ridiculous philosophical juggling. Instead, he argues for a simple affirmation of what came to be called *consubstantiation*—that the real body and blood of Christ are present together with the real bread and wine. Although all the Protestant Reformers were to follow Luther in his rejection of transubstantiation, most would not endorse his somewhat overreaching attacks on scholastic metaphysics, and indeed the Reformed came to think that the consubstantiation view led to no less nonsensical conclusions than transubstantiation.

In attacking "the third captivity of this sacrament," the sacrificial conception of the mass, which Luther calls "the most wicked of all," he gets to the real heart of the matter, offering a comprehensive rethink of the meaning of the Eucharist, and the sacraments in general. He is well aware of the consequences—that he will "alter almost the entire external form of the churches and introduce, or rather reintroduce, a totally different kind of ceremonies" and will "overturn the practice and teaching of all the churches and monasteries, by virtue of which they have flourished all these centuries." At its root, he argues, the Eucharist is nothing else than Christ's promise of the forgiveness of sins (and thus, simply the Gospel itself in visible form) received by faith by believing communicants. In this last section, Luther's genius for distilling his doctrine to clear and beautifully simple explanations shines through, such as his example of the rich lord bequeathing his inheritance to a beggar. If the gospel heart of the sacrament is recognized and preserved, Luther has no objection to embellishing the ceremony with outward pomp. But we must not, he says (now adopting scholastic metaphysical terms for his own use) confuse the gospel substance with the outward accidents.

Although inspiring to his growing body of sympathizers, the *Babylonian Captivity* was shocking and scandalous to orthodox Catholic ears. Indeed, it was so much so that one of his bitterest opponents, Thomas Murner, did Luther the favor of translating his Latin treatise into German, assuming that it would be self-refuting,[1] a scheme that backfired rather badly.

1 Martin Luther, *Three Treatises*, 2nd ed. (Minneapolis: Fortress Press, 1990), 120.

THE BABYLONIAN CAPTIVITY OF THE CHURCH

Martin Luther

TRANSLATED BY ALBERT T. W. STEINHAEUSER,

MODERNIZED BY ROBERT E. SMITH

EXCERPT: THE SACRAMENT OF THE ALTAR

2.1 Now, about the Sacrament of the Bread, the most important of all sacraments:

2.2 Let me tell you what progress I have made in my studies on the administration of this sacrament. For when I published my treatise on the Eucharist, I clung to the common usage, being in no way concerned with the question whether the papacy was right or wrong. But now, challenged and attacked, no, forcibly thrust into the arena, I shall freely speak my mind, let all the papists laugh or weep together.

2.3 In the first place, John 6 is to be entirely excluded from this discussion, since it does not refer in a single syllable to the sacrament. For not only was the sacrament not yet instituted, but the whole context plainly shows that Christ is speaking of faith in the Word made flesh, as I have said above. For He says, "My words are spirit, and they are life," which shows that He is speaking of a spiritual eating, whereby whoever eats has life, while the Jews understood Him to be speaking of bodily eating and therefore disputed with Him. But no eating can give life save the eating which is by faith, for that is the truly spiritual and living eating. As Augustine also says: "Why make ready teeth and stomach? Believe, and you have eaten." For the sacramental eating does not give life, since many eat unworthily. Therefore, He cannot be understood as speaking of the sacrament in this passage.

2.4 These words have indeed been wrongly applied to the sacrament, as in the decretal Dudum and often elsewhere. But it is one thing to misapply the Scriptures, it is quite another to understand them in their proper meaning. But if Christ in this passage enjoined the sacramental eating, then by saying, "Except you eat my flesh and drink my blood, you have no life in you," He would condemn all infants, invalids and those absent or in any way hindered from the sacramental eating, however strong their faith might be. Thus Augustine, in the second book of his Contra Julianum, proves from Innocent that even infants eat the flesh and drink the blood of Christ, without the sacrament, that is, they partake of them through the faith of the Church. Let this then be accepted as proved—John 6 does not belong here. For this reason I have elsewhere written that the Bohemians have no right to rely on this passage in support of their use of the sacrament in both kinds.

2.5 Now there are two passages that do clearly bear upon this matter—the Gospel narratives of the institution of the Lord's Supper,and Paul in 1 Corinthians 11. Let us examine these. Matthew, Mark and Luke agree that Christ gave the whole sacrament to all the disciples, and it is certain that Paul delivered both kinds. No one has ever had the temerity to assert the contrary. Further, Matthew reports that Christ did not say of the bread, "All of you, eat of it," but of the cup, "Drink of it all of you." Mark likewise does not say, "They all ate from it," but, "They all drank from it."

Both Matthew and Mark attach the note of universality to the cup, not to the bread, as though the Spirit saw this schism coming, by which some would be forbidden to partake of the cup, which Christ desired should be common to all. How furiously, do you think, would they rave against us, if they had found the word "all" attached to the bread instead of the cup! They would not leave us a loophole to escape, they would cry out against us and set us down as heretics, they would damn us for schismatics. But now, since it stands on our side and against them, they will not be bound by any force of logic—these men of the most free will, who change and change again even the things that are God's, and throw everything into confusion.

2.6 But imagine me standing over against them and interrogating my lords the papists. In the Lord's Supper, I say, the whole sacrament, or communion in both kinds, is given only to the priests or else it is given also to the laity. If it is given only to the priests, as they would have it, then it is not right to give it to the laity in either kind. It must not be rashly given to any to whom Christ did not give it when He instituted it. For if we permit one institution of Christ to be changed, we make all of His laws invalid, and every one will boldly claim that he is not bound by any law or institution of His. For a single exception, especially in the Scriptures, invalidates the whole. But if it is given also to the laity, then it inevitably follows that it ought not to be withheld from them in either form. And if any do withhold it from them when they desire it, they act impiously and contrary to the work, example and institution of Christ.

2.7 I confess that I am conquered by this, to me, unanswerable argument, and that I have neither read nor heard nor found anything to advance against it. For here the word and example of Christ stand firm, when He says, not by way of permission but of command, "All of you, drink from it." For if all are to drink, and the words cannot be understood as addressed to the priests alone, then it is certainly an impious act to withhold the cup from laymen who desire it, even though an angel from heaven were to do it. For when they say that the distribution of both kinds was left to the judgment of the Church, they make this assertion without giving any reason for it and put it forth without any authority. It is ignored just as readily as it is proved, and does not stand up against an opponent who confronts us with the word and work of Christ. such a one must be refuted with a word of Christ, but this we do not possess.

2.8 But if one kind may be withheld from the laity, then with equal right and reason a portion of baptism and penance might also be taken from them by this same authority of the Church. Therefore, just as baptism and absolution must be administered in their entirety, so the Sacrament of the Bread must be given in its entirety to all laymen, if they desire it. I am amazed to find them asserting that the priests may never receive only the one kind, in the mass, on pain of committing a mortal sin—that for no other reason, as they unanimously say, than that both kinds constitute the one complete sacrament, which may not be divided. I beg them to tell me why it may be divided in the case of the laity, and why to them alone the whole sacrament may not be given. Do they not acknowledge, by their own testimony, either that both kinds are to be given to the laity, or that it is not a valid sacrament when only one kind is given to them?

How can the one kind be a complete sacrament for the laity and not a complete sacrament for the priests? Why do they flaunt the authority of the Church and the power of the pope in my face? These do not make void the Word of God and the testimony of the truth.

2.9 But further, if the Church can withhold the wine from the laity, it can also withhold the bread from them. It could, therefore, withhold the entire Sacrament of the Altar from the laity and completely annul Christ's institution so far as they are concerned. I ask, by what authority? But if the Church cannot withhold the bread, or both kinds, neither can it withhold the wine. This cannot possibly be contradicted. For the Church's power must be the same over either kind as over both kinds, and if she has no power over both kinds, she has none over either kind. I am curious to hear what the Roman flatterers will have to say to this.

2.10 What carries most weight with me, however, and quite decides the matter for me is this. Christ says: "This is my blood, which is shed for you and for many for the remission of sins." Here we see very plainly that the blood is given to all those for whose sins it was shed. But who will dare to say it was not shed for the laity? Do you not see whom He addresses when He gives the cup? Doesn't He give it to all? Doesn't He say that it is shed for all? "For you," He says—Well, we will let these be the priests— "and for many"—these cannot be priests. Yet He says, "All of you, drink of it." I too could easily trifle here and with my words make a mockery of Christ's words, as my dear trifler does. But they who rely on the Scriptures in opposing us, must be refuted by the Scriptures.

2.11 This is what has prevented me from condemning the Bohemians, who, whether they are wicked men or good, certainly have the word and act of Christ on their side, while we have neither, but only that hollow device of men—"the Church has appointed it." It was not the Church that appointed these things, but the tyrants of the churches, without the consent of the Church, which is the people of God.

2.12 But where in all the world is the necessity, where the religious duty, where the practical use, of denying both kinds, i.e., the visible sign, to the laity, when everyone concedes to them the grace of the sacrament without the sign? If they concede the grace, which is the greater, why not the sign, which is the lesser? For in every sacrament the sign as such is of far less importance than the thing signified.What then is to prevent them from conceding the lesser, when they concede the greater? I can see but one reason. It has come about by the permission of an angry God in order to give occasion for a schism in the Church. It is to bring home to us how, having long ago lost the grace of the sacrament, we contend for the sign, which is the lesser, against that which is the most important and the chief thing, just as some men for the sake of ceremonies contend against love. No, this monstrous perversion seems to date from the time when we began for the sake of the riches of this world to rage against Christian love. Thus God would show us, by this terrible sign, how we esteem signs more than the things they signify.

How preposterous would it be to admit that the faith of baptism is granted the candidate for baptism, and yet to deny him the sign of this faith, namely, the water!

2.13 Finally, Paul stands invincible and stops every mouth, when he says in 1 Corinthians 11, "I have received from the Lord what I also delivered to you." He does not say, "I permitted to you," as that friar lyingly asserts. Nor is it true that Paul delivered both kinds on account of the contention in the Corinthian congregation. For, first, the text shows that their contention was not about both kinds, but about the contempt and envy among rich and poor, as it is clearly stated: "One is hungry, and another is drunken, and you put to shame those that have nothing." Again, Paul is not speaking of the time when he first delivered the sacrament to them, for he does not say, "I receive from the Lord and give to you," but, "I received and delivered"—namely, when he first began to preach among them, a long while before this contention. This shows that he delivered both kinds to them. "Delivered" means the same as "commanded," for elsewhere he uses the word in this sense. Consequently there is nothing in the friar's fuming about permission. It is an assortment of arguments without Scripture, reason or sense. His opponents do not ask what he has dreamed, but what the Scriptures decree in this matter. Out of the Scriptures he cannot adduce one dot of an I or cross of a T in support of his dreams, while they can bring forward mighty thunderbolts in support of their faith.

2.14 Come here then, popish flatterers, one and all! Fall in line and defend yourselves against the charge of godlessness, tyranny, treason against the Gospel, and the crime of slandering your brethren. You decry as heretics those who will not be wise after the vaporings of your own brains, in the face of such patent and potent words of Scripture. If any are to be called heretics and schismatics, it is not the Bohemians nor the Greeks, for they take their stand upon the Gospel. But you Romans are the heretics and godless schismatics, for you presume upon your own fictions and fly in the face of the clear Scriptures of God. Parry that stroke, if you can!

2.15 But what could be more ridiculous, and more worthy of this friar's brain, than his saying that the Apostle wrote these words and gave this permission, not to the Church universal, but to a particular church, that is, the Corinthian? Where does he get his proof? Out of his one storehouse, his own impious head. If the Church universal receives, reads and follows this epistle in all points as written for itself, why should it not do the same with this portion of it? If we admit that any epistle, or any part of any epistle, of Paul does not apply to the Church universal, then the whole authority of Paul falls to the ground. Then the Corinthians will say that what he teaches about faith in the epistle to the Romans does not apply to them. What greater blasphemy and madness can be imagined than this!

God forbid that there should be one dot of an I or cross of a T in all of Paul which the whole Church universal is not bound to follow and keep! Not so did the Fathers hold, down to these perilous times, in which Paul foretold there should be blasphemers and blind and foolish men, of whom this friar is one, no, the chief of them.

2.16 However, suppose we grant the truth of this intolerable madness. If Paul gave his permission to a particular church, then, even from your own point of view, the Greeks and Bohemians are in the right, for they are particular churches. Hence it is sufficient that they do not act contrary to Paul, who at least gave permission. Moreover, Paul could not permit anything contrary to Christ's institution. Therefore I throw in your face, O Rome, and in the face of all you flatterers, these sayings of Christ and Paul, on behalf of the Greeks and the Bohemians. You cannot prove that you have received any authority to change them, much less to accuse others of heresy for disregarding your arrogance. Rather you deserve to be charged with the crime of godlessness and despotism.

2.17 Furthermore, Cyprian, who alone is strong enough to hold all the Romanists at bay, bears witness, in the fifth book of his treatise On the Lapsed, that it was a wide-spread custom in his church to administer both kinds to the laity, and even to children, yes, to give the body of the Lord into their hands, of which he cites many instances. He condemns, for example, certain members of the congregation as follows: "The sacrilegious man is angered at the priests because he does not receive the body of the Lord right away with unclean hands, or drink the blood of the Lord with defiled lips." He is speaking, as you see, of laymen, and irreverent laymen, who desired to receive the body and the blood from the priests. Do you find anything to snarl at here, wretched flatterer? Say that even this holy martyr, a Church Father preeminent for his apostolic spirit, was a heretic and used that permission in a particular church.

2.18 In the same place, Cyprian narrates an incident that came under his own observation. He describes at length how a deacon was administering the cup to a little girl, who drew away from him, whereupon he poured the blood of the Lord into her mouth. We read the same of St.Donatus, whose broken chalice this wretched flatterer so lightly disposes of. "I read of a broken chalice," he says, "but I do not read that the blood was given." It is no wonder! He who finds what he pleases in the Scriptures will also read what he pleases in histories. But will the authority of the Church be established, or will heretics be refuted, in this way?

2.19 Enough of this! I did not undertake this work to reply to him who is not worth replying to, but to bring the truth of the matter to light.

2.20 I conclude, then, that it is wicked and despotic to deny both kinds to the laity, and that this is not in the power of any angel, much less of any pope or council.

Nor does the Council of Constance give me pause, for if its authority carries weight, why does not that of the Council of Basel also carry weight? For the latter council decided, on the contrary, after much disputing, that the Bohemians might use both kinds, as the extant records and documents of the council prove. And to that council this ignorant flatterer refers in support of his dream. In such wisdom does his whole treatise abound.

2.21 The first captivity of this sacrament, therefore, concerns its substance or completeness, of which we have been deprived by the despotism of Rome. Not that they sin against Christ, who use the one kind, for Christ did not command the use of either kind, but left it to everyone's free will, when He said: "As often as you do this, do it in remembrance of me." But they sin who forbid the giving of both kinds to such as desire to exercise this free will. The fault lies not with the laity, but with the priests. The sacrament does not belong to the priests, but to all, and the priests are not lords but ministers, in duty bound to administer both kinds to those who desire them, and as often as they desire them. If they wrest this right from the laity and forcibly withhold it, they are tyrants. But the laity are without fault, whether they lack one kind or both kinds. They must meanwhile be sustained by their faith and by their desire for the complete sacrament. The priests, being ministers, are bound to administer baptism and absolution to whoever seeks them, because he has a right to them. But if they do not administer them, he that seeks them has at least the full merit of his faith, while they will be accused before Christ as wicked servants. In like manner the holy Fathers of old who dwelt in the desert did not receive the sacrament in any form for many years together.

2.22 Therefore I do not urge that both kinds be seized by force, as though we were bound to this form by a rigorous command. But I instruct men's consciences that they may endure the Roman tyranny, knowing well they have been deprived of their rightful share in the sacrament because of their own sin. This only do I desire—that no one justify the tyranny of Rome, as though it did well to forbid one of the two kinds to the laity. We ought rather to abhor it, withhold our consent, and endure it just as we should do if we were held captive by the Turk and not permitted to use either kind. That is what I meant by saying it seemed well to me that this captivity should be ended by the decree of a general council, our Christian liberty restored to us out of the hands of the Roman tyrant, and every one left free to seek and receive this sacrament, just as he is free to receive baptism and penance. But now they compel us, by the same tyranny, to receive the one kind year after year. So utterly lost is the liberty which Christ has given us. This is but the due reward of our godless ingratitude.

2.23 The second captivity of this sacrament is less grievous so far as the conscience is concerned, yet the very gravest danger threatens the man who would attack it, to say nothing of condemning it. Here I shall be called a Wycliffite and a heretic a thousand times over. But what of that? Since the Roman bishop has ceased to be a bishop and become a tyrant, I fear none of his decrees, for I know that it is not in his power, nor even in that of a general council, to make new articles of faith. Years ago, when I was delving into scholastic theology, the Cardinal of Cambrai gave me food for thought, in his comments on the fourth Book of the Sentences, where he argues with great acumen that to hold that real bread and real wine, and not their accidents only, are present on the altar, is much more probable and requires fewer unnecessary miracles—if only the Church had not decreed otherwise. When I learned later what church it was that had decreed this—namely, the Church of Thomas, i.e., of Aristotle—I waxed bolder, and after floating in a sea of doubt, at last found rest for my conscience in the above view—namely, that it is real bread and real wine, in which Christ's real flesh and blood are present, not otherwise and not less really than they assume to be the case under their accidents. I reached this conclusion because I saw that the opinions of the Thomists, though approved by pope and council, remain but opinions and do not become articles of faith, even though an angel from heaven were to decree otherwise. For what is asserted without Scripture or an approved revelation, may be held as an opinion, but need not be believed. But this opinion of Thomas hangs so completely in the air, devoid of Scripture and reason, that he seems here to have forgotten both his philosophy and his logic. For Aristotle writes about subject and accidents so very differently from St. Thomas, that I think this great man is to be pitied, not only for drawing his opinions in matters of faith from Aristotle, but for attempting to base them on him without understanding his meaning—an unfortunate superstructure upon an unfortunate foundation.

2.24 I therefore permit every man to hold either of these views, as he chooses. My one concern at present is to remove all scruples of conscience, so that no one may fear to become guilty of heresy if he should believe in the presence of real bread and real wine on the altar, and that everyone may feel at liberty to ponder, hold and believe either one view or the other, without endangering his salvation. However, I shall now more fully set forth my own view. In the first place, I do not intend to listen or attach the least importance to those who will cry out that this teaching of mine is Wycliffite, Hussite, heretical, and contrary to the decision of the Church, for they are the very persons whom I have convicted of manifold heresies in the matter of indulgences, the freedom of the will and the grace of God, good works and sin, etc. If Wycliffe was once a heretic, they are heretics ten times over, and it is a pleasure to be suspected and accused by such heretics and perverse sophists, whom to please is the height of godlessness. Besides, the only way in which they can prove their opinions and disprove those of others, is by saying, "That is Wycliffite, Hussite, heretical!" They have this feeble retort always on their tongue, and they have nothing else. If you demand a Scripture passage, they say, "This is our opinion, and the decision of the Church—that is, of ourselves!" Thus these men, "reprobate concerning the faith" and untrustworthy, have the audacity to set their own fancies before us in the name of the Church as articles of faith.

2.25 But there are good grounds for my view, and this above all—no violence is to be done to the words of God, whether by man or angel. But they are to be retained in their simplest meaning wherever possible, and to be understood in their grammatical and literal sense unless the context plainly forbids, lest we give our adversaries occasion to make a mockery of all the Scriptures. Thus Origen was repudiated, in ancient times, because he despised the grammatical sense and turned the trees, and all things else written concerning Paradise, into allegories. For it might be concluded from this that God did not create trees. Even so here, when the Evangelists plainly write that Christ took bread and broke it, and the book of Acts and Paul, in their turn, call it bread, we have to think of real bread and real wine, just as we do of a real cup. For even they do not maintain that the cup is transubstantiated. But since it is not necessary to assume a transubstantiation wrought by Divine power, it is to be regarded as a figment of the human mind, for it rests neither on Scripture nor on reason, as we shall see.

2.26 Therefore it is an absurd and unheard-of juggling with words, to understand "bread" to mean "the form, or accidents of bread," and "wine" to mean "the form, or accidents of wine." Why do they not also understand all other things to mean their forms, or accidents? Even if this might be done with all other things, it would yet not be right thus to emasculate the words of God and arbitrarily to empty them of their meaning.

2.27 Moreover, the Church had the true faith for more than twelve hundred years, during which time the holy Fathers never once mentioned this transubstantiation—certainly, a monstrous word for a monstrous idea—until the pseudo-philosophy of Aristotle became rampant in the Church these last three hundred years. During these centuries many other things have been wrongly defined, for example, that the Divine essence neither is begotten nor begets, that the soul is the substantial form of the human body, and the like assertions, which are made without reason or sense, as the Cardinal of Cambray himself admits.

2.28 Perhaps they will say that the danger of idolatry demands that bread and wine be not really present. How ridiculous! The laymen have never become familiar with their subtle philosophy of substance and accidents, and could not grasp it if it were taught them.

Besides, there is the same danger in the case of the accidents which remain and which they see, as in the case of the substance which they do not see. For if they do not adore the accidents, but Christ hidden under them, why should they adore the bread, which they do not see?

2.29 But why could not Christ include His body in the substance of the bread just as well as in the accidents? The two substances of fire and iron are so mingled in the heated iron that every part is both iron and fire. Why could not much rather Christ's body be thus contained in every part of the substance of the bread?

2.30 What will they say? We believe that in His birth Christ came forth out of the unopened womb of His mother. Let them say here too that the flesh of the Virgin was meanwhile annihilated, or as they would more aptly say, transubstantiated, so that Christ, after being enfolded in its accidents, finally came forth through the accidents! The same thing will have to be said of the shut door and of the closed opening of the tomb, through which He went in and out without disturbing them. Hence has risen that Babylonian philosophy of constant quantity distinct from the substance, until it has come to such a pass that they themselves no longer know what are accidents and what is substance. For who has ever proved beyond the shadow of a doubt that heat, color, cold, light, weight or shape are mere accidents? Finally, they have been driven to the fancy that a new substance is created by God for their accidents on the altar—all on account of Aristotle, who says, "It is the essence of an accident to be in something," and endless other monstrosities, all of which they would be rid if they simply permitted real bread to be present. And I rejoice greatly that the simple faith of this sacrament is still to be found at least among the common people. They do not understand, so they do not dispute, whether accidents are present or substance, but believe with a simple faith that Christ's body and blood are truly contained in whatever is there, and leave to those who have nothing else to do the business of disputing about that which contains them.

2.31 But perhaps they will say: From Aristotle we learn that in an affirmative proposition subject and predicate must be identical, or, to set down the beast's own words, in the sixth book of his Metaphysics: "An affirmative proposition demands the agreement of subject and predicate," which they interpret as above. Hence, when it is said, "This is my body," the subject cannot be identical with the bread, but must be identical with the body of Christ.

2.32 What shall we say when Aristotle and the doctrines of men are made to be the arbiters of these lofty and divine matters? Why do we not put aside such curiosity, and cling simply to the word of Christ, willing to remain in ignorance of what here takes place, and content with this, that the real body of Christ is present by virtue of the words? Or is it necessary to comprehend the manner of the divine working in every detail?

2.33 But what do they say to Aristotle's assigning a subject to whatever is predicated of the attributes, although he holds that the substance is the chief subject? Hence for him, "this white," "this large," etc., are subjects of which something is predicated. If that is correct, I ask: If a transubstantiation must be assumed in order that Christ's body is not predicated of the bread, why not also a transaccidentation in order that it be not predicated of the accidents? For the same danger remains if one understands the subject to be "this white" or "this round" is my body, and for the same reason that a transubstantiation is assumed, a transaccidentation must also be assumed, because of this identity of subject and predicate.

2.34 If, however, going beyond our understanding, you get rid of accidents, and therefore refuse to understand that accidents are included in the subject when you say, "This is my body," then why do you not, with the same ease, ignore the substance of bread, so that you do not include the bread as the subject, and, therefore "this is my body" includes the substance no less than the accident? Especially, seeing that this is a divine work, accomplished with all powerful might, and can work in the same manner and to the same extent in the substance as much as in the accident.[2]

2.35 Let us not, however, dabble too much in philosophy. Does not Christ appear to have admirably anticipated such curiosity by saying of the wine, not, "Hoc est sanguis meus," but "Hic est sanguis meus"?[3] And yet more clearly, by bringing in the word "cup," when He said, "This cup is the new testament in my blood." Does it not seem as though He desired to keep us in a simple faith, so that we might but believe His blood to be in the cup? For my part, if I cannot fathom how the bread is the body of Christ, I will take my reason captive to the obedience of Christ, and clinging simply to His word, firmly believe not only that the body of Christ is in the bread, but that the bread is the body of Christ. For this is proved by the words, "He took bread, and giving thanks, He broke it and said, Take, eat; this [i.e., this bread which He took and broke] is my body." And Paul says: "The bread which we break, is it not the communion of the body of Christ?" He says not, in the bread, but the bread itself, is the communion of the body

2 This portion (2.34) originally left in Latin. Translated by Jonathan Roberts.

3 "Hoc" meaning "this," "hic" meaning "here." "Sanguis meus" meaning "my blood."

of Christ. What does it matter if philosophy cannot fathom this? The Holy Spirit is greater than Aristotle. Does philosophy fathom their transubstantiation, of which they themselves admit that here all philosophy breaks down? But the agreement of the pronoun "this" with "body," in Greek and Latin, is owing to the fact that in these languages the two words are of the same gender. But in the Hebrew language, which has no neuter gender, "this" agrees with "bread," so that it would be proper to say, "Hic est corpus meum." This is proved also by the use of language and by common sense. The subject, certainly, points to the bread, not to the body, when He says, "Hoc est corpus meum," "Das ist mein Leib,"—i.e., This bread is my body.

2.36 Therefore it is with the sacrament even as it is with Christ. In order that divinity may dwell in Him, it is not necessary that the human nature be transubstantiated and divinity be contained under its accidents. But both natures are there in their entirety, and it is truly said, "This man is God," and "This God is man." Even though philosophy cannot grasp this, faith grasps it, and the authority of God's Word is greater than the grasp of our intellect. Even so, in order that the real body and the real blood of Christ may be present in the sacrament, it is not necessary that the bread and wine be transubstantiated and Christ be contained under their accidents. But both remain there together, and it is truly said, "This bread is my body, this wine is my blood," and vice versa. Thus I will for now understand it, for the honor of the holy words of God, which I will not allow any petty human argument to override or give to them meanings foreign to them. At the same time, I permit other men to follow the other opinion, which is laid down in the decree Firmiter. Only let them not press us to accept their opinions as articles of faith, as I said above.

2.37 The third captivity of this sacrament is that most wicked abuse of all, in consequence of which there is today no more generally accepted and firmly believed opinion in the Church than this—that the mass is a good work and a sacrifice. This abuse has brought an endless host of others in its wake, so that the faith of this sacrament has become utterly extinct and the holy sacrament has truly been turned into a fair, tavern, and place of merchandise. Hence participations, brotherhoods, intercessions, merits, anniversaries, memorial days, and the like wares are bought and sold, traded and bartered in the Church, and from this priests and monks derive their whole living.

2.38 I am attacking a difficult matter, and one perhaps impossible to abate, since it has become so firmly entrenched through century-long custom and the common consent of men that it would be necessary to abolish most of the books now in vogue, to alter almost the whole external form of the churches, and to introduce, or rather re-introduce, a totally different kind of ceremony. But my Christ lives, and we must be careful to give more heed to the Word of God than to all the thoughts of men and of angels. I will perform the duties of my office, and uncover the facts in the case. I will give the truth as I have received it, freely and without malice. For the rest let every man look to his own salvation. I will faithfully do my part that none may cast on me the blame for his lack of faith and knowledge of the truth, when we appear before the judgment seat of Christ.

2.39 IN THE FIRST PLACE, in order to grasp safely and fortunately a true and unbiased knowledge of this sacrament, we must above all else be careful to put aside whatever has been added by the zeal and devotion of men to the original, simple institution of this sacrament—such things as vestments, ornaments, chants, prayers, organs, candles, and the whole pageantry of outward things. We must turn our eyes and hearts simply to the institution of Christ and to this alone, and put nothing before us but the very word of Christ by which He instituted this sacrament, made it perfect, and committed it to us. For in that word, and in that word alone, reside the power, the nature, and the whole substance of the mass. All else is the work of man, added to the word of Christ. And the mass can be held and remain a mass just as well without it. Now the words of Christ, in which He instituted this sacrament, are these:

2.40 "And while they were at supper, Jesus took bread, and blessed, and broke it: and gave to His disciples, and said: "Take it and eat. This is my body, which shall be given for you." And taking the chalice, He gave thanks, and gave to them, saying: "All of you, drink of this. This is the chalice, the new testament in my blood, which shall be shed for you and for many the remission of sins. This do to commemorate me.""

2.41 These words the Apostle also delivers and more fully expounds in 1 Corinthians 11. On them we must lean and build as on a firm foundation, if we would not be carried about with every wind of doctrine, even as we have until now been carried about by the wicked doctrines of men, who turn aside the truth. For in these words nothing is omitted that concerns the completeness, the use and the blessing of this sacrament and nothing is included that is superfluous and not necessary for us to know. Whoever sets them aside and meditates or teaches concerning the mass, will teach monstrous and wicked doctrines, as they have done who made of the sacrament an opus operatum and a sacrifice.

2.42 Therefore let this stand at the outset as our infallibly certain proposition—the mass, or Sacrament of the Altar, is Christ's testament which He left behind Him at His death, to be distributed among His believers. For that is the meaning of His word—"This is the chalice, the new testament in my blood." Let this truth stand, I say, as the immovable foundation on which we shall base all that we have to say, for we are going to overthrow, as you will see, all the godless opinions of men imported into this most precious sacrament. Christ, Who is the Truth, said truly that this is the new testament in His blood, which is shed for us. Not without reason do I dwell on this sentence. The matter is not at all trivial, and must be most deeply impressed upon us.

2.43 Let us inquire, therefore, what a testament is, and we shall learn at the same time what the mass is, what its use is,what its blessing is, and what its abuse is.

2.44 A testament, as everyone knows, is a promise made by one about to die, in which he designates his bequest and appoints his heirs. Therefore a testament involves, first, the death of the testator, and secondly, the promise of the bequest and the naming of the heir. Thus St. Paul discusses at length the nature of a testament in Romans 4, Galatians 3 and 4, and Hebrews 9. The same thing is also clearly seen in these words of Christ. Christ testifies concerning His death when He says: "This is my body, which shall be given; this is my blood, which shall be shed." He designates the bequest when He says: "For remission of sins." And He appoints the heirs when He says: "For you, and for many"—i.e., for such as accept and believe the promise of the testator. For here it is faith that makes men heirs, as we shall see.

2.45 You see, therefore, that what we call the mass is the promise of remission of sins made to us by God—the kind of promise that has been confirmed by the death of the Son of God. For the one difference between a promise and a testament is that a testament is a promise which implies the death of him who makes it. A testator is a man who is about to die making a promise. While he that makes a promise is, if I may so put it, a testator who is not about to die. This testament of Christ was foreshadowed in all the promises of God from the beginning of the world. Yes, whatever value those ancient promises possessed was altogether derived from this new promise that was to come in Christ. This is why the words "covenant" and "testament of the Lord" occur so frequently in the Scriptures, which words signified that God would one day die. For where there is a testament, the death of the testator must follow (Hebrews 9). Now God made a testament. Therefore it was necessary that He should die. But God could not die unless He became man. Thus both the incarnation and the death of Christ are briefly understood in this one word "testament."

2.46 From the above it will at once be seen what is the right and what is the wrong use of the mass, what is the worthy and what is the unworthy preparation for it. If the mass is a promise, as has been said, it is to be approached, not with any work, strength or merit, but with faith alone. For where there is the word of God Who makes the promise, there must be the faith of man who takes it. It is plain, therefore, that the first step in our salvation is faith, which clings to the word of the promise made by God, Who without any effort on our part, in free and unmerited mercy makes a beginning and offers us the word of His promise. For He sent His Word, and by it healed them. He did not accept our work and thus heal us. God's Word is the beginning of all. Faith follows it, and love follows faith. Then love works every good work, for it does not cause harm, no, it is the fulfilling of the law. In no other way can man come to God and deal with Him than through faith. That is, not man, by any work of his, but God, by His promise, is the author of salvation, so that all things depend on the word of His power, and are upheld and preserved by it, with which word He conceived us, that we should be a kind of firstfruits of His creatures.

2.47 Thus, in order to raise up Adam after the fall, God gave him this promise, addressing the serpent: "I will put hostility between you and the woman, and your seed and her seed. She shall crush your head, and you will lie in wait for her heel." In this word of promise Adam, with his descendants, was carried as it were in God's arms, and by faith in it he was preserved, patiently waiting for the woman who should crush the serpent's head, as God had promised. And in that faith and expectation he died, not knowing when or in what form she would come, yet never doubting that she would come. For such a promise, being the truth of God, preserves, even in hell, those who believe it and wait for it. After this came another promise, made to Noah—to last until the time of Abraham—when a rainbow was set as a sign in the clouds, by faith in which Noah and his descendants found a gracious God. After that He promised Abraham that all nations should be blessed in his seed. This is Abraham's arms, in which his posterity was carried. Then to Moses and the children of Israel, and especially to David, He gave the plain promise of Christ, thereby at last making clear what was meant by the ancient promise to them.

2.48 So it came finally to the most complete promise of the new testament, in which with plain words life and salvation are freely promised, and granted to such as believe the promise. He distinguished this testament by a particular mark from the old, calling it the "new testament." For the old testament, which He gave by Moses, was a promise not of remission of sins or of eternal things, but of temporal things—namely, the land of Canaan—by which no man was renewed in his spirit, to lay hold of the heavenly inheritance. Therefore it was also necessary that irrational beasts should be slain, as types of Christ, that by their blood the testament might be confirmed. So the testament was like the blood, and the promise like the sacrifice. But here He says: "The new testament in my blood"—not in another's, but in His own. By this blood grace is promised, through the Spirit, for the remission of sins, that we may obtain the inheritance.

2.49 The mass, according to its substance, is, therefore, nothing else than the words of Christ mentioned above—"Take and eat." It is as if He said: "Behold, condemned, sinful man, in the pure and unmerited love with which I love you, and by the will of the Father of all mercies, I promise you in these words, even though you do not desire or deserve them, the forgiveness of all your sins and life everlasting. And, so that you may be most certainly assured of this my irrevocable promise, I give my body and shed my blood, thus by my very death confirming this promise, and leaving my body and blood to you as a sign and memorial of this same promise. As often, therefore, as you partake of them, remember me, and praise, magnify, and give thanks for my love and bounty for you."

2.50 From this you will see that nothing else is needed to have a worthy mass than a faith that confidently relies on this promise, believes these words of Christ are true, and does not doubt that these infinite blessings have been bestowed upon it. Following closely behind this faith there follows, by itself, a most sweet stirring of the heart, by which the spirit of man is enlarged and grows fat—that is love, given by the Holy Spirit through faith in Christ—so that he is drawn to Christ, that gracious and good Testator, and made quite another and a new man. Who would not shed tears of gladness, no, nearly faint for the joy he has for Christ, if he believed with unshaken faith that this inestimable promise of Christ belonged to him!

How could one help loving so great a Benefactor, who offers, promises and grants, all unasked, such great riches, and this eternal inheritance, to someone unworthy and deserving of something far different?

2.51 Therefore, it is our one misfortune, that we have many masses in the world, and yet none or but the fewest of us recognize, consider and receive these promises and riches that are offered, although truly we should do nothing else in the mass with greater zeal (yes, it demands all our zeal) than set before our eyes, meditate, and ponder these words, these promises of Christ, which truly are the mass itself, in order to exercise, nourish, increase, and strengthen our faith by such daily remembrance. For this is what He commands, saying, "This do in remembrance of me." This should be done by the preachers of the Gospel, in order that this promise might be faithfully impressed upon the people and commended to them, to the awakening of faith in the same.

2.52 But how many are there now who know that the mass is the promise of Christ? I will say nothing of those godless preachers of fables, who teach human traditions instead of this promise. And even if they teach these words of Christ, they do not teach them as a promise or testament, and, therefore, not to the awakening of faith.

2.53 O the pity of it! Under this captivity, they take every precaution that no layman should hear these words of Christ, as if they were too sacred to be delivered to the common people. So mad are we priests that we arrogantly claim that the so-called words of consecration may be said by ourselves alone, as secret words, yet so that they do not profit even us, for we too fail to regard them as promises or as a testament, for the strengthening of faith. Instead of believing them, we reverence them with I know not what superstitious and godless fancies. This misery of ours, what is it but a device of Satan to remove every trace of the mass out of the Church? Although he is meanwhile at work filling every nook and corner on earth with masses, that is, abuses and mockeries of God's testament, and burdening the world more and more heavily with grievous sins of idolatry, to its deeper condemnation. For what worse idolatry can there be than to abuse God's promises with perverse opinions and to neglect or extinguish faith in them?

2.54 For God does not deal, nor has He ever dealt, with man otherwise than through a word of promise, as I have said. Again, we cannot deal with God otherwise than through faith in the word of His promise. He does not desire works, nor has He need of them. We deal with men and with ourselves on the basis of works. But He has need of this—that we deem Him true to His promises, wait patiently for Him, and thus worship Him with faith, hope and love. Thus He obtains His glory among us, since it is not of ourselves who run, but of God who shows mercy, promises and gives, that we have and hold every blessing. That is the true worship and service of God which we must perform in the mass. But if the words of promise are not proclaimed, what exercise of faith can there be? And without faith, who can have hope or love? Without faith, hope and love, what service can there be? There is no doubt, therefore, that in our day all priests and monks, together with all their bishops and superiors, are idolaters and in a most perilous state, by reason of this ignorance, abuse and mockery of the mass, or sacrament, or testament of God.

2.55 For any one can easily see that these two—the promise and faith—must go together. For without the promise there is nothing to believe, while without faith the promise remains without effect, for it is established and fulfilled through faith. From this everyone will readily gather that the mass, which is nothing else than the promise, is approached and observed only in this faith, without which whatever prayers, preparations, works, signs of the cross, or genuflections are brought to it, are incitements to impiety rather than exercises of piety. For they who come thus prepared are likely to imagine themselves on that account justly entitled to approach the altar, when in reality they are less prepared than at any other time and in any other work, by reason of the unbelief which they bring with them. How many priests will you find every day offering the sacrifice of the mass, who accuse themselves of a horrible crime if they—wretched men!—commit a trifling blunder—such as putting on the wrong robe or forgetting to wash their hands or stumbling over their prayers—but that they neither regard nor believe the mass itself, namely, the divine promise. This causes them not the slightest qualms of conscience.

O worthless religion of this our age, the most godless and thankless of all ages!

2.56 Hence the only worthy preparation and proper use of the mass is faith in the mass, that is to say, in the divine promise. Whoever, therefore, is minded to approach the altar and to receive the sacrament, let him beware of appearing empty before the Lord God. But he will appear empty unless he has faith in the mass, or this new testament. What godless work that he could commit would be a more grievous crime against the truth of God, than this unbelief of his, by which, as much as in him lies, he convicts God of being a liar and a maker of empty promises? The safest course, therefore, will be to go to mass in the same spirit in which you would go to hear any other promise of God, that is, not to be ready to perform and bring many works, but to believe and receive all that is there promised, or proclaimed by the priest as having been promised to you. If you do not go in this spirit, beware of going at all. You will surely go to your condemnation.

2.57 I was right, then, in saying that the whole power of the mass consists in the words of Christ, in which He testifies that the remission of sins is bestowed on all those who believe that His body is given and His blood shed for them. For this reason nothing is more important for those who go to hear mass than diligently and in full faith to ponder these words. Unless they do this, all else that they do is in vain. But while the mass is the word of Christ, it is also true that God usually adds to nearly every one of His promises a certain sign as a mark or memorial of His promise, so that we may thereby the more faithfully hold to His promise and be the more forcibly admonished by it. Thus, to his promise to Noah that He would not again destroy the world by a flood, He added His rainbow in the clouds, to show that He would be mindful of His covenant. And after promising Abraham the inheritance in his seed, He gave him the sign of circumcision as the seal of his righteousness by faith. Thus, to Gideon He granted the sign of the dry and the wet fleece, to confirm His promise of victory over the Midianites. And to Ahaz He offered a sign through Isaiah concerning his victory over the kings of Syria and Samaria, to strengthen his faith in the promise. And many such signs of the promises of God do we find in the Scriptures.

2.58 Thus also to the mass, that crown of all His promises, He adds His body and blood in the bread and wine, as a memorial sign of this great promise, as He says, "This do in remembrance of me." Even so in baptism He adds to the words of the promise, the sign of immersion in water. We learn from this that in every promise of God two things are presented to us—the word and the sign—so that we are to understand the word to be the testament, but the sign to be the sacrament. Thus, in the mass, the word of Christ is the testament, and the bread and wine are the sacrament. And as there is greater power in the word than in the sign, so there is greater power in the testament than in the sacrament. For a man can have and use the word, or testament, apart from the sign, or sacrament. "Believe," says Augustine, "and you have eaten." But what does one believe save the word of promise? Therefore I can hold mass every day, yes, every hour, for I can set the words of Christ before me, and with them refresh and strengthen my faith, as often as I choose. That is a truly spiritual eating and drinking.

2.59 Here you may see what great things our theologians of the Sentences have produced. That which is the principal and chief thing, namely, the testament and word of promise, is not treated by one of them. Thus they have obliterated faith and the whole power of the mass. But the second part of the mass—the sign, or sacrament—this alone do they discuss, yet in such a manner that here too they teach not faith but their preparations and opera operata, participations and fruits, as though these were the mass, until they have fallen to babbling of transubstantiation and endless other metaphysical quibbles, and have destroyed the proper understanding and use of both sacrament and testament, altogether abolished faith, and caused Christ's people to forget their God, as the prophet says, days without number. Let the others count the manifold fruits of hearing mass. Focus your attention on this: say and believe with the prophet, that God prepares a table before you in the presence of your enemies, at which your soul may eat and grow fat. But your faith is fed only with the word of divine promise, for "not by bread alone does man live, but by every word that proceeds from the mouth of God." Hence, in the mass you must above all things pay closest heed to the word of promise, as to your rich banquet, green pasture, and sacred refreshment. You must esteem this word higher than all else, trust in it above all things, and cling firmly to it even through the midst of death and all sins. By thus doing you will attain not merely to those tiny drops and crumbs of "fruits of the mass," which some have superstitiously imagined, but to the very fountainhead of life, which is faith in the word, from which every blessing flows. As it is said in John 4: "He who believes in me, out of his heart will flow rivers of living water" and again: "He who will drink of the water that I will give him, it shall become in him a fountain of living water, springing up to life everlasting."

2.60 Now there are two roadblocks that commonly prevent us from gathering the fruits of the mass. First, the fact that we are sinners and unworthy of such great things because of our exceeding vileness. Secondly, the fact that, even if we were worthy, these things are so high that our faint-hearted nature dare not aspire to them or ever hope to attain to them. For to have God for our Father, to be His sons and heirs of all His goods—these are the great blessings that come to us through the forgiveness of sins and life everlasting. If you see these things clearly, aren't you more likely to stand in awe before them than to desire to possess them? Against this twofold faintness of ours we must lay hold on the word of Christ and fix our gaze on it much more firmly than on those thoughts of our weakness. For "great are the works of the Lord; all who enjoy them study them," "who is able to do exceeding abundantly above all that we ask or think." If they did not surpass our worthiness, our grasp and all our thoughts, they would not be divine. Thus Christ also encourages us when He says: "Fear not, little flock, for your Father is pleased to give you a kingdom." For it is just this overflowing goodness of the incomprehensible God, lavished upon us through Christ, that moves us to love Him again with our whole heart above all things, to be drawn to Him with all confidence, to despise all things else, and be ready to suffer all things for Him. For this reason, this sacrament is correctly called "a fount of love."

2.61 Let us take an illustration of this from human experience. If a thousand gold coins were bequeathed by a rich lord to a beggar or an unworthy and wicked servant, it is certain that he would boldly claim and take them regardless of his unworthiness and the greatness of the bequest. And if anyone should seek to oppose him by pointing out his unworthiness and the large amount of the legacy, what do you suppose he would say? Certainly, he would say: "What is that to you? What I accept, I accept not on my merits or by any right that I may personally have to it. I know that I am unworthy and receive more than I have deserved, no, I have deserved the very opposite. But I claim it because it is so written in the will, and on the account of another's goodness. If it was not an unworthy thing for him to bequeath so great a sum to an unworthy person, why should I refuse to accept this other man's gracious gift?" With such thoughts we need to fortify the consciences of men against all qualms and scruples, that they may lay hold of the promise of Christ with unwavering faith, and take the greatest care to approach the sacrament, not trusting in their confession, prayer and preparation, but rather despairing of these and with a proud confidence in Christ Who gives the promise. For, as we have said again and again, the word of promise must here reign supreme in a pure and unalloyed faith, and such faith is the one and all-sufficient preparation.

2.62 Hence we see how angry God is with us, in that he has permitted godless teachers to conceal the words of this testament from us, and thereby, as much as in them lay, to extinguish faith. And the inevitable result of this extinguishing of faith is even now plainly to be seen—namely, the most godless superstition of works. For when faith dies and the word of faith is silent, works and the traditions of works immediately crowd into their place. By them we have been carried away out of our own land, as in a Babylonian captivity, and despoiled of all our precious possessions. This has been the fate of the mass. It has been converted by the teaching of godless men into a good work, which they themselves call an *opus operatum* and by which they presumptuously imagine themselves all-powerful with God. Thereupon they proceeded to the very height of madness, and having invented the lie that the mass works *ex opere operato*, they asserted further that it is none the less profitable to others, even if it be harmful to the wicked priest celebrating it. On such a foundation of sand they base their applications, participations, sodalities, anniversaries and numberless other money-making schemes.

2.63 These lures are so powerful, widespread and firmly entrenched that you will scarcely be able to prevail against them unless you keep before you with unremitting care the real meaning of the mass, and bear well in mind what has been said above. We have seen that the mass is nothing else than the divine promise or testament of Christ, sealed with the sacrament of His body and blood. If that is true, you will understand that it cannot possibly be a work, and that there is nothing to do in it, nor can it be dealt within any other way than by faith alone. And faith is not a work, but the mistress and the life of all works. Where in all the world is there a man so foolish as to regard a promise made to him, or a testament given to him, as a good work which by his acceptance of it he renders to the testator? What heir will imagine he is doing his departed father a kindness by accepting the terms of the will and the inheritance bequeathed to him? What godless audacity is it, therefore, when we who are to receive the testament of God come as those who would perform a good work for Him! This ignorance of the testament, this captivity of the sacrament—are they not too sad for tears? When we ought to be grateful for benefits received, we come in our pride to give that which we ought to take, mocking with unheard-of perversity the mercy of the Giver by giving as a work the thing we receive as a gift. So the testator, instead of being the dispenser of His own goods, becomes the recipient of ours. What sacrilege!

2.64 Who has ever been so mad as to regard baptism as a good work, or to believe that by being baptised he was performing a work which he might offer to God for himself and communicate to others? If, therefore, there is no good work that can be communicated to others in this one sacrament or testament, neither will there be any in the mass, since it too is nothing else than a testament and sacrament. Hence it is a manifest and wicked error to offer or apply masses for sins, for satisfactions, for the dead, or for any necessity whatsoever of one's own or of others. You will readily see the obvious truth of this if you but hold firmly that the mass is a divine promise, which can profit no one, be applied to no one, intercede for no one, and be communicated to no one, save him alone who believes with a faith of his own. Who can receive or apply, in behalf of another, the promise of God, which demands the personal faith of every individual? Can I give to another what God has promised, even if he does not believe? Can I believe for another, or cause another to believe? But this is what I must do if I am able to apply and communicate the mass to others. For there are but two things in the mass—the promise of God, and the faith of man which takes that which the promise offers. But if it is true that I can do this, then I can also hear and believe the Gospel for others, I can be baptised for another, I can be absolved from sins for another, I can also partake of the Sacrament of the Altar for another, and—to run the gamut of their sacraments also—I can marry a wife for another, be ordained for another, receive confirmation and extreme unction for another!

2.65 So, then, why didn't Abraham believe for all the Jews? Why was faith in the promise made to Abraham demanded of every individual Jew? Therefore, let this irrefutable truth stand fast. Where there is a divine promise everyone must stand upon his own feet, every one's personal faith is demanded, everyone will give an account for himself and will bear his own burden, as it is said in the last chapter of Mark: "He that believes and is baptised, shall be saved. But he that does not believe, shall be damned." Even so everyone may derive a blessing from the mass for himself alone and only by his own faith, and no one can commune for any other. Just as the priest cannot administer the sacrament to any one in another's place, but administers the same sacrament to each individual by himself. For in consecrating and administering, the priests are our ministers, through whom we do not offer a good work or commune (in the active), but receive the promises and the sign and are communed (in the passive). That has remained to this day the custom among the laity, for they are not said to do good, but to receive it. But the priests have departed into godless ways. Out of the sacrament and testament of God, the source of blessings to be received, they have made a good work which they may communicate and offer to others.

2.66 But you will say: "How is this? Will you not overturn the practice and teaching of all the churches and monasteries, by virtue of which they have flourished these many centuries? For the mass is the foundation of their anniversaries, intercessions, applications, communications, etc.—that is to say, of their fat income." I answer: This is the very thing that has constrained me to write of the captivity of the Church, for in this manner the adorable testament of God has been subjected to the bondage of a godless traffic, through the opinions and traditions of wicked men, who, passing over the Word of God, have put forth the thoughts of their own hearts and misled the whole world. What do I care for the number and influence of those who are in this error? The truth is mightier than they all. If you are able to refute Christ, according to Whom the mass is a testament and sacrament, then I will admit that they are right. Or if you can bring yourself to say that you are doing a good work, when you receive the benefit of the testament, or when you use this sacrament of promise in order to receive it, then I will gladly condemn my teachings. But since you can do neither, why do you hesitate to turn your back on the multitude who go after evil, and to give God the glory and confess His truth? Which is, indeed, that all priests today are perversely mistaken, who regard the mass as a work whereby they may relieve their own necessities and those of others, dead or alive. I am uttering unheard-of and startling things. But if you will consider the meaning of the mass, you will realize that I have spoken the truth. The fault lies with our false sense of security, in which we have become blind to the wrath of God that is raging against us.

2.67 I am ready, however, to admit that the prayers which we pour out before God when we are gathered together to partake of the mass, are good works or benefits, which we impart, apply and communicate to one another, and which we offer for one another. As James teaches us to pray for one another that we may be saved, and as Paul, in 1 Timothy 2, commands that supplications, prayers and intercessions be made for all men, for kings, and for all that are in high station. These are not the mass, but works of the mass—if the prayers of heart and lips may be called works—for they flow from the faith that is kindled or increased in the sacrament. For the mass, being the promise of God, is not fulfilled by praying, but only by believing. But when we believe, we shall also pray and perform every good work. But what priest offers the sacrifice of the mass in this sense and believes that he is offering up nothing but the prayers? They all imagine themselves to be offering up Christ Himself, as all-sufficient sacrifice, to God the Father, and to be performing a good work for all whom they have the intention to benefit. For they put their trust in the work which the mass accomplishes, and they do not ascribe this work to prayer. Thus, gradually, the error has grown, until they have come to ascribe to the sacrament what belongs to the prayers, and to offer to God what should be received as a benefit.

2.68 It is necessary, therefore, to make a sharp distinction between the testament or sacrament itself and the prayers which are there offered. And it is no less necessary to bear in mind that the prayers avail nothing, either for him who offers them or for those for whom they are offered, unless the sacrament be first received in faith, so that it is faith that offers the prayers, for it alone is heard, as James teaches in his first chapter. So great is the difference between prayer and the mass. The prayer may be extended to as many persons as one desires. But the mass is received by none but the person who believes for himself, and only in proportion to his faith. It cannot be given either to God or to men, but God alone gives it, by the ministration of the priest, to such men as receive it by faith alone, without any works or merits. For no one would dare to make the mad assertion that a ragged beggar does a good work when he comes to receive a gift from a rich man. But the mass is, as has been said, the gift and promise of God, offered to all men by the hand of the priest.

2.69 It is certain, therefore, that the mass is not a work which may be communicated to others, but it is the object, as it is called, of faith, for the strengthening and nourishing of the personal faith of each individual. But there is yet another stumbling-block that must be removed, and this is much greater and the most dangerous of all. It is the common belief that the mass is a sacrifice, which is offered to God. Even the words of the canon tend in this direction, when they speak of "these gifts," "these offerings," "this holy sacrifice," and farther on, of "this offering." Prayer also is made, in so many words, "that the sacrifice may be accepted even as the sacrifice of Abel," etc., and hence Christ is termed the "Sacrifice of the altar." In addition to this there are the sayings of the holy Fathers, the great number of examples, and the constant usage and custom of all the world.

2.70 We must resolutely oppose all of this, firmly entrenched as it is, with the words and example of Christ. For unless we hold fast to the truth, that the mass is the promise or testament of Christ, as the words clearly say, we shall lose the whole Gospel and all our comfort. Let us permit nothing to prevail against these words, even though an angel from heaven should teach otherwise. For there is nothing said in them of a work or a sacrifice. Moreover, we have also the example of Christ on our side. For at the Last Supper, when He instituted this sacrament and established this testament, Christ did not offer Himself to God the Father, nor did He perform a good work on behalf of others, but He set this testament before each of them that sat at table with Him and offered him the sign. Now, the more closely our mass resembles that first mass of all, which Christ performed at the Last Supper, the more Christian will it be. But Christ's mass was most simple, without the pageantry of vestments, genuflections, chants and other ceremonies. Indeed, if it were necessary to offer the mass as a sacrifice, then Christ's institution of it was not complete.

2.71 Not that anyone should condemn the Church universal for embellishing and amplifying the mass with many additional rites and ceremonies. But this is what we contend for: no one should be deceived by the glamour of the ceremonies and entangled in the multitude of pompous forms, and thus lose the simplicity of the mass itself, and indeed practice a sort of transubstantiation—losing sight of the simple substance of the mass and clinging to the manifold accidents of outward pomp. For whatever has been added to the word and example of Christ, is an accident of the mass, and ought to be regarded just as we regard the so-called monstrances and corporal cloths in which the host itself is contained. Therefore, as distributing a testament, or accepting a promise, differs diametrically from offering a sacrifice, so it is a contradiction in terms to call the mass a sacrifice. The former is something that we receive, while the latter is something that we offer. The same thing cannot be received and offered at the same time, nor can it be both given and taken by the same person. Just as little as our prayer can be the same as that which our prayer obtains, or the act of praying the same as the act of receiving the answer to our prayer.

2.72 What shall we say, then, about the canon of the mass and the sayings of the Fathers? First of all, if there were nothing at all to be said against them, it would yet be the safer course to reject them all rather than admit that the mass is a work or a sacrifice, lest we deny the word of Christ and overthrow faith together with the mass. Nevertheless, not to reject altogether the canons and the Fathers, we shall say the following: The Apostle instructs us in 1 Corinthians 11 that it was customary for Christ's believers, when they came together to mass, to bring with them meat and drink, which they called "collections" and distributed among all who were in need, after the example of the apostles in Acts 4. From this store was taken the portion of bread and wine that was consecrated for use in the sacrament. And since all this store of meat and drink was sanctified by the word and by prayer, being "lifted up" according to the Hebrew rite of which we read in Moses, the words and the rite of this lifting up, or offering, have come down to us, although the custom of collecting that which was offered, or lifted up, has fallen long since into disuse. Thus, in Isaiah 37,

Hezekiah commanded Isaiah to lift up his prayer in the sight of God for the remnant. The Psalmist sings: "Lift up your hands to the holy places" and "To you will I lift up my hands." And in 1 Timothy 2 we read: "Lifting up pure hands in every place." For this reason the words "sacrifice" and "offering" must be taken to refer, not to the sacrament and testament, but to these collections, from this also the word "collect" has come down to us, as meaning the prayers said in the mass.

2.73 The same thing is indicated when the priest elevates the bread and the chalice immediately after the consecration, whereby he shows that he is not offering anything to God, for he does not say a single word here about a victim or an offering. But this elevation is either a survival of that Hebrew rite of lifting up what was received with thanksgiving and returned to God, or else it is an admonition to us, to provoke us to faith in this testament which the priest has set forth and exhibited in the words of Christ, so that now he shows us also the sign of the testament. Thus the offering of the bread properly accompanies the demonstrative this in the words, "This is my body," by which sign the priest addresses us gathered about him. In like manner the offering of the chalice accompanies the demonstrative this in the words, "This chalice is the new testament, etc." For it is faith that the priest ought to awaken in us by this act of elevation. I wish that, as he elevates the sign, or sacrament, openly before our eyes, he might also sound in our ears the words of the testament with a loud, clear voice, and in the language of the people, whatever it may be, in order that faith may be the more effectively awakened. For why may mass be said in Greek and Latin and Hebrew, and not also in German or in any other language?

2.74 Let the priests, therefore, who in these corrupt and perilous times offer the sacrifice of the mass, take heed, first, that the words of the greater and the lesser canon together with the collects, which smack too strongly of sacrifice, be not referred by them to the sacrament, but to the bread and wine which they consecrate, or to the prayers which they say.

For the bread and wine are offered at the first, in order that they may be blessed and thus sanctified by the Word and by prayer. But after they have been blessed and consecrated, they are no longer offered, but received as a gift from God. And let the priest bear in mind that the Gospel is to be set above all canons and collects devised by men. The Gospel does not sanction the calling of the mass a sacrifice, as has been shown.

2.75 Further, when a priest celebrates a public mass, he should determine to do nothing else through the mass than to commune himself and others. Yet he may at the same time offer prayers for himself and for others, but he must beware lest he presume to offer the mass. But let him determine to commune himself, if he holds a private mass. The private mass does not differ in the least from the ordinary communion which any layman receives at the hand of the priest, and has no greater effect, apart from the special prayers and the fact that the priest consecrates the elements for himself and administers them to himself. So far as the blessing of the mass and sacrament is concerned, we are all of us on an equal footing, whether we be priests or laymen.

2.76 If a priest be requested by others to celebrate so-called "votive" masses, let him beware of accepting a reward for the mass, or of presuming to offer a votive sacrifice. He should be careful to refer all to the prayers which he offers for the dead or the living, saying within himself, "I will go and partake of the sacrament for myself alone, and while partaking I will say a prayer for this one and that." Thus he will take his reward—to buy him food and clothing—not for the mass, but for the prayers. And let him not be disturbed because all the world holds and practices the contrary. You have the most sure Gospel, and relying on this you may well despise the opinions of men. But if you despise me and insist upon offering the mass and not the prayers alone, know that I have faithfully warned you and will be without blame on the day of judgment. You will have to bear your sin alone. I have said what I was bound to say as brother to brother for his soul's salvation. Yours will be the gain if you observe it, yours the loss if you neglect it. And if some should even condemn what I have said, I reply in the words of Paul: "But evil men and seducers shall grow worse and worse: erring and driving into error."

2.77 From the above every one will readily understand what there is in that often quoted saying of Gregory's: "A mass celebrated by a wicked priest is not to be considered of less effect than one celebrated by any godly priest. St. Peter's mass would not have been better than Judas the traitor's, if they had offered the sacrifice of the mass." This saying has served many as a cloak to cover their godless doings, and because of it they have invented the distinction between *opus operati* and *opus operantis*, so as to be free to lead wicked lives themselves and yet to benefit other men. Gregory speaks truth, but they misunderstand and pervert his words. For it is true beyond a question, that the testament or sacrament is given and received through the ministration of wicked priests no less completely than through the ministration of the most saintly. For who has any doubt that the Gospel is preached by the ungodly? Now the mass is part of the Gospel, no, its sum and substance. For what is the whole Gospel but the good tidings of the forgiveness of sins? But whatever can be said of the forgiveness of sins and the mercy of God, is all briefly comprehended in the word of this testament.

So popular sermons ought to be nothing else than expositions of the mass, that is, a setting forth of the divine promise of this testament. Doing this teaches faith and truly edifies the Church. But in our day the expounders of the mass play with the allegories of human rites and make it a joke to people.

2.78 Therefore, just as a wicked priest may baptise, that is, apply the word of promise and the sign of the water to a candidate for baptism, so he may also set forth the promise of this sacrament and administer it to those who partake, and even himself partake, like Judas the traitor, at the Lord's Supper. It still remains always the same sacrament and testament, which works in the believer its own work, in the unbeliever a "strange work." But when it comes to offering a sacrifice the case is quite different. For not the mass but the prayers are offered to God, and therefore it is as plain as day that the offerings of a wicked priest avail nothing, but, as Gregory says again, when an unworthy intercessor is chosen, the heart of the judge is moved to greater displeasure. We must, therefore, not confound these two—the mass and the prayers, the sacrament and the work, the testament and the sacrifice. For the one comes from God to us, through the ministration of the priest, and demands our faith, the other proceeds from our faith to God, through the priest, and demands His answer. The former descends, the latter ascends. Therefore the former does not necessarily require a worthy and godly minister, but the latter does indeed require such a priest, because "God does not hear sinners." He knows how to send down blessings through evildoers, but He does not accept the work of any evildoer, as He showed in the case of Cain, and as it is said in Proverbs 15, "The victims of the wicked are abominable to the Lord" and in Romans 14, "All that is not of faith is sin."

2.79 But in order to make an end of this first part, we must take up one remaining point against which an opponent might arise. From all that has been said we conclude that the mass was provided only for such as have a sad, afflicted, disturbed, perplexed and erring conscience, and that they alone commune worthily. For, since the word of divine promise in this sacrament sets forth the remission of sins, that man may fearlessly draw near, whoever he be, whose sins distress him, either with remorse for past or with temptation to future wrongdoing. For this testament of Christ is the one remedy against sins, past, present and future, if you but cling to it with unwavering faith and believe that what the words of the testament declare is freely granted to you. But if you do not believe this, you will never, nowhere, and by no works or efforts of your own, find peace of conscience. For faith alone sets the conscience at peace, and unbelief alone keeps the conscience troubled.

INTRODUCTION TO
Martin Luther
THE FREEDOM OF THE CHRISTIAN

With Luther's luminous and at times almost lyrical summary of the Christian life, *The Freedom of the Christian*, we finally encounter the Protestant manifesto that was missing in his earlier works: a statement no longer of what Luther was against, but of what he was *for*, the joyful rediscovery of the gospel that he wanted to share with Western Christendom. Having leveled a devastating critique of the captivity of believers perpetuated by Rome's sacramental system in *The Babylonian Captivity*, Luther here proclaimed the freedom that believers have in Christ and which no church authority can take away from them. In fact, the whole work breathes a very different tone than most of his earlier writings, especially his conciliatory letter to Pope Leo X that served as the preface to the work (not included here). There he insisted he had never meant to attack Leo personally, considering him to be a well-intentioned pope surrounded by wicked advisors, and offering his own advice on what Leo should do about them. Needless to say, Leo would not be impressed by the letter, and his bull of excommunication was in any case already on its way, destroying the aspirations of would-be peacemaker Karl von Miltitz, who had convinced Luther to write the letter.

Luther's theology would continue to develop after 1520, but we find here in *The Freedom of the Christian* in succinct and admirably clear form the central themes that were to dominate his mature theology and that of all the Protestant reformers who followed him. These include the famous dualities of *simul justus et peccator* (that a believer is at the same time righteous and a sinner), of Law and Gospel (that Scripture must be read as consisting of commandments and promises), of faith and works, of the imputation of sin and righteousness ("the believing soul can boast of and glory in whatever Christ has as though it were its own, and whatever the soul has Christ claims as his own"), and of the two kingdoms—the inward man, alive by faith, and the outward man, animated by love. Each set of dualities was to be nuanced in various ways by later reformers and sometimes by Luther himself, but Luther's formulations of them here may still be taken as broadly representative for the Protestant movement.

Luther's penchant for paradox is on full display in the book, above all in his summary statement: "A Christian is a perfectly free lord of all, subject to none. A Christian is a perfectly dutiful servant of all, subject to all." Luther goes on to explain that in his inward character, before God, the Christian is entirely free because he is justified by faith; outwardly, before men, he is enslaved by love to serve all. Only by virtue of such a radical distinction between the inward and the outward, Luther believes, can the freedom of a Christian conscience before God be guaranteed, for if the Christian is led to believe that his justification before God depends on any outward works, rather than the free gift of faith, he is in bondage. By this means Luther attacks the whole array of Catholic ceremonies, saying,

> It does not help the soul if the body is adorned with the sacred robes of priests or dwells in sacred places or is occupied with sacred duties or prays, fasts, abstains from certain kinds of food, or does any work that can be done by the body and in the body. The righteousness and the freedom of the soul require something far different.

That something, he says, is the "the most holy Word of God, the gospel of Christ."

It is crucial to understand that the purpose of this radical distinction is not to attack outward works *per se*, but merely to establish the priority of the inward, which is faith: the outward must never determine the inward, grace must never be conditioned upon works, but the inward life of grace will determine the outward, issuing forth in good works. The freedom of justification results in an overflow of love that willingly obeys the laws of Scripture and the needs of the neighbor without allowing such works to reign over his conscience: "A man does not live for himself alone in this mortal body to work for it alone, but he lives also for all men on earth; rather he lives only for others and not for himself."

The freedom of a Christian is thus not, as it was quickly twisted by some of Luther's more radical followers, a freedom *for* oneself, but a freedom *from* oneself, a liberation from the preoccupation with one's own salvation and merit, from fear that one is not toeing the line and meeting the standards; instead, the believer can actually focus on serving his neighbor.

But although Luther offers a compelling account of the relation of faith and works in this treatise, it is certainly not without tensions or ambiguities. Luther clearly states toward the end of the treatise that just because the Christian is freed in conscience from considering Catholic ceremonies as necessary to salvation, he need not reject all such ceremonies out of hand. But the guidance he offers for how to handle such ceremonies was not easy to follow. He argued that toward "wolves" who urge ceremonies upon us as necessary, we "must resist, do the very opposite, and offend them boldly." He himself was later to provide a particularly shocking example of such bold offense by his 1525 marriage to Katerina von Bora, a former monk marrying a former nun. But in the same passage, Luther goes on to advise just the opposite course of action before the weak in faith who needed to be initiated slowly into Gospel liberty—continuing to practice fasts and ceremonies that they were accustomed to. The challenge of discerning when one was dealing with wolves or sheep, Pharisees or weaker brethren, was to result in sharply differing approaches to the practice of traditional Catholic ceremonies that continue to create conflicts among Protestants today.

THE FREEDOM OF THE CHRISTIAN

Martin Luther

TRANSLATED BY C. A. BUCHHEIM

CONCERNING CHRISTIAN LIBERTY

CHRISTIAN faith has appeared to many an easy thing; nay, not a few even reckon it among the social virtues, as it were; and this they do, because they have not made proof of it experimentally, and have never tasted of what efficacy it is. For it is not possible for any man to write well about it, or to understand well what is rightly written, who has not at some time tasted of its spirit, under the pressure of tribulation. While he who has tasted of it, even to a very small extent, can never write, speak, think, or hear about it sufficiently. For it is a living fountain, springing up unto eternal life, as Christ calls it in the 4th chapter of St. John.

Now, though I cannot boast of my abundance, and though I know how poorly I am furnished, yet I hope that, after having been vexed by various temptations, I have attained some little drop of faith, and that I can speak of this matter, if not with more elegance, certainly with more solidity than those literal and too subtle disputants who have hitherto discoursed upon it, without understanding their own words. That I may open, then, an easier way for the ignorant—for these alone I am trying to serve—I first lay down these two propositions, concerning spiritual liberty and servitude.

A Christian man is the most free lord of all, and subject to none; a Christian man is the most dutiful servant of all, and subject to every one.

Although these statements appear contradictory, yet, when they are found to agree together, they will be highly serviceable to my purpose. They are both the statements of Paul himself, who says: "Though I be free from all men, yet have I made myself servant unto all" (1 Cor. ix. 19), and: "Owe no man anything, but to love one another." (Rom. xiii. 8.) Now love is by its own nature dutiful and obedient to the beloved object. Thus even Christ, though Lord of all things, was yet made of a woman; made under the law; at once free and a servant; at once in the form of God and in the form of a servant.

Let us examine the subject on a deeper and less simple principle. Man is composed of a twofold nature, a spiritual and a bodily. As regards the spiritual nature, which they name the soul, he is called the spiritual, inward, new man; as regards the bodily nature, which they name the flesh, he is called the fleshly, outward, old man. The Apostle speaks of this: "Though our outward man perish, yet the inward man is relieved day by day." (2 Cor. iv. 16.) The result of this diversity is, that in the Scriptures opposing statements are made concerning the same man; the fact being that in the same man these two men are opposed to one another; the flesh lusting against the spirit, and the spirit against the flesh. (Gal. v. 17.)

We first approach the subject of the inward man, that we may see by what means a man becomes justified, free, and a true Christian; that is, a spiritual, new, and inward man. It is certain that absolutely none among outward things, under whatever name they may be reckoned, has any weight in producing a state of justification and Christian liberty, nor, on the other hand an unjustified state and one of slavery. This can be shown by an easy course of argument.

What can it profit the soul, that the body should be in good condition, free, and full of life; that it should eat, drink, and act according to its pleasure; when even the most impious slaves of every kind of vice are prosperous in these matters? Again, what harm can ill-health, bondage, hunger, thirst, or any other outward evil, do to the soul, when even the most pious of men, and the freest in the purity of their conscience are harassed by these things? Neither of these states of things has to do with the liberty or the slavery of the soul.

And so it will profit nothing that the body should be adorned with sacred vestments, or dwell in holy places, or be occupied in sacred offices, or pray, fast, and abstain from certain meats, or do whatever works can be done through the body and in the body. Something widely different will be necessary for the justification and liberty of the soul, since the things I have spoken of can be done by any impious person, and only hypocrites are produced by devotion to these things. On the other hand, it will not at all injure the soul that the body should be clothed in profane raiment, should dwell in profane places, should eat and drink in the ordinary fashion, should not pray aloud, and should leave undone all the things abovementioned, which may be done by hypocrites.

And, to cast everything aside, even speculations, meditations and whatever things can be performed by the exertions of the soul itself, are of no profit. One thing, and one alone, is necessary for life, justification, and Christian liberty; and that is the most holy word of God, the Gospel of Christ, as He says: "I am the resurrection and the life; he that believeth in me shall not die eternally" (John xi. 25); and also (John viii. 36) "If the Son shall make you free, ye shall be free indeed"; and (Matt. iv. 4), "Man shall not live by bread alone, but by every word that proceedeth out of the mouth of God."

Let us therefore hold it for certain and firmly established, that the soul can do without everything, except the word of God, without which none at all of its wants are provided for. But, having the word, it is rich and want for nothing; since that is the word of life, of truth, of light, of peace, of justification, of salvation, of joy, of liberty, of wisdom, of virtue, of grace, of glory, and of every good thing. It is on this account that the prophet in a whole psalm (Ps. cxix.), and in many other places, sighs for and calls upon the word of God with so many groanings and words.

Again, there is no more cruel stroke of the wrath of God than when He sends a famine of hearing His words (Amos viii. 11); just as there is no greater favour from Him than the sending forth of His word, as it is said: "He sent his word and healed them, and delivered them from their destructions." (Ps. cvii. 20.) Christ was sent for no other office than that of the word, and the order of apostles, that of bishops, and that of the whole body of the clergy, have been called and instituted for no object but the ministry of the word.

But you will ask, "What is this word, and by what means is it to be used, since there are so many words of God?" I answer, the Apostle Paul (Rom. i.) explains what it is, namely, the Gospel of God, concerning His Son, incarnate, suffering, risen, and glorified through the Spirit, the sanctifier. To preach Christ is to feed the soul, to justify it, to set it free, and to save it, if it believes the preaching. For faith alone, and the efficacious use of the word of God, bring salvation. "If thou shalt confess with thy mouth the Lord Jesus, and shalt believe in thine heart that God hath raised him from the dead, thou shalt be saved." (Rom. x. 9.) And again: "Christ is the end of the law for righteousness to every one that believeth" (Rom. x. 4); and "The just shall live by faith." (Rom. i. 17.) For the word of God cannot be received and honoured by any works, but by faith alone. Hence it is clear that, as the soul needs the word alone for life and justification, so it is justified by faith alone and not by any works. For if it could be justified by any other means, it would have no need of the word, nor consequently of faith.

But this faith cannot consist at all with works; that is, if you imagine that you can be justified by those works, whatever they are, along with it. For this would be to halt between two opinions, to worship Baal, and to kiss the hand to him, which is a very great iniquity, as Job says. Therefore, when you begin to believe, you learn at the same time that all that is in you is utterly guilty, sinful, and damnable; according to that saying: "All have sinned, and come short of the glory of God." (Rom. iii. 23.) And also: "There is none righteous, no, not one; they are all gone out of the way; they are together become unprofitable; there is none that doth good, no, not one." (Rom. iii. 10–12.) When you have learnt this, you will know that Christ is necessary for you, since He has suffered and risen again for you, that, believing on Him, you might by this faith become another man, all your sins being remitted, and you being justified by the merits of another, namely, of Christ alone.

Since then this faith can reign only in the inward man, as it is said: "With the heart man believeth unto righteousness" (Rom. x. 10); and since it alone justifies, it is evident that by no outward work or labour can the inward man be at all justified, made free, and saved; and that no works whatever have any relation to him. And so, on the other hand, it is solely by impiety and incredulity of heart that he becomes guilty, and a slave of sin, deserving condemnation; not by any outward sin or work. Therefore the first care of every Christian ought to be, to lay aside all reliance on works, and strengthen his faith alone more and more, and by it grow in the knowledge, not of works, but of Christ Jesus, who has suffered and risen again for him; as Peter teaches, when he makes no other work to be a Christian one. Thus Christ, when the Jews asked Him what they should do that they might work the works of God, rejected the multitude of works, with which He saw that they were puffed up, and commanded them one thing only, saying: "This is the work of God, that ye believe on him whom He hath sent, for him hath God the Father sealed." (John vi. 27, 29.)

Hence a right faith in Christ is an incomparable treasure, carrying with it universal salvation, and preserving from all evil, as it is said: "He that believeth and is baptized shall be saved; but he that believeth not shall be damned." (Mark xvi. 16.) Isaiah, looking to this treasure, predicted: "The consumption decreed shall overflow with righteousness. For the Lord God of hosts shall make a consumption, even determined, in the midst of the land." (Is. x. 22, 23.) As if he said, "Faith, which is the brief and complete fulfilling of the law, will fill those who believe with such righteousness, that they will need nothing else for justification." Thus too Paul says: "For with the heart man believeth unto righteousness." (Rom. x. 10.)

But you ask how it can be the fact that faith alone justifies, and affords without works so great a treasure of good things, when so many works, ceremonies, and laws are prescribed to us in the Scriptures. I answer: before all things bear in mind what I have said, that faith alone without works justifies, sets free, and saves, as I shall show more clearly below.

Meanwhile it is to be noted, that the whole Scripture of God is divided into two parts, precepts and promises. The precepts certainly teach us what is good, but what they teach is not forthwith done. For they show us what we ought to do, but do not give us the power to do it. They were ordained, however, for the purpose of showing man to himself; that through them he may learn his own impotence for good, and may despair of his own strength. For this reason they are called the Old Testament, and are so.

For example: "thou shalt not covet," is a precept by which we are all convicted of sin; since no man can help coveting, whatever efforts to the contrary he may make. In order therefore that he may fulfill the precept, and not covet, he is constrained to despair of himself and to seek elsewhere and through another the help which he cannot find in himself; as it is said: "O Israel, thou hast destroyed thyself; but in me is thine help." (Hosea xiii. 9.) Now what is done by this one precept, is done by all; for all are equally impossible of fulfilment by us.

Now when a man has through the precepts been taught his own impotence, and become anxious by what means he may satisfy the law—for the law must be satisfied, so that no jot or tittle of it may pass away; otherwise he must be hopelessly condemned—then, being truly humbled and brought to nothing in his own eyes, he finds in himself no resource for justification and salvation.

Then comes in that other part of Scripture, the promises of God, which declare the glory of God, and say: "If you wish to fulfill the law, and, as the law requires, not to covet, lo! believe in Christ, in whom are promised to you grace, justification, peace, and liberty." All these things you shall have, if you believe, and shall be without them, if you do not believe. For what is impossible for you by all the works of the law, which are many and yet useless, you shall fulfill in an easy and summary way through faith; because God the Father has made everything to depend on faith, so that whosoever has it, has all things, and he who has it not, has nothing. "For God hath concluded them all in unbelief, that He might have mercy upon all." (Rom. xi. 32.) Thus the promises of God give that which the precepts exact, and, fulfill what the law commands; so that all is of God alone, both the precepts and their fulfilment. He alone commands. He alone also fulfils. Hence the promises of God belong to the New Testament; nay, are the New Testament.

Now since these promises of God are words of holiness, truth, righteousness, liberty, and peace, and are full of universal goodness; the soul, which cleaves to them with a firm faith, is so united to them, nay, thoroughly absorbed by them, that it not only partakes in, but is penetrated and saturated by, all their virtue. For if the touch of Christ was healing, how much more does that most tender spiritual touch, nay, absorption of the word, communicate to the soul all that belongs to the word. In this way, therefore, the soul, through faith alone, without works, is from the word of God justified, sanctified, endued with truth, peace, and liberty, and filled full with every good thing, and is truly made the child of God; as it is said: "To them gave he power to become the sons of God, even to them that believe on his name." (John i. 12.)

From all this it is easy to understand why faith has such great power, and why no good works, nor even all good works put together, can compare with it; since no work can cleave to the word of God, or be in the soul. Faith alone and the word reign in it; and such as is the word, such is the soul made by it; just as iron exposed to fire glows like fire, on account of its union with the fire. It is clear then that to a Christian man his faith suffices for everything, and that he has no need of works for justification. But if he has no need of works, neither has he need of the law; and, if he has no need of the law, he is certainly free from the law, and the saying is true: "The law is not made for a righteous man." (1 Tim. i. 9.) This is that Christian liberty, our faith, the effect of which is, not that we should be careless or lead a bad life, but that no one should need the law or works for justification and salvation.

Let us consider this as the first virtue of faith; and let us look also to the second. This also is an office of faith, that it honours with the utmost veneration and the highest reputation him in whom it believes, inasmuch as it holds him to be truthful and worthy of belief. For there is no honour like that reputation of truth and righteousness, with which we honour him, in whom we believe. What higher credit can we attribute to any one than truth and righteousness, and absolute goodness? On the other hand, it is the greatest insult to brand any one with the reputation of falsehood and unrighteousness, or to suspect him of these, as we do when we disbelieve him.

Thus the soul, in firmly believing the promises of God, holds Him to be true and righteous; and it can attribute to God no higher glory than the credit of being so. The highest worship of God is to ascribe to Him truth, righteousness, and whatever qualities we must ascribe to one in whom we believe. In doing this the soul shows itself prepared to do His whole will; in doing this it hallows His, name, and gives itself up to be dealt with as it may please God. For it cleaves to His promises, and never doubts that He is true, just, and wise, and will do, dispose, and provide for all things in the best way. Is not such a soul, in this its faith, most obedient to God in all things? What commandment does there remain which has not been amply fulfilled by such an obedience? what fulfilment can be more full than universal obedience? Now this is not accomplished by works, but by faith alone.

On the other hand, what greater rebellion, impiety, or insult to God can there be, than not to believe His promises? What else is this, than either to make God a liar, or to doubt His truth—that is, to attribute truth to ourselves, but to God falsehood and levity? In doing this, is not a man denying God and setting himself up as an idol in his own heart? What then can works, done in such a state of impiety, profit us, were they even angelic or apostolic works? Rightly hath God shut up all—not in wrath nor in lust—but in unbelief; in order that those who pretend that they are fulfilling the law by works of purity and benevolence (which are social and human virtues), may not presume that they will therefore be saved;

but, being included in the sin of unbelief, may either seek mercy, or be justly condemned.

But when God sees that truth is ascribed to Him, and that in the faith of our hearts He is honoured with all the honour of which He is worthy; then in return He honours us on account of that faith; attributing to us truth and righteousness. For faith produces truth and righteousness, in rendering to God what is His; and therefore in return God gives glory to our righteousness. It is a true and righteous thing, that God is true and righteous; and to confess this, and ascribe these attributes to Him, is to be ourselves true and righteous. Thus He says: "Them that honour me I will honour, and they that despise me shall be lightly esteemed." (1 Sam. ii. 30.) And so Paul, says that Abraham's faith was imputed to him for righteousness, because by it he gave glory to God; and that to us also, for the same reason, it shall be reputed for righteousness, if we believe. (Rom. iv.)

The third incomparable grace of faith is this, that it unites the soul to Christ, as the wife to the husband; by which mystery, as the Apostle teaches, Christ and the soul are made one flesh. Now if they are one flesh, and if a true marriage—nay, by far the most perfect of all marriages—is accomplished between them (for human marriages are but feeble types of this one great marriage), then it follows that all they have becomes theirs in common, as well good things as evil things; so that whatsoever Christ possesses, that the believing soul may take to itself and boast of as its own, and whatever belongs to the soul, that Christ claims as his.

If we compare these possessions, we shall see how inestimable is the gain. Christ is full of grace, life, and salvation; the soul is full of sin, death, and condemnation. Let faith step in, and then sin, death, and hell will belong to Christ, and grace, life, and salvation to the soul. For, if he is a husband, he must needs take to himself that which is his wife's, and, at the same time, impart to his wife that which is his. For, in giving her his own body and himself, how can he but give her all that is his? And, in taking to himself the body of his wife, how can he but take to himself all that is hers?

In this is displayed the delightful sight, not only of communion, but of a prosperous warfare, of victory, salvation, and redemption.

For since Christ is God and man, and is such a person as neither has sinned, nor dies, nor is condemned,—nay, cannot sin, die, or be condemned; and since his righteousness, life, and salvation are invincible, eternal, and almighty; when, I say, such a person, by the wedding-ring of faith, takes a share in the sins, death, and hell of his wife, nay, makes them his own, and deals with them no otherwise than as if they were his, and as if he himself had sinned; and when he suffers, dies, and descends to hell, that he may overcome all things, since sin, death, and hell cannot swallow him up, they must needs be swallowed up by him in stupendous conflict. For his righteousness rises above the sins of all men; his life is more powerful than all death; his salvation is more unconquerable than all hell.

Thus the believing soul, by the pledge of its faith in Christ, becomes free from all sin, fearless of death, safe from hell, and endowed with the eternal righteousness, life, and salvation of its husband Christ. Thus he presents to himself a glorious bride, without spot or wrinkle, cleansing her with the washing of water by the word; that is, by faith in the word of life, righteousness, and salvation. Thus he betrothes her unto himself "in faithfulness, in righteousness, and in judgment, and in lovingkindness, and in mercies." (Hosea ii. 19, 20.)

Who then can value highly enough these royal nuptials? Who can comprehend the riches of the glory of this grace?

Christ, that rich and pious husband, takes as a wife a needy and impious harlot, redeeming her from all her evils, and supplying her with all his good things. It is impossible now that her sins should destroy her, since they have been laid upon Christ and swallowed up in Him, and since she has in her husband Christ a righteousness which she may claim as her own, and which she can set up with confidence against all her sins, against death and hell, saying: "If I have sinned, my Christ, in whom I believe, has not sinned; all mine is His, and all His is mine"; as it is written, "My beloved is mine, and I am his. (Cant. ii. 16.) This is what Paul says: "Thanks be to God, which giveth us the victory through our Lord Jesus Christ"; victory over sin and death, as he says: "The sting of death is sin, and the strength of sin is the law." (I Cor. xv. 56, 57.)

From all this you will again understand, why so much importance is attributed to faith, so that it alone can fulfill the law, and justify without any works. For you see that the first commandment, which says, "Thou shalt worship one God only," is fulfilled by faith alone. If you were nothing but good works from the soles of your feet to the crown of your head, you would not be worshipping God, nor fulfilling the first commandment. since it is impossible to worship God, without ascribing to Him the glory of truth and of universal goodness, as it ought in truth to be ascribed. Now this is not done by works, but only by faith of heart. It is not by working, but by believing, that we glorify God, and confess Him to be true. On this ground faith is the sole righteousness of a Christian man, and the fulfilling of all the commandments. For to him who fulfils the first, the task of fulfilling all the rest is easy.

Works, since the are irrational things, cannot glorify God; although they may be done to the glory of God, if faith be present. But at present we are enquiring, not into the quality of the works done, but into him who does them, who glorifies God, and brings forth good works. This is faith of heart, the head and the substance of all our righteousness. Hence that is a blind and perilous doctrine which teaches that the commandments are fulfilled by works. The commandments must have been fulfilled, previous to any good works, and good works follow their fulfilment, as we shall see.

But, that we may have a wider view of that grace which our inner man has in Christ, we must know that in the Old Testament God sanctified to Himself every first-born male. The birthright was of great value, giving a superiority over the rest by the double honour of priesthood and kingship. For the first-born brother was priest and lord of all the rest.

Under this figure was foreshown Christ, the true and only first-born of God the Father and of the Virgin Mary, and a true king and priest, not in a fleshly and earthly sense. For His kingdom is not of this world; it is in heavenly and spiritual things that He reigns and acts as priest; and these are righteousness, truth, wisdom, peace, salvation, etc. Not but that all things, even those of earth and hell, are subject to Him for otherwise how could He defend and save us from them?—but it is not in these, nor by these, that His kingdom stands.

So too His priesthood does not consist in the outward display of vestments and gestures, as did the human priesthood of Aaron and our ecclesiastical priesthood at this day, but in spiritual things, wherein, in His invisible office, He intercedes for us with God in heaven, and there offers Himself, and performs all the duties of a priest; as Paul describes Him to the Hebrews under the figure of Melchizedek. Nor does He only pray and intercede for us; He also teaches us inwardly in the spirit with the living teachings of His Spirit. Now those are the two special offices of a priest, as is figured to us in the case of fleshly priests, by visible prayers and sermons.

As Christ by His birthright has obtained these two dignities, so He imparts and communicates them to every believer in Him, under that law of matrimony of which we have spoken above, by which all that is the husband's is also the wife's. Hence all we who believe on Christ are kings and priests in Christ, as it is said: "Ye are a chosen generation, a royal priesthood, an holy nation, a peculiar people; that ye should shew forth the praises of him who hath called you out of darkness into his marvellous light." (1 Pet. ii. 9.)

These two things stand thus. First, as regards kingship, every Christian is by faith so exalted above all things, that, in spiritual power, he is completely lord of all things; so that nothing whatever can do him any hurt; yea, all things are subject to him, and are compelled to be subservient to his salvation. Thus Paul says: "All things work together for good to them who are the called" (Rom. viii. 28); and also; "Whether life, or death, or things present, or things to come: all are yours; and ye are Christ's." (I Cor. iii. 22, 23.)

Not that in the sense of corporeal power any one among Christians has been appointed to possess and rule all things, according to the mad and senseless idea of certain ecclesiastics. That is the office of kings, princes, and men upon earth. In the experience of life we see that we subjected to all things, and suffer many things, even death. Yea, the more of a Christian any man is, to so many the more evils, sufferings, and deaths is he subject; as we see in the first place in Christ the first-born, and in all His holy brethren.

This is a spiritual power, which rules in the midst of enemies, and is powerful in the midst of distress. And this is nothing else than that strength is made perfect in my weakness, and that I can turn all things to the profit of my salvation; so that even the cross and death are compelled to serve me and to work together for my salvation. This is a lofty and eminent dignity, a true and almighty dominion, a spiritual empire, in which there is nothing so good, nothing so bad, as not to work together for my good, if only I believe. And yet there is nothing of which I have need—for faith alone suffices for my salvation—unless that, in it, faith may exercise the power and empire of its liberty. This is the inestimable power and liberty of Christians.

Nor are we only kings and the freest of all men, but also priests for ever, a dignity far higher than kinship, because by that priesthood we are worthy to appear before God, to pray for others, and to teach one another mutually the things which are of God. For these are the duties of priests, and they cannot possibly be permitted to any unbeliever. Christ has obtained for us this favour, if we believe in Him, that, just as we are His brethren, and co-heirs and fellow kings with Him, so we should be also fellow priests with Him, and venture with confidence, through the spirit of faith, to come into the presence of God, and cry "Abba, Father! "and to pray for one another, and to do all things which we see done and figured in the visible and corporeal office of priesthood. But to an unbelieving person nothing renders service or works for good. He himself is in servitude to all things, and all things turn out for evil to him, because he uses all things in an impious way for his own advantage. and not for the glory of God. And thus he is not a priest, but a profane person, whose prayers are turned into sin; nor does he ever appear in the presence of God, because God does not hear sinners.

Who then can comprehend the loftiness of that Christian dignity which, by its royal power, rules over all things, even over death, life, and sin, and, by its priestly glory, is all powerful with God;

since God does what He Himself seeks and wishes; as it is written: "He will fulfill the desire of them that fear Him: He also will hear their cry, and will save them"? (Ps. cxlv. 19.) This glory certainly cannot be attained by any works, but by faith only.

From these considerations any one may clearly see how a Christian man is free from all things; so that he needs no works in order to be justified and saved, but receives these gifts in abundance from faith alone. Nay, were he so foolish as to pretend to be justified, set free, saved, and made a Christian, by means of any good work, he would immediately lose faith with all its benefits. Such folly is prettily represented in the fable, where a dog, running along in the water, and carrying in his mouth a real piece of meat, is deceived by the reflection of the meat in the water, and, in trying with open mouth to seize it, loses the meat and its image at the same time.

Here you will ask: "If all who are in the Church are priests by what character are those, whom we now call priests, to be distinguished from the laity?" I reply: By the use of these words, "priest," "clergy," "spiritual person," "ecclesiastic," an injustice has been done, since they have been transferred from the remaining body of Christians to those few, who are now, by a hurtful custom, called ecclesiastics. For Holy Scripture makes no distinction between them, except that those, who are now boastfully called popes, bishops, and lords, it calls ministers, servants, and stewards, who are to serve the rest in the ministry of the Word, for teaching the faith of Christ and the liberty of believers. For though it is true that we are all equally priests, yet we cannot, nor, if we could, ought we all to minister and teach publicly. Thus Paul says "Let a man so account of us as of the ministers of Christ, and stewards of the mysteries of God." (1 Cor. iv. 1.)

This bad system has now issued in such a pompous display of power, and such a terrible tyranny, that no earthly government can be compared to it, as if the laity were something else than Christians. Through this perversion of things it has happened that the knowledge of Christian grace, of faith, of liberty, and altogether of Christ, has utterly perished, and has been succeeded by an intolerable bondage to human works and laws; and, according to the Lamentations of Jeremiah, we have become the slaves of the vilest men on earth, who abuse our misery to all the disgraceful and ignominious purposes of their own will.

Returning to the subject which we had begun, I think it is made clear by these considerations that it is not sufficient, nor a Christian course, to preach the works, life, and words of Christ in a historic manner, as facts which it suffices to know as an example how to frame our life; as do those who are now held the best preachers: and much less so, to keep silence altogether on these and to teach in their stead the laws of men and the decrees of the Fathers. There are now not a few persons who preach and read about Christ with the object of moving the human affections to sympathise with Christ, to indignation against the Jews, and other childish and womanish absurdities of that kind.

Now preaching ought to have the object of promoting faith in Him, so that He may not only be Christ, but a Christ for you and for me, and that what is said of Him, and what He is called, may work in us. And this faith is produced and is maintained by preaching why Christ came, what He has brought us and given to us, and to what profit and advantage He is to be received. This is done, when the Christian liberty which we have from Christ Himself is rightly taught, and we are shown in what manner all we Christians are kings and priests, and how we are lords of all things, and may be confident that whatever we do in the presence of God is pleasing and acceptable to Him. Whose heart would not rejoice in its inmost core at hearing these things? Whose heart, on receiving so great a consolation, would not become sweet with the love of Christ, a love to which it can never attain by any laws or works? Who can injure such a heart, or make it afraid? If the consciousness of sin, or the horror of death, rush in upon it, it is prepared to hope in the Lord, and is fearless of such evils, and undisturbed, until it shall look down upon its enemies. For it believes that the righteousness of Christ is its own, and that its sin is no longer its own, but that of Christ, for, on account of its faith in Christ, all its sin must needs be swallowed up from before the face of the righteousness of Christ, as I have said above. It learns too, with the Apostle, to scoff at death and sin, and to say: "O death, where is thy sting? O grave, where is thy victory? The sting of death is sin, and the strength of sin is the law. But thanks be to God, which giveth us the victory through our Lord Jesus Christ." (1 Cor. xv. 55–57.) For death is swallowed up in victory; not only the victory of Christ, but ours also; since by faith it becomes ours, and in it we too conquer.

Let it suffice to say this concerning the inner man and its liberty, and concerning that righteousness of faith, which needs neither laws nor good works; nay, they are even hurtful to it, if any one pretends to be justified by them.

And now let us turn to the other part, to the outward man. Here we shall give an answer to all those who, taking offence at the word of faith and at what I have asserted, say: "If faith does everything, and by itself suffices for justification, why then are good works commanded? Are we then to take our ease and do no works, content with faith?" Not so, impious man, I reply; not so. That would indeed really be the case, if we were thoroughly and completely inner and spiritual persons; but that will not happen until the last day, when the dead shall be raised. As long as we live in the flesh, we are but beginning and making advances in that which shall be completed in a future life. On this account the Apostle calls that which we have in this life, the first-fruits of the Spirit. (Rom. viii. 23.) In future we shall have the tenths, and the fulness of the Spirit. To this part belongs the fact I have stated before, that the Christian is the servant of all and subject to all. For in that part in which he is free, he does no works, but in that in which he is a servant, he does all works. Let us see on what principle this is so.

Although, as I have said, inwardly, and according to the spirit, a man is amply enough justified by faith, having all that lie requires to have, except that this very faith and abundance ought to increase from day to day, even till the future life; still he remains in this mortal life upon earth, in which it is necessary that he should rule his own body, and have intercourse with men. Here then works begin; here he must not take his ease; here he must give heed to exercise his body by fastings, watchings, labour, and other moderate discipline, so that it may be subdued to the spirit, and obey and conform itself to the inner man and faith, and not rebel against them nor hinder them, as is its nature to do if it is not kept under. For the inner man, being conformed to God, and created after the image of God through faith, rejoices and delights itself in Christ, in whom such blessings have been conferred on it; and hence has only this task before it, to serve God with joy and for nought in free love.

In doing this he offends that contrary will in his own flesh, which is striving to serve the world, and to seek its own gratification. This the spirit of faith cannot and will not bear; but applies itself with cheerfulness and zeal to keep it down and restrain it; as Paul says: "I delight in the law of God after the inward man; but I see another law in my members, warring against the law of my mind, and bringing me into captivity to the law of sin." (Rom. vii. 22, 23.) And again: "I keep under my body, and bring it into subjection, lost that by any means, when I have preached to others, I myself should be a castaway." (1 Cor. ix. 27.) And: "They that are Christ's have crucified the flesh with the affections and lusts." (Gal. v. 24.)

These works, however, must not be done with any notion that by them a man can be justified before God—for faith, which alone is righteousness before God, will not bear with this false notion—but solely with this purpose, that the body may be brought into subjection, and be purified from its evil lusts, so that our eyes may be turned only to purging away those lusts. For when the soul has been cleansed by faith and made to love God, it would have all things to be cleansed in like manner; and especially in its own body, so that all things might unite with it in the love and praise of God. Thus it comes that from the requirements of his own body a man cannot take his ease, but is compelled on its account to do many good works, that he may bring it into subjection. Yet these works are not the means of his justification before God, he does them out of disinterested love to the service of God; looking to no other end than to do what is well-pleasing to Him whom he desires to obey dutifully in all things.

On this principle every man may easily instruct himself in what measure, and with what distinctions, he ought to chasten his own body. He will fast, watch, and labour, just as much as he sees to suffice for keeping down the wantonness and concupiscence of the body. But those who pretend to be justified by works are looking, not to the mortification of their lusts, but only to the works themselves; thinking that, if they can accomplish as many works and as great ones as possible, all is well with them, and they are justified. Sometimes they even injure their brain, and extinguish nature, or at least make it useless. This is enormous folly, and ignorance of Christian life and faith, when a man seeks, without faith, to be justified and saved by works.

To make what we have said more easily understood, let us set it forth under a figure. The works of a Christian man, who is justified and saved by his faith out of the pure and unbought mercy of God, ought to be regarded in the same light as would have been those of Adam and Eve in Paradise, and of all their posterity, if they had not sinned. Of them it is said: "The Lord God took the man, and put him into the garden of Eden to dress it and to keep it." (Gen. ii. 15.) Now Adam had been created by God just and righteous, so that he could not have needed to be justified and made righteous by keeping the garden and working in it; but, that he might not be unemployed, God gave him the business of keeping and cultivating Paradise. These would have indeed been works of perfect freedom, being done for no object but that of pleasing God, and not in order to obtain justification, which he already had to the full, and which would have been innate in us all.

So it is with the works of a believer. Being by his faith replaced afresh in Paradise and created anew, he does not need works for his justification, but that he may not be idle, but may keep his own body and work upon it. His works are to be done freely, with the sole object of pleasing God. Only we are not yet fully created anew in perfect faith and love; these require to be increased, not however through works, but through themselves.

A bishop, when he consecrates a church, confirms children, or performs any other duty of his office, is not consecrated as bishop by these works; nay, unless he had been previously consecrated as bishop, not one of those works would have any validity; they would be foolish, childish, and ridiculous. Thus a Christian, being consecrated by his faith, does good works; but he is not by these works made a more sacred person, or more a Christian. That is the effect of faith alone; nay, unless he were previously a believer and a Christian, none of his works would have any value at all; they would really be impious and damnable sins.

True then are these two sayings: Good works do not make a good man, but a good man does good works. Bad works do not make a bad man, but a bad man does bad works. Thus it is always necessary that the substance or person should be good before any good works can be done, and that good works should follow and proceed from a good person. As Christ says: "A good tree cannot bring forth evil fruit, neither can a corrupt tree bring forth good fruit." (Matt. vii. 18) Now it is clear that the fruit does not bear the tree, nor does the tree grow on the fruit; but, on the contrary, the trees bear the fruit and the fruit grows on the trees.

As then trees must exist before their fruit, and as the fruit does not make the tree either good or bad, but, on the contrary, a tree of either kind produces fruit of the same kind; so must first the person of the man be good or bad, before he can do either a good or a bad work; and his works do not make him tad or good, but he himself makes his works either bad or good.

We may see the same thing in all handicrafts. A bad or good house does not make a bad or good builder, but a good or bad builder makes a good or bad house. And in general, no work makes the workman such as it is itself; but the workman makes the work such as he is himself. Such is the case too with the works of men. Such as the man himself is, whether in faith or in unbelief, such is his work; good if it be done in faith, bad if in unbelief. But the converse is not true—that, such as the work is, such the man becomes in faith or in unbelief For as works do not make a believing man, so neither do they make a justified man; but faith, as it makes a man a believer and justified, so also it makes his works good.

Since, then, works justify no man, but a man must be justified before he can do any good work, it is most evident that it is faith alone which, by the mere mercy of God through Christ, and by means of His word, can worthily and sufficiently justify and save the person; and that a Christian man needs no work, no law, for his salvation; for by faith be is free from all law, and in perfect freedom does gratuitously all that he does, seeking nothing either of profit or of salvation—since by the grace of God he is already saved and rich in all things through his faith—but solely that which is well-pleasing to God.

So too no good work can profit an unbeliever to justification and salvation; and on the other hand no evil work makes him an evil and condemned person, but that unbelief, which makes the person and the tree bad, makes his works evil and condemned. Wherefore, when any man is made good or bad, this does not arise from his works, but from his faith or unbelief, as the wise man says: "The beginning of sin is to fall away from God"; that is, not to believe. Paul says: "He that cometh to God must believe" (Heb. xi. 6); and Christ says the same thing: "Either make the tree good, and his fruit good; or else make the tree corrupt, and his fruit corrupt." (Matt. xii. 33.) As much as to say: He who wishes to have good fruit, will begin with the tree, and plant a good one; even so he who wishes, to do good works must begin, not by working, but by believing, since it is this which makes the person good. For nothing makes the person good but faith, nor bad but unbelief.

It is certainly true that, in the sight of men, a man becomes good or evil by his works; but here 'becoming" means that it is thus shown and recognised who is good or evil; as Christ says: "By their fruits ye shall know them." (Matt.. vii. 20.) But all this stops at appearances and externals; and in this matter very many deceive themselves, when they presume to write and teach that we are to be justified by good works, and meanwhile make no mention even of faith, walking in their own ways, ever deceived and deceiving, going from bad to worse, blind leaders of the blind, wearying themselves with many works, and yet never attaining to true righteousness; of whom Paul says: "Having a form of godliness, but denying the power thereof; ever learning, and never able to come to the knowledge of the truth." (2 Tim. iii. 5, 7.)

He then, who does not wish to go astray with these blind ones, must look further than to the works of the law or the doctrine of works; nay, must turn away his spirit from works, and look to the person, and to the manner in which it may be justified. Now it is justified and saved, not by works or laws, but by the word of God, that is, by the promise of His grace; so that the glory may be to the Divine majesty, which has saved us who believe, not by works of righteousness which we have done, but according to His mercy, by the word of His grace.

From all this it is easy to perceive on what principle good works are to be cast aside or embraced, and by what rule all teachings put forth concerning works are to be understood. For if works are brought forward as grounds of justification, and are done under the false persuasion that we can pretend to be justified by them, they lay on us the yoke of necessity, and extinguish liberty along with faith, and by this very addition to their use, they become no longer good, but really worthy of condemnation. For such works are not free, but blaspheme the grace of God, to which alone it belongs to justify and save through faith. Works cannot accomplish this, and yet, with impious presumption, through our folly, they take it on themselves to do so; and thus break in with violence upon the office and glory of grace.

We do not then reject good works; nay, we embrace them and teach them in the highest degree. It is not on their own account that we condemn them, but on account of this impious addition to them, and the perverse notion of seeking justification by them. These things cause them to be only good in outward show, but in reality not good; since by them men are deceived and deceive others, like ravening wolves in sheep's clothing.

Now this Leviathan, this perverted notion about works, is invincible, when sincere faith is wanting. For those sanctified doers of works cannot but hold it, till faith, which destroys it, comes and reigns in the heart. Nature cannot expel it by her own power; nay, cannot even see it for what it is, but considers it as a most holy will. And when custom steps in besides, and strengthens this pravity of nature, as has happened by means of impious teachers, then the evil is incurable, and leads astray multitudes to irreparable ruin. Therefore, though it is good to preach and write about penitence, confession, and satisfaction, yet if we stop there, and do not go on to teach faith, such teaching is without doubt deceitful and devilish. For Christ, speaking by His servant John, not only said: "Repent ye"; but added: "for the kingdom of heaven is at hand." (Matt. iii. 2.)

For not one word of God only, but both, should be preached; new and old things should be brought out of the treasury, as well the voice of the law, as the word of grace. The voice of the law should be brought forward, that men may be terrified and brought to a knowledge of their sins, and thence be converted to penitence and to a better manner of life. But we must not stop here; that would be to wound only and not to bind up, to strike and not to heal, to kill and not to make alive, to bring down to hell and not to bring back, to humble and not to exalt. Therefore the word of grace, and of the promised remission of sin, must also be preached, in order to teach and set up faith; since, without that word, contrition, penitence, and all other duties, are performed and taught in vain.

There still remain, it is true, preachers of repentance and grace, but they do not explain the law and the promises of God to such an end, and in such a spirit, that men may learn whence repentance and grace are to come. For repentance comes from the law of God, but faith or grace from the promises of God, as it is said: "Faith cometh by hearing, and hearing by the word of God." (Rom. x. 17.) Whence it comes, that a man, when humbled and brought to the knowledge of himself by the threatenings and terrors of the law, is consoled and raised up by faith in the Divine promise. Thus "weeping may endure for a night, but joy cometh in the morning." (Ps. xxx. 5.) Thus much we say concerning works in general, and also concerning those which the Christian practises with regard to his own body.

Lastly, we will speak also of those works which he performs towards his neighbor. For man does not live for himself alone in this mortal body, in order to work on its account, but also for all men on earth; nay, he lives only for others and not for himself. For it is to this end that he brings his own body into subjection, that he may be able to serve others more sincerely and more freely; as Paul says: "None of us liveth to himself, and no man dieth to himself. For whether we live, we live unto the Lord; and whether we die, we die unto the Lord." (Rom. xiv. 7, 8.) Thus it is impossible that he should take his ease in this life, and not work for the good of his neighbors; since he must needs speak, act, and converse among men; just is Christ was made in the likeness of men, and found in fashion as a man, and had His conversation among men.

Yet a Christian has need of none of these things for justification and salvation, but in all his works he ought to entertain this view, and look only to this object, that he may serve and be useful to others in all that he does; having nothing before his eyes but the necessities and the advantage of his neighbor. Thus the Apostle commands us to work with our own hands, that we may have to give to those that need. He might have said, that we may support ourselves; but he tells us to give to those that need. It is the part of a Christian to take care of his own body for the very purpose that, by its soundness and wellbeing, be may be enabled to labour, and to acquire and preserve property, for the aid of those who are in want; that thus the stronger member may serve the weaker member, and we may be children of God, thoughtful and busy one for another, bearing one another's burdens, and so fulfilling the law of Christ.

Here is the truly Christian life; here is faith really working by love; when a man applies himself with joy and love to the works of that freest servitude, in which he serves others voluntarily and for nought; himself abundantly satisfied in the fulness and riches of his own faith.

Thus, when Paul had taught the Philippians how they had been made rich by that faith in Christ, in which they had obtained all things, he teaches them further in these words—"If there be therefore any consolation in Christ, if any comfort of love, if any fellowship of the Spirit, if any bowels and mercies, fulfill ye my joy, that ye be like-minded, having the same love, being of one accord, of one mind. Let nothing be done through strife or vainglory; but in lowliness of mind let each esteem other better than themselves. Look not every man on his own things, but every man also on the things of others." (Phil. ii. 1–4.)

In this we see clearly that the Apostle lays down this rule for a Christian life, that all our works should be directed to the advantage of others; since every Christian has such abundance through his faith, that all his other works and his whole life remain over and above, wherewith to serve and benefit his neighbor of spontaneous good will.

To this end he brings forward Christ as an example, saying: "Let this mind be in you, which was also in Christ Jesus: who, being in the form of God, thought it not robbery to be equal with God: but made himself of no reputation, and took upon him the form of a servant, and was made in the likeness of men; and being found in fashion as a man, he humbled himself, and became obedient unto death." (Phil. ii. 5–8.) This most wholesome saying of the Apostle has been darkened to us by men who, totally misunderstanding the expressions: "form of God," "form of a servant," "fashion," "likeness of men," have transferred them to the natures of Godhead and manhood. Paul's meaning is this: Christ, when He was full of the form of God, and abounded in all good things, so that He had no need of works or sufferings to be justified and saved—for all those things He had from the very beginning—yet was not puffed up with these things, and did not raise Himself above us, and arrogate to Himself power over us, though He might lawfully have done so, but on the contrary so acted in labouring, working, suffering, and dying, as to be like the rest of men, and no otherwise than a man in fashion and in conduct, as if he were in want of all things, and had nothing of the form of God; and yet all this He did for our sakes, that He might serve us, and that all the works He should do under that form of a servant, might become ours.

Thus a Christian, like Christ his head, being full and in abundance through his faith, ought to be content with this form of God, obtained by faith; except that, as I have said, he ought to increase this faith, till it be perfected. For this faith is his life, justification, and salvation, preserving his person itself and making it pleasing to God, and bestowing on him all that Christ has; as I have said above, and as Paul affirms: "The life which I now live in the flesh I live by the faith of the Son of God." (Gal. ii. 20.) Though he is thus free from all works, yet he ought to empty himself of this liberty, take on him the form of a servant, be made in the likeness of men, be found in fashion as a man, serve, help, and in every way act towards his neighbor as be sees that God through Christ has acted and is acting towards him. All this he should do freely, and with regard to nothing but the good pleasure of God, and he should reason thus:

Lo! my God, without merit on my part, of His pure and free mercy, has given to me, an unworthy, condemned, and contemptible creature, all the riches of justification and salvation in Christ, so that I no longer am in want of anything, except of faith to believe that this is so. For such a Father then, who has overwhelmed me with these inestimable riches of His, why should I not freely, cheerfully, and with my whole heart and from voluntary zeal, do all that I know will be pleasing to Him, and acceptable in His sight? I will therefore give myself, as a sort of Christ, to my neighbor, as Christ has given Himself to me; and will do nothing in this life, except what I see will be needful, advantageous, and wholesome for my neighbor, since by faith I abound in all good things in Christ.

Thus from faith flow forth love and joy in the Lord, and from love a cheerful, willing, free spirit, disposed to serve our neighbor voluntarily, without taking any account of gratitude or ingratitude, praise or blame, gain or loss. Its object is not to lay men under obligations, nor does it distinguish between friends and enemies, or look to gratitude or ingratitude, but most freely and willingly spends itself and its goods, whether it loses them through ingratitude, or gains good will. For thus did its Father, distributing all things to all men abundantly and freely; making His sun to rise upon the just and the unjust. Thus too the child does and endures nothing, except from the free joy with which it delights through Christ in God, the giver of such great gifts.

You see then that, if we recognise those great and precious gifts, as Peter says, which have been given to us, love is quickly diffused in our hearts through the Spirit, and by love we are made free, joyful, all-powerful, active workers, victors over all our tribulations, servants to our neighbor, and nevertheless lords of all things. But for those who do not recognize the good things given to them through Christ, Christ has been born in vain; such persons walk by works, and will never attain the taste and feeling of these great things. Therefore, just as our neighbor is in want, and has need of our abundance, so we too in the sight of God were in want, and bad need of His mercy. And as our heavenly Father has freely helped us in Christ, so ought we freely to help our neighbor by our body and works, and each should become to other a sort of Christ, so that we may be mutually Christs, and that the same Christ may be in all of us; that is, that we may be truly Christians.

Who then can comprehend the riches and glory of the Christian life? It can do all things, has all things, and is in want of nothing; is lord over sin, death, and hell, and at the same time is the obedient and useful servant of all. But alas! it is at this day unknown throughout the world; it is neither preached nor sought after, so that we are quite ignorant about our own name, why we are and are called Christians. We are certainly called so from Christ, who is not absent, but dwells among us, provided, that is, that we believe in Him, and are reciprocally and mutually one the Christ of the other, doing to our neighbor as Christ does to us. But now, in the doctrine of men, we are taught only to seek after merits, rewards, and things which are already ours, and we have made of Christ a taskmaster far more severe than Moses.

The Blessed Virgin, beyond all others, affords us an example of the same faith, in that she was purified according to the law of Moses, and like all other women, though she was bound by no such law, and had no need of purification. Still she submitted to the law voluntarily and of free love, making herself like the rest of women, that she might not offend or throw contempt on them. She was not justified by doing this; but, being already justified, she did it freely and gratuitously. Thus ought our works too to be done, and not in order to be justified by them; for, being first justified by faith, we ought to do all our works freely and cheerfully for the sake of others.

St. Paul circumcised his disciple Timothy, not because he needed circumcision for his justification, but that he might not offend or contemn those Jews, weak in the faith, who had not yet been able to comprehend the liberty of faith. On the other hand, when they contemned liberty, and urged that circumcision was necessary for justification, he resisted them, and would not allow Titus to be circumcised. For as he would not offend or contemn any one's weakness in faith, but yielded for the time to their will, so again he would not have the liberty of faith offended or contemned by hardened self-justifiers, but walked in a middle path, sparing the weak for the time, and always resisting the hardened, that he might convert all to the liberty of faith. On the same principle we ought to act, receiving those that are weak in the faith, but boldly resisting these hardened teachers of works, of whom we shall hereafter speak at more length.

Christ also, when His disciples were asked for the tribute money, asked of Peter, whether the children of a king were not free from taxes. Peter agreed to this; yet Jesus commanded him to go to the sea, saying: "Lest we should offend them, go thou to the sea, and cast a hook, and take up the fish that first cometh up; and when thou bast opened his mouth, thou shalt find a piece of money; that take, and give unto them for me and thee." (Matt. xvii. 27.)

This example is very much to our purpose; for here Christ calls Himself and His disciples free men, and children of a king, in want of nothing; and yet He voluntarily submits and pays the tax. Just as far then as this work was necessary or useful to Christ for justification or salvation, so far do all His other works or those of His disciples avail for justification. They are really free and subsequent to justification, and only done to serve others and set them an example.

Such are the works which Paul inculcated; that Christians should be subject to principalities and powers, and ready to every good work (Tit. iii. 1); not that they may be justified by these things, for they are already justified by faith, but that in liberty of spirit they may thus be the servants of others, and subject to powers, obeying their will out of gratuitous love.

Such too ought to have been the works of all colleges, monasteries, and priests; every one doing the works of his own profession and state of life, not in order to be justified by them, but in order to bring his own body into subjection, as an example to others, who themselves also need to keep under their bodies; and also in order to accommodate himself to the will of others, out of free love. But we must always guard most carefully against any vain confidence or presumption of being justified, gaining merit, or being saved by these works; this being the part of faith alone, as I have so often said.

Any man possessing this knowledge may easily keep clear of danger among those innumerable commands and precepts of the pope, of bishops, of monasteries, of churches, of princes, and of magistrates, which some foolish pastors urge on us as being necessary for justification and salvation, calling them precepts of the Church, when they are not so at all. For the Christian freeman will speak thus: I will fast, I will pray, I will do this or that, which is commanded me by men, not as having any need of these things for justification or salvation, but that I may thus comply with the will of the pope, of the bishop, of such a community or such a magistrate, or of my neighbor as an example to him; for this cause I will do and suffer all things, just as Christ did and suffered much more for me, though He needed not at all to do so on His own account, and made Himself for my sake under the law, when he was not under the law. And although tyrants may do me violence or wrong in requiring obedience to these things, yet it will not hurt me to do them, so long as they are not done against God.

From all this every man will be able to attain a sure judgment and faithful discrimination between all works and laws, and to know who are blind and foolish pastors, and who are true and good ones. For whatsoever work is not directed to the sole end, either of keeping under the body, or of doing service to our neighbor—provided he require nothing contrary to the will of God—is no good or Christian work. Hence I greatly fear that at this day few or no colleges, monasteries, altars, or ecclesiastical functions are Christian ones; and the same may be said of fasts and special prayers to certain Saints. I fear that in all these nothing is being sought but what is already ours; While we fancy that by these things our sins are purged away and salvation is attained, and thus utterly do away with Christian liberty. This comes from ignorance of Christian faith and liberty.

This ignorance, and this crushing of liberty, are diligently promoted by the teaching of very many blind pastors, who stir up and urge the people to a zeal for these things, praising such zeal and puffing up men with their indulgences, but never teaching faith. Now I would advise you, if you have any wish to pray, to fast, or to make foundations in churches, as they call it, to take care not to do so with the object of gaining any advantage, either temporal or eternal. You will thus wrong your faith which alone bestows all things on you, and the increase of which, either by working or by suffering, is alone to be cared for. What you give, give freely and without price, that others may prosper and have increase from you and from your goodness. Thus you will be a truly good man and a Christian. For what do you want with your goods and your works, which are done over and above for the subjection of the body, since you have abundance for yourself through your faith, in which God has given you all things?

We give this rule: the good things which we have from God ought to flow from one to another, and become common to all, so that every one of us may, as it were, put on his neighbor, and so behave towards him as if he were himself in his place. They flowed and do flow from Christ to us; he put us on, and acted for us as if he himself were what we are. From us they flow to those who have need of them; so that my faith and righteousness ought to be laid down before God as a covering and intercession for the sins of my neighbor, which I am to take on myself, and so labour and endure servitude in them, as if they were my own; for thus has Christ done for us. This is true love and the genuine truth of Christian life. But only there is it true and genuine, where there is true and genuine faith. Hence the Apostle attributes to Charity this quality, that she seeketh not her own.

We conclude therefore that a Christian man does not live in himself, but in Christ, and in his neighbor, or else is no Christian; in Christ by faith, in his neighbor by love. By faith he is carried upwards above himself to God, and by love he sinks back below himself to his neighbor, still always abiding in God and His love, as Christ says: "verily I say unto you, hereafter ye shall see heaven open, and the angels of God ascending and descending upon the Son of man." (John i. 51.)

Thus much concerning liberty, which, as you see, is a true and spiritual liberty, making our hearts free from all sins, laws, and commandments; as Paul says: "The law is not made for a righteous man" (1 Tim. i. 9); and one which surpasses every other and outward liberty, as far as heaven is above earth. May Christ make us to understand and preserve this liberty. Amen.

Finally, for the sake of those to whom nothing can be stated so well but that they misunderstand and distort it, we must add a word, in case they can understand even that. There are very many persons, who, when they hear of this liberty of faith, straightway turn it into an occasion of licence. They think that everything is now lawful for them, and do not choose to show themselves free men and Christians in any other way than by their contempt and reprehension of ceremonies, of traditions of human laws; as if they were Christians merely because they refuse to fast on stated days, or eat flesh when others fast, or omit the customary prayers; scoffing at the precepts of men, but utterly passing over all the rest that belongs to the Christian religion. On the other hand, they are most pertinaciously resisted by those who strive after salvation solely by their observance of and reverence for ceremonies; as if they would be saved merely because they fast on stated days, or abstain from flesh, or make formal prayers talking loudly of the precepts of the Church and of the Fathers, and not caring a straw about those things which belong to our genuine faith. Both these parties are plainly culpable, in that, while they neglect matters which are of weight and necessary for salvation, they contend noisily about such as are without weight and not necessary.

How much more rightly does the Apostle Paul teach us to walk in the middle path, condemning either extreme, and saying: "Let not him that eateth despise him that eateth not; and let not him which eateth not judge him that eateth." (Rom. xiv. 3.) You see here how the Apostle blames those who, not from religious feeling, but in mere contempt, neglect and rail at ceremonial observances; and teaches them not to despise, since this "knowledge puffeth up." Again he teaches the pertinacious upholders of these things not to judge their opponents. For neither party observes towards the other that charity which edifieth. In this matter we must listen to Scripture, which teaches us to turn aside neither to the right hand nor to the left, but to follow those right precepts of the Lord which rejoice the heart. For just as a man is not righteous merely because be serves and devotes himself to works and ceremonial rites, so neither will be accounted righteous, merely because he neglects and despises them.

It is not from works that we are set free by the faith of Christ, but from the belief in works, that is, from foolishly presuming to seek justification through works. Faith redeems our consciences, makes them upright and preserves them, since by it we recognise the truth that justification does not depend on our works, although good works neither can nor ought to be wanting to it; just as we cannot exist without food and drink and all the functions of this mortal body. Still it is not on them that our justification is based, but on faith; and yet they ought not on that account to be despised or neglected. Thus in this world we are compelled by the needs of this bodily life; but we are not hereby justified. "My kingdom is not hence, nor of this world," says Christ; but He does not say: "My kingdom is not here, nor in this world." Paul too says "Though we walk in the flesh, we do not war after the flesh" (2 Cor. x. 3); and: "The life which I now live in the flesh I live by the faith of the Son of God." (Gal. ii. 20.) Thus our doings, life, and being, in works and ceremonies, are done from the necessities of this life, and with the motive of governing our bodies; but yet we are not justified by these things, but by the faith of the Son of God.

The Christian must therefore walk in the middle path, and meet these two classes of men before his eyes. He may meet with hardened and obstinate ceremonialists, who, like deaf adders, refuse to listen to the truth of liberty, and cry up, enjoin, and urge on us their ceremonies, as if they could justify us without faith. Such were the Jews of old, who would not understand, that they might act well. These men we must resist, do just the contrary to what they do, and be bold to give them offence; lest by this impious notion of theirs they should deceive many along with themselves. In the sight of these men it is expedient to eat flesh, to break fasts, and to do in behalf of the liberty of faith things which they hold to be the greatest sins. We must say of them: "Let them alone; they be blind leaders of the blind." (Matt. xv. 14.) In this way Paul also would not have Titus circumcised, though these men urged it; and Christ defended the Apostles, who had plucked ears of corn on the Sabbath day; and many like instances.

Or else we may meet with simple-minded and ignorant persons, weak in the faith, as the Apostle calls them, who are as yet unable to apprehend that liberty of faith, even if willing to do so. These we must spare, lest they should be offended. We must bear with their infirmity, till they shall be more fully instructed. For since these men do not act thus from hardened malice, but only from weakness of faith, therefore, in order to avoid giving them offence, we must keep fasts and do other things which they consider necessary. This is required of us by charity, which injures no one, but serves all men. It is not the fault of these persons that they are weak, but that of their pastors, who by the snares and weapons of their own traditions have brought them into bondage, and wounded their souls, when they ought to have been set free and healed by the teaching of faith and liberty. Thus the Apostle says: "If meat make my brother to offend, I will eat no flesh while the world standeth." (I Cor. viii. 13.) And again: "I know, and am persuaded by the Lord Jesus, that there is nothing unclean of itself; but to him that esteemeth anything to be unclean, to him it is unclean. It is evil for that man who eateth with offence." (Rom. xiv. 14, 20.)

Thus, though we ought boldly to resist those teachers of tradition, and though those laws of the pontiffs, by which they make aggressions on the people of God, deserve sharp reproof, yet we must spare the timid crowd, who are held captive by the laws of those impious tyrants, till they are set free. Fight vigorously against the wolves, but on behalf of the sheep, not against the sheep. And this you may do by inveighing against the laws and lawgivers, and yet at the same time observing these laws with the weak, lest they be offended; until they shall themselves recognise the tyranny as such, and understand their own liberty. If you wish to use your liberty, do it secretly, as Paul says: "Hast thou faith? have it to thyself before God." (Rom. xiv. 22) But take care not to use it in the presence of the weak. On the other hand, in the presence of tyrants and obstinate opposers, use your liberty in their despite, and with, the utmost pertinacity, that they too may understand that they themselves are tyrants, and their laws useless for justification; nay, that they had not right to establish such laws.

Since, then, we cannot live in this world without ceremonies and works; since the hot and inexperienced period of youth has need of being restrained and protected by such bonds; and since everyone is bound to keep under his own body by attention to these things; therefore the minister of Christ must be prudent and faithful in so ruling and teaching the people of Christ in all these matters that no root of bitterness may spring up among them, and so many be defiled, as Paul warned the Hebrews; that is, that they may not lose the faith, and begin to be defiled by a belief in works, as the means of justification. This is a thing which easily happens, and defiles very many, unless faith be constantly inculcated along with works. It is impossible to avoid this evil, when faith is passed over in silence, and only the ordinances of men are taught, as has been done hitherto by the pestilent, impious, and soul-destroying traditions of our pontiffs, and opinions of our theologians. An infinite number of souls have been drawn down to hell by these snares, so that you may recognise the work of Antichrist.

In brief, as poverty is imperilled amid riches, honesty amid business, humility amid honours, abstinence amid feasting, purity amid pleasures, so is justification by faith imperilled among ceremonies. Solomon says: "Can a man take fire in his bosom, and his clothes not be burned?" (Prov. vi. 27.) And yet, as we must live among riches, business, honours, pleasures, feastings, so must we among ceremonies, that is, among perils. Just as infant boys have the greatest need of being cherished in the bosoms and by the care of girls, that they may not die and yet, when they are grown, there is peril to their salvation in living among girls; so inexperienced and fervid young men require to be kept in and restrained by the barriers of ceremonies, even were they of iron, lest their weak mind should rush headlong into vice. And yet it would be death to them to persevere in believing that they can be justified by these things. They must rather be taught that they have been thus imprisoned, not with the purpose of their being justified or gaining merit in this way, but in order that they might avoid wrong doing, and be more easily instructed in that righteousness which is by faith; a thing which the headlong character of youth would not bear, unless it were put under restraint.

Hence in the Christian life ceremonies are to be no otherwise looked upon than builders and workmen look upon those preparations for building or working which are not made with any view of being permanent or anything in themselves, but only because without them there could be no building and no work. When the structure is completed, they are laid aside. Here you see that we do not contemn these preparations, but set the highest value on them; a belief in them we do contemn, because no one thinks that they constitute a real and permanent structure. If any one were so manifestly out of his senses as to have no other object in life but that of setting up these preparations with all possible expense, diligence, and perseverance, while he never thought of the structure itself, but pleased himself and made his boast of these useless preparations and props; should we not all pity his madness, and think that, at the cost thus thrown away, some great building might have been raised?

Thus too we do not contemn works and ceremonies; nay, we set the highest value on them; but we contemn the belief in works, which no one should consider to constitute true righteousness; as do those hypocrites who employ and throw away their whole life in the pursuit of works, and yet never attain to that for the sake of which the works are done. As the Apostle says, they are "ever learning, and never able to come to the knowledge of the truth." (2 Tim. iii. 7). They appear to wish to build, they make preparations, and yet they never do build; and thus they continue in a show of godliness, but never attain to its power.

Meanwhile they please themselves with this zealous pursuit, and even dare to judge all others, whom they do not see adorned with such a glittering display of works; while, if they had been imbued with faith, they might have done great things for their own and others' salvation, at the same cost which they now waste in abuse of the gifts of God. But since human nature and natural reason, as they call it, are naturally superstitious, and quick to believe that justification can be attained by any laws or works proposed to them; and since nature is also exercised and confirmed in the same view by the practice of all earthly lawgivers, she can never, of her own power, free herself from this bondage to works, and come to a recognition of the liberty of faith.

We have therefore need to pray that God will lead us, and make us taught of God, that is, ready to learn from God; and will Himself, as He has promised, write His law in our hearts; otherwise there is no hope for us. For unless He himself teach us inwardly this wisdom hidden in a mystery, nature cannot but condemn it and judge it to be heretical. She takes offence at it and it seems folly to her; just as we see that it happened of old in the case of the prophets and apostles; and just as blind and impious pontiffs, with their flatterers, do now in my case and that of those who are like me; upon whom, together with ourselves, may God at length have mercy, and lift up the light of His countenance upon them, that we may know His way upon earth and His saving health among all nations, Who is blessed for evermore. Amen. In the year of the Lord MDXX.

INTRODUCTION TO
Michael Sattler
THE SCHLEITHEIM ARTICLES

Despite Luther's constant attempts to guard against misunderstanding, his fulminations against the unbiblical corruptions of the Roman church and proclamation of Christian freedom were readily misappropriated in the tumultuous context of the early Reformation. Whereas Luther had insisted that unbiblical ceremonies and practices did not necessarily have to be discarded, so long as they were recognized as merely human institutions and were not sources of superstitions, some began to preach that all such ceremonies be purged right away. And although Luther had insisted that the freedom of a Christian was inward, compatible with outward bondage to lawful government as a form of loving one's neighbor, more radical followers taught that the true Christian had no need of civil government at all, and that civil government, accordingly, had nothing to do with the church. Such ideas, which became known as the "radical Reformation" in contrast to the "magisterial Reformation," initially appeared in Germany—first in the radical reforms of Luther's former associate, Andreas Karlstadt, in 1522–23, and then in the apocalyptic theology of Thomas Müntzer and the associated disastrous peasant uprising of 1525.

The most enduring form of the Radical Reformation, however, was the movement known as Anabaptism, which, although a squabbling family of disparate groups and ideas rather than one united movement, is most associated with teachings that emerged in and around Zurich between 1523 and 1525. Since 1519, Zurich had been undergoing a sweeping reformation of its own under the influential leadership of Ulrich Zwingli, often considered the father of the Reformed branch of the Reformation. Zurich had embraced a particularly thoroughgoing partnership between the reforming ministers and the city magistrates, and although the Reformation there was real and resulted in the conversion of many, it proceeded at the pace of politics. Ministers such as Conrad Grebel and Balthasar Hubmaier were appalled by the slow pace of reform and the nominalism of so much of the populace. The Church in Zurich was self-evidently not identical with the city's whole population, and Grebel and Hubmaier did not think that such an ambiguous state of affairs should be tolerated. Anabaptism is best known for its insistence on re-baptism and its critique of civil authority, but both of these positions must be understood against the larger background of the Anabaptist aim to establish a visible congregation of saints that truly was the Church and nothing but the Church. This soon led to the practice of limiting church membership to those who voluntarily committed themselves by baptism (hence the name Anabaptist, or "re-baptizer"), but also to an insistence on policing church membership by rigorous discipline ("the ban") to remove false Christians from the fellowship. Despite the complexity and variety of the Anabaptist movements, this emphasis on discipline was a consistent theme.

Perhaps the most famous Anabaptist teaching, however, that of pacifism or non-resistance (and the corresponding notion that Christians must have nothing to do with civil government) came slightly later. It does not seem to have really emerged until after Grebel and Hubmaier's movement failed to gain public support and instead became the object of bitter persecution.[1] In the chaotic situation that followed the outbreak of such persecution

1 James M. Stayer, "Swiss-South German Anabaptism," in John D. Roth and James M. Stayer, eds., *A Companion to Anabaptism and Spiritualism* (Leiden: Brill, 2007), 84.

in 1526, an Anabaptist preacher named Michael Sattler tried to bring unity to the movement by convening a gathering at the Swiss town of Schleitheim. There he gained general support for the document he penned, the *Brotherly Union of a number of children of God concerning Seven Articles*, which has since become known simply as the Schleitheim Articles or the Schleitheim Confession. In it we find the already-established emphasis on rebaptism and the ban (articles 1 and 2), and a treatment of the Lord's Supper that emphasizes the need to restrict it only to true believers (article 3). Articles 4 and 6, on the necessity for a strict separation between church and world, and the rejection of any use of the "the sword," though reflecting existing Anabaptist themes, were the first explicit declaration of them. Article 7, forbidding oaths and thus further separating Anabaptist believers from participation in the legal affairs of the broader society, seems to have been a new contribution of Sattler.[2]

As an attempt to establish something like an Anabaptist confession of faith, the Schleitheim Articles were only partially successful. A dizzying variety of sometimes contradictory expressions of the movement long persisted, but the principles of Schleitheim quickly became broadly influential in Swiss and South German Anabaptist communities, and in most of their present-day descendants, such as the Mennonites.

2 Stayer 89–91.

THE SCHLEITHEIM ARTICLES

Michael Sattler

TRANSLATED BY J. C. WENGER

First. Observe concerning baptism: Baptism shall be given to all those who have learned repentance and amendment of life, and who believe truly that their sins are taken away by Christ, and to all those who walk in the resurrection of Jesus Christ, and wish to be buried with Him in death, so that they may be resurrected with Him, and to all those who with this significance request it [baptism] of us and demand it for themselves. This excludes all infant baptism, the highest and chief abomination of the pope. In this you have the foundation and testimony of the apostles. Mt. 28, Mk. 16, Acts 2, 8, 16, 19. This we wish to hold simply, yet firmly and with assurance.

Second. On the Ban [Excommunication]. We are agreed as follows The ban shall be employed with all those who have given themselves to the Lord, to walk in His commandments, and with all those who are baptized into the one body of Christ and who are called brethren or sisters, and yet who slip sometimes and fall into error and sin, being inadvertently overtaken. The same shall be admonished twice in secret and the third time openly disciplined or banned according to the command of Christ (Mt 18). But this shall be done according to the regulation of the Spirit (Mt. 5) before the breaking of bread, so that we may break and eat one bread, with one mind and in one love, and may drink of one cup.

Third. Eucharist or Communion: In the breaking of bread we are of one mind and are agreed [as follows]: All those who wish to break one bread in remembrance of the broken body of Christ, and all who wish to drink of one drink as a remembrance of the shed blood of Christ, shall be united beforehand by baptism in one body of Christ which is the church of God and whose Head is Christ. For as Paul points out we cannot at the same time be partakers of the Lord's table and the table of devils; we cannot at the same time drink the cup of the Lord and the cup of the devil. That is, all those who have fellowship with the dead works of darkness have no part in the light Therefore all who follow the devil and the world have no part with those who are called unto God out of the world. All who lie in evil have no part in the good. Therefore it is and must be [thus]: Whoever has not been called by one God to one faith, to one baptism, to one Spirit, to one body, with all the children of God's church, cannot be made [into] one bread with them, as indeed must be done if one is truly to break bread according to the command of Christ.

Fourth. On separation of the saved: A separation shall be made from the evil and from the wickedness which the devil planted in the world; in this manner, simply that we shall not have fellowship with them [the wicked] and not run with them in the multitude of their abominations. This is the way it is: Since all who do not walk in the obedience of faith, and have not united themselves with God so that they wish to do His will, are a great abomination before God, it is not possible for anything to grow or issue from them except abominable things. For truly all creatures are in but two classes, good and bad, believing and unbelieving, darkness and light, the world and those who [have come] out of the world, God's temple and idols, Christ and Belial; and none can have part with the other.

To us then the command of the Lord is clear when He calls upon us to be separate from the evil and thus He will be our God and we shall be His sons and daughters. He further admonishes us to withdraw from Babylon and the earthly Egypt that we may not be partakers of the pain and suffering which the Lord will bring upon them. From this we should learn that everything which is not united with our God and Christ cannot be other than an abomination which we should shun and flee from. By this is meant all popish and antipopish works and church services, meetings and church attendance, drinking houses, civic affairs, the commitments [made in] unbelief and other things of that kind, which are highly regarded by the world and yet are carried on in flat contradiction to the command of God, in accordance with all the unrighteouness which is in the world. From all these things we shall be separated and have no part with them for they are nothing but an abomination, and they are the cause of our being hated before our Christ Jesus, Who has set us free from the slavery of the flesh and fitted us for the service of God through the Spirit Whom He has given us.

Therefore there will also unquestionably fall from us the unchristian, devilish weapons of force—such as sword, armor and the like, and all their use [either] for friends or against one's enemies I would like the records—by virtue of the word of Christ, Resist not [him that is] evil.

Fifth. On pastors in the church of God: The pastor in the church of God shall, as Paul has prescribed, be one who out-and-out has a good report of those who are outside the faith. This office shall be to read, to admonish and teach, to warn, to discipline, to ban in the church, to lead out in prayer for the advancement of all the brethren and sisters, to lift up the bread when it is to be broken, and in all things to see to the care of the body of Christ, in order that it may be built up and developed, and the mouth of the slanderer be stopped.

This one moreover shall be supported of the church which has chosen him, wherein he may be in need, so that he who serves the Gospel may live of the Gospel as the Lord has ordained. But if a pastor should do something requiring discipline, he shall not be dealt with except [on the testimony of] two or three witnesses. And when they sin they shall be disciplined before all in order that the others may fear.

But should it happen that through the cross this pastor should be banished or led to the Lord [through martyrdom] another shall be ordained in his place in the same hour so that God's little flock and people may not be destroyed.

Sixth. Concerning the sword: The sword is ordained of God outside the perfection of Christ. It punishes and puts to death the wicked, and guards and protects the good. In the Law the sword was ordained for the punishment of the wicked and for their death, and the same [sword] is [now] ordained to be used by the worldly magistrates. In the perfection of Christ, however, only the ban is used for a warning and for the excommunication of the one who has sinned, without putting the flesh to death—simply the warning and the command to sin no more.

Now it will be asked by many who do not recognize [this as] the will of Christ for us, whether a Christian may or should employ the sword against the wicked for the defence and protection of the good, or for the sake of love.

Our reply is unanimously as follows: Christ teaches and commands us to learn of Him, for He is meek and lowly in heart and so shall we find rest to our souls. Also Christ says to the heathenish woman who was taken in adultery, not that one should stone her according to the law of His Father (and yet He says, As the Father has commanded me, thus I do), but in mercy and forgiveness and warning, to sin no more. Such [an attitude] we also ought to take completely according to the rule of the ban.

Secondly, it will be asked, whether a Christian shall pass sentence in worldly disputes and strife such as unbelievers have with one another. This is our united answer: Christ did not wish to decide or pass judgment between brother and brother in the case of the inheritance, but refused to do so. Therefore we should do likewise.

Thirdly, it will be asked concerning the sword, Shall one be a magistrate if one should be chosen as such? The answer is as follows: They wished to make Christ king, but He fled and did not view it as the arrangement of His Father. Thus shall we do as He did, and follow Him, and so shall we not walk in darkness. For He Himself says, He who wishes to come after me, let him deny himself and take up his cross and follow me. Also, He Himself forbids the [employment of] the force of the sword saying, The worldly princes lord it over them, etc., but not so shall it be with you. Further, Paul says, Whom God did foreknow He also did predestinate to be conformed to the image of His Son, etc. Also Peter says, Christ has suffered (not ruled) and left us an example, that ye should follow His steps.

Finally it will be observed that it is not appropriate for a Christian to serve as a magistrate because of these points: The government magistracy is according to the flesh, but the Christians' is according to the Spirit; their houses and dwelling remain in this world, but the Christians' are in heaven; their citizenship is in this world, but the Christians' citizenship is in heaven; the weapons of their conflict and war are carnal and against the flesh only, but the Christians' weapons are spiritual, against the fortification of the devil. The worldlings are armed with steel and iron, but the Christians are armed with the armor of God, with truth, righteousness, peace, faith, salvation and the Word of God. ...

Seventh Concerning the oath: The oath is a confirmation among those who are quarreling or making promises. In the Law it is commanded to be performed in God's Name, but only in truth, not falsely. Christ, who teaches the perfection of the Law, prohibits all swearing to His [followers], whether true or false—neither by heaven, nor by the earth, nor by Jerusalem, nor by our head—and that for the reason which He shortly thereafter gives. For you are not able to make one hair white or black. So you see it is for this reason that all swearing is forbidden: we cannot fulfill that which we promise when we swear, for we cannot change [even] the very least thing on us.

Christ also taught us along the same line when He said, Let your communication be Yea, yea; Nay, nay; for whatsoever is more than these cometh of evil. He says, Your speech or word shall be yea and nay. [However] when one does not wish to understand, he remains closed to the meaning. Christ is simply Yea and Nay, and all those who seek Him simply will understand His Word. Amen.

INTRODUCTION TO
Philip Melanchthon
APOLOGY OF THE AUGSBURG CONFESSION

Despite internal tensions and numerous setbacks, the Lutheran reform movement in Germany gained far more traction than might have been expected, given the Catholic Church's history of brutal efficiency in suppressing many heresies of recent centuries. Politics had worked in their favor. True, the new Holy Roman Emperor, Charles V, was devoutly loyal to the Roman Church and, on paper, the most powerful man that Europe had seen in centuries. In practice, though, he was distracted from dealing with Protestantism both by ongoing political rivalries with the French and the Papacy, and by the growing power of the Ottoman Turks. Under Suleiman the Magnificent, the Turks had won a crushing victory over King of Hungary, Charles's cousin, at the Battle of Mohacs in 1526, and in 1529 besieged Vienna itself with seemingly unstoppable momentum.

Though the siege failed, the Turkish threat remained dire, and Charles recognized the urgent need to bring unity within Germany if he was to successfully oppose it. Accordingly, in 1530 he convened an Imperial Diet (that is to say, an assembly of all the representatives in the realm) at Augsburg to try to re-establish religious peace and political unity. The Protestant princes of Germany, for their part, saw an unprecedented opportunity to win formal toleration for their cause, or even persuade the Emperor of its righteousness. Although both hopes proved over-optimistic, the Diet did represent a huge milestone for the new movement, as the Lutherans were invited to publicly present a confession of their faith before the Emperor, a confession that was to become the foundational document of the new movement: the Augsburg Confession.

Consisting of twenty-one articles of faith and seven articles rehearsing the abuses of Catholic practice that had been reformed, corrected, or abolished in the Protestant churches, the Confession was a remarkably irenic document. Its author was Philipp Melanchthon, Luther's close friend and colleague, who knew much better than Luther how to moderate his words when circumstances required, as they certainly did in this case. The twenty-one articles of faith focused on the positive content of Protestant faith (which on several points was identical with Catholic orthodoxy) rather than the errors of Catholic doctrine, and took care to condemn the excesses and erros of the Anabaptist radicals. But conciliatory as it may have been, the forthrightly Protestant character of the Confession was unmistakable: just four articles in, after declaring the doctrines of God, of sin, and of Christ, the Confession offered a succinct formulation of the Protestant doctrine of justification by faith:

> Also they [Protestants] teach that men cannot be justified before God by their own strength, merits, or works, but are freely justified for Christ's sake, through faith, when they believe that they are received into favor, and that their sins are forgiven for Christ's sake, who, by His death, has made satisfaction for our sins. This faith God imputes for righteousness in His sight.

A confutation of the confession was soon prepared by theologians loyal to Rome, with the implacable Johann Eck again in a leading role. In response, Melanchthon penned a lengthy *Apology* (or Defense) *of the Augsburg Confession*, offering what was at that point the fullest systematic articulation and defense of central Protestant doctrines. Particularly important was his thorough explanation of the article on justification, which appears in full here. Although there is a fair bit of inside baseball here, with Melanchthon taking scholastic theologians to task on their use of distinctions such as "condign merit" and "congruent merit," to defend meritorious works while opposing Pelagianism, there is also a barrage of forthrightly biblical argumentation, particularly in the final section.

Melanchthon goes to some lengths to correct several key misunderstandings of the Protestant doctrine which are as common today as they were then. First, in the opening section he explains why it is that our righteousness cannot please God. It is not that we cannot do things outwardly just (what Melanchthon calls "civil righteousness," or "the righteousness of reason"), whether by reason alone or by unregenerate attention to the Law given in Scripture. We can, for instance, avoid theft, killing, and adultery, and many do. But, says Melanchthon, the Decalog[ue] requires not only outward civil works, which reason can in some way produce, but it also requires other things placed far above reason, namely, truly to fear God, truly to love God, truly to call upon God, truly to be convinced that God hears us, and to expect the aid of God in death and in all afflictions; finally, it requires obedience to God, in death and all afflictions.

Confronted with the demands of such a heart-obedience, our sinful souls balk or despair, and can only enjoy fellowship with God by clinging to the promises given in Christ.

Melanchthon also corrects the misunderstanding that such saving faith is merely historical knowledge, accepting as true propositions about God and Christ's redeeming work in history. Rather, in perhaps the most beautiful passages of this whole section, Melanchthon declares, saving faith is

> the certainty or the certain trust in the heart, when, with my whole heart, I regard the promises of God as certain and true, through which there are offered me, without my merit, the forgiveness of sins, grace, and all salvation, through Christ the Mediator. . . . Faith is that my whole heart takes to itself this treasure. It is not my doing, not my presenting or giving, not my work or preparation, but that a heart comforts itself, and

> is perfectly confident with respect to this, namely, that God makes a present and gift to us, and not we to Him, that He sheds upon us every treasure of grace in Christ.

Thus Melanchthon also guards against the misconception that for Protestantism, faith itself becomes a meritorious work, as if justification by faith meant, "do this one meritorious thing, faith, and God will justify you." Rather, he clarifies, faith is no active work but a passive receiving of Christ's finished work: "For faith justifies and saves, not on the ground that it is a work in itself worthy, but only because it receives the promised mercy."

The *Apology* was certainly not to be the last word on the subject. But by crystallizing Protestant doctrine, especially on key points like justification, in lucid and systematic form, Melanchthon was to play almost as important a role in the new movement as Luther himself.

APOLOGY OF THE AUGSBURG CONFESSION

Philip Melanchthon

ARTICLE IV (II): OF JUSTIFICATION.

In the Fourth, Fifth, Sixth, and, below, in the Twentieth Article, they condemn us, for teaching that men obtain remission of sins not because of their own merits, but freely for Christ's sake, through faith in Christ. For they condemn us both for denying that men obtain remission of sins because of their own merits, and for affirming that, through faith, men obtain remission of sins, and through faith in Christ are justified. But since in this controversy the chief topic of Christian doctrine is treated, which, understood aright, illumines and amplifies the honor of Christ, and brings necessary and most abundant consolation to devout consciences, we ask His Imperial Majesty to hear us with forbearance in regard to matters of such importance. For since the adversaries understand neither what the remission of sins, nor what faith, nor what grace, nor what righteousness is, they sadly corrupt this topic, and obscure the glory and benefits of Christ, and rob devout consciences of the consolations offered in Christ. But that we may strengthen the position of our Confession, and also remove the charges which the adversaries advance against us, certain things are to be premised in the beginning, in order that the sources of both kinds of doctrine, i.e., both that of our adversaries and our own, may be known.

All Scripture ought to be distributed into these two principal topics, the Law and the promises. For in some places it presents the Law, and in others the promise concerning Christ, namely, either when it promises that Christ will come, and offers, for His sake, the remission of sins justification, and life eternal, or when, in the Gospel, Christ Himself, since He has appeared, promises the remission of sins, justification, and life eternal. Moreover, in this discussion, by Law we designate the Ten Commandments, wherever they are read in the Scriptures. Of the ceremonies and judicial laws of Moses we say nothing at present.

Of these two parts the adversaries select the Law, because human reason naturally understands, in some way, the Law (for it has the same judgment divinely written in the mind); and by the Law they seek the remission of sins and justification. Now, the Decalog requires not only outward civil works, which reason can in some way produce, but it also requires other things placed far above reason, namely, truly to fear God, truly to love God, truly to call upon God, truly to be convinced that God hears us, and to expect the aid of God in death and in all afflictions; finally, it requires obedience to God, in death and all afflictions, so that we may not flee from these or refuse them when God imposes them.

Here the scholastics, having followed the philosophers, teach only a righteousness of reason, namely, civil works, and fabricate besides that without the Holy Ghost reason can love God above all things. For, as long as the human mind is at ease, and does not feel the wrath or judgment of God, it can imagine that it wishes to love God, that it wishes to do good for God's sake. In this manner they teach that men merit the remission of sins by doing what is in them, i.e., if reason, grieving over sin, elicit an act of love to God, or for God's sake be active in that which is good. And because this opinion naturally flatters men, it has brought forth and multiplied in the Church many services, monastic vows, abuses of the mass;

and, with this opinion the one has, in the course of time, devised this act of worship and observances, the other that. And in order that they might nourish and increase confidence in such works, they have affirmed that God necessarily gives grace to one thus working, by the necessity not of constraint but of immutability.

In this opinion there are many great and pernicious errors, which it would be tedious to enumerate. Let the discreet reader think only of this: If this be Christian righteousness, what difference is there between philosophy and the doctrine of Christ? If we merit the remission of sins by these elicit acts, of what benefit is Christ? If we can be justified by reason and the works of reason, wherefore is there need of Christ or regeneration[1]? And from these opinions the matter has now come to such a pass that many ridicule us because we teach that an other than the philosophic righteousness must be sought after. We have heard that some after setting aside the Gospel, have, instead of a sermon, explained the ethics of Aristotle. Nor did such men err if those things are true which the adversaries defend. For Aristotle wrote concerning civil morals so learnedly that nothing further concerning this need be demanded. We see books extant in which certain sayings of Christ are compared with the sayings of Socrates, Zeno, and others, as though Christ had come for the purpose of delivering certain laws through which we might merit the remission of sins, as though we did not receive this gratuitously because of His merits. Therefore, if we here receive the doctrine of the adversaries, that by the works of reason we merit the remission of sins and justification, there will be no difference between philosophic, or certainly pharisaic, and Christian righteousness.

Although the adversaries, not to pass by Christ altogether, require a knowledge of the history concerning Christ, and ascribe to Him that it is His merit that a habit is given us or, as they say, prima gratia, "first grace," which they understand as a habit, inclining us the more readily to love God; yet, what they ascribe to this habit is of little importance, because they imagine that the acts of the will are of the same kind before and after this habit. They imagine that

1 As Peter declares, 1 Pet. 1:18ff

the will can love God; but nevertheless this habit stimulates it to do the same the more cheerfully. And they bid us first merit this habit by preceding merits; then they bid us merit by the works of the Law an increase of this habit and life eternal. Thus they bury Christ, so that men may not avail themselves of Him as a Mediator, and believe that for His sake they freely receive remission of sins and reconciliation, but may dream that by their own fulfilment of the Law they merit the remission of sins, and that by their own fulfilment of the Law they are accounted righteous before God; while, nevertheless, the Law is never satisfied, since reason does nothing except certain civil works, and, in the mean time, neither fears God, nor truly believes that God cares for it. And although they speak of this habit, yet, without the righteousness of faith, neither the love of God can exist in man, nor can it be understood what the love of God is.

Their feigning a distinction between *meritum congrui*[2] and *meritum condigni*[3] is only an artifice in order not to appear openly to Pelagianize. For, if God necessarily gives grace for the *meritum congrui*, it is no longer *meritum congrui*, but *meritum condigni*. But they do not know what they are saying. After this habit of love, they imagine that man can acquire merit *de condigno*. And yet they bid us doubt whether there be a habit present. How, therefore, do they know whether they acquire merit *de congruo* or *de condigno*?[4] But this whole matter was fabricated by idle men, who did not know how the remission of sins occurs, and how, in the judgment of God and terrors of conscience, trust in works is driven out of us. Secure hypocrites always judge that they acquire merit de condigno, whether the habit be present or be not present, because men naturally trust in their own righteousness; but terrified consciences waver and hesitate, and then seek and accumulate other works in order to find rest. Such consciences never think that they acquire merit *de condigno*, and they rush into despair unless they hear, in addition to the doctrine of the

2 Quasi-merit, or half-merit.

3 Desert of merit, of full merit.

4 In full, or half.

Law, the Gospel concerning the gratuitous remission of sins and the righteousness of faith.

Thus the adversaries teach nothing but the righteousness of reason, or certainly of the Law, upon which they look just as the Jews upon the veiled face of Moses; and, in secure hypocrites who think that they satisfy the Law, they excite presumption and empty confidence in works and contempt of the grace of Christ. On the contrary, they drive timid consciences to despair, which laboring with doubt, never can experience what faith is, and how efficacious it is; thus, at last they utterly despair.

Now, we think concerning the righteousness of reason thus, namely, that God requires it, and that, because of God's commandment, the honorable works which the Decalog commands must necessarily be performed, according to the passage Gal. 3:24: The Law was our schoolmaster; likewise 1 Tim. 1:9: The Law is made for the ungodly. For God wishes those who are carnal to be restrained by civil discipline, and to maintain this, He has given laws, letters, doctrine, magistrates, penalties. And this righteousness reason, by its own strength, can, to a certain extent, work, although it is often overcome by natural weakness, and by the devil impelling it to manifest crimes. Now, although we cheerfully assign this righteousness of reason the praises that are due it (for this corrupt nature has no greater good, and Aristotle says aright: Neither the evening star nor the morning star is more beautiful than righteousness, and God also honors it with bodily rewards), yet it ought not to be praised with reproach to Christ.

For it is false that we merit the remission of sins by our works.

False also is this, that men are accounted righteous before God because of the righteousness of reason.

False also is this that reason, by its own strength, is able to love God above all things, and to fulfill God's Law, namely, truly to fear God, to be truly confident that God hears prayer, to be willing to obey God in death and other dispensations of God, not to covet what belongs to others, etc.; although reason can work civil works.

False also and dishonoring Christ is this, that men do not sin who, without grace, do the commandments of God.

We have testimonies for this our belief, not only from the Scriptures, but also from the Fathers. For in opposition to the Pelagians, Augustine contends at great length that grace is not given because of our merits. And in *De Natura et Gratia* he says: If natural ability, through the free will, suffice both for learning to know how one ought to live and for living aright, then Christ has died in vain, then the offense of the Cross is made void. Why may I not also here cry out? Yea, I will cry out, and, with Christian grief, will chide them: Christ has become of no effect unto you whosoever of you are justified by the Law; ye are fallen from grace. Gal. 5:4; cf. 2:21. For they, being ignorant of God's righteousness, and going about to establish their own righteousness, have not submitted themselves unto the righteousness of God. For Christ is the end of the Law for righteousness to every one that believeth. Rom. 10:3,4. And John 8:36: If the Son therefore shall make you free, ye shall be free indeed. Therefore by reason we cannot be freed from sins and merit the remission of sins. And in John 3:5 it is written: Except a man be born of water and of the Spirit, he cannot enter into the kingdom of God. But if it is necessary to be born again of the Holy Ghost, the righteousness of reason does not justify us before God, and does not fulfill the Law, Rom. 3:23: All have come short of the glory of God, i.e., are destitute of the wisdom and righteousness of God, which acknowledges and glorifies God. Likewise Rom. 8:7–8: The carnal mind is enmity against God; for it is not subject to the Law of God, neither indeed can be. So then they that are in the flesh cannot please God. These testimonies are so manifest that, to use the words of Augustine which he employed in this case, they do not need an acute understanding, but only an attentive hearer. If the carnal mind is enmity against God, the flesh certainly does not love God; if it cannot be subject to the Law of God, it cannot love God. If the carnal mind is enmity against God, the flesh sins, even when we do external civil works. If it cannot be subject to the Law of God, it certainly sins even when, according to human judgment, it possesses deeds that are excellent and worthy of praise. The adversaries consider only the precepts of the Second Table which contain civil righteousness that reason understands. Content with this, they think that they satisfy the Law of God. In the mean time they do not see the First Table which commands that we love God, that we declare as certain that God is angry with sin, that we truly fear God, that we declare as certain that God hears prayer. But the human heart without the Holy Ghost either in security despises God's judgment, or in punishment flees from, and hates, God when He judges. Therefore it does not obey the First Table. Since, therefore, contempt of God, and doubt concerning the Word of God, and concerning the threats and promises, inhere in human nature, men truly sin, even when, without the Holy Ghost, they do virtuous works, because they do them with a wicked heart, according to Rom. 14:23: Whatsoever is not of faith is sin. For such persons perform their works with contempt of God, just as Epicurus does not believe that God cares for him, or that he is regarded or heard by God. This contempt vitiates works seemingly virtuous, because God judges the heart.

Lastly, it was very foolish for the adversaries to write that men who are under eternal wrath merit the remission of sins by an act of love, which springs from their mind since it is impossible to love God, unless the remission of sins be apprehended first by faith. For the heart, truly feeling that God is angry, cannot love God, unless He be shown to have been reconciled. As long as He terrifies us, and seems to cast us into eternal death, human nature is not able to take courage, so as to love a wrathful, judging, and punishing God. It is easy for idle men to feign such dreams concerning love, as, that a person guilty of mortal sin can love God above all things, because they do not feel what the wrath or judgment of God is. But in agony of conscience and in conflicts conscience experiences the emptiness of these philosophical speculations. Paul says, Rom. 4:15: The Law worketh wrath. He does not say that by the Law men merit the remission of sins. For the Law always accuses and terrifies consciences. Therefore it does not justify, because conscience terrified by the Law flees from the judgment of God. Therefore they err who trust that by the Law, by their own works, they merit the remission of sins. It is sufficient for us to have said these things concerning the righteousness of reason or of the Law, which the adversaries teach. For after a while, when we will declare our belief concerning the righteousness of faith, the subject itself will compel us to adduce more testimonies, which also will be of service in overthrowing the errors of the adversaries which we have thus far reviewed.

Because, therefore, men by their own strength cannot fulfill the Law of God, and all are under sin, and subject to eternal wrath and death, on this account we cannot be freed by the Law from sin and be justified, but the promise of the remission of sins and of justification has been given us for Christ's sake, who was given for us in order that He might make satisfaction for the sins of the world, and has been appointed as the Mediator and Propitiator. And this promise has not the condition of our merits, but freely offers the remission of sins and justification as Paul says Rom. 11:6: If it be of works, then is it no more grace. And in another place, Rom. 3:21: The righteousness of God without the Law is manifested, i.e., the remission of sins is freely offered. Nor does reconciliation depend upon our merits. Because if the remission of sins were to depend upon our merits, and reconciliation were from the Law, it would be useless. For as we do not fulfill the Law, it would also follow that we would never obtain the promise of reconciliation. Thus Paul reasons, Rom. 4:14: For if they which are of the Law be heirs, faith is made void, and the promise made of none effect. For if the promise would require the condition of our merits and the Law, which we never fulfill, it would follow that the promise would be useless.

But since justification is obtained through the free promise it follows that we cannot justify ourselves. Otherwise wherefore would there be need to promise? For since the promise cannot be received except by faith, the Gospel which is properly the promise of the remission of sins and of justification for Christ's sake, proclaims the righteousness of faith in Christ, which the Law does not teach. Nor is this the righteousness of the Law. For the Law requires of us our works and our perfection. But the Gospel freely offers, for Christ's sake, to us, who have been vanquished by sin and death, reconciliation which is received not by works, but by faith alone. This faith brings to God not confidence in one's own merits, but only confidence in the promise, or the mercy promised in Christ. This special faith, therefore, by which an individual believes that for Christ's sake his sins are remitted him, and that for Christ's sake God is reconciled and propitious, obtains remission of sins and justifies us. And because in repentance, i.e. in terrors, it comforts and encourages hearts, it regenerates us and brings the Holy Ghost that then we may be able to fulfill God's Law, namely, to love God, truly to fear God, truly to be confident that God hears prayer, and to obey God in all afflictions; it mortifies concupiscence etc. Thus, because faith, which freely receives the remission of sins, sets Christ, the Mediator and Propitiator, against God's wrath, it does not present our merits or our love. This faith is the true knowledge of Christ, and avails itself of the benefits of Christ, and regenerates hearts, and precedes the fulfilling of the Law. And of this faith not a syllable exists in the doctrine of our adversaries. Hence we find fault with the adversaries, equally because they teach only the righteousness of the Law, and because they do not teach the righteousness of the Gospel, which proclaims the righteousness of faith in Christ.

WHAT IS JUSTIFYING FAITH?

The adversaries feign that faith is only a knowledge of the history, and therefore teach that it can coexist with mortal sin. Hence they say nothing concerning faith, by which Paul so frequently says that men are justified, because those who are accounted righteous before God do not live in mortal sin. But that faith which justifies is not merely a knowledge of history, but it is to assent to the promise of God, in which, for Christ's sake, the remission of sins and justification are freely offered. And that no one may suppose that it is mere knowledge, we will add further: it is to wish and to receive the offered promise of the remission of sins and of justification. And the difference between this faith and the righteousness of the Law can be easily discerned. Faith is the *latreiva*,[5] which receives the benefits offered by God; the righteousness of the Law is the *latreiva* which offers to God our merits. By faith God wishes to be worshiped in this way, that we receive from Him those things which He promises and offers.

Now, that faith signifies, not only a knowledge of the history, but such faith as assents to the promise, Paul plainly testifies when he says, Rom. 4:16: Therefore it is of faith, to the end the promise might be sure. For he judges that the promise cannot be received unless by faith. Wherefore he puts them together as things that belong to one another, and connects promise and faith. Although it will be easy to decide what faith is if we consider the Creed, where this article certainly stands: The forgiveness of sins. Therefore it is not enough to believe that Christ was born, suffered, was raised again, unless we add also this article, which is the purpose of the history: The forgiveness of sins. To this article the rest must be referred, namely, that for Christ's sake, and not for the sake of our merits, forgiveness of sins is given us. For what need was there that Christ was given for our sins if for our sins our merits can make satisfaction?

As often, therefore, as we speak of justifying faith, we must keep in mind that these three objects concur: the promise, and that, too, gratuitous, and the merits of Christ, as the price and propitiation. The promise is received by faith; the "gratuitous" excludes our merits, and signifies that the benefit is offered only through mercy; the merits of Christ are the price, because there must be a certain propitiation for our sins. Scripture frequently implores mercy; and the holy Fathers often say that we are saved by mercy. As often, therefore, as mention is made of mercy, we must keep in mind that faith is there required, which receives the promise of mercy. And, again, as often as we speak of faith, we wish an object to be understood, namely, the promised mercy. For faith justifies and saves, not on the ground that it is a work in itself worthy, but only because it receives the promised mercy.

5 Divine service.

And throughout the prophets and the psalms this worship, this *latreiva*, is highly praised, although the Law does not teach the gratuitous remission of sins. But the Fathers knew the promise concerning Christ, that God for Christ's sake wished to remit sins. Therefore, since they understood that Christ would be the price for our sins, they knew that our works are not a price for so great a matter. Accordingly, they received gratuitous mercy and remission of sins by faith, just as the saints in the New Testament. Here belong those frequent repetitions concerning mercy and faith, in the psalms and the prophets, as this, Ps. 130:3: If Thou, Lord, shouldest mark iniquities, O Lord, who shall stand? Here David confesses his sins, and does not recount his merits. He adds: But there is forgiveness with Thee. Here he comforts himself by his trust in God's mercy, and he cites the promise: My soul doth wait, and in His Word do I hope, i.e., because Thou hast promised the remission of sins, I am sustained by this Thy promise. Therefore the fathers also were justified, not by the Law, but by the promise and faith. And it is amazing that the adversaries extenuate faith to such a degree, although they see that it is everywhere praised as an eminent service, as in Ps. 50:15: Call upon Me in the day of trouble: I will deliver thee. Thus God wishes Himself to be known, thus He wishes Himself to be worshiped, that from Him we receive benefits, and receive them, too, because of His mercy, and not because of our merits. This is the richest consolation in all afflictions. And such consolations the adversaries abolish when they extenuate and disparage faith, and teach only that by means of works and merits men treat with God.

THAT FAITH IN CHRIST JUSTIFIES.

In the first place, lest any one may think that we speak concerning an idle knowledge of the history, we must declare how faith is obtained. Afterward we will show both that it justifies, and how this ought to be understood, and we will explain the objections of the adversaries. Christ, in the last chapter of Luke 24:47, commands that repentance and remission of sins should be preached in His name. For the Gospel convicts all men that they are under sin, that they all are subject to eternal wrath and death, and offers, for Christ's sake, remission of sin and justification, which is received by faith. The preaching of repentance, which accuses us, terrifies consciences with true and grave terrors. In these, hearts ought again to receive consolation. This happens if they believe the promise of Christ, that for His sake we have remission of sins. This faith, encouraging and consoling in these fears, receives remission of sins, justifies and quickens. For this consolation is a new and spiritual life. These things are plain and clear, and can be understood by the pious, and have testimonies of the Church. The adversaries nowhere can say how the Holy Ghost is given. They imagine that the Sacraments confer the Holy Ghost *ex opere operato*, without a good emotion in the recipient, as though indeed, the gift of the Holy Ghost were an idle matter.

But since we speak of such faith as is not an idle thought, but of that which liberates from death and produces a new life in hearts, and is the work of the Holy Ghost; this does not coexist with mortal sin, but as long as it is present, produces good fruits, as we will say after a while. For concerning the conversion of the wicked, or concerning the mode of regeneration, what can be said that is more simple and more clear? Let them, from so great an array of writers, adduce a single commentary upon the *Sententiae* that speaks of the mode of regeneration. When they speak of the habit of love, they imagine that men merit it through works, and they do not teach that it is received through the Word, precisely as also the Anabaptists teach at this time. But God cannot be treated with, God cannot be apprehended, except through the Word. Accordingly, justification occurs through the Word, just as Paul says, Rom. 1:16: The Gospel is the power of God unto salvation to every one that believeth. Likewise Rom. 10:17: Faith cometh by hearing. And proof can be derived even from this that faith justifies, because, if justification occurs only through the Word, and the Word is apprehended only by faith, it follows that faith justifies. But there are other and more important reasons. We have said these things thus far in order that we might show the mode of regeneration, and that the nature of faith, concerning which we speak, might be understood.

Now we will show that faith justifies. Here, in the first place, readers must be admonished of this, that just as it is necessary to maintain this sentence: Christ is Mediator, so is it necessary to defend that faith justifies. For how will Christ be Mediator if in justification we do not use Him as Mediator; if we do not hold that for His sake we are accounted righteous? But to believe is to trust in the merits of Christ, that for His sake God certainly wishes to be reconciled with us. Likewise, just as we ought to maintain that, apart from the Law, the promise of Christ is necessary, so also is it needful to maintain that faith justifies. For the Law cannot be performed unless the Holy Ghost be first received. It is, therefore, needful to maintain that the promise of Christ is necessary. But this cannot be received except by faith. Therefore, those who deny that faith justifies, teach nothing but the Law, both Christ and the Gospel being set aside.

But when it is said that faith justifies, some perhaps understand it of the beginning, namely, that faith is the beginning of justification or preparation for justification, so that not faith itself is that through which we are accepted by God, but the works which follow; and they dream, accordingly, that faith is highly praised, because it is the beginning. For great is the importance of the beginning, as they commonly say, The beginning is half of everything; just as if one would say that grammar makes the teachers of all arts, because it prepares for other arts, although in fact it is his own art that renders every one an artist. We do not believe thus concerning faith, but we maintain this, that properly and truly, by faith itself, we are for Christ's sake accounted righteous, or are acceptable to God. And because "to be justified" means that out of unjust men just men are made, or born again, it means also that they are pronounced or accounted just. For Scripture speaks in both ways. Accordingly we wish first to show this, that faith alone makes of an unjust, a just man, i.e., receives remission of sins.

The particle alone offends some, although even Paul says, Rom. 3:28: We conclude that a man is justified by faith, without the deeds of the Law. Again, Eph. 2:8: It is the gift of God; not of works, lest any man should boast. Again, Rom. 3:24: Being justified freely. If the exclusive alone displeases, let them remove from Paul also the exclusives freely, not of works, it is the gift, etc. For these also are exclusives. It is, however, the opinion of merit that we exclude. We do not exclude the Word or Sacraments, as the adversaries falsely charge us. For we have said above that faith is conceived from the Word, and we honor the ministry of the Word in the highest degree. Love also and works must follow faith. Wherefore, they are not excluded so as not to follow, but confidence in the merit of love or of works is excluded in justification. And this we will clearly show.

THAT WE OBTAIN REMISSION OF SINS BY FAITH ALONE IN CHRIST.

We think that even the adversaries acknowledge that, in justification, the remission of sins is necessary first. For we all are under sin. Wherefore we reason thus:

To attain the remission of sins is to be justified, according to Ps. 32:1: Blessed is he whose transgression is forgiven. By faith alone in Christ, not through love, not because of love or works, do we acquire the remission of sins, although love follows faith. Therefore by faith alone we are justified, understanding justification as the making of a righteous man out of an unrighteous, or that he be regenerated.

It will thus become easy to declare the minor premise if we know how the remission of sins occurs. The adversaries with great indifference dispute whether the remission of sins and the infusion of grace are the same change. Being idle men, they did not know what to answer. In the remission of sins, the terrors of sin and of eternal death, in the heart, must be overcome, as Paul testifies, 1 Cor. 15:56: The sting of death is sin, and the strength of sin is the Law. But thanks be to God, which giveth us the victory through our Lord Jesus Christ. That is, sin terrifies consciences, this occurs through the Law, which shows the wrath of God against sin; but we gain the victory through Christ. How? By faith, when we comfort ourselves by confidence in the mercy promised for Christ's sake. Thus, therefore, we prove the minor proposition. The wrath of God cannot be appeased if we set against it our own works, because Christ has been set forth as a Propitiator, so that for His sake, the Father may become reconciled to us. But Christ is not apprehended as a Mediator except by faith. Therefore, by faith alone we obtain remission of sins, when we comfort our hearts with confidence in the mercy promised for Christ's sake. Likewise Paul, Rom. 5:2, says: By whom also we have access, and adds, by faith. Thus, therefore, we are reconciled to the Father, and receive remission of sins when we are comforted with confidence in the mercy promised for Christ's sake. The adversaries regard Christ as Mediator and Propitiator for this reason, namely, that He has merited the habit of love; they do not urge us to use Him now as Mediator, but, as though Christ were altogether buried, they imagine that we have access through our own works, and, through these, merit this habit, and afterwards, by this love, come to God. Is not this to bury Christ altogether, and to take away the entire doctrine of faith? Paul on the contrary, teaches that we have access, i.e., reconciliation, through Christ. And to show how this occurs, he adds that we have access by faith. By faith, therefore, for Christ's sake, we receive remission of sins. We cannot set our own love and our own works over against God's wrath.

Secondly. It is certain that sins are forgiven for the sake of Christ, as Propitiator, Rom. 3:25: Whom God hath set forth to be a propitiation. Moreover, Paul adds: through faith. Therefore this Propitiator thus benefits us, when by faith we apprehend the mercy promised in Him, and set it against the wrath and judgment of God. And to the same effect it is written, Heb. 4:14,16: Seeing, then, that we have a great High Priest, etc., let us therefore come with confidence. For the Apostle bids us come to God, not with confidence in our own merits, but with confidence in Christ as a High Priest; therefore he requires faith.

Thirdly. Peter, in Acts 10:43, says: To Him give all the prophets witness that through His name, whosoever believeth on Him, shall receive remission of sins. How could this be said more clearly? We receive remission of sins, he says, through His name, i.e., for His sake; therefore, not for the sake of our merits, not for the sake of our contrition, attrition, love, worship, works. And he adds: When we believe in Him. Therefore he requires faith. For we cannot apprehend the name of Christ except by faith. Besides he cites the agreement of all the prophets. This is truly to cite the authority of the Church. But of this topic we will speak again after a while, when treating of "Repentance."

Fourthly. Remission of sins is something promised for Christ's sake. Therefore it cannot be received except by faith alone. For a promise cannot be received except by faith alone. Rom. 4:16: Therefore it is of faith that it might be by grace, to the end that the promise might be sure; as though he were to say: "If the matter were to depend upon our merits, the promise would be uncertain and useless, because we never could determine when we would have sufficient merit." And this, experienced consciences can easily understand. Accordingly, Paul says, Gal. 3:22: But the Scripture hath concluded all under sin, that the promise by faith of Jesus Christ might be given to them that believe. He takes merit away from us, because he says that all are guilty and concluded under sin; then he adds that the promise, namely, of the remission of sins and of justification, is given, and adds how the promise can be received, namely, by faith. And this reasoning, derived from the nature of a promise, is the chief reasoning in Paul, and is often repeated. Nor can anything be devised or imagined whereby this argument of Paul can be overthrown. Wherefore let not good minds suffer themselves to be forced from the conviction that we receive remission of sins for Christ's sake, only through faith. In this they have sure and firm consolation against the terrors of sin, and against eternal death, and against all the gates of hell.

But since we receive remission of sins and the Holy Ghost by faith alone, faith alone justifies, because those reconciled are accounted righteous and children of God, not on account of their own purity, but through mercy for Christ's sake, provided only they by faith apprehend this mercy. Accordingly, Scripture testifies that by faith we are accounted righteous, Rom. 3:26. We, therefore, will add testimonies which clearly declare that faith is that very righteousness by which we are accounted righteous before God, namely, not because it is a work that is in itself worthy, but because it receives the promise by which God has promised that for Christ's sake He wishes to be propitious to those believing in Him, or because He knows that Christ of God is made unto us wisdom, and righteousness, and sanctification, and redemption, 1 Cor. 1:30.

In the Epistle to the Romans, Paul discusses this topic especially, and declares that, when we believe that God, for Christ's sake, is reconciled to us, we are justified freely by faith. And this proposition, which contains the statement of the entire discussion, he maintains in the third chapter: We conclude that a man is justified by faith, without the deeds of the Law, Rom. 3:28. Here the adversaries interpret that this refers to Levitical ceremonies. But Paul speaks not only of the ceremonies, but of the whole Law. For he quotes afterward (7:7) from the Decalog: Thou shalt not covet. And if moral works would merit the remission of sins and justification, there would also be no need of Christ and the promise, and all that Paul speaks of the promise would be overthrown. He would also have been wrong in writing to the Ephesians 2:8: By grace are ye saved through faith, and that not of yourselves; it is the gift of God, not of works. Paul likewise refers to Abraham and David, Rom. 4:1,6. But they had the command of God concerning circumcision. Therefore, if any works justified, these works must also have justified at the time that they had a command. But Augustine teaches correctly that Paul speaks of the entire Law, as he discusses at length in his book, Of the Spirit and Letter, where he says finally: These matters, therefore having been considered and treated, according to the ability that the Lord has thought worthy to give us, we infer that man is not justified by the precepts of a good life, but by faith in Jesus Christ.

And lest we may think that the sentence that faith justifies, fell from Paul inconsiderately, he fortifies and confirms this by a long discussion in the fourth chapter to the Romans, and afterwards repeats it in all his epistles. Thus he says, Rom. 4:4,5: To him that worketh is the reward not reckoned of grace, but of debt. But to him that worketh not, but believeth on Him that justifieth the ungodly, his faith is counted for righteousness. Here he clearly says that faith itself is imputed for righteousness. Faith, therefore, is that thing which God declares to be righteousness, and he adds that it is imputed freely, and says that it could not be imputed freely, if it were due on account of works. Wherefore he excludes also the merit of moral works. For if justification before God were due to these, faith would not be imputed for righteousness without works. And afterwards, Rom. 4:9: For we say that faith was reckoned to Abraham for righteousness. Romans 5:1 says: Being justified by faith, we have peace with God, i.e., we have consciences that are tranquil and joyful before God. Rom. 10:10: With the heart man believeth unto righteousness. Here he declares that faith is the righteousness of the heart. Gal. 2:16: We have believed in Christ Jesus that we might be justified by the faith of Christ, and not by the works of the Law. Eph. 2:8: For by grace are ye saved through faith, and that not of yourselves; it is the gift of God; not of works, lest any man should boast.

John 1:12: To them gave He power to become the sons of God, even to them that believe on His name; which were born, not of blood, nor of the will of the flesh, nor of the will of man, but of God. John 3:14,15: As Moses lifted up the serpent in the wilderness, even so must the Son of man be lifted up, that whosoever believeth in Him should not perish. Likewise, 3:17: For God sent not His Son into the world to condemn the world, but that the world through Him might be saved. He that believeth on Him is not condemned.

Acts 13:38–39: Be it known unto you therefore, men and brethren, that through this Man is preached unto you the forgiveness of sins; and by Him all that believe are justified from all things from which ye could not be justified by the Law of Moses. How could the office of Christ and justification be declared more clearly? The Law, he says, did not justify. Therefore Christ was given, that we may believe that for His sake we are justified. He plainly denies justification to the Law. Hence, for Christ's sake we are accounted righteous when we believe that God, for His sake, has been reconciled to us. Acts 4:11–12: This is the stone which was set at naught of you builders, which is become the head of the corner. Neither is there salvation in any other; for there is none other name under heaven given among men whereby we must be saved.

But the name of Christ is apprehended only by faith. Therefore, by confidence in the name of Christ, and not by confidence in our works, we are saved. For "the name" here signifies the cause which is mentioned, because of which salvation is attained. And to call upon the name of Christ is to trust in the name of Christ, as the cause or price because of which we are saved. Acts 15:9: Purifying their hearts by faith. Wherefore that faith of which the Apostles speak is not idle knowledge, but a reality, receiving the Holy Ghost and justifying us.

Hab. 2:4: The just shall live by his faith. Here he says, first, that men are just by faith, by which they believe that God is propitious, and he adds that the same faith quickens, because this faith produces in the heart peace and joy and eternal life.

Is. 53:11: By His knowledge shall He justify many. But what is the knowledge of Christ unless to know the benefits of Christ, the promises which by the Gospel He has scattered broadcast in the world? And to know these benefits is properly and truly to believe in Christ, to believe that that which God has promised for Christ's sake He will certainly fulfill.

But Scripture is full of such testimonies since, in some places, it presents the Law and in others the promises concerning Christ, and the remission of sins, and the free acceptance of the sinner for Christ's sake.

Here and there among the Fathers similar testimonies are extant. For Ambrose says in his letter to a certain Irenaeus: Moreover, the world was subject to Him by the Law for the reason that, according to the command of the Law, all are indicted, and yet, by the works of the Law, no one is justified, i.e., because, by the Law, sin is perceived, but guilt is not discharged. The Law, which made all sinners, seemed to have done injury, but when the Lord Jesus Christ came, He forgave to all sin which no one could avoid, and, by the shedding of His own blood, blotted out the handwriting which was against us. This is what he says in Rom. 5:20: "The Law entered that the offense might abound. But where sin abounded, grace did much more abound." Because after the whole world became subject, He took away the sin of the whole world, as he

[John] testified, saying in John 1:29: "Behold the Lamb of God, which taketh away the sin of the world." And on this account let no one boast of works, because no one is justified by his deeds. But he who is righteous has it given him because he was justified after the laver. Faith, therefore, is that which frees through the blood of Christ, because he is blessed "whose transgression is forgiven, whose sin is covered," Ps. 32:1. These are the words of Ambrose, which clearly favor our doctrine; he denies justification to works, and ascribes to faith that it sets us free through the blood of Christ. Let all the Sententiarists, who are adorned with magnificent titles, be collected into one heap. For some are called angelic; others, subtile, and others irrefragable. When all these have been read and reread, they will not be of as much aid for understanding Paul as is this one passage of Ambrose.

To the same effect, Augustine writes many things against the Pelagians. In Of the Spirit and Letter he says: The righteousness of the Law, namely, that he who has fulfilled it shall live in it, is set forth for this reason that when any one has recognized his infirmity he may attain and work the same and live in it, conciliating the Justifier not by his own strength nor by the letter of the Law itself (which cannot be done), but by faith. Except in a justified man, there is no right work wherein he who does it may live. But justification is obtained by faith. Here he clearly says that the Justifier is conciliated by faith, and that justification is obtained by faith. And a little after: By the Law we fear God; by faith we hope in God. But to those fearing punishment grace is hidden; and the soul laboring, etc., under this fear betakes itself by faith to God's mercy, in order that He may give what He commands. Here he teaches that by the Law hearts are terrified, but by faith they receive consolation. He also teaches us to apprehend, by faith, mercy, before we attempt to fulfill the Law. We will shortly cite certain other passages.

Truly, it is amazing that the adversaries are in no way moved by so many passages of Scripture, which clearly ascribe justification to faith, and, indeed, deny it to works. Do they think that the same is repeated so often for no purpose? Do they think that these words fell inconsiderately from the Holy Ghost? But they have also devised sophistry whereby they elude them. They say that these passages of Scripture, (which speak of faith,) ought to be received as referring to a *fides formata*, i.e., they do not ascribe justification to faith except on account of love. Yea, they do not, in any way, ascribe justification to faith, but only to love, because they dream that faith can coexist with mortal sin. Whither does this tend, unless that they again abolish the promise and return to the Law? If faith receive the remission of sins on account of love, the remission of sins will always be uncertain, because we never love as much as we ought, yea, we do not love unless our hearts are firmly convinced that the remission of sins has been granted us. Thus the adversaries, while they require in the remission of sins and justification confidence in one's own love, altogether abolish the Gospel concerning the free remission of sins; although, at the same time, they neither render this love nor understand it, unless they believe that the remission of sins is freely received.

We also say that love ought to follow faith, as Paul also says, Gal. 5:6: For in Jesus Christ neither circumcision availeth anything, nor uncircumcision, but faith which worketh by love. And yet we must not think on that account that by confidence in this love or on account of this love we receive the remission of sins and reconciliation, just as we do not receive the remission of sins because of other works that follow. But the remission of sins is received by faith alone, and, indeed, by faith properly so called, because the promise cannot be received except by faith. But faith, properly so called, is that which assents to the promise. Of this faith Scripture speaks. And because it receives the remission of sins, and reconciles us to God, by this faith we are accounted righteous for Christ's sake before we love and do the works of the Law, although love necessarily follows. Nor, indeed, is this faith an idle knowledge, neither can it coexist with mortal sin, but it is a work of the Holy Ghost, whereby we are freed from death, and terrified minds are encouraged and quickened. And because this faith alone receives the remission of sins, and renders us acceptable to God, and brings the Holy Ghost, it could be more correctly called gratia gratum faciens, grace rendering one pleasing to God, than an effect following, namely, love.

Thus far, in order that the subject might be made quite clear, we have shown with sufficient fulness, both from testimonies of Scripture, and arguments derived from Scripture, that by faith alone we obtain the remission of sins for Christ's sake, and that by faith alone we are justified, i.e., of unrighteous men made righteous, or regenerated. But how necessary the knowledge of this faith is, can be easily judged, because in this alone the office of Christ is recognized, by this alone we receive the benefits of Christ; this alone brings sure and firm consolation to pious minds. And in the Church it is necessary that there should be the doctrine from which the pious may receive the sure hope of salvation. For the adversaries give men bad advice when they bid them doubt whether they obtain remission of sins. For how will such persons sustain themselves in death who have heard nothing of this faith, and think that they ought to doubt whether they obtain the remission of sins? Besides, it is necessary that in the Church of Christ the Gospel be retained, i.e., the promise that for Christ's sake sins are freely remitted. Those who teach nothing of this faith, concerning which we speak, altogether abolish the Gospel. But the scholastics mention not even a word concerning this faith. Our adversaries follow them, and reject this faith. Nor do they see that, by rejecting this faith they abolish the entire promise concerning the free remission of sins and the righteousness of Christ.

INTRODUCTION TO
John Calvin,
INSTITUTES OF THE CHRISTIAN RELIGION

While the struggles for Reformation intensified in Germany, other parts of Europe did not remain free from the contagion of unrest that Luther's writings were spreading. France, in particular, had long harbored reformist sympathies, both on account of that country's long history of conflict with the Papacy, and from the new flowering of the humanist movement. Emphasizing a return to the original sources—both the original text of Scripture, and the writings of the Church Fathers—the humanists found in these sources a stark contrast to the tangle of ceremonies, corruptions, and scholastic logic-chopping that dominated the late medieval church.

In the early 1520s, a circle gathered around the humanist leader Jacques Lefevre d'Etaples in the diocese of Meaux who was involved in the translation of the Bible into French and the teaching of doctrines quite similar to those being devloped at the same time by Luther. This naturally invited suspicion and hostility from conservative theologians, but as the movement enjoyed the enthusiastic patronage of King Francis's sister, Marguerite d'Angouleme, it escaped persecution until the early 1530s. By that time it had been joined by a brilliant young lawyer, Jean Calvin, who had studied theology and philosophy before switching to law at the insistence of his father. The date of Calvin's conversion to full-fledged

Protestant faith is not entirely clear, but he does write of it as a "sudden conversion," and it was complete enough by 1533 that he was forced to flee Paris in the midst of a crackdown on Protestant sympathizers. Taking refuge with several friends for a time in the small kingdom of Navarre in the south of France, where Marguerite was now Queen, Calvin began a period of focused study and writing, and in 1534 resigned his salaried position in the Catholic church, signalling his full commitment to the Protestant cause. By 1535 he was in Basel, Switzerland, hard at work on a book that was to become a landmark of Protestant theology and an enduring classic of Christian thought: *The Institutes of the Christian Religion*. Completed in August of that year, it was not published until early in 1536, but immediately made a name for its young author (then just 26 years old). It was a relatively short volume (only a fraction of the length of the final 1559 edition, having been significantly expanded along the way in editions of 1539 and 1543), but composed with extraordinary clarity, stylistic beauty, and logical order, qualities it was to maintain through all subsequent expansions.

It should be noted that Calvin did not at this stage (nor indeed ever) view himself as the founder of a distinct "Reformed" tradition of Protestantism over against Lutheranism. The 1536 edition certainly contains differences of detail and emphasis from Luther's theology, but so did the work of Luther's friend and collaborator Melanchthon, and Calvin certainly identified more closely with Luther's flavor of Protestantism than Zwingli's at this point. In fact, he did not hesitate to later subscribe to the *Augsburg Confession*, and it was only polemical developments within the 1550s that set Calvin at odds with more stubborn defenders of Luther's theology within Germany.

What is clear is that Calvin viewed himself as a Frenchman, with a passionate lifelong concern to see the Protestant cause flourish in his homeland, from which he was exiled for the last three decades of his life. The prefatory letter to King Francis, which he penned in 1535 but retained in all subsequent editions of the *Institutes* as a symbol of his hopes for France, even after the death of Francis, was no mere rhetorical flattery of a hoped-for powerful patron. It was an earnest plea for the King to hear out the true nature of the Protestant confession (of which the *Institutes* was meant to serve as an outline for the King) and to stop listening to its slanderers, who infected the ear of the king against it. In particular, events of 1534 and 1535 had not been favorable to the public perception of Protestantism. A radical Anabaptist sect under the leadership of the fanatic John of Leiden had seized the west German city of Munster and proclaimed the New Jerusalem. Combining the disdain for established civil authorities that other Anabaptists shared with an embrace of violence that many did not, this radical group preached polygamy and other alarming practices before being destroyed by an imperial army in 1535. Catholic leaders were quick to try and paint such rebels and radicals as the natural fruit of Protestantism, and Francis was naturally alarmed. Still, political considerations had led him to seek an alliance with the German Protestant princes, and at the time of Calvin's writing of the *Institutes*, he had real reason to be optimistic that Francis might respond favorably to the book. In any event, it is unclear whether Francis ever read even the preface, and French royal policy was to remain mostly hostile to Protestantism until an official toleration was declared, after much bloodshed, in 1598.

Calvin's theology, as the excerpt here from the first six chapters of the 1559 *Institutes* shows, revolved not around the hidden and inscrutable decree of predestination, as often imagined, but around God's self-revelation. God is so near to us that we cannot scarcely begin to think without being drawn to consider God, and can have no true knowledge of ourselves without considering ourselves in relation to Him. Calvin's theology is informed throughout by what he called the *duplex cognitio Dei*, the twofold knowledge of God—as Creator and as Redeemer. The first, Calvin argued, was made known even to the natural man by virtue of creation itself: "there is no portion of the world, however minute, that does not exhibit at least some sparks of beauty." Calvin discusses at some length how even pagan philosophers attained to some understanding of God and his greatness. However, he emphasizes no less, especially in chapter 4, how readily this knowledge is smothered by sin and turned to superstition and hypocrisy (no doubt having some of the Catholicism of his day in mind, although these opening chapters are free of any direct reference to 16th-century conflicts). Accordingly, we need Scripture to show us how to rightly understand God and His works even as Creator—of God as Redeemer in Christ, the natural man knows nothing, and Calvin does not turn to consider this subject until Book II of the *Institutes*. Book III of the *Institutes* then expounds the inward and hidden means by which we receive the redeeming work of Christ, and Book IV the external and visible aids—the ministry of the church and the support of the godly magistrate. Although Calvin was to massively expand the treatment of the church's ministry in later editions of the *Institutes*, laying more stress on it than Luther ever did, the persistence of the internal/external division of Books III and IV reveals the ongoing influence of Luther's two-kingdoms framework.

INSTITUTES OF THE CHRISTIAN RELIGION

John Calvin

TRANSLATED BY HENRY BEVERIDGE

PREFATORY ADDRESS

TO

HIS MOST CHRISTIAN MAJESTY,

THE MOST MIGHTY AND ILLUSTRIOUS MONARCH,

FRANCIS, KING OF THE FRENCH,

HIS SOVEREIGN;

JOHN CALVIN PRAYS PEACE AND SALVATION IN CHRIST.

Sire,

When I first engaged in this work, nothing was farther from my thoughts than to write what should afterwards be presented to your Majesty. My intention was only to furnish a kind of rudiments, by which those who feel some interest in religion might be trained to true godliness. And I toiled at the task chiefly for the sake of my countrymen the French, multitudes of whom I perceived to be hungering and thirsting after Christ, while very few seemed to have been duly imbued with even a slender knowledge of him. That this was the object which I had in view is apparent from the work itself, which is written in a simple and elementary form adapted for instruction.

But when I perceived that the fury of certain bad men had risen to such a height in your realm, that there was no place in it for sound doctrine, I thought it might be of service if I were in the same work both to give instruction to my countrymen, and also lay before your Majesty a Confession, from which you may learn what the doctrine is that so inflames the rage of those madmen who are this day, with fire and sword, troubling your kingdom. For I fear not to declare, that what I have here given may be regarded as a summary of the very doctrine which, they vociferate, ought to be punished with confiscation, exile, imprisonment, and flames, as well as exterminated by land and sea.

I am aware, indeed, how, in order to render our cause as hateful to your Majesty as possible, they have filled your ears and mind with atrocious insinuations; but you will be pleased, of your clemency, to reflect, that neither in word nor deed could there be any innocence, were it sufficient merely to accuse. When any one, with the view of exciting prejudice, observes that this doctrine, of which I am endeavouring to give your Majesty an account, has been condemned by the suffrages of all the estates, and was long ago stabbed again and again by partial sentences of courts of law, he undoubtedly says nothing more than that it has sometimes been violently oppressed by the power and faction of adversaries, and sometimes fraudulently and insidiously overwhelmed by lies, cavils, and calumny. While a cause is unheard, it is violence to pass sanguinary sentences against it; it is fraud to charge it, contrary to its deserts, with sedition and mischief.

That no one may suppose we are unjust in thus complaining, you yourself, most illustrious Sovereign, can bear us witness with what lying calumnies it is daily traduced in your presence, as aiming at nothing else than to wrest the sceptres of kings out of their hands, to overturn all tribunals and seats of justice, to subvert all order and government, to disturb the peace and quiet of society, to abolish all laws, destroy the distinctions of rank and property, and, in short, turn all things upside down. And yet, that which you hear is but the smallest portion of what is said; for among the common people are disseminated certain horrible insinuations—insinuations which, if well founded, would justify the whole world in condemning the doctrine with its authors to a thousand fires and gibbets. Who can wonder that the popular hatred is inflamed against it, when credit is given to those most iniquitous accusations? See, why all ranks unite with one accord in condemning our persons and our doctrine!

Carried away by this feeling, those who sit in judgment merely give utterance to the prejudices which they have imbibed at home, and think they have duly performed their part if they do not order punishment to be inflicted on any one until convicted, either on his own confession, or on legal evidence. But of what crime convicted? "Of that condemned doctrine," is the answer. But with what justice condemned? The very essence of the defence was, not to abjure the doctrine itself, but to maintain its truth. On this subject, however, not a whisper is allowed!

Justice, then, most invincible Sovereign, entitles me to demand that you will undertake a thorough investigation of this cause, which has hitherto been tossed about in any kind of way, and handled in the most irregular manner, without any order of law, and with passionate heat rather than judicial gravity.

Let it not be imagined that I am here framing my own private defence, with the view of obtaining a safe return to my native land. Though I cherish towards it the feelings which become me as a man, still, as matters now are, I can be absent from it without regret. The cause which I plead is the common cause of all the godly, and therefore the very cause of Christ—a cause which, throughout your realm, now lies, as it were, in despair, torn and trampled upon in all kinds of ways, and that more through the tyranny of certain Pharisees than any sanction from yourself. But it matters not to inquire how the thing is done; the fact that it is done cannot be denied. For so far have the wicked prevailed, that the truth of Christ, if not utterly routed and dispersed, lurks as if it were ignobly buried; while the poor Church, either wasted by cruel slaughter or driven into exile, or intimidated and terror-struck, scarcely ventures to breathe. Still her enemies press on with their wonted rage and fury over the ruins which they have made, strenuously assaulting the wall, which is already giving way. Meanwhile, no man comes forth to offer his protection against such furies. Any who would be thought most favourable to the truth, merely talk of pardoning the error and imprudence of ignorant men. For so those modest personages speak; giving the name of error and imprudence to that which they know to be the infallible truth of God, and of ignorant men to those whose intellect they see that Christ has not despised, seeing he has deigned to intrust them with the mysteries of his heavenly wisdom. Thus all are ashamed of the Gospel.

Your duty, most serene Prince, is, not to shut either your ears or mind against a cause involving such mighty interests as these: how the glory of God is to be maintained on the earth inviolate, how the truth of God is to preserve its dignity, how the kingdom of Christ is to continue amongst us compact and secure. The cause is worthy of your ear, worthy of your investigation, worthy of your throne.

The characteristic of a true sovereign is, to acknowledge that, in the administration of his kingdom, he is a minister of God. He who does not make his reign subservient to the divine glory, acts the part not of a king, but a robber. He, moreover, deceives himself who anticipates long prosperity to any kingdom which is not ruled by the sceptre of God, that is, by his divine word. For the heavenly oracle is infallible which has declared, that "where there is no vision the people perish" (Prov. 29:18).

Let not a contemptuous idea of our insignificance dissuade you from the investigation of this cause. We, indeed, are perfectly conscious how poor and abject we are: in the presence of God we are miserable sinners, and in the sight of men most despised—we are (if you will) the mere dregs and off—scourings of the world, or worse, if worse can be named: so that before God there remains nothing of which we can glory save only his mercy, by which, without any merit of our own, we are admitted to the hope of eternal salvation: and before men not even this much remains, since we can glory only in our infirmity, a thing which, in the estimation of men, it is the greatest ignominy even tacitly to confess. But our doctrine must stand sublime above all the glory of the world, and invincible by all its power, because it is not ours, but that of the living God and his Anointed, whom the Father has appointed King, that he may rule from sea to sea, and from the rivers even to the ends of the earth; and so rule as to smite the whole earth and its strength of iron and brass, its splendour of gold and silver, with the mere rod of his mouth, and break them in pieces like a potter's vessel; according to the magnificent predictions of the prophets respecting his kingdom (Dan. 2:34; Isaiah 11:4; Psalm 2:9).

Our adversaries, indeed, clamorously maintain that our appeal to the word of God is a mere pretext,—that we are, in fact, its worst corrupters. How far this is not only malicious calumny, but also shameless effrontery, you will be able to decide, of your own knowledge, by reading our Confession. Here, however, it may be necessary to make some observations which may dispose, or at least assist, you to read and study it with attention.

When Paul declared that all prophecy ought to be according to the analogy of faith (Rom. 12:6), he laid down the surest rule for determining the meaning of Scripture. Let our doctrine be tested by this rule and our victory is secure. For what accords better and more aptly with faith than to acknowledge ourselves divested of all virtue that we may be clothed by God, devoid of all goodness that we may be filled by Him, the slaves of sin that he may give us freedom, blind that he may enlighten, lame that he may cure, and feeble that he may sustain us; to strip ourselves of all ground of glorying that he alone may shine forth glorious, and we be glorified in him? When these things, and others to the same effect, are said by us, they interpose, and querulously complain, that in this way we overturn some blind light of nature, fancied preparatives, free will, and works meritorious of eternal salvation, with their own supererogations also; because they cannot bear that the entire praise and glory of all goodness, virtue, justice, and wisdom, should remain with God. But we read not of any having been blamed for drinking too much of the fountain of living water; on the contrary, those are severely reprimanded who "have hewed them out cisterns, broken cisterns, that can hold no water" (Jer. 2:13). Again, what more agreeable to faith than to feel assured that God is a propitious Father when Christ is acknowledged as a brother and propitiator, than confidently to expect all prosperity and gladness from Him, whose ineffable love towards us was such that He "spared not his own Son, but delivered him up for us all" (Rom. 8:32), than to rest in the sure hope of salvation and eternal life whenever Christ, in whom such treasures are hid, is conceived to have been given by the Father? Here they attack us, and loudly maintain that this sure confidence is not free from arrogance and presumption. But as nothing is to be presumed of ourselves, so all things are to be presumed of God; nor are we stript of vainglory for any other reason than that we may learn to glory in the Lord. Why go farther? Take but a cursory view, most valiant King, of all the parts of our cause, and count us of all wicked men the most iniquitous, if you do not discover plainly, that "therefore we both labour and suffer reproach because we trust in the living God" (1 Tim. 4:10); because we believe it to be "life eternal" to know "the only true God, and Jesus Christ," whom he has sent (John 17:3). For this hope some of us are in bonds, some beaten with rods, some made a gazing-stock, some proscribed, some most cruelly tortured, some obliged to flee; we are all pressed with straits, loaded with dire execrations, lacerated by slanders, and treated with the greatest indignity.

Look now to our adversaries (I mean the priesthood, at whose beck and pleasure others ply their enmity against us), and consider with me for a little by what zeal they are actuated. The true religion which is delivered in the Scriptures, and which all ought to hold, they readily permit both themselves and others to be ignorant of, to neglect and despise; and they deem it of little moment what each man believes concerning God and Christ, or disbelieves, provided he submits to the judgment of the Church with what they call implicit faith; nor are they greatly concerned though they should see the glow of God dishonoured by open blasphemies, provided not a finger is raised against the primacy of the Apostolic See and the authority of holy mother Church. Why, then, do they war for the mass, purgatory, pilgrimage, and similar follies, with such fierceness and acerbity, that though they cannot prove one of them from the word of God, they deny godliness can be safe without faith in these things—faith drawn out, if I may so express it, to its utmost stretch? Why? just because their belly is their God, and their kitchen their religion; and they believe, that if these were away they would not only not be Christians, but not even men. For although some wallow in luxury, and others feed on slender crusts, still they all live by the same pot, which without that fuel might not only cool, but altogether freeze. He, accordingly, who is most anxious about his stomach, proves the fiercest champion of his faith. In short, the object on which all to a man are bent, is to keep their kingdom safe or their belly filled; not one gives even the smallest sign of sincere zeal.

Nevertheless, they cease not to assail our doctrine, and to accuse and defame it in what terms they may, in order to render it either hated or suspected. They call it new, and of recent birth; they carp at it as doubtful and uncertain; they bid us tell by what miracles it has been confirmed; they ask if it be fair to receive it against the consent of so many holy Fathers and the most ancient custom; they urge us to confess either that it is schismatical in giving battle to the Church, or that the Church must have been without life during the many centuries in which nothing of the kind was heard. Lastly, they say there is little need of argument, for its quality may be known by its fruits, namely, the large number of sects, the many seditious disturbances, and the great licentiousness which it has produced. No doubt, it is a very easy matter for them, in presence of an ignorant and credulous multitude, to insult over an undefended cause; but were an opportunity of mutual discussion afforded, that acrimony which they now pour out upon us in frothy torrents, with as much license as impunity, would assuredly boil dry.

1. First, in calling it new, they are exceedingly injurious to God, whose sacred word deserved not to be charged with novelty. To them, indeed, I very little doubt it is new, as Christ is new, and the Gospel new; but those who are acquainted with the old saying of Paul, that Christ Jesus "died for our sins, and rose again for our justification" (Rom. 4:25), will not detect any novelty in us. That it long lay buried and unknown is the guilty consequence of man's impiety; but now when, by the kindness of God, it is restored to us, it ought to resume its antiquity just as the returning citizen resumes his rights.

2. It is owing to the same ignorance that they hold it to be doubtful and uncertain; for this is the very thing of which the Lord complains by his prophet, "The ox knoweth his owner, and the ass his master's crib; but Israel doth not know, my people doth not consider" (Isaiah 1:3). But however they may sport with its uncertainty, had they to seal their own doctrine with their blood, and at the expense of life, it would be seen what value they put upon it. Very different is our confidence—a confidence which is not appalled by the terrors of death, and therefore not even by the judgment—seat of God.

3. In demanding miracles from us, they act dishonestly; for we have not coined some new gospel, but retain the very one the truth of which is confirmed by all the miracles which Christ and the apostles ever wrought. But they have a peculiarity which we have not—they can confirm their faith by constant miracles down to the present day! Way rather, they allege miracles which might produce wavering in minds otherwise well disposed; they are so frivolous and ridiculous, so vain and false. But were they even exceedingly wonderful, they could have no effect against the truth of God, whose name ought to be hallowed always, and everywhere, whether by miracles, or by the natural course of events. The deception would perhaps be more specious if Scripture did not admonish us of the legitimate end and use of miracles. Mark tells us (Mark 16:20) that the signs which followed the preaching of the apostles were wrought in confirmation of it; so Luke also relates that the Lord "gave testimony to the word of his grace, and granted signs

and wonders to be done" by the hands of the apostles (Acts 14:3). Very much to the same effect are those words of the apostle, that salvation by a preached gospel was confirmed, "The Lord bearing witness with signs and wonders, and with divers miracles" (Heb. 2:4). Those things which we are told are seals of the gospel, shall we pervert to the subversion of the gospel? What was destined only to confirm the truth, shall we misapply to the confirmation of lies? The proper course, therefore, is, in the first instance, to ascertain and examine the doctrine which is said by the Evangelist to precede; then after it has been proved, but not till then, it may receive confirmation from miracles. But the mark of sound doctrine given by our Saviour himself is its tendency to promote the glory not of men, but of God (John 7:18; 8:50). Our Saviour having declared this to be test of doctrine, we are in error if we regard as miraculous, works which are used for any other purpose than to magnify the name of God. And it becomes us to remember that Satan has his miracles, which, although they are tricks rather than true wonders, are still such as to delude the ignorant and unwary. Magicians and enchanters have always been famous for miracles, and miracles of an astonishing description have given support to idolatry: these, however, do not make us converts to the superstitions either of magicians or idolaters. In old times, too, the Donatists used their power of working miracles as a battering-ram, with which they shook the simplicity of the common people. We now give to our opponents the answer which Augustine then gave to the Donatists (in Joan. Tract. 23), "The Lord put us on our guard against those wonder—workers, when he foretold that false prophets would arise, who, by lying signs and divers wonders, would, if it were possible, deceive the very elect" (Mt. 24:24). Paul, too, gave warning that the reign of antichrist would be "withall power, and signs, and lying wonders" (2 Thess. 2:9).

But our opponents tell us that their miracles are wrought not by idols, not by sorcerers, not by false prophets, but by saints: as if we did not know it to be one of Satan's wiles to transform himself "into an angel of light" (2 Cor. 11:14). The Egyptians, in whose neighbourhood Jeremiah was buried, anciently sacrificed and paid other divine honours to him (Hieron. in Praef. Jerem). Did they not abuse of the holy prophet of God? and yet, in recompense for so venerating his tomb, they thought that they were cured of the bite of serpents. What, then, shall we say but that it has been, and always will be, a most just punishment of God, to send on those who do not receive the truth in the love of it, "strong delusion, that they should believe a lie"? (2 Thess. 2:11). We, then, have no lack of miracles, sure miracles, that cannot be gainsaid; but those to which our opponents lay claim are mere delusions of Satan, inasmuch as they draw off the people from the true worship of God to vanity.

4. It is a calumny to represent us as opposed to the Fathers (I mean the ancient writers of a purer age), as if the Fathers were supporters of their impiety. Were the contest to be decided by such authority (to speak in the most moderate terms), the better part of the victory would be ours. While there is much that is admirable and wise in the writings of those Fathers, and while in some things it has fared with them as with ordinary men; these pious sons, forsooth, with the peculiar acuteness of intellect, and judgment, and soul, which belongs to them, adore only their slips and errors, while those things which are well said they either overlook, or disguise, or corrupt; so that it may be truly said their only care has been to gather dross among gold. Then, with dishonest clamour, they assail us as enemies and despisers of the Fathers. So far are we from despising them, that if this were the proper place, it would give us no trouble to support the greater part of the doctrines which we now hold by their suffrages. Still, in studying their writings, we have endeavoured to remember (1 Cor. 3:21–23; see also Augustin. Ep. 28), that all things are ours, to serve, not lord it over us, but that we axe Christ's only, and must obey him in all things without exception. He who does not draw this distinction will not have any fixed principles in religion; for those holy men were ignorant of many things, are often opposed to each other, and are sometimes at variance with themselves.

It is not without cause (remark our opponents) we are thus warned by Solomon, "Remove not the ancient landmarks which thy fathers have set" (Prov. 22:28). But the same rule applies not to the measuring of fields and the obedience of faith. The rule applicable to the latter is, "Forget also thine own people, and thy father's house" (Ps. 45:10). But if they are so fond of allegory, why do they not understand the apostles, rather than any other class of Fathers, to be meant by those whose landmarks it is unlawful to remove? This is the interpretation of Jerome, whose words they have quoted in their canons. But as regards those to whom they apply the passage, if they wish the landmarks to be fixed, why do they, whenever it suits their purpose, so freely overleap them?

Among the Fathers there were two, the one of whom said, "Our God neither eats nor drinks, and therefore has no need of chalices and salvers"; and the other "Sacred rites do not require gold, and things which are not bought with gold, please not by gold." They step beyond the boundary, therefore, when in sacred matters they are so much delighted with gold, driver, ivory, marble, gems, and silks, that unless everything is overlaid with costly show, or rather insane luxury , they think God is not duly worshipped.

It was a Father who said, "He ate flesh freely on the day on which others abstained from it, because he was a Christian." They overleap the boundaries, therefore, when they doom to perdition every soul that, during Lent, shall have tasted flesh.

There were two Fathers, the one of whom said, "A monk not labouring with his own hands is no better than a violent man and a robber"; and the other, "Monks, however assiduous they may be in study, meditation, and prayer, must not live by others." This boundary, too, they transgressed, when they placed lazy gormandising monks in dens and stews, to gorge themselves on other men's substance.

It was a Father who said, "It is a horrid abomination to see in Christian temples a painted image either of Christ or of any saint." Nor was this pronounced by the voice of a single individual; but an Ecclesiastical Council also decreed, "Let nought that is worshipped be depicted on walls." Very far are they from keeping within these boundaries when they leave not a corner without images.

Another Father counselled, "That after performing the office of humanity to the dead in their burial, we should leave them at rest." These limits they burst through when they keep up a perpetual anxiety about the dead.

It is a Father who testifies, "That the substance of bread and wine in the Eucharist does not cease but remains, just as the nature and substance of man remains united to the Godhead in the Lord Jesus Christ." This boundary they pass in pretending that, as soon as the words of our Lord are pronounced, the substance of bread and wine ceases, and is transubstantiated into body and blood.

They were Fathers, who, as they exhibited only one Eucharist to the whole Church, and kept back from it the profane and flagitious; so they, in the severest terms, censured all those who, being present, did not communicate How far have they removed these landmarks, in filling not churches only, but also private houses, with their masses, admitting all and sundry to be present, each the more willingly the more largely he pays, however wicked and impure he may be,—not inviting any one to faith in Christ and faithful communion in the sacraments, but rather vending their own work for the grace and merits of Christ!

There were two Fathers, the one of whom decided that those were to be excluded altogether from partaking of Christ's sacred supper, who, contented with communion in one kind, abstained from the other; while the other Father strongly contends that the blood of the Lord ought not to be denied to the Christian people, who, in confessing him, are enjoined to shed their own blood. These landmarks, also, they removed, when, by an unalterable law, they ordered the very thing which the former Father punished with excommunication, and the latter condemned for a valid reason.

It was a Father who pronounced it rashness, in an obscure question, to decide in either way without clear and evident authority from Scripture. They forgot this landmark when they enacted so many constitutions, so many canons, and so many dogmatical decisions, without sanction from the word of God.

It was a Father who reproved Montanus, among other heresies, for being the first who imposed laws of fasting. They have gone far beyond this landmark also in enjoining fasting under the strictest laws.

It was a Father who denied that the ministers of the Church should be interdicted from marrying, and pronounced married life to be a state of chastity; and there were other Fathers who assented to his decision. These boundaries they overstepped in rigidly binding their priests to celibacy.

It was a Father who thought that Christ only should be listened to, from its being said, "hear him"; and that regard is due not to what others before us have said or done, but only to what Christ, the head of all, has commanded. This landmark they neither observe themselves nor allow to be observed by others, while they subject themselves and others to any master whatever, rather than Christ.

There is a Father who contends that the Church ought not to prefer herself to Christ, who always judges truly, whereas ecclesiastical judges, who are but men, are generally deceived. Having burst through this barrier also, they hesitate not to suspend the whole authority of Scripture on the judgment of the Church.

All the Fathers with one heart execrated, and with one mouth protested against, contaminating the word of God with the subtleties sophists, and involving it in the brawls of dialecticians. Do they keep within these limits when the sole occupation of their lives is to entwine and entangle the simplicity of Scripture with endless disputes, and worse than sophistical jargon? So much so, that were the Fathers to rise from their graves, and listen to the brawling art which bears the name of speculative theology, there is nothing they would suppose it less to be than a discussion of a religious nature.

But my discourse would far exceed its just limits were I to show, in detail, how petulantly those men shake off the yoke of the Fathers, while they wish to be thought their most obedient sons. Months, nay, years would fail me; and yet so deplorable and desperate is their effrontery, that they presume to chastise us for overstepping the ancient landmarks!

5. Then, again, it is to no purpose they call us to the bar of custom. To make everything yield to custom would be to do the

greatest injustice. Were the judgments of mankind correct, custom would be regulated by the good. But it is often far otherwise in point of fact; for, whatever the many are seen to do, forthwith obtains the force of custom. But human affairs have scarcely ever been so happily constituted as that the better course pleased the greater number. Hence the private vices of the multitude have generally resulted in public error, or rather that common consent in vice which these worthy men would have to be law. Any one with eyes may perceive that it is not one flood of evils which has deluged us; that many fatal plagues have invaded the globe; that all things rush headlong; so that either the affairs of men must be altogether despaired of, or we must not only resist, but boldly attack prevailing evils. The cure is prevented by no other cause than the length of time during which we have been accustomed to the disease. But be it so that public error must have a place in human society, still, in the kingdom of God, we must look and listen only to his eternal truth, against which no series of years, no custom, no conspiracy, can plead prescription. Thus Isaiah formerly taught the people of God, "Say ye not, A confederacy, to all to whom this people shall say, A confederacy"; i.e. do not unite with the people in an impious consent; "neither fear ye their fear, nor be afraid. Sanctify the Lord of hosts himself; and let him be your fear, and let him be your dread" (Is. 8:12). Now, therefore, let them, if they will, object to us both past ages and present examples; if we sanctify the Lord of hosts, we shall not be greatly afraid. Though many ages should have consented to like ungodliness, He is strong who taketh vengeance to the third and fourth generation; or the whole world should league together in the same iniquity. He taught experimentally what the end is of those who sin with the multitude, when He destroyed the whole human race with a flood, saving Noah with his little family, who, by putting his faith in Him alone, "condemned the world" (Heb. 11:7). In short, depraved custom is just a kind of general pestilence in which men perish not the less that they fall in a crowd. It were well, moreover, to ponder the observation of Cyprian, that those who sin in ignorance, though they cannot be entirely exculpated, seem, however, to be, in some sense, excusable;

whereas those who obstinately reject the truth, when presented to them by the kindness of God, have no defence to offer.

6. Their dilemma does not push us so violently as to oblige us to confess, either that the Church was a considerable time without life, or that we have now a quarrel with the Church. The Church of Christ assuredly has lived, and will live, as long as Christ shall reign at the right hand of the Father. By his hand it is sustained, by his protection defended, by his mighty power preserved in safety. For what he once undertook he will undoubtedly perform, he will be with his people always, "even to the end of the world" (Mt. 28:20). With the Church we wage no war, since, with one consent, in common with the whole body of the faithful, we worship and adore one God, and Christ Jesus the Lord, as all the pious have always adored him. But they themselves err not a little from the truth in not recognising any church but that which they behold with the bodily eye, and in endeavouring to circumscribe it by limits, within which it cannot be confined.

The hinges on which the controversy turns are these: first, in their contending that the form of the Church is always visible and apparent; and, secondly, in their placing this form in the see of the Church of Rome and its hierarchy. We, on the contrary, maintain, both that the Church may exist without any apparent form, and, moreover, that the form is not ascertained by that external splendour which they foolishly admire, but by a very different mark, namely, by the pure preaching of the word of God, and the due administration of the sacraments. They make an outcry whenever the Church cannot be pointed to with the finger. But how oft was it the fate of the Church among the Jews to be so defaced that no comeliness appeared? What do we suppose to have been the splendid form when Elijah complained that he was left alone? (1 Kings 19:14). How long after the advent of Christ did it lie hid without form? How often since has it been so oppressed by wars, seditions, and heresies, that it was nowhere seen in splendour? Had they lived at that time, would they have believed there was any Church? But Elijah learned that there remained seven thousand men who had not bowed the knee to Baal; nor ought we to doubt that Christ has always reigned on earth ever since he ascended to heaven. Had the faithful at that time required some discernible form, must they not have forthwith given way to despondency? And, indeed, Hilary accounted it a very great fault in his day, that men were so possessed with a foolish admiration of Episcopal dignity as not to perceive the deadly hydra lurking under that mask. His words are (Cont. Auxentium), "One advice I give: Beware of Antichrist; for, unhappily, a love of walls has seized you; unhappily, the Church of God which you venerate exists in houses and buildings; unhappily, under these you find the name of peace. Is it doubtful that in these Antichrist will have his seat? Safer to me are mountains, and woods, and lakes, and dungeons, and whirlpools; since in these prophets, dwelling or immersed, did prophesy."

And what is it at the present day that the world venerates in its horned bishops, unless that it imagines those who are seen presiding over celebrated cities to be holy prelates of religion? Away, then, with this absurd mode of judging! Let us rather reverently admit, that as God alone knows who are his, so he may sometimes withdraw the external manifestation of his Church from the view of men. This, I allow, is a fearful punishment which God sends on the earth; but if the wickedness of men so deserves, why do we strive to oppose the just vengeance of God? It was thus that God, in past ages, punished the ingratitude of men; for after they had refused to obey his truth, and had extinguished his light, he allowed them, when blinded by sense, both to be deluded by lying vanities and plunged in thick darkness, so that no face of a true Church appeared. Meanwhile, however, though his own people were dispersed and concealed amidst errors and darkness, he saved them from destruction. No wonder; for he knew how to preserve them even in the confusion of Babylon and the flame of the fiery furnace.

But as to the wish that the form of the Church should be ascertained by some kind of vain pomp, how perilous it is I will briefly indicate, rather than explain, that I may not exceed all bounds.

What they say is, that the Pontiff, who holds the apostolic see, and the priests who are anointed and consecrated by him, provided they have the insignia of fillets and mitres, represent the Church, and ought to be considered as in the place of the Church, and therefore cannot err. Why so? because they are pastors of the Church, and consecrated to the Lord. And were not Aaron and other prefects of Israel pastors? But Aaron and his sons, though already set apart to the priesthood, erred notwithstanding when they made the calf (Exod. 32:4). Why, according to this view, should not the four hundred prophets who lied to Ahab represent the Church? (1 Kings 22:11, etc.). The Church, however, stood on the side of Micaiah. He was alone, indeed, and despised, but from his mouth the truth proceeded. Did not the prophets also exhibit both the name and face of the Church, when, with one accord, they rose up against Jeremiah, and with menaces boasted of it as a thing impossible that the law should perish from the priest, or counsel from the wise, or the word from the prophet? (Jer. 18:18). In opposition to the whole body of the prophets, Jeremiah is sent alone to declare from the Lord (Jer. 4:9), that a time would come when the law would perish from the priest, counsel from the wise, and the word from the prophet. Was not like splendour displayed in that council when the chief priests, scribes, and Pharisees assembled to consult how they might put Jesus to death? Let them go, then, and cling to the external mask, while they make Christ and all the prophets of God schismatics, and, on the other hand, make Satan's ministers the organs of the Holy Spirit!

But if they are sincere, let them answer me in good faith,—in what place, and among whom, do they think the Church resided, after the Council of Basle degraded and deposed Eugenius from the popedom, and substituted Amadeus in his place? Do their utmost, they cannot deny that that Council was legitimate as far as regards external forms, and was summoned not only by one Pontiff, but by two. Eugenius, with the whole herd of cardinals and bishops who had joined him in plotting the dissolution of the Council, was there condemned of contumacy, rebellion, and schism. Afterwards, however, aided by the favour of princes, he got back his popedom safe. The election of Amadeus, duly made by the authority of a general holy synod, went to smoke; only he himself was appeased with a cardinal's cap, like a piece of offal thrown to a barking dog. Out of the lap of these rebellious and contumacious schismatics proceeded all future popes, cardinals, bishops, abbots, and presbyters. Here they are caught, and cannot escape. For, on which party will they bestow the name of Church? Will they deny it to have been a general Council, though it lacked nothing as regards external majesty, having been solemnly called by two bulls, consecrated by the legate of the Roman See as its president, constituted regularly in all respects, and continuing in possession of all its honours to the last? Will they admit that Eugenius, and his whole train, through whom they have all been consecrated, were schismatical? Let them, then, either define the form of the Church differently, or, however numerous they are, we will hold them all to be schismatics in having knowingly and willingly received ordination from heretics. But had it never been discovered before that the Church is not tied to external pomp, we are furnished with a lengthened proof in their own conduct, in proudly vending themselves to the world under the specious title of Church, notwithstanding that they are the deadly pests of the Church. I speak not of their manners and of those tragical atrocities with which their whole life teems, since it is said that they are Pharisees who should be heard, not imitated. By devoting some portion of your leisure to our writings, you will see, not obscurely, that their doctrine—the very doctrine to which they say it is owing that they are the Church—is a deadly murderer of souls, the firebrand, ruin, and destruction of the Church.

7. Lastly, they are far from candid when they invidiously number up the disturbances, tumults, and disputes, which the preaching of our doctrine has brought in its train, and the fruits which, in many instances, it now produces; for the doctrine itself is undeservedly charged with evils which ought to be ascribed to the malice of Satan. It is one of the characteristics of the divine word, that whenever it appears, Satan ceases to slumber and sleep. This is the surest and most unerring test for distinguishing it from false

doctrines which readily betray themselves, while they are received by all with willing ears, and welcomed by an applauding world. Accordingly, for several ages, during which all things were immersed in profound darkness, almost all mankind were mere jest and sport to the god of this world, who, like any Sardanapalus, idled and luxuriated undisturbed. For what else could he do but laugh and sport while in tranquil and undisputed possession of his kingdom? But when light beaming from above somewhat dissipated the darkness—when the strong man arose and aimed a blow at his kingdom—then, indeed, he began to shake off his wonted torpor, and rush to arms. And first he stirred up the hands of men, that by them he might violently suppress the dawning truth; but when this availed him not, he turned to snares, exciting dissensions and disputes about doctrine by means of his Catabaptists, and other portentous miscreants, that he might thus obscure, and, at length, extinguish the truth. And now he persists in assailing it with both engines, endeavouring to pluck up the true seed by the violent hand of man, and striving, as much as in him lies, to choke it with his tares, that it may not grow and bear knit. But it will be in vain, if we listen to the admonition of the Lord, who long ago disclosed his wiles, that we might not be taken unawares, and armed us with full protection against all his machinations. But how malignant to throw upon the word of God itself the blame either of the seditions which wicked men and rebels, or of the sects which impostors stir up against it! The example, however, is not new. Elijah was interrogated whether it were not he that troubled Israel. Christ was seditious, according to the Jews; and the apostles were charged with the crime of popular commotion. What else do those who, in the present day, impute to us all the disturbances, tumults, and contentions which break out against us? Elijah, however, has taught us our answer (1 Kings 18:17, 18). It is not we who disseminate errors or stir up tumults, but they who resist the mighty power of God.

But while this single answer is sufficient to rebut the rash charges of these men, it is necessary, on the other hand, to consult for the weakness of those who take the alarm at such scandals, and not unfrequently waver in perplexity. But that they may not fall away in this perplexity, and forfeit their good degree, let them know that the apostles in their day experienced the very things which now befall us. There were then unlearned and unstable men who, as Peter tells us (2 Pet. 3:16), wrested the inspired writings of Paul to their own destruction. There were despisers of God, who, when they heard that sin abounded in order that grace might more abound, immediately inferred, "We will continue in sin that grace may abound" (Rom. 6:1); when they heard that believers were not under the law, but under grace, forthwith sung out, "We will sin because we are not under the law, but under grace" (Rom. 6:15). There were some who charged the apostle with being the minister of sin. Many false prophets entered in privily to pull down the churches which he had reared. Some preached the gospel through envy and strife, not sincerely (Phil. 1:15)—maliciously even—thinking to add affliction to his bonds. Elsewhere the gospel made little progress. All sought their own, not the things which were Jesus Christ's. Others went back like the dog to his vomit, or the sow that was washed to her wallowing in the mire. Great numbers perverted their spiritual freedom to carnal licentiousness. False brethren crept in to the imminent danger of the faithful. Among the brethren themselves various quarrels arose. What, then, were the apostles to do? Were they either to dissemble for the time, or rather lay aside and abandon that gospel which they saw to be the seed-bed of so many strifes, the source of so many perils, the occasion of so many scandals? In straits of this kind, they remembered that "Christ was a stone of stumbling, and a rock of offence," "set up for the fall and rising again of many," and "for a sign to be spoken against" (Luke 2:34); and, armed with this assurance, they proceeded boldly through all perils from tumults and scandals. It becomes us to be supported by the same consideration, since Paul declares that it is a neverfailing characteristic of the gospel to be a "savour of death unto death in them that perish" (2 Cor. 2:16), although rather destined to us for the purpose of being a savour of life unto life, and the power of God for the salvation of believers. This we should certainly experience it to be, did we not by our ingratitude corrupt this unspeakable gift of God, and turn to our destruction what ought to be our only saving defence.

But to return, Sire. Be not moved by the absurd insinuations with which our adversaries are striving to frighten you into the belief that nothing else is wished and aimed at by this new gospel (for so they term it), than opportunity for sedition and impunity for all kinds of vice. Our God is not the author of division, but of peace; and the Son of God, who came to destroy the works of the devil, is not the minister of sin. We, too, are undeservedly charged with desires of a kind for which we have never given even the smallest suspicion. We, forsooth, meditate the subversion of kingdoms; we, whose voice was never heard in faction, and whose life, while passed under you, is known to have been always quiet and simple; even now, when exiled from our home, we nevertheless cease not to pray for all prosperity to your person and your kingdom. We, forsooth, are aiming after an unchecked indulgence in vice, in whose manners, though there is much to be blamed, there is nothing which deserves such an imputation; nor (thank God) have we profited so little in the gospel that our life may not be to these slanderers an example of chastity, kindness, pity, temperance, patience, moderation, or any other virtue. It is plain, indeed, that we fear God sincerely, and worship him in truth, since, whether by life or by death, we desire his name to be hallowed; and hatred herself has been forced to bear testimony to the innocence and civil integrity of some of our people on whom death was inflicted for the very thing which deserved the highest praise. But if any, under pretext of the gospel, excite tumults (none such have as yet been detected in your realm), if any use the liberty of the grace of God as a cloak for licentiousness (I know of numbers who do), there are laws and legal punishments by which they may be punished up to the measure of their deserts—only, in the mean time, let not the gospel of God be evil spoken of because of the iniquities of evil men.

Sire, That you may not lend too credulous an ear to the accusations of our enemies, their virulent injustice has been set before you at sufficient length; I fear even more than sufficient, since this preface has grown almost to the bulk of a full apology. My object, however, was not to frame a defence, but only with a view to the hearing of our cause, to mollify your mind, now indeed turned away and estranged from us—I add, even inflamed against us—but whose good will, we are confident, we should regain, would you but once, with calmness and composure, read this our Confession, which we desire your Majesty to accept instead of a defence. But if the whispers of the malevolent so possess your ear, that the accused are to have no opportunity of pleading their cause; if those vindictive furies, with your connivance, are always to rage with bonds, scourgings, tortures, maimings, and burnings, we, indeed, like sheep doomed to slaughter, shall be reduced to every extremity; yet so that, in our patience, we will possess our souls, and wait for the strong hand of the Lord, which, doubtless, will appear in its own time, and show itself armed, both to rescue the poor from affliction, and also take vengeance on the despisers, who are now exulting so securely.

Most illustrious King, may the Lord, the King of kings, establish your throne in righteousness, and your sceptre in equity.

Basle, 1st August 1536.

BOOK I

Chapter 1. The Knowledge of God and of Ourselves Mutually Connected. Nature of the Connection.

1. Our wisdom, in so far as it ought to be deemed true and solid Wisdom, consists almost entirely of two parts: the knowledge of God and of ourselves. But as these are connected together by many ties, it is not easy to determine which of the two precedes and gives birth to the other. For, in the first place, no man can survey himself without forthwith turning his thoughts towards the God in whom he lives and moves; because it is perfectly obvious, that the endowments which we possess cannot possibly be from ourselves; nay, that our very being is nothing else than subsistence in God alone. In the second place, those blessings which

unceasingly distil to us from heaven, are like streams conducting us to the fountain. Here, again, the infinitude of good which resides in God becomes more apparent from our poverty. In particular, the miserable ruin into which the revolt of the first man has plunged us, compels us to turn our eyes upwards; not only that while hungry and famishing we may thence ask what we want, but being aroused by fear may learn humility. For as there exists in man something like a world of misery, and ever since we were stript of the divine attire our naked shame discloses an immense series of disgraceful properties every man, being stung by the consciousness of his own unhappiness, in this way necessarily obtains at least some knowledge of God. Thus, our feeling of ignorance, vanity, want, weakness, in short, depravity and corruption, reminds us (see Calvin on John 4:10), that in the Lord, and none but He, dwell the true light of wisdom, solid virtue, exuberant goodness. We are accordingly urged by our own evil things to consider the good things of God; and, indeed, we cannot aspire to Him in earnest until we have begun to be displeased with ourselves. For what man is not disposed to rest in himself? Who, in fact, does not thus rest, so long as he is unknown to himself; that is, so long as he is contented with his own endowments, and unconscious or unmindful of his misery? Every person, therefore, on coming to the knowledge of himself, is not only urged to seek God, but is also led as by the hand to find him.

2. On the other hand, it is evident that man never attains to a true self-knowledge until he has previously contemplated the face of God, and come down after such contemplation to look into himself. For (such is our innate pride) we always seem to ourselves just, and upright, and wise, and holy, until we are convinced, by clear evidence, of our injustice, vileness, folly, and impurity. Convinced, however, we are not, if we look to ourselves only, and not to the Lord also —He being the only standard by the application of which this conviction can be produced. For, since we are all naturally prone to hypocrisy, any empty semblance of righteousness is quite enough to satisfy us instead of righteousness itself. And since nothing appears within us or around us that is not tainted

with very great impurity, so long as we keep our mind within the confines of human pollution, anything which is in some small degree less defiled delights us as if it were most pure just as an eye, to which nothing but black had been previously presented, deems an object of a whitish, or even of a brownish hue, to be perfectly white. Nay, the bodily sense may furnish a still stronger illustration of the extent to which we are deluded in estimating the powers of the mind. If, at mid-day, we either look down to the ground, or on the surrounding objects which lie open to our view, we think ourselves endued with a very strong and piercing eyesight; but when we look up to the sun, and gaze at it unveiled, the sight which did excellently well for the earth is instantly so dazzled and confounded by the refulgence, as to oblige us to confess that our acuteness in discerning terrestrial objects is mere dimness when applied to the sun. Thus too, it happens in estimating our spiritual qualities. So long as we do not look beyond the earth, we are quite pleased with our own righteousness, wisdom, and virtue; we address ourselves in the most flattering terms, and seem only less than demigods. But should we once begin to raise our thoughts to God, and reflect what kind of Being he is, and how absolute the perfection of that righteousness, and wisdom, and virtue, to which, as a standard, we are bound to be conformed, what formerly delighted us by its false show of righteousness will become polluted with the greatest iniquity; what strangely imposed upon us under the name of wisdom will disgust by its extreme folly; and what presented the appearance of virtuous energy will be condemned as the most miserable impotence. So far are those qualities in us, which seem most perfect, from corresponding to the divine purity.

3. Hence that dread and amazement with which as Scripture uniformly relates, holy men were struck and overwhelmed whenever they beheld the presence of God. When we see those who previously stood firm and secure so quaking with terror, that the fear of death takes hold of them, nay, they are, in a manner, swallowed up and annihilated, the inference to be drawn is that men are never duly touched and impressed with a conviction of their

insignificance, until they have contrasted themselves with the majesty of God. Frequent examples of this consternation occur both in the Book of Judges and the Prophetical Writings; so much so, that it was a common expression among the people of God, "We shall die, for we have seen the Lord." Hence the Book of Job, also, in humbling men under a conviction of their folly, feebleness, and pollution, always derives its chief argument from descriptions of the Divine wisdom, virtue, and purity. Nor without cause: for we see Abraham the readier to acknowledge himself but dust and ashes the nearer he approaches to behold the glory of the Lord, and Elijah unable to wait with unveiled face for His approach; so dreadful is the sight. And what can man do, man who is but rottenness and a worm, when even the Cherubim themselves must veil their faces in very terror? To this, undoubtedly, the Prophet Isaiah refers, when he says (Isaiah 24:23), "The moon shall be confounded, and the sun ashamed, when the Lord of Hosts shall reign"; i.e., when he shall exhibit his refulgence, and give a nearer view of it, the brightest objects will, in comparison, be covered with darkness.

But though the knowledge of God and the knowledge of ourselves are bound together by a mutual tie, due arrangement requires that we treat of the former in the first place, and then descend to the latter.

Chapter 2. What It Is to Know God. Tendency of This Knowledge.

1. By the knowledge of God, I understand that by which we not only conceive that there is some God, but also apprehend what it is for our interest, and conducive to his glory, what, in short, it is befitting to know concerning him. For, properly speaking, we cannot say that God is known where there is no religion or piety. I am not now referring to that species of knowledge by which men, in themselves lost and under curse, apprehend God as a Redeemer in Christ the Mediator. I speak only of that simple and primitive knowledge, to which the mere course of nature would have conducted us, had Adam stood upright. For although no man will now, in the present ruin of the human race, perceive

God to be either a father, or the author of salvation, or propitious in any respect, until Christ interpose to make our peace; still it is one thing to perceive that God our Maker supports us by his power, rules us by his providence, fosters us by his goodness, and visits us with all kinds of blessings, and another thing to embrace the grace of reconciliation offered to us in Christ. Since, then, the Lord first appears, as well in the creation of the world as in the general doctrine of Scripture, simply as a Creator, and afterwards as a Redeemer in Christ—a twofold knowledge of him hence arises: of these the former is now to be considered, the latter will afterwards follow in its order. But although our mind cannot conceive of God, without rendering some worship to him, it will not, however, be sufficient simply to hold that he is the only being whom all ought to worship and adore, unless we are also persuaded that he is the fountain of all goodness, and that we must seek everything in him, and in none but him. My meaning is: we must be persuaded not only that as he once formed the world, so he sustains it by his boundless power, governs it by his wisdom, preserves it by his goodness, in particular, rules the human race with justice and judgment, bears with them in mercy, shields them by his protection; but also that not a particle of light, or wisdom, or justice, or power, or rectitude, or genuine truth, will anywhere be found, which does not flow from him, and of which he is not the cause; in this way we must learn to expect and ask all things from him, and thankfully ascribe to him whatever we receive. For this sense of the divine perfections is the proper master to teach us piety, out of which religion springs. By piety I mean that union of reverence and love to God which the knowledge of his benefits inspires. For, until men feel that they owe everything to God, that they are cherished by his paternal care, and that he is the author of all their blessings, so that nought is to be looked for away from him, they will never submit to him in voluntary obedience; nay, unless they place their entire happiness in him, they will never yield up their whole selves to him in truth and sincerity.

2. Those, therefore, who, in considering this question, propose to inquire what the essence of God is, only delude us with frigid

speculations—it being much more our interest to know what kind of being God is, and what things are agreeable to his nature. For, of what use is it to join Epicures in acknowledging some God who has cast off the care of the world, and only delights himself in ease? What avails it, in short, to know a God with whom we have nothing to do? The effect of our knowledge rather ought to be, first, to teach us reverence and fear; and, secondly, to induce us, under its guidance and teaching, to ask every good thing from him, and, when it is received, ascribe it to him. For how can the idea of God enter your mind without instantly giving rise to the thought, that since you are his workmanship, you are bound, by the very law of creation, to submit to his authority?—that your life is due to him?—that whatever you do ought to have reference to him? If so, it undoubtedly follows that your life is sadly corrupted, if it is not framed in obedience to him, since his will ought to be the law of our lives. On the other hand, your idea of his nature is not clear unless you acknowledge him to be the origin and fountain of all goodness. Hence would arise both confidence in him, and a desire of cleaving to him, did not the depravity of the human mind lead it away from the proper course of investigation.

For, first of all, the pious mind does not devise for itself any kind of God, but looks alone to the one true God; nor does it feign for him any character it pleases, but is contented to have him in the character in which he manifests himself always guarding, with the utmost diligences against transgressing his will, and wandering, with daring presumptions from the right path. He by whom God is thus known perceiving how he governs all things, confides in him as his guardian and protector, and casts himself entirely upon his faithfulness,—perceiving him to be the source of every blessing, if he is in any strait or feels any want, he instantly recurs to his protection and trusts to his aid,—persuaded that he is good and merciful, he reclines upon him with sure confidence, and doubts not that, in the divine clemency, a remedy will be provided for his every time of need,—acknowledging him as his Father and his Lord he considers himself bound to have respect to his authority in all things, to reverence his majesty, aim at the advancement of his glory, and obey his commands,—regarding him as a just judge, armed with severity to punish crimes, he keeps the judgment-seat always in his view. Standing in awe of it, he curbs himself, and fears to provoke his anger. Nevertheless, he is not so terrified by an apprehension of judgment as to wish he could withdraw himself, even if the means of escape lay before him; nay, he embraces him not less as the avenger of wickedness than as the rewarder of the righteous; because he perceives that it equally appertains to his glory to store up punishment for the one, and eternal life for the other. Besides, it is not the mere fear of punishment that restrains him from sin. Loving and revering God as his father, honouring and obeying him as his master, although there were no hell, he would revolt at the very idea of offending him.

Such is pure and genuine religion, namely, confidence in God coupled with serious fear—fear, which both includes in it willing reverence, and brings along with it such legitimate worship as is prescribed by the law. And it ought to be more carefully considered that all men promiscuously do homage to God, but very few truly reverence him. On all hands there is abundance of ostentatious ceremonies, but sincerity of heart is rare.

Chapter 3. The Knowledge of God Naturally Implanted in the Human Mind.

1. That there exists in the human minds and indeed by natural instinct, some sense of Deity, we hold to be beyond dispute, since God himself, to prevent any man from pretending ignorance, has endued all men with some idea of his Godhead, the memory of which he constantly renews and occasionally enlarges, that all to a man being aware that there is a God, and that he is their Maker, may be condemned by their own conscience when they neither worship him nor consecrate their lives to his service. Certainly, if there is any quarter where it may be supposed that God is unknown, the most likely for such an instance to exist is among the dullest tribes farthest removed from civilisation. But, as a heathen tells us, there is no nation so barbarous, no race so brutish, as not to be imbued with the conviction that there is a God. Even those

who, in other respects, seem to differ least from the lower animals, constantly retain some sense of religion; so thoroughly has this common conviction possessed the mind, so firmly is it stamped on the breasts of all men. Since, then, there never has been, from the very first, any quarter of the globe, any city, any household even, without religion, this amounts to a tacit confession, that a sense of Deity is inscribed on every heart. Nay, even idolatry is ample evidence of this fact. For we know how reluctant man is to lower himself, in order to set other creatures above him. Therefore, when he chooses to worship wood and stone rather than be thought to have no God, it is evident how very strong this impression of a Deity must be; since it is more difficult to obliterate it from the mind of man, than to break down the feelings of his nature,—these certainly being broken down, when, in opposition to his natural haughtiness, he spontaneously humbles himself before the meanest object as an act of reverence to God.

2. It is most absurd, therefore, to maintain, as some do, that religion was devised by the cunning and craft of a few individuals, as a means of keeping the body of the people in due subjection, while there was nothing which those very individuals, while teaching others to worship God, less believed than the existence of a God. I readily acknowledge, that designing men have introduced a vast number of fictions into religion, with the view of inspiring the populace with reverence or striking them with terror, and thereby rendering them more obsequious; but they never could have succeeded in this, had the minds of men not been previously imbued with that uniform belief in God, from which, as from its seed, the religious propensity springs. And it is altogether incredible that those who, in the matter of religion, cunningly imposed on their ruder neighbours, were altogether devoid of a knowledge of God. For though in old times there were some, and in the present day not a few are found who deny the being of a God, yet, whether they will or not, they occasionally feel the truth which they are desirous not to know. We do not read of any man who broke out into more unbridled and audacious contempt of the Deity than C. Caligula, and yet none showed greater dread when any indication

of divine wrath was manifested. Thus, however unwilling, he shook with terror before the God whom he professedly studied to condemn. You may every day see the same thing happening to his modern imitators. The most audacious despiser of God is most easily disturbed, trembling at the sound of a falling leaf. How so, unless in vindication of the divine majesty, which smites their consciences the more strongly the more they endeavour to flee from it. They all, indeed, look out for hiding-places where they may conceal themselves from the presence of the Lord, and again efface it from their mind; but after all their efforts they remain caught within the net. Though the conviction may occasionally seem to vanish for a moment, it immediately returns, and rushes in with new impetuosity, so that any interval of relief from the gnawing of conscience is not unlike the slumber of the intoxicated or the insane, who have no quiet rest in sleep, but are continually haunted with dire horrific dreams. Even the wicked themselves, therefore, are an example of the fact that some idea of God always exists in every human mind.

3. All men of sound judgment will therefore hold, that a sense of Deity is indelibly engraven on the human heart. And that this belief is naturally engendered in all, and thoroughly fixed as it were in our very bones, is strikingly attested by the contumacy of the wicked, who, though they struggle furiously, are unable to extricate themselves from the fear of God. Though Diagoras, and others of like stamps make themselves merry with whatever has been believed in all ages concerning religion, and Dionysus scoffs at the judgment of heaven, it is but a Sardonian grin; for the worm of conscience, keener than burning steel, is gnawing them within. I do not say with Cicero, that errors wear out by age, and that religion increases and grows better day by day. For the world (as will be shortly seen) labours as much as it can to shake off all knowledge of God, and corrupts his worship in innumerable ways. I only say, that, when the stupid hardness of heart, which the wicked eagerly court as a means of despising God, becomes enfeebled, the sense of Deity, which of all things they wished most to be extinguished, is still in vigour, and now and then breaks forth. Whence

we infer, that this is not a doctrine which is first learned at school, but one as to which every man is, from the womb, his own master; one which nature herself allows no individual to forget, though many, with all their might, strive to do so. Moreover, if all are born and live for the express purpose of learning to know God, and if the knowledge of God, in so far as it fails to produce this effect, is fleeting and vain, it is clear that all those who do not direct the whole thoughts and actions of their lives to this end fail to fulfill the law of their being. This did not escape the observation even of philosophers. For it is the very thing which Plato meant (in *Phaedo* and *Theactetus*) when he taught, as he often does, that the chief good of the soul consists in resemblance to God; i.e., when, by means of knowing him, she is wholly transformed into him. Thus Gryllus, also, in Plutarch (lib. *Bruta animalia ratione uti*), reasons most skilfully, when he affirms that, if once religion is banished from the lives of men, they not only in no respect excel, but are, in many respects, much more wretched than the brutes, since, being exposed to so many forms of evil, they continually drag on a troubled and restless existence: that the only thing, therefore, which makes them superior is the worship of God, through which alone they aspire to immortality.

Chapter 4. The Knowledge of God Stifled or Corrupted, Ignorantly or Maliciously.

1. But though experience testifies that a seed of religion is divinely sown in all, scarcely one in a hundred is found who cherishes it in his heart, and not one in whom it grows to maturity so far is it from yielding fruit in its season. Moreover, while some lose themselves in superstitious observances, and others, of set purpose, wickedly revolt from God, the result is that, in regard to the true knowledge of him, all are so degenerate, that in no part of the world can genuine godliness be found. In saying that some fall away into superstition, I mean not to insinuate that their excessive absurdity frees them from guilt; for the blindness under which they labour is almost invariably accompanied with vain pride and stubbornness. Mingled vanity and pride appear in this, that when

miserable men do seek after God, instead of ascending higher than themselves as they ought to do, they measure him by their own carnal stupidity, and, neglecting solid inquiry, fly off to indulge their curiosity in vain speculation. Hence, they do not conceive of him in the character in which he is manifested, but imagine him to be whatever their own rashness has devised. This abyss standing open, they cannot move one footstep without rushing headlong to destruction. With such an idea of God, nothing which they may attempt to offer in the way of worship or obedience can have any value in his sight, because it is not him they worship, but, instead of him, the dream and figment of their own heart. This corrupt procedure is admirably described by Paul, when he says, that "thinking to be wise, they became fools" (Rom. 1:22). He had previously said that "they became vain in their imaginations," but lest any should suppose them blameless, he afterwards adds that they were deservedly blinded, because, not contented with sober inquiry, because, arrogating to themselves more than they have any title to do, they of their own accord court darkness, nay, bewitch themselves with perverse, empty show. Hence it is that their folly, the result not only of vain curiosity, but of licentious desire and overweening confidence in the pursuit of forbidden knowledge, cannot be excused.

2. The expression of David (Psalm 14:1, 53:1), "The fool hath said in his heart, There is no God," is primarily applied to those who, as will shortly farther appear, stifle the light of nature, and intentionally stupefy themselves. We see many, after they have become hardened in a daring course of sin, madly banishing all remembrance of God, though spontaneously suggested to them from within, by natural sense. To show how detestable this madness is, the Psalmist introduces them as distinctly denying that there is a God, because although they do not disown his essence, they rob him of his justice and providence, and represent him as sitting idly in heaven. Nothing being less accordant with the nature of God than to cast off the government of the world, leaving it to chance, and so to wink at the crimes of men that they may wanton with impunity in evil courses; it follows, that every man who

indulges in security, after extinguishing all fear of divine Judgment, virtually denies that there is a God. As a just punishment of the wicked, after they have closed their own eyes, God makes their hearts dull and heavy, and hence, seeing, they see not. David, indeed, is the best interpreter of his own meaning, when he says elsewhere, the wicked has "no fear of God before his eyes," (Psalm 36:1); and, again, "He has said in his heart, God has forgotten; he hideth his face; he will never see it." Thus although they are forced to acknowledge that there is some God, they, however, rob him of his glory by denying his power. For, as Paul declares, "If we believe not, he abideth faithful, he cannot deny himself," (2 Tim. 2:13); so those who feign to themselves a dead and dumb idol, are truly said to deny God. It is, moreover, to be observed, that though they struggle with their own convictions, and would fain not only banish God from their minds, but from heaven also, their stupefaction is never so complete as to secure them from being occasionally dragged before the divine tribunal. Still, as no fear restrains them from rushing violently in the face of God, so long as they are hurried on by that blind impulse, it cannot be denied that their prevailing state of mind in regard to him is brutish oblivion.

3. In this way, the vain pretext which many employ to clothe their superstition is overthrown. They deem it enough that they have some kind of zeal for religion, how preposterous soever it may be, not observing that true religion must be conformable to the will of God as its unerring standard; that he can never deny himself, and is no spectra or phantom, to be metamorphosed at each individual's caprice. It is easy to see how superstition, with its false glosses, mocks God, while it tries to please him. Usually fastening merely on things on which he has declared he sets no value, it either contemptuously overlooks, or even undisguisedly rejects, the things which he expressly enjoins, or in which we are assured that he takes pleasure. Those, therefore, who set up a fictitious worship, merely worship and adore their own delirious fancies; indeed, they would never dare so to trifle with God, had they not previously fashioned him after their own childish conceits. Hence that vague and wandering opinion of Deity is

declared by an apostle to be ignorance of God: "Howbeit, then, when ye knew not God, ye did service unto them which by nature are no gods." And he elsewhere declares, that the Ephesians were "without God" (Eph. 2:12) at the time when they wandered without any correct knowledge of him. It makes little difference, at least in this respect, whether you hold the existence of one God, or a plurality of gods, since, in both cases alike, by departing from the true God, you have nothing left but an execrable idol. It remains, therefore, to conclude with Lactantius (Instit. Div. lib 1:2, 6), "No religion is genuine that is not in accordance with truth."

4. To this fault they add a second—viz. that when they do think of God it is against their will; never approaching him without being dragged into his presence, and when there, instead of the voluntary fear flowing from reverence of the divine majesty, feeling only that forced and servile fear which divine judgment extorts judgment which, from the impossibility of escape, they are compelled to dread, but which, while they dread, they at the same time also hate. To impiety, and to it alone, the saying of Statius properly applies: "Fear first brought gods into the world," (Theb. lib. 1). Those whose inclinations are at variance with the justice of God, knowing that his tribunal has been erected for the punishment of transgression, earnestly wish that that tribunal were overthrown. Under the influence of this feeling they are actually warring against God, justice being one of his essential attributes. Perceiving that they are always within reach of his power, that resistance and evasion are alike impossible, they fear and tremble. Accordingly, to avoid the appearance of condemning a majesty by which all are overawed, they have recourse to some species of religious observance, never ceasing meanwhile to defile themselves with every kind of vice, and add crime to crime, until they have broken the holy law of the Lord in every one of its requirements, and set his whole righteousness at nought; at all events, they are not so restrained by their semblance of fear as not to luxuriate and take pleasure in iniquity, choosing rather to indulge their carnal propensities than to curb them with the bridle of the Holy Spirit. But since this shadow of religion (it scarcely even deserves to be

called a shadow) is false and vain, it is easy to infer how much this confused knowledge of God differs from that piety which is instilled into the breasts of believers, and from which alone true religion springs. And yet hypocrites would fain, by means of tortuous windings, make a show of being near to God at the very time they are fleeing from him. For while the whole life ought to be one perpetual course of obedience, they rebel without fear in almost all their actions, and seek to appease him with a few paltry sacrifices; while they ought to serve him with integrity of heart and holiness of life, they endeavour to procure his favour by means of frivolous devices and punctilios of no value. Nay, they take greater license in their grovelling indulgences, because they imagine that they can fulfill their duty to him by preposterous expiations; in short, while their confidence ought to have been fixed upon him, they put him aside, and rest in themselves or the creatures. At length they bewilder themselves in such a maze of error, that the darkness of ignorance obscures, and ultimately extinguishes, those sparks which were designed to show them the glory of God. Still, however, the conviction that there is some Deity continues to exist, like a plant which can never be completely eradicated, though so corrupt, that it is only capable of producing the worst of fruit. Nay, we have still stronger evidence of the proposition for which I now contend—viz. that a sense of Deity is naturally engraven on the human heart, in the fact, that the very reprobate are forced to acknowledge it. When at their ease, they can jest about God, and talk pertly and loquaciously in disparagement of his power; but should despair, from any cause, overtake them, it will stimulate them to seek him, and dictate ejaculatory prayers, proving that they were not entirely ignorant of God, but had perversely suppressed feelings which ought to have been earlier manifested.

Chapter 5. The Knowledge of God Conspicuous in the Creation, and Continual Government of the World.

1. Since the perfection of blessedness consists in the knowledge of God, he has been pleased, in order that none might be excluded from the means of obtaining felicity, not only to deposit in our

minds that seed of religion of which we have already spoken, but so to manifest his perfections in the whole structure of the universe, and daily place himself in our view, that we cannot open our eyes without being compelled to behold him. His essence, indeed, is incomprehensible, utterly transcending all human thought; but on each of his works his glory is engraven in characters so bright, so distinct, and so illustrious, that none, however dull and illiterate, can plead ignorance as their excuse. Hence, with perfect truth, the Psalmist exclaims, "He covereth himself with light as with a garment," (Psalm 104:2); as if he had said, that God for the first time was arrayed in visible attire when, in the creation of the world, he displayed those glorious banners, on which, to whatever side we turn, we behold his perfections visibly portrayed. In the same place, the Psalmist aptly compares the expanded heavens to his royal tent, and says, "He layeth the beams of his chambers in the waters, maketh the clouds his chariot, and walketh upon the wings of the wind," sending forth the winds and lightnings as his swift messengers. And because the glory of his power and wisdom is more refulgent in the firmament, it is frequently designated as his palace. And, first, wherever you turn your eyes, there is no portion of the world, however minute, that does not exhibit at least some sparks of beauty; while it is impossible to contemplate the vast and beautiful fabric as it extends around, without being overwhelmed by the immense weight of glory. Hence, the author of the Epistle to the Hebrews elegantly describes the visible worlds as images of the invisible (Heb. 11:3), the elegant structure of the world serving us as a kind of mirror, in which we may behold God, though otherwise invisible. For the same reason, the Psalmist attributes language to celestial objects, a language which all nations understand (Psalm 19:1), the manifestation of the Godhead being too clear to escape the notice of any people, however obtuse. The apostle Paul, stating this still more clearly, says, "That which may be known of God is manifest in them, for God has showed it unto them. For the invisible things of him from the creation of the world are clearly seen, being understood by the things that are made, even his eternal power and Godhead," (Rom. 1:20).

2. In attestation of his wondrous wisdom, both the heavens and the earth present us with innumerable proofs not only those more recondite proofs which astronomy, medicine, and all the natural sciences, are designed to illustrate, but proofs which force themselves on the notice of the most illiterate peasant, who cannot open his eyes without beholding them. It is true, indeed, that those who are more or less intimately acquainted with those liberal studies are thereby assisted and enabled to obtain a deeper insight into the secret workings of divine wisdom. No man, however, though he be ignorant of these, is incapacitated for discerning such proofs of creative wisdom as may well cause him to break forth in admiration of the Creator. To investigate the motions of the heavenly bodies, to determine their positions, measure their distances, and ascertain their properties, demands skill, and a more careful examination; and where these are so employed, as the providence of God is thereby more fully unfolded, so it is reasonable to suppose that the mind takes a loftier flight, and obtains brighter views of his glory. Still, none who have the use of their eyes can be ignorant of the divine skill manifested so conspicuously in the endless variety, yet distinct and well ordered array, of the heavenly host; and, therefore, it is plain that the Lord has furnished every man with abundant proofs of his wisdom. The same is true in regard to the structure of the human frame. To determine the connection of its parts, its symmetry and beauty, with the skill of a Galen (lib. *De Usu Partium*), requires singular acuteness; and yet all men acknowledge that the human body bears on its face such proofs of ingenious contrivance as are sufficient to proclaim the admirable wisdom of its Maker.

3. Hence certain of the philosophers have not improperly called man a microcosm (miniature world), as being a rare specimen of divine power, wisdom, and goodness, and containing within himself wonders sufficient to occupy our minds, if we are willing so to employ them. Paul, accordingly, after reminding the Athenians that they "might feel after God and find him," immediately adds, that "he is not far from every one of us," (Acts 17:27); every man having within himself undoubted evidence of the heavenly grace

by which he lives, and moves, and has his being. But if, in order to apprehend God, it is unnecessary to go farther than ourselves, what excuse can there be for the sloth of any man who will not take the trouble of descending into himself that he may find Him? For the same reason, too, David, after briefly celebrating the wonderful name and glory of God, as everywhere displayed, immediately exclaims, "What is man, that thou art mindful of him?" and again, "Out of the mouths of babes and sucklings thou hast ordained strength," (Psalm 8:2, 4). Thus he declares not only that the human race are a bright mirror of the Creator's works, but that infants hanging on their mothers' breasts have tongues eloquent enough to proclaim his glory without the aid of other orators. Accordingly, he hesitates not to bring them forward as fully instructed to refute the madness of those who, from devilish pride, would fain extinguish the name of God. Hence, too, the passage which Paul quotes from Aratus, "We are his offspring," (Acts 17:28), the excellent gifts with which he has endued us attesting that he is our Father. In the same way also, from natural instinct, and, as it were, at the dictation of experience, heathen poets call him the father of men. No one, indeed, will voluntarily and willingly devote himself to the service of God unless he has previously tasted his paternal love, and been thereby allured to love and reverence Him.

4. But herein appears the shameful ingratitude of men. Though they have in their own persons a factory where innumerable operations of God are carried on, and a magazine stored with treasures of inestimable value—instead of bursting forth in his praise, as they are bound to do, they, on the contrary, are the more inflated and swelled with pride. They feel how wonderfully God is working in them, and their own experience tells them of the vast variety of gifts which they owe to his liberality. Whether they will or not, they cannot but know that these are proofs of his Godhead, and yet they inwardly suppress them. They have no occasion to go farther than themselves, provided they do not, by appropriating as their own that which has been given them from heaven, put out the light intended to exhibit God clearly to their minds. At this day, however, the earth sustains on her bosom many

monster minds—minds which are not afraid to employ the seed of Deity deposited in human nature as a means of suppressing the name of God. Can any thing be more detestable than this madness in man, who, finding God a hundred times both in his body and his soul, makes his excellence in this respect a pretext for denying that there is a God? He will not say that chance has made him differ from the brutes that perish; but, substituting nature as the architect of the universe, he suppresses the name of God. The swift motions of the soul, its noble faculties and rare endowments, bespeak the agency of God in a manner which would make the suppression of it impossible, did not the Epicureans, like so many Cyclops, use it as a vantage-ground, from which to wage more audacious war with God. Are so many treasures of heavenly wisdom employed in the guidance of such a worm as man, and shall the whole universe be denied the same privilege? To hold that there are organs in the soul corresponding to each of its faculties, is so far from obscuring the glory of God, that it rather illustrates it. Let Epicurus tell what concourse of atoms, cooking meat and drink, can form one portion into refuse and another portion into blood, and make all the members separately perform their office as carefully as if they were so many souls acting with common consent in the superintendence of one body.

5. But my business at present is not with that stye: I wish rather to deal with those who, led away by absurd subtleties, are inclined, by giving an indirect turn to the frigid doctrine of Aristotle, to employ it for the purpose both of disproving the immortality of the soul, and robbing God of his rights. Under the pretext that the faculties of the soul are organised, they chain it to the body as if it were incapable of a separate existence, while they endeavour as much as in them lies, by pronouncing eulogiums on nature, to suppress the name of God. But there is no ground for maintaining that the powers of the soul are confined to the performance of bodily functions. What has the body to do with your measuring the heavens, counting the number of the stars, ascertaining their magnitudes, their relative distances, the rate at which they move, and the orbits which they describe? I deny not that Astronomy has its use; all I

mean to show is, that these lofty investigations are not conducted by organised symmetry, but by the faculties of the soul itself apart altogether from the body. The single example I have given will suggest many others to the reader. The swift and versatile movements of the soul in glancing from heaven to earth, connecting the future with the past, retaining the remembrance of former years, nay, forming creations of its own—its skill, moreover, in making astonishing discoveries, and inventing so many wonderful arts, are sure indications of the agency of God in man. What shall we say of its activity when the body is asleep, its many revolving thoughts, its many useful suggestions, its many solid arguments, nay, its presentiment of things yet to come? What shall we say but that man bears about with him a stamp of immortality which can never be effaced? But how is it possible for man to be divine, and yet not acknowledge his Creator? Shall we, by means of a power of judging implanted in our breast, distinguish between justice and injustice, and yet there be no judge in heaven? Shall some remains of intelligence continue with us in sleep, and yet no God keep watch in heaven? Shall we be deemed the inventors of so many arts and useful properties that God may be defrauded of his praise, though experience tells us plainly enough, that whatever we possess is dispensed to us in unequal measures by another hand? The talk of certain persons concerning a secret inspiration quickening the whole world, is not only silly, but altogether profane. Such persons are delighted with the following celebrated passage of Virgil:

> "Know, first, that heaven, and earth's compacted frame,
> And flowing waters, and the starry flame,
> And both the radiant lights, one common soul
> Inspires and feeds—and animates the whole.
> This active mind, infused through all the space,
> Unites and mingles with the mighty mass:
> Hence, men and beasts the breath of life obtain,
> And birds of air, and monsters of the main.
> Th' ethereal vigour is in all the same,
> And every soul is filled with equal flame."

The meaning of all this is, that the world, which was made to display the glory of God, is its own creator. For the same poet has, in another place, adopted a view common to both Greeks and Latins:

> Hence to the bee some sages have assigned
> A portion of the God, and heavenly mind;
> For God goes forth, and spreads throughout the whole,
> Heaven, earth, and sea, the universal soul;
> Each, at its birth, from him all beings share,
> Both man and brute, the breath of vital air;
> To him return, and, loosed from earthly chain,
> Fly whence they sprung, and rest in God again;
> Spurn at the grave, and, fearless of decay,
> Dwell in high heaven, art star th' ethereal way.

Here we see how far that jejune speculation, of a universal mind animating and invigorating the world, is fitted to beget and foster piety in our minds. We have a still clearer proof of this in the profane verses which the licentious Lucretius has written as a deduction from the same principle. The plain object is to form an unsubstantial deity, and thereby banish the true God whom we ought to fear and worship. I admit, indeed that the expressions "Nature is God," may be piously used, if dictated by a pious mind; but as it is inaccurate and harsh (Nature being more properly the order which has been established by God), in matters which are so very important, and in regard to which special reverence is due, it does harm to confound the Deity with the inferior operations of his hands.

6. Let each of us, therefore, in contemplating his own nature, remember that there is one God who governs all natures, and, in governing, wishes us to have respect to himself, to make him the object of our faith, worship, and adoration. Nothing, indeed, can be more preposterous than to enjoy those noble endowments which bespeak the divine presence within us, and to neglect him who, of his own good pleasure, bestows them upon us. In regard to his power, how glorious the manifestations by which he urges

us to the contemplation of himself; unless, indeed, we pretend not to know whose energy it is that by a word sustains the boundless fabric of the universe—at one time making heaven reverberate with thunder, sending forth the scorching lightning, and setting the whole atmosphere in a blaze; at another, causing the raging tempests to blow, and forthwith, in one moment, when it so pleases him, making a perfect calm; keeping the sea, which seems constantly threatening the earth with devastation, suspended as it were in air; at one time, lashing it into fury by the impetuosity of the winds; at another, appeasing its rage, and stilling all its waves. Here we might refer to those glowing descriptions of divine power, as illustrated by natural events, which occur throughout Scripture; but more especially in the book of Job, and the prophecies of Isaiah. These, however, I purposely omit, because a better opportunity of introducing them will be found when I come to treat of the Scriptural account of the creation. (Infra, chap. 14 s. 1, 2, 20, sq). I only wish to observe here, that this method of investigating the divine perfections, by tracing the lineaments of his countenance as shadowed forth in the firmament and on the earth, is common both to those within and to those without the pale of the Church. From the power of God we are naturally led to consider his eternity since that from which all other things derive their origin must necessarily be selfexistent and eternal. Moreover, if it be asked what cause induced him to create all things at first, and now inclines him to preserve them, we shall find that there could be no other cause than his own goodness. But if this is the only cause, nothing more should be required to draw forth our love towards him; every creature, as the Psalmist reminds us, participating in his mercy. "His tender mercies are over all his works," (Ps. 145:9).

7. In the second class of God's works, namely those which are above the ordinary course of nature, the evidence of his perfections are in every respect equally clear. For in conducting the affairs of men, he so arranges the course of his providence, as daily to declare, by the clearest manifestations, that though all are in innumerable ways the partakers of his bounty, the righteous are the special objects of his favour, the wicked and profane the special

objects of his severity. It is impossible to doubt his punishment of crimes; while at the same time he, in no unequivocal manner, declares that he is the protector, and even the avenger of innocence, by shedding blessings on the good, helping their necessities, soothing and solacing their griefs, relieving their sufferings, and in all ways providing for their safety. And though he often permits the guilty to exult for a time with impunity, and the innocent to be driven to and fro in adversity, nay, even to be wickedly and iniquitously oppressed, this ought not to produce any uncertainty as to the uniform justice of all his procedure. Nay, an opposite inference should be drawn. When any one crime calls forth visible manifestations of his anger, it must be because he hates all crimes; and, on the other hand, his leaving many crimes unpunished, only proves that there is a judgment in reserve, when the punishment now delayed shall be inflicted. In like manner, how richly does he supply us with the means of contemplating his mercy when, as frequently happens, he continues to visit miserable sinners with unwearied kindness, until he subdues their depravity, and woos them back with more than a parent's fondness?

8. To this purpose the Psalmist (Ps. 107) mentioning how God, in a wondrous manner, often brings sudden and unexpected succour to the miserable when almost on the brink of despair, whether in protecting them when they stray in deserts, and at length leading them back into the right path, or supplying them with food when famishing for want, or delivering them when captive from iron fetters and foul dungeons, or conducting them safe into harbour after shipwreck, or bringing them back from the gates of death by curing their diseases, or, after burning up the fields with heat and drought, fertilising them with the river of his grace, or exalting the meanest of the people, and casting down the mighty from their lofty seats—the Psalmist, after bringing forward examples of this description, infers that those things which men call fortuitous events, are so many proofs of divine providence, and more especially of paternal clemency, furnishing ground of joy to the righteous, and at the same time stopping the mouths of the ungodly. But as the greater part of mankind, enslaved by error,

walk blindfold in this glorious theatre, he exclaims that it is a rare and singular wisdom to meditate carefully on these works of God, which many, who seem most sharp-sighted in other respects, behold without profit. It is indeed true, that the brightest manifestation of divine glory finds not one genuine spectator among a hundred. Still, neither his power nor his wisdom is shrouded in darkness. His power is strikingly displayed when the rage of the wicked, to all appearance irresistible, is crushed in a single moment; their arrogance subdued, their strongest bulwarks overthrown, their armour dashed to pieces, their strength broken, their schemes defeated without an effort, and audacity which set itself above the heavens is precipitated to the lowest depths of the earth. On the other hand, the poor are raised up out of the dust, and the needy lifted out of the dung hill (Ps. 113:7), the oppressed and afflicted are rescued in extremity, the despairing animated with hope, the unarmed defeat the armed, the few the many, the weak the strong. The excellence of the divine wisdom is manifested in distributing everything in due season, confounding the wisdom of the world, and taking the wise in their own craftiness (1 Cor. 3:19); in short, conducting all things in perfect accordance with reason.

9. We see there is no need of a long and laborious train of argument in order to obtain proofs which illustrate and assert the Divine Majesty. The few which we have merely touched, show them to be so immediately within our reach in every quarter, that we can trace them with the eye, or point to them with the finger. And here we must observe again (see chap. 2 s. 2), that the knowledge of God which we are invited to cultivate is not that which, resting satisfied with empty speculation, only flutters in the brain, but a knowledge which will prove substantial and fruitful wherever it is duly perceived, and rooted in the heart. The Lord is manifested by his perfections. When we feel their power within us, and are conscious of their benefits, the knowledge must impress us much more vividly than if we merely imagined a God whose presence we never felt. Hence it is obvious, that in seeking God, the most direct path and the fittest method is, not to attempt with presumptuous

curiosity to pry into his essence, which is rather to be adored than minutely discussed, but to contemplate him in his works, by which he draws near, becomes familiar, and in a manner communicates himself to us. To this the Apostle referred when he said, that we need not go far in search of him (Acts 17:27), because, by the continual working of his power, he dwells in every one of us. Accordingly, David (Psalm 145), after acknowledging that his greatness is unsearchable, proceeds to enumerate his works, declaring that his greatness will thereby be unfolded. It therefore becomes us also diligently to prosecute that investigation of God which so enraptures the soul with admiration as, at the same time, to make an efficacious impression on it. And, as Augustine expresses it (in Psalm 144), since we are unable to comprehend Him, and are, as it were, overpowered by his greatness, our proper course is to contemplate his works, and so refresh ourselves with his goodness.

10. By the knowledge thus acquired, we ought not only to be stimulated to worship God, but also aroused and elevated to the hope of future life. For, observing that the manifestations which the Lord gives both of his mercy and severity are only begun and incomplete, we ought to infer that these are doubtless only a prelude to higher manifestations, of which the full display is reserved for another state. Conversely, when we see the righteous brought into affliction by the ungodly, assailed with injuries, overwhelmed with calumnies, and lacerated by insult and contumely, while, on the contrary, the wicked flourish, prosper, acquire ease and honour, and all these with impunity, we ought forthwith to infer, that there will be a future life in which iniquity shall receive its punishment, and righteousness its reward. Moreover, when we observe that the Lord often lays his chastening rod on the righteous, we may the more surely conclude, that far less will the unrighteous ultimately escape the scourges of his anger. There is a well-known passage in Augustine (*De Civitate Dei [The City of God]*, lib. 1 c. 8), "Were all sin now visited with open punishment, it might be thought that nothing was reserved for the final Judgment; and, on the other hand, were no sin now openly punished, it might be supposed there was no divine providence." It must be

acknowledged, therefore, that in each of the works of God, and more especially in the whole of them taken together, the divine perfections are delineated as in a picture, and the whole human race thereby invited and allured to acquire the knowledge of God, and, in consequence of this knowledge, true and complete felicity. Moreover, while his perfections are thus most vividly displayed, the only means of ascertaining their practical operation and tendency is to descend into ourselves, and consider how it is that the Lord there manifests his wisdom, power, and energy,—how he there displays his justice, goodness, and mercy. For although David (Psalm 92:6) justly complains of the extreme infatuation of the ungodly in not pondering the deep counsels of God, as exhibited in the government of the human race, what he elsewhere says (Psalm 40) is most true, that the wonders of the divine wisdom in this respect are more in number than the hairs of our head. But I leave this topic at present, as it will be more fully considered afterwards in its own place (Book I. c. 16, see. 6–9).

11. Bright, however, as is the manifestation which God gives both of himself and his immortal kingdom in the mirror of his works, so great is our stupidity, so dull are we in regard to these bright manifestations, that we derive no benefit from them. For in regard to the fabric and admirable arrangement of the universe, how few of us are there who, in lifting our eyes to the heavens, or looking abroad on the various regions of the earth, ever think of the Creator? Do we not rather overlook Him, and sluggishly content ourselves with a view of his works? And then in regard to supernatural events, though these are occurring every day, how few are there who ascribe them to the ruling providence of God—how many who imagine that they are casual results produced by the blind evolutions of the wheel of chance? Even when under the guidance and direction of these events, we are in a manner forced to the contemplation of God (a circumstance which all must occasionally experience), and are thus led to form some impressions of Deity, we immediately fly off to carnal dreams and depraved fictions, and so by our vanity corrupt heavenly truth. This far, indeed, we differ from each other, in that every one appropriates

to himself some peculiar error; but we are all alike in this, that we substitute monstrous fictions for the one living and true God—a disease not confined to obtuse and vulgar minds, but affecting the noblest, and those who, in other respects, are singularly acute. How lavishly in this respect have the whole body of philosophers betrayed their stupidity and want of sense? To say nothing of the others whose absurdities are of a still grosser description, how completely does Plato, the soberest and most religious of them all, lose himself in his round globe? What must be the case with the rest, when the leaders, who ought to have set them an example, commit such blunders, and labour under such hallucinations? In like manner, while the government of the world places the doctrine of providence beyond dispute, the practical result is the same as if it were believed that all things were carried hither and thither at the caprice of chance; so prone are we to vanity and error. I am still referring to the most distinguished of the philosophers, and not to the common herd, whose madness in profaning the truth of God exceeds all bounds.

12. Hence that immense flood of error with which the whole world is overflowed. Every individual mind being a kind of labyrinth, it is not wonderful, not only that each nation has adopted a variety of fictions, but that almost every man has had his own god. To the darkness of ignorance have been added presumption and wantonness, and hence there is scarcely an individual to be found without some idol or phantom as a substitute for Deity. Like water gushing forth from a large and copious spring, immense crowds of gods have issued from the human mind, every man giving himself full license, and devising some peculiar form of divinity, to meet his own views. It is unnecessary here to attempt a catalogue of the superstitions with which the world was overspread. The thing were endless; and the corruptions themselves, though not a word should be said, furnish abundant evidence of the blindness of the human mind. I say nothing of the rude and illiterate vulgar; but among the philosophers who attempted, by reason and learning, to pierce the heavens, what shameful disagreement! The higher any one was endued with genius, and the more he was polished

by science and art, the more specious was the colouring which he gave to his opinions. All these, however, if examined more closely, will be found to be vain show. The Stoics plumed themselves on their acuteness, when they said that the various names of God might be extracted from all the parts of nature, and yet that his unity was not thereby divided: as if we were not already too prone to vanity, and had no need of being presented with an endless multiplicity of gods, to lead us further and more grossly into error. The mystic theology of the Egyptians shows how sedulously they laboured to be thought rational on this subject. And, perhaps, at the first glance, some show of probability might deceive the simple and unwary; but never did any mortal devise a scheme by which religion was not foully corrupted. This endless variety and confusion emboldened the Epicureans, and other gross despisers of piety, to cut off all sense of God. For when they saw that the wisest contradicted each others they hesitated not to infer from their dissensions, and from the frivolous and absurd doctrines of each, that men foolishly, and to no purpose, brought torment upon themselves by searching for a God, there being none: and they thought this inference safe, because it was better at once to deny God altogether, than to feign uncertain gods, and thereafter engage in quarrels without end. They, indeed, argue absurdly, or rather weave a cloak for their impiety out of human ignorance; though ignorance surely cannot derogate from the prerogatives of God. But since all confess that there is no topic on which such difference exists, both among learned and unlearned, the proper inference is, that the human mind, which thus errs in inquiring after God, is dull and blind in heavenly mysteries. Some praise the answer of Simonides, who being asked by King Hero what God was, asked a day to consider. When the king next day repeated the question, he asked two days; and after repeatedly doubling the number of days, at length replied, "The longer I consider, the darker the subject appears." He, no doubt, wisely suspended his opinion, when he did not see clearly: still his answer shows, that if men are only naturally taught, instead of having any distinct, solid, or certain knowledge, they fasten only on contradictory principles, and, in consequence, worship an unknown God.

13. Hence we must hold, that whosoever adulterates pure religion (and this must be the case with all who cling to their own views), make a departure from the one God. No doubt, they will allege that they have a different intention; but it is of little consequence what they intend or persuade themselves to believe, since the Holy Spirit pronounces all to be apostates, who, in the blindness of their minds, substitute demons in the place of God. For this reason Paul declares that the Ephesians were "without God," (Eph. 2:12), until they had learned from the Gospel what it is to worship the true God. Nor must this be restricted to one people only, since, in another place, he declares in general, that all men "became vain in their imaginations," after the majesty of the Creator was manifested to them in the structure of the world. Accordingly, in order to make way for the only true God, he condemns all the gods celebrated among the Gentiles as lying and false, leaving no Deity anywhere but in Mount Zion where the special knowledge of God was professed (Hab. 2:18, 20). Among the Gentiles in the time of Christ, the Samaritans undoubtedly made the nearest approach to true piety; yet we hear from his own mouth that they worshipped they knew not what (John 4:22); whence it follows that they were deluded by vain errors. In short, though all did not give way to gross vice, or rush headlong into open idolatry, there was no pure and authentic religion founded merely on common belief. A few individuals may not have gone all insane lengths with the vulgar; still Paul's declaration remains true, that the wisdom of God was not apprehended by the princes of this world (1 Cor. 2:8). But if the most distinguished wandered in darkness, what shall we say of the refuse? No wonder, therefore, that all worship of man's device is repudiated by the Holy Spirit as degenerate. Any opinion which man can form in heavenly mysteries, though it may not beget a long train of errors, is still the parent of error. And though nothing worse should happen, even this is no light sin—to worship an unknown God at random. Of this sin, however, we hear from our Saviour's own mouth (John 4:22), that all

are guilty who have not been taught out of the law who the God is whom they ought to worship. Nay, even Socrates in Xenophon (lib. 1 *Memorabilia*), lauds the response of Apollo enjoining every man to worship the gods according to the rites of his country, and the particular practice of his own city. But what right have mortals thus to decide of their own authority in a matter which is far above the world; or who can so acquiesce in the will of his forefathers, or the decrees of the people, as unhesitatingly to receive a god at their hands? Every one will adhere to his own judgment, sooner than submit to the dictation of others. Since, therefore, in regulating the worship of God, the custom of a city, or the consent of antiquity, is a too feeble and fragile bond of piety; it remains that God himself must bear witness to himself from heaven.

14. In vain for us, therefore, does creation exhibit so many bright lamps lighted up to show forth the glory of its Author. Though they beam upon us from every quarter, they are altogether insufficient of themselves to lead us into the right path. Some sparks, undoubtedly, they do throw out; but these are quenched before they can give forth a brighter effulgence. Wherefore, the apostle, in the very place where he says that the worlds are images of invisible things, adds that it is by faith we understand that they were framed by the word of God (Heb. 11:3); thereby intimating that the invisible Godhead is indeed represented by such displays, but that we have no eyes to perceive it until they are enlightened through faith by internal revelation from God. When Paul says that that which may be known of God is manifested by the creation of the world, he does not mean such a manifestation as may be comprehended by the wit of man (Rom. 1:19); on the contrary, he shows that it has no further effect than to render us inexcusable (Acts 17:27). And though he says, elsewhere, that we have not far to seek for God, inasmuch as he dwells within us, he shows, in another passage, to what extent this nearness to God is availing. God, says he, "in times past, suffered all nations to walk in their own ways. Nevertheless, he left not himself without witness, in that he did good, and gave us rain from heaven, and fruitful seasons, filling our hearts with food and gladness," (Acts 14:16, 17). But though God is not left without

a witness, while, with numberless varied acts of kindness, he woos men to the knowledge of himself, yet they cease not to follow their own ways, in other words, deadly errors.

15. But though we are deficient in natural powers which might enable us to rise to a pure and clear knowledge of God, still, as the dullness which prevents us is within, there is no room for excuse. We cannot plead ignorance, without being at the same time convicted by our own consciences both of sloth and ingratitude. It were, indeed, a strange defence for man to pretend that he has no ears to hear the truth, while dumb creatures have voices loud enough to declare it; to allege that he is unable to see that which creatures without eyes demonstrate, to excuse himself on the ground of weakness of mind, while all creatures without reason are able to teach. Wherefore, when we wander and go astray, we are justly shut out from every species of excuse, because all things point to the right path. But while man must bear the guilt of corrupting the seed of divine knowledge so wondrously deposited in his mind, and preventing it from bearing good and genuine fruit, it is still most true that we are not sufficiently instructed by that bare and simple, but magnificent testimony which the creatures bear to the glory of their Creator. For no sooner do we, from a survey of the world, obtain some slight knowledge of Deity, than we pass by the true God, and set up in his stead the dream and phantom of our own brain, drawing away the praise of justice, wisdom, and goodness, from the fountain-head, and transferring it to some other quarter. Moreover, by the erroneous estimate we form, we either so obscure or pervert his daily works, as at once to rob them of their glory and the author of them of his just praise.

Chapter 6. The Need of Scripture, as a Guide and Teacher, in Coming to God as a Creator.

1. Therefore, though the effulgence which is presented to every eye, both in the heavens and on the earth, leaves the ingratitude of man without excuse, since God, in order to bring the whole human race under the same condemnation, holds forth to all, without exception, a mirror of his Deity in his works, another

and better help must be given to guide us properly to God as a Creator. Not in vain, therefore, has he added the light of his Word in order that he might make himself known unto salvation, and bestowed the privilege on those whom he was pleased to bring into nearer and more familiar relation to himself. For, seeing how the minds of men were carried to and fro, and found no certain resting-place, he chose the Jews for a peculiar people, and then hedged them in that they might not, like others, go astray. And not in vain does he, by the same means, retain us in his knowledge, since but for this, even those who, in comparison of others, seem to stand strong, would quickly fall away. For as the aged, or those whose sight is defective, when any books however fair, is set before them, though they perceive that there is something written are scarcely able to make out two consecutive words, but, when aided by glasses, begin to read distinctly, so Scripture, gathering together the impressions of Deity, which, till then, lay confused in our minds, dissipates the darkness, and shows us the true God clearly. God therefore bestows a gift of singular value, when, for the instruction of the Church, he employs not dumb teachers merely, but opens his own sacred mouth; when he not only proclaims that some God must be worshipped, but at the same time declares that He is the God to whom worship is due; when he not only teaches his elect to have respect to God, but manifests himself as the God to whom this respect should be paid.

The course which God followed towards his Church from the very first, was to supplement these common proofs by the addition of his Word, as a surer and more direct means of discovering himself. And there can be no doubt that it was by this help, Adam, Noah, Abraham, and the other patriarchs, attained to that familiar knowledge which, in a manner, distinguished them from unbelievers. I am not now speaking of the peculiar doctrines of faith by which they were elevated to the hope of eternal blessedness. It was necessary, in passing from death unto life, that they should know God, not only as a Creator, but as a Redeemer also; and both kinds of knowledge they certainly did obtain from the Word. In point of order, however, the knowledge first given was that which made them acquainted with the God by whom the world was made and is governed. To this first knowledge was afterwards added the more intimate knowledge which alone quickens dead souls, and by which God is known not only as the Creator of the worlds and the sole author and disposer of all events, but also as a Redeemer, in the person of the Mediator. But as the fall and the corruption of nature have not yet been considered, I now postpone the consideration of the remedy (for which, see Book 2 c. 6 etc). Let the reader then remember, that I am not now treating of the covenant by which God adopted the children of Abraham, or of that branch of doctrine by which, as founded in Christ, believers have, properly speaking, been in all ages separated from the profane heathen. I am only showing that it is necessary to apply to Scripture, in order to learn the sure marks which distinguish God, as the Creator of the world, from the whole herd of fictitious gods. We shall afterward, in due course, consider the work of Redemption. In the meantime, though we shall adduce many passages from the New Testament, and some also from the Law and the Prophets, in which express mention is made of Christ, the only object will be to show that God, the Maker of the world, is manifested to us in Scripture, and his true character expounded, so as to save us from wandering up and down, as in a labyrinth, in search of some doubtful deity.

2. Whether God revealed himself to the fathers by oracles and visions, or, by the instrumentality and ministry of men, suggested what they were to hand down to posterity, there cannot be a doubt that the certainty of what he taught them was firmly engraven on their hearts, so that they felt assured and knew that the things which they learnt came forth from God, who invariably accompanied his word with a sure testimony, infinitely superior to mere opinion. At length, in order that, while doctrine was continually enlarged, its truth might subsist in the world during all ages, it was his pleasure that the same oracles which he had deposited with the fathers should be consigned, as it were, to public records. With this view the law was promulgated, and prophets were afterwards added to be its interpreters. For though the uses of the law were

manifold (Book 2 c. 7 and 8), and the special office assigned to Moses and all the prophets was to teach the method of reconciliation between God and man (whence Paul calls Christ "the end of the law," Rom. 10:4); still I repeat that, in addition to the proper doctrine of faith and repentance in which Christ is set forth as a Mediator, the Scriptures employ certain marks and tokens to distinguish the only wise and true God, considered as the Creator and Governor of the world, and thereby guard against his being confounded with the herd of false deities. Therefore, while it becomes man seriously to employ his eyes in considering the works of God, since a place has been assigned him in this most glorious theatre that he may be a spectator of them, his special duty is to give ear to the Word, that he may the better profit. Hence it is not strange that those who are born in darkness become more and more hardened in their stupidity; because the vast majority instead of confining themselves within due bounds by listening with docility to the Word, exult in their own vanity. If true religion is to beam upon us, our principle must be, that it is necessary to begin with heavenly teaching, and that it is impossible for any man to obtain even the minutest portion of right and sound doctrine without being a disciple of Scripture. Hence, the first step in true knowledge is taken, when we reverently embrace the testimony which God has been pleased therein to give of himself. For not only does faith, full and perfect faith, but all correct knowledge of God, originate in obedience. And surely in this respect God has with singular Providence provided for mankind in all ages.

3. For if we reflect how prone the human mind is to lapse into forgetfulness of God, how readily inclined to every kind of error, how bent every now and then on devising new and fictitious religions, it will be easy to understand how necessary it was to make such a depository of doctrine as would secure it from either perishing by the neglect, vanishing away amid the errors, or being corrupted by the presumptuous audacity of men. It being thus manifest that God, foreseeing the inefficiency of his image imprinted on the fair form of the universe, has given the assistance of his Word to all whom he has ever been pleased to instruct effectually,

we, too, must pursue this straight path, if we aspire in earnest to a genuine contemplation of God;—we must go, I say, to the Word, where the character of God, drawn from his works is described accurately and to the life; these works being estimated, not by our depraved judgment, but by the standard of eternal truth. If, as I lately said, we turn aside from it, how great soever the speed with which we move, we shall never reach the goal, because we are off the course. We should consider that the brightness of the Divine countenance, which even an apostle declares to be inaccessible (1 Tim. 6:16), is a kind of labyrinth,—a labyrinth to us inextricable, if the Word do not serve us as a thread to guide our path; and that it is better to limp in the way, than run with the greatest swiftness out of it. Hence the Psalmist, after repeatedly declaring (Psalm 93, 96, 97, 99, etc). that superstition should be banished from the world in order that pure religion may flourish, introduces God as reigning; meaning by the term, not the power which he possesses and which he exerts in the government of universal nature, but the doctrine by which he maintains his due supremacy: because error never can be eradicated from the heart of man until the true knowledge of God has been implanted in it.

4. Accordingly, the same prophet, after mentioning that the heavens declare the glory of God, that the firmament sheweth forth the works of his hands, that the regular succession of day and night proclaim his Majesty, proceeds to make mention of the Word: "The law of the Lord," says he, "is perfect, converting the soul; the testimony of the Lord is sure, making wise the simple. The statutes of the Lord are right, rejoicing the heart; the commandment of the Lord is pure, enlightening the eyes," (Psalm 19:1–9). For though the law has other uses besides (as to which, see Book 2 c. 7, sec. 6, 10, 12), the general meaning is, that it is the proper school for training the children of God; the invitation given to all nations, to behold him in the heavens and earth, proving of no avail. The same view is taken in the 29th Psalm, where the Psalmist, after discoursing on the dreadful voice of God, which, in thunder, wind, rain, whirlwind, and tempest, shakes the earth, makes the mountains tremble, and breaks the cedars, concludes

by saying, "that in his temple does every one speak of his glory," unbelievers being deaf to all God's words when they echo in the air. In like manner another Psalm, after describing the raging billows of the sea, thus concludes, "Thy testimonies are very sure; holiness becometh thine house for ever," (Psalm 93:5). To the same effect are the words of our Saviour to the Samaritan woman, when he told her that her nation and all other nations worshipped they knew not what; and that the Jews alone gave worship to the true God (John 4:22). Since the human mind, through its weakness, was altogether unable to come to God if not aided and upheld by his sacred word, it necessarily followed that all mankind, the Jews excepted, inasmuch as they sought God without the Word, were labouring under vanity and error.

INTRODUCTION TO
the Council of Trent
DECREE ON JUSTIFICATION

Just a couple of years into the Reformation, Luther had appealed his cause to a General Council of the Church. And although there were many in Rome who preferred to silence him by papal fiat or imperial force, his call for a Council found sympathetic ears throughout Christendom. Not only was the memory of the reforming councils of the previous century still relatively fresh, but it was clear to the majority of church leaders that Luther had gained such a large following because there was more than a kernel of truth in his denunciations of the Roman Church. Corruptions of both doctrine and practice were rife. Even many staunch traditionalists welcomed a council if it meant an opportunity to crystallize once and for all disputed and ambiguous Catholic teachings.

However, the interminable three-way political squabbles (and intermittent all-out wars) between the pope, the French king Francis, and Emperor Charles V delayed a council over and over. An abortive effort at Mantua in 1537 almost materialized, but soon dissolved. Meanwhile, remarkable reforming energies began to be felt within Italy itself, the heart of the Catholic Church. Moved partly by reading translations of Luther's writings and partly by their own religious experiences and reflections on the Augustinian legacy of the medieval Church, many prominent Italian churchmen came to views not too distant from Luther's doctrine of justification. When one of them, Gasparo Contarini, was chosen as papal representative to a conference with Protestant leaders, including Melanchthon and Bucer, at Regensburg in 1541, hopes were accordingly high for some sort of settlement. The Colloquy backfired, however, as Contarini's willingness to make concessions confirmed the suspicions of hardline traditionalists in Rome, leading to the arrest of Contarini and the launch of the Roman Inquisition in 1542.

It was thus in a climate exceedingly unfavorable to any concessions that a Council was at last convened at Trent after further negotiations, arguments, and delays in 1545. But though the pope had obtained the grudging support of Charles for the Council, Francis still opposed it, and it was hardly the great General Council of Christendom that had been hoped for or that the moment required. Only a few dozen of the 600 bishops invited appeared, and almost all of them from Italy. Reform-minded bishops from Germany and France generally kept a wary distance, as did Protestant leaders.

This did not mean that no significant reforms were undertaken by the Council; on the contrary, it saw many important changes to the Church, including a purging of many of the worldly corruptions of the clergy that had made the church such a laughingstock to men like Erasmus and had earned Luther such a wide hearing. But the purpose of these reforms was to shore up the authority of the church, and when it came to doctrine, the result of the Council was to render the gap between Rome and Protestantism unbridgeable. To be sure, Trent condemned some of the more seriously aberrant formulations of church doctrine that had invited Protestant opposition, but they also set out to clarify many traditional teachings in such a way as to allow no more wiggle room, anathematizing errors on every side. Most significant in this regard were the fourth session of the Council, affirming the equal authority of church tradition alongside Scripture, and the sixth session of the Council, on justification.

The decree on justification proved the most trying and contentious of the Council, involving more than six months of debate and including a violent personal confrontation between one bishop who affirmed justification by faith alone and another who denounced him as "either a knave or a fool."[1] The final doctrinal statement epitomizes the legacy of Trent, on the one hand affirming much of what Protestants sought to affirm—the necessity of God's grace for every step of salvation—but at the same time conceiving justification as the infusion of a gracious power into the soul which then enabled the sinner to merit salvation by subsequent good works. Justification is by faith then only in the sense that faith is essential to begin the process. While Protestants of course would agree that the initial justifying faith is only a beginning, they stressed that the subsequent steps of the process must be understood as *sanctification*, the working out of a finished work of justification, and that even these sanctified works did not merit God's favor, but, being imperfect, were only accepted for the sake of Christ. Trent was particularly adamant in rejecting this view, insisting that once justified, the believer could offer up to God a truly acceptable sacrifice of obedience.

The decree itself is structured as a series of sixteen short chapters, followed by thirty-three much shorter canons, each of which pronounces a summary anathema against any who teach contrary to the canon. Both the chapters and the canons intentionally agree with the Protestants in some matters—canons 1–3, 10, 22, 23a, 28, and 29a all seem to fall under this heading. Moreover, a large portion of the decree is directed against statements which, although apparently considered to be standard Protestant teachings, seem to have been largely misunderstood, so that most Protestant theologians would have said that the condemnations did not apply to them. Canons 4–6, 8, 14, 18–21, 26, and 31 seem to fall under this heading. There are also points where the Council attacks teachings that do seem to have been voiced by some Protestant writers and confessions, but which were disputed within the movement both

1 John W. O'Malley, *Trent: What Happened at the Council* (Cambridge, MA: The Belknap Press of Harvard University Press, 2013), 109.

in the 16th century and beyond. In particular, the Council was eager to refute the notion that the saved necessarily experienced full assurance of salvation, such that failure to do so was a sign that one was not saved. While Protestants did insist, contra Catholic orthodoxy, that full assurance of salvation was possible, there were disputes as to whether it was necessary, or whether doubting was to be expected. The Council also clearly asserts the possibility of temporary justification—that is, that some might receive genuine grace through faith but not persevere. This was and remains a point of persistent disagreement among Protestants. Canons 13, 15, 16, 17, and 23b concerns such issues. This leaves Canons 7, 9, 11–12, 24, 25, 27, 29b, 30, and 32 as all reflecting a more or less accurate understanding of what the Protestants intended to teach, and forthrightly rejecting it. By declaring these statements *anathema*, or damnable errors, the Council closed the door to any likelihood of reunion with the Protestant reform movement.

DECREE ON JUSTIFICATION

Council of Trent

TRANSLATED BY J. WATERWORTH

PROEM.

Whereas there is, at this time, not without the shipwreck of many souls, and grievous detriment to the unity of the Church, a certain erroneous doctrine disseminated touching justification; the sacred and holy, ecumenical and general Synod of Trent, lawfully assembled in the Holy Ghost,—the most reverend lords, Giammaria del Monte, bishop of Palaestrina, and Marcellus of the title of the Holy Cross in Jerusalem, priest, cardinals of the holy Roman Church, and legates apostolic *a latere*, presiding therein, in the name of our most holy father and lord in Christ, Paul III., by the providence of God, Pope, purposes, unto the praise and glory of Almighty God, the tranquillising of the Church, and the salvation of souls, to expound to all the faithful of Christ the true and sound doctrine touching the said justification; which (doctrine) the sun of justice, Christ Jesus, the author and finisher of our faith, taught, which the apostles transmitted, and which the Catholic Church, the Holy Ghost reminding her thereof, has always retained; most strictly forbidding that any henceforth presume to believe, preach, or teach, otherwise than as by this present decree is defined and declared.

CHAPTER I.

ON THE INABILITY OF NATURE AND OF THE LAW TO JUSTIFY MAN.

The holy Synod declares first, that, for the correct and sound understanding of the doctrine of justification, it is necessary that each one recognise and confess, that, whereas all men had lost their innocence in the prevarication of Adam—having become unclean, and, as the apostle says, by nature children of wrath, as (this Synod) has set forth in the decree on original sin—they were so far the servants of sin, and under the power of the devil and of death, that not the Gentiles only by the force of nature, but not even the Jews by the very letter itself of the law of Moses, were able to be liberated, or to arise, therefrom; although free will, attenuated as it was in its powers, and bent down, was by no means extinguished in them.

CHAPTER II.

ON THE DISPENSATION AND MYSTERY OF CHRIST'S ADVENT.

Whence it came to pass, that the heavenly Father, the father of mercies and the God of all comfort, when that blessed fulness of the time was come, sent unto men, Jesus Christ, His own Son-who had been, both before the Law, and during the time of the Law, to many of the holy fathers announced and promised-that He might both redeem the Jews who were under the Law, and that the Gentiles, who followed not after justice, might attain to justice, and that all men might receive the adoption of sons. Him God hath proposed as a propitiator, through faith in his blood, for our sins, and not for our sins only, but also for those of the whole world.

CHAPTER III.

WHO ARE JUSTIFIED THROUGH CHRIST.

But, though He died for all, yet do not all receive the benefit of His death, but those only unto whom the merit of His passion is communicated. For as in truth men, if they were not born propagated of the seed of Adam, would not be born unjust—seeing that, by that propagation, they contract through him, when they are conceived, injustice as their own—so, if they were not born again in Christ, they never would be justified; seeing that, in that new birth, there is bestowed upon them, through the merit of His passion, the grace whereby they are made just. For this benefit the apostle exhorts us, evermore to give thanks to the Father, who hath made us worthy to be partakers of the lot of the saints in light, and hath delivered us from the power of darkness, and hath translated us into the Kingdom of the Son of his love, in whom we have redemption, and remission of sins.

CHAPTER IV.

A DESCRIPTION IS INTRODUCED OF THE JUSTIFICATION OF THE IMPIOUS, AND OF THE MANNER THEREOF UNDER THE LAW OF GRACE.

By which words, a description of the justification of the impious is indicated—as being a translation, from that state wherein man is born a child of the first Adam, to the state of grace, and of the adoption of the sons of God, through the second Adam, Jesus Christ, our Saviour. And this translation, since the promulgation of the Gospel, cannot be effected, without the laver of regeneration, or the desire thereof, as it is written; unless a man be born again of water and the Holy Ghost, he cannot enter into the Kingdom of God.

CHAPTER V.

ON THE NECESSITY, IN ADULTS, OF PREPARATION FOR JUSTIFICATION, AND WHENCE IT PROCEEDS.

The Synod furthermore declares, that in adults, the beginning of the said justification is to be derived from the prevenient grace of God, through Jesus Christ, that is to say, from His vocation, whereby, without any merits existing on their parts, they are called; that so they, who by sins were alienated from God, may be disposed through His quickening and assisting grace, to convert themselves to their own justification, by freely assenting to and co-operating with that said grace: in such sort that, while God touches the heart of man by the illumination of the Holy Ghost, neither is man himself utterly without doing anything while he receives that inspiration, forasmuch as he is also able to reject it; yet is he not able, by his own free will, without the grace of God, to move himself unto justice in His sight. Whence, when it is said in the sacred writings: Turn ye to me, and I will turn to you, we are admonished of our liberty; and when we answer; Convert us, O Lord, to thee, and we shall be converted, we confess that we are prevented by the grace of God.

CHAPTER VI.

THE MANNER OF PREPARATION.

Now they (adults) are disposed unto the said justice, when, excited and assisted by divine grace, conceiving faith by hearing, they are freely moved towards God, believing those things to be true which God has revealed and promised—and this especially, that God justifies the impious by His grace, through the redemption that is in Christ Jesus; and when, understanding themselves to be sinners, they, by turning themselves, from the fear of divine justice whereby they are profitably agitated, to consider the mercy of God, are raised unto hope, confiding that God will be propitious to them for Christ's sake; and they begin to love Him as the fountain of all justice; and are therefore moved against sins by a certain hatred and detestation, to wit, by that penitence which must be performed before baptism: lastly, when they purpose to receive baptism, to begin a new life, and to keep the commandments of God. Concerning this disposition it is written; He that cometh to God, must believe that he is, and is a rewarder to them that seek him; and, Be of good faith, son, thy sins are forgiven thee; and, The fear of the Lord driveth out sin; and, Do penance, and be baptized every one of you in the name of Jesus Christ, for the remission of your sins, and you shall receive the gift of the Holy Ghost; and, Going, therefore, teach ye all nations, baptizing them in the name of the Father, and of the Son, and of the Holy Ghost; finally, Prepare your hearts unto the Lord.

CHAPTER VII.

WHAT THE JUSTIFICATION OF THE IMPIOUS IS, AND WHAT ARE THE CAUSES THEREOF.

This disposition, or preparation, is followed by justification itself, which is not remission of sins merely, but also the sanctification and renewal of the inward man, through the voluntary reception of the grace, and of the gifts, whereby man of unjust becomes just, and of an enemy a friend, that so he may be an heir according to hope of life everlasting.

Of this justification the causes are these: the final cause indeed is the glory of God and of Jesus Christ, and life everlasting; while the efficient cause is a merciful God who washes and sanctifies gratuitously, signing, and anointing with the holy Spirit of promise, who is the pledge of our inheritance; but the meritorious cause is His most beloved only-begotten, our Lord Jesus Christ, who, when we were enemies, for the exceeding charity wherewith he loved us, merited justification for us by His most holy Passion on the wood of the cross, and made satisfaction for us unto God the Father; the instrumental cause is the sacrament of baptism, which is the sacrament of faith, without which (faith) no man was ever justified; lastly, the alone formal cause is the justice of God, not that whereby He Himself is just, but that whereby He maketh us just, that, to wit, with which we being endowed by Him, are renewed in the spirit of our mind, and we are not only reputed, but are truly called, and are, just, receiving justice within us, each one according to his own measure, which the Holy Ghost distributes to every one as He wills, and according to each one's proper disposition and co-operation. For, although no one can be just, but he to whom the merits of the Passion of our Lord Jesus Christ are communicated, yet is this done in the said justification of the impious, when by the merit of that same most holy Passion, the charity of God is poured forth, by the Holy Spirit, in the hearts of those that are justified, and is inherent therein: whence, man, through Jesus Christ, in whom he is ingrafted, receives, in the said justification, together with the remission of sins, all these (gifts) infused at once, faith, hope, and charity. For faith, unless hope and charity be added thereto, neither unites man perfectly with Christ, nor makes him a living member of His body. For which reason it is most truly said, that Faith without works is dead and profitless; and, In Christ Jesus neither circumcision, availeth anything, nor uncircumcision, but faith which worketh by charity. This faith, Catechumen's beg of the Church—agreeably to a tradition of the apostles—previously to the sacrament of Baptism; when they beg for the faith which bestows life everlasting, which, without hope and charity, faith cannot bestow: whence also do they immediately hear that word of Christ; If thou wilt enter into life, keep the commandments. Wherefore, when receiving true and Christian justice, they are bidden, immediately on being born again, to preserve it pure and spotless, as the first robe given them through Jesus Christ in lieu of that which Adam, by his disobedience, lost for himself and for us, that so they may bear it before the judgment-seat of our Lord Jesus Christ, and may have life everlasting.

CHAPTER VIII.

IN WHAT MANNER IT IS TO BE UNDERSTOOD, THAT THE IMPIOUS IS JUSTIFIED BY FAITH, AND GRATUITOUSLY.

And whereas the Apostle saith, that man is justified by faith and freely, those words are to be understood in that sense which the perpetual consent of the Catholic Church hath held and expressed; to wit, that we are therefore said to be justified by faith, because faith is the beginning of human salvation, the foundation, and the root of all justification; without which it is impossible to please God, and to come unto the fellowship of His sons: but we are therefore said to be justified freely, because that none of those things which precede justification—whether faith or works—merit the grace itself of justification. For, if it be a grace, it is not now by works, otherwise, as the same Apostle says, grace is no more grace.

CHAPTER IX.

AGAINST THE VAIN CONFIDENCE OF HERETICS.

But, although it is necessary to believe that sins neither are remitted, nor ever were remitted save gratuitously by the mercy of

God for Christ's sake; yet is it not to be said, that sins are forgiven, or have been forgiven, to any one who boasts of his confidence and certainty of the remission of his sins, and rests on that alone; seeing that it may exist, yea does in our day exist, amongst heretics and schismatics; and with great vehemence is this vain confidence, and one alien from all godliness, preached up in opposition to the Catholic Church. But neither is this to be asserted, that they who are truly justified must needs, without any doubting whatever, settle within themselves that they are justified, and that no one is absolved from sins and justified, but he that believes for certain that he is absolved and justified; and that absolution and justification are effected by this faith alone: as though whoso has not this belief, doubts of the promises of God, and of the efficacy of the death and resurrection of Christ. For even as no pious person ought to doubt of the mercy of God, of the merit of Christ, and of the virtue and efficacy of the sacraments, even so each one, when he regards himself, and his own weakness and indisposition, may have fear and apprehension touching his own grace; seeing that no one can know with a certainty of faith, which cannot be subject to error, that he has obtained the grace of God.

CHAPTER X.

ON THE INCREASE OF JUSTIFICATION RECEIVED.

Having, therefore, been thus justified, and made the friends and domestics of God, advancing from virtue to virtue, they are renewed, as the Apostle says, day by day; that is, by mortifying the members of their own flesh, and by presenting them as instruments of justice unto sanctification, they, through the observance of the commandments of God and of the Church, faith co-operating with good works, increase in that justice which they have received through the grace of Christ, and are still further justified, as it is written; He that is just, let him be justified still; and again, Be not afraid to be justified even to death; and also, Do you see that by works a man is justified, and not by faith only. And this increase of justification holy Church begs, when she prays, "Give unto us, O Lord, increase of faith, hope, and charity."

CHAPTER XI.

ON KEEPING THE COMMANDMENTS, AND ON THE NECESSITY AND POSSIBILITY THEREOF.

But no one, how much soever justified, ought to think himself exempt from the observance of the commandments; no one ought to make use of that rash saying, one prohibited by the Fathers under an anathema—that the observance of the commandments of God is impossible for one that is justified. For God commands not impossibilities, but, by commanding, both admonishes thee to do what thou are able, and to pray for what thou art not able (to do), and aids thee that thou mayest be able; whose commandments are not heavy; whose yoke is sweet and whose burthen light. For, whoso are the sons of God, love Christ; but they who love him, keep his commandments, as Himself testifies; which, assuredly, with the divine help, they can do. For, although, during this mortal life, men, how holy and just soever, at times fall into at least light and daily sins, which are also called venial, not therefore do they cease to be just. For that cry of the just, Forgive us our trespasses, is both humble and true. And for this cause, the just themselves ought to feel themselves the more obligated to walk in the way of justice, in that, being already freed from sins, but made servants of God, they are able, living soberly, justly, and godly, to proceed onwards through Jesus Christ, by whom they have had access unto this grace. For God forsakes not those who have been once justified by His grace, unless he be first forsaken by them. Wherefore, no one ought to flatter himself up with faith alone, fancying that by faith alone he is made an heir, and will obtain the inheritance, even though he suffer not with Christ, that so he may be also glorified with him. For even Christ Himself, as the Apostle saith, Whereas he was the son of God, learned obedience by the things which he suffered, and being consummated, he became, to all who obey him, the cause of eternal salvation. For which cause the same Apostle admonishes the justified, saying; Know you not that they that run in the race, all run indeed, but one receiveth the prize? So run that you may obtain. I therefore so run, not as at an uncertainty: I so fight, not as one beating the air, but I chastise my body, and bring it into subjection; lest perhaps, when I have preached to others, I myself should become a cast-away. So also the prince of the apostles, Peter; Labour the more that by good works you may make sure your calling and election. For doing those things, you shall not sin at any time. From which it is plain, that those are opposed to the orthodox doctrine of religion, who assert that the just man sins, venially at least, in every good work; or, which is yet more insupportable, that he merits eternal punishments; as also those who state, that the just sin in all their works, if, in those works, they, together with this aim principally that God may be gloried, have in view also the eternal reward, in order to excite their sloth, and to encourage themselves to run in the course: whereas it is written, I have inclined my heart to do all thy justifications for the reward: and, concerning Moses, the Apostle saith, that he looked unto the reward.

CHAPTER XII.

THAT A RASH PRESUMPTUOUSNESS IN THE MATTER OF PREDESTINATION IS TO BE AVOIDED.

No one, moreover, so long as he is in this mortal life, ought so far to presume as regards the secret mystery of divine predestination, as to determine for certain that he is assuredly in the number of the predestinate; as if it were true, that he that is justified, either cannot sin any more, or, if he do sin, that he ought to promise himself an assured repentance; for except by special revelation, it cannot be known whom God hath chosen unto Himself.

CHAPTER XIII.

ON THE GIFT OF PERSEVERANCE.

So also as regards the gift of perseverance, of which it is written, He that shall persevere to the end, he shall be saved—which gift cannot be derived from any other but Him, who is able to establish him who standeth that he stand perseveringly, and to restore him who falleth: let no one herein promise himself any thing as certain with an absolute certainty; though all ought to place and repose a most firm hope in God's help. For God, unless men be themselves wanting to His grace, as he has begun the good work, so will he perfect it, working (in them) to will and to accomplish. Nevertheless, let those who think themselves to stand, take heed lest they fall, and, with fear and trembling work out their salvation, in labours, in watchings, in almsdeeds, in prayers and oblations, in fastings and chastity: for, knowing that they are born again unto a hope of glory, but not as yet unto glory, they ought to fear for the combat which yet remains with the flesh, with the world, with the devil, wherein they cannot be victorious, unless they be with God's grace, obedient to the Apostle, who says, We are debtors, not to the flesh, to live according to the flesh; for if you live according to the flesh, you shall die; but if by the spirit you mortify the deeds of the flesh, you shall live.

CHAPTER XIV.

ON THE FALLEN, AND THEIR RESTORATION.

As regards those who, by sin, have fallen from the received grace of justification, they may be again justified, when, God exciting them, through the sacrament of Penance they shall have attained to the recovery, by the merit of Christ, of the grace lost: for this manner of justification is of the fallen the reparation: which the holy Fathers have aptly called a second plank after the shipwreck of grace lost. For, on behalf of those who fall into sins after baptism, Christ Jesus instituted the sacrament of Penance, when He said, Receive ye the Holy Ghost, whose sins you shall forgive, they are forgiven them, and whose sins you shall retain, they are retained. Whence it is to be taught, that the penitence of a Christian, after his fall, is very different from that at (his) baptism; and that therein are included not only a cessation from sins, and a detestation thereof, or, a contrite and humble heart, but also the sacramental confession of the said sins—at least in desire, and to be made in its season—and sacerdotal absolution; and likewise satisfaction by fasts, alms, prayers, and the other pious exercises of a spiritual life; not indeed for the eternal punishment—which is, together with the guilt, remitted, either by the sacrament, or by the desire of the sacrament—but for the temporal punishment, which, as the sacred writings teach, is not always wholly remitted, as is done in baptism, to those who, ungrateful to the grace of God which they have received, have grieved the Holy Spirit, and have not feared to violate the temple of God. Concerning which penitence it is written; Be mindful whence thou art fallen; do penance, and do the first works. And again; The sorrow that is according to God worketh penance steadfast unto salvation. And again; Do penance, and bring forth fruits worthy of penance.

CHAPTER XV.

THAT, BY EVERY MORTAL SIN, GRACE IS LOST, BUT NOT FAITH.

In opposition also to the subtle wits of certain men, who, by pleasing speeches and good words, seduce the hearts of the innocent, it is to be maintained, that the received grace of justification is lost, not only by infidelity whereby even faith itself is lost, but also by any other mortal sin whatever, though faith be not lost; thus defending the doctrine of the divine law, which excludes from the kingdom of God not only the unbelieving, but the faithful also (who are) fornicators, adulterers, effeminate, liers with mankind, thieves, covetous, drunkards, railers, extortioners, and all others who commit deadly sins; from which, with the help of divine grace, they can refrain, and on account of which they are separated from the grace of Christ.

CHAPTER XVI.

ON THE FRUIT OF JUSTIFICATION, THAT IS, ON THE MERIT OF GOOD WORKS, AND ON THE NATURE OF THAT MERIT.

Before men, therefore, who have been justified in this manner—whether they have preserved uninterruptedly the grace received, or whether they have recovered it when lost—are to be set the words of the Apostle: Abound in every good work, knowing that your labour is not in vain in the Lord; for God is not unjust, that he should forget your work, and the love which you have shown in his name; and, do not lose your confidence, which hath a great reward. And, for this cause, life eternal is to be proposed to those working well unto the end, and hoping in God, both as a grace mercifully promised to the sons of God through Jesus Christ, and as a reward which is according to the promise of God Himself, to be faithfully rendered to their good works and merits. For this is that crown of justice which the Apostle declared was, after his fight and course, laid up for him, to be rendered to him by the just judge, and not only to him, but also to all that love his coming. For, whereas Jesus Christ Himself continually infuses his virtue into the said justified—as the head into the members, and the vine into the branches—and this virtue always precedes and accompanies and follows their good works, which without it could not in any wise be pleasing and meritorious before God—we must believe that nothing further is wanting to the justified, to prevent their being accounted to have, by those very works which have been done in God, fully satisfied the divine law according to the state of this life, and to have truly merited eternal life, to be obtained also in its (due) time, if so be, however, that they depart in grace: seeing that Christ, our Saviour, saith: If any one shall drink of the water that I will give him, he shall not thirst for ever; but it shall become in him a fountain of water springing up unto life everlasting. Thus, neither is our own justice established as our own as from ourselves; nor is the justice of God ignored or repudiated: for that justice which is called ours, because that we are justified from its being inherent in us, that same is (the justice) of God, because that it is infused into us of God, through the merit of Christ. Neither is this to be omitted—that although, in the sacred writings, so much is attributed to good works, that Christ promises, that even he that shall give a drink of cold water to one of his least ones, shall not lose his reward; and the Apostle testifies that, That which is at present momentary and light of our tribulation, worketh for us above measure exceedingly an eternal weight of glory; nevertheless God forbid that a Christian should either trust or glory in himself, and not in the Lord, whose bounty towards all men is so great, that He will have the things which are His own gifts be their merits. And forasmuch as in many things we all offend, each one ought to have before his eyes, as well the severity and judgment, as the mercy and goodness (of God); neither ought any one to judge himself, even though he be not conscious to himself of anything; because the whole life of man is to be examined and judged, not by the judgment of man, but of God, who will bring to light the hidden things of darkness, and will make manifest the counsels of the hearts, and then shall every man have praise from God, who, as it is written, will render to every man according to his works. After this Catholic doctrine on justification, which whoso receiveth not faithfully and firmly cannot be justified, it hath seemed good to the holy Synod to subjoin these canons, that all may know not only what they ought to hold and follow, but also what to avoid and shun.

ON JUSTIFICATION

Canon I. If any one saith, that man may be justified before God by his own works, whether done through the teaching of human nature, or that of the law, without the grace of God through Jesus Christ; let him be anathema.

Canon II. If any one saith, that the grace of God, through Jesus Christ, is given only for this, that man may be able more easily to live justly, and to merit eternal life, as if, by free will without grace, he were able to do both, though hardly indeed and with difficulty; let him be anathema.

Canon III. If any one saith, that without the prevenient inspiration of the Holy Ghost, and without his help, man can believe, hope, love, or be penitent as he ought, so as that the grace of justification may be bestowed upon him; let him be anathema.

Canon IV. If any one saith, that man's free will moved and excited by God, by assenting to God exciting and calling, nowise co-operates towards disposing and preparing itself for obtaining the grace of justification; that it cannot refuse its consent, if it would, but that, as something inanimate, it does nothing whatever and is merely passive; let him be anathema.

Canon V. If any one saith, that, since Adam's sin, the free will of man is lost and extinguished; or, that it is a thing with only a name, yea a name without a reality, a figment, in fine, introduced into the Church by Satan; let him be anathema.

Canon VI. If any one saith, that it is not in man's power to make his ways evil, but that the works that are evil God worketh as well as those that are good, not permissively only, but properly, and of Himself, in such wise that the treason of Judas is no less His own proper work than the vocation of Paul; let him be anathema.

Canon VII. If any one saith, that all works done before justification, in whatsoever way they be done, are truly sins, or merit the hatred of God; or that the more earnestly one strives to dispose himself for grace, the more grievously he sins: let him be anathema.

Canon VIII. If any one saith, that the fear of hell, whereby, by grieving for our sins, we flee unto the mercy of God, or refrain from sinning—is a sin, or makes sinners worse; let him be anathema.

Canon IX. If any one saith, that by faith alone the impious is justified; in such wise as to mean, that nothing else is required to co-operate in order to the obtaining the grace of justification, and that it is not in any way necessary, that he be prepared and disposed by the movement of his own will; let him be anathema.

Canon X. If any one saith, that men are just without the justice of Christ, whereby He merited for us to be justified; or that it is by that justice itself that they are formally just; let him be anathema.

Canon XI. If any one saith, that men are justified, either by the sole imputation of the justice of Christ, or by the sole remission of sins, to the exclusion of the grace and the charity which is poured forth in their hearts by the Holy Ghost, and is inherent in them; or even that the grace, whereby we are justified, is only the favour of God; let him be anathema.

Canon XII. If any one saith, that justifying faith is nothing else but confidence in the divine mercy which remits sins for Christ's sake; or, that this confidence alone is that whereby we are justified; let him be anathema.

Canon XIII. If any one saith, that it is necessary for every one, for the obtaining the remission of sins, that he believe for certain, and without any wavering arising from his own infirmity and disposition, that his sins are forgiven him; let him be anathema.

Canon XIV. If any one saith, that man is truly absolved from his sins and justified, because that he assuredly believed himself absolved and justified; or, that no one is truly justified but he who believes himself justified; and that, by this faith alone, absolution and justification are effected; let him be anathema.

Canon XV. If any one saith, that a man, who is born again and justified, is bound of faith to believe that he is assuredly in the number of the predestinate; let him be anathema.

Canon XVI. If any one saith, that he will for certain, of an absolute and infallible certainty, have that great gift of perseverance unto the end—unless he have learned this by special revelation; let him be anathema.

Canon XVII. If any one saith, that the grace of justification is only attained to by those who are predestined unto life; but that all others who are called, are called indeed, but receive not grace, as being, by the divine power, predestined unto evil; let him be anathema.

Canon XVIII. If any one saith, that the commandments of God are, even for one that is justified and constituted in grace, impossible to keep; let him be anathema.

Canon XIX. If any one saith, that nothing besides faith is commanded in the Gospel; that other things are indifferent, neither commanded nor prohibited, but free; or, that the ten commandments nowise appertain to Christians; let him be anathema.

Canon XX. If any one saith, that the man who is justified and how perfect soever, is not bound to observe the commandments of God and of the Church, but only to believe; as if indeed the Gospel were a bare and absolute promise of eternal life, without the condition of observing the commandments; let him be anathema.

Canon XXI. If any one saith, that Christ Jesus was given of God to men, as a redeemer in whom to trust, and not also as a legislator whom to obey; let him be anathema.

Canon XXII. If any one saith, that the justified, either is able to persevere, without the special help of God, in the justice received; or that, with that help, he is not able; let him be anathema.

Canon XXIII. If any one saith, that a man once justified can sin no more, nor lose grace, and that therefore he that falls and sins was never truly justified; or, on the other hand, that he is able, during his whole life, to avoid all sins, even those that are venial—except by a special privilege from God, as the Church holds in regard of the Blessed Virgin; let him be anathema.

Canon XXIV. If any one saith, that the justice received is not preserved and also increased before God through good works; but that the said works are merely the fruits and signs of justification obtained, but not a cause of the increase thereof; let him be anathema.

Canon XXV. If any one saith, that, in every good work, the just sins venially at least, or-which is more intolerable still-mortally, and consequently deserves eternal punishments; and that for this cause only he is not damned, that God does not impute those works unto damnation; let him be anathema.

Canon XXVI. If any one saith, that the just ought not, for their good works done in God, to expect and hope for an eternal recompense from God, through His mercy and the merit of Jesus Christ, if so be that they persevere to the end in well doing and in keeping the divine commandments; let him be anathema.

Canon XXVII. If any one saith, that there is no mortal sin but that of infidelity; or, that grace once received is not lost by any other sin, however grievous and enormous, save by that of infidelity; let him be anathema.

Canon XXVIII. If any one saith, that, grace being lost through sin, faith also is always lost with it; or, that the faith which remains, though it be not a lively faith, is not a true faith; or, that he, who has faith without charity, is not a Chris taught; let him be anathema.

Canon XXIX. If any one saith, that he, who has fallen after baptism, is not able by the grace of God to rise again; or, that he is able indeed to recover the justice which he has lost, but by faith alone without the sacrament of Penance, contrary to what the holy Roman and universal Church—instructed by Christ and his Apostles—has hitherto professed, observed, and taught; let him be anathema.

Canon XXX. If any one saith, that, after the grace of justification has been received, to every penitent sinner the guilt is remitted, and the debt of eternal punishment is blotted out in such wise, that there remains not any debt of temporal punishment to be discharged either in this world, or in the next in Purgatory, before the entrance to the kingdom of heaven can be opened (to him); let him be anathema.

Canon XXXI. If any one saith, that the justified sins when he performs good works with a view to an eternal recompense; let him be anathema.

Canon XXXII. If any one saith, that the good works of one that is justified are in such manner the gifts of God, as that they are not also the good merits of him that is justified; or, that the said justified, by the good works which he performs through the grace of God and the merit of Jesus Christ, whose living member he is, does not truly merit increase of grace, eternal life, and the attainment of that eternal life—if so be, however, that he depart in grace—and also an increase of glory; let him be anathema.

Canon XXXIII. If any one saith that, by the Catholic doctrine touching justification, by this holy Synod inset forth in this present decree, the glory of God, or the merits of our Lord Jesus Christ are in any way derogated from, and not rather that the truth of our faith, and the glory in fine of God and of Jesus Christ are rendered (more) illustrious; let him be anathema.

INTRODUCTION TO
Ignatius of Loyola
SPIRITUAL EXERCISES

It is important to keep in mind what we mean by the Catholic Counter-Reformation which ramped up in the 1540s. It was not merely—indeed, not even primarily—a "Counter-Reformation" in the sense of "something that counteracted, or sought to resist, the Reformation." Rather, it was very much a "Counter-Reformation" in the same sense of a "counter-attack"—it was itself a reformation which sought to respond to that which the Protestants had undertaken, an internal reform and renewal movement that was, however, fiercely loyal to the Pope. Of course, what shape such internal reform and renewal should take was hotly contested, and all but the most traditionalist advocates of reform ran the risk of being accused of Protestant sympathizers.

So it was with probably the most famous and influential of all Counter-Reformation leaders, Ignatius of Loyola, founder of Society of Jesus, or Jesuit order. From its humble beginnings as a band of friends trying to travel to Jerusalem in the late 1530s, the order was nearly ubiquitous a century later, with well-established mission centers not only across Europe but in South America, North America, and East Asia.

No group did more to slow and in some places, such as Poland, to roll back the progress of the Reformation as the Jesuits. Key to their success was their imitation of key features of Protestantism. They stressed the importance of teaching and catechesis, realizing that ordinary Catholic laypeople could hardly be expected to just "shut up and obey the Pope" when presented with persuasive arguments from Protestant preachers. They also downplayed the barrier between clergy and laity that had been such a crucial part of Luther's early protest, acting neither as parish priests nor as monks living in their separated communities, but instead working closely with ordinary people. Indeed, their courageous and dedicated mission work in the Americas and Asia won countless converts from heathenism and set a model that later Protestant foreign missionaries were to seek to imitate. The Jesuits also laid great stress on individual religious experience and the discipleship of the soul, thus helping to rebut Protestant critiques of hypocritical outward ceremonialism.

This last emphasis grew directly out of Ignatius's own deep religious experience. Born in northern Spain under the name Íñigo de Loyola (his later name, Ignatius, was the result of a scribal error),[1] he aspired to rise to a position in the nobility and joined the army. Seriously wounded in the battle of Pamplona, he spent several months convalescing with little around to read but medieval devotional texts. The result was a powerful conversion experience that led Ignatius to commit himself to a missionary life. Although he was passionately devoted to the service of the Roman Church, Ignatius's emphasis on personal religious experience savored a little too much of Protestantism and other heresies for the Spanish Inquisition, and he left Spain in 1528.

After a period of study in Paris, Ignatius and a group of companions vowed to make a pilgrimage to Jerusalem, but were thwarted in 1537 by a war with the Turks that shut down all shipping. Stranded in Italy, Ignatius and his companions went to Rome and determined to serve Jesus and His Church in whatever ways He called them to, and began calling themselves the Society of Jesus. In 1540, Ignatius succeeded in winning papal

1 Diarmaid MacCulloch, *Reformation: Europe's House Divided, 1490–1700* (London: Penguin, 2003), 220.

approval to formalize the Society as a religious order of the Catholic Church. Ignatius and his associates still faced suspicion and opposition from many members of the Roman hierarchy, however, and his devotional guide, the *Spiritual Exercises*, was carefully screened by the Roman Inquisition before being approved for publication in 1548.

The *Exercises* is a curious book—not meant for reading so much as for use as a how-to manual by spiritual directors, which Ignatius trained his followers to be. Rather than playing the passive role of confessor that most parish priests did before the Reformation, Jesuit spiritual directors would lead believers in a prolonged process of self-examination, meditation, and contemplation of Christ to help them leave behind sin and strengthen their faith. Indeed, in their emphasis on the depth of our depravity that must be confessed, the *Exercises* are reminiscent of aspects of Luther's theology, particularly those that earned early condemnation in the bull *Exsurge Domine*. However, the difference between Reformation and Counter-Reformation spirituality is also clear in the excerpt below. For Luther, although awareness of one's deep sinfulness and helplessness was necessary to truly receive the grace of God, one was not supposed to wallow in self-examination, grief, or fear, but to turn immediately from it to the comfort of Christ's mercy. To be sure, the "First Week" excerpted here is followed by meditations on Christ's life, on his death, and on his resurrection; introspection and repentance is only the beginning. Still, it is a beginning that is never wholly left behind, since in Ignatian spirituality, as in all Roman Catholic spirituality, there is no room for the firm and confident assurance of salvation that Protestants proclaimed; indeed, as we saw in the last reading, such assurance was explicitly anathematized.

SPIRITUAL EXERCISES

Ignatius of Loyola

TRANSLATED BY ELDER MULLAN, S.J.

GENERAL EXAMEN OF CONSCIENCE TO PURIFY ONESELF AND TO MAKE ONE'S CONFESSION BETTER

I presuppose that there are three kinds of thoughts in me: that is, one my own, which springs from my mere liberty and will; and two others, which come from without, one from the good spirit, and the other from the bad.

Thought

There are two ways of meriting in the bad thought which comes from without, namely:

First Way. A thought of committing a mortal sin, which thought I resist immediately and it remains conquered.

Second Way. The second way of meriting is: When that same bad thought comes to me and I resist it, and it returns to me again and again, and I always resist, until it is conquered.

This second way is more meritorious than the first.

A venial sin is committed when the same thought comes of sinning mortally and one gives ear to it, making some little delay, or receiving some sensual pleasure, or when there is some negligence in rejecting such thought.

There are two ways of sinning mortally:

First Way. The first is, when one gives consent to the bad thought, to act afterwards as he has consented, or to put it in act if he could.

Second Way. The second way of sinning mortally is when that sin is put in act.

This is a greater sin for three reasons: first, because of the greater time; second, because of the greater intensity; third, because of the greater harm to the two persons.

Word

One must not swear, either by Creator or creature, if it be not with truth, necessity and reverence.

By necessity I mean, not when any truth whatever is affirmed with oath, but when it is of some importance for the good of the soul, or the body, or for temporal goods.

By reverence I mean when, in naming the Creator and Lord, one acts with consideration, so as to render Him the honor and reverence due.

It is to be noted that, though in an idle oath one sins more when he swears by the Creator than by the creature, it is more difficult to swear in the right way with truth, necessity and reverence by the creature than by the Creator, for the following reasons.

First Reason. The first: When we want to swear by some creature, wanting to name the creature does not make us so attentive or circumspect as to telling the truth, or as to affirming it with necessity, as would wanting to name the Lord and Creator of all things.

Second Reason. The second is that in swearing by the creature it is not so easy to show reverence and respect to the Creator, as in swearing and naming the same Creator and Lord, because wanting to name God our Lord brings with it more respect and reverence than wanting to name the created thing. Therefore swearing by the creature is more allowable to the perfect than to the imperfect, because the perfect, through continued contemplation and enlightenment of intellect, consider, meditate and contemplate more that God our Lord is in every creature, according to His own essence, presence and power, and so in swearing by the creature they are more apt and prepared than the imperfect to show respect and reverence to their Creator and Lord.

Third Reason. The third is that in continually swearing by the creature, idolatry is to be more feared in the imperfect than in the perfect.

One must not speak an idle word. By idle word I mean one which does not benefit either me or another, and is not directed to that intention. Hence words spoken for any useful purpose, or meant to profit one's own or another's soul, the body or temporal goods, are never idle, not even if one were to speak of something foreign to one's state of life, as, for instance, if a religious speaks of wars or articles of trade; but in all that is said there is merit in directing well, and sin in directing badly, or in speaking idly.

Nothing must be said to injure another's character or to find fault, because if I reveal a mortal sin that is not public, I sin mortally; if a venial sin, venially; and if a defect, I show a defect of my own.

But if the intention is right, in two ways one can speak of the sin or fault of another:

First Way. The first: When the sin is public, as in the case of a public prostitute, and of a sentence given in judgment, or of a public error which is infecting the souls with whom one comes in contact.

Second Way. Second: When the hidden sin is revealed to some person that he may help to raise him who is in sin—supposing, however, that he has some probable conjectures or grounds for thinking that he will be able to help him.

Act

Taking the Ten Commandments, the Precepts of the Church and the recommendations of Superiors, every act done against any of these three heads is, according to its greater or less nature, a greater or a lesser sin.

By recommendations of Superiors I mean such things as Bulls de Cruzadas and other Indulgences, as for instance for peace, granted under condition of going to Confession and receiving the Blessed Sacrament. For one commits no little sin in being the cause of others acting contrary to such pious exhortations and recommendations of our Superiors, or in doing so oneself.

Method For Making The General Examen

It contains in it five Points.

First Point. The first Point is to give thanks to God our Lord for the benefits received.

Second Point. The second, to ask grace to know our sins and cast them out.

Third Point. The third, to ask account of our soul from the hour that we rose up to the present Examen, hour by hour, or period by period: and first as to thoughts, and then as to words, and then as to acts, in the same order as was mentioned in the Particular Examen.

Fourth Point. The fourth, to ask pardon of God our Lord for the faults.

Fifth Point. The fifth, to purpose amendment with His grace.

OUR FATHER.

GENERAL CONFESSION WITH COMMUNION

Whoever, of his own accord, wants to make a General Confession, will, among many other advantages, find three in making it here.

First. The first: Though whoever goes to Confession every year is not obliged to make a General Confession, by making it there is greater profit and merit, because of the greater actual sorrow for all the sins and wickedness of his whole life.

Second. The second: In the Spiritual Exercises, sins and their malice are understood more intimately, than in the time when one was not so giving himself to interior things. Gaining now more knowledge of and sorrow for them, he will have greater profit and merit than he had before.

Third. The third is: In consequence, having made a better Confession and being better disposed, one finds himself in condition and prepared to receive the Blessed Sacrament: the reception of which is an aid not only not to fall into sin, but also to preserve the increase of grace.

This General Confession will be best made immediately after the Exercises of the First Week.

FIRST EXERCISE

It Is a Meditation with the Three Powers on the First, the Second and the Third Sin

It contains in it, after one Preparatory Prayer and two Preludes, three chief Points and one *Colloquy*.

Prayer. The Preparatory Prayer is to ask grace of God our Lord that all my intentions, actions and operations may be directed purely to the service and praise of His Divine Majesty.

First Prelude. The First Prelude is a composition, seeing the place.

Here it is to be noted that, in a visible contemplation or meditation—as, for instance, when one contemplates Christ our Lord, Who is visible—the composition will be to see with the sight of the imagination the corporeal place where the thing is found which I want to contemplate. I say the corporeal place, as for instance, a Temple or Mountain where Jesus Christ or Our Lady is found, according to what I want to contemplate. In an invisible contemplation or meditation—as here on the Sins—the composition will be to see with the sight of the imagination and consider that my soul is imprisoned in this corruptible body, and all the compound in this valley, as exiled among brute beasts: I say all the compound of soul and body.

Second Prelude. The second is to ask God our Lord for what I want and desire.

The petition has to be according to the subject matter; that is, if the contemplation is on the Resurrection, one is to ask for joy with Christ in joy; if it is on the Passion, he is to ask for pain, tears and torment with Christ in torment.

Here it will be to ask shame and confusion at myself, seeing how many have been damned for only one mortal sin, and how many times I deserved to be condemned forever for my so many sins.

Note. Before all Contemplations or Meditations, there ought always to be made the Preparatory Prayer, which is not changed, and the two Preludes already mentioned, which are sometimes changed, according to the subject matter.

First Point. The first Point will be to bring the memory on the First Sin, which was that of the Angels, and then to bring the intellect on the same, discussing it; then the will, wanting to recall and understand all this in order to make me more ashamed and confound me more, bringing into comparison with the one sin of the Angels my so many sins, and reflecting, while they for one sin were cast into Hell, how often I have deserved it for so many.

I say to bring to memory the sin of the Angels, how they, being created in grace, not wanting to help themselves with their liberty to reverence and obey their Creator and Lord, coming to pride, were changed from grace to malice, and hurled from Heaven to Hell; and so then to discuss more in detail with the intellect: and then to move the feelings more with the will.

Second Point. The second is to do the same—that is, to bring the Three Powers—on the sin of Adam and Eve, bringing to memory how on account of that sin they did penance for so long a time, and how much corruption came on the human race, so many people going the way to Hell.

I say to bring to memory the Second Sin, that of our First Parents; how after Adam was created in the field of Damascus and placed in the Terrestrial Paradise, and Eve was created from his rib, being forbidden to eat of the Tree of Knowledge, they ate and so sinned, and afterwards clothed in tunics of skins and cast from Paradise, they lived, all their life, without the original justice which they had lost, and in many labors and much penance. And then to discuss with the understanding more in detail; and to use the will as has been said.

Third Point. The third is likewise to do the same on the Third particular Sin of any one who for one mortal sin is gone to Hell—and many others without number, for fewer sins than I have committed.

I say to do the same on the Third particular Sin, bringing to memory the gravity and malice of the sin against one's Creator and

Lord; to discuss with the understanding how in sinning and acting against the Infinite Goodness, he has been justly condemned forever; and to finish with the will as has been said.

Colloquy. Imagining Christ our Lord present and placed on the Cross, let me make a Colloquy, how from Creator He is come to making Himself man, and from life eternal is come to temporal death, and so to die for my sins.

Likewise, looking at myself, what I have done for Christ, what I am doing for Christ, what I ought to do for Christ.

And so, seeing Him such, and so nailed on the Cross, to go over that which will present itself.

The Colloquy is made, properly speaking, as one friend speaks to another, or as a servant to his master; now asking some grace, now blaming oneself for some misdeed, now communicating one's affairs, and asking advice in them.

And let me say an OUR FATHER.

SECOND EXERCISE

It Is a Meditation on the Sins and Contains in It after the Preparatory Prayer and Two Preludes, Five Points and One Colloquy

Prayer. Let the Preparatory Prayer be the same.

First Prelude. The First Prelude will be the same composition.

Second Prelude. The second is to ask for what I want. It will be here to beg a great and intense sorrow and tears for my sins.

First Point. The first Point is the statement of the sins; that is to say, to bring to memory all the sins of life, looking from year to year, or from period to period. For this three things are helpful: first, to look at the place and the house where I have lived; second, the relations I have had with others; third, the occupation in which I have lived.

Second Point. The second, to weigh the sins, looking at the foulness and the malice which any mortal sin committed has in it, even supposing it were not forbidden.

Third Point. The third, to look at who I am, lessening myself by examples:

First, how much I am in comparison to all men;

Second, what men are in comparison to all the Angels and Saints of Paradise;

Third, what all Creation is in comparison to God: (Then I alone, what can I be?)

Fourth, to see all my bodily corruption and foulness;

Fifth, to look at myself as a sore and ulcer, from which have sprung so many sins and so many iniquities and so very vile poison.

Fourth Point. The fourth, to consider what God is, against Whom I have sinned, according to His attributes; comparing them with their contraries in me—His Wisdom with my ignorance; His Omnipotence with my weakness; His Justice with my iniquity; His Goodness with my malice.

Fifth Point. The fifth, an exclamation of wonder with deep feeling, going through all creatures, how they have left me in life and preserved me in it; the Angels, how, though they are the sword of the Divine Justice, they have endured me, and guarded me, and prayed for me; the Saints, how they have been engaged in interceding and praying for me; and the heavens, sun, moon, stars, and elements, fruits, birds, fishes and animals—and the earth, how it has not opened to swallow me up, creating new Hells for me to suffer in them forever!

Colloquy. Let me finish with a Colloquy of mercy, pondering and giving thanks to God our Lord that He has given me life up to now, proposing amendment, with His grace, for the future.

OUR FATHER.

THIRD EXERCISE

It Is a Repetition of the First and Second Exercise, Making Three Colloquies

After the Preparatory Prayer and two Preludes, it will be to repeat the First and Second Exercise, marking and dwelling on the Points in which I have felt greater consolation or desolation, or greater spiritual feeling.

After this I will make three Colloquies in the following manner:

First Colloquy. The first Colloquy to Our Lady, that she may get me grace from Her Son and Lord for three things: first, that I may feel an interior knowledge of my sins, and hatred of them; second, that I may feel the disorder of my actions, so that, hating them, I may correct myself and put myself in order; third, to ask knowledge of the world, in order that, hating it, I may put away from me worldly and vain things.

And with that a HAIL MARY.

Second Colloquy. The second: The same to the Son, begging Him to get it for me from the Father.

And with that the SOUL OF CHRIST.

Third Colloquy. The third: The same to the Father, that the Eternal Lord Himself may grant it to me.

And with that an OUR FATHER.

FOURTH EXERCISE

It Is a Summary of This Same Third

I said a summary, that the understanding, without wandering, may assiduously go through the memory of the things contemplated in the preceding Exercises.

I will make the same three Colloquies.

FIFTH EXERCISE

It Is a Meditation on Hell

It contains in it, after the Preparatory Prayer and two Preludes, five Points and one Colloquy:

Prayer. Let the Preparatory Prayer be the usual one.

First Prelude. The first Prelude is the composition, which is here to see with the sight of the imagination the length, breadth and depth of Hell.

Second Prelude. The second, to ask for what I want: it will be here to ask for interior sense of the pain which the damned suffer, in order that, if, through my faults, I should forget the love of the Eternal Lord, at least the fear of the pains may help me not to come into sin.

First Point. The first Point will be to see with the sight of the imagination the great fires, and the souls as in bodies of fire.

Second Point. The second, to hear with the ears wailings, howlings, cries, blasphemies against Christ our Lord and against all His Saints.

Third Point. The third, to smell with the smell smoke, sulphur, dregs and putrid things.

Fourth Point. The fourth, to taste with the taste bitter things, like tears, sadness and the worm of conscience.

Fifth Point. The fifth, to touch with the touch; that is to say, how the fires touch and burn the souls.

Colloquy. Making a Colloquy to Christ our Lord, I will bring to memory the souls that are in Hell, some because they did not believe the Coming, others because, believing, they did not act according to His Commandments; making three divisions:

First, Second, and Third Divisions. The first, before the Coming; the second, during His life; the third, after His life in this world; and with this I will give Him thanks that He has not let me fall into any of these divisions, ending my life.

Likewise, I will consider how up to now He has always had so great pity and mercy on me.

I will end with an OUR FATHER.

Note. The first Exercise will be made at midnight; the second immediately on rising in the morning; the third, before or after Mass; in any case, before dinner; the fourth at the hour of Vespers; the fifth, an hour before supper.

This arrangement of hours, more or less, I always mean in all the four Weeks, according as his age, disposition and physical condition help the person who is exercising himself to make five Exercises or fewer.

ADDITIONS

To Make the Exercises Better and to Find Better What One Desires

First Addition. The first Addition is, after going to bed, just when I want to go asleep, to think, for the space of a HAIL MARY, of the hour that I have to rise and for what, making a resume of the Exercise which I have to make.

Second Addition. The second: When I wake up, not giving place to any other thought, to turn my attention immediately to what I am going to contemplate in the first Exercise, at midnight, bringing myself to confusion for my so many sins, setting examples, as, for instance, if a knight found himself before his king and all his court, ashamed and confused at having much offended him, from whom he had first received many gifts and many favors: in the same way, in the second Exercise, making myself a great sinner and in chains; that is to say going to appear bound as in chains before the Supreme Eternal Judge; taking for an example how prisoners in chains and already deserving death, appear before their temporal judge. And I will dress with these thoughts or with others, according to the subject matter.

Third Addition. The third: A step or two before the place where I have to contemplate or meditate, I will put myself standing for the space of an OUR FATHER, my intellect raised on high, considering how God our Lord is looking at me, etc.; and will make an act of reverence or humility.

Fourth Addition. The fourth: To enter on the contemplation now on my knees, now prostrate on the earth, now lying face upwards, now seated, now standing, always intent on seeking what I want.

We will attend to two things. The first is, that if I find what I want kneeling, I will not pass on; and if prostrate, likewise, etc. The second; in the Point in which I find what I want, there I will rest, without being anxious to pass on, until I content myself.

Fifth Addition. The fifth: After finishing the Exercise, I will, during the space of a quarter of an hour, seated or walking leisurely, look how it went with me in the Contemplation or Meditation; and if badly, I will look for the cause from which it proceeds, and having so seen it, will be sorry, in order to correct myself in future; and if well, I will give thanks to God our Lord, and will do in like manner another time.

Sixth Addition. The sixth: Not to want to think on things of pleasure or joy, such as heavenly glory, the Resurrection, etc. Because whatever consideration of joy and gladness hinders our feeling pain and grief and shedding tears for our sins: but to keep before me that I want to grieve and feel pain, bringing to memory rather Death and Judgment.

Seventh Addition. The seventh: For the same end, to deprive myself of all light, closing the blinds and doors while I am in the room, if it be not to recite prayers, to read and eat.

Eighth Addition. The eighth: Not to laugh nor say a thing provocative of laughter.

Ninth Addition. The ninth: To restrain my sight, except in receiving or dismissing the person with whom I have spoken.

Tenth Addition. The tenth Addition is penance.

This is divided into interior and exterior. The interior is to grieve for one's sins, with a firm purpose of not committing them nor any others. The exterior, or fruit of the first, is chastisement for the sins committed, and is chiefly taken in three ways.

First Way. The first is as to eating. That is to say, when we leave off the superfluous, it is not penance, but temperance. It is penance when we leave off from the suitable; and the more and more, the greater and better—provided that the person does not injure himself, and that no notable illness follows.

Second Way. The second, as to the manner of sleeping. Here too it is not penance to leave off the superfluous of delicate or soft things, but it is penance when one leaves off from the suitable in the manner: and the more and more, the better—provided that the person does not injure himself and no notable illness follows. Besides, let not anything of the suitable sleep be left off, unless in order to come to the mean, if one has a bad habit of sleeping too much.

Third Way. The third, to chastise the flesh, that is, giving it sensible pain, which is given by wearing haircloth or cords or iron chains next to the flesh, by scourging or wounding oneself, and by other kinds of austerity.

Note. What appears most suitable and most secure with regard to penance is that the pain should be sensible in the flesh and not enter within the bones, so that it give pain and not illness. For this it appears to be more suitable to scourge oneself with thin cords, which give pain exteriorly, rather than in another way which would cause notable illness within.

First Note. The first Note is that the exterior penances are done chiefly for three ends: First, as satisfaction for the sins committed;

Second, to conquer oneself—that is, to make sensuality obey reason and all inferior parts be more subject to the superior;

Third, to seek and find some grace or gift which the person wants and desires; as, for instance, if he desires to have interior contrition for his sins, or to weep much over them, or over the pains and sufferings which Christ our Lord suffered in His Passion, or to settle some doubt in which the person finds himself.

Second Note. The second: It is to be noted that the first and second Addition have to be made for the Exercises of midnight and at daybreak, but not for those which will be made at other times; and the fourth Addition will never be made in church in the presence of others, but in private, as at home, etc.

Third Note. The third: When the person who is exercising himself does not yet find what he desires—as tears, consolations, etc.,—it often helps for him to make a change in food, in sleep and in other ways of doing penance, so that he change himself, doing penance two or three days, and two or three others not. For it suits some to do more penance and others less, and we often omit doing penance from sensual love and from an erroneous judgment that the human system will not be able to bear it without notable illness; and sometimes, on the contrary, we do too much, thinking that the body can bear it; and as God our Lord knows our nature infinitely better, often in such changes He gives each one to perceive what is suitable for him.

Fourth Note. The fourth: Let the Particular Examen be made to rid oneself of defects and negligences on the Exercises and Additions. And so in the SECOND, THIRD AND FOURTH WEEKS.

INTRODUCTION TO
Zacharias Ursinus
COMMENTARY ON THE HEIDELBERG CATECHISM

We noted in the introduction to the preceding selection that the one note that most differentiated Reformation from Counter-Reformation spirituality was that of comfort or assurance. Although Catholic apologists frequently chided the Reformers, as Enlightenment intellectuals were later to do also, for an overemphasis on the depth of human sin and depravity, the focal point of all good Protestant theology was always calm comfort in the mercy of Christ. This sentiment was given its most memorable expression in the great words of Question 1 of the Heidelberg Catechism:

> *Q. What is your only comfort in life and in death?*
>
> That I am not my own, but belong, body and soul, in life and in death, to my faithful Savior Jesus Christ, who has fully paid for all my sins and delivered me from the dominion of the devil. He also watches over me in such a way that not a hair can fall from my head without the will of my father in heaven; in fact, all things must work together for my salvation. Because I belong to him, Christ, by his Holy Spirit, assures me of eternal life, and makes me wholeheartedly willing and ready from now on to live for him.

This document, however, was to emerge out of a decidedly uncomfortable moment in the history of Protestantism: the moment when the Lutheran and Reformed branches of the Reformation began to draw clear battle lines as opposing parties. There had, to be sure, been different teachings and emphases among the leading Reformers from the beginning, and on the matter of the Lord's Supper in particular, the early disagreement between Luther and Zwingli in the 1520s, although largely ironed out, or papered over (depending on your perspective) in the 1530s and 1540s, remained a source of tension between churches more influenced by Wittenberg and those more influenced by Zurich.

However, conflict did not seriously erupt until the 1550s, precipitated chiefly by intra-Lutheran squabbles as to who represented the truer heirs of Luther's theology. Melanchthon had always reserved the right to disagree with Luther when necessary, and as his own thinking on the matter of the Lord's Supper in particular evolved, he taught a doctrine that had clear affinities with that of Calvin, prompting loud denunciations from a party that came to be called Gnesio (that is, "authentic")-Lutherans. Still, until Melanchthon's death in 1560, there was a fair bit of wiggle room between the emerging confessional boundaries.

It was into this fast-disappearing wiggle room that Elector Frederick III of the Palatinate, an important principality in western Germany, tried to squeeze in the late 1550s and early 1560s. Frederick was determined to make the Palatinate, and especially the university in his capital city, Heidelberg, a beacon of the Reformation. To that end, he surrounded himself with leading disciples of Melanchthon and also some theologians trained in Zurich and Geneva, inviting increasing condemnations from Gnesio-Lutheran leaders around Germany. Seeking a full confessional statement that would highlight the common ground among Protestants, and that would serve as an effective teaching tool for his people, Frederick commissioned the Heidelberg Catechism, which appeared in 1563.

Its lead author, Zacharias Ursinus, epitomized the middle way Frederick was seeking to forge. Born in 1534, he had trained in theology at Wittenberg under the tutelage of Melanchthon, quickly becoming one of his star students and developing a close friendship with the great teacher. As intra-Lutheran conflict became more fierce, however, he went to Zurich in 1560 to study with one of the giants of the emerging Reformed tradition, Peter Martyr Vermigli. A year later he was called to Heidelberg to teach in the University, and the next year, appointed to the drafting committee of the Catechism, in which he seems to have taken the leading role. Despite his success in producing a document which breathes the spirit of Melanchthon and Calvin equally, not to mention showing the influence of other leading theologians, the Heidelberg Catechism was to provoke even sharper opposition than Frederick had faced before, and the Palatinate found itself increasingly isolated from other territories in Lutheran Germany.

Indeed, when Frederick died in 1576, his son Louis sought to align the Palatinate fully with the Gnesio-Lutherans, and drove out Ursinus and the other theologians at Heidelberg, an effort that was cut short by his own death in 1583. Ursinus, sadly, died that same year when only 48 years old, too soon to return to Heidelberg. Fortunately, however, he had succeeded before his death in producing, alongside many other brilliant works of theology, a series of lectures comprising a complete commentary on the Catechism, thoroughly elaborating the doctrines so succinctly stated in it. This text was edited into publishable form by his student David Pareus, who was subsequently to become one of the brightest luminaries of German Reformed theology. The Catechism itself, meanwhile, was to find before long a much wider sphere of influence than the Palatinate, being officially adopted by the Dutch Reformed Church in 1618 as one of their Three Forms of Unity, and has continued to serve as the official catechism of the Dutch and German Reformed down to the present.

The following excerpt provides the text of questions 86–91 of the Catechism, together with Ursinus's commentary. In this section, Ursinus turns to consider the role of good works in the life of a Christian as the fruits of gratitude which the justified believer should display to God and neighbor. This reflects a growing emphasis within the second generation of the Reformation, as well as within the Reformed tradition generally, which sought to counteract concerns that the proclamation of justification by faith alone might lead to an aimless antinomianism, rather than a disciplined and holy life.

However, Ursinus does not in any way back down from the affirmation that works in no way contribute to justification. In a theological *tour de force* that is particularly on display in his lengthy treatment of Q. 91, he answers such vexing questions and objections as these:

- In what sense are good works necessary to salvation?
- Are all our works before justification displeasing to God?
- If so, how can we still distinguish between moral and immoral works of the unregenerate?
- Are all our works after justification still tainted with sin?
- If so, how can they be pleasing to God?

Ursinus's careful answers to these questions represent a powerful clarification and defense of the Protestant position against Roman Catholic critiques that had been voiced from *Exsurge Domine* down to the Council of Trent and beyond.

COMMENTARY ON THE HEIDELBERG CATECHISM

Zacharias Ursinus

TRANSLATED BY GEORGE W. WILLIARD

THIRTY-SECOND LORD'S DAY

Question 86. Since then we are delivered from our misery, merely of grace through Christ, without any merit of ours, why must we still do good works?

Answer. Because that Christ, having redeemed and delivered us by his blood, also renews us by his Holy Spirit, after his own image; that so we may testify, by the whole of our conduct, our gratitude to God for his blessings, and that he may be praised by us; also, that every one may be assured in himself of his faith, by the fruits thereof; and that by our godly conversation others may be gained to Christ.

Exposition. This Question, with respect to the moving causes of good works, is placed first, even before the Question relating to man's conversion, not because good works precede conversion, but because the things which follow are in this way more strikingly connected with what precedes. Human reason argues in this way from the doctrine of free satisfaction: He is not bound to make satisfaction, for whom another has already satisfied.

Christ has satisfied for us. Therefore, there is no need that we should perform good works. We reply, that there is more in the conclusion than in the premises. All that legitimately follows, is: Therefore, we ourselves are not bound to make satisfaction, which we grant, 1. In respect to the justice of (God, which does not demand a double payment. 2. In respect to our salvation, which, in other respects, would be no salvation. Yet we are, nevertheless, bound to render obedience, and perform good works, for the reasons which are referred to, and explained in the above Question of the Catechism:

1. Because good works are the fruits of our regeneration by the Holy Spirit, which are always connected with our free justification. "Whom he called, them he also justified, and whom he justified, them he also glorified." "Such were some of you; but ye are washed; but ye are sanctified; but ye are justified," etc. (Rom. 8:30. 1 Cor. 6:11.) Those, therefore, who do not perform good works, show that they are neither regenerated by the Spirit of God, nor redeemed by the blood of Christ.

2. That we may express our gratitude to God for the benefit of redemption. "Yield your members as instruments of righteousness unto God." "That ye present your bodies, a living sacrifice, holy, acceptable unto God, which is your reasonable service," etc. (Rom. 6:13; 12:1.)

3. That God may be glorified by us. "Let your light so shine before men, that they may see your good works, and glorify your Father which is in heaven." "That they may, by your good works, which they shall behold, glorify God in the day of visitation." (Matt. 5:16. 1 Pet. 2:12.)

4. Because they are the fruits of faith—that by which our own faith, as well as the faith of others is judged of. "Give diligence, to make your calling and election sure"; after which certain copies add the words, by good works. "Every good tree bringeth forth good fruit; but a corrupt tree bringeth forth evil fruit." "Faith worketh by love." "But the fruit of the Spirit is love, joy, peace, long-suffering, gentleness, goodness, faith, meekness, temperance." (2 Pet. 1:10. Matt. 7:17. Gal. 5:6, 22.)

5. That we may bring others to Christ. "When thou art converted, strengthen thy brethren." "Ye wives, be in subjection to your own husbands; that, if any obey not the word, they also may, without the word, be won by the conversation of their wives." "Let us follow after the things which make for peace, and things wherewith one may edify another." (Luke 22:32. 1 Pet. 3:1. Rom. 14:19.) These causes, now, must be explained and urged with great diligence, in our sermons and exhortations to the people; and here we may cite, as being in point, the whole of the sixth chapter, and the first part of the eighth chapter of Paul's epistle to the Romans, down to the sixteenth verse.

For a further explanation of the first cause, we may remark, that the benefit of justification is not given without regeneration: 1. Because Christ has merited both; viz., the remission of sins, and the habitation of God within us by the Holy Spirit. The Holy Spirit, now, is never inactive, but is always efficacious, and so brings it to pass that those in whom he dwells are made conformable to God. 2. Because the heart is purified by faith: for in all those to whom the merits of Christ are applied by faith, there is kindled the love of God, and a desire to do those things which are pleasing in his sight. 3. Because God bestows the benefit of justification upon none, but such as render true gratitude. But no one ever renders true gratitude except those who receive the benefit of regeneration. Therefore, neither of these can be separated from the other.

We must also observe the difference which exists between the first and second causes. The first shows what Christ effects in us by virtue of his death; whilst the second teaches to what we are bound in view of the benefits received.

Question 87. Cannot they then be saved, who, continuing in their wicked and ungrateful lives, are not converted to God?

Answer. By no means; for the holy Scripture declares that no unchaste person, idolater, adulterer, thief, covetous man, drunkard, slanderer, robber, or any such like shall inherit the kingdom of God.

Exposition. This Question naturally grows out of the preceding one; for since good works are the fruits of our regeneration—since they are the expression of our thankfulness to God, and the evidences of true faith; and since none are saved but those in whom these things are found; it follows, on the other hand, that evil works are the fruits of the flesh—that they are manifestations of ingratitude, and evidences of unbelief, so that no one that continues to produce them can be saved. Hence, all those who are not converted to God from their evil works, but continue in their sins, are condemned for ever, according to the following declarations of the word of God: "Know ye not that the unrighteous shall not inherit the kingdom of God? be not deceived; neither fornicators, nor idolaters, nor adulterers, nor effeminate, etc., shall inherit the kingdom of God." "Of the which I have told you in times past that they which do such things, shall not inherit the kingdom of God." "For this ye know; that no whoremonger, nor unclean person, nor covetous man, who is an idolater, hath any inheritance in the kingdom of Christ and of God; for because of these things cometh the wrath of God upon the children of disobedience." "He that loveth not his brother abideth in death." (1 Cor. 6:9. Gal. 5:21. Eph. 5:5, 6. 1 John 3:14.)

We may also observe, that another reason for good works may be deduced from the consequence which results from evil works; viz., that all those who perform evil works, and continue in their wicked and ungrateful lives, cannot be saved, inasmuch as they are destitute of true faith, and conversion.

THIRTY-THIRD LORD'S DAY

Question 88. In how many parts doth the true conversion of man consist?

Answer. In two parts; in the mortification of the old, and in the quickening of the new man.

Question 89. What is the mortification of the old man?

Answer. It is a sincere sorrow of heart, that we have provoked God by our sins; and more and more to hate and flee from them.

Question 90. What is the quickening of the new man?

Answer. It is a sincere joy of heart in God, through Christ, and with love and delight to live according to the will of God in all good works.

Exposition. The doctrine touching man's conversion to God now claims our attention, concerning which we must inquire:

I. Is conversion necessary?

II. What is it?

III. Of how many parts does it consist?

IV. What are the causes of it?

V. What are the effects of it?

VI. Is it perfect in this life?

VII. In what does the conversion of the godly differ from the repentance of the wicked?

I. IS THE CONVERSION OF MAN TO GOD NECESSARY?

Man's conversion in this life is so necessary, that without it no one can obtain everlasting life in the world to come, according to what the Scriptures teach: "Except a man be born of water and of the Spirit, he cannot enter into the kingdom of God." "Except ye repent, ye shall all likewise perish." "They which do such things shall not inherit the kingdom of God." "If so be that being clothed we shall not be found naked." (John 3:5. Luke 13:3. 1 Cor. 6:9. 2 Cor. 5:3.) The example of the foolish virgins (Matt. 25:1–10) who were excluded from the marriage, because they had not their lamps burning and filled with oil, is here in point. We may also here cite the following declarations of Christ: "Let your loins be girded about, and your lights burning." "Be ye ready also; for the Son of man cometh at an hour when ye think not." "The Lord of that servant will come in a day when he looketh not for him, and at an hour when he is not aware, and will cut him in sunder, and will appoint him his portion with the unbelievers." (Luke 12:35, 40, 46.) We may here also quote the notable saying of Cyprian against Demetrius: "When we have once departed this life, there is no more room for repentance, or work of satisfaction. Here life is either lost or gained: here we secure our eternal salvation by the worship of God and the fruit of faith. Nor let any one be hindered, either by sin or external opposition, from coming to obtain salvation. No repentance is too late for any one still remaining in the world," etc. From this it appears how necessary conversion is for those who are to be saved. Hence all our exhortations to repentance must be based upon the absolute necessity of conversion to God, in all those who are to be justified.

II. WHAT IS MAN'S CONVERSION TO GOD?

The Hebrew expresses the idea of conversion by the word *Teschubah*; the Greek by *μετανοια* and *μεταμελεια*. There are some who affirm that these Greek words differ from each other in this: that the former is used only in reference to the repentance of the godly, whilst the latter is used also in reference to the repentance of the ungodly. Of Judas it is said, that he repented himself (Matt. 27:3), where the word *μεταμεληθας*, is used. Of Esau it is said, he found no place of repentance (*μετανοιας*). (Heb. 12:17.) Of God it is said (Rom. 11:29), the gifts of God are without repentance, where the word *αμεταμελητα* is used; that is, they are of such a kind that he himself cannot repent of them. The Septuagint, in speaking of God, uses both words without making any distinction. It repents me (*μεταμελομα*) that I have set up Saul to be king. (1 Sam. 15:11.) The Strength of Israel will not lie nor repent (*ου μετανοησει*). The difference, therefore, is either very small, or none at all, unless that the former Greek word above mentioned properly signifies a change of the mind, whilst the latter expresses a change of the will or purpose. In conversion, however, there is a change both of the understanding and the will.

The Latins have a number of words by which they express the same thing. They call it *regeneratio*, *renovatio*, *resipiscentia*, *conversio*, *pœnitentia*. *Resipiscentia* seems properly to correspond with the Greek *μετανοια*; for as *resipiscentia* is derived from *resipisco*, which means to become wise after having done a thing; so *μετανοια* is from *μετανοεω*, which means to become wise after having committed something wrong; to change the mind, and to alter the purpose. *Pœnitenia* is said to be derived either from *pœnitet* or from *pœna*, because the sorrow which is in repentance is, as it were, a punishment. Or else, as Erasmus supposes, it is from *pone tenendo*, as if to repent were to lay hold of a later purpose, or to understand a thing after it is done. But whatever may be the derivation of the word *pœnitentia* or repentance, it is more obscure than the term conversion. For repentance does not comprehend the whole extent of the subject—it does not express from what, and to what we are changed, but merely signifies the sorrow which is felt after the commission of some sin. Conversion, on the other hand, embraces the whole, as it adds that which is the beginning of a new life by faith.

The term repentance is, moreover, of a broader signification than conversion: for conversion is spoken of only in reference to the godly, who alone are converted to God. The same thing may be said of *μετανοια* and *resipiscentia*,—that they refer merely to the godly; for by these three terms the new life of the godly is signified. But *pœnitentia* is spoken of the ungodly also, as of Judas, who did indeed repent of his wicked deed, but was not converted; because the ungodly, when they sorrow, are not converted or reformed. Thus far we have spoken of the terms which have reference to this subject; we must now proceed to inquire into the thing itself.

A definition, with respect to the parts of conversion, may be obtained from the 88th Question of the Catechism, where it is defined to be the mortification of the old, and the quickening of the new man. It is more fully expressed in the following definition: Man's conversion to God consists in a change of the corrupt mind and will into that which is good, produced by the Holy Ghost through the preaching of the law and the gospel, which is followed by a sincere desire to produce the fruits of repentance, and a conformity of the life to all the commands of God. This definition is confirmed by the following passages of Scripture: "If thou wilt return, return unto me." "Wash you, make you clean." "But ye are washed; but ye are sanctified in the name of the Lord

Jesus, and by the Spirit of our God." "Depart from evil, and do good." (Jer. 4:1. Is. 1:16. 1 Cor. 6:11. Ps. 34:14.) The whole definition is expressed in Acts 26:18, 20: "I send thee to open their eyes, and to turn them from darkness to light, and from the power of Satan unto God, that they may receive forgiveness of sins, and inheritance among them which are sanctified by faith that is in me." "But shewed that they should repent, and turn to God, and do works meet for repentance."

III. OF HOW MANY PARTS DOES CONVERSION CONSIST?

Conversion consists of two parts: the mortification of the old man, and the quickening of the new man. We speak more properly in this way, using the language of Paul, than if we were, as some do, to make conversion consist in contrition and faith. By contrition they understand mortification; and by faith the joy which follows the desire of righteousness and new obedience, which are indeed effects of faith, but not faith itself. Contrition also precedes conversion, but is not conversion itself, nor any part of it, being only a preparation, or that which leads to conversion; and that only in the elect. The old man which is mortified is the sinner only, or the corrupt nature of man. The new man which is quickened is he who begins to depart from sin, or it is the nature of man as regenerated. The mortification of the old man, or of the flesh, consists in the laying off and subduing of the corruption of our nature, and includes, 1. A knowledge of sin, and of the wrath of God. 2. Sorrow for sin, and on account of having offended God. 3. Hatred of sin, and an earnest desire to avoid it. The Scriptures speak of this mortification of sin in the following places: "If ye through the Spirit do mortify the deeds of the body, ye shall live." "Rend your hearts, and not your garments." "Come and let us return unto the Lord; for he hath torn, and he will heal us; he hath smitten, and he will bind us up." (Rom. 8:13. Joel 2:13. Hosea 6:1.) From this it appears that mortification, or conversion, is very improperly attributed to the wicked, in whom there is no hatred or shunning of sin, nor sorrow for sin, all of which is embraced in the mortification of the old man. A knowledge of sin precedes sorrow, because the affections of the heart follow knowledge. Sorrow may follow a knowledge of sin on the part of the ungodly, from a sense of present, and from a fear of future evil, viz: of temporal and eternal punishment; yet this sorrow is not properly a part of conversion, nor a preparation to it; but rather a flight and turning away from God, and a rushing into desperation, as in the case of Cain, Saul, Judas, etc. It is called a sorrow, not unto salvation—the sorrow of the world, working death—a sorrow not after a godly sort, etc. In the godly, however, this sorrow arises from a sense of the displeasure of God, which they sincerely acknowledge and lament, and is connected with a hatred and abhorrence of all past sins, and with a shunning or turning away from all present and future sin. This sorrow is a part of conversion, or at least a preparation to it, and is called a sorrow unto salvation—a sorrow which is after a godly sort, working repentance unto salvation. The knowledge of sin, sorrow for sin, and a flying from it, differ in their subject, or as it respects that part of our being in which they have their proper seat. The knowledge of sin is in the mind, sorrow for sin in the heart, and fleeing from it in the will. The turning, which is included in conversion, is in the heart and will, and is a turning from one thing to another—from evil to good, according to what the Psalmist says: "Depart from evil and do good." (Ps. 34:14.)

It is called in Scripture mortification, 1. Because, as one that is dead cannot perform the actions of a living man, so our nature, when its corruption is once removed, no more performs the actions peculiar to it in its corrupt state; that is, it does not produce actual sin when original sin is once circumscribed and kept under proper restraint. "For he that is dead as freed from sin." (Rom. 6:7.) 2. Because, this mortification is not without wrestling and pain: "for the flesh lusteth against the Spirit." (Gal. 5:17.) It is for this reason that this mortification is called a crucifixion of the flesh. "They that are Christ's have crucified the flesh with the affections and lusts." (Gal. 5:24.) 3. Because, it is a ceasing from sin. It is, moreover, not simply called mortification, but the mortification of the old man, because, by it not the substance of man, but sin in man, is destroyed. The expression, old man, is also added for the purpose of distinguishing between the repentance of the godly and ungodly; for in the godly, not the man, but the old man is destroyed, whilst in the ungodly it is not the old man, but the man.

The quickening of the new man is a true joy and delight in God, through Christ, and an earnest and sincere desire to regulate the life according to the will of God, and to perform all good works. It embraces three things which are different from what is included in mortification: 1. A knowledge of the mercy of God, and an application of it in Christ. 2. Joy and delight arising from the fact that God is reconciled to us through Christ, and that obedience is begun in us and shall be perfected. 3. An ardent desire to perform new obedience, or to sin no more, but to render gratitude to God during our whole life, and to retain his love, which desire is itself new obedience according to the following declarations of Scripture: "Being justified by faith we have peace with God through our Lord Jesus Christ." "The kingdom of God is righteousness, and peace, and joy in the Holy Ghost." "I dwell in the high and holy place; with him also that is of a contrite and humble spirit to revive the spirit of the humble, and to revive the heart of the contrite ones." "Likewise, reckon ye also yourselves to be dead indeed unto sin, but alive unto God through Jesus Christ our Lord." "Nevertheless I live; yet not I, but Christ liveth in me; and the life which I now live in the flesh, I live by the faith of the Son of God, who loved me and gave himself for me." (Rom. 5:1; 14:17. Is. 57:15. Rom. 6:11. Gal. 2:20.)

This part of conversion is called quickening, 1. Because, as a living man performs the actions of one that is alive, so this quickening includes the kindling of new light in the understanding, and the producing of new qualities and activities in the will and heart, from which a new life and new works proceed. 2. Because, it includes on the part of those who are converted, joy and delight in God, which affords great comfort and consolation. It is added through Christ, because we cannot rejoice in God, unless he be reconciled unto us. It is now only through Christ that God is reconciled unto us. Hence, we only rejoice in God through Christ.

These two parts of conversion spring from faith. The reason is, because no one can hate sin and draw nigh to God, unless he loves God. But no one loves God who is not possessed of faith. Hence, although there is no express mention made of faith in either part of conversion, this is done, not because faith is excluded from conversion, but because the whole doctrine of conversion and thankfulness presupposes it, as a cause is presupposed from the presence of its own peculiar effect.

OBJECTION: But faith produces joy. Therefore, it does not produce grief and mortification. ANSWER: It is not absurd to affirm that the same cause produces different effects by a different kind of operation and in different respects. So faith produces grief, not of itself, but by an accident, which is sin, by which we offend God our kind and gracious father. Of itself it produces joy, because it assures us of God's fatherly will towards us, by and for the sake of Christ. REPLY: The preaching of the law precedes faith, since the preaching of repentance commences with the law. But the preaching of the law works sorrow and wrath. Therefore, there is a certain sorrow before faith. ANSWER: We grant that there is a certain sorrow before faith, but not such as constitutes a part of conversion; for the sorrow of the ungodly which is before and without faith, is rather a turning away from God, than a return to him, which being contrary, cannot agree neither wholly nor in part. But the contrition and sorrow which the elect experience is a certain preparation, leading to conversion, as we have already shown.

IV. WHAT ARE THE CAUSES OF CONVERSION?

The Holy Spirit, or God himself, is the chief efficient cause of our conversion. Hence, it is that the saints pray that God would convert them, and that repentance is frequently called in the Scriptures the gift of God. "Turn thou me and I shall be turned, for thou art the Lord my God." "Turn thou us unto thee, O Lord, and we shall be turned." "Him hath God exalted with his right hand to be a Prince and a Saviour to give repentance to Israel, and forgiveness of sins"; from which we may draw a most forcible argument in proof of the Divinity of Christ, inasmuch as it is peculiar to God alone to grant repentance and forgiveness of sins. "Then hath God also to the Gentiles granted repentance unto life." "If God, peradventure, will give them repentance to the acknowledging of the truth, and that they may recover themselves out of the snare of the devil," etc. (Jer. 31:18. Lamen. 5:21. Acts 5:31; 11:18. 2 Tim. 2:25.)

The means or instrumental causes of conversion are the law—the gospel, and again, the doctrine of the law after that of the gospel. For the preaching of the law goes before, preparing and leading us to a knowledge of the gospel: "for by the law is the knowledge of sin." (Rom. 3:20.) Hence, there can be no sorrow for sin without the law. After the sinner has once been led to a knowledge of sin, then the preaching of the gospel follows, encouraging contrite hearts by the assurance of the mercy of God through Christ. Without this preaching there is no faith, and without faith there is no love to God, and hence no conversion to him. After the preaching of the gospel, the preaching of the law again follows, that it may be the rule of our thankfulness and of our life. The law, therefore, precedes, and follows conversion. It precedes that it may lead to a knowledge and sorrow for sin: it follows that it may serve as a rule of life to the converted. It is for this reason that the prophets first charge sin upon the ungodly, threaten punishment, and exhort to repentance; then comfort and promise pardon and forgiveness; and lastly, again exhort and prescribe the duties of piety and godliness. Such was, also, the character of the preaching of John the Baptist. It is in this way, that the preaching of repentance comprehends the law and the gospel, although in effecting conversion each has a part to perform peculiar to itself.

The next instrumental and internal cause of conversion, is faith. Without faith there is no love to God, and unless we know what the will of God towards us is; viz., that he will remit unto us our sins by and for the sake of Christ, conversion will never be begun in us, neither as its respects the mortification of the old man, nor as it respects the quickening of the new: for by faith the heart is purified. (Acts 15:9.) Without faith we can have no true joy or delight in God; without faith we cannot love God; and whatsoever is not of faith, is sin. (Rom. 14:23.) All good works proceed from faith, as their fountain. "Being justified by faith, we have peace with God through our Lord Jesus Christ." (Rom. 5:1.)

The causes which contribute to our conversion are the cross, with the chastisements inflicted upon ourselves and others; also the benefits, punishments and example of others, etc. "Thou hast chastised me, and I was chastised, as a bullock unaccustomed to the yoke." "It is good for me that I have been afflicted, that I might learn thy statutes." "Let your light so shine before men, that they may see your good works and glorify your Father which is in heaven." (Jer. 31:18. Ps. 119:71. Matt. 5:16.) The subject, or matter in which conversion is grounded, is the understanding, the will, the heart, and all the affections of man in which a change is produced.

The form of conversion is the turning itself with all the circumstances that are connected with it, which includes, 1. As it respects the mind and understanding, a correct judgment of God, together with his will and works. 2. As it respects the will, a sincere and earnest desire to avoid those falls and things which offend God, with a steady purpose to obey him, according to all his commandments. 3. As it respects the heart, new and holy desires and affections in accordance with the divine law. 4. As it respects the external actions and life, rectitude and obedience begun, according to the law of God. The object of conversion is, 1. Sin, or disobedience, which is the thing from which we are converted. 2. Righteousness, or new obedience, which is the thing to which we are converted. The chief end of conversion is the glory of God; the next end, which is subordinate to the glory of God, is our good, which consists in our blessedness and enjoyment of eternal life. The conversion of others is another end, still less principal, than those just mentioned. "And when thou art converted, strengthen thy brethren." "Let your light so shine before men, that they may see your good works and glorify your Father which is in heaven." (Luke 22:32. Matt. 5:16.)

The questions respecting Pelagianism are here properly in place; Whether a man can convert himself without the grace of the Holy Spirit: and, Whether a man can, by the exercise of his free power of choice, prepare himself for the reception of divine grace. Pelagius maintained the first, in opposition to what the Scriptures most plainly affirm. "Turn thou me, and I shall be turned." "It is God which worketh in you, both to will and to do, of his good pleasure." "A corrupt tree cannot bring forth good fruit." (Jer. 31:18. Phil. 2:13. Matt. 7:18.) The Schoolmen and Papists at this day defend the last proposition respecting Pelagianism, in opposition to the explicit declarations of the word of God just cited, and also in contradiction to what Christ himself affirms, when he says, "No man can come to me, except the Father which hath sent me draw him." (John 6:44.) Thomas Aquinas attributes a certain preparation to the free-will of man, but not conversion. He speaks however of this preparation, as though it contributed to the grace of conversion, which it does by the gracious aid of God, moving us inwardly. See *Summa Theologica*, I-II, Q109, A 6.

V. WHAT ARE THE EFFECTS OF CONVERSION?

The effects of conversion are, 1. A true and ardent love to God, and our neighbor. 2. An earnest desire to obey God, without any exception, according to all his commandments. 3. All good works, or new obedience itself. 4. A desire to convert others, and bring them in the way of salvation. In a word, the fruits of true repentance are the duties of piety towards God, and of charity towards our neighbor.

VI. IS CONVERSION PERFECT IN THIS LIFE?

Our conversion to God is not perfect in this life, but is here continually advancing, until it reaches the perfection which is proposed in the life to come. "We know in part." (1 Cor. 13:9.) All the complaints and prayers of the saints are confirmations of this truth. "Cleanse thou me from secret faults." "O wretched man that I am, who shall deliver me from the body of this death." (Ps. 19:13. Rom. 7:24.) The conflict which is continually going on in those who are converted, bears testimony to the same truth. "The flesh lusteth against the Spirit, and the Spirit against the flesh," etc. (Gal. 5:17.) The same thing may be said of the exhortations of the prophets and apostles, in which they exhort those who are converted to turn more fully unto God. "He that is righteous, let him be righteous still, and he that is holy, let him be holy still." (Rev. 22:11.) We may also establish the same thing in the following manner: Neither the mortification of the flesh, nor the quickening of the Spirit, is absolute or perfect in the saints in this life. Therefore, neither is conversion, which consists of these two parts, perfect. As it respects the mortification of the old man, the case is clear, and does not admit of doubt that it is not perfect in this life; because the saints do not only continually strive against the lust of the flesh, but they also often for a time yield, and give over in this conflict—often do they sin, fall and offend God, although they do not defend their sins, but detest, deplore, and endeavor to avoid them. As it regards the imperfection of the quickening of the new man, the same conflict is a sufficient testimony; and surely as our knowledge is now only in part, the renovation of the will and heart must also be imperfect: for the will follows the knowledge which we have.

There are two plain reasons why the will, in the case of those who are converted, tends imperfectly to the good in this life: 1. Because the renovation of our nature is never made perfect in this life, neither as it respects our knowledge of God, nor the inclination which we have to obey him. The single complaint and acknowledgment which the apostle Paul made is a sufficient proof of what we have just said. "I know that in me, that is, in my flesh dwelleth no good thing," etc. (Rom. 7:18, 19.) 2. Because those who are converted are not always governed by the Holy Spirit, but are sometimes for a season deserted by God, either for the purpose of trying, or chastising, or humbling them; yet they are nevertheless brought to repentance, so as not to perish. "Lord, I believe, help thou mine unbelief." (Mark 9:24.)

But why does God not perfect conversion in the case of his people in this life, seeing that he is able to effect it? The reasons are, 1. That the saints may be humbled and exercised in faith, patience, prayer and wrestling against the flesh, and that they may not boast of their perfection, thinking of themselves more highly than they ought, but daily pray; "Enter not into judgment with thy servant." "Forgive us our sins." (Ps. 143:2. Matt. 6:12.) 2. That they may press forward more and more unto perfection, and desire it more earnestly. That, trampling the world under their feet, they may run with greater alacrity in the Christian course, and aspire after those joys that are laid up in heaven, knowing that it will not be until then that they shall fully enjoy their promised inheritance. "Set your affection on things above, not on things on the earth, for ye are dead, and your life is hid with Christ in God." "Mortify, therefore, your members which are upon the earth." "It doth not yet appear what we shall be; but we know that when he shall appear, we shall be like him." (Col. 3:2, 3, 5. John 3:2.)

Concerning this imperfection Calvin writes in the following expressive language: "This restoration is not accomplished in a single moment, or day, or year; but by continual, and sometimes even slow advances, the Lord destroys the carnal corruptions of his chosen, purifies them from all pollution, and consecrates them as temples to himself; renewing all their senses to real purity, that they may employ their whole life in the exercise of repentance, and know that this warfare will be terminated only in death." Inst. lib. 3. cap. 3. sec. 9. The sections following the one from which we have quoted, down to the fifteenth, may also be read to advantage, in which there is a disputation learnedly set forth against the Cathari and Anabaptists, in reference to the remains of sin which cleave to the godly as long as they remain in the flesh.

VII. IN WHAT DOES THE CONVERSION OF THE GODLY DIFFER FROM THE REPENTANCE OF THE UNGODLY?

The term repentance is used in reference to the ungodly as well as to the godly, because there are certain things in which they agree, as in a knowledge of sin, and sorrow on account of it. As it respects other things, however, there is a wide difference. They differ, 1. In the moving cause of repentance, or in the sorrow which is felt. The wicked are sorrowful, not on account of having offended God, but merely because of the punishment which they have brought upon themselves, and which necessarily attaches itself to the violation of God's law. If it were not for this, they would never manifest any sorrow for sin. So Cain was sorrowful merely on account of the punishment which God inflicted upon him for his sin. "My iniquity" (that is the punishment of my iniquity) "is greater than I can bear. Behold thou hast driven me out this day from the face of the earth," etc. The godly, however, do, indeed, dread the punishment of sin, but they are pained and grieved more particularly on account of sin itself, and the offence which they have committed against God. So it was in the case of David: "Against thee, thee only have I sinned: my sin is ever before me." (Ps. 51:3, 4.) So it was also in the case of Peter, who wept bitterly on account of having offended Christ. The sorrow of Judas, however, did not arise on account of the evil of sin, but merely on account of the punishment which followed his crime. Horace expresses this distinction in the following language: (lib. 1. epist. 16.)

Oderunt peccare boni, virtutis amore,
Tu nihil admittes in te, formidine pœnæ.[1]

2. The repentance of the godly differs from that of the ungodly as it respects the efficient cause of it. The repentance of the ungodly proceeds from distrust and despair, so that their despair, disquietude and hatred to God increases. The repentance of the godly, however, proceeds from faith, or the confidence which they have in the mercy of God, and in a gracious reconciliation with him by and for the sake of Christ.

3. They differ in form. The repentance of the godly is a turning to God from the devil, sin and their old nature; because they do not only sorrow, but also encourage themselves by exercising confidence in the mediator—they confide in Christ, rejoice in God, and trust in him saying with David, "Purge me with hyssop, and I shall be clean." (Ps. 51:7.) The repentance of the ungodly is a turning away from God to the devil, to hatred and repining against God, and to despair.

1 Good men hate to sin from their love of goodness; bad men hate to sin from their fear of punishment.

4. They differ in their effects. The repentance of the godly is followed by new obedience; and in proportion to the depth of their repentance is the old man mortified in them, and the desire of righteousness increased. But the repentance of the ungodly is not followed by new obedience; but they continue in sin and return to their vomit, although for a time they feigned to repent of their sins, as Ahab did. They are, indeed, mortified, and destroyed, but the corruption of their nature is not subdued: yea, by how much the more they repent, by so much the more is hatred, distrust, and aversion to God increased in them, so that they are continually being brought more and more under the power and dominion of Satan.

Question 91. But what are good works?

Answer. Only those which proceed from a true faith, are performed according to the law of God, and to his glory, and not such as are founded on our imaginations, or the institutions of men.

Exposition. The doctrine concerning good works belongs properly to this Question of the Catechism, concerning which we must enquire particularly:

I. What are good works?

II. How may they be performed?

III. Are the works of the saints pure and perfectly good?

IV. How can our works please God since they are only imperfectly good?

V. Why must we perform good works?

VI. Do your good works merit any thing in the sight of God?

I. WHAT ARE GOOD WORKS?

Good works are such as are performed according to the law of God, such as proceed from a true faith, and are directed to the glory of God. Three things, therefore, claim our attention in the exposition of this question: 1. The conditions necessary to constitute a work good in the sight of God. 2. The difference between the works of the regenerate and the unregenerate. 3. In what respect, or how far the moral works of the ungodly are sins.

First, that a work may be good and pleasing in the sight of God these three conditions are necessary:

1. It must be commanded by God. No creature has the right, or power to institute the worship of God. But good works (we speak of moral good) and the worship of God are the same. Moral good differs widely from natural good, inasmuch as all actions, in as far as they are actions, including even those of the wicked, are naturally good; but all actions are not morally good, or in accordance with the justice of God. This condition excludes all will-worship, as well as the figment of good intentions, as when men do evil that good may come, or when they perform works founded upon their own imaginations, which they endeavor to thrust upon God in the place of worship, which, indeed, are not evil in themselves, but yet are not commanded by God. It is not sufficient for the worship of God, that a work be not evil, or not prohibited: it must also be commanded by God, according to what the Scriptures declare, "To obey is better than sacrifice, and to hearken than the fat of rams." "Walk in my statutes." "In vain do they worship me, teaching for doctrines the commandments of men." (1 Sam. 15:22. Ez. 20:19. Matt. 15:9.)

But someone may object and say, that works of indifference, such as may be done, or left undone, are not commanded by God, and yet many of them are pleasing to him; to which we reply that they are not pleasing to God in themselves, but by an accident, in as far as they partake of the general nature of love, and in as far as they are performed for the purpose of avoiding offence, and for the sake of contributing to the salvation of our fellow men. In this respect they are commanded by God in general, although not specially.

2. That a work may be good it must proceed from a true faith, which rests upon the merit and intercession of Christ, and from which we may know that we, together with our works, are acceptable to God for the sake of the mediator. To do any thing from a true faith is, 1. To believe that we are acceptable to God for the sake of the satisfaction of Christ. 2. That our obedience itself is pleasing to God, both because it is commanded by him, and because the imperfection which attaches itself to it is made

acceptable to God for the sake of the same satisfaction of Christ on account of which God is well pleased with us. Without faith it is impossible for any one to please God. Nor is the faith, by which any one may assure himself, that God wills and commands any particular work sufficient; for if this were all that is necessary, then the wicked, who know and do what God wills, would also act from faith. To act from a true faith, however, includes much more than this, because it includes in itself historical faith, and what is the most important of all, it applies unto itself the promise of the gospel. The Scriptures speak of this true faith in the following references: "Whatsoever is not of faith is sin." "Without faith it is impossible to please God." (Rom. 14:23. Heb. 11:6.) Nor is it difficult to perceive the reason and force of what is here affirmed; because without faith there is no love to God, and consequently no love to our neighbor. Every work now that does not proceed from love to God is hypocrisy, yea a reproach and contempt of God; for he who has the presumption to do any thing, whether it be pleasing to God or not, despises God, and casts a reproach upon him. Nor is it possible for us to have a good conscience without faith; and what is not done with a good conscience cannot please God.

3. That a work may be good, it must be referred principally to the honor and glory of God. Honor embraces love, reverence, obedience and gratitude. Hence, to do any thing to the honor of God, is to do it, that we may testify our love, reverence and obedience to God, and that for the sake of showing our thankfulness for the benefits which we have received. There is a necessity that our works, in order that they may be good and acceptable to God, should be referred to the divine glory, and not to our own praise or advantage; otherwise they will not proceed from the love of God, but from a desire to advance our own selfish interests, and will thus be mere hypocrisy. God must, therefore, be respected first whenever we do any thing: nor must we care what men may say, whether they praise or reproach us, if we have the assurance that we please God in what we do, according to what the Apostle says, "Do all to the glory of God." (1 Cor. 10:31.) Yet we may at the same time lawfully and profitably desire and seek true glory, according as it is written, "Let your

light so shine before men that they may see your good works, and glorify your Father which is in heaven." (Matt. 5:16.)

Briefly, faith is required in good works, because if we are not firmly persuaded that our works are pleasing to God, they proceed from contempt of God. The divine command is necessary, because faith has respect to the word of God. Inasmuch, therefore, as there cannot be any faith apart from the word, there can likewise be no good works independent of it. Finally, it is necessary that whatever we do, be referred to the glory of God, because, if we seek our own praise, or advantage in what we do, our works cannot please God.

By these conditions we exclude from the category of good works all those works, 1. Which are sins in themselves, being contrary to the divine law, and the will of God as revealed in his word. 2. Also those which are not opposed to the divine law, which in themselves are neither good nor evil, being actions of indifference, but which may, nevertheless, become evil by an accident. For works which are not opposed to the divine law, and which are not commanded by God, but by men, become evil and sinful when they are done with the conceit and expectation of worshipping God, or with offence and injury to our neighbor. Works of this character are deficient as it respects the first two conditions which we have specified as being indispensably necessary to constitute an action good in the sight of God. 3. Those works which are good in themselves, and which are commanded by God; but which, nevertheless, become sins by accident, in that they are not performed lawfully, not being done in the manner, nor with the design which God requires; that is, they do not proceed from a true faith, and are not done with the end that God may be glorified thereby. Works of this character are deficient in the last two conditions specified as necessary in order that our action may be pleasing to God.

Secondly, the works of the regenerate and the unregenerate differ, in this, that the good works of the regenerate are done according to the conditions which we have here specified; whilst those of the unregenerate, although God may have commanded them, do, nevertheless, not proceed from faith, and are not joined with internal obedience; but are done without sincerity, and are, therefore, works of hypocrisy: and, as they do not spring from a right cause, which is faith, so they are nor directed to the glory of God which is the chief end to which all our actions ought to be referred. The actions of the unregenerate do not, therefore, deserve to be called good works.

Thirdly, the difference which exists between the works of the righteous and the wicked, goes to prove that the moral works of the wicked are sins, but yet not such sins as those which are in their own nature opposed to the law of God: for these are sins in themselves, and according to their very nature, whilst the moral works of the wicked are sins merely by an accident; viz., on account of some defect, either because they do not proceed from a true faith, or are not done to the glory of God. This consequence, therefore, is of no force: The good works of the heathen and such as are unregenerate are sins. Therefore they are all to be avoided and condemned: this consequence, we say, is not legitimate, because it is only the defects which attach themselves to these works, that are to be avoided and guarded against, as we have shown, in the former part of this work, when treating the subject of sin.

II. HOW MAY GOOD WORKS BE PERFORMED?

The explanation of this question is necessary on account of the Pelagians, who affirm that the unregenerate may also, as well as the regenerate, perform good works; and also on account of the Papists and semi-Pelagians who imagine certain preparatory works of free-will. Good works are possible only by the grace and assistance of the Holy Spirit, and that by the regenerate alone, whose hearts have been truly regenerated by the Spirit of God, through the preaching of the gospel, and that not only in their first conversion and regeneration, but also by the perpetual and constant influence and direction of the same Spirit, who works in them a knowledge of sin, faith and a desire of new obedience, and also daily increases and confirms more and more the same gifts in them. St. Jerome endorses this doctrine when he says, "Let him be accursed, who says that it is possible to render obedience to the law, without the grace of the Holy Spirit." Without the grace and continual direction of the Holy Spirit, even the most holy persons on earth can do nothing but sin, as is evident from the examples of David, Peter, and others. Yea, without regeneration, no part of any work that is good in the sight of God, can ever be begun, inasmuch as we are all by nature evil and dead in sin. (Matt. 7:11. Eph. 2:1.) "All our righteousnesses," says the prophet Isaiah, in which declaration he comprehends both himself and the most holy amongst men, "are as filthy rags." (Is. 64:6.) Now if nothing but sin is found before God in the saints, what will that be which is found in those who are unregenerated? What good these are able to perform, the apostle Paul describes in a most graphic manner, in the first and second chapters of his Epistle to the Romans. That the unregenerate are unable to perform such works as are acceptable to God, is also taught in the following passages of Scripture: "A corrupt tree cannot bring forth good fruit." "Can the Ethiopian change his skin, or the leopard his spots? then may ye also do good, that are accustomed to do evil." "Without me ye can do nothing." "It is God, which worketh in you, both to will and to do of his good pleasure." (Matt. 7:18. Jer. 13:23. John, 15:5. Phil. 2:13.) Without the righteousness of Christ imputed unto us, we are altogether unclean and abominable in the sight of God, and all our works are as dung. But the righteousness of Christ is not imputed unto us before our conversion. It is impossible, therefore, either that we, or our works should be pleasing to God before our conversion. Faith is the cause of good works. Faith comes from God: Therefore good works which are the fruits of faith, are from God; neither can they be before faith and conversion, or else the effect would be before its cause.

It is asked by some, in connection with this subject, are there not works that are preparatory to conversion? To which we reply, that if by preparatory works are meant such as are the occasion of repentance, or which God uses for the purpose of effecting repentance in us, which may be said to be true of the outward deportment and discipline of the life, in as far as it is in accordance with the divine law; hearing, reading and meditating upon the word of God; also the cross, and adverse circumstances;—if such works as these are meant, we may admit that there are such works as are preparatory. But if by preparatory works are meant works which are performed according to the law before conversion, by which, as by men's good efforts, God is enticed and moved to grant true conversion, as well as his other gifts, to those who do these things, we deny that there are any such works; because, according to the declaration of the Apostle Paul, "Whatsoever is not of faith is sin." (Rom. 14:23.) The Papists call such works merits of congruity, as if they would say that they are indeed such as are imperfect in themselves and deserve nothing, but on account of which it may seem proper for the mercy of God to grant unto men conversion and eternal life. But God hath mercy on whom he will have mercy, and not upon those who deserve mercy. (Rom. 9:18.) No one deserves anything of God, but punishment, and banishment from his presence. "When ye shall have done all those things which are commanded you, say, We are unprofitable servants; for we have done that which was our duty to do." (Luke 17:10.)

III. ARE THE WORKS OF THE REGENERATE PERFECTLY GOOD?

The works of the saints are not perfectly good or pure in this life: 1. Because even those who are regenerated do many things which are evil, which are sins in themselves, on account of which they are guilty in the sight of God, and deserve to be cast into everlasting punishment. Thus, Peter denied Christ thrice; David committed adultery, slew Uriah, attempted to conceal his wickedness, numbered the children of Israel, etc. The law now declares, "Cursed be he that confirmeth not all the words of this law to do them." (Deut. 27:26.). 2. Because they omit doing many good things which they ought to do according to the law. 3. Because the good works which they perform are not so perfectly good and pure as the law requires; for they are always marred with defects, and polluted with sins. The perfect righteousness which the law requires is wanting, even in the best works of the saints.

The reason of this is easily understood, inasmuch as faith, regeneration, and the love of God and our neighbor, from which good works proceed, continue imperfect in us in this life. As the cause is, therefore, imperfect, it is impossible that the effects which flow from this cause should be perfect. "I see another law in my members, warring against the law of my mind." (Rom. 7:23.) This is the reason why the works of the godly cannot stand in the judgment of God. "Enter not into judgment with thy servant; for in thy sight shall no man living be justified." "Cursed be he that confirmeth not all the words of this law to do them." (Ps. 143:2. Deut. 27:26.) Inasmuch, therefore, as all our works are imperfect, it becomes us to acknowledge and lament our sinfulness and infirmity, and press forward so much the more towards perfection.

From what has now been said, it is evident that the figment, or conceit of the Monks in reference to works of supererogation—by which they understand such works as are done over and above what God and the law require from them, is full of impiety; for it makes God a debtor to man. Yea, it is a blasphemous doctrine; for Christ himself has said: "When ye shall have done all those things which are commanded you, say, We are unprofitable servants; for we have done that which was our duty to do." (Luke 17:10.)

OBJECTION 1: But is is said, Luke 10:35: "Whatsoever thou spendest more, when I came again I will repay thee." Therefore there are at least some works of supererogation. Ans. It is a sufficient reply to this objection to remark, that in the interpretation of parables we must be careful not to press every minute circumstance too closely: for that which is similar is not altogether the same. The Samaritan says, Whatsoever thou spendest more, not in reference to God, but to the man that was bruised and wounded.

OBJECTION 2: Paul says, 1 Cor. 7:25: "Concerning virgins I have no commandment of the Lord, yet I give my judgment." Therefore judgment or advice may be given concerning things not commanded or required. Ans. But Paul's meaning is, I give my advice, that it is suitable and profitable for this life, but not that it merits eternal life.

OBJECTION 3: But Christ said, Matt. 19:21: "If thou wilt be perfect, go and sell what thou hast," etc. Therefore there are certain directions, which, being followed, make those who comply therewith perfect. Ans. This is a special command, by which Christ designed to call this proud young man to humility, to the love of his neighbor, and to the office of an apostle in Judea. We may also remark, that Christ did not require from him supererogation, but perfection; which requirement he made in order that he might bring him to see his great deficiency.

IV. HOW CAN OUR GOOD WORKS PLEASE GOD, SINCE THEY ARE ONLY IMPERFECTLY GOOD?

If our works were not pleasing to God, they would be performed to no purpose. We must, therefore, know in what way it is that they please God. As they are imperfect in themselves, and defiled in many respects, they cannot of themselves please God, on account of his extreme justice and rectitude. Yet they are, nevertheless, acceptable to God in Christ the Mediator, through faith, or on account of the merit and satisfaction of Christ imputed unto us by faith, and on account of his intercession with the Father in our behalf. For just as we ourselves do not please God in ourselves, but in his Son, so our works being imperfect and unholy in themselves, are acceptable to God on account of the righteousness of Christ, which covers all their imperfection or impurity, so that it does not appear before God. It is necessary that the person who performs good works should be acceptable to God; then the works of the person are also accepted; otherwise, when the person is without faith, the best works are but an abomination before God, inasmuch as they are altogether hypocritical. As now the person is acceptable to God, so are the works. But the person is acceptable to God on account of the Mediator; that is, by the imputation of the merit and righteousness of Christ, with which the person is covered as with a garment in the presence of God. Hence the works of the person are also pleasing to God, for the sake of the Mediator. God does not look upon and examine our righteousness and imperfect works as they are in themselves, according to the rigor of his law in respect to which he would rather condemn them; but he beholds and considers them in his Son. It is for this reason that God is said to have had respect to Abel and his offering, viz: in his Son, in whom Abel believed; for it was by faith that he presented his sacrifice. (Gen. 4:4. Heb. 11:4.) So Christ is also called our High Priest, by whom our works are offered unto God. He is also called the altar, on which our prayers and works being placed, they are acceptable unto God, which otherwise would be detestable in his sight. It follows, therefore, that every defect and every imperfection respecting ourselves and our works is covered, and, as it were, repaired in the judgment of God, by the perfect satisfaction of Christ. It is in view of this that Paul says, "That I may be found in him, not having mine own righteousness, which is of the law, but that which is through the faith of Christ, the righteousness which is of God by faith." (Phil. 3:9.)

V. WHY GOOD WORKS ARE TO BE DONE, OR WHY ARE THEY NECESSARY?

We have already, under the 86th Question, enumerated certain moving causes of good works which properly belong here; such as the connection which holds necessarily between regeneration and justification, the glory of God, the proof of our faith and election, and a good example by which others are won to Christ. These causes may be very appropriately dwelt upon to a much greater extent, if, having reduced them to three principal heads, we say that good works are to be performed by us for the sake of God, ourselves and our neighbor.

I. Good works are to be done in respect to God, 1. That the glory of God our heavenly Father, may be manifested. The manifestation of the glory of God is the chief end why God commands and wills that good works should be performed by us, that we may honor him by our good works, and that others seeing them may glorify our Father which is in heaven, as it is said, "Let your light so shine before men that they may see your good works, and glorify your Father which is in heaven." (Matt. 5:16.)

2. That we may render unto God the obedience which he requires, or on account of the command of God. God requires the

commencement of obedience in this life, and the perfection of it in the life to come. "This is my commandment, That ye love one another." "This is the will of God even your sanctification." "Being then made free from sin, ye became the servants of righteousness." "Yield your members as instruments of righteousness unto God." (John 15:12. 1 Thes. 4:3. Rom. 6:18, 13.)

3. That we may thus render unto God the gratitude which we owe unto him. It is just and proper that we should love, worship and reverence him by whom we have been redeemed, and from whom we have received the greatest benefits, and that we should declare our love and gratitude by our obedience and good works. God deserves our obedience and worship on account of the benefits which he confers upon us. We do not merit his benefits by anything that we do. Hence our gratitude, which shows itself by our obedience and good works, is due unto God for his great benefits. "I beseech you, brethren, by the mercies of God, that ye present your bodies a living sacrifice, holy, acceptable unto God, which is your reasonable service." "Ye are an holy priesthood to offer up spiritual sacrifices acceptable to God by Jesus Christ. (Rom. 12:1. Pet. 2:5, 9, 20.)

II. Good works are to be done on our own account, 1. That we may thereby testify our faith, and be assured of its existence in us by the fruits which we produce in our lives. "Every good tree bringeth forth good fruit." "Being filled with the fruits of righteousness which are by Jesus Christ, unto the praise and glory of God." "Faith without works is dead." (Matt. 7:17. Phil. 1:11. James 2:17.) It is by our good works, therefore, that we know that we possess true faith, because the effect is not without its own proper cause, which is always known by its effect; so that if we are destitute of good works and new obedience, we are hypocrites, and have an evil conscience instead of true faith; for true faith (which is never wanting in all the fruits which are peculiar to it,) as a fruitful tree produces good works, obedience and repentance; which fruits distinguish true faith from that faith which is merely historical and temporary, as well as from hypocrisy itself.

2. That we may be assured of the fact that we have obtained the forgiveness of sins through Christ, and that we are justified

for his sake. Justification and regeneration are benefits which are connected and knit together in such a way as never to be separated from each other. Christ obtained both for us at the same time, viz: the forgiveness of sins and the Holy Spirit, who through faith excites in us the desire of good works and new obedience.

3. That we may be assured of our election and salvation. "Give diligence to make your calling and election sure." (2 Pet. 1:10.) This cause naturally grows out of the preceding one; for God out of his mercy chose from everlasting only those who are justified on account of the merit of his Son. "Whom he did predestinate, them he also called; and whom he called, them he also justified." (Rom. 8:30.) We are, therefore, assured of our election by our justification; and that we are justified in Christ, (which benefit is never granted unto the elect without sanctification,) we know from faith; of which we are, again, assured by the fruits of faith, which are good works, new obedience and true repentance.

4. That our faith may be exercised, nourished, strengthened and increased by good works. Those who indulge in unclean lusts and desires against their consciences cannot have faith, and so are destitute of a good conscience and of confidence in God as reconciled and gracious; for it is only by faith that we obtain a sense of the divine favor towards us and a good conscience. "If ye live after the flesh, ye shall die." "I put thee in remembrance, that thou stir up the gift of God, which is in thee." (Rom. 8:13. 2 Tim. 1:6.)

5. That we may adorn and commend our profession, life and calling by our good works. "I beseech you, that ye walk worthy of the vocation wherewith ye are called." (Eph. 4:1.)

6. That we may escape temporal and eternal punishment. "Every tree that bringeth not forth good fruit is hewn down and cast into the fire." "If ye live after the flesh ye shall die." "Thou with rebukes dost correct man for iniquity." (Matt. 7:19. Rom. 8:13. Ps. 39:11.)

7. That we may obtain from God those temporal and spiritual rewards, which, according to the divine promise, accompany good works both in this and in a future life. "Godliness is profitable unto all things, having promise of the life that now is, and

of that which is to come." (1 Tim. 4:8.) And if God did not desire that the hope of reward, and the fear of punishment should be moving causes of good works, he would not use them as arguments in the promises and threatenings which he addresses unto us in his word.

III Good works are to be done for the sake of our neighbor, 1. That we may be profitable unto our neighbor, and edify him by our example and godly conversation. "All things are for your sakes, that the abundant grace might, through the thanksgiving of many, redound to the glory of God," etc. "Nevertheless to abide in the flesh is more needful for you." (2 Cor. 4:15. Phil. 1:24.)

2. That we may not be the occasion of offences and scandal to the cause of Christ. "Woe to that man by whom the offence cometh." "The name of God is blasphemed among the Gentiles through you." (Matt. 18:7. Rom. 2:24.)

3. That we may win the unbelieving to Christ. "And when thou art converted, strengthen thy brethren." (Luke 22:32.) The question, whether good works are necessary to salvation, belongs properly to this place. There have been some who have maintained simply and positively, that good works are necessary to salvation, whilst others, again, have held that they are pernicious and injurious to salvation. Both forms of speech are ambiguous and inappropriate, especially the latter; because it seems not only to condemn confidence, but also the desire of performing good works. It is, therefore, to be rejected. The former expression must be explained in this way; that good works are necessary to salvation, not as a cause to an effect, or as if they merited a reward, but as a part of salvation itself, or as an antecedent to a consequent, or as a means without which we cannot obtain the end. In the same way we may also say, that good works are necessary to righteousness or justification, or in them that are to be justified, viz: as a consequence of justification, with which regeneration is inseparably connected. But yet we would prefer not to use these forms of speech, 1. Because they are ambiguous. 2. Because they breed contentions, and give our enemies room for caviling. 3. Because these expressions are not used in the Scriptures with which our

forms of speech should conform as nearly as possible. We may more safely and correctly say that good works are necessary in them that are justified, and that are to be saved. To say that good works are necessary in them that are to be justified, is to speak ambiguously, because it may be so understood as if they were required before justification, and so become a cause of our justification. Augustine has correctly said: "Good works do not precede them that are to be justified, but follow them that are justified." We may, therefore, easily return an answer to the following objection: That is necessary to salvation without which no one can be saved. But no one who is destitute of good works can be saved, as it is said in the 87th Question. Therefore, good works are necessary to salvation. We reply to the major proposition, by making the following distinction: That without which no one can be saved is necessary to salvation, viz: as a part of salvation, or as a certain antecedent necessary to salvation, in which sense we admit the conclusion; but not as a cause, or as a merit of salvation. We, therefore, grant the conclusion of the major proposition if understood in the sense in which we have just explained it. For good works are necessary to salvation, or, to speak more properly, in them that are to be saved (for it is better thus to speak for the sake of avoiding ambiguity,) as a part of salvation itself; or, as an antecedent of salvation, but not as a cause or merit of salvation.

VI. DO OUR GOOD WORKS MERIT ANY THING IN THE SIGHT OF GOD?

This question naturally grows out of the preceding one, as the fourth grew out of the third. For when we say that we obtain rewards from God by our own good works, men immediately conclude that our good works must merit something at the hands of God. We must know, therefore, that our good works are necessary, and that they are also to be done for the rewards which are consequent thereon; but that they are, nevertheless, not meritorious, by which we mean that they deserve nothing from God, not even the smallest particle of spiritual or temporal blessings. The reasons of this are most true and evident.

1. Our works are imperfect, both in respect to their parts and degrees. As it respects the parts of our works, they are imperfect, for the reason that we omit many good things which the law prescribes, and do many evil things which the law prohibits; and always mingle much that is evil with the good we do, as both Scripture and experience testify. "The flesh lusteth against the Spirit and the Spirit against the flesh; and these are contrary, the one to the other; so that ye cannot do the things that ye would." (Gal. 5:17.) Works, now, that are imperfect not only merit nothing, but are even condemned in the judgment of God. "Cursed be he that confirmeth not all the words of this law to do them. (Deut. 27:26.) Our works are also imperfect in degree, because the best works of the saints are unclean and defiled in the sight of God, not being performed by those who are perfectly regenerated, nor with that love to God and our neighbor which the law requires. The prophet Isaiah declares even in reference to good works, "We are all as an unclean thing, and all our righteousnesses are as filthy rags." (Is. 64:6.) So the apostle Paul passes the same judgment in regard to his own works, saying, "I count all things but loss, for the excellency of the knowledge of Christ Jesus my Lord; for whom I have suffered the loss of all things; and do count them but dung that I may win Christ." (Phil. 3:8.) It is in this way, now, that all the saints speak and judge concerning their own righteousness and merits.

2. No creature, performing even the best works, can merit any thing at the hand of God, or bind him to give any thing as though it were due from him, and according to the order of divine justice. The Apostle assigns the reason of this when he says, "Who hath first given to him, and it shall be recompensed unto him again." "Is it not lawful for me to do what I will with mine own." (Rom. 11:35. Matt. 20:15.) We deserve our preservation no more than we did our creation. God was not bound to create us; nor is he bound to preserve those whom he has created. But he did, and does, both of his own free-will and good pleasure. God receives no benefit from us, nor can we confer any thing upon our Creator.

Now, where there is no benefit, there is no merit; for merit presupposes some benefit received.

3. Our works are all due unto God; for all creatures are bound to render worship and gratitude to the Creator, so that if we were even never to sin, yet we could not render unto God the worship and gratitude which is due from us. "When ye have done all those things which are commanded you, say, We are unprofitable servants; we have done that which was our duty to do." (Luke 17:10.)

4. If we do any works which are good, these works are not ours, but God's, who produces them in us by his Holy Spirit. "It is God which worketh in you, both to will and to do, of his good pleasure." "What hast thou, that thou didst not receive?" (Phil. 2:13. 1 Cor. 4:7.) We are by nature the children of wrath—dead in trespasses and sins—evil trees, which cannot produce good fruit. (Eph. 2:1, 3. Matt. 7:18.) If we are by nature evil trees, God must by his grace make us good trees, and produce good fruit in us, as it is said; "We are his workmanship, created in Christ Jesus unto good works, which God hath before ordained, that we should walk in them." (Eph. 2:10.) Hence, if we perform any thing that is good, it is the gift of God, and not any merit on our part. It would, indeed, be foolish on the part of any one, if, when he were to receive a hundred florins as a present from a rich man, he should think he deserved a thousand for receiving the hundred, seeing that he is under obligations to the rich man for the gift which he has received, and not the rich man to him.

5. There is no proportion between our works, which are altogether imperfect, and those exceedingly great benefits which the Father freely grants unto us in his Son.

6. "He that glorieth, let him glory in the Lord." (1 Cor. 1:31.) But if we deserve the remission of our sins by our good works, we should then have something whereof to glory; nor should we attribute the glory of our salvation to God, as it is said, "If Abraham were justified by works, he hath whereof to glory, but not before God." (Rom. 4:2.)

7. We are justified before we perform good works. "For the children being not yet born, neither having done any good or evil,

that the purpose of God according to election might stand, not of works, but of him that calleth; it was said unto her, the elder shall serve the younger: As it is written, "Jacob have I loved, but Esau have I hated." (Rom. 9:11–14.) We are, therefore, not justified before God at the time when we do good works, but we perform good works when we are justified.

8. The conceit of merit and justification by our good works is calculated to shake true Christian consolation, to disturb the conscience and lead men to doubt and despair in reference to their salvation. For when they hear the denunciation of the law, cursed be he that confirmeth not all the words of this law to do them, and consider their own imperfection, their conscience tells them that they can never perform all these things, so that they are continually led to cherish doubts, and to live in dread of the curse of the law. Faith, however, imparts sure and solid comfort to the conscience, because it grounds itself in the promise of God, which cannot disappoint the soul. "The inheritance is of faith, that it might be by grace, to the end the promise might be sure to all the seed." (Rom. 4:16.)

9. If we were to obtain righteousness by our own works, the promise would then be made of none effect, and Christ would have died in vain.

10. If the conceit concerning the merit of good works be admitted, then there would not be one and the same method of salvation. Abraham and the Thief on the cross would have been justified differently, which might also be said of us. But there is only one way of salvation: "I am the Way, and the Truth, and the Life; no man cometh unto the Father, but by me." "There is one Mediator between God and men." "There is one Lord, one faith, one baptism." "Jesus Christ the same yesterday, to-day, and forever." "There is none other name under heaven given among men, whereby we must be saved." (John 14:6. 1 Tim. 2:5. Eph. 4:5. Heb. 13:8. Acts 4:12.)

11. Christ would not accomplish the whole of our salvation, and thus would not be a perfect Saviour if any thing were to be added by us to our righteousness by way of merit; for there would be as

much detracted from his merit as would be added thereto from our merit. But Christ is our perfect Saviour, as the Scriptures sufficiently testify. "In whom we have redemption through his blood, the forgiveness of sins, according to the riches of his grace." "By grace are ye saved, through faith, and that not of yourselves; it is the gift of God; not of works, lest any man should boast." "The blood of Jesus Christ his Son cleanseth us from all sin." "Neither is there salvation in any other." (Eph. 1:7; 2:8, 9. 1 John 1:7. Acts 4:12.)

Obj. Reward presupposes merit. God also calls those good things which he promises, and grants unto them that perform good works, rewards. Therefore good works presuppose merit, and are meritorious in the sight of God. Ans. The major proposition, sometimes, holds true among men, but never with God; because no creature can merit any thing at the hands of God, seeing that he is indebted to no one. Yet they are, nevertheless, called the rewards of our good works in respect to God, because he, out of his mere grace, recompenses them. This recompense, however, is not due; for we can add nothing to God, neither does he stand in need of our works. Yea, something is rather added unto us by our good works; because they are a conformity of ourselves with God, and his benefits, by which we are bound to render gratitude to God, and not God to us. It is, therefore, not less absurd to say that we merit salvation at the hands of God, than if a certain one should say, Thou hast given me one hundred florins. Therefore thou oughtest to give me a thousand florins. Yet God commands us to perform good works, and promises a gracious reward to those who do them, as a father promises rewards to his children.

INTRODUCTION TO
The Church of England
THE BOOK OF COMMON PRAYER (1559)

The Reformation was not a straightforward affair anywhere in Europe where it took root, but it encountered a particularly rocky and tortuous road in England. Nurtured in its earliest stages by a king (Henry VIII) who was temperamental, paranoid, autocratic, and deeply attached to the old Roman Catholic religion himself, the English Reformation seemed unlikely to amount to much for its first twenty years. Its leading architects, foremost among them the unlikely Archbishop of Canterbury, Thomas Cranmer (who was appointed to this lofty position in the Roman Catholic Church while himself a closet Protestant, with a closet wife to boot!) had to learn nothing so much as the art of diplomacy, and several met untimely deaths by misjudging the king's religious mood. Still, the authority of the Pope in England had been decisively rejected in 1533 and 1534, and Cranmer carefully laid the groundwork for deeper and more fully Protestant reform in the years that followed.

When Henry died in 1547 and left the throne to his nine-year-old son, Edward VI, who was hailed as a "new Josiah," reform accelerated rapidly. Edward himself was devoutly Protestant, as were several of his most influential councillors. In 1548 communion was offered for the first time in both kinds (that is, both bread and wine), and in 1549, a full Book of Common Prayer in English was published and prescribed for use throughout the country. Cranmer himself was the primary composer of the new text, though he made substantial use of existing liturgies; the peculiar beauty of expression that the new English texts displayed was to make an enduring impact on the development of the English language and centuries of Anglican worshippers. Although the orders of service in this book were relatively conservative, maintaining significant continuity with centuries of Catholic practice and even many points of theology, the mere fact of a liturgy celebrated entirely in English was a dramatic change. Worship was no longer to be a mere ceremonial display by the priests, with ordinary parishioners gawking on while the clergy mumbled in Latin. Now it was to be an opportunity for the whole congregation to gather together and worship the Lord, and to be instructed in the truth of Scripture through the readings and prayers.

However, the 1549 Prayer Book was only a beginning. With the Protestant cause on the Continent in a tenuous position after important military victories by Charles V, Cranmer was able to invite leading reformers such as Martin Bucer and Peter Martyr Vermigli to England to help advance the cause of the Reformation there. Bolstered by their support, he was able to begin work on a much more dramatic revision of the liturgy in a simpler, more biblical direction. Moreover, as all of these reformers had a more Reformed than Lutheran bent, Cranmer's own thought seems to have progressively evolved in that direction, particularly on the matter of the Eucharist. Given that transubstantiation was the greatest bulwark of the old Catholic religion, Cranmer encountered fiercer resistance here than anywhere, but in perhaps the boldest change of all in the new 1552 Book of Common Prayer, he changed the Words of Administration in Holy Communion as follows:

1549 version:

"The body of our Lord Jesus Christ which was given for thee, preserve thy body and soul unto everlasting life."

"The blood of our Lord Jesus Christ which was shed for thee, preserve thy body and soul unto everlasting life."

1552 version:

"Take and eat this, in remembrance that Christ died for thee, and feed on him in thy heart by faith, with thanksgiving."

"Drink this in remembrance that Christ's blood was shed for thee, and be thankful."

Still, the 1552 Prayer Book did not satisfy everyone. Some of the more zealous reformers, especially the fiery Scotsman John Knox, newly-arrived at court, felt that it was still much too popish, and they particularly decried the continuation of the practice of kneeling at communion. Whatever the words said, they complained, this physical practice would continue to encourage the common people in the superstition of transubstantiation. Accordingly, a last-minute change was made to include a rubric (the so-called "black rubric," because it was not printed in red like all the others) offering an explanation to worshippers that the kneeling signalled the penitent heart of the worshipper, not any adoration of Christ's flesh physically present in the consecrated elements. It was a compromise that was to please no one, and with the accession of Queen Elizabeth in 1559, it was tossed out to avoid antagonizing the conservatives. Indeed, the revision of 1559 attempted another compromise, fusing the Words of Administration from the 1549 and 1552 editions, so that different theologies of the Eucharist could all find a place in this most intimate moment of worship. Aside from these small but significant changes, and a few other minor alterations, the 1559 Prayer Book was substantially identical to that of 1552, and was to remain in use in the English Reformed church (the term "Anglican" was not to come till much later) for over a century, although maligned by Puritans as still too full of popish abuses.

The excerpts below comprise the original Preface and "On Ceremonies" that first appeared in the 1552 Prayer Book, as well as the Order for Holy Communion as it was crystallized in 1559. A couple points are worth highlighting from each.

The Preface emphasizes in good Protestant fashion the importance of people hearing the Word of God in their own tongue and lays considerable stress on the reform of the lectionary so as to ensure that as much of Scripture as possible be publicly read and understood. However, it also emphasizes, in very English fashion, the importance of uniformity in worship, a uniformity that was to prove so contentious in later decades. Anticipating already some of these contentions, the brief essay "On Ceremonies" seeks to offer a rationale for which old Catholic ceremonies were to be abolished, which reformed, and which retained. The focus was on edification, and readers were warned "to be more studious of unity and concord than of innovations and newfangledness," recognizing that antiquity deserved respect.

The Order for Holy Communion, it should be noted, was not simply an order of worship for the communion part of the service, but for a full worship service, one that was envisioned as only taking place a few times a year (no less than three, the Prayer Book prescribed). Although the Reformers by and large wanted to see much more frequent communion, the late medieval practice had been increasingly to commune only once per year, and it proved unrealistic to revise this practice too dramatically. Once we realize this, we may be a bit more forgiving of what may seem the excessively wordy and laborious explanations and warnings that the priest is to offer to the congregants before communing. Moreover, Cranmer intended the Prayer Book to be not merely a form of worship, but an opportunity to instruct the common people in the basics of Protestant theology, especially as there were few parish priests capable of preaching competently on their own. Centuries later, the extraordinary theological richness that he managed to pack into many of the prayers remains a source of instruction and inspiration to worshippers today.

THE BOOK OF COMMON PRAYER (1559)

Church of England

SPELLING MODERNIZED BY BRIAN MARR

PREFACE

There was never anything by the wit of man so well devised or so sure established which in continuance of time hath not been corrupted, as among other things it may plainly appear by the common prayers in the church, commonly called divine service, the first original and ground whereof, if a man would search out by ancient fathers, he shall find that the same was not ordained but of a good purpose and for a great advancement of godliness. For they so ordered the matter that all the whole Bible (or the greatest part thereof) should be read over once in the year, intending thereby that the clergy and especially such as were Ministers of the congregation, should by often reading and [by the] meditation of God's word be stirred up to godliness themselves, and be more able also to exhort other[s] by wholesome doctrine, and to confute them that were adversaries to the truth. And further, that the people by daily hearing of holy scripture read in the Church should continually profit more and more in the knowledge of God and be the more inflamed with the love of

His true religion. But, these many years [having] passed, those godly and decent order[s] of the ancient fathers hath been so altered, broken, and neglected by planting in uncertain stories, legends, responses, verses, vain repetitions, commemorations, and synodals that commonly when any book of the Bible was begun before three or four Chapters were read out, all the rest were unread. And in this sort the book of Isaiah was begun in Advent, and the book of Genesis in Septuagesima, but they were only begun, and never read through. After like sort were other books of holy scripture used. And moreover, whereas St. Paul would have such language spoken to the people in the Church as they might understand and have profit by hearing the same, the service in this church of England these many years hath been read in Latin to the people, which they understood not, so that they have heard with their ears only, and their hearts, spirit, and mind have not been edified thereby. And furthermore, notwithstanding that the ancient fathers have divided the Psalms into seven portions, whereof every one was called a nocturn, now of late time, a few of them have been daily said (and oft repeated) and the rest utterly omitted. Moreover, the number and hardness of the rules, called the Pie, and the manifold changings of the service was the cause that to turn the book only was so hard and intricate a matter that many times there was more business to find out what should be read than to read it when it was found out.

These inconveniences therefore considered, here is set forth such an order whereby the same shall be redressed. And for a readiness in this matter, here is drawn out a calendar for that purpose, which is plain and easy to be understood, wherein (so much as may be) the reading of holy scriptures is so set forth that all things shall be done in order, without breaking one piece thereof from another. For this cause be cut off anthems, responds, invitatories, and such like things as did break the continual course of the reading of the scripture. Yet because there is no remedy but that of necessity there must be some rules, therefore certain rules are here set forth, which as they be few in number, so they be plain and easy to be understand. So that here you have an order for prayer (as touching the reading of holy scripture) much agreeable to the mind and purpose of the old fathers, and a great deal more profitable and commodious than that which of late was used. It is more profitable, because here are left out many things, whereof some be untrue, some uncertain, some vain and superstitious, and is ordained nothing to be read but the very pure word of God, the holy scriptures, or that which is evidently grounded upon the same, and that in such a language and order as is most easy and plain for the understanding both of the readers and hearers. It is also more commodious, both for the shortness thereof and for the plainness of the order, and for that the rules be few and easy. Furthermore, by this order the Curates shall need none other books for their public service, but this book and the Bible, by the means whereof the people shall not be at so great charge for books, as in time paste they have been.

And where heretofore there hath been great diversity in saying and singing in churches within this realm—some following Salisbury use, some Hereford use, some the use of Bangor, some of York, and some of Lincoln—now from henceforth all the whole realm shall have but one use. And if any would judge this way more painful because that all things must be read upon the book, whereas before by the reason of so often repetition they could say many things by heart, if those men will weigh their labor, with the profit and knowledge which daily they shall obtain by reading upon the book, they will not refuse the pain in consideration of the great profit that shall ensue thereof.

And forasmuch as nothing can almost be so plainly set forth, but doubts may rise in the use and practicing of the same, to appease all such diversity (if any arise) and for the resolution of all doubts concerning the manner how to understand, do, and execute the things contained in this book, the parties that so doubt or diversely take anything shall always resort to the Bishop of the diocese, who by his discretion shall take order for the quieting and appeasing of the same, so that the same order be not contrary to anything contained in this book. And if the Bishop of the diocese be in any doubt, then may he send for the resolution thereof unto the Archbishop.

Though it be appointed in the afore written Preface that all things shall be read and sung in the Church, in the English tongue to the end that the congregation may be thereby edified, yet it is not meant, but when men say morning and evening prayer privately, they may say the same in any language that they themselves do understand.

And all priests and deacons shall be bound to say daily, the morning and evening prayer, either privately or openly, except they be letted[1] by preaching, studying of divinity, or by some other urgent cause.

And the curate that ministereth in every parish church or chapel, being at home and not being otherwise reasonably letted[2] shall say the same in the parish church or chapel where he ministereth and shall toll a bell thereto a convenient time before he begin that such as be disposed may come to hear God's word and to pray with him.

OF CEREMONIES

Of such ceremonies as be used in the church and have had their beginning by the institution of man, some at the first were of godly intent and purpose devised, and yet at length turned to vanity and superstition; some entered into the Church by undiscrete devotion and such a zeal as was without knowledge, and for because they were winked at in the beginning, they grew daily to more and more abuses, which not only for their unprofitableness, but also because they have much blinded the people and obscured the glory of God are worthy to be cut away and clean rejected; other there be which, although they have been devised by man, yet it is thought good to reserve them still, as well for a decent order in the church (for the which they were first devised) as because they pertain to edification, whereunto all things done in the Church (as the Apostle teaches) ought to be referred. And although the keeping or omitting of a ceremony (in itself considered) is but a small thing, yet the willful and contemptuous transgression and breaking of a common order and discipline is no small offence before God.

1 Prevented

2 Prevented

Let all things be done among you (saith St. Paul) in a seemly and due order. The appointment of the which order pertaineth not to private men, therefore no man ought to take in hand, nor presume to appoint or alter any public or common order in Christ's Church, except he be lawfully called and authorized thereunto.

And whereas as in this our time, the minds of men are so diverse that some think it a great matter of conscience to depart from a piece of the least of their ceremonies (they be so addicted to their old customs), and again on the other side some be so newfangled that they would innovate all thing[s] and so do despise the old that nothing can like them but that is new, it was thought expedient not so much to have respect how to please and satisfy either of these parties as how to please God and profit them both. And yet, lest any man should be offended (whom good reason might satisfy), here be certain causes rendered why some of the accustomed ceremonies be put away, and some retained and kept still.

Some are put away because the great excess and multitude of them hath so increased in these latter days that the burden of them was intolerable, whereof St. Augustine in his time complained that they were grown to such a number that the state of Christian people was in worse case (concerning that matter) than were the Jews. And he counselled that such [a] yoke and burden should be taken away, as time would serve quietly to do it.

But what would St. Augustine have said if he had seen the ceremonies of late days used among us, whereunto the multitude used in his time was not to be compared? This our excessive multitude of ceremonies was so great and many of them so dark that they did more confound and darken than declare and set forth Christ's benefits unto us.

And besides this, Christ's Gospel is not a ceremonial law (as much of Moses' law was) but it is a religion to serve God, not in bondage of the figure or shadow, but in the freedom of spirit, being content only with those ceremonies which do serve to a decent order and godly discipline, and such as be apt to stir up the dull mind of man to the remembrance of his duty to God by some notable and special signification whereby he might be edified.

Furthermore, the most weighty cause of the abolishment of certain ceremonies was that they were so far abused, partly by the superstitious blindness of the rude and unlearned, and partly by the insatiable avarice of such as sought more their own lucre than the glory of God that the abuses could not well be taken away, the thing remaining still. But now as concerning those persons, which peradventure will be offended, for that some of the old ceremonies are retained still, if they consider that without some ceremonies it is not possible to keep any order or quiet discipline in the Church, they shall easily perceive just cause to reform their judgements. And if they think much that any of the old do remain and would rather have all devised new, then such men granting some ceremonies convenient to be had, surely where the old may be well used, there they cannot reasonably reprove the old only for their age without betraying of their own folly. For in such a case, they ought rather to have reverence unto them for their antiquity, if they will declare themselves to be more studious of unity and concord than of innovations and newfangledness, which, as much as may be with the true setting forth of Christ's religion, is always to be eschewed. Furthermore, such shall have no just cause with the ceremonies reserved to be offended, for as those be taken away which were most abused and did burden men's consciences without any cause, so the other that remain are retained for a discipline and order which (upon just causes) may be altered and changed, and therefore are not to be esteemed equal with God's law. And moreover they be neither dark nor dumb ceremonies, but are so set forth that every man may understand what they do mean and to what use they do serve so that it is not like that they in time to come should be abused, as the other have been. And in these our doings, we condemn no other nations, nor prescribe anything but to our own people only. For we think it convenient that every country should use such ceremonies as they shall think best to the setting forth of God's honor or glory, and to the reducing of the people to a most perfect and godly living, without error or superstition. And that they should put away other things, which from time to time, they perceive to be most abused, as in men's ordinances, it often chanceth diversely in divers countries.

THE ORDER FOR THE ADMINISTRATION OF THE LORD'S SUPPER OR HOLY COMMUNION

So many as intend to be partakers of the Holy Communion shall signify their names to the curate over night, or else in the morning afore the beginning of morning prayer or immediately after.

And if any of those be an open and notorious evil liver, so that the congregation by him is offended, or have done any wrong to his neighbors by word or deed, the curate having knowledge thereof, shall call him and advertise him in any wise not to presume to the Lord's table until he have openly declared himself to have truly repented and amended his former naughty life, that the congregation may thereby be satisfied which afore were offended, and that he have recompensed the parties who he hath done wrong unto, or at the least declare himself to be in full purpose so to do, as soon as he conveniently may.

The same order shall the Curate use with those betwixt whom he perceiveth malice and hatred to reign, not suffering them to be partakers of the Lord's table until he know them to be reconciled. And if one of the parties so at variance, he content to forgive from the bottom of his heart all that the other hath trespassed against him and to make amends for that he himself hath offended, and the other party will not be persuaded to a godly unity, but remain still in his frowardness and malice, the Minister in that case ought to admit the penitent person to the Holy Communion, and not him that is obstinate.

The table, having at the Communion time a fair white linen cloth upon it, shall stand in the body of the church or in the chancel where morning prayer and evening prayer be appointed to be said. And the priest, standing at the north side of the table, shall say the Lord's prayer with this collect following:

Almighty God, unto whom all hearts be open, all desires known, and from whom no secrets are hid, cleanse the thoughts of our hearts by the inspiration of thy Holy Spirit, that we may perfectly love Thee and worthily magnify Thy holy name, through Christ our Lord. Amen.

Then shall the Priest rehearse distinctly at the ten commandments, and the people kneeling shall after every commandment ask God's mercy for their transgression of the same, after this sort:

MINISTER: God spake these words and said, "I am the Lord thy God, thou shalt have none other gods but me."

PEOPLE: Lord have mercy upon us, and incline our hearts to keep this law.

MINISTER: "Thou shalt not make to thyself any graven image, nor the likeness of anything that is in heaven above, or in the earth beneath, or in the water under the earth. Thou shalt not bow down to them, nor worship them, for I the Lord thy God am a jealous God and visit the sin of the fathers upon the children unto the third and fourth generation of them that hate me, and shew mercy unto thousands, in them that love me and keep my commandments."

PEOPLE: Lord have mercy upon us, and incline our hearts to keep this law.

MINISTER: "Thou shalt not take the name of the Lord thy God in vain, for the Lord will not hold him guiltless that taketh His name in vain."

PEOPLE: Lord have mercy upon us, and incline our hearts to keep this law.

MINISTER: "Remember that thou keep holy the Sabbath day: six days shalt thou labor and do all that thou hast to do, but the seventh day is the Sabbath of the Lord thy God. In it thou shalt do no manner of work, thou and thy son and thy daughter, thy manservant, and thy maidservant, thy cattle, and the stranger that is within thy gates, for in six days the Lord made heaven and earth, the sea and all that in them is, and rested the seventh day. Wherefore the Lord blessed the seventh day and hallowed it."

PEOPLE: Lord have mercy upon us, and incline our hearts to keep this law.

MINISTER: "Honor thy father and thy mother, that thy days may be long in the land which the Lord thy God giveth thee."

PEOPLE: Lord have mercy upon us, and incline our hearts to keep this law.

MINISTER: "Thou shalt not do murder."

PEOPLE: Lord have mercy upon us, and incline our hearts to keep this law.

MINISTER: "Thou shalt not commit adultery."

PEOPLE: Lord have mercy upon us, and incline our hearts to keep this law.

MINISTER: "Thou shalt not steal."

PEOPLE: Lord have mercy upon us, and incline our hearts to keep this law.

MINISTER: "Thou shalt not bear false witness against thy neighbor."

PEOPLE: Lord have mercy upon us, and incline our hearts to keep this law.

MINISTER: "Thou shalt not covet thy neighbor's house. Thou shalt not covet thy neighbor's wife, nor his servant, nor his maid, nor his ox, nor his ass, nor any thing that is his."

PEOPLE: Lord have mercy upon us, and write all these thy laws in our hearts we beseech thee.

Then shall follow the Collect of the day with one of these two Collects following for the Queen, the Priest standing up and saying,

Let us pray. Almighty God, whose kingdom is everlasting and power infinite, have mercy upon the whole congregation, and so rule the heart of thy chosen servant Elizabeth our Queen and governor that she (knowing whose minister she is) may above all things seek Thy honor and glory, and that we her subjects (duly considering whose authority she hath) may faithfully serve, honor, and humbly obey her in Thee and for Thee, according to Thy blessed word and ordinance, through Jesus Christ our Lord, who with Thee and the Holy Ghost liveth and reigneth ever one God, world without end. Amen.

Almighty and everlasting God, we be taught by Thy holy word that the hearts of Princes are in Thy rule and governance and that thou dost dispose and turn them as it seemeth best to Thy Godly wisdom: we humbly beseech Thee so to dispose and govern the heart of Elizabeth, Thy servant, our Queen and governor, that in all her thoughts, words, and works she may ever seek Thy honor and glory, and study to preserve Thy people committed to her charge, in wealth, peace, and godliness. Grant this, O merciful Father, for Thy dear Son's sake Jesus Christ our Lord. Amen.

Immediately after the Collects, the Priest shall read the Epistle beginning thus:

The Epistle written in the __th chapter of _______.

And the Epistle ended, he shall say the Gospel, beginning thus:

The Gospel written in the __th chapter of _______.

And the Epistle and Gospel being ended, shall be said the Creed:

I believe in one God, the Father Almighty, maker of heaven and earth, and of all things visible and invisible, and in one Lord Jesus Christ, the only-begotten Son of God, begotten of His Father before all worlds, God of God, light of light, very God of very God, gotten, not made, being of one substance with the Father, by whom all things were made, who for us men, and for our salvation came down from heaven, and was incarnate by the Holy Ghost, of the Virgin Mary, and was made man, and was crucified also for us, under Pontius Pilate. He suffered and was buried, and the third day he rose again, according to the Scriptures, and ascended into heaven, and sitteth at the right hand of the Father, and He shall come again with glory, to judge both the quick and the dead, whose kingdom shall have no end; and I believe in the Holy Ghost, the Lord and giver of life, who proceedeth from the Father and the Son, who with the Father and the Son together is worshipped and glorified, who spake by the Prophets; and I believe one catholic and Apostolic Church. I acknowledge one Baptism, for the remission of sins. And I look for the resurrection of the dead, and the life of the world to come. Amen.

After the Creed, if there be no sermon, shall follow one of the homilies already set forth, or hereafter to he set forth by common authority.

After such sermon, homily, or exhortation, the curate shall declare unto the people whether there be any holy days or fasting days the week following, and earnestly exhort them to remember the poor, saying one, or more of these sentences following, as he thinketh most convenient by his discretion:

"Let your light so shine before men that they may see your good works and glorify your Father which is in heaven" (Matt. 5:16).

"Lay not up yourselves treasure upon the earth, where the rust and moth doth corrupt, and where thieves break through and steal, but lay up for yourselves treasures in heaven, where neither rust, nor moth doth corrupt, and where thieves do not break through and steal" (Matt. 6:19–20).

"Whatsoever you would that men should do unto you, even so do unto them, for this is the law and the Prophets" (Matt. 7:12).

"Not everyone that sayeth unto me, 'Lord, Lord,' shall enter into the Kingdom of heaven; but he that doth the will of my Father which is in heaven" (Matt. 7:21).

"Zacchaeus stood forth and said unto the Lord, 'behold Lord, the half of my goods I give to the poor, and if I have done any wrong to any man, I restore fourfold'" (Luke 19:8).

"Who goeth a warfare at any time of his own cost? Who planteth a vineyard and eateth not of the fruit thereof? Or who feedeth a flock, and eateth not of the milk of the flock?" (1 Cor. 9:7).

"If we have sown unto you spiritual things, is it a great matter if we shall reap your worldly things?" (1 Cor. 9:11).

"Do ye not know that they which minister about holy things, live off the sacrifice? Which wait off the altar are partakers with the altar. Even so hath the Lord also ordained that they which preach the Gospel should live off the gospel" (1 Cor. 9:13).

"He which soweth little shall reap little, and he that soweth plenteously shall reap plenteously. Let every man do according as he is disposed in his heart, not grudgingly or of necessity, for God loveth a cheerful giver" (2 Cor. 9:6–7).

"Let him that is taught in the word minister unto him that teaches in all good things. Be not deceived: God is not mocked, for whatsoever a man soweth, that shall he reap" (Gal. 6:6).

"While we have time, let us do good unto all men, and specially unto them which are of the household of faith" (Gal. 6:10).

"Godliness is great riches if a man be content with that he hath, for we brought nothing into the world, neither may we carry anything out" (1 Tim. 6:6).

"Charge them which are rich in this world that they be ready to give and glad to distribute, laying up in store for themselves a good foundation against the time to come, that they may attain eternal life" (1 Tim. 6:17).

"God is not unrighteous that He will forget your works and labor that proceedeth of love, which love ye have shewed for His name's sake which have ministered unto saints, and yet do minister" (Heb. 6:10).

"To do good and to distribute, forget not, for with such sacrifices God is pleased" (Heb. 13:16).

"Whoso hath this world's good and seeth his brother have need and shutteth up his compassion from him, how dwelleth the love of God in him?" (1 Jn. 3:17).

"Give alms of thy goodness, and turn never thy face from any poor man, and then the face of the Lord shall not be turned away from thee" (Tob. 4:5).

"Be merciful after thy power. If thou hast much, give plenteously; if thou hast little, do thy diligence gladly to give of that little, for so gatherest thou thyself a good reward in the day of necessity" (Tob. 4:8).

"He that hath pity upon the poor lendeth unto the Lord, and look what he layeth out: it shall be paid him again" (Prov. 19:17).

"Blessed be the man that provideth for the sick and needy, the Lord shall deliver him, in the time of trouble" (Ps. 41:1).

Then shall the Church wardens, or some other by them appointed, gather the devotion of the people and put the same into the poor men's box, and upon the offering days appointed, every man and woman shall pay to the Curate the due and accustomed offerings, after which done, the Priest shall say:

Let us pray for the whole estate of Christ's Church militant here in earth.

Almighty and everliving God, which by Thy holy Apostle hast taught us to make prayers and supplications and to give thanks for all men, we humbly beseech thee most mercifully (to accept our alms) and to receive these our prayers which we offer unto thy divine majesty, beseeching Thee to inspire continually the universal Church with the spirit of truth, unity, and concord, and grant that all they that do confess Thy holy name may agree in the truth of Thy holy word and live in unity and godly love. We beseech Thee also to save and defend all Christian kings, princes, and governors, and specially thy servant, Elizabeth our Queen that under her we may be godly and quietly governed, and grant unto her whole Counsel and to all that be put in authority under her that they may truly and indifferently[3] minister justice to the punishment of wickedness and vice, and to the maintenance of God's true religion and virtue. Give grace, O heavenly Father, to all Bishops, Pastors and Curates that they may both by their life and doctrine set forth Thy true and lively word and rightly and duly administer Thy holy Sacraments, and to all Thy people give thy heavenly grace, and especially to this congregation here present, that with meek heart and due reverence they may hear and receive thy holy word, truly serving Thee in holiness and righteousness all the days of their life. And we most humbly beseech Thee of Thy goodness, O Lord, to comfort and succor all them which in this transitory life be in trouble, sorrow, need, sickness, or any other adversity. Grant this, O father, for Jesus Christ's sake our only Mediator and advocate. Amen.

3 Impartially

Then shall follow this exhortation at certain times when the Curate shall see the people negligent to come to the holy Communion:

We be come together at this time, dearly beloved brethren, to feed at the Lord's supper, unto the which in God's behalf I bid you all that be here present, and beseech you for the Lord Jesus Christ's sake that ye will not refuse to come thereto, being so lovingly called and bidden of God Himself. Ye know how grievous and unkind a thing it is when a man hath prepared a rich feast, decked his table with all kind of provision so that there lacketh nothing but the guests to sit down, and yet they which be called without any cause most unthankfully refuse to come. Which of you in such a case would not be moved? Who would not think a great injury and wrong done unto him? Wherefore, most dearly beloved in Christ, take ye good heed lest ye, withdrawing yourselves from this holy supper, provoke God's indignation against you; it is an easy matter for a man to say, 'I will not communicate, because I am otherwise letted[4] with worldly business', but such excuses be not so easily accepted and allowed before God. If any man say, 'I am a grievous sinner, and therefore am afraid to come', wherefore then do ye not repent and amend? When God calleth you, be you not ashamed to say ye will not come? When you should return to God, will you excuse yourself and say that you be not ready? Consider earnestly with yourselves how little such feigned excuses shall avail before God. They that refused the feast in the Gospel, because they had bought a farm, or would try their yokes of oxen, or because they were married, were not so excused, but counted unworthy of the heavenly feast. I for my part am here present and according to mine office I bid you in the name of God; I call you in Christ's behalf; I exhort you, as you love your own Salvation that ye will be partakers of this holy Communion. And as the Son of God did vouchsafe to yield up His soul by death upon the cross for your health, even so it is your duty to receive the Communion together in the remembrance of His death as He Himself commanded. Now, if ye

4 Hindered

will in no wise thus do, consider with yourselves how great injury ye do unto God, and how sore punishment hangeth over your heads for the same. And whereas ye offend God so sore in refusing this holy banquet, I admonish, exhort, and beseech you that unto this unkindness ye will not add anymore, which thing ye shall do if ye stand by as gazers and lookers of them that do Communicate, and be no partakers of the same yourselves. For what thing can this be accounted else than a further contempt and unkindness unto God? Truly it is a great unthankfulness to say nay when ye be called, but the fault is much greater when men stand by, and yet will neither eat, nor drink this holy Communion with other[s]. I pray you what can this be else but even to have the mysteries of Christ in derision. It is said unto all: Take ye and eat, take and drink ye all of this, do this in remembrance of me. With what face then, or with what countenance shall ye hear these words? What will this be else, but a neglecting, a despising, and mocking of the Testament of Christ? Wherefore rather than you should so do, depart you hence, and give place to them that be godly disposed. But when you depart, I beseech you ponder with yourselves from whom ye depart: ye depart from the Lord's Table: ye depart from your brethren, and from the banquet of most heavenly food. These things, if ye earnestly consider, ye shall by God's grace return to a better mind, for the obtaining whereof we shall make our humble petitions while we shall receive the holy Communion.

And some time shall be said this also, at the discretion of the Curate:

Dearly beloved, forasmuch as our duty is to render to almighty God our heavenly Father most hearty thanks for that He hath given His Son our Savior Jesus Christ, not only to die for us, but also to be our Spiritual food and sustenance, as it is declared unto us, as well by God's word as by the holy sacraments of His blessed body and blood, the which being so comfortable a thing to them which receive it worthily and so dangerous to them that will presume to receive it unworthily, my duty is to exhort you to consider the dignity of the holy mystery, and the great peril of the unworthy receiving thereof, and so to search and examine your own consciences, as you should come holy and clean to a most godly and heavenly feast. So that in no wise you come but in the marriage garment, required of God in holy scripture, and so come and be received as worthy partakers of such a heavenly Table, the way and means thereto is:

First to examine your lives and conversation by the rule of God's commandments and whereinsoever ye shall perceive yourselves to have offended either by will, word, or deed, there bewail your own sinful lives, confess yourselves to almighty God, with full purpose of amendment of life. And if ye shall perceive your offenses to be such as be not only against God, but also against your neighbors, then ye shall reconcile yourselves unto them, ready to make restitution and satisfaction according to the uttermost of your powers for all injuries and wrongs done by you to any other, and likewise being ready to forgive other[s] that have offended you as you would have forgiveness of your offenses at God's hand. For otherwise the receiving of the holy Communion doth nothing else, but increase your damnation.

And because it is requisite that no man should come to the holy Communion but with a full trust in God's mercy and with a quiet conscience, therefore if there be any of you which by the means aforesaid cannot quiet his own conscience, but requireth further comfort or counsel, then let him come to me, or some other discrete and learned minister of God's word, and open his grief, that he may receive such Ghostly counsel, advice, and comfort as his conscience may be relieved, and that by the ministry of God's word, he may receive comfort, and the benefit of absolution, to the quieting of his conscience and avoiding of all scruple and doubtfulness.

Then shall the Priest say this exhortation:

Dearly beloved in the Lord, ye that mind to come to the holy Communion of the body and blood of our savior Christ must consider what St. Paul writeth unto the Corinthians, how he exhorteth all persons diligently to try and examine themselves before they presume to eat of that bread and drink of that cup. For as the benefit is great, if with a truly penitent heart and lively faith we receive that holy sacrament (for then we spiritually eat the flesh of Christ, and drink His blood, then we dwell in Christ and Christ in us, we be one with Christ, and Christ with us), so is the danger great if we receive the same unworthily. For then we be guilty of the body and blood of Christ our savior. We eat and drink our own damnation, not considering the Lord's body. We kindle God's wrath against us. We provoke him to plague us with diverse diseases and sundry kinds of death. Therefore if any of you be a blasphemer of God, a hinderer or slanderer of His word, an adulterer, or be in malice or envy, or in any other grievous crime, bewail your sins and come not to this holy table, lest after the taking of that holy sacrament, the devil enter into you, as he entered into Judas, and fill you full of all iniquities and bring you to destruction both of body and soul. Judge therefore yourselves, brethren, that ye be not judged of the Lord. Repent you truly for your sins past, have a lively and steadfast faith in Christ our savior. Amend your lives, and be in perfect charity with all men, so shall ye be meet partakers of those holy mysteries. And above all things ye must give most humble and hearty thanks to God the Father, the Son, and the Holy Ghost, for the redemption of the world by the death and passion of our savior Christ, both God and man, who did humble himself, even to the death upon the cross for us miserable sinners which lay in darkness and shadow of death that He might make us the children of God and exalt us to everlasting life. And to the end that we should always remember the exceeding great love of our master and only savior Jesus Christ, thus dying for us, and the innumerable benefits which by His precious bloodshedding He hath obtained to us, He hath instituted and ordained holy mysteries as pledges of His love, and continual remembrance of His death, to our great and endless comfort. To Him therefore with the Father and the Holy Ghost, let us give (as we are most bounden) continual thanks, submitting ourselves wholly to His holy will and pleasure, and studying to serve Him in true holiness and righteousness, all the days of our life. Amen.

Then shall the Priest say to them that come to receive the holy Communion:

You that do truly and earnestly repent you of your sins and be in love and charity with your neighbors and intend to lead a new life, following the commandments of God, and walking from hence further in His holy ways, draw near and take this holy Sacrament, to your comfort make your humble confession to almighty God, before this congregation here gathered together in His holy name, meekly kneeling upon your knees.

Then shall this general confession be made in the name of all those that are minded to receive this holy Communion, either by one of them, or else by one of the ministers, or by the priest himself, all kneeling humbly upon their knees.

Almighty God, Father of our Lord Jesus Christ, maker of all things, Judge of all men, we acknowledge and bewail our manifold sins and wickedness, which we from time to time most grievously have committed, by thought, word, and deed, against Thy divine Majesty, provoking most justly Thy wrath and indignation against us. We do earnestly repent and be heartily sorry for these our misdoings. The remembrance of them is grievous unto us; the burden of them is intolerable. Have mercy upon us, have mercy upon us, most merciful Father. For Thy Son our Lord Jesus Christ's sake, forgive us all that is past and grant that we may ever hereafter serve and please Thee in newness of life, to the honor and glory of Thy name, through Jesus Christ our Lord. Amen.

Then shall the priest or the Bishop, being present, stand up and, turning himself to the people, shall say thus:

Almighty God, our Heavenly Father, who of His great mercy hath promised forgiveness of sins to all them which with hearty repentance and true faith turn to him, have mercy upon you, pardon and deliver you from all your sins, confirm and strengthen you in all goodness, and bring you to everlasting life, through Jesus Christ our Lord. Amen.

Then shall the Priest also say:

Hear what comfortable words our savior Christ saith to all them that truly turn to him:

"Come unto me all that travail and be heavy laden, and I shall refresh you. So God loved the world that he gave His only begotten Son, to the end that all that believe in Him should not perish but have life everlasting" (Matt. 11:28; Jn. 3:16).

Hear also what St. Paul saith:

"This is a true saying, and worthy of all men to be received: that Jesus Christ came into the world to save sinners" (1 Tim. 1:15).

Hear also what St. John sayeth:

"If any man sin, we have an advocate with the Father, Jesus Christ the righteous, and He is the propitiation for our sins" (1 Jn. 2:1).

After the which the priest shall proceed saying:

MINISTER: Lift up your hearts.

PEOPLE: We lift them up unto the Lord.

MINISTER: Let us give thanks unto our Lord God.

PEOPLE: It is meet and right so to do.

MINISTER: It is very meet, right, and our bounden duty that we should at all times and in all places give thanks to Thee, O Lord holy Father, almighty, everlasting God.

Here shall follow the proper prefaces, according to the time, if there be any specially appointed, or else immediately shall follow:

Therefore with Angels and Archangels, and with all the company of heaven, we laud and magnify Thy glorious name, evermore praising Thee, and saying: Holy, holy, holy, Lord God of hosts, heaven and earth are full of Thy glory, glory be to Thee, O Lord most high.

PROPER PREFACES

Upon Christmas day and seven days after:

Because thou didst give Jesus Christ, Thine only Son, to be born as this day for us, who by the operation of the Holy Ghost was made very man of the substance of the virgin Mary His mother, and that without spot of sin, to make us clean from all sin. Therefore with Angels and Archangels, and with all the company of heaven, we laud and magnify Thy glorious name, evermore praising Thee, and saying: Holy, holy, holy, Lord God of hosts, heaven and earth are full of Thy glory, glory be to Thee, O Lord most high.

Upon Easter day, and seven days after:

But chiefly are we bound to praise Thee for the glorious resurrection of Thy Son Jesus Christ our Lord, for He is the very paschal lamb which was offered for us and hath taken away the sin of the world, who by His death hath destroyed death, and by His rising to life again hath restored to us everlasting life. Therefore with Angels and Archangels, and with all the company of heaven, we laud and magnify Thy glorious name, evermore praising Thee, and saying: Holy, holy, holy, Lord God of hosts, heaven and earth are full of Thy glory, glory be to Thee, O Lord most high.

Upon the Ascension day, and seven days after:

Through Thy most dear beloved Son, Jesus Christ our Lord, who after His most glorious resurrection, manifestly appeared to all His Apostles, and in their sight ascended up into heaven to prepare a place for us, that, where He is, thither might we also ascend and reign with Him in glory. Therefore with Angels and Archangels, and with all the company of heaven, we laud and magnify Thy glorious name, evermore praising Thee, and saying: Holy, holy, holy, Lord God of hosts, heaven and earth are full of Thy glory, glory be to Thee, O Lord most high.

Upon Whitsunday, and six days after:

Through Jesus Christ our Lord, according to whose most true promise, the Holy Ghost came down this day from heaven, with a sudden great sound, as it had been a mighty wind in the likeness of fiery tongues lighting upon the Apostles, to teach them, and to lead them to all truth, giving them both the gift of divers languages, and also boldness with fervent zeal, constantly to preach the gospel unto all nations, whereby we are brought out of darkness and error into the clear light and true knowledge of Thee, and of thy Son Jesus Christ. Therefore with Angels and Archangels, and with all the company of heaven, we laud and magnify Thy glorious name, evermore praising Thee, and saying: Holy, holy, holy, Lord God of hosts, heaven and earth are full of Thy glory, glory be to Thee, O Lord most high.

Upon the feast of Trinity only:

It is very meet, right, and our bounden duty that we should at all times and in all places give thanks to Thee, O Lord, almighty and everlasting God, which art one God, one Lord, not one only person, but three persons in one substance, for that which we believe of the glory of the Father, the same we believe of the Son, and of the Holy Ghost, without any difference or inequality.

After which preface, shall follow immediately.

Therefore with Angels and Archangels, and with all the company of heaven, we laud and magnify Thy glorious name, evermore praising Thee, and saying: Holy, holy, holy, Lord God of hosts, heaven and earth are full of Thy glory, glory be to Thee, O Lord most high.

Then shall the priest, kneeling down at God's board, say in the name of all them that shall receive the communion, this prayer following:

We do not presume to come to this Thy table, O merciful Lord, trusting in our own righteousness, but in Thy manifold and great mercies, we be not worthy so much as to gather up the crumbs under Thy Table, but Thou art the same Lord, whose property is always to have mercy. Grant us therefore, gracious Lord, so to eat the flesh of Thy dear Son Jesus Christ, and to drink His blood that our sinful bodies may be made clean by His body, and our souls washed through his most precious blood, and that we may evermore dwell in Him, and He in us.

Then the priest standing up, shall say as followeth:

Almighty God, our heavenly Father which of thy tender mercy didst give thine only Son Jesus Christ to suffer death upon the Cross for our redemption, who made there (by His one oblation of Himself once offered) a full, perfect, and sufficient sacrifice, oblation, and satisfaction for the sins of the whole world, and did institute and, in His holy gospel, command us to continue a perpetual memory of that His precious death, until his coming again, hear us O merciful father, we beseech Thee, and grant that we receiving these Thy creatures of bread and wine, according to Thy Son our savior Jesus Christ's holy institution, in remembrance of His death and passion, may be partakers of His most blessed body and blood, who in the same night that He was betrayed, took bread, and when He had given thanks, He brake it, and gave it to His disciples, saying: "Take, eat, this is my body, which is given for you. Do this in remembrance of me." Likewise after supper he took the cup, and when He had given thanks, He gave it to them, saying: "Drink ye all of this, for this is my blood of the new Testament, which is shed for you and for many, for remission of sins. Do this as oft as ye shall drink it in remembrance of me."

Then shall the minister first receive the Communion in both kinds himself, and next deliver it to other Ministers (if any be there present that they may help the chief minister) and after to the people in their hands kneeling. And when he delivereth the bread, he shall say:

The body of our Lord Jesus Christ, which was given for thee, preserve thy body and soul into everlasting life, and take and eat this in remembrance that Christ died for thee: feed on Him in thine heart by faith, with thanksgiving.

And the minister that delivereth the cup shall say:

The blood of our Lord Jesus Christ, which was shed for thee, preserve thy body and soul into everlasting life, and drink this in remembrance that Christ's blood was shed for thee, and be thankful.

Then shall the priest say the Lord's prayer, the people repeating after him every petition.

After shall be said as followeth:

O Lord and heavenly Father, we thy humble servants, entirely desire Thy fatherly goodness mercifully to accept this our Sacrifice of praise and thanksgiving most humbly beseeching thee to grant that by the merits and death of thy Son Jesus Christ, and through faith in His blood, we (and all thy whole church) may obtain remission of our sins, and all other benefits of His passion. And here we offer and present unto Thee, O Lord, ourselves, our souls and bodies, to be a reasonable, holy, and lively sacrifice unto Thee, humbly beseeching Thee that all we which be partakers of this holy communion may be filled with Thy grace and heavenly benediction. And although we be unworthy through our manifold sins to offer unto Thee any sacrifice, yet we beseech Thee to accept this our bounden duty and service, not weighing our merits, but pardoning our offenses through Jesus Christ our Lord, by whom and with whom, in the unity of the Holy Ghost, all honor and glory be unto Thee, O Father Almighty, world without end. Amen.

Or this:

Almighty and everlasting God, we most heartily thank Thee, for that Thou dost vouchsafe to feed us which have duly received these holy mysteries with the spiritual food of the most precious body and blood of Thy Son, our savior Jesus Christ, and dost assure us thereby of Thy favor and goodness toward us, and that we be very members incorporate in Thy mystical body, which is the blessed company of all faithful people, and be also heirs through hope of Thy everlasting kingdom, by the merits of the most precious death and passion of Thy dear Son. We now most humbly beseech Thee, O heavenly Father, so to assist us with Thy grace that we may continue in that holy fellowship and do all such good works as Thou hast prepared for us to walk in, through Jesus Christ our Lord, to whom with Thee and the Holy Ghost be all honor and glory, world without end. Amen.

Then shall be said or sung:

Glory be to God on high, and in earth peace, goodwill towards men. We praise Thee, we bless Thee, we worship Thee, we glorify Thee, we give thanks to Thee, for Thy great glory. O Lord God, heavenly King, God the Father Almighty. O Lord the only-begotten Son Jesus Christ. O Lord God, Lamb of God, Son of the Father, that takest away the sins of the world, have mercy upon us: Thou that takest away the sins of the world, have mercy upon us. Thou that takest away the sins of the world, receive our prayer. Thou that sittest at the right hand of God the Father, have mercy upon us. For thou only art holy: Thou only art the Lord, thou only O Christ with the Holy Ghost art most high in the Glory of God the Father. Amen.

Then the Priest or the Bishop, if he be present, shall let them depart with this blessing:

The peace of God, which passeth all understanding, keep your hearts and minds in the knowledge and love of God, and of His Son Jesus Christ, our Lord. And the blessing of God almighty, the Father, the Son, and the Holy Ghost, be among you, and remain with you always. Amen.

Collects to be said after the offertory when there is no Communion; every such day one. And the same may be said also as often as occasion shall serve after the Collects, either of Morning and Evening Prayer, Communion, or Littany, by the discretion of the minister.

Assist us mercifully, O Lord, in these our Supplications and Prayers, and dispose the way of Thy servants toward the attainment of everlasting salvation, that among all the changes and chances of this mortal life they may ever be defended by Thy most gracious and ready help, through Christ our Lord. Amen.

O Almighty Lord and everliving God, vouchsafe we beseech Thee, to direct, sanctify, and govern both our hearts and bodies in the ways of Thy laws, and in the works of Thy commandments, that through Thy most mighty protection, both here and ever, we may be preserved in body and soul, through our Lord and Savior Jesus Christ. Amen.

Grant, we beseech Thee, almighty God, that the words which we have heard this day with our outward ears, may through Thy grace be so grafted inwardly in our hearts that they may bring forth in us the fruit of good living, to the honor and praise of Thy name, through Jesus Christ our Lord. Amen.

Prevent[5] us, O Lord, in all our doings, with Thy most gracious favor, and further us with Thy continual help that in all our works begun, continued, and ended in Thee, we may glorify Thy holy name, and finally by Thy mercy, obtain everlasting life, through Jesus Christ our Lord. Amen.

Almighty God, the fountain of all wisdom, which knowest our necessities before we ask and our ignorance in asking, we beseech Thee to have compassion upon our infirmities and those things which for our unworthiness we dare not, and for our blindness we cannot ask, vouchsafe to give us for the worthiness of Thy Son Jesus Christ our Lord. Amen.

Almighty God, which hast promised to hear the petitions of them that ask in Thy Son's name, we beseech Thee mercifully to incline Thine ears to us that have made known now our prayers and supplications unto Thee, and grant that those things which we have faithfully asked, according to Thy will, may effectually be obtained to the relief of our necessity, and to the setting forth of Thy glory through Jesus Christ our Lord. Amen.

Upon the holy days (if there be no Communion) shall be said that that is appointed at the Communion, until the end of the homily, concluding with the general prayer for the whole estate of Christ's Church militant

5 Direct

here in earth, and one, or more of these Collects before rehearsed, as occasion shall serve.

And there shall be no celebration of the Lord's supper except there be a good number to Communicate with the Priest, according to his discretion.

And if there be not above twenty persons in the parish of discretion to receive the Communion, yet there shall be no communion except four or three at the least communicate with the priest And in cathedral and collegiate churches, where be many Priests and Deacons, they shall all receive the communion with the minister every Sunday at the least, except they have a reasonable cause to the contrary.

And to take away the superstition which any person hath or might have in the bread and wine, it shall suffice that the bread be such as is usual to be eaten at the table with other meats, but the best and purest wheat bread that conveniently may be gotten. And if any of the bread or wine remain, the Curate shall have it to his own use.

The bread and wine for the Communion shall be provided by the Curate, and the church wardens, at the charges of the Parish, and the parish shall be discharged of such sums of money or other duties which hitherto they have paid for the same by order of their houses every Sunday.

And note that every Parishioner shall communicate at the least three times in the year, of which Easter to be one, and shall also receive the sacraments and other rites according to the order in this book appointed. And yearly at Easter, every Parishioner shall reckon with his Parson, Vicar or Curate, or his or their deputy or deputies, and pay to them or him all ecclesiastical duties, accustomably due then and at that time to be paid.

THE FORM OF SOLEMNIZATION OF MATRIMONY

First, the banns[6] *must be given three separate Sundays or holy days, at the time of service, the people being present, after the accustomed manner. And if the persons that would be married dwell in diverse Parishes, the banns must be asked in both Parishes and the Curate of the one Parish shall not solemnize matrimony betwixt them without a certificate*

6 Proclamation or notice given in a church of an intended marriage.

of the banns being thrice asked, from the Curate of the other Parish. At the date appointed for solemnization of Matrimony, the persons to be married shall come into the body of the Church, with their friends and neighbors. And there the Minister shall thus say:

Dearly beloved friends, we are gathered together here in the sight of God, and in the face of his congregation, to join together this man and this woman in holy matrimony, which is an honorable state, instituted of God in Paradise, in the time of man's innocence, signifying unto us the mystical union that is betwixt Christ and his Church: which holy state Christ adorned and beautified with his presence and first miracle that he wrought in Cana of Galilee, and is commended of Saint Paul to be honourable among all men, and therefore is not to be enterprised, nor taken in hande unadvisedly, lightly or wantonly, to satisfy mans carnal lusts and appetites, like brute beasts that have no understanding; but reverently, discretely, advisedly, soberly, and in the fear of God, duly considering the causes for the which matrimony was ordained. One was the procreation of children, to be brought up in the fear and nurture of the Lord, and praise of God. Secondly, it was ordained for a remedy against sin and to avoid fornication, that such persons as have not the gift of continence might marry, and keep themselves undefiled members of Christ's body. Thirdly, for the mutual society, help, and comfort, that the one ought to have of the other, both in prosperity and adversity, into the which holy state these two persons present, come now to be joined. Therefore if any man can show any just cause, why they may not lawfully be joined together let him now speak, or else hereafter for ever hold his peace.

And also speaking to the persons that shall be marred, he shall say:

I require and charge you (as you will answer at the dreadful day of judgment, when the secrets of all hearts shall be disclosed) that if either of you does know any impediment, why ye may not be lawfully joined together in Matrimony, that ye confess it. For be ye well assured, that so many as be coupled together, otherwise than God's word doth allow, are not joined together by God, neither is their Matrimony lawful.

At which day of marriage, if any man do allege and declare any impediment, why they may not be coupled together in matrimony by Gods law, or the laws of this realm, and will be bound, and sufficient sureties with him to the parties, or else put in a caution to the full value of such charges, as the persons to be married do sustain to prove his allegation: then the solemnization must be deferred unto such time as the truth be tried. If no impediment be alleged, then shall the curate say unto the man,

N. Wilt thou have this woman to thy wedded wife, to love together after God's ordinance in the holy estate of Matrimony? Wilt thou love her, comfort her, honour, and keep her, in sickness, and in health? And forsaking all others, keep thee only to her, so long as you both shall live?

The man shall answer,

I will.

Then shall the Minister say to the woman,

N. Wilt thou have this man to thy wedded husband, to love together after God's ordinance in the holy estate of matrimony? Wilt thou obey him and serve him, love, honour, and keep him, in sickness and in health? And forsaking all others, keep thee only to him so long as ye both shall live

The woman shall answer,

I will.

Then shall the Minister say,

Who giveth this woman to be married unto this man?

And the Minister receiving the woman at her father's or friend's hands, shall cause the man to take the woman by the right hand, and so either to give their troth to other, the man first saying.

I ***N.*** take thee ***N.*** to my wedded wife, to have and to hold from this day forward, for better, for worse, for richer, for poorer, in sickness, and in health, to love and to cherish, till death us depart; according to God's holy ordinance, and thereto I plight thee my troth.

Then shall they loose their hands, and the woman taking again the man by the right hand, shall say.

I ***N.*** take thee ***N.*** to my wedded husband, to have and to hold, from this day forward, for better, for worse, for richer, for poorer, in sickness, ad in health, to love, cherish, and to obey, till death us depart, according to god's holy ordinance: and thereto I give thee my troth.

Then shall they again loose their hands, and the man shall give unto the woman a ring, laying the same upon the book, with the accustomed duty to the Minister and Clerk. And the Minister taking the ring, shall deliver it unto the man, to put it upon the fourth finger of the woman's left hand. And the man taught by the Minister, shall say.

With this ring I thee wed: with my body I thee worship: and with all my worldly goods, I thee endow. In the name of the Father, and of the Son, and of the Holy Ghost. Amen.

Then the man leaving the ring upon the fourth finger of the womans left hand, the Minister shall say.

O Eternal God, creator and preserver of all mankind, giver of all spiritual grace, the author of everlasting life: send thy blessing upon these thy servants, this man and this woman, whom we bless in thy name, that as Isaac and Rebecca lived faithfully together: So these persons may surely perform and keep the vow and covenant betwixt them made, whereof this ring given, and received, is a token and pledge, and may ever remain in perfect love and peace together, and live according unto thy laws, thorough Jesus Christ our Lord. Amen.

Then shall the Minister join their right hands together and say.

Those whom God hath joined together, let no man put asunder.

Then shall the Minister speak unto the people.

FOR as much as ***N.*** and ***N.*** have consented together in holy wedlock, and have witnessed the same before God, and this company, and thereto have given and pledged, their troth one to the other, and have declared the same by giving and receiving of a ring, and by joining of hands I pronounce that they be man and wife together. In the name of the father, of the son and of the holy Ghost. Amen.

And the Minister shall add this blessing.

God the Father, God the Son, God the holy Ghost, bless, preserve, and keep you, the Lord mercifully with his favour look upon you, and so fill you with all spiritual benediction, and grace, that you may so love together in this life, that in the world to come, you may have life everlasting. Amen.

Then the Ministers or Clerks going to the Lord's table, shall say, or sing this Psalm following Beati omnes.

Blessed are all they that fear the Lord, and walk in his ways.
For thou shalt eat the labour of thy hands, O well is thee, and happy shalt thou be.
Thy wife shall be as the fruitfull vine upon the walls of thy house.
Thy children like the olive branches round about thy table.
Lo thus shall the man be blessed: that feareth the lord.
The Lord from out of Sion shall bless thee: that thou shalt see Jerusalem in prosperity, all thy life long:
Yea, that thou shalt see thy children's children, and peace upon Israel.
Glory be to the. etc.
As it was. etc.

Or else this Psalm following Deus misereatur.

GOD be merciful unto us and bless us: and show us the light of his countenance, and be merciful unto us.
That thy way may be known upon the earth: thy sayings health among all nations.
Let the people praise thee (O God) yea, let all the people praise thee.
O let the nations rejoice and be glad, for thou shalt judge the folk righteously, and govern the nations upon the earth.

Let the people praise thee (O God) let all the people praise thee.
Then shall the earthe bring forth her increase, and God, even our God, shall give us his blessing.
God shall bless us, and all the ends of the world shall fear him.
Glory be to the Father. etc. As it was in the be. etc.

The Psalm ended, and the man and the woman kneeling before the Lord's table: The Minister standing at the Table, and turning his face toward them, shall say,

Lord have mercy upon us.

PEOPLE: Christ have mercy upon us.

MINISTER: Lord have mercy upon us.
OUR FATHER which art. etc.
And lead us not into temptation.

PEOPLE: But deliver us from evil. Amen.

MINISTER: O Lord, save thy servant, and thy handmaiden.

PEOPLE: Which put their trust in the.

MINISTER: O Lord send them help from thy holy place.

PEOPLE: And evermore defend them.

MINISTER: Be unto them a tower of strength.

PEOPLE: From the face of their enemies.

MINISTER: O Lord hear our prayer.

PEOPLE: And let our cries come unto thee.

The Minister:

O GOD of Abraham, God of Isaac, God of Jacob, bless these thy servants, and sow the seed of eternal life in their minds, that whatsoever in thy holy word they shall profitably learn, they may in deed fulfill the same. Look, O Lord, mercifully upon them from heaven, and bless them. And as thou didst send thy blessing upon Abraham and Sara to their great comfort: so vouchsafe to send thy blessing upon these thy servants, that they obeying thy will, and alway being in safety under thy protection, may abide in thy love unto their lives end, through Jesus Christ our Lord. Amen.

This prayer next following shall be omitted where the woman is past child birth.

O MERCIFUL Lord, and heavenly Father, by whose gracious gift mankind is increased, we beseech thee assist with thy blessing these two persons, that they may both be fruitful in procreation of children, also live together so long in godly love and honesty, that they may see their children's children, unto the third and fourth generation unto thy praise and honour: through Jesus Christ our Lord. Amen.

O GOD which by thy mighty power hast made all things of naught, which also after other things set in order, didst appoint that out of man (created after thine own image and similitude) woman should take her beginning, and knitting them together, didst teach that it should never be lawful to put asunder those, whom thou by matrimony hadst made one: O God which haste consecrated the state of matrimony to such an excellent ministry, that in it is signified and represented the spiritual marriage and unity betwixt Christ and his Church: Look mercifully upon these thy servants, that both this man may love his wife, according to thy word (as Christ did love his spouse the Church, who gave himself for it, loving and cherishing it, even as his own flesh). And also that this woman may be loving and amiable to her husband as Rachel, wise as Rebecca, faithful and obedient as Sara, and in all quietness, sobriety, and peace, be a follower of holy and Godly matrons, O Lord bless them both, and grant them to inherit thy everlasting kingdom: through Jesus Christ our Lord. Amen.

Then shall the Minister say,

ALMIGHTY God, which, at the beginning did create our first parents Adam and Eve, and did sanctify and join them together in marriage, pour upon you the riches of his grace, sanctify, and bless you, that ye may please him both in body and soul, and live together in holy love, unto your lives end. Amen.

Then shall begin the Communion, and after the Gospel shall be said a Sermon, wherein ordinarily (so oft as there is any marriage) the office of a man and wife shall be declared, according to holy Scripture, or if there be no sermon, the Minister shall read this that follows.

ALL ye which be married, and which entered to take the holy estate of Matrimony upon you: hear what holy scripture doth say, as touching the duties of husbands toward their wives, and wives toward their husbands.

Saint Paul (in his Epistle to the Ephesians, the fifth Chapter) doth give this commandment to all married men.

Ye husbands love your wives, even as Christ loved the Church, and hath given himself for it, to sanctify it, purging it in the fountain of water, through the word, that he might make it unto himself a glorious congregation, not having spot or wrinkle, or any such thing, but that it should be holy and blameless. So men are bound to love their own wives, as their own bodies. He that loveth his own wife loveth himself. For never did any man hate his own flesh, but nourisheth and cherisheth it, even as the Lord doth the congregation, for we are members of his body: of his flesh and of his bones.

For this cause shall a man leave father and mother, and shall be joined unto his wife, and they two shall be one flesh. This mystery is great, but I speak of Christ and of the congregation. Nevertheless, let every one of you so love his own wife, even as himself.

Likewise the same Saint Paul (writing to the Colossians) speaks thus to all men that be married. Ye men, love your wives, and be not bitter unto them.

Hear also what saint Peter the Apostle of Christ, which was him self a married man (saith unto all men) that are married. Ye husbands, dwell with your wives according to knowledge. Giving honour unto the wife as unto the weaker vessel, and as heirs together of the grace of life, so that your prayers be not hindered.

Hitherto ye have heard the duties of the husband toward the wife.

Now likewise ye wives hear and learn your duties toward your husbands, even as it is plainly set forth in holy scripture.

Saint Paul (in the forenamed Epistle to the Ephesians) teaches you thus: Ye women, submit yourselves unto your own husbands as unto the Lord: for the husband is the wife's head, even as Christ is the head of the Church. And he is also the saviour of the whole body. Therefore as the Church or congregation, is subject unto Christ. So likewise let wives also be in subjection unto their own husbands in all things. And again he sayeth: Let the wife reverence her husband. And (in his Epistle to the Colossians) Saint Paul giveth you this short lesson, Ye wives submit yourselves unto your own husbands, as it is convenient in the Lord.

Saint Peter also doth instruct you very godly, thus saying, Let wives be subject to their own husbands, so that if any obey not the worde, they may be won without the word, by the conversation of the wives, while they behold your chaste conversation coupled with fear, whose apparel let it not be outward, with braided hair and trimming about with gold, neither in putting on of gorgeous apparel, but let the hid man which is in the heart, be without all corruption, so that the spirit be mild and quiet, which is a precious thing in the sight of God. For after this manner (in the old time) did the holy women which trusted in God apparel themselves, being subject to their own husbands, as Sara obeyed Abraham callyng him Lord; whose daughters ye are made, doing well, and being not dismayed with any fear.

The new married persons (the same day of their marriage) must receive the holy Communion.

INTRODUCTION TO
John Foxe
FOXE'S BOOK OF MARTYRS

The English Reformation nearly came to a sudden and violent end with the untimely death of Edward VI in the summer of 1553. Next in line for the succession was Mary, the daughter of Catherine of Aragon, Henry VIII's first wife, from whom he had sought the divorce that had begun the English Reformation twenty years before. Mary had every reason to want to roll back the progress of Protestantism in England: not only was she anxious to revenge the insult upon her mother, but she had been raised a devout Catholic, and felt it her religious duty to return England to the obedience of the Pope as quickly as possible. Protestant leaders recognized the danger, and hastily scrambled to rewrite the laws of succession so as to bring Edward's young Protestant cousin, Lady Jane Grey, to the throne. Unfortunately, popular support for Mary as the rightful heir proved irresistible, and the leaders such as Cranmer had succeeded only in adding the stigma of treason to that of heresy.

Many made their way in haste to safety on the Continent, including many who were to be later bishops in Queen Elizabeth's church, but Cranmer himself did not. Devoutly loyal to the English crown and deeply conflicted about the treason he had been involved in, he determined to remain, hoping for the best and preparing for the worst. The worst was indeed to soon fall on many of his co-religionists. By late 1554, Mary had bent Parliament largely to her will and began trying many Protestants for heresy. Beginning early in 1555, hundreds were burned at the stake. Cranmer, however, was left to wait in increasing psychological agony under arrest in Oxford.

The delay in executing Cranmer was due to a number of factors. Some were simply legal and procedural; he was after all the Archbishop of Canterbury, and he had to be duly deprived by both authorities in church and state before judicial proceedings could commence. There was also some hope by the Catholic authorities that he might be brought to publicly recant his Protestant opinions and profess again his obedience to the Pope. Even those determined to see him executed hoped to achieve this result first, thus winning a public relations victory for the Roman cause unlike any that they had yet managed anywhere in Europe. This was indeed the plan that was soon put into action, and with cunning persistence and precision.

Cranmer was confined in increasing isolation for a year, brought out only to witness the excruciating execution of his friends, Bishops Ridley and Latimer, and to undergo various interrogations and mock trials, all the while his resolve being slowly worn down. At the end of 1555, a Spanish friar, Juan de Villagarcia, began meeting with him to persuade him of his errors and convince him to repent. Skillfully playing on Cranmer's gnawing guilt and loneliness, Villagarcia and his allies eventually succeeded in eliciting a series of increasingly abject recantations from Cranmer's pen, so that by March 1556 he seemed ready to fully return to the bosom of the Roman Catholic Church and the obedience of the pope.

His execution, however, was not to be stayed even by such repentance. But before he was brought to the stake, the authorities were determined to make a public show of his recantation, thus crushing, they hoped, all psychological resistance by remaining Protestants in England. Instead, the elaborate event on March 21st must go down as one of the greatest public-relations catastrophes of history. Cranmer, marshaling all his courage, recanted his recantation in the most dramatic manner, and went to the stake with dignity, dying in the Protestant faith in which he had so long lived. The result was a strengthening of growing popular resistance to Mary, which helped Elizabeth rapidly re-establish Protestant religion at Mary's death in 1558.

The account below of Cranmer's final weeks and death is taken from the book traditionally known as *Foxe's Book of Martyrs*, which became a classic of English religious literature. John Foxe was an English Protestant scholar who had, with many others, taken flight to the Continent at Mary's accession, to return when Elizabeth took the throne. Seeking to memorialize the lives and deaths of the Marian martyrs, and set them alongside classic stories of martyrs from earlier ages of the church, Foxe composed the massive tome *Acts and Monuments* in 1563. It was to prove matchless as a piece of propaganda for the Protestant cause in an England that, although now formally Protestant, still harbored many lukewarm or Catholic holdouts. Subsequently expanded still further and reprinted (often in abridgments) many times, it was instrumental in framing the self-understanding of the Protestant English Church as a continuation of the faithful testimony of the early Christians against tyrannical persecutors.

Although blatantly one-sided, it has been generally recognized as a relatively reliable source at least for its core subject matter, the English Reformation. For Cranmer's martyrdom in particular, so public were the events surrounding it that there was little room for either Catholic or Protestant propagandists to distort it, and the following account may be taken as substantially accurate.[1]

1 For the fullest modern scholarly account, see Diarmaid MacCulloch, *Thomas Cranmer: A Life* (New Haven: Yale University Press, 1996), ch. 13.

FOXE'S BOOK OF MARTYRS

John Foxe

THE MARTYRDOM OF THOMAS CRANMER

Dr. Thomas Cranmer was descended from an ancient family, and was born at the village of Arselacton, in the county of Northampton. After the usual school education he was sent to Cambridge, and was chosen fellow of Jesus College. Here he married a gentleman's daughter, by which he forfeited his fellowship, and became a reader in Buckingham college, placing his wife at the Dolphin inn, the landlady of which was a relation of hers, whence arose the idle report that he was an ostler. His lady shortly after dying in childbed, to his credit he was re-chosen a fellow of the college before mentioned. In a few years after, he was promoted to be Divinity Lecturer, and appointed one of the examiners over those who were ripe to become Bachelors or Doctors in Divinity. It was his principle to judge of their qualifications by the knowledge they possessed of the Scriptures, rather than of the ancient fathers, and hence many popish priests were rejected, and others rendered much improved.

He was strongly solicited by Dr. Capon to be one of the fellows on the foundation of Cardinal Wolsey's college, Oxford, of which he hazarded the refusal. While he continued in Cambridge, the question of Henry VIII.'s divorce with Catharine was agitated. At that time, on account of the plague, Dr. Cranmer removed to the house of a Mr. Cressy, at Waltham Abbey, whose two sons were then educating under him. The affair of divorce, contrary to the king's approbation, had remained undecided above two or three years, from the intrigues of the canonists and civilians, and though the cardinals Campeius and Wolsey were commissioned from Rome to decide the question, they purposely protracted the sentence. It happened that Dr. Gardiner (secretary) and Dr. Fox, defenders of the king in the above suit, came to the house of Mr. Cressy to lodge, while the king removed to Greenwich. At supper, a conversation ensued with Dr. Cranmer, who suggested that the question, whether a man may marry his brother's wife or not, could be easily and speedily decided by the word of God, and this as well in the English courts as in those of any foreign nation. The king, uneasy at the delay, sent for Dr. Gardiner and Dr. Foxe, to consult them, regretting that a new commission must be sent to Rome, and the suit be endlessly protracted. Upon relating to the king the conversation which had passed on the previous evening with Dr. Cranmer, his majesty sent for him, and opened the tenderness of conscience upon the near affinity of the queen. Dr. Cranmer advised that the matter should be referred to the most learned divines of Cambridge and Oxford, as he was unwilling to meddle in an affair of such weight; but the king enjoined him to deliver his sentiments in writing, and to repair for that purpose to the Earl of Wiltshire's, who would accommodate him with books, and every thing requisite for the occasion. This Dr. Cranmer immediately did, and in his declaration, not only quoted the authority of the Scriptures, of general councils and the ancient writers, but maintained that the bishop of Rome had no authority whatever to dispense with the word of God. The king asked him if he would stand by this bold declaration; to which replying in the affirmative, he was deputed ambassador to Rome, in conjunction with the Earl of Wiltshire, Dr. Stokesley, Dr. Carne, Dr. Bennet, and others, previous to which, the marriage was discussed in most of the universities of Christendom and at Rome; when the pope presented his toe to be kissed, as customary, the Earl of Wiltshire and his party refused. Indeed, it is affirmed, that a spaniel of the Earl's, attracted by the glitter of the pope's toe, made a snap at it, whence his holiness drew in his sacred foot, and kicked at the offender with the other. Upon the pope demanding the cause of their embassy, the Earl presented Dr. Cranmer's book, declaring that his learned friends had come to defend it. The pope treated the embassy honourably, and appointed a day for the discussion, which he delayed, as if afraid of the issue of the investigation. The Earl returned, and Dr. Cranmer, by the king's desire, visited the emperor, and was successful in bringing him over to his opinion. Upon the Doctor's return to England, Dr. Warham, archbishop of Canterbury, having quitted this transitory life, Dr. Cranmer was deservedly, and by Dr. Warham's desire, elevated to that eminent station.

In this function, it may be said that he followed closely the charge of St. Paul. Diligent in duty, he rose at five in the morning, and continued in study and prayer till nine: between then and dinner, he devoted to temporal affairs. After dinner, if any suitors wanted hearing, he would determine their business with such an affability, that even the defaulters were scarcely displeased. Then he would play at chess for an hour, or see others play, and at five o'clock he heard the Common Prayer read, and from this till supper he took the recreation of walking. At supper his conversation was lively and entertaining; again he walked or amused himself till nine o'clock, and then entered his study.

He ranked high in favour with king Henry and ever had the purity and the interest of the English church deeply at heart. His mild and forgiving disposition is recorded in the following instance—An ignorant priest, in the country, had called Cranmer an ostler, and spoken very derogatory of his learning. Lord Cromwell receiving information of it, the man was sent to the fleet, and his case was told to the archbishop by a Mr. Chertsey, a grocer, and a relation of the priest's. His grace, having sent for the offender, reasoned with him, and solicited the priest to question him on any learned subject. This the man, overcome by the bishop's good nature, and knowing his own glaring incapacity, declined, and entreated his forgiveness, which was immediately granted, with a charge to employ his time better when he returned to his parish. Cromwell was much vexed at the lenity displayed, but the bishop was ever more ready to receive injury than to retaliate in any other manner than by good advice and good offices.

At the time that Cranmer was raised to be archbishop, he was king's chaplain, and archdeacon of Taunton; he was also constituted by the pope, penitentiary general of England. It was considered by the king that Cranmer would be obsequious; hence the latter married the king to Anne Boleyn, performed her coronation, stood godfather to Elizabeth, the first child, and divorced the king from Catharine. Though Cranmer received a confirmation of his dignity from the pope, he always protested against acknowledging any other authority than the king's, and he persisted in the same independent sentiments when before Mary's commissioners in 1555. One of the first steps after the divorce was to prevent preaching throughout his dioceses, but this narrow measure had rather a political view than a religious one, as there were many who inveighed against the king's conduct. In his new dignity Cranmer agitated the question of supremacy, and by his powerful and just arguments induced the parliament to "render to Cæsar the things which are Cæsar's." During Cranmer's residence in Germany, 1531, he became acquainted with Ossiander, at Nurenburgh, and married his niece, but left her with him while on his return to England; after a season he sent for her privately, and she remained with him till the year 1539, when the Six Articles compelled him to return her to her friends for a time.

It should be remembered that Ossiander, having obtained the approbation of his friend Cranmer, published the laborious work of the Harmony of the Gospels in 1537. In 1534 the archbishop completed the dearest wish of his heart, the removal of every obstacle to the perfection of the Reformation, by the subscription of the nobles and bishops to the king's sole supremacy. Only bishop Fisher and Sir Thomas More made objection; and their agreement not to oppose the succession, Cranmer was willing to consider as sufficient, but the monarch would have no other than an entire concession. Not long after, Gardiner, in a private interview with the king, spoke inimically of Cranmer, (whom he maliciously hated) for assuming the title of Primate of all England, as derogatory to the supremacy of the king, this created much jealousy against Cranmer, and his translation of the Bible was strongly opposed by Stokesley, bishop of London. It is said, upon the demise of queen Catharine, that her successor Anne Boleyn rejoiced—a lesson this to show how shallow is the human judgment! since her own execution took place in the spring of the following year, and the king, on the day following the beheading of this sacrificed lady, married the beautiful Jane Seymour, a maid of honour to the late queen. Cranmer was ever the friend of Anne Boleyn, but it was dangerous to oppose the will of the carnal tyrannical monarch.

In 1538, the holy Scriptures were openly exposed to sale; and the places of worship overflowed every where to hear its holy doctrines expounded. Upon the king's passing into a law the famous Six Articles, which went nearly again to establish the essential tenets of the Romish creed, Cranmer shone forth with all the lustre of a Christian patriot, in resisting the doctrines they contained, and in which he was supported by the bishops of Sarum, Worcester, Ely, and Rochester, the two former of whom resigned their bishoprics. The king, though now in opposition to Cranmer, still revered the sincerity that marked his conduct. The death of Lord Cromwell in the Tower, in 1540, the good friend of Cranmer, was a severe blow to the wavering protestant cause, but even now Cranmer, when he saw the tide directly adverse to the truth, boldly waited on the king in person, and by his manly and heartfelt pleading, caused the book of Articles to be passed on his side, to the great confusion of his enemies, who had contemplated his fall as inevitable.

Cranmer now lived in as secluded a manner as possible, till the rancour of Winchester preferred some articles against him, relative to the dangerous opinion he taught in his family, joined to other treasonable charges. These the king delivered himself to Cranmer, and believing firmly the fidelity and assertions of innocence of the accused prelate, he caused the matter to be deeply investigated, and Winchester and Dr. Lenden, with Thornton and Barber, of the bishop's household, were found by the papers to be the real conspirators. The mild forgiving Cranmer would have interceded for all remission of punishment, had not Henry, pleased with the subsidy voted by parliament, let them be discharged; these nefarious men, however, again renewing their plots against Cranmer, fell victims to Henry's resentment, and Gardiner forever lost his confidence. Sir G. Gostwick soon after laid charges against the archbishop, which Henry quashed, and the primate was willing to forgive.

In 1544, the archbishop's palace at Canterbury was burnt, and his brother-in-law with others perished in it. These various afflictions may serve to reconcile us to an humble state; for of what happiness could this great and good man boast? since his life was constantly harassed either by political, religious, or natural crosses. Again the inveterate Gardiner laid high charges against the meek archbishop and would have sent him to the tower; but the king was his friend, gave him his signet that he would defend him, and in the council not only declared the bishop one of the best affected men in his realm, but sharply rebuked his accusers for their calumny.

A peace having been made, Henry, and the French king Henry the Great, were unanimous to have the mass abolished in their kingdom, and Cranmer set about this great work; but the death of the English monarch, in 1546, suspended the procedure, and king Edward his successor continued Cranmer in the same functions, upon whose coronation he delivered a charge that will ever honour his memory, for its purity, freedom, and truth. During this reign he prosecuted the glorious reformation with unabated zeal, even in the year 1552, when he was seized with a severe ague, from which it pleased God to restore him that he might testify by his death the truth of that seed he had diligently sown.

The death of Edward, in 1553, exposed Cranmer to all the rage of his enemies. Though the archbishop was among those who supported Mary's accession, he was attainted at the meeting of parliament, and in November adjudged guilty of high treason at Guildhall, and degraded from his dignities. He sent an humble letter to Mary, explaining the cause of his signing the will in favor of Edward, and in 1554 he wrote to the council, whom he pressed to obtain a pardon from the queen, by a letter delivered to Dr. Weston, but which the latter opened, and on seeing its contents, basely returned. Treason was a charge quite inapplicable to Cranmer, who supported the queen's right; while others, who had favoured Lady Jane, upon paying a small fine were dismissed. A calumny was now spread against Cranmer, that he complied with some of the popish ceremonies to ingratiate himself with the queen, which he dared publicly to disavow, and justified his articles of faith. The active part which the prelate had taken in the divorce of Mary's mother had ever rankled deeply in the heart of the queen, and revenge formed a prominent feature in the death of Cranmer. We have in this work, noticed the public disputations at Oxford, in which the talents of Cranmer, Ridley, and Latimer, shone so conspicuously, and tended to their condemnation.—The first sentence was illegal, inasmuch as the usurped power of the pope had not yet been re-established by law. Being kept in prison till this was effected, a commission was despatched from Rome, appointing Dr. Brooks to sit as the representative of his Holiness, and Drs. Story and Martin as those of the queen. Cranmer was willing to bow to the authority of Drs. Story and Martin, but against that of Dr. Brooks he protested. Such were the remarks and replies of Cranmer, after a long examination, that Dr. Brooks observed, "We come to examine you, and methinks you examine us." Being sent back to confinement, he received a citation to appear at Rome within eighteen days, but this was impracticable, as he was imprisoned in England; and as he stated, even had he been at liberty, he was too poor to employ an advocate. Absurd as it must appear, Cranmer was condemned at Rome, and February 14, 1556, a new commission was appointed by which, Thirdly, bishop of Ely, and Bonner, of London, were deputed to sit in judgment at Christ-church, Oxford. By virtue of this instrument, Cranmer was gradually degraded, by putting mere rags on him to represent the dress of an archbishop; then stripping him of his attire, they took off his own gown, and put an old worn one upon him instead. This he bore unmoved, and his enemies, finding that severity only rendered him more determined, tried the opposite course, and placed him in the house of the dean of Christ-church, where he was treated with every indulgence. This presented such a contrast to the three years hard imprisonment he had received, that it threw him off his guard. His open, generous nature was more easily to be seduced by a liberal conduct than by threats and fetters. When satan finds the christian proof against one mode of attack, he tries another; and what form is so seductive as smiles, rewards, and power, after a long, painful imprisonment? Thus it was with Cranmer: his enemies promised him his former greatness if he would but recant, as well as the queen's favour, and this at the very time they knew that his death was determined in council. To soften the path to apostacy, the first paper brought for his signature was conceived in general terms; this one signed, five others were obtained as explanatory of the first, till finally he put his hand to the following detestable instrument:

"I, Thomas Cranmer, late archbishop of Canterbury, do renounce, abhor, and detest all manner of heresies and errors of Luther and Zuinglius, and all other teachings which are contrary to sound and true doctrine. And I believe most constantly in my heart, and with my mouth I confess one holy and catholic church visible, without which there is no salvation; and therefore I acknowledge the bishop of Rome to be supreme head on earth, whom I acknowledge to be the highest bishop and pope, and Christ's vicar, unto whom all christian people ought to be subject.

"And as concerning the sacraments, I believe and worship in the sacrament of the altar the body and blood of Christ, being contained most truly under the forms of bread and wine; the bread, through the mighty power of God being turned into the body of our Saviour Jesus Christ, and the wine into his blood.

"And in the other six sacraments, also, (alike as in this) I believe and hold as the universal church holdeth, and the church of Rome judgeth and determineth.

"Furthermore, I believe that there is a place of purgatory, where souls departed be punished for a time, for whom the church doth godlily and wholesomely pray, like as it doth honour saints and make prayers to them.

"Finally, in all things I profess, that I do not otherwise believe than the catholic church and the church of Rome holdeth and teaches.—I am sorry that I ever held or thought otherwise. And I beseech Almighty God, that of his mercy he will vouchsafe to forgive me whatsoever I have offended against God or his church, and also I desire and beseech all christian people to pray for me.

"And all such as have been deceived either by mine example of doctrine, I require them by the blood of Jesus Christ that they will return to the unity of the church, that we may be all of one mind, without schism or division.

"And to conclude, as I submit myself to the catholic church of Christ, and to the supreme head thereof, so I submit myself unto the most excellent majesties of Philip and Mary, king and queen of this realm of England, etc. and to all other their laws and ordinances, being ready always as a faithful subject ever to obey them. And God is my witness, that I have not done this for favour or fear of any person, but willingly and of mine own conscience, as to the instruction of others."

"Let him that standeth take heed lest he fall!" said the apostle, and here was a falling off indeed! The papists now triumphed in their turn: they had acquired all they wanted short of his life. His recantation was immediately printed and dispersed, that it might have its due effect upon the astonished protestants; but God counter-worked all the designs of the catholics by the extent to which they carried the implacable persecution of their prey. Doubtless, the love of life induced Cranmer to sign the above declaration; yet death may be said to have been preferable to life to him who lay under the stings of a goaded conscience and the contempt of every gospel christian; this principle he strongly felt in all its force and anguish.

The queen's revenge was only to be satiated in Cranmer's blood, and therefore she wrote an order to Dr. Cole, to prepare a sermon to be preached March 21, directly before his martyrdom, at St. Mary's, Oxford; Dr. Cole visited him the day previous, and was induced to believe that he would publicly deliver his sentiments in confirmation of the articles to which he had subscribed. About nine in the morning of the day of sacrifice, the queen's commissioners, attended by the magistrates, conducted the amiable unfortunate to St. Mary's church. His torn, dirty garb, the same in which they habited him upon his degradation, excited the commisseration of the people. In the church he found a low, mean stage, erected opposite to the pulpit, on which being placed, he turned his face, and fervently prayed to God. The church was crowded with persons of both persuasions, expecting to hear the justification of the late apostacy: the catholics rejoicing, and the protestants deeply wounded in spirit at the deceit of the human heart. Dr. Cole, in his sermon, represented Cranmer as having been guilty of the most atrocious crimes; encouraged the deluded sufferer not to fear death, not to doubt the support of God in his torments, nor that masses would be said in all the churches of Oxford for the repose of his soul. The Doctor then noticed his conversion, and which he ascribed to the evident working of Almighty Power, and in order that the people might be convinced of its reality, asked the prisoner to give them a sign. This Cranmer did, and begged the congregation to pray for him, for he had committed many and grievous sins; but, of all, there was one which awfully lay upon his mind, of which he would speak shortly.

During the sermon Cranmer wept bitter tears: lifting up his hands and eyes to heaven, and letting them fall, as if unworthy to live: his grief now found vent in words: before his confession he fell upon his knees, and, in the following words unveiled the deep contrition and agitation which harrowed up his soul.

"O Father of heaven! O Son of God, Redeemer of the world! O Holy Ghost, three persons and one God! have mercy on me, most wretched caitiff and miserable sinner. I have offended both against heaven and earth, more than my tongue can express. Whither then may I go, or whither may I flee? To heaven I may be ashamed to lift up mine eyes, and in earth I find no place of refuge or succour. To thee, therefore, O Lord, do I run; to thee do I humble myself, saying, O Lord, my God, my sins be great, but yet have mercy upon me for thy great mercy. The great mystery that God became man, was not wrought for little or few offences. Thou didst not give thy Son, O Heavenly Father, unto death for small sins only, but for all the greatest sins of the world, so that the sinner return to thee with his whole heart, as I do at present. Wherefore, have mercy on me, O God, whose property is always to have mercy, have mercy upon me, O Lord, for thy great mercy. I crave nothing for my own merits, but for thy name's sake, that it may be hallowed thereby, and for thy dear Son Jesus Christ's sake. And now therefore, O Father of Heaven, hallowed be thy name," etc.

Then rising, he said he was desirous before his death to give them some pious exhortations by which God might be glorified and themselves edified. He then descanted upon the danger of a love for the world, the duty of obedience to their majesties of love to one another and the necessity of the rich administering to the wants of the poor. He quoted the three verses of the fifth chapter of James, and then proceeded, "Let them that be rich ponder well these three sentences: for if they ever had occasion to show their charity, they have it now at this present, the poor people being so many, and victual so dear.

"And now forasmuch as I am come to the last end of my life, whereupon hangeth all my life past, and all my life to come, either to live with my master Christ for ever in joy, or else to be in pain for ever with the wicked in hell, and I see before mine eyes presently, either heaven ready to receive me, or else hell ready to swallow me up; I shall therefore declare unto you my very faith how I believe, without any colour of dissimulation: for now is no time to dissemble, whatsoever I have said or written in times past.

"First, I believe in God the Father Almighty, maker of heaven and earth, etc. And I believe every article of the Catholic faith, every word and sentence taught by our Saviour Jesus Christ, his apostles and prophets, in the New and Old Testament.

"And now I come to the great thing which so much troubleth my conscience, more than any thing that ever I did or said in my whole life, and that is the setting abroad of a writing contrary to the truth, which now here I renounce and refuse, as things written with my hand contrary to the truth which I thought in my heart, and written for fear of death, and to save my life, if it might be; and that is, all such bills or papers which I have written or signed with my hand since my degradation, wherein I have written many things untrue. And forasmuch as my hand hath offended, writing contrary to my heart, therefore my hand shall first be punished; for when I come to the fire, it shall first be burned.

"And as for the Pope, I refuse him as Christ's enemy, and antichrist, with all his false doctrine.

"And as for the sacrament, I believe as I have taught in my book against the bishop of Winchester, which my book teaches so true a doctrine of the sacrament, that it shall stand in the last day before the judgment of God, where the papistical doctrines contrary thereto shall be ashamed to show their face."

Upon the conclusion of this unexpected declaration, amazement and indignation were conspicuous in every part of the church. The catholics were completely foiled, their object being frustrated; Cranmer, like Sampson, having completed a greater ruin upon his enemies in the hour of death, than he did in his life.

Cranmer would have proceeded in the exposure of the popish doctrines, but the murmurs of the idolaters drowned his voice, and the preacher gave an order to lead the heretic away! The savage command was directly obeyed, and the lamb about to suffer was torn from his stand to the place of slaughter, insulted all the way by the revilings and taunts of the pestilent monks and friars. With thoughts intent upon a far higher object than the empty threats of man, he reached the spot dyed with the blood of Ridley and Latimer. There he knelt for a short time in earnest devotion, and then arose, that he might undress and prepare for the fire. Two friars who had been parties in prevailing upon him to abjure, now endeavoured to draw him off again from the truth, but he was steadfast and immoveable in what he had just professed, and before publicly taught. A chain was provided to bind him to the stake, and after it had tightly encircled him, fire was put to the fuel, and the flames began soon to ascend. Then were the glorious sentiments of the martyr made manifest;—then it was, that stretching out his right hand, he held it unshrinkingly in the fire till it was burnt to a cinder, even before his body was injured, frequently exclaiming, "This unworthy right hand!" Apparently insensible of pain, with a countenance of venerable resignation, and eyes directed to Him for whose cause he suffered, he continued, like St. Stephen, to say, "Lord Jesus receive my spirit!" till the fury of the flames terminated his powers of utterance and existence. He closed a life of high sublunary elevation, of constant uneasiness, and of glorious martyrdom, on March 21, 1556.

Thus perished the illustrious Cranmer, the man whom king Henry's capricious soul esteemed for his virtues above all other men. Cranmer's example is an endless testimony that fraud and cruelty are the leading characteristics of the catholic hierarchy. They first seduced him to live by recantation, and then doomed him to perish, using perhaps the sophistical arguments, that, being brought again within the catholic pale, he was then most fit to die. His gradual change from darkness to the light of the truth, proved that he had a mind open to conviction. Though mild and forgiving in temper, he was severe in church discipline, and it is only on this ground that one act of cruelty of his can in any way be excused. A poor woman was in Edward's reign condemned to be burnt for her religious opinions; the pious young monarch reasoned with the archbishop upon the impropriety of protestants resorting to the same cruel means they censured in papists, adding humanely, "What! would you have me send her quick to the devil in her error?" The prelate however was not to be softened, and the king signed the death warrant with eyes steeped in tears. There is however a shade in the greatest characters, and few characters, whether political or religious, were greater than Cranmer's.

INTRODUCTION TO

John Field and Thomas Wilcox
AN ADMONITION TO PARLIAMENT

Elizabeth's restoration of Protestant worship and doctrine in 1558-9 was initially hailed by Protestant leaders and ministers throughout England and abroad as a God-sent deliverance from the tyranny and superstition of Mary's reign. But it was not long before dissatisfaction began to fester in the young Church of England. The sources of the trouble are not hard to find; as we saw in the introduction to the Book of Common Prayer selection, there were some tensions even in Edward's reign between those who felt that many traditional liturgical elements could be harmlessly retained and those who favored a simplified and, as they saw it, more biblical liturgy. When many Protestant leaders fled abroad during Mary's reign, they had the freedom to improvise their own forms of worship, and many came to prefer the pared-down and more word-centered liturgies of Reformed churches on the Continent. In a series of contentious episodes in Frankfurt, different parties within the English exile community there quarreled over whether or not to retain the liturgies of the 1552 Book of Common Prayer, and the city magistrates had to intervene.

Although both parties to this dispute happily re-united in England after Elizabeth took the throne, the liturgy she established was in certain respects even more conservative than the 1552 Prayer Book, concerned as she was to avoid antagonizing too much Catholic nobles at home and Catholic monarchs abroad. Indeed, many churchmen, including high-ranking bishops such as John Jewel of Salisbury and Edmund Grindal of London, who had been in exile and seen Continental models of worship first-hand, expected that there would be considerable leeway in the actual practice of the liturgy, and that more progressive-minded ministers would be free to leave out portions that they considered too tainted with the popish past.

But while most bishops might have been fine with a more flexible policy, Queen Elizabeth certainly was not. Although her own commitment to Protestant faith cannot be doubted, her personal sense of piety was still relatively traditional, and she was a shrewd enough politician to recognize her position would become tenuous indeed if she appeared too openly anti-Catholic. Accordingly, as the 1560s went on, she made clear to her Archbishop of Canterbury, Matthew Parker, that she expected him to enforce full conformity to the Book of Common Prayer, including in the matter of clerical vestments (the various ceremonial garments that priests and bishops were expected to wear). These were a particular sticking point among more reform-minded Protestants, who saw them as the uniform of Antichrist, and a series of conflicts known as the Vestiarian Controversy broke out from 1564 to 1567. However, the anti-Vestiarian party lost a lot of steam when they appealed for advice to the Reformed leader Heinrich Bullinger in Zurich and were exhorted to conform to the law, such vestments being "things indifferent"—neither commanded nor forbidden in Scripture.

Between 1567 and 1572, however, the Elizabethan Church entered upon a decisive new stage, engendering a movement which was to leave a wide and lasting legacy on the Reformed world over succeeding centuries, particularly in Britain and America, a movement traditionally known as "puritanism." A great deal seems to have changed between the conclusion of this controversy in 1567 and the outbreak of the Admonition Controversy in 1572, when young radicals John Field and Thomas Wilcox, frustrated by the lack of official response to reforming overtures and complaints, published and disseminated a scandalously rancorous Admonition to Parliament.

The document, although framed as a petition to the Parliament that was then assembling (Parliament meeting, back then, only every few years) was clearly intended as a piece of public propaganda;[1] indeed, Elizabeth had already made clear, and would make increasingly clear over the next couple decades, that she did not see it as Parliament's task to deliberate on matters of church government. Unsurprisingly, the document ignited a firestorm of controversy: Field and Wilcox were imprisoned, an official *Answere* by John Whitgift was commissioned, and battle lines were drawn as pamphlets and counter-pamphlets, treatises and counter-treatises, began to multiply. The immediate literary controversy, in which Whitgift emerged as the spokesman for the establishment, and Thomas Cartwright as the spokesman for the puritans, lasted until 1577. However, the movement that the *Admonition* called into being lasted in organized form until the early 1590s, when it had grown so militant that the bishops and Privy Council took dramatic steps to quash it. The cast of this new act in the drama, however, were quite different from those who had fought it out with the bishops over vestments in 1565–67, most of whom had grudgingly submitted when it was clear the policy was inflexible. Of the twenty scrupulous Protestants who presented a supplication to the bishops over vestments in 1565, only three, says Puritan scholar Patrick Collinson, "remained staunch to the radical cause until their deaths," and most "at once dissociated themselves from the new extremism." So much so, in fact, that from 1572 on, "we are evidently witnessing the beginnings of a new movement rather than the conversion of the old."[2]

And indeed, the issues at stake in the Admonition Controversy are far different, and broader, than those in the Vestiarian. No longer is the question one of when scrupulous consciences can legitimately

1 Patrick Collinson, *The Elizabethan Puritan Movement* (Berkeley: University of California Press, 1967), 118–120.

2 Collinson, *Elizabethan Puritan Movement*, 75, 120.

resist imposition of certain ceremonies, a dispute on the margins of the Elizabethan settlement. Instead, the new dispute concerned the basic validity of that settlement in its essential features. "We in England are so far off from having a church rightly reformed, according to the prescript of God's word, that as yet we are not come to the outward face of the same," the *Admonition* fulminates, throwing down a gauntlet to the bishops and the government.[3] At stake now is not whether the bishops should enforce strict conformity, but whether the bishops have power to govern the church at all; not whether civil law should presume to bind ministers to wear the cap and surplice, but whether civil authority has any role in determining ceremonies. A fundamental platform of the *Admonition* is the presbyterian doctrine of church government, which, aside from a general sense that lower clergy ought to have more authority in determining church affairs, had been nowhere on the radar in the earlier controversy. This system of polity is not presented as a suggestion, as that best suited to the edification and good government of the churches, but as a biblical requirement. This emphasis reflects a shift in attitudes toward "things indifferent" across the board, with the new Admonitionists suggesting not so much that indifferent ceremonies were being used unedifyingly, but that they were not indifferent in the first place. Indeed, it was no longer enough for ceremonies not to be forbidden by Scriptural teaching, as Catholic rites had been considered by earlier Protestants, but they must be positively affirmed and required by Scripture. Such was the principle that Thomas Cartwright was to hammer out in conflict with Whitgift, a principle that has since become known as the "regulative principle of worship" and has exercised great influence on the Presbyterian and Reformed traditions through the centuries.

3 John Field and Thomas Wilcox, *An Admonition to Parliament*, in W. H. Frere and C. E. Douglas, eds., *Puritan Manifestoes: A Study of the Origin of the Puritan Revolt* (London: SPCK, 1907), 9. This sentence was quickly amended in the second edition of the *Admonition* to the somewhat more moderate, "as yet we are *scarce* come to the outward face of the same"; but the damage was done—conformists would hereafter charge the Presbyterians with denying that the Church of England was a true church.

AN ADMONITION TO THE PARLIAMENT

John Field and Thomas Wilcox

Seeing that nothing in this mortal life is more diligently to be sought for and carefully to be looked unto than the restitution of true religion and reformation of God's church, it shall be your parts, dearly beloved, in this present Parliament assembled, as much as in you lieth to promote the same, and to employ your whole labor and study, not only in abandoning all popish remnants, both in ceremonies and regiment, but also in bringing in and placing in God's church those things only which the Lord himself in His word commandeth, because it is not enough to take pains in taking away evil, but also to be occupied in placing good in the stead thereof. Now because many men see not all things, and the world in this respect is marvelously blinded, it hath been thought good to proffer to your godly considerations a true platform of a church reformed, to the end that, it being laid before your eyes to behold the great unlikeness betwixt it and this our English Church, you may learn either with perfect hatred to detest the same, and with singular love to embrace and carefully endeavor to plant the other, or else to be without excuse before the majesty of our God, who, for the discharge of our conscience and manifestation of his truth, hath by us revealed unto you, at this present, the sincerity and simplicity of his Gospel. Not that you should either willfully withstand or ungraciously tread the same under your feet, for God doth not disclose His will to any such end, but that you should yet now at the length with all your main and might endeavor that Christ, whose easy yoke and light burthen we have of long time cast off from us, might rule and reign in his church by the scepter of His word only.

May it therefore please your wisdoms to understand that we in England are so far off from having a church rightly reformed according to the prescript of God's word that, as yet, we are scarce come to the outward face of the same. For to speak of that wherein the best consent, and whereupon all good writers accord the outward marks whereby a true Christian church is known are preaching of the word purely, ministering of the sacraments sincerely, and ecclesiastical discipline, which consisteth in admonition and correction of faults severely. Touching the first, namely the ministry of the word, although it must be confessed that the substance of doctrine by many delivered is sound and good, yet herein it faileth: that neither the ministers thereof are according to God's word proved, elected, called, or ordained, nor the function in such sort so narrowly looked unto as of right it ought and is of necessity required. For whereas in the old church a trial was had, both of their ability to instruct and of their godly conversation also, now by the letters commendatory of some one man, noble or other, tag and rag, learned and unlearned, of the basest sort of the people (to the slander of the gospel in the mouths of the adversaries are freely received. In those days no idolatrous sacrificers or heathenish priests were appointed to be preachers of the Gospel, but we allow and like well of popish mass-mongers, men for all seasons, King Henry's priests, Queen Mary's priests, who of a truth (if God's word were precisely followed) should from the same be utterly removed. Then they taught others; now they must be instructed themselves, and therefore like young children they must learn catechisms, and so first they consecrate them and make them ministers, and then they set them to school. Then election was made by the elders with the common consent of the whole church; now everyone picketh out for himself some notable good benefice, he obtaineth the next advowson[1], by money or by favor and so thinketh himself to be sufficiently chosen. Then the congregation had authority to call ministers; in stead thereof now they run, they ride, and by unlawful suite and buying, prevent other suiters also. Then no minister placed in any congregation but by the consent of the people; now, that authority is given into the hands of the bishop alone, who by his sole authority thrusteth upon them such as they many times as well for unhonest life, as also for lack of learning may and do [instantly] dislike. Then, none admitted to the ministery but a place was void beforehand to which he should be called, but now bishops (to whom the right of ordering ministers doth at no hand appertain) do make sixty, eighty, or a hundred at a clap, and send them abroad into the country like masterless men. Then, after just trial and vocation they were admitted to their function by laying on of the hands of the company of the eldership only; now there is (neither of these being looked unto) required a surplice, a vestment, a pastoral staff, beside that ridiculous and (as they use it to their new creatures) blasphemous saying: "receive the Holy Ghost." Then every pastor had his flock, and every flock his shepherd, or else shepherds; now they do not only run fisking[2] from place to place (a miserable disorder in God's church), but covetously join living to living, making shipwreck of their own consciences, and being but one shepherd (nay, would to God they were shepherds and not wolves) have many flocks. Then the ministers were preachers; now bare readers. And if any be so well disposed to preach in their own charges, they may not without my lord's license. In those days known by voice, learning, and doctrine; now they must be discerned from other by popish and Antichristian apparel, as cap, gown, tipper and etc. Then, as God gave utterance they preached the word only; now they read homilies, articles, injunctions, etc. Then it was painful; now gainful. Then poor and ignominious

1 patronage

2 scampering

in the eyes of the world; now rich and glorious. And therefore titles, livings, and offices by Antichrist devised are given to them, as metropolitan, archbishop, lord's grace, lord bishop, suffragan, dean, archdeacon, prelate of the garter, earl, county palatine, honor, high commissioners, justices of peace and quorum, etc.—all which, together with their offices, as they are strange and unheard of in Christ's church, nay plainly in God's word forbidden, so are they utterly with speed out of the same to be renounced. Then ministers were not so tied to any one form of prayers but as the spirit moved them and as necessity of time required, so they might pour forth hearty supplications to the Lord. Now they are bound of necessity to a prescript order of service and book of common prayer in which a great number of things contrary to God's word are contained, as baptism by women private, communions, Jewish purifyings, observing of holy days, etc. patched (if not all together, yet the greatest piece) out of the Popes' portius.[3] Then, feeding the flock diligently; now, teaching quarterly. Then, preaching in season and out of season; now once in a month is thought of some sufficient, if twice, it is judged a work of supererogation. Then, nothing taught but Gods word; now princes' pleasures, men's devices, popish ceremonies, and Antichristian rites in public pulpits descended. Then they sought them; now they seek theirs.

These, and a great many other abuses are in the ministry remaining, which unless they be removed and the truth brought in, not only God's justice shall be poured forth, but also God's church in this realm shall never be built. For if they which seem to be workmen are no workmen in deed, but in name, or else work not so diligently and in such order as the workmaster commandeth, it is not only unlikely that the building shall go forward, but altogether impossible that ever it shall be preferred. The way therefore to avoid these inconveniences and to reform these deformities is this: your wisdoms have to remove advowsons, patronages, impropriations, and bishops' authority, claiming to themselves thereby right to ordain ministers and to bring in the old and true election which was accustomed to be made by the congregation.

3 manual

You must displace those ignorant and unable ministers already placed, and in their rooms appoint such as both can and will by God's assistance feed the flock. You must pluck down and utterly overthrow without hope of restitution the court of faculties, from whence not only licenses to enjoy many benefices are obtained, as pluralities, trialities, totquots[4], etc., but all things for the most part, as in the court of Rome are set on sale: licenses to marry, to eat flesh in times prohibited, to live from benefices and charges, and a great number beside of such like abominations. Appoint to every congregation a learned and diligent preacher. Remove homilies, articles, injunctions, and that prescript order of service made out of the mass-book. Take away the lordship, the loitering, the pomp, the idleness, and livings of bishops, but yet employ them to such ends as they were in the old church appointed for. Let a lawful and a godly seignory[5] look that they preach, not quarterly or monthly, but continually, not for filthy lucre's sake, but of a ready mind. So God shall be glorified, your consciences discharged, and the flock of Christ, purchased with his own blood, edified.

Now to the second point, which concerneth ministration of sacraments: in the old time, the word was preached before they were ministered; now it is supposed to be sufficient if it be read. Then they were ministered in public assemblies; now in private houses. Then by ministers only; now by midwives, and deacons equally. But because in treating of both the sacraments together, we should deal confusedly, we will therefore speak of them severally. And first for the Lord's supper, or holy communion.

They had no introite, for Celestinus a pope brought it in, about the year 430; but we have borrowed a piece of one out of the mass-book. They read no fragments of the Epistle and Gospel; we use both. The Nicene Creed was not read in their communion; we have it in ours. There was then accustomed to be an examination of the communicants, which now is neglected. Then they ministered the sacrament with common and usual bread; now with

4 dispensation permitting one man to hold an unlimited number of church appointments

5 lord, i.e., a bishop or someone else high up in the church hierarchy

wafer cakes, brought in by Pope Alexander, being in form, fashion, and substance, like their god of the altar. They received it sitting; we, kneeling, according to Honorius' Decree. Then it was delivered generally and indefinitely, "Take ye and eat ye"; we particularly, and singularly, "Take thou, and eat thou." They used no other words but such as Christ left; we borrow from papists, "The body of our Lord Jesus Christ which was given for thee." They had no *Gloria in excelsis* in the ministry of the Sacrament then, for it was put to afterward; we have now. They took it with conscience; we without. They shut men by reason of their sins from the Lord's Supper; we thrust them in their sin to the Lord's Supper. They ministered the sacrament plainly; we, pompously with singing, piping, surplice and cope wearing. They simply, as they received it from the Lord; we sinfully, mixed with man's inventions and devices. And as for baptism, it was enough with them if they had water and the party to be baptized, faith, and the minister to preach the word and minister the sacraments.

Now, we must have surplices devised by Pope Aidan, interrogatories ministered to the infant, holy sorts invented by Pope Pius, crossing and such like pieces of Popery which the church of God in the Apostles' times never knew (and therfore not to be used), nay, which we are sure of, were and are man's devices, brought in long after the purity of the primitive church. To redress these, your wisdoms have to remove (as before) ignorant ministers, to take away private communions and baptisms, to enjoin deacons and midwives not to meddle in ministers' matters, [and] if they do, to see them sharply punished; to join assistance of elders and other officers that, seeing men will not examine themselves, they may be examined and brought to render a reason of their hope; that the statute against wafer-cakes may more prevail than an Injunction; that people be appointed to receive the Sacrament, rather sitting for avoiding of superstition than kneeling, having in it the outward show of evil, from which we must abstain; that excommunication be restored to his old former force; that papists, nor other, neither constrainedly nor customably communicate in the mysteries of salvation; that both the sacrament of the Lord's supper and Baptism also may be ministered according to the ancient purity and simplicity; that the parties to be baptized, if they be of the years of discretion, by themselves and in their own persons, or if they be infants, by their parents (in whose room if upon necessary occasions and businesses they be absent, some of the congregation knowing the good behavior and sound faith of the parents) may both make rehearsal of their faith, and also if their faith be sound and agreeable to holy scriptures, desire to be in the same baptized; and finally that nothing be done in this or any other thing but that which you have the express warrant of God's word for.

Let us come now to the third part, which concerneth ecclesiastical discipline: the officers that have to deal in this charge are chiefly three: ministers, preachers, or pastors of whom before; seniors or elders; and deacons. Concerning seniors, not only their office but their name also is out of this English church utterly removed. Their office was to govern the church with the rest of the ministers, to consult, to admonish, to correct, and to order all things appertaining to the state of the congregation. Instead of these seigniors in every church, the pope hath brought in and we yet maintain the Lordship of one men over many churches, yea over sundry Shires. These seigniors then did execute their offices in their own persons without substitutes. Our lord bishops have their under-officers, as suffragans, chancellors, archdeacons, officials, commissaries, and such like. Touching deacons, though their names be remaining, yet is the office foully perverted and turned upside down, for their duty in the primitive church was to gather the alms diligently and to distribute it faithfully, also for the sick and impotent persons to provide painfully, having ever a diligent care that the charity of godly men were not wasted upon loiterers and idle vagabonds. Now it is the first step to the ministry, nay, rather a mere order of priesthood. For they may baptize in the presence of a bishop or priest, or in their absence (if necessity so require) minister the other Sacrament, likewise read the holy Scriptures and homilies in the congregation, instruct the youth in the catechism, and also preach, if he be commanded by the bishop. Again, in the old church, every congregation had their deacons; now they are tied to cathedral churches only, and what do they there? Gather the alms and distribute to the poor? Nay, that is the least piece or rather no part of their function. What then? To sing a gospel when the bishop ministereth the communion. If this be not a perverting of this office and charge, let everyone judge. And yet, lest the reformers of our time should seem utterly to take out of God's church this necessary function, they appoint somewhat to it concerning the poor, and that is, to search for the sick, needy, and impotent people of the parish, and to intimate their estates, names, and places where they dwell to the curate, that by his exhortation they may be relieved by the parish or other convenient alms. And this as you see is the nighest part of his office, and yet you must understand it to be in such places where there is a curate and a deacon, every parish cannot be at that cost to have both, nay, no parish so far as can be gathered as this present hath. Now then, if you will restore the church to his ancient officers, this you must do: instead of an archbishop or lord bishop, you must make equality of ministers. Instead of chancellors, archdeacons, officials, commissaries, proctors, summoners, church wardens, and such like, you have to put in every congregation a lawful and godly seigniory. The deaconship must not be confounded with the ministry, nor the collectors for the poor may not usurp the deacon's office, but he that hath an office must look to his office, and every man must keep himself within the bounds and limits of his own vocation. And to these three jointly, that is, the ministers, seniors, and deacons, is the whole regiment of the church to be committed. This regiment consisteth especially in ecclesiastical discipline, which is an order left by God unto his church, whereby men learn to frame their wills and doings according to the law of God, instructing and admonishing one another, yea and by correcting and punishing all willful persons and contemners of the same. Of this discipline there is two kinds, one private, wherewith we will not, because it is impertinent to our purpose, another public, which although it hath been long banished, yet if it might now at the length be restored, would be very necessary and profitable for the building up of God's house. The final end of this discipline is the reframing of the disordered, and to bring them to repentance, and to bridle such as would offend. The chiefest part and last punishment of this discipline is excommunication, by the consent of the church determined if the offender be obstinate, which how miserably it hath been by the pope's proctors, and is by our new canonists abused, who seeth not? In the primitive church it was in many men's hands; now one alone excommunicateth. In those days it was the last censure of the church, and never went forth but for notorious crimes; now it is pronounced for every light trifle. Then excommunication was greatly regarded and feared; now because it is a money matter, no whit at all esteemed. Then for great sins, severe punishment, and for small offenses, censures according. Now great sins either not at all punished, as blasphemy, usury, drunkenness, etc., or else slightly passed over with pricking in a blanket, or pinning in a sheet, as adultery, whoredom, etc. Again, such as are no sins (as if a man conform not himself to popish orders and ceremonies, if he come not at the whistle of him who hath by God's word no authority to call, we mean, chancellors, officials, and all that rule) are grievously punished, not only by excommunication, suspension, deprivation and other (as they term it) spiritual coercion, but also by banishing, imprisoning, revilings, taunting, and what not? Then the sentence was tempered according to the notoriousness of the fact; now on the one side either hatred against some persons carrieth men headlong into rash and cruel judgment, or else favor, affection, or money mitigateth the rigor of the same, and all this cometh to pass because the regiment left of Christ to his church is committed into one man's hands, whom alone it shall be more easy for the wicked by bribing to pervert than to ouerthrow the faith and piety of zealous and godly company, for such manner of men in deed should the seigniors be. Then it was said, "tell the church"; now it is spoken, "complain to my lord's grace, primate, and metropolitan of all England, or to his inferior, my lord bishop of the diocese, [and] if not to him, show the chancellor or official, or commissary." Again, whereas the excommunicate were never received till they had publicly confessed their offense, now for paying the fees of the court, they shall by master official or chancellor easily be absolved in some private place. Then the congregation, by the wickedness of the offender grieved, was by his public penance satisfied. Now absolution shall be pronounced, though that be not accomplished. Then the party offending should in his own person hear the sentence of absolution pronounced; now, bishops, archdeacons, chancellors, officials, commissaries and such like absolve one man for another. And this is that order of ecclesiastical discipline which all godly wish to be restored, to the end that everyone by the same may be kept within the limits of his vocation, and a great number be brought to line in godly conversation. Not that we mean to take away the authority of the civil magistrate and chief governor, to whom we wish all blessedness, and for the increase of whose godliness we daily pray, but that, Christ being restored into his kingdom, to rule in the same by the scepter of his word and severe discipline, the prince may be better obeyed, the realm more flourish in godliness, and the Lord himself more sincerely and purely according to His revealed will served than heretofore He hath been, or yet at this present is. Amend therefore these horrible abuses, and reform God's church, and the Lord is on your right hand, you shall not be removed forever. For He will deliver and defend you from all your enemies, either at home or abroad, as He did faithful Jacob and good Jehoshaphat. Let these things alone, and God is a righteous judge; He will one day call you to your reckoning. Is a reformation good for France, and can it be evil for England? Is discipline meet for Scotland and is it unprofitable for this realm? Surely God hath set these examples before your eyes to encourage you to go forward to a thorough and a speedy reformation. You may not do as heretofore you have done, patch and piece, nay rather go backward, and never labor or contend to perfection. But altogether remove whole Antichrist, both head and tail, and perfectly plant that purity of the word, that simplicity of the sacraments, and severity of discipline which Christ hath commanded and commended to His church. And here to end, we desire all to suppose that we have not attempted this enterprise for vainglory, gain, preferment, or any other worldly respect; neither yet judging ourselves so exactly to have set out the state of a church reformed as that nothing more could be added, or a more perfect form and order drawn, for that were great presumption to arrogate so much unto ourselves, seeing that, as we are but weak and simple souls, so God hath raised up men of profound judgment and notable learning. But thereby to declare our good wills towards the setting forth of God's glory, and the building up of his church, accounting this, as it were, but an entrance into further matter, hoping that our God, who hath in us begun this good work, will not only in time hereafter make us strong and able to go forward therein, but also move other[s], upon whom he hath bestowed greater measure of his gifts and graces, to labor more thoroughly and fully in the same.

The God of all glory so open your eyes to see His truth that you may not only be inflamed with a love thereof, but with a continual care seek to promote, plant, and place the same amongst us, that we the English people and our posterity, enjoying the sincerity of God's gospel forever, may say always: "The Lord be praised!" To whom, with Christ Jesus His Son, our only Savior, and the Holy Ghost, our alone comforter, be honor, praise, and glory, forever and ever. Amen.

INTRODUCTION TO
Richard Hooker
LAWS OF ECCLESIASTICAL POLITY

The conflict provoked by the *Admonition to Parliament* was not only heated but prolonged, lasting until at least 1593, though there were more dormant phases within the ongoing rounds of controversy. The first round lasted until 1577, as Puritan champion Thomas Cartwright duked it out in print with John Whitgift, an unbending defender of the establishment. After a few years of relative quiet, in which some bishops were tolerant toward Puritan dissenters in their dioceses, Whitgift was appointed the new Archbishop of Canterbury in 1583 and wasted little time in doing the bidding of his royal mistress by trying to enforce complete uniformity on the Church of England. His somewhat harsh measures, however, backfired by helping the Puritans win support from sympathetic noblemen. They also provoked the more militant to map out a blueprint for a complete overhaul of the Church of England along Presbyterian lines, and even to begin putting certain elements in practice despite the bishops' opposition.

It is difficult to understand why this might have been such a radical notion from our 21st-century standpoint, but it bears remembering that at the time, it had scarcely occurred to anyone that a society could accommodate multiple churches (what we would now call "denominations") within a single political unit. If you lived in Geneva, you were expected to be a member of the

Church of Geneva, with a single city-wide church government. If you lived in England, you were expected to be a member of the Church of England, with a single nation-wide church government. To either replace that single government against the will of the Queen, or to carve out a separate church within the one nation, was seen by some defenders of the Church as scarcely less treasonous than the plots of English Catholics to bring back in papal authority.

As a result, a new burst of publishing war ramped up from 1585 onward, but the turning point was 1588, when a group of radical Puritans ghostwriting under the name Martin Marprelate published a series of satirical pamphlets impugning the character of the bishops that were seen even by many Puritan leaders as a shocking violation of propriety. Public opinion started to swing against the presbyterians, particularly when a somewhat deranged fanatic named William Hacket in 1591 declared himself a prophet anointed by God for the task of overthrowing the Queen and establishing presbyterianism. By 1593, the authorities had largely quashed the presbyterian movement. However, the deep-seated dissatisfaction with the Church's structure and liturgy that had prompted the movement remained unresolved.

Enter Richard Hooker. Born in 1553 near the city of Exeter, he was a student in Oxford during the years of the Admonition Controversy and a teacher during the uneasy peace that followed it. With friends among both Puritan sympathizers and more moderate bishops (and with Walter Travers as his brother-in-law), Hooker sought to chart a middle course until the late 1580s, when the increasing stridency of the presbyterian rhetoric seems to have prompted him to decisively reject the movement. He recognized, however, that the Church would scarcely succeed in its mission of bringing the grace and peace of Christ to the people of England unless it addressed the root cause of the complaints, and persuaded Puritan dissenters that the Prayer Book worship, and government by bishops, were biblically acceptable and spiritually upbuilding.

Hooker realized that this task would require a much more systematic analysis of the dispute than anyone had yet offered, an analysis he undertook in his *magnum opus*, *The Laws of Ecclesiastical Polity*, the first part of which appeared in 1593. In the lengthy Preface, he sought to understand the psychology behind the Puritan complaint: legitimate dissatisfaction with imperfections in the Church led to the search for a scapegoat—the bishops—and a comprehensive solution—Scriptural rules. But this was not, he contended, how Scripture functioned; just because it tells us all we need to be saved does not mean it contains the answer for every question we might want answered. After all, God gave us rational minds for the purpose of making wise judgments in the absence of direct revelations of his will (Books I and II). Hooker argued in Book III that many matters of church government fell within this absence, since they were certainly not matters necessary to salvation. Moreover, many Puritan complaints were motivated by irrational fear of anything tainted with "popery," as if, just because some practice had been followed in the medieval Catholic church, that alone meant it could not be followed in a Protestant church (Book IV). Hooker went on in Books V through VIII to offer a detailed defense of the rationale behind various Prayer Book ceremonies and the governmental structure of the English church, arguing that even if not always perfect, they were more than adequate to foster a godly and faithful church.

Hooker's work retains a startling relevance right down to the 21st century, as both of the tendencies that he particularly singles out—an insistence on finding detailed rules in Scripture even for relatively minor questions, and a fear of doing anything that Catholics do—remain alive and well in Protestant churches today. Unfortunately, his original prose, though masterful ("for its purpose, perhaps the most perfect in English" according to C. S. Lewis)[1] was challenging to read even in its time and is nearly impossible today, given how much the language has evolved. The following text therefore represents part of a project to "translate" Hooker's *Laws* into modern English that I am currently pursuing with colleagues at The Davenant Trust.

1 C. S. Lewis, *English Literature in the Sixteenth Century, Excluding Drama*, The Oxford History of English Literature, vol. 3 (Oxford: Clarendon Press, 1954), 462.

OF THE LAWS OF ECCLESIASTICAL POLITY

Richard Hooker

MODERNIZED TEXT BY DR. W. BRADFORD LITTLEJOHN AND THE DAVENANT TRUST

PREFACE

1. The cause and occasion for writing this work and what is hoped for from those for whom such pains are taken

(1.) THOUGH for no other cause, yet for this—that posterity may know we have not loosely through silence permitted things to pass away as in a dream—for this I write, offering to posterity an account of the present state and legal establishment of the Church of England, and a vindication of those who have fought so hard to preserve and uphold it. I know I have little reason, beloved, to expect from you anything but your usual harshness and bitterness toward all who disagree with you, but this bitterness will never drown the love which we have for all who claim the name of Christ. Man is naturally impatient when it comes to insults and slanders, but we hope that the God of peace will give us the grace to be patient, for the sake of the work which we desire to complete.

(2.) I first decided to undertake this project when I saw how fervently you presbyterians protested against the established government and liturgy of our church; was it true, as all your books insisted, that all good Christians were obliged to join with you in promoting this new church government, which you call "the Lord's Discipline"? I will confess that, initially, I was disposed to think there must be some very strong reasons why so many well-intentioned and pious men were so worked up about this issue. Unfortunately, however, when I looked into the matter (at least, as far as my own poor abilities would permit) in obedience to St. Paul's admonition to "prove all things" and to "hold fast that which is good," (1 Thess. 5:21), I had no choice but to conclude otherwise. Specifically, I arrived at two conclusions. First, no law of God nor reason of man has yet been offered that would prove we do ill to stubbornly resist the alteration of the present form of church-government which the laws of this land have established. Second, the new presbyterian scheme which you propose in its place has no compelling claim to be called "the ordinance of Jesus Christ," since you have at least thus far offered no clear proof to this effect.

(3.) In this book, I have undertaken to offer for you a proof of these two theses. I heartily beseech you, for the love you have for Jesus Christ, that if you really care for the peace and quietness of this church, if you have in you that gracious humility which is the crown of Christian virtues, if you care, as I am sure you do, for the integrity of your souls, hearts, and consciences (which cannot with integrity refuse to acknowledge truth merely on account of personal animus), you will "hold not the faith of our Lord Jesus Christ, the Lord of glory, with respect of persons" (Jas. 2:1) and you will regard the truth of what I am writing, not the fact that it is I who am writing it. Please do not think that you are reading the words of someone who is out to oppose the truths that you have embraced, but rather the words of someone who is eager to embrace the same truths, insofar as they are indeed truths. God knows this is the only reason that I have undertaken such a laborious and painstaking project as this. [...]

4 What Has Made the More Learned Approve This Discipline

(1.) AS FOR those of you who are a lantern to the rest and mold the hearts of others (not seeking to manipulate, but because you have already been swayed by greater men), it is your burden to defend this cause by argument. For this you bring forth many verses from Scripture, but such that those things which you say logically and necessarily follow from Scripture, turn out to be cobbled together only by poor and slight conjecture. I need not bring up any particular example of you doing this, since it would in fact be hard to find any examples of you doing otherwise. It is rather peculiar that your presbyterian government, should be so clearly taught by Christ and His Apostles in Scripture, but never discovered by any church until now, while the sort of church government, which you so resolutely oppose, has been observed by Christians everywhere and none of them noticed that it was forbidden by Scripture. I challenge you to find one church upon the face of the earth that has had such a church government, or that has not been episcopally-governed since the time of the Apostles!

(2.) You offer many examples from history trying to show that the early church followed this discipline in this way and that it remains a pattern for us, a mirror of what Scripture supposedly teaches. But you do not really mean it, and only say this because everybody else does; you complain whenever someone brings up the example of antiquity that anyone should look for examples of church government from prior times. You plainly think that, from the time of the Apostles to the present age, when you have at last discovered the truth, no age is a safe example to follow.[1] You then cite from Eusebius the report of Hegesippus that "until then the Church had remained a virgin, pure and uncorrupted. ... But when the sacred band of the apostles and the generation of those who heard the divine wisdom with their own ears passed on, then godless error began."[2] Clement also confirms

1 Thomas Cartwright, A Replye to an Answere made of M. doctor Whitgifte [Hemel Hepstead: J. Shroud, 1573], 97; John Whitgift, *The Works of John Whitgift*, ed. John Ayre (Cambridge: The University Press, 1851–53), 2:181–84.

2 Eusebius, The Church History, translated by Paul L. Maier (Grand Rapids: Kregel Publications, 2007), 106–107.

that there was corruption immediately after the Apostles' time, quoting the old proverb that "few sons are like their fathers,"[3] and Socrates says that around 430 AD the Roman and Alexandrian bishops stopped being sacred rulers, and fell to the level of merely secular rulers.[4] From this you conclude that no form of church government is safe to follow except for that from the Apostolic age.

(3.) By the way, note that when you propose the pattern of the Apostolic church as a pattern for all times, although you all agree about church government, you do not all have the same intentions. Laymen who are anxious for reform want the clergy to follow the pattern of Apostolic poverty and be poor just as they were. This sort would be happy if the church was led by none but a company of begging friars! If it did add to the glory of God for His clergy to be as bare as the Apostles when they had neither staff nor purse, then I hope that God also would give them the accompanying spirit, which Paul describes when he says he knew "both to abound and to be in want" (Phil. 4:12). This would be a fit mark of true episcopacy. The Church of Christ is a mystical body, and a body cannot stand unless all the parts are properly fitted and proportioned to one another. Please apply the same standard to both sides: if the clergy are to be poor like the Apostles, let the laity be poor like those who were under them! There might be little wisdom in such an arrangement, but at least fairness.

(4.) But you who are clergy (if you still do not mind me calling you clergy!) sometimes seem to want more than even this. You think that perfect reform of the church means making the church just as it was in the time of the Apostles, which is neither possible, nor certain, nor fitting. Not possible, because Scripture does not fully describe what form of church government existed in the time of the Apostles, so you are setting up a standard that cannot be known, and thus certainly cannot be practiced. Not certain, because even within the apostolic period, later times saw policies that

3 Clement of Alexandria, Stromateis: Books 1–3, trans. Paul Ferguson, vol. 85 of The Fathers of the Church (Washington, DC: Catholic University of America Press, 1991), 30.

4 Socrates, Ecclesiastical History 7.11.

had not been anticipated in earlier times, so that a general appeal to "apostolic practice" is much too vague, especially given that you yourselves waver in defining when the authoritative apostolic period ends. You say that, although the frame of Antichrist's building was not yet set up, the foundations were secretly laid for it even in the Apostle's times! So you reject all times except the Apostolic period, yet you only half-heartedly approve of even that period, leaving it rather doubtful by what principles we should follow their example. Finally, your appeal to the apostolic standard is not fitting for our present time. While the masses often go astray by favoring whatever is traditional, insisting that we return to it if things are going badly, and do not attempt to examine why things have changed, we can hardly tolerate such naiveté in learned men like you, who should understand well enough how the church must sometimes adapt itself to changing circumstances.

To be sure, it is a good general rule, as Arnobius says, that the older a ceremony, the better; not as an absolute rule, however, but only so far as the good intention behind such rites, orders, and ceremonies continues to apply in different times and circumstances.[5] For instance, there are certain Apostolic customs, which if we tried to revive would be scandalous, such as the holy kiss (Rom. 16:16), and others, such as the love feasts (Jude 12), which no one now thinks needful. Conversely, there are many things not found in apostolic times, such as providing for the clergy by tithes, building almshouses for the poor, sorting people into parishes, and so forth, not practical in the Apostles' times, which are much more convenient and fitting for the church to retain than to remove merely for the sake of better conforming to the most ancient practice.

(5.) The Apostolic order of the church should not be put forward as a sufficient or necessary rule for all churches. Even if it were, you still have to prove that your discipline was the Apostolic form of church government. You have even failed to prove those things which you say are all-important, concerning the authority of lay elders and the distinction between doctors and pastors. In short,

5 Minucius Felix, Octavius, Loeb Classcial Library 250 (Cambridge: CUP, 1931), 328–329.

we can conclude that with the exception of our own time, one in which insolence, pride, and contempt of all authority are at their worst, there has been no time when the complete form, or even the basic substance of your model of church government was practiced.

(6.) When this argument from antiquity fails you, you appeal to learned men that seem to claim all Christians should abandon our form of church government and adopt yours. While you mention many men worthy of respect, there are others whom you cite, it would seem, only to impress the more gullible who judge by quantity, not quality. Yet surely those who know the quality and value of these men will think you are scraping from the bottom of the barrel! But even if every one of them were as good as the best of them, their opinions and conjectures should not overrule the laws of the Church of England. This is doubly true since they do not in fact all agree, and those few who do agree do so because they followed one man as their guide, and that one himself is not unlikely to have strayed. But if anybody happens to say that in the Apostles' time there were probably lay-elders, or does not dislike having them in the church today, or says that "bishop" was at first merely a synonym for "presbyter," or in any way praises churches without an Episcopal government, or attacks those bishops that abuse their office—all these, you claim, are just as convinced as you that the law of God obligates every Christian church to remove Bishops and replace them with elders. Anyone who thinks that all the names you invoke are on your side is greatly deceived indeed.

(7.) On some of the main points about your church government, I concede that there is a general agreement among many of the Reformed churches abroad. Certainly, the learned in other churches were inclined to do as did the Church of Geneva, since the tedious workings of public authority made reform come a little too slowly for a people eager to change everything right away. They had no time to think up a form of church government other than that form which had been already been devised and was ready to hand, had already been tried in similar situations, could be established without delay, and easily pleased the people because of the power it gave them. Therefore since the example of this one church was followed by the rest, due to the necessity of circumstances, it should not surprise us to find among them all a remarkable consensus about the key points of church-order. We should not marvel greatly when people who do the same thing agree about why they are doing it.

(8.) Consider also what Galen once said about philosophy, in which people decide their beliefs in the same way they evaluate rumors.[6] People will often be persuaded by a credible man, but when two, three, or four good men agree about something, the issue is thought to be beyond debate, and thus often they are all led astray, either by all erring in judgment at the same point, or by too credulously deferring to the testimony of one. Even if ten people offer the same testimony, if it turns out that their knowledge comes from only one of them, then we should treat their testimony as if there had only been one of them. It is the same in the issue at hand, when daughter churches speak their mother church's dialect, when many sing one song because their choirmaster sings it (a man whose authority amongst the greatest divines we have already described).

You might very well ask why so many learned men follow one man's judgment, without being compelled by an argument.[7] To ask the question is to answer it. You are reluctant to imagine that those who have, in matters of doctrine, achieved a knowledge unsurpassed since the time of the Apostles, should err when it comes to church government. Such is our human tendency, that whenever we admire somebody for their achievements in great things, it is hard to persuade us that they err in anything. The reason for this is that "Dead flies cause the oil of the perfumer to send forth an evil odor; so doth a little folly outweigh wisdom and honor" (Eccles. 10:1). In virtually every profession, this has given the opinions of a few undue influence, so that Luther can do no wrong in the eyes of the Germans, and Calvin none in the eyes of many of the Reformed churches. We see, however, that God presents many models of virtue in Scripture, yet none of them is totally

6 Cf. Galen, *Concerning the Diagnosis and Cure of the Errors of Every Soul in Opera*, ed. C. G. Kuhn (Leipzig: in officina Libraria C. Cnoblochii, 1821–33), 5:96–97.
7 A Petition Directed to Her most excellent Majesty [Middleburg: R. Schilders], 14.

without sin, in order that to Him alone we might say, "Thou only art holy, thou only art just." Thus it is not up to us whether God in His wisdom might permit some worthy vessels of His glory to be blemished with the stain of human frailty so that we would not esteem anyone more than he deserves.

BOOK III

2. Whether it is necessary that some particular form of Church government be set down in Scripture, since the things belonging to such a form are not necessary for salvation

Just because someone might point out that speech is necessary for all men throughout the world, this does not mean that all men must speak the same language. In the same way, while all churches need a polity and order of some sort, not all need have exactly the same sort. Of course, any form of polity that is good must have God is its author. As Tertullian says, "They obviously cannot come from anyone else if they are not from God, because those things which are not of God must be of His rival."[8] Whatever be in the Church of God, if it is not of God, we hate it. It must come from God in one of two ways: either as supernaturally revealed by God, like those things delivered by Moses for the government of the commonwealth of Israel, or as something which men can discover with the light of reason given to them by God for that purpose. No one can deny that the Law of Nature itself is instituted by God, which it cannot be unless God be considered to speak in the latter way as well as in the former. Therefore, since our opponents say that no form of Church Polity is lawful, or of God, unless God has set it down in Scripture, I cannot help but ask whether they mean set down in Scripture in whole or in part. If they say in whole, I challenge them to show any form of Polity that ever was so set down. They will not dare to claim that their own is indeed comprehensively laid out in Scripture, nor will they deny that even ours, which they so detest, is at least in part taken from

8 Tertullian, *On the Apparel of Women*, trans. Edwin A. Quain, in *Tertullian: Disciplinary, Moral, and Ascetical Works*, vol. 40 of *The Fathers of the Church* (Washington DC: Catholic University of America Press, 1959), 126 [section 8].

Scripture. I must also ask whether, when they speak of a polity "taken from Scripture," do they mean explicitly and specifically set down there, or simply that the general principles and rules can be found in Scripture? They cannot pretend the former, since not every part of their own discipline is spelled out in Scripture; and as for the latter, if this is all they mean, they can hardly object against other forms of polity! After all, such general principles do not prescribe any one particular form of polity, but allow for many different sorts which may all embody these principles in different ways.

(2.) However, let us cut them some slack and try to give their objections as fair a hearing as possible, when they earnestly resist all who deny that we need to find a complete form of Church Polity in Scripture. We have already established [in Book II, ch. 8] that matters of faith and salvation are in a completely different category than matters having to do with ceremonies, order, and the kind of church government. The former are necessarily contained in the word of God, either explicitly or by clear deduction; the latter are not. We may not accept anything in the former category unless it is found in Scripture, but we may accept anything in the latter unless it is denied in Scripture. Although I do not see any just or reasonable cause for questioning this distinction, it is hard to satisfy minds that are so brainsick in their errors that they always find something to take issue with. We are here rebuked for two things: first for failing to rightly distinguish (since they say that matters of discipline and church government are "matters necessary to salvation and of faith," while we distinguish them) and second for demeaning Scripture as if it contained only "the principal points of religion, some rude and unfashioned matter of building the Church, but had left out that which belongeth unto the form and fashion of it; as if there were in the Scripture no more than only to cover the Church's nakedness, and not chains, bracelets, rings, and jewels, to adorn her; sufficient to quench her thirst, to kill her hunger, but not to minister a more liberal, and (as it were) a more delicious and dainty diet."[9] If this is all they have to say, our response will be an easy one.

9 Thomas Cartwright, *First Replie*, page 26.

3. Matters of Church government are different from matters of Faith and Salvation, and even our opponents teach this

To lump together in speech things which are different in reality is the mother of all error. To remove error-breeding confusions, it is necessary to distinguish, and to rightly distinguish, the mind must sever things of different natures and discern how they are different. If we imagine a difference where there is none because we distinguish where we ought not to, we obviously misdistinguish. The only way to know whether we are committing this error is by comparing our conceptions with the nature of things as they actually are.

(2.)Things having to do with the Church of Christ are not all of the same sort. Some things are matters of faith, which we must merely know and believe; others are matters of action, which must be both known and done. The doctrine of the Trinity is simply a matter of faith to be believed. Precepts concerning works of charity are matters of action, and we must not only know them, but practice them. Since this is obvious to all men, I marvel that our opponents find it ridiculous for us to distinguish Church government, clearly a matter of action, from matters of faith, since they themselves distinguish between "doctrine" and "discipline."[10] For if they rightly distinguish matters of discipline from matters of doctrine, why may we not reasonably distinguish matters of government from matters of faith? Do not they include under doctrine what we call matters of faith? Do they not include church government under discipline? When they blame us for doing what they themselves do, it is hard to avoid the conclusion that their protests are motivated by something besides reason.

(3.) We learn what God's Church is obligated to know or do partly from nature. But Nature teaches this only incompletely—neither as fully nor as clearly as we need in order to have knowledge sufficient for salvation. Therefore, God has revealed in Scripture that which we need for salvation and could never know without supernatural revelation, and also restated more clearly the most important truths that nature teaches. So then Scripture contains

10 Cartwright, *Second Replie*, book 2, pp. 1, 5.

all that is needful for the Church, and even the chief of those things that are not needful, yet we are still charged with error. We all teach that whatever is said to be necessary for salvation—whatever all men must know or do to be saved, so that to not believe or not do it is eternal death and damnation, such as the articles of the Christian faith and the sacraments of the Church—these things must be contained in Scripture for God's church to be able to measure the length and breadth of the way in which she must walk. But unlike them we also teach that those things which are mere aids to sanctification may be changed, just as a gravel path, if it is then paved with stone, still remains the same path. Since discretion may teach the Church what is beneficial in these matters, Scripture here only binds the church in this sense: that whatever it forbids, the church must not permit, lest the path which should always be clear become overgrown with brambles and thorns.

(4.) If this is not a sound argument, where does it go astray? It cannot be that we make some things necessary and others mere aids, for our Lord and Savior Himself makes such a distinction by calling justice and mercy and faith "the weightier matters of the law" (Matt. 23:23). Is our mistake then counting ceremonies as mere aids, not as things necessary to salvation? (Note that by "ceremonies," we do not mean sacraments or other means of grace, but only the external rites which accompany them.) Let those who blame us for this carefully consider their words. Do not they themselves plainly compare things necessary for salvation to garments which cover the body of the Church, and those that are merely accessory to rings, bracelets, and jewels that adorn it? Do they not compare the one to the food by which the Church lives, and the other to that which makes her diet liberal, dainty, and delicious?[11] Is dainty fare necessary for sustenance? Is rich attire necessary to clothe the body? If not, how can they urge as necessary the very things which their own metaphors imply are not necessary? What logician is there who can show us how these similes can be true while our distinction is untrue, a distinction between external aids and things necessary to salvation?

11 Travers footnote. A rare moment of Hookerian liberties taken in translation.

4. By saying this we in no way lessen the truth of Scripture

It is no insult to nature to say, as Plato and Aristotle have, that she provides all living creatures with sufficient nourishment and that she brings forth no kind of creature who needs that which she cannot provide, even if we do not so magnify her bounty as to say she brings sons of men into the world adorned with dazzling attire or that she makes costly buildings to spring up out of the earth for them.[12] In the same way, to say that Scripture leaves some things at the Church's discretion in no way diminishes the perfection of Scripture and the honor due to it. All we are saying is that Scripture must teach the Church whatever is necessary for salvation, and it is no disgrace for Scripture to leave some things at the Church's liberty, just as nature has left it to men to design his own attire, instead of providing coverings for them as it does for the beasts of the field. Therefore let them show where it is that we say, as they accuse us, that Scripture contains no more than the bare essentials. We admit that infinite treasures of wisdom are found in it, including for particular application to the myriad circumstances of life, and indeed that there is scarcely any noble branch of knowledge worthy of study to which it does not give direction and light. Not only that, but even in the disputed matter of church government, although Scripture not prescribe a particular form of church polity, it gives many general precepts for how to govern rightly, and many examples of good governance even in particulars; indeed, that it even contains those things which are of principal weight in determining the particular form of church polity (though, it should be added, these things point more to our episcopal form than to the form that they imagine). If we so willingly grant all this, why do they accuse us of so narrowing the scope of Scripture that it can only direct us in the principal points of our religion, or as if Scripture gave us only a rough and unfinished framework of the Church and left out everything pertaining to its form and fashion? Let such accusers judge in their consciences whether this accusation be deserved.

12 Cf. Plato, *Menexenus* [237E]; Aristotle, *Poetics*, book 1, section 8 [1258a]; *On the Soul* book 3, sections 4, 5 [415a, 434a].

BOOK IV

1. What great use ceremonies have in the Church

Such ancient simplicity and gentleness of spirit once prevailed in the world that those leaders highly esteemed among men were always reluctant to pass judgment against anything that was publicly received by the Church of God, unless it was obviously evil. They were not so much inclined to a severity that delights to find fault with the least thing it sees wrong as they were to that charity which wants to give everything the benefit of the doubt. In this present age, zeal has conquered charity; and rhetoric has drowned meekness. Anybody can criticize anything, and nobody is surprised by it. The rites and ceremonies of the Church—the very same ones that holy and virtuous men defended in face of profane and scornful foes—are now mocked by her own children! Whether they have done so justly or not will become apparent once we have heard everything they have to say about the established rituals of our church. Since they themselves compare them to "mint and cumin,"[13] thereby admitting that they are not weighty matters of polity, we hope that their wrangling over small things will be neither earnest nor long.

(2.) Here we will not consider their particular objections against the orders of the church. Instead, we will discuss merely those general objections which have been raised against them. Let us plainly discern the nature and use of these ceremonies, so that we may better know their different qualities. First we must take note that every public duty which God requires the Church to perform has not only essential, defining elements, but also a particular outward manner in which they are properly administered. The substance of all religious actions is declared to us by God Himself in few words; for example, in the case of the sacraments. Of these, St. Augustine says, "The word is added to the elemental substance, and it becomes a sacrament."[14] Baptism is given by the element of

13 Thomas Cartwright, *The Rest of the Second Replie*, 171.

14 Saint Augustine, *Tractates on the Gospel of John 55–111*, trans. John W. Rettig, vol. 90 of *The Fathers of the Church* (Washington DC: Catholic University of America Press, 1994), 117 [Tractate 80, section 3].

water and with the prescribed words which the Church of Christ uses. The sacrament of the body and blood of Christ is administered in the elements of bread and wine, if the mystical words are added to them. However, a great deal more is necessary to properly administer these holy sacraments.

(3.) In determining the outward form of any religious action, our chief goal should be the edification of the church. Men are edified either when their minds are taught about something that all men should consider, or when their hearts are moved with any suitable affection—when they are in any way stirred up to the appropriate reverence, devotion, attention, and due regard. Therefore, not only speech, but also many different sensible means have always been thought necessary for this purpose. Of these, the eye is the liveliest and most receptive of all our senses, the organ by which to best make a deep and lasting impression, and therefore we have not only prayers, readings, questions, and exhortations, but also visible signs, which are very effective at helping men to carefully know and remember the purpose for which they carry out such ceremonies. Nature itself must teach this, for do not men always mark any public actions of great weight (whether civil or sacred) with pomp and ceremony? Such visible solemnity, setting them apart from common deeds, draws the eyes of the people to give them close attention. Words, both because they are commonly used and do not so strongly move man's imagination, often fail to engage our attention, and so God has wisely provided that the public deeds of men should be marked not only with words, but also with certain visible actions, which make an easier and more memorable impression than mere speech does.

Let us not presume to condemn as follies the things which the long experience of all ages has proven profitable, just because we do not always know the reason for them. A mind disposed to mock whatever it does not understand might ask why Abraham told his servant to put his hand under his thigh and swear (Gen. 24:9), instead of simply showing the strength of his oath by naming the Lord God of heaven and earth without that strange ceremony. In contracts and bargains, a man's word is sufficient to express his will. However, "Now this was the custom in former time in Israel concerning redeeming and concerning exchanging, to confirm all things: a man drew off his shoe, and gave it to his neighbor; and this was the manner of attestation in Israel" (Ruth 4:7). The Romans had a similarly strange ceremony when freeing a slave: the master presented his slave in a court, took him by the hand, and not only said before the public magistrate, "I will that this man become free," but also struck him on the cheek, turned him around, and shaved off his hair, before the magistrate touched him three times with a rod, and he was given a cap and white garment. What was the point of all these things? How strange and seemingly unreasonable it was for the Hebrews, when someone wanted to make himself a perpetual servant, he was not only to testify in the presence of a judge, but, as a visible token of it he was to have his ear bored through with an awl! There are innumerable examples of such things in both civil and religious actions, for they have use and force in both. "Sacred symbols are actually the perceptible tokens of the conceptual things. They show the way to them and lead to them."[15]

(4.) Someone might object that to add to religious duties significant rites and ceremonies is to institute new sacraments. However, I am sure they will not say that Numa Pompilius ordained a sacrament when he commanded the priests to "make sacrifices with their hands wrapped as far as the fingers, thus signifying that faith must be kept and that when men clasp hands, there too is the sacred temple of faith."[16] Again, we must remind them that they themselves do not think that all significant ceremonies are sacraments, since they deny that laying on of hands is a sacrament, yet they still deem it a forceful sign and reminder, as they say: "The party ordained by this ceremony was reminded that he

15 *Pseudo-Dionysius: The Complete Works*, trans. Colm Luibheid (New York: Paulist Press, 1987), 205 [2.2]. Hooker translated it as "the sensible things which religion hath hallowed, are resemblances framed according to things spiritually understood, whereunto they serve as a hand to lead, and a way to direct."

16 Livy, *The History of Rome, Books 1–5*, trans. Valerie M. Warrior (Indianapolis: Hackett Publishing, 2006), 33 [1.21].

had been separated to the work of the Lord, and so that he might remember that he had been taken as it were by the hand of God from among others and learn not to account himself his own, nor to act according to his own will, but to consider that God has set him to a duty. If he discharges and accomplish this duty, he can rest assured of a reward at the hands of God, but if not, he can expect vengeance."[17] Among great ceremonies, some of them are sacraments, some are only like sacraments. Sacraments are the signs and tokens of some general promised grace, which always truly descends from God to the soul that duly receives them. Other significant tokens are only like sacraments, yet not sacraments: which is not our distinction, but theirs. For concerning the Apostles' laying on of hands these are their own words: "they used this sign, or as it were sacrament."[18]

2. First, they accuse our ceremonies of not having the Apostolic simplicity, and having instead greater pomp and stateliness

Rites and ceremonies may be faulted, for being of the wrong sort or being too numerous. The first charge leveled at our ceremonies is that they are of the wrong sort: that we have departed from the ancient simplicity of Christ and His apostles, replacing it with outward stateliness, so that we now have rituals which those who pleased God best and served Him most devoutly never had.[19] For our opponents take it for granted the first condition of the church was the best, that the faith of the Christian religion was soundest in its beginning, that God's Scriptures were then best understood by all men, and that all manner of godliness then abounded. Thus they conclude that the customs, laws, and ordinances devised since then must not be as good for the Church of Christ, and that we ought to sweep away all later innovations to return the Church to its former condition. We consider this principle to be either uncertain, or at the very least insufficient, if not both.

17 Travers, *Ecclesiastical Discipline*, fol. 51

18 Travers, fol. 52.

19 Travers, fols. 1–2, 11, 12, 98, and Thomas Cartwright, *The Rest of the Second Replie*, 181.

(2.) For if this principle were certain, then they should have no difficulty showing us where it is so spelled out that we can say without dispute 'these were all the ceremonies and customs of the Apostle's times, and none other, neither more nor less than these'. It is true that many things of this sort are alluded to in Scripture—indeed, many things are either explicitly declared in or necessarily deduced from the Apostles' writings—but must all the customs of the Church then in use to be found in their books? Surely not, for if one closely observes the scope of their writings, it is clear that they mentioned no more details than particular occasions required. So will our opponents admit any other record besides the apostolic writings? Obviously not. Whereas St. Augustine says that those things done by the whole Church may be thought apostolic, even though they are not written, they utterly condemn his judgment.[20] I will not here defend St. Augustine's opinion, which is actually that such universal practices were either of apostolic origin or else rooted in the decrees of a general council (he could imagine no other source of positive laws and orders received by the Christian world besides these two).[21] But, putting aside St. Augustine, those who condemn his opinion here must confess that it is very uncertain what the customs of the Church were in the times of the Apostles, since the Scriptures do not mention them and our opponents utterly reject all other sources. Therefore, by tying the Church to the orders of the Apostolic times, they tie it to a remarkably vague standard, unless they require that no orders be observed except for those found in the writings of the Apostles themselves, in which case their standard hardly suffices as a benchmark against which to measure the church's ceremonies forever after.

(3.) Our end must always be the same; our ways and means to reaching that end, need not be. The Apostles were pursuing the glory of God, and the good of His Church, and therefore these are the marks at which we too must aim. However, since

20 Augustine, *On Baptism, Against the Donatists* 5.23. Cartwright condemns it in *The First Replie*, 31.

21 Augustine, 118.

rites and orders may be better suited to one time than to another, why should we insist on one age as the ideal for the rest to follow? I am quite sure that they do not mean that we must worship God in secret meetings; or that we should use common brooks and rivers for baptism; or that the Eucharist should be administered after mealtime; or that we must reinstitute love feasts; or that ministers should no longer have regular salaries and must become dependent on voluntary donations. In such cases, they easily enough perceive how what was fitting enough for the first age of the church is unfit for the present. We rightly honor the faith, zeal, and godliness of former times, but does this prove that our Church orders must be identical to theirs or that we may lawfully add nothing or subtract nothing from their practices? Those who call for the Church to return to its former state cannot help but limit their claims. If any practice has appeared which violates the spirit of what was first established in the Church, then we must return to the former things. However, where the new practice is consistent with the principles old, our respect for the ancient practice need not cause us to reject the new.

(4.) If we compare the people of God when they served God in the house of bondage in a strange land with what they did in the land of Canaan and Jerusalem, then who will not admit what a great difference there was between the two conditions? In Egypt, they were perhaps glad to take some corner of a poor hovel and serve God upon their knees, perhaps covered in dust and straw. Yet their worship was just as accepted by God, whose deliverance of them from bondage showed that they had not served Him in vain. Nonetheless, no sooner do they have any possessions to call their own in the desert, than the Lord requires a tabernacle of them. Having planted them in the land, God gave them David as their king and gave him rest from all his enemies. Then it grieved David's pious mind to contrast the flourishing of his palace with the lowly state of the house of worship. "See now, I dwell in a house of cedar, but the ark of God dwelleth within curtains" (2 Sam. 7:2). But it was God's pleasure for Solomon his son to carry out this purpose, and to do so in a manner consistent not with their ancient poverty, but with their present prosperity. For this reason Solomon writes to the king of Tyre, "And the house which I build is great; for great is our God above all gods" (2 Chr. 2:5). From this it is clear that the orders of the Church may be equally acceptable to God, whether they are framed for the splendor of later times, or for the reverent simplicity of former times. Therefore, the mere fact that our orders differ from those of the Apostles is no proof that they are defective.

3. Second, they accuse many of our ceremonies of being the same as those which the church of Rome uses, and for this reason being blameworthy

And yet, our opponents say, we have accommodated ourselves to the customs of the church of Rome, and our orders and ceremonies are popish![22] They note that the founders of our church were not as careful in this matter as they should have been and were content with practices taken from the church of Rome, and we should correct their error by abolishing all popish ceremonies. They say we must have no communion or fellowship with Papists, neither in doctrine, nor ceremonies, nor government.[23] It is not enough for us to be divided from the church of Rome by a wall of doctrine alone while retaining part of their ceremonies and almost all of their form of government—away with all such government and ceremonies! They demand nothing less than the utter rejection all things popish.

We must answer them according to the plain meaning of their words, not allowing for any ambiguity which may cause endless disputes. If their main position is simply that "nothing should be placed in the Church except what God has commanded in His word,"[24] then everything Rome does beyond this they must call popish. And therefore, anything of this sort that our church retains, they call popish, even if it is lawful and consistent with the word of God. For they plainly affirm that, "Even if the forms and ceremonies

22 Travers, *Ecclesiastical discipline*, fol. 12. Cartwright, *The First Replie*, 131.

23 Cartwright, *The First Replie*, 20.

24 Cartwright, *The First Replie*, 25.

which the church of Rome used were not unlawful and contained nothing contrary to the word of God, nonetheless neither the word of God, nor reason, nor the examples of the oldest Jewish and Christian churches permit us to use the same forms and ceremonies, since they are neither commanded by God, and there are always better ones that could be put in their place."[25] Therefore, the question is whether we may follow the church of Rome in its orders, rites, and ceremonies as long as they are not defective, or whether we must always devise others, and have no conformity with Rome even in minor things. If this, then, is what they mean by saying that we should abrogate whatever is popish, we wholeheartedly reject their argument.

(2.) Their arguments proving that in general all popish orders and ceremonies should be utterly abolished are these in short: "First, we do respect St. Augustine's judgment that where nothing is commanded or forbidden in Scripture, we must observe the custom of the people of God and the decree of our forefathers. But why should we retain the customs and constitutions of the papists in such things, since they were neither the people of God nor our forefathers?"[26] Second, "even if the forms and ceremonies which the church of Rome used were not unlawful and contained nothing contrary to the word of God, nonetheless neither the word of God, nor reason, nor the examples of the oldest churches permit us to use the same forms and ceremonies"—especially since the papists are heretics and so close at hand—"since they are neither commanded by God, and there are always better ones that could be put in their place. It is against the word of God to be in agreement with the church of Rome in such things . . . ."[27]

4. When they explain which Popish ceremonies they are referring to, they contradict their own arguments against Popish ceremonies

Before, we answer our opponents' further arguments, we must cut off that escape route which they so often use when the

25 Cartwright, *The First Replie*, p. 131.

26 Cartwright, *The First Replie*, p. 30.

27 Cartwright, *The First Replie*, p. 131.

strength of their arguments fails. For since we only retain such ceremonies as appear to us good and profitable (indeed, so good and profitable that it would have been worse to replace them with others), then the plainest and most direct way for them to counter this would be to prove that the ceremonies in question are in fact harmful to the church (or at least worse than some alternative). However, when they saw how difficult it would be to prove this, they took the easy way out, deriding the ceremonies of our church as "popish." They preferred this way because the term "popery" is to the common people more odious than paganism itself, so that whenever they hear something called "popish," they come to loathe it, imagining that nothing can merit that label without being detestable. They have therefore filled the ears of the people with a great clamor: 'The Church of England is fraught with popish ceremonies! Those who favor the cause of reformation do nothing more than maintain the sincerity of the Gospel of Jesus Christ and all who resist them fight for the laws of Jesus' sworn enemy, upholding the filthy relics of Antichrist by defending that which is popish." These are the notes which draw so many sighs from the hearts of the multitude; these are the tunes that so exasperate their minds against the lawful guides and governors of their souls; these are the voices that fill them with a general discontent, as if the bosom of the famous church in which they lived reeked more than any dungeon. However, when the authors of such seductive speeches are examined and asked to answer directly whether it is lawful for us to retain any ceremonies not commanded in the word of God and used by the church of Rome, they equivocate. Since they cannot deny that some such ceremonies must be lawful, they try to convince us that they agree with us and they only think such ceremonies must be avoided when they are unprofitable or "when ones that are just as good or better may be established."[28] This answer adds nothing to what we already believe, and seems to contradict their own arguments.

(2.) It adds nothing to our convictions, because they know that any ceremonies we have kept in common with the church

28 Cartwright, *The Rest of the Second Replie*, 171.

of Rome, we retain because we judge them to be profitable and better than alternatives. So when they say that we should abolish any Romish ceremonies that are unprofitable or could be improved upon, they are tilting at windmills, unless they mean that we should abolish all Romish ceremonies which in their judgment are unprofitable. But then they must show who authorized them to be the judges in such matters and why we are required to agree with them. Otherwise, they will not get much of a hearing when they oppose their "It seems to me..." to the orders of the church of England, as in the question of surplices[29] one of them does: "It seems to me black is a more decent color, and a garment down to the foot is a great deal more comely."[30] If they think that the burden of proof is on us to show that these ceremonies are best, they are sadly deceived. For it is only right and fair that anything long received and formally approved of in the Church should be presumed good until proven otherwise. If we as defendants answer that the ceremonies in question are godly, comely, decent, and profitable for the Church, it is childish and disorderly when they reply that we are begging the question and thereby reveal the weakness of our cause.[31] On the contrary, orderly proceeding demands that we answer this way; the burden of proof rests on them. It is hardly fair for them to first say that we must not use the bad ceremonies of the church of Rome, and then to presume that all which they happen to dislike are bad until proven otherwise.

(3.) Moreover, it contradicts their own arguments. For they often appeal to the mere fact that the church of Rome uses a certain ceremony to prove that it cannot be good and profitable for us. This manner of arguing shows that they not only exclude those Romish ceremonies that are unprofitable, but that they judge all to be unprofitable which are Romish—that is, any either devised by the church of Rome, or used in it without Scriptural command. Indeed, only by this clarification can they render this exclusion consistent with their other positions. For they do think it lawful to

29 A white vestment worn over the cassock.

30 Travers, *Ecclesiastical Discipline*, fol. 100.

31 Cartwright, *The Rest of the Second Replie*, 176.

retain certain good doctrines and customs of discipline which they have in common with the church of Rome as long as those good things are "perpetual commandments in whose place no other can come," while ceremonies, they say, are changeable.[32] So in reality, their judgment is that anything the church of Rome practices, except for what is immutably commanded by God, reformed Churches have reason enough to change it and to think it neither good nor profitable. Lest we seem to be attributing to them something that they do not believe, let them read their own words in which they complain that "our church is forced to be like the Papists in any of their ceremonies" and urge that this alone should make them do away with them "inasmuch as these are their ceremonies," and that the writings of Bishop John Jewel justify their complaint.[33] Their appeal to Bishop Jewel is false, but their words here at least show that we do them no wrong in identifying that the point of contention between us is whether we should abolish all orders, rites, and ceremonies in the church of England that are used in the Church of Rome and not prescribed in the word of God. . . .

32 Cartwright, *The Rest of the Second Replie*, 174.

33 Cartwright, *The Rest of the Second Replie*, 177.

THE FAERIE QUEENE

Edmund Spenser

BOOK I
THE LEGENDE OF THE KNIGHT OF THE RED CROSSE, OR OF HOLINESSE

I

Lo I the man, whose Muse whilome did maske,
As time her taught, in lowly Shepheards weeds,
Am now enforst a far unfitter taske,
For trumpets sterne to chaunge mine Oaten reeds,
And sing of Knights and Ladies gentle deeds;
Whose prayses having slept in silence long,
Me, all too meane, the sacred Muse areeds
To blazon broade emongst her learned throng:
Fierce warres and faithful loves shall moralize my song.

II

Helpe then, O holy Virgin chiefe of nine,
Thy weaker Novice to perform thy will;
Lay forth out of thine everlasting scryne
The antique rolles, which there lye hidden still,
Of Faerie knights and fairest Tanaquill,

Whom that most noble Briton Prince so long
Sought through the world, and suffered so much ill,
That I must rue his undeserved wrong:
O helpe thou my weake wit, and sharpen my dull tong.

III

And thou most dreaded impe of highest Jove,
Faire Venus son, that with thy cruell dart
At that good knight so cunningly didst rove,
That glorious fire it kindled in his hart,
Lay now thy deadly Heben bow apart,
And with thy mother milde come to mine ayde;
Come both, and with you bring triumphant Mart,
In loves and gentle jollities arrayd,
After his murdrous spoiles and bloudy rage allayd.

IV

And with them eke, O Goddesse heavenly bright,
Mirrour of grace and Majestie divine,
Great Lady of the greatest Isle, whose light
Like Phoebus lampe throughout the world doth shine,
Shed thy faire beames into my feeble eyne,
And raise my thoughts, too humble and too vile,
To thinke of that true glorious type of thine,
The argument of mine afflicted stile:
The which to hear, vouchsafe, O dearest dred, a-while.

CANTO I

The Patron of true Holinesse
foule Errour doth defeate;
Hypocrisie him to entrappe
doth to his home entreate.

I

A GENTLE Knight was pricking on the plaine,
Ycladd in mighty armes and silver shielde,
Wherein old dints of deepe wounds did remaine,

The cruel markes of many'a bloudy fielde;
Yet armes till that time did he never wield:
His angry steede did chide his foming bitt,
As much disdayning to the curbe to yield:
Full jolly knight he seemd, and faire did sitt,
As one for knightly giusts and fierce encounters fitt.

II

And on his brest a bloudie Crosse he bore,
The deare remembrance of his dying Lord,
For whose sweete sake that glorious badge he wore,
And dead as living ever him ador'd:
Upon his shield the like was also scor'd,
For soveraine hope, which in his helpe he had:
Right faithful true he was in deede and word,
But of his cheere did seeme too solemne sad;
Yet nothing did he dread, but ever was ydrad.

III

Upon a great adventure he was bond,
That greatest Gloriana to him gave,
That greatest Glorious Queene of Faerie lond,
To winne him worship, and her grace to have,
Which of all earthly things he most did crave;
And ever as he rode, his hart did earne
To prove his puissance in battell brave
Upon his foe, and his new force to learn;
Upon his foe, a Dragon horrible and stearne.

IV

A lovely Ladie rode him faire beside,
Upon a lowly Asse more white then snow,
Yet she much whiter, but the same did hide
Under a vele, that wimpled was full low,
And over all a blacke stole she did throw,
As one that inly mournd: so was she sad,
And heavie sat upon her palfrey slow;

Seemed in heart some hidden care she had,
And by her in a line a milke white lambe she lad.

V

So pure and innocent, as that same lambe,
She was in life and every vertuous lore,
And by descent from Royall lynage came
Of ancient Kings and Queenes, that had of yore
Their scepters stretcht from East to Westerne shore,
And all the world in their subjection held;
Till that infernall feend with foule uprore
Forwasted all their land, and them expeld:
Whom to avenge, she had this Knight from far compeld.

VI

Behind her farre away a Dwarfe did lag,
That lasie seemd in being ever last,
Or wearied with bearing of her bag
Of needments at his backe. Thus as they past,
The day with cloudes was suddeine overcast,
And angry Jove an hideous storme of raine
Did poure into his Lemans lap so fast,
That everie wight to shrowd it did constrain,
And this faire couple eke to shroud themselves were fain.

VII

Enforst to seeke some covert nigh at hand,
A shadie grove not far away they spide,
That promist ayde the tempest to withstand:
Whose loftie trees yclad with sommers pride
Did spred so broad, that heavens light did hide,
Not perceable with power of any starre:
And all within were pathes and alleies wide,
With footing worne, and leading inward farre:
Faire harbour that them seemes; so in they entred arre.

VIII

And foorth they passe, with pleasure forward led,
Joying to hear the birdes sweete harmony,

Which therein shrouded from the tempest dred,
Seemd in their song to scorne the cruell sky.
Much can they prayse the trees so straight and hy,
The sayling Pine, the Cedar proud and tall,
The vine-prop Elme, the Poplar never dry,
The builder Oake, sole king of forrests all,
The Aspine good for staves, the Cypresse funerall.

IX

The Laurell, meed of mighty Conquerours
And Poets sage, the firre that weepeth still,
The Willow worne of forlorne Paramours,
The Eugh obedient to the benders will,
The Birch for shaftes, the Sallow for the mill,
The Mirrhe sweete bleeding in the bitter wound,
The warlike Beech, the Ash for nothing ill,
The fruitfull Olive, and the Platane round,
The carver Holme, the Maple seeldom inward sound.

X

Led with delight, they thus beguile the way,
Untill the blustring storme is overblowne;
When weening to returne, whence they did stray,
They cannot finde that path, which first was showne,
But wander too and fro in wayes unknowne,
Furthest from end then, when they neerest weene,
That makes them doubt their wits be not their own:
So many pathes, so many turnings seene,
That which of them to take, in diverse doubt they been.

XI

At last resolving forward still to fare,
Till that some end they finde or in or out,
That path they take, that beaten seemd most bare,
And like to lead the labyrinth about;
Which when by tract they hunted had throughout,
At length it brought them to a hollow cave

Amid the thickest woods. The Champion stout
Eftsoones dismounted from his courser brave,
And to the Dwarfe awhile his needlesse spere he gave.

XII

Be well aware, quoth then that Ladie milde,
Least suddaine mischiefe ye too rash provoke:
The danger hid, the place unknowne and wilde,
Breedes dreadfull doubts: Oft fire is without smoke,
And perill without show: therefore your stroke,
Sir Knight, with-hold, till further triall made.
Ah Ladie, (said he) shame were to revoke
The forward footing for an hidden shade:
Vertue gives her selfe light, through darkenesse for to wade.

XIII

Yea but (quoth she) the perill of this place
I better wot then you, though now too late
To wish you backe returne with foule disgrace,
Yet wisedome warnes, whilest foot is in the gate,
To stay the steppe, ere forced to retrate.
This is the wandring wood, this Errours den,
A monster vile, whom God and man does hate:
Therefore I read beware. Fly fly (quoth then
The fearefull Dwarfe) this is no place for living men.

XIV

But full of fire and greedy hardiment,
The youthfull knight could not for ought be staide,
But forth unto the darksome hole he went,
And looked in: his glistring armor made
A litle glooming light, much like a shade,
By which he saw the ugly monster plaine,
Halfe like a serpent horribly displaide,
But th'other halfe did womans shape retaine,
Most lothsom, filthie, foule, and full of vile disdaine.

XV

And as she lay upon the durtie ground,
Her huge long taile her den all overspred,
Yet was in knots and many boughtes upwound,
Pointed with mortall sting. Of her there bred
A thousand yong ones, which she dayly fed,
Sucking upon her poisnous dugs, eachone
Of sundry shapes, yet all ill favored:
Soone as that uncouth light upon them shone,
Into her mouth they crept, and suddain all were gone.

XVI

Their dam upstart, out of her den effraide,
And rushed forth, hurling her hideous taile
About her cursed head, whose folds displaid
Were stretcht now forth at length without entraile.
She lookt about, and seeing one in mayle
Armed to point, sought backe to turne again;
For light she hated as the deadly bale,
Ay wont in desert darknesse to remaine,
Where plain none might her see, nor she see any plaine.

XVII

Which when the valiant Elfe perceiv'd, he lept
As Lyon fierce upon the flying pray,
And with his trenchand blade her boldly kept
From turning backe, and forced her to stay:
Therewith enrag'd she loudly gan to bray,
And turning fierce, her speckled taile advaunst,
Threatning her angry sting, him to dismay:
Who nought aghast his mighty hand enhaunst:
The stroke down from her head unto her shoulder glaunst.

XVIII

Much daunted with that dint, her sence was dazd,
Yet kindling rage, her selfe she gathered round,
And all attonce her beastly body raizd

With doubled forces high above the ground:
Tho wrapping up her wrethed sterne arownd,
Lept fierce upon his shield, and her huge traine
All suddenly about his body wound,
That hand or foot to stirre he strove in vaine:
God helpe the man so wrapt in Errours endlesse traine.

XIX

His Lady sad to see his sore constraint,
Cride out, Now now Sir knight, shew what ye bee,
Add faith unto your force, and be not faint:
Strangle her, else she sure will strangle thee.
That when he heard, in great perplexitie,
His gall did grate for griefe and high disdaine,
And knitting all his force got one hand free,
Wherewith he grypt her gorge with so great paine,
That soone to loose her wicked bands did her constraine.

XX

Therewith she spewd out of her filthy maw
A floud of poyson horrible and blacke,
Full of great lumpes of flesh and gobbets raw,
Which stunck so vildly, that it forst him slacke
His grasping hold, and from her turne him backe:
Her vomit full of bookes and papers was,
With loathly frogs and toades, which eyes did lacke,
And creeping sought way in the weedy gras:
Her filthy parbreake all the place defiled has.

XXI

As when old father Nilus gins to swell
With timely pride above the Aegyptian vale,
His fattie waves do fertile slime outwell,
And overflow each plaine and lowly dale:
But when his later spring gins to avale,
Huge heapes of mudd he leaves, wherein there breed
Ten thousand kindes of creatures, partly male

And partly female of his fruitful seed;
Such ugly monstrous shapes elswhere may no man reed.

XXII

The same so sore annoyed has the knight,
That welnigh choked with the deadly stinke,
His forces faile, ne can no lenger fight.
Whose corage when the feend perceiv'd to shrinke,
She poured forth out of her hellish sinke
Her fruitfull cursed spawne of serpents small,
Deformed monsters, fowle, and blacke as inke,
With swarming all about his legs did crall,
And him encombred sore, but could not hurt at all.

XXIII

As gentle Shepheard in sweete even-tide,
When ruddy Phoebus gins to welke in west,
High on an hill, his flocke to vewen wide,
Markes which do byte their hasty supper best,
A cloud of combrous gnattes do him molest,
All striving to infixe their feeble stings,
That from their noyance he no where can rest,
But with his clownish hands their tender wings
He brusheth oft, and oft doth mar their murmurings.

XXIV

Thus ill bestedd, and fearefull more of shame,
Then of the certeine perill he stood in,
Halfe furious unto his foe he came,
Resolv'd in minde all suddenly to win,
Or soone to lose, before he once would lin
And strooke at her with more then manly force,
That from her body full of filthie sin
He raft her hatefull head without remorse;
A streame of cole black bloud forth gushed from her corse.

XXV

Her scattred brood, soone as their Parent deare
They saw so rudely falling to the ground,

Groning full deadly, all with troublous feare,
Gathred themselves about her body round,
Weening their wonted entrance to have found
At her wide mouth: but being there withstood
They flocked all about her bleeding wound,
And sucked up their dying mothers blood,
Making her death their life, and eke her hurt their good.

XXVI

That detestable sight him much amazde,
To see th' unkindly Impes, of heaven accurst,
Devoure their dam; on whom while so he gazd,
Having all satisfide their bloudy thurst,
Their bellies swolne he saw with fulnesse burst,
And bowels gushing forth: well worthy end
Of such as drunke her life, the which them nurst;
Now needeth him no lenger labour spend,
His foes have slaine themselves, with whom he should contend.

XXVII

His Ladie seeing all that chaunst, from farre
Approcht in hast to greet his victorie,
And said, Faire knight, borne under happy starre,
Who see your vanquisht foes before you lye:
Well worthie be you of that Armorie,
Wherein ye have great glory wonne this day,
And proov'd your strength on a strong enimie,
Your first adventure: many such I pray,
And henceforth ever wish that like succeed it may.

XXVIII

Then mounted he upon his Steede again,
And with the Lady backward sought to wend;
That path he kept which beaten was most plaine,
Ne ever would to any by-way bend,
But still did follow one unto the end,
The which at last out of the wood them brought.

So forward on his way (with God to frend)
He passed forth, and new adventure sought;
Long way he travelled, before he heard of ought.

XXIX

At length they chaunst to meet upon the way
An aged Sire, in long blacke weedes yclad,
His feete all bare, his beard all hoarie gray
And by his belt his book he hanging had;
Sober he seemde, and very sagely sad,
And to the ground his eyes were lowly bent,
Simple in shew, and voyde of malice bad,
And all the way he prayed, as he went,
And often knockt his brest, as one that did repent.

XXX

He faire the knight saluted, louting low,
Who faire him quited, as that courteous was:
And after asked him, if he did know
Of straunge adventures, which abroad did pas.
Ah my deare Son (quoth he) how should, alas,
Silly old man, that lives in hidden cell,
Bidding his beades all day for his trespas,
Tydings of warre and worldly trouble tell?
With holy father sits not with such things to mell.

XXXI

But if of daunger which hereby doth dwell,
And homebred evil ye desire to hear,
Of a straunge man I can you tidings tell,
That wasteth all this countrey farre and neare.
Of such (said he) I chiefly do inquere,
And shall you well reward to shew the place,
In which that wicked wight his dayes doth weare:
For to all knighthood it is foule disgrace,
That such a cursed creature lives so long a space.

XXXII

Far hence (quoth he) in wastfull wildernesse
His dwelling is, by which no living wight
May ever passe, but thorough great distresse.
Now (sayd the Lady) draweth toward night,
And well I wote, that of your later fight
Ye all forwearied be: for what so strong,
But wanting rest will also want of might?
The Sunne that measures heaven all day long,
At night doth baite his steedes the Ocean waves emong.

XXXIII

Then with the Sunne take Sir, your timely rest,
And with new day new worke at once begin:
Untroubled night they say gives counsell best.
Right well Sir knight ye have advised bin,
(Quoth then that aged man;) the way to win
Is wisely to advise: now day is spent;
Therefore with me ye may take up your In
For this same night. The knight was well content:
So with that godly father to his home they went.

XXXIV

A little lowly Hermitage it was,
Downe in a dale, hard by a forests side,
Far from resort of people, that did pas
In travell to and froe: a little wyde
There was an holy Chappell edifyde,
Wherein the Hermite dewly wont to say
His holy things each morne and eventyde:
Thereby a Christall streame did gently play,
Which from a sacred fountain welled forth alway.

XXXV

Arrived there, the little house they fill,
Ne looke for entertainement, where none was:
Rest is their feast, and all things at their will:

The noblest mind the best contentment has.
With faire discourse the evening so they pas:
For that old man of pleasing wordes had store,
And well could file his tongue as smooth as glas,
He told of Saintes and Popes, and evermore
He strowd an Ave-Mary after and before.

XXXVI

The drouping Night thus creepeth on them fast,
And the sad humour loading their eye liddes,
As messenger of Morpheus on them cast
Sweet slombring deaw, the which to sleepe them biddes.
Unto their lodgings then his guestes he riddes:
Where when all drownd in deadly sleepe he findes,
He to this study goes, and there amiddes
His Magick bookes and artes of sundry kindes,
He seekes out mighty charmes, to trouble sleepy minds.

XXXVII

Then choosing out few words most horrible,
(Let none them read) thereof did verses frame,
With which and other spelles like terrible,
He bad awake blacke Plutoes griesly Dame,
And cursed heaven and spake reprochfull shame
Of highest God, the Lord of life and light;
A bold bad man, that dar'd to call by name
Great Gorgon, Prince of darknesse and dead night,
At which Cocytus quakes, and Styx is put to flight.

XXXVIII

And forth he cald out of deepe darknesse dred
Legions of Sprights, the which like little flyes
Fluttring about his ever damned hed,
Awaite whereto their service he applyes,
To aide his friends, or fray his enimies:
Of those he chose out two, the falsest twoo,
And fittest for to forge true-seeming lyes;

The one of them he gave a message too,
The other by him selfe staide other worke to doo.

XXXIX

He making speedy way through spersed ayre,
And through the world of waters wide and deepe,
To Morpheus house doth hastily repaire.
Amid the bowels of the earth full steepe,
And low, where dawning day doth never peepe,
His dwelling is; there Tethys his wet bed
Doth ever wash, and Cynthia still doth steepe
In silver deaw his ever-drouping hed,
Whiles sad Night over him her mantle black doth spred.

XL

Whose double gates he findeth locked fast,
The one faire fram'd of burnisht Yvory,
The other all with silver overcast;
And wakeful dogges before them farre do lye,
Watching to banish Care their enimy,
Who oft is wont to trouble gentle Sleepe.
By them the Sprite doth passe in quietly,
And unto Morpheus comes, whom drowned deepe
In drowsie fit he findes: of nothing he takes keepe.

XLI

And more, to lulle him in his slumber soft,
A trickling streame from high rock tumbling downe,
And ever-drizling raine upon the loft,
Mixt with a murmuring winde, much like the sowne
Of swarming Bees, did cast him in a swowne:
No other noyse, nor peoples troublous cryes,
As still are wont t'annoy the walled towne,
Might there be heard: but carelesse Quiet lyes,
Wrapt in eternall silence farre from enemyes.

XLII

The messenger approching to him spake,
But his wast wordes returnd to him in vaine:

So sound he slept, that nought mought him awake.
Then rudely he him thrust, and pusht with paine
Whereat he gan to stretch: but he again
Shooke him so hard, that forced him to speak.
As one then in a dreame, whose dryer braine
Is tost with troubled sights and fancies weake,
He mumbled soft, but would not all his silence breake.

XLIII

The Sprite then gan more boldly him to wake,
And threatned unto him the dreaded name
Of Hecate: whereat he gan to quake,
And lifting up his lumpish head, with blame
Halfe angry asked him, for what he came.
Hither (quoth he) me Archimago sent,
He that the stubborne Sprites can wisely tame,
He bids thee to him send for his intent
A fit false dreame, that can delude the sleepers sent.

XLIV

The God obayde, and, calling forth straightway
A diverse dreame out of his prison darke,
Delivered it to him, and downe did lay
His heavie head, devoide of carefull carke,
Whose sences all were straight benumbed and starke.
He backe returning by the Yvorie dore,
Remounted up as light as chearefull Larke,
And on his litle winges the dreame he bore
In hast unto his Lord, where he him left afore.

XLV

Who all this while with charmes and hidden artes,
Had made a Lady of that other Spright,
And fram'd of liquid ayre her tender partes
So lively, and so like in all mens sight,
That weaker sence it could have ravisht quight:
The maker selfe, for all his wondrous witt,

Was nigh beguiled with so goodly sight:
Her all in white he clad, and over it
Cast a black stole, most like to seeme for Una fit.

XLVI

Now when that ydle dreame was to him brought,
Unto that Elfin knight he bad him fly,
Where he slept soundly void of evill thought,
And with false shewes abuse his fantasy,
In sort as he him schooled privily:
And that new creature, borne without her dew,
Full of the makers guile, with usage sly
He taught to imitate that Lady trew,
Whose semblance she did carrie under feigned hew.

XLVII

Thus well instructed, to their worke they hast,
And coming where the knight in slomber lay,
The one upon his hardy head him plast
And made him dreame of loves and lustfull play,
That nigh his manly hart did melt away,
Bathed in wanton blis and wicked joy:
Then seemed him his Lady by him lay,
And to him playnd, how that false winged boy,
Her chast hart had subdewd, to learn Dame Pleasures toy.

XLVIII

And she herselfe of beautie soveraigne Queene,
Fayre Venus seemde unto his bed to bring
Her, whom he waking evermore did weene,
To bee the chastest flowre, that ay did spring
On earthly braunch, the daughter of a king,
Now a loose Leman to vile service bound:
And eke the Graces seemed all to sing,
Hymen Iö Hymen dauncing all around,
Whilst freshest Flora her with Yvie girlond crownd.

XLIX

In this great passion of unwonted lust,
Or wonted feare of doing ought amis,
He started up, as seeming to mistrust
Some secret ill, or hidden foe of his:
Lo there before his face his Lady is,
Under blake stole hyding her bayted hooke;
And as halfe blushing offred him to kis,
With gentle blandishment and lovely looke,
Most like that virgin true, which for her knight him took.

L

All cleane dismayd to see so uncouth sight,
And half enraged at her shamelesse guise,
He thought have slaine her in his fierce despight:
But hasty heat tempring with suffrance wise,
He stayde his hand, and gan himself advise
To prove his sense, and tempt her faigned truth.
Wringing her hands in womans pitteous wise,
Tho can she weepe, to stirre up gentle ruth,
Both for her noble bloud, and for her tender youth.

LI

And said, Ah Sir, my liege Lord and my love,
Shall I accuse the hidden cruell fate,
And mighty causes wrought in heaven above,
Or the blind God, that doth me thus amate,
For hoped love to winne me certaine hate?
Yet thus perforce he bids me do, or die.
Die is my dew; yet rew my wretched state
You, whom my hard avenging destinie
Hath made judge of my life or death indifferently.

LII

Your own deare sake forst me at first to leave
My Fathers kingdome—There she stopt with teares;
Her swollen hart her speech seemd to bereave,

And then again begun; My weaker yeares
Captiv'd to fortune and frayle worldly feares,
Fly to your fayth for succour and sure ayde:
Let me not dye in languor and long teares.
Why Dame (quoth he) what hath ye thus dismayd?
What frayes ye, that were wont to comfort me affrayd?

LIII

Love of your selfe, she saide, and deare constraint,
Lets me not sleepe, but wast the wearie night
In secret anguish and unpittied plaint,
Whiles you in carelesse sleepe are drowned quight.
Her doubtfull words made that redoubted knight
Suspect her truth: yet since no' untruth he knew,
Her fawning love with foule disdainefull spight
He would not shend; but said, Deare dame I rew,
That for my sake unknowne such griefe unto you grew.

LIV

Assure your selfe, it fell not all to ground;
For all so deare as life is to my hart,
I deeme your love, and hold me to you bound:
Ne let vaine feares procure your needlesse smart,
Where cause is none, but to your rest depart.
Not all content, yet seemd she to appease
Her mournefull plaintes, beguiled of her art,
And fed with words that could not chuse but please,
So slyding softly forth, she turned as to her ease.

LV

Long after lay he musing at her mood,
Much griev'd to thinke that gentle Dame so light,
For whose defence he was to shed his blood.
At last, dull wearinesse of former fight
Having yrockt asleepe his irkesome spright,
That troublous dreame gan freshly tosse his braine,
With bowres, and beds, and Ladies deare delight:

But when he saw his labour all was vaine,
With that misformed spright he backe returnd again.

CANTO II

In Canto II, not included in this volume,

The guilefull great Enchaunter parts
the Redcrosse Knight from truth,
Into whose stead faire Falshood steps,
and workes him wofull ruth.

CANTO III

In Canto III, not included in this volume,

Forsaken Truth long seekes her love,
and makes the Lyon mylde,
Marres blind Devotions mart, and fals
in hand of leachour vylde.

CANTO IV

To sinfull house of Pride, Duessa
guides the faithful knight,
Where brother's death to wreak Sansjoy
doth chalenge him to fight.

I

YOUNG knight whatever that dost armes professe,
And through long labours huntest after fame,
Beware of fraud, beware of ficklenesse,
In choice, and change of thy deare loved Dame,
Least thou of her beleeve too lightly blame,
And rash misweening doe thy hart remove:
For unto knight there is no greater shame,
Then lightnesse and inconstancie in love;
That doth this Redcrosse knights ensample plainly prove.

II

Who after that he had faire Una lorne,
Through light misdeeming of her loialtie,
And false Duessa in her sted had borne,
Called Fidess', and so supposd to bee;
Long with her traveild, till at last they see
A goodly building, bravely garnished,
The house of mighty Prince it seemd to bee:
And towards it a broad high way that led,
All bare through peoples feet, which thither traveiled.

III

Great troupes of people traveild thitherward
Both day and night, of each degree and place,
But few returned, having scaped hard,
With balefull beggerie, or foule disgrace;
Which ever after in most wretched case,
Like loathsome lazars, by the hedges lay.
Thither Duessa bad him bend his pace:
For she is wearie of the toilesome way,
And also nigh consumed is the lingring day.

IV

A stately Pallace built of squared bricke,
Which cunningly was without morter laid,
Whose wals were high, but nothing strong, nor thick,
And golden foile all over them displaid,
That purest skye with brightnesse they dismaid:
High lifted up were many loftie towres,
And goodly galleries farre over laid,
Full of faire windowes and delightful bowres;
And on the top a Diall told the timely howres.

V

It was a goodly heape for to behould,
And spake the praises of the workmans wit;
But full great pittie, that so faire a mould

Did on so weake foundation ever sit:
For on a sandie hill, that still did flit
And fall away, it mounted was full hie,
That every breath of heaven shaked it:
And all the hinder parts, that few could spie,
Were ruinous and old, but painted cunningly.

VI

Arrived there, they passed in forth right;
For still to all the gates stood open wide:
Yet charge of them was to a Porter hight
Cald Malvenù, who entrance none denide:
Thence to the hall, which was on every side
With rich array and costly arras dight:
Infinite sorts of people did abide
There waiting long, to win the wished sight
Of her that was the Lady of that Pallace bright.

VII

By them they passe, all gazing on them round,
And to the Presence mount; whose glorious vew
Their frayle amazed senses did confound:
In living Princes court none ever knew
Such endlesse richesse, and so sumptuous shew;
Ne Persia selfe, the nourse of pompous pride
Like ever saw. And there a noble crew
Of Lord's and Ladies stood on every side,
Which with their presence faire the place much beautifide.

VIII

High above all a cloth of State was spred,
And a rich throne, as bright as sunny day,
On which there sate most brave embellished
With royall robes and gorgeous array,
A mayden Queene, that shone as Titans ray,
In glistring gold, and peerelesse pretious stone:
Yet her bright blazing beautie did assay

To dim the brightnesse of her glorious throne,
As envying her selfe, that too exceeding shone.

IX

Exceeding shone, like Phœbus fairest childe,
That did presume his fathers firie wayne,
And flaming mouthes of steedes unwonted wilde
Through highest heaven with weaker hand to rayne;
Proud of such glory and advancement vaine,
While flashing beames do daze his feeble eyen,
He leaves the welkin way most beaten plaine,
And rapt with whirling wheeles, inflames the skyen,
With fire not made to burne, but fairely for to shyne.

X

So proud she shyned in her Princely state,
Looking to heaven; for earth she did disdayne:
And sitting high; for lowly she did hate:
Lo underneath her scornefull feete was layne
A dreadfull Dragon with an hideous trayne,
And in her hand she held a mirrhour bright,
Wherein her face she often vewed fayne,
And in her selfe-lov'd semblance tooke delight;
For she was wondrous faire, as any living wight.

XI

Of griesly Pluto she the daughter was,
And sad Proserpina the Queene of hell;
Yet did she thinke her pearlesse worth to pas
That parentage, with pride so did she swell;
And thundring Jove, that high in heaven doth dwell,
And wield the world, she claymed for her syre,
Or if that any else did Jove excell:
For to the highest she did still aspyre,
Or if ought higher were then that, did it desyre.

XII

And proud Lucifera men did her call,
That made her selfe a Queene, and crownd to be,

Yet rightfull kingdome she had none at all,
Ne heritage of native soveraintie,
But did usurpe with wrong and tyrannie
Upon the scepter, which she now did hold:
Ne ruld her Realmes with laws, but pollicie,
And strong advizement of six wisards old,
That with their counsels bad her kingdome did uphold.

XIII

Soone as the Elfin knight in presence came,
And false Duessa seeming Lady faire,
A gentle Husher, Vanitie by name
Made rowme, and passage for them did prepaire:
So goodly brought them to the lowest staire
Of her high throne, where they on humble knee
Making obeyssance, did the cause declare,
Why they were come, her royall state to see,
To prove the wide report of her great Majestee.

XIV

With loftie eyes, halfe loth to looke so low,
She thanked them in her disdainefull wise;
Ne other grace vouchsafed them to show
Of Princesse worthy, scarse them bad arise.
Her Lord's and Ladies all this while devise
Themselves to setten forth to straungers sight:
Some frounce their curled haire in courtly guise,
Some prancke their ruffes, and others trimly dight
Their gay attire: each others greater pride does spight.

XV

Goodly they all that knight do entertaine,
Right glad with him to have increast their crew:
But to Duess' each one himself did paine
All kindnesse and faire courtesie to shew;
For in that court whylome her well they knew:
Yet the stout Faerie mongst the middest crowd

Thought all their glorie vaine in knightly vew,
And that great Princesse too exceeding prowd,
That to strange knight no better countenance allowd.

XVI

Suddein upriseth from her stately place
The royall Dame, and for her coche did call:
All hurtlen forth, and she with Princely pace,
As faire Aurora in her purple pall,
Out of the east the dawning day doth call:
So forth she comes: her brightnesse brode doth blaze;
The heapes of people thronging in the hall,
Do ride each other, upon her to gaze:
Her glorious glitterand light doth all mens eyes amaze.

XVII

So forth she comes, and to her coche does clyme,
Adorned all with gold, and girlonds gay,
That seemd as fresh as Flora in her prime,
And strove to match, in royall rich array,
Great Junoes golden chaire, the which they say
The Gods stand gazing on, when she does ride
To Joves high house through heavens bras-paved way
Drawne of faire Pecocks, that excell in pride,
And full of Argus eyes their tailes dispredden wide.

XVIII

But this was drawne of six unequall beasts,
On which her six sage Counsellours did ryde,
Taught to obay their bestiall beheasts,
With like conditions to their kinds applyde:
Of which the first, that all the rest did guyde,
Was sluggish Idlenesse the nourse of sin;
Upon a slouthful Asse he chose to ryde,
Arayd in habit blacke, and amis thin,
Like to an holy Monck, the service to begin.

XIX

And in his hand his Portesse still he bare,
That much was worne, but therein little red,
For of devotion he had little care,
Still drownd in sleepe, and most of his dayes ded;
Scarse could he once uphold his heavie hed,
To looken, whether it were night or day:
May seeme the wayne was very evill led,
When such an one had guiding of the way,
That knew not, whether right he went, or else astray.

XX

From worldly cares himself he did esloyne,
And greatly shunned manly exercise,
From every worke he chalenged essoyne,
For contemplation sake: yet otherwise,
His life he led in lawlesse riotise;
By which he grew to grievous malady;
For in his lustlesse limbs through evill guise
A shaking fever raignd continually:
Such one was Idlenesse, first of this company.

XXI

And by his side rode loathsome Gluttony,
Deformed creature, on a filthie swyne;
His belly was up-blowne with luxury,
And eke with fatnesse swollen were his eyne,
And like a Crane his necke was long and fyne,
With which he swallowed up excessive feast,
For want whereof poore people oft did pyne;
And all the way, most like a brutish beast,
He spued up his gorge, that all did him deteast.

XXII

In greene vine leaves he was right fitly clad;
For other clothes he could not weare for heat,
And on his head an yvie girland had,

From under which fast trickled downe the sweat:
Still as he rode, he somewhat still did eat,
And in his hand did beare a bouzing can,
Of which he supt so oft, that on his seat
His dronken corse he scarse upholden can,
In shape and life more like a monster, then a man.

XXIII

Unfit he was for any worldly thing,
And eke unhable once to stirre or go,
Not meet to be of counsell to a king,
Whose mind in meat and drinke was drowned so,
That from his friend he seldome knew his fo:
Full of diseases was his carcas blew,
And a dry dropsie through his flesh did flow:
Which by misdiet daily greater grew:
Such one was Gluttony, the second of that crew.

XXIV

And next to him rode lustfull Lechery,
Upon a bearded Goat, whose rugged haire,
And whally eyes (the signe of gelosy),
Was like the person selfe, whom he did beare:
Who rough, and blacke, and filthy did appeare,
Unseemely man to please faire Ladies eye;
Yet he of Ladies oft was loved deare,
When fairer faces were bid standen by:
O who does know the bent of womens fantasy?

XXV

In a greene gowne he clothed was full faire,
Which underneath did hide his filthinesse,
And in his hand a burning hart he bare,
Full of vaine follies, and new fanglenesse,
For he was false, and fraught with ficklenesse;
And learned had to love with secret lookes;
And well could daunce, and sing with ruefulnesse,

And fortunes tell, and read in loving bookes,
And thousand other wayes, to bait his fleshly hookes.

XXVI

Inconstant man, that loved all he saw,
And lusted after all that he did love;
Ne would his looser life be tide to law,
But joyd weak wemens hearts to tempt and prove,
If from their loyall loves he might them move;
Which lewdnesse fild him with reprochfull paine
Of that fowle evill, which all men reprove,
That rots the marrow and consumes the braine:
Such one was Lecherie, the third of all this traine.

XXVII

And greedy Avarice by him did ride,
Upon a Camell loaden all with gold;
Two iron coffers hong on either side,
With precious mettall full as they might hold;
And in his lap an heape of coine he told;
For of his wicked pelfe his God he made,
And unto hell him selfe for money sold;
Accursed usurie was all his trade,
And right and wrong ylike in equall ballaunce waide.

XXVIII

His life was nigh unto deaths doore yplast,
And thred-bare cote, and cobled shoes he ware,
Ne scarse good morsell all his life did tast,
But both from backe and belly still did spare,
To fill his bags, and richesse to compare;
Yet chylde ne kinsman living had he none
To leave them to; but thorough daily care
To get, and nightly feare to lose his own,
He led a wretched life unto him selfe unknowne.

XXIX

Most wretched wight, whom nothing might suffise,
Whose greedy lust did lacke in greatest store,

Whose need had end, but no end covetise,
Whose wealth was want, whose plenty made him pore,
Who had enough, yet wished ever more;
A vile disease, and eke in foote and hand
A grievous gout tormented him full sore,
That well he could not touch, nor go, nor stand;
Such one was Avarice, the fourth of this faire band.

XXX

And next to him malicious Envie rode,
Upon a ravenous wolfe, and still did chaw
Betweene his cankred teeth a venemous tode,
That all the poison ran about his chaw;
But inwardly he chawed his own maw
At neighbours wealth, that made him ever sad;
For death it was when any good he saw,
And wept, that cause of weeping none he had,
But when he heard of harme, he wexed wondrous glad.

XXXI

All in a kirtle of discolourd say
He clothed was, ypainted full of eyes;
And in his bosome secretly there lay
An hatefull Snake, the which his taile uptyes
In many folds, and mortall sting implyes.
Still as he rode, he gnasht his teeth, to see
Those heapes of gold with griple Covetyse;
And grudged at the great felicitie
Of proud Lucifera, and his own companie.

XXXII

He hated all good workes and vertuous deeds,
And him no lesse, that any like did use,
And who with gracious bread the hungry feeds,
His almes for want of faith he doth accuse;
So every good to bad he doth abuse:
And eke the verse of famous Poets witt

He does backebite, and spightfull poison spues
From leprous mouth on all that ever writt:
Such one vile Envie was, that fifte in row did sitt.

XXXIII

And him beside rides fierce revenging Wrath,
Upon a Lion, loth for to be led;
And in his hand a burning brond he hath,
The which he brandisheth about his hed;
His eyes did hurle forth sparkles fiery red,
And stared sterne on all that him beheld,
As ashes pale of hew and seeming ded;
And on his dagger still his hand he held,
Trembling through hasty rage, when choler in him sweld.

XXXIV

His ruffin raiment all was staind with blood,
Which he had spilt, and all to rags yrent,
Through unadvized rashnesse woxen wood;
For of his hands he had no governement,
Ne car'd for bloud in his avengement:
But when the furious fit was overpast,
His cruell facts he often would repent;
Yet wilfull man he never would forecast,
How many mischieves should ensue his heedlesse hast.

XXXV

Full many mischiefes follow cruell Wrath;
Abhorred bloodshed and tumultuous strife,
Unmanly murder, and unthrifty scath,
Bitter despight, with rancours rusty knife,
And fretting griefe the enemy of life;
All these, and many evils moe haunt ire,
The swelling Splene, and Frenzy raging rife,
The shaking Palsey, and Saint Fraunces fire:
Such one was Wrath, the last of this ungodly tire.

XXXVI

And after all, upon the wagon beame
Rode Sathan, with a smarting whip in hand,
With which he forward lasht the laesie teme,
So oft as Slowth still in the mire did stand.
Hugh routs of people did about them band,
Showting for joy, and still before their way
A foggy mist had covered all the land;
And underneath their feet, all scattered lay
Dead sculs and bones of men, whose life had gone astray.

XXXVII

So forth they marchen in this goodly sort,
To take the solace of the open aire,
And in fresh flowring fields themselves to sport;
Emongst the rest rode that false Lady faire,
The foule Duessa, next unto the chaire
Of proud Lucifera, as one of the traine:
But that good knight would not so nigh repaire,
Him selfe estraunging from their joyaunce vaine,
Whose fellowship seemd far unfit for warlike swaine.

XXXVIII

So having solaced themselves a space
With pleasaunce of the breathing fields yfed,
They backe retourned to the Princely Place;
Whereas an errant knight in armes ycled,
And heathnish shield, wherein with letters red
Was writ Sans joy, they new arrived find:
Enflam'd with fury and fiers hardy-hed
He seemd in hart to harbour thoughts unkind,
And nourish bloudy vengeaunce in his bitter mind.

XXXIX

Who when the shamed shield of slaine Sansfoy
He spide with that same Faery champions page,
Bewraying him, that did of late destroy

His eldest brother, burning all with rage
He to him leapt, and that same envious gage
Of victors glory from him snatcht away:
But th' Elfin knight, which ought that warlike wage
Disdaind to loose the meed he wonne in fray,
And him rencountring fierce, reskewd the noble pray.

XL

Therewith they gan to hurtlen greedily,
Redoubted battaile ready to darrayne,
And clash their shields, and shake their swords on hy,
That with their sturre they troubled all the traine;
Till that great Queene upon eternall paine
Of high displeasure that ensewen might,
Commaunded them their fury to refraine,
And if that either to that shield had right,
In equall lists they should the morrow next it fight.

XLI

Ah dearest Dame, (quoth then the Paynim bold,)
Pardon the error of enraged wight,
Whom great griefe made forget the raines to hold
Of reasons rule, to see this recreant knight,
No knight, but treachour full of false despight
And shamefull treason, who through guile hath slayn
The prowest knight that ever field did fight,
Even stout Sansfoy (O who can then refrayn?)
Whose shield he beares renverst, the more to heape disdayn.

XLII

And to augment the glorie of his guile,
His dearest love, the faire Fidessa, loe
Is there possessed of the traytour vile,
Who reapes the harvest sowen by his foe,
Sowen in bloudy field, and bought with woe:
That brothers hand shall dearely well requight,

So be, O Queene, you equall favour showe.
Him litle answerd th' angry Elfin knight;
He never meant with words, but swords to plead his right.

XLIII

But threw his gauntlet as a sacred pledge,
His cause in combat the next day to try:
So been they parted both, with harts on edge
To be aveng'd each on his enimy.
That night they pas in joy and jollity,
Feasting and courting both in bowre and hall;
For Steward was excessive Gluttonie,
That of his plenty poured forth to all;
Which doen, the Chamberlain Slowth did to rest them call.

XLIV

Now whenas darkesome night had all displayed
Her coleblacke curtein over brightest skye,
The warlike youthes on dayntie couches layd,
Did chace away sweet sleepe from sluggish eye,
To muse on meanes of hoped victory.
But whenas Morpheus had with leaden mace
Arrested all that courtly company,
Up-rose Duessa from her resting place,
And to the Paynims lodging comes with silent pace.

XLV

Whom broad awake she finds, in troublous fit,
Forecasting, how his foe he might annoy,
And him amoves with speaches seeming fit:
Ah deare Sansjoy, next dearest to Sansfoy,
Cause of my new griefe, cause of my new joy,
Joyous, to see his image in mine eye,
And greev'd, to thinke how foe did him destroy,
That was the flowre of grace and chevalrye;
Lo his Fidessa to thy secret faith I flye.

XLVI

With gentle wordes he can her fairely greet,
And bad say on the secret of her hart.
Then sighing soft, I learn that litle sweet
Oft tempred is (quoth she) with muchell smart:
For since my brest was launcht with lovely dart
Of deare Sans foy, I never joyed howre,
But in eternall woes my weaker hart
Have wasted, loving him with all my powre,
And for his sake have felt full many an heavie stowre.

XLVII

At last when perils all I weened past,
And hop'd to reape the crop of all my care,
Into new woes unweeting I was cast,
By this false faytor, who unworthy ware
His worthy shield, whom he with guilefull snare
Entrapped slew, and brought to shamefull grave.
Me silly maid away with him he bare,
And ever since hath kept in darksome cave,
For that I would not yeeld, that to Sans foy I gave.

XLVIII

But since faire Sunne hath sperst that lowring clowd,
And to my loathed life now shewes some light,
Under your beames I will me safely shrowd,
From dreaded storme of his disdainfull spight:
To you th' inheritance belongs by right
Of brothers prayse, to you eke longs his love.
Let not his love, let not his restlesse spright,
Be unreveng'd, that calles to you above
From wandring Stygian shores, where it doth endlesse move.

XLIX

Thereto said he, Faire Dame, be nought dismaid
For sorrowes past; their griefe is with them gone:

Ne yet of present perill be affraid;
For needlesse feare did never vantage none
And helplesse hap it booteth not to mone.
Dead is Sansfoy, his vitall paines are past,
Though greeved ghost for vengeance deepe do grone:
He lives, that shall him pay his dewties last,
And guiltie Elfin blood shall sacrifice in hast.

L

O but I feare the fickle freakes (quoth shee)
Of fortune false, and oddes of armes in field.
Why Dame (quoth he) what oddes can ever bee,
Where both do fight alike, to win or yield?
Yea but (quoth she) he beares a charmed shield,
And eke enchaunted armes, that none can perce,
Ne none can wound the man that does them wield.
Charmd or enchaunted (answerd he then ferce)
I no whit reck, ne you the like need to reherce.

LI

But faire Fidessa, sithens fortunes guile,
Or enimies powre, hath now captived you,
Returne from whence ye came, and rest a while
Till morrow next, that I the Elfe subdew,
And with Sansfoyes dead dowry you endew.
Ay me, that is a double death (she said)
With proud foes sight my sorrow to renew:
Where ever yet I be, my secret aid
Shall follow you. So passing forth she him obaid.

CANTO V

In Canto V, not included in this volume,

The faithful knight in equall field
subdewes his faithlesse foe,
Whom false Duessa saves, and for
his cure to hell does goe.

CANTO VI

In Canto VI, not included in this volume,

From lawlesse lust by wondrous grace
fayre Una is releast:
Whom salvage nation does adore,
and learnes her wise beheast.

CANTO VII

The Redcrosse knight is captive made
by Gyaunt proud opprest,
Prince Arthur meets with Una great-
ly with those newes distrest.

I

WHAT man so wise, what earthly wit so ware,
As to discry the crafty cunning traine,
By which deceipt doth maske in visour faire,
And cast her colours dyed deepe in graine,
To seeme like Truth, whose shape she well can faine,
And fitting gestures to her purpose frame;
The guiltlesse man with guile to entertaine?
Great maistresse of her art was that false Dame,
The false Duessa, cloked with Fidessaes name.

II

Who when returning from the drery Night,
She fownd not in that perilous house of Pryde,
Where she had left, the noble Redcrosse knight,
Her hoped pray; she would no lenger bide,
But forth she went, to seeke him far and wide.
Ere long she fownd, whereas he wearie sate
To rest him selfe, foreby a fountain side,
Disarmed all of yron-coted Plate,
And by his side his steed the grassy forage ate.

III

He feedes upon the cooling shade, and bayes
His sweatie forehead in the breathing wind,
Which through the trembling leaves full gently playes,
Wherein the cherefull birds of sundry kind
Do chaunt sweet musick, to delight his mind:
The Witch approaching gan him fairely greet,
And with reproch of carelesnesse unkind
Upbrayd, for leaving her in place unmeet,
With fowle words tempring faire, soure gall with hony sweet.

IV

Unkindnesse past, they gan of solace treat,
And bathe in pleasaunce of the joyous shade,
Which shielded them against the boyling heat,
And with greene boughes decking a gloomy glade,
About the fountain like a girlond made;
Whose bubbling wave did ever freshly well,
Ne ever would through fervent sommer fade:
The sacred Nymph, which therein wont to dwell,
Was out of Dianes favour, as it then befell.

V

The cause was this: One day, when Phœbe fayre
With all her band was following the chace,
This Nymph, quite tyr'd with heat of scorching ayre,
Sat downe to rest in middest of the race:
The goddesse wroth gan fowly her disgrace,
And bad the waters, which from her did flow,
Be such as she her selfe was then in place.
Thenceforth her waters waxed dull and slow,
And all that drinke thereof do faint and feeble grow.

VI

Hereof this gentle knight unweeting was,
And lying downe upon the sandie graile,
Drunke of the streame, as cleare as cristall glas:

Eftsoones his manly forces gan to faile,
And mighty strong was turned to feeble fraile.
His chaunged powres at first them selves not felt,
Till crudled cold his corage gan assaile,
And cheareful bloud in faintnesse chill did melt,
Which like a fever fit through all his body swelt.

VII

Yet goodly court he made still to his Dame,
Pourd out in loosnesse on the grassy grownd,
Both carelesse of his health, and of his fame:
Till at the last he heard a dreadfull sownd,
Which through the wood loud bellowing did rebownd,
That all the earth for terrour seemd to shake,
And trees did tremble. Th' Elfe therewith astownd,
Upstarted lightly from his looser make,
And his unready weapons gan in hand to take.

VIII

But ere he could his armour on him dight,
Or get his shield, his monstrous enimy
With sturdie steps came stalking in his sight,
An hideous Geant, horrible and hye,
That with his tallnesse seemd to threat the skye,
The ground eke groned under him for dreed;
His living like saw never living eye,
Ne durst behold: his stature did exceed
The hight of three the tallest sonnes of mortall seed.

IX

The greatest Earth his uncouth mother was,
And blustering Æolus his boasted syre,
Brought forth this monstrous masse of earthly slime
Puft up with emptie wind, and fild with sinfull crime.

X

So growen great through arrogant delight
Of th' high descent, whereof he was yborne,

And through presumption of his matchlesse might,
All other powres and knighthood he did scorne.
Such now he marcheth to this man forlorne,
And left to losse: his stalking steps are stayde
Upon a snaggy Oke, which he had torne
Out of his mothers bowelles, and it made
His mortall mace, wherewith his foeman he dismayde.

XI

That when the knight he spide, he gan advance
With huge force and insupportable mayne,
And towardes him with dreadfull fury praunce;
Who haplesse, and eke hopelesse, all in vaine
Did to him pace, sad battaile to darrayne,
Disarmd, disgrast, and inwardly dismayde,
And eke so faint in every joynt and vaine,
Through that fraile fountain, which him feeble made,
That scarsely could he weeld his bootlesse single blade.

XII

The Geaunt strooke so maynly mercilesse,
That could have overthrowne a stony tower,
And were not heavenly grace, that did him bless,
He had beene pouldred all, as thin as flowre:
But he was wary of that deadly stowre,
And lightly lept from underneath the blow:
Yet so exceeding was the villeins powre,
That with the wind it did him overthrow,
And all his sences stound, that still he lay full low.

XIII

As when that divelish yron Engin wrought
In deepest Hell, and framd by Furies skill,
With windy Nitre and quick Sulphur fraught,
And ramd with bullet round, ordaind to kill,
Conceiveth fire, the heavens it doth fill
With thundring noyse, and all the ayre doth choke,

That none can breath, nor see, nor hear at will,
Through smouldry cloud of duskish stincking smoke,
That th' only breath him daunts, who hath escapt the stroke.

XIV

So daunted when the Geaunt saw the knight,
His heavie hand he heaved up on hye,
And him to dust thought to have battred quight,
Untill Duessa loud to him gan crye;
O great Orgoglio, greatest under skye,
O hold thy mortall hand for Ladies sake,
Hold for my sake, and do him not to dye,
But vanquisht thine eternall bondslave make,
And me, thy worthy meed, unto thy Leman take.

XV

He hearkned, and did stay from further harmes,
To gayne so goodly guerdon, as she spake:
So willingly she came into his armes,
Who her as willingly to grace did take,
And was possessed of his new found make.
Then up he tooke the slombred sencelesse corse,
And ere he could out of his swowne awake,
Him to his castle brought with hastie forse,
And in a Dongeon deepe him threw without remorse.

XVI

From that day forth Duessa was his deare,
And highly honourd in his haughtie eye,
He gave her gold and purple pall to weare,
And triple crowne set on her head full hye,
And her endowd with royall majestye:
Then for to make her dreaded more of men,
And peoples harts with awfull terrour tye,
A monstrous beast ybred in filthy fen
He chose, which he had kept long time in darksome den.

XVII

Such one it was, as that renowmed Snake
Which great Alcides in Stremona slew,
Long fostred in the filth of Lerna lake,
Whose many heads out budding ever new
Did breed him endlesse labour to subdew:
But this same Monster much more ugly was;
For seven great heads out of his body grew,
An yron brest, and back of scaly bras,
And all embrewd in bloud, his eyes did shine as glas.

XVIII

His tayle was stretched out in wondrous length,
That to the house of heavenly gods it raught,
And with extorted powre, and borrow'd strength,
The ever-burning lamps from thence it braught,
And prowdly threw to ground, as things of naught;
And underneath his filthy feet did tread
The sacred things, and holy heasts foretaught.
Upon this dreadfull Beast with sevenfold head
He sett the false Duessa, for more aw and dread.

XIX

The wofull Dwarfe, which saw his maisters fall,
Whiles he had keeping of his grasing steed,
And valiant knight become a caytive thrall,
When all was past, tooke up his forlorne weed,
His mighty armour, missing most at need;
His silver shield, now idle maisterlesse;
His poynant speare, that many made to bleed,
The rueful moniments of heavinesse,
And with them all departes, to tell his great distresse.

XX

He had not travaild long, when on the way
He wofull Ladie, wofull Una met,
Fast flying from that Paynims greedy pray,

Whilest Satyrane him from pursuit did let:
Who when her eyes she on the Dwarfe had set,
And saw the signes, that deadly tydings spake,
She fell to ground for sorrowfull regret,
And lively breath her sad brest did forsake,
Yet might her pitteous hart be seene to pant and quake.

XXI

The messenger of so unhappie newes,
Would faine have dyde: dead was his hart within,
Yet outwardly some little comfort shewes:
At last recovering hart, he does begin
To rub her temples, and to chaufe her chin,
And everie tender part does tosse and turne.
So hardly he the flitted life does win,
Unto her native prison to retourne:
Then gins her grieved ghost thus to lament and mourne.

XXII

Ye dreary instruments of dolefull sight,
That doe this deadly spectacle behold,
Why do ye lenger feed on loathed light,
Or liking find to gaze on earthly mould,
Sith cruell fates the carefull threeds unfould,
The which my life and love together tyde?
Now let the stony dart of senselesse cold
Perce to my hart, and pas through every side,
And let eternall night so sad sight fro me hide.

XXIII

O lightsome day, the lampe of highest Jove,
First made by him, mens wandring wayes to guyde,
When darkenesse he in deepest dongeon drove,
Henceforth thy hated face for ever hyde,
And shut up heavens windowes shyning wyde:
For earthly sight can nought but sorrow breed,
And late repentance, which shall long abyde.

Mine eyes no more on vanitie shall feed,
But seeled up with death, shall have their deadly meed.

XXIV

Then downe again she fell unto the ground;
But he her quickly reared up again:
Thrise did she sinke adowne in deadly swownd
And thrise he her reviv'd with busie paine,
At last when life recover'd had the raine,
And over-wrestled his strong enemies,
With foltring tong, and trembling every vaine,
Tell on (quoth she) the wofull Tragedie,
The which these reliques sad present unto mine eie.

XXV

Tempestuous fortune hath spent all her spight,
And thrilling sorrow throwne his utmost dart;
Thy sad tongue cannot tell more heavy plight,
Then that I feele, and harbour in mine hart:
Who hath endur'd the whole, can beare each part.
If death it be, it is not the first wound,
That launched hath my brest with bleeding smart.
Begin, and end the bitter balefull stound;
If lesse then that I feare, more favour I have found.

XXVI

Then gan the Dwarfe the whole discourse declare,
The subtill traines of Archimago old;
The wanton loves of false Fidessa faire,
Bought with the blood of vanquisht Paynim bold;
The wretched payre transformed to treen mould;
The house of Pride, and perils round about;
The combat, which he with Sansjoy did hould;
The lucklesse conflict with the Gyant stout,
Wherein captiv'd, of life or death he stood in doubt.

XXVII

She heard with patience all unto the end,
And strove to maister sorrowfull assay,

Which greater grew, the more she did contend,
And almost rent her tender hart in tway;
And love fresh coles unto her fire did lay:
For greater love, the greater is the losse.
Was never Lady loved dearer day,
Then she did love the knight of the Redcrosse;
For whose deare sake so many troubles her did tosse.

XXVIII
At last when fervent sorrow slaked was,
She up arose, resolving him to find
Alive or dead: and forward forth doth pas,
All as the Dwarfe the way to her assynd:
And evermore, in constant carefull mind,
She fed her wound with fresh renewed bale;
Long tost with stormes, and bet with bitter wind,
High over hills, and low adowne the dale,
She wandred many a wood, and measurd many a vale.

XXIX
At last she chaunced by good hap to meet
A goodly knight, faire marching by the way
Together with his Squire, arrayed meet:
His glitterand armour shined farre away,
Like glauncing light of Phœbus brightest ray;
From top to toe no place appeared bare,
That deadly dint of steele endanger may:
Athwart his brest a bauldrick brave he ware,
That shynd, like twinkling stars, with stons most pretious rare.

XXX
And in the midst thereof one pretious stone
Of wondrous worth, and eke of wondrous mights,
Shapt like a Ladies head, exceeding shone,
Like Hesperus emongst the lesser lights,
And strove for to amaze the weaker sights:
Thereby his mortall blade full comely hong

In yvory sheath, ycarv'd with curious slights;
Whose hilts were burnisht gold, and handle strong
Of mother pearle, and buckled with a golden tong.

XXXI

His haughtie helmet, horrid all with gold,
Both glorious brightnesse, and great terrour bred;
For all the crest a Dragon did enfold
With greedie pawes, and over all did spred
His golden wings: his dreadfull hideous hed
Close couched on the bever, seem'd to throw
From flaming mouth bright sparkles fierie red,
That suddeine horror to faint harts did show,
And scaly tayle was stretcht adowne his backe full low.

XXXII

Upon the top of all his loftie crest,
A bunch of haires discolourd diversly,
With sprincled pearle, and gold full richly drest,
Did shake, and seemd to daunce for jollity,
Like to an Almond tree ymounted hye
On top of greene Selinis all alone,
With blossoms brave bedecked daintily;
Whose tender locks do tremble every one
At every little breath that under heaven is blowne.

XXXIII

His warlike shield all closely cover'd was,
Ne might of mortall eye be ever seene;
Not made of steele, nor of enduring bras,
Such earthly mettals soone consumed beene;
But all of Diamond perfect pure and cleene
It framed was, one massie entire mould,
Hewen out of Adamant rocke with engines keene,
That point of speare it never percen could,
Ne dint of direfull sword divide the substance would.

XXXIV

The same to wight he never wont disclose,
But when as monsters huge he would dismay,
Or daunt unequall armies of his foes,
Or when the flying heavens he would affray;
For so exceeding shone his glistring ray,
That Phœbus golden face it did attaint,
As when a cloud his beames doth over-lay;
And silver Cynthia wexed pale and faint,
As when her face is staynd with magicke arts constraint.

XXXV

No magicke arts hereof had any might,
Nor bloudie wordes of bold Enchaunters call;
But all that was not such as seemd in sight,
Before that shield did fade, and suddeine fall;
And, when him list the raskall routes appall,
Men into stones therewith he could transmew,
And stones to dust, and dust to nought at all;
And when him list the prouder lookes subdew,
He would them gazing blind, or turne to other hew.

XXXVI

Ne let it seeme, that credence this exceedes,
For he that made the same, was knowne right well
To have done much more admirable deedes.
It Merlin was, which whylome did excell
All living wightes in might of magicke spell:
Both shield, and sword, and armour all he wrought
For this young Prince, when first to armes he fell;
But when he dyde, the Faerie Queene it brought
To Faerie lond, where yet it may be seene, if sought.

XXXVII

A gentle youth, his dearely loved Squire,
His speare of heben wood behind him bare,
Whose harmefull head, thrice heated in the fire,

Had riven many a brest with pikehead square:
A goodly person, and could menage faire
His stubborne steed with curbed canon bit,
Who under him did trample as the aire,
And chauft, that any on his backe should sit;
The yron rowels into frothy fome he bit.

XXXVIII

When as this knight nigh to the Ladie drew,
With lovely court he gan her entertaine;
But when he heard her answeres loth, he knew
Some secret sorrow did her heart distraine:
Which to allay, and calme her storming paine,
Faire feeling words he wisely gan display,
And for her humour fitting purpose faine,
To tempt the cause it selfe for to bewray;
Wherewith emmov'd, these bleeding words she gan to say.

XXXIX

What worlds delight, or joy of living speach
Can heart, so plung'd in sea of sorrowes deep,
And heaped with so huge misfortunes, reach?
The carefull cold beginneth for to creepe,
And in my heart his yron arrow steepe,
Soone as I thinke upon my bitter bale:
Such helplesse harmes yts better hidden keepe,
Then rip up griefe, where it may not availe,
My last left comfort is, my woes to weepe and waile.

XL

Ah Ladie deare, quoth then the gentle knight,
Well may I weene your griefe is wondrous great;
For wondrous great griefe groneth in my spright,
Whiles thus I hear you of your sorrowes treat.
But wofull Ladie, let me you intrete
For to unfold the anguish of your hart:
Mishaps are maistred by advice discrete,

And counsell mittigates the greatest smart;
Found never helpe who never would his hurts impart.

XLI

O but (quoth she) great griefe will not be tould,
And can more easily be thought then said.
Right so (quoth he), but he that never would,
Could never: will to might gives greatest aid.
But griefe (quoth she) does greater grow displaid,
If then it find not helpe, and breedes despaire.
Despaire breedes not (quoth he) where faith is staid.
No faith so fast (quoth she) but flesh does paire.
Flesh may empaire (quoth he) but reason can repaire.

XLII

His goodly reason, and well guided speach,
So deepe did settle in her gracious thought,
That her perswaded to disclose the breach,
Which love and fortune in her heart had wrought,
And said; Faire Sir, I hope good hap hath brought
You to inquire the secrets of my griefe,
Or that your wisedome will direct my thought,
Or that your prowesse can me yield reliefe:
Then hear the storie sad, which I shall tell you briefe.

XLIII

The forlorne Maiden, whom your eyes have seene
The laughing stocke of fortunes mockeries,
Am th' only daughter of a King and Queene,
Whose parents deare, whilest equal destinies
Did runne about, and their felicities
The favourable heavens did not envy,
Did spread their rule through all the territories,
Which Phison and Euphrates floweth by,
And Gehons golden waves doe wash continually.

XLIV

Till that their cruell cursed enemy,
An huge great Dragon horrible in sight,

Bred in the loathly lakes of Tartary,
With murdrous ravine, and devouring might
Their kingdome spoild, and countrey wasted quight:
Themselves, for feare into his jawes to fall,
He forst to castle strong to take their flight,
Where fast embard in mighty brasen wall,
He has them now foure yeres besiegd to make them thrall.

XLV

Full many knights adventurous and stout
Have enterpriz'd that Monster to subdew;
From every coast that heaven walks about,
Have thither come the noble Martiall crew,
That famous hard atchievements still pursew;
Yet never any could that girlond win,
But all still shronke, and still he greater grew:
All they for want of faith, or guilt of sin,
The pitteous pray of his fierce crueltie have bin.

XLVI

At last yledd with farre reported praise,
Which flying fame throughout the world had spred,
Of doughty knights, whom Faery land did raise,
That noble order hight of Maidenhed,
Forthwith to court of Gloriane I sped
Of Gloriane great Queene of glory bright,
Whose Kingdomes seat Cleopolis is red,
There to obtaine some such redoubted knight,
The Parents deare from tyrants powre deliver might.

XLVII

It was my chance (my chance was faire and good)
There for to find a fresh unproved knight,
Whose manly hands imbrew'd in guiltie blood
Had never bene, ne ever by his might
Had throwne to ground the unregarded right:
Yet of his prowesse proofe he since hath made

(I witnesse am) in many a cruell fight;
The groning ghosts of many one dismaide
Have felt the bitter dint of his avenging blade.

XLVIII

And ye the forlorne reliques of his powre,
His byting sword, and his devouring speare,
Which have endured many a dreadfull stowre,
Can speak his prowesse, that did earst you beare,
And well could rule: now he hath left you hear
To be the record of his ruefull losse,
And of my dolefull disaventurous deare:
O heavie record of the good Redcrosse,
Where have you left your Lord, that could so well you tosse?

XLIX

Well hoped I, and faire beginnings had,
That he my captive languor should redeeme,
Till all unweeting, an Enchaunter bad
His sence abusd, and made him to misdeeme
My loyalty, not such as it did seeme;
That rather death desire, then such despight.
Be judge ye heavens, that all things right esteeme,
How I him lov'd, and love with all my might,
So thought I eke of him, and thinke I thought aright.

L

Thenceforth me desolate he quite forsooke,
To wander, where wilde fortune would me lead,
And other bywaies he himself betooke,
Where never foot of living wight did tread,
That brought not backe the balefull body dead;
In which him chaunced false Duessa meete,
Mine only foe, mine only deadly dread,
Who with her witchcraft, and misseeming sweete,
Inveigled him to follow her desires unmeete.

LI

At last by subtill sleights she him betraid
Unto his foe, a Gyant huge and tall,
Who him disarmed, dissolute, dismaid,
Unwares surprised, and with mighty mall
The monster mercilesse him made to fall,
Whose fall did never foe before behold;
And now in darkesome dungeon, wretched thrall,
Remedilesse, for aie he doth him hold;
This is my cause of griefe, more great then may be told.

LII

Ere she had ended all, she gan to faint:
But he her comforted and faire bespake,
Certes, Madame, ye have great cause of plaint,
The stoutest heart, I weene, could cause to quake.
But be of cheare, and comfort to you take:
For till I have acquit your captive knight,
Assure your selfe, I will you not forsake.
His chearefull wordes reviv'd her chearelesse spright,
So forth they went, the Dwarfe them guiding ever right.

CANTO VIII

In Canto VIII, not included in this volume,

Faire virgin, to redeeme her deare
brings Arthur to the fight:
Who slayes that Gyant, woundes the beast,
and strips Duessa quight.

CANTO IX

His loves and lignage Arthur tells:
the Knights knit friendly hands:
Sir Trevisan flies from Despayre,
whom Redcrosse Knight withstands.

I

O GOODLY golden chaine, wherewith yfere
The vertues linked are in lovely wize:
And noble minds of yore allyed were,
In brave poursuit of chevalrous emprize,
That none did others safety despize,
Nor aid envy to him, in need that stands,
But friendly each did others prayse devize,
How to advaunce with favourable hands,
As this good Prince redeemd the Redcrosse knight from bands.

II

Who when their powres empaird through labour long,
With dew repast they had recured well,
And that weake captive wight now wexed strong,
Them list no lenger there at leasure dwell,
But forward fare, as their adventures fell,
But ere they parted, Una faire besought
That straunger knight his name and nation tell;
Least so great good, as he for her had wrought,
Should die unknown, and buried be in thanklesse thought.

III

Faire virgin (said the Prince) ye me require
A thing without the compas of my wit:
For both the lignage and the certain Sire,
From which I sprong, from me are hidden yit.
For all so soone as life did me admit
Into this world, and shewed heavens light,
From mothers pap I taken was unfit:
And streight deliver'd to a Faery knight,
To be upbrought in gentle thewes and martiall might.

IV

Unto old Timon he me brought bylive,
Old Timon, who in youthly yeares hath beene
In warlike feates th'expertest man alive,

And is the wisest now on earth I weene;
His dwelling is low in a valley greene,
Under the foot of Rauran mossy hore,
From whence the river Dee as silver cleene,
His tombling billowes roll with gentle rore:
There all my dayes he traind me up in vertuous lore.

V

Thither the great magicien Merlin came,
As was his use, ofttimes to visit me:
For he had charge my discipline to frame,
And Tutours nouriture to oversee.
Him oft and oft I askt in privitie,
Of what loines and what lignage I did spring:
Whose answer bad me still assured bee,
That I was son and heire unto a king,
As time in her just terme the truth to light should bring.

VI

Well worthy impe, said then the Lady gent,
And pupill fit for such a Tutours hand.
But what adventure, or what high intent
Hath brought you hither into Faery land,
Aread Prince Arthur, crowne of Martiall band?
Full hard it is (quoth he) to read aright
The course of heavenly cause, or understand
The secret meaning of th' eternall might,
That rules mens wayes, and rules the thoughts of living wight.

VII

For whether he through fatall deepe foresight
Me hither sent, for cause to me unghest,
Or that fresh bleeding wound, which day and night
Whilome doth rancle in my riven brest,
With forced fury following his behest,
Me hither brought by wayes yet never found;
You to have helpt I hold myself yet blest.

Ah curteous knight (quoth she) what secret wound
Could ever find, to grieve the gentlest hart on ground?

VIII
Deare dame (quoth he) you sleeping sparkes awake,
Which troubled once, into huge flames will grow,
Ne ever will their fervent fury slake,
Till living moysture into smoke do flow,
And wasted life do lye in ashes low.
Yet sithens silence lesseneth not my fire,
But told it flames, and hidden it does glow;
I will revele what ye so much desire:
Ah Love, lay down thy bow, the whiles I may respire.

IX
It was in freshest flowre of youthly yeares,
When courage first does creepe in manly chest,
Then first the coale of kindly heat appeares
To kindle love in every living brest;
But me had warnd old Timons wise behest,
Those creeping flames by reason to subdew,
Before their rage grew to so great unrest,
As miserable lovers use to rew,
Which still wex old in woe, whiles woe still wexeth new.

X
That idle name of love, and lovers life,
As losse of time, and vertues enimy,
I ever scornd, and joyd to stirre up strife,
In middest of their mournfull Tragedy,
Ay wont to laugh, when them I heard to cry,
And blow the fire, which them to ashes brent:
Their God himself, griev'd at my libertie,
Shot many a dart at me with fiers intent,
But I them warded all with wary government.

XI
But all in vaine: no fort can be so strong,
Ne fleshly brest can armed be so sound,

But will at last be wonne with battrie long,
Or unawares at disadvantage found:
Nothing is sure, that growes on earthly ground:
And who most trustes in arme of fleshly might,
And boasts in beauties chaine not to be bound,
Doth soonest fall in disaventrous fight,
And yeeldes his caytive neck to victours most despight.

XII

Ensample make of him your haplesse joy,
And of my selfe now mated, as ye see;
Whose prouder vaunt that proud avenging boy
Did soone pluck downe and curbd my libertie.
For on a day, prickt forth with jollitie
Of looser life, and heat of hardiment,
Raunging the forest wide on courser free,
The fields, the floods, the heavens with one consent
Did seeme to laugh on me, and favour mine intent.

XIII

For-wearied with my sports, I did alight
From loftie steed, and downe to sleepe me layd;
The verdant gras my couch did goodly dight,
And pillow was my helmet faire displayd:
Whiles every sence the humour sweet embayd,
And slombring soft my hart did steale away,
Me seemed, by my side a royall Mayd
Her daintie limbes full softly down did lay:
So faire a creature yet saw never sunny day.

XIV

Most goodly glee and lovely blandishment
She to me made, and bad me love her deare;
For dearely sure her love was to me bent,
As when just time expired should appeare.
But whether dreames delude, or true it were,
Was never hart so ravisht with delight,

Ne living man like words did ever hear,
As she to me delivered all that night;
And at her parting said, She Queene of Faeries hight.

XV

When I awoke, and found her place devoyd,
And nought but pressed gras, where she had lyen,
I sorrowed all so much as earst I joyd,
And washed all her place with watry eyen.
From that day forth I lov'd that face divine;
From that day forth I cast in carefull mind
To seeke her out with labour, and long tyne,
And never vowd to rest till her I find,
Nine monethes I seeke in vain, yet ni'll that vow unbind.

XVI

Thus as he spake, his visage wexed pale,
And chaunge of hew great passion did bewray;
Yet still he strove to cloke his inward bale,
And hide the smoke that did his fire display,
Till gentle Una thus to him gan say;
O happy Queene of Faeries, that has found
Mongst many, one that with his prowesse may
Defend thine honour, and thy foes confound:
True Loves are often sown, but seldom grow on ground.

XVII

Thine, O then, said the gentle Recrosse knight,
Next to that Ladies love, shall be the place,
O fairest virgin, full of heavenly light,
Whose wondrous faith exceeding earthly race,
Was firmest fixt in mine extremest case.
And you, my Lord, the Patrone of my life,
Of that great Queene may well gaine worthy grace:
For only worthy you through prowes priefe,
Yf living man mote worthie be, to be her liefe.

XVIII

So diversly discoursing of their loves,
The golden Sunne his glistring head gan shew,
And sad remembraunce now the Prince amoves
With fresh desire his voyage to pursew;
Als Una earnd her traveill to renew.
Then those two knights, fast friendship for to bynd,
And love establish each to other trew,
Gave goodly gifts, the signes of gratefull mynd,
And eke the pledges firme, right hands together joynd.

XIX

Prince Arthur gave a boxe of Diamond sure,
Embowd with gold and gorgeous ornament,
Wherein were closd few drops of liquor pure,
Of wondrous worth, and vertue excellent,
That any wound could heale incontinent:
Which to requite, the Redcrosse knight him gave
A book, wherein his Saveours testament
Was writ with golden letters rich and brave;
A worke of wondrous grace, and able soules to save.

XX

Thus beene they parted, Arthur on his way
To seeke his love, and th' other for to fight
With Unaes foe, that all her realm did pray.
But she now weighing the decayed plight,
And shrunken synewes of her chosen knight,
Would not a while her forward course pursew,
Ne bring him forth in face of dreadfull fight,
Till he recovered had his former hew:
For him to be yet weake and wearie well she knew.

XXI

So as they traveild, lo they gan espy
An armed knight towards them gallop fast,
That seemed from some feared foe to fly,

Or other griesly thing, that him aghast.
Still as he fled, his eye was backward cast,
As if his feare still followed him behind;
Als flew his steed, as he his bands had brast,
And with his winged heeles did tread the wind,
As he had beene a fole of Pegasus his kind.

XXII

Nigh as he drew, they might perceive his head
To be unarmd, and curld uncombed heares
Upstaring stiffe, dismayd with uncouth dread;
Nor drop of bloud in all his face appeares
Nor life in limbe: and to increase his feares
In fowle reproch of knighthoods faire degree,
About his neck an hempen rope he weares,
That with his glistring armes does ill agree;
But he of rope or armes has now no memoree.

XXIII

The Redcrosse knight toward him crossed fast,
To weet, what mister wight was so dismayd:
There him he finds all sencelesse and aghast,
That of him selfe he seemd to be afrayd;
Whom hardly he from flying forward stayd,
Till he these wordes to him deliver might;
Sir knight, aread who hath ye thus arayd,
And eke from whom make ye this hasty flight:
For never knight I saw in such misseeming plight.

XXIV

He answerd nought at all, but adding new
Feare to his first amazment, staring wide
With stony eyes, and hartlesse hollow hew,
Astonisht stood, as one that had aspide
Infernall furies, with their chaines untide.
Him yet again, and yet again bespake
The gentle knight; who nought to him replide,

But trembling every joint did inly quake,
And foltring tongue at last these words seemd forth to shake.

XXV

For Gods deare love, Sir knight, do me not stay;
For loe he comes, he comes fast after mee.
Eft looking back would faine have runne away;
But he him forst to stay, and tellen free
The secret cause of his perplexitie:
Yet nathemore by his bold hartie speach
Could his bloud-frosen hart emboldned bee,
But through his boldnesse rather feare did reach,
Yet forst, at last he made through silence suddein breach.

XXVI

And am I now in safetie sure (quoth he)
From him, that would have forced me to dye?
And is the point of death now turnd fro mee,
That I may tell this haplesse history?
Feare nought: (quoth he) no daunger now is nye.
Then shall I you recount a ruefull cace,
(Said he) the which with this unlucky eye
I late beheld, and had not greater grace
Me reft from it, had bene partaker of the place.

XXVII

I lately chaunst (would I had never chaunst)
With a faire knight to keepen companee,
Sir Terwin hight, that well himself advaunst
In all affaires, and was both bold and free,
But not so happy as mote happy bee:
He lov'd, as was his lot, a Ladie gent,
That him again lov'd in the least degree:
For she was proud, and of too high intent,
And joyd to see her lover languish and lament.

XXVIII

From whom returning sad and comfortlesse,
As on the way together we did fare,

We met that villen (God from him me bless)
That cursed wight, from whom I scapt whyleare,
A man of hell, that cals himself Despaire:
Who first us greets, and after faire areedes
Of tydings strange, and of adventures rare:
So creeping close, as Snake in hidden weedes,
Inquireth of our states, and of our knightly deedes.

XXIX
Which when he knew, and felt our feeble harts
Embost with bale, and bitter byting griefe,
Which love had launched with his deadly darts,
With wounding words and termes of foule repriefe,
He pluckt from us all hope of due reliefe,
That earst us held in love of lingring life;
Then hopelesse hartlesse, gan the cunning thiefe
Perswade us die, to stint all further strife:
To me he lent this rope, to him a rustie knife.

XXX
With which sad instrument of hasty death,
That wofull lover, loathing lenger light,
A wide way made to let forth living breath.
But I more fearfull, or more luckie wight,
Dismayd with that deformed dismall sight,
Fled fast away, halfe dead with dying feare:
Ne yet assur'd of life by you, Sir knight,
Whose like infirmitie like chaunce may beare:
But God you never let his charmed speeches hear.

XXXI
How may a man (said he) with idle speach
Be wonne, to spoyle the Castle of his health?
I wote (quoth he) whom triall late did teach,
That like would not for all this worldes wealth:
His subtill tongue, like dropping honny, mealt'h
Into the hart, and searcheth every vaine;

That ere one be aware, by secret stealth
His powre is reft, and weaknesse doth remaine.
O never Sir desire to try his guilefull traine.

XXXII

Certes (said he) hence shall I never rest,
Till I that treacherours art have heard and tride;
And you Sir knight, whose name mote I request,
Of grace do me unto his cabin guide.
I that hight Trevisan (quoth he) will ride,
Against my liking backe, to do you grace:
But not for gold nor glee will I abide
By you, when ye arrive in that same place
For lever had I die, then see his deadly face.

XXXIII

Ere long they come, where that same wicked wight
His dwelling has, low in an hollow cave,
Farre underneath a craggie clift ypight,
Darke, dolefull, drearie, like a greedy grave,
That still for carrion carcases doth crave:
On top whereof aye dwelt the ghastly Owle,
Shrieking his balefull note, which ever drave
Far from that haunt all other chearefull fowle;
And all about it wandring ghostes did waile and howle.

XXXIV

And all about old stockes and stubs of trees,
Whereon nor fruit nor leafe was ever seene,
Did hang upon the ragged rocky knees;
On which had many wretches hanged beene,
Whose carcases were scattered on the greene,
And throwne about the clifts. Arrived there,
That bare-head knight for dread and dolefull teene,
Would faine have fled, ne durst approchen neare,
But th' other forst him stay, and comforted in feare.

XXXV

That darkesome cave they enter, where they find
That cursed man, low sitting on the ground,
Musing full sadly in his sullein mind;
His griesie lockes, long growen, and unbound,
Disordred hong about his shoulders round,
And hid his face; through which his hollow eyne
Lookt deadly dull, and stared as astound;
His raw-bone cheekes, through penurie and pine,
Were shronke into his jawes, as he did never dine.

XXXVI

His garment nought but many ragged clouts,
With thornes together pind and patched was,
The which his naked sides he wrapt abouts;
And him beside there lay upon the gras
A drearie corse, whose life away did pas,
All wallowed in his own yet luke-warme blood,
That from his wound yet welled fresh alas;
In which a rustie knife fast fixed stood,
And made an open passage for the gushing flood.

XXXVII

Which piteous spectacle, approving trew
The wofull tale that Trevisan had told,
When as the gentle Redcrosse knight did vew,
With firie zeale he burnt in courage bold,
Him to avenge, before his bloud were cold,
And to the villein said, Thou damned wight,
The author of this fact we here behold,
What justice can but judge against thee right,
With thine own bloud to price his bloud, here shed in sight.

XXXVIII

What franticke fit (quoth he) hath thus distraught
Thee, foolish man, so rash a doome to give?
What justice ever other judgment taught,

But he should die, who merites not to live?
None else to death this man despayring drive,
But his own guiltie mind deserving death.
Is then unjust to each his due to give?
Or let him die, that loatheth living breath?
Or let him die at ease, that liveth here uneath?

XXXIX

Who travels by the wearie wandring way,
To come unto his wished home in haste,
And meetes a flood, that doth his passage stay,
Is not great grace to helpe him over past,
Or free his feet that in the myre sticke fast?
Most envious man, that grieves at neighbours good,
And fond, that joyest in the woe thou hast,
Why wilt not let him passe, that long hath stood
Upon the banke, yet wilt thy selfe not passe the flood?

XL

He there does now enjoy eternall rest
And happy ease, which thou dost want and crave,
And further from it daily wanderest:
What if some little paine the passage have,
That makes fraile flesh to feare the bitter wave?
Is not short paine well borne, that brings long ease,
And layes the soul to sleepe in quiet grave?
Sleepe after toyle, port after stormie seas,
Ease after warre, death after life does greatly please.

XLI

The knight much wondred at his suddeine wit,
And said, The terme of life is limited,
Ne may a man prolong, nor shorten it;
The souldier may not move from watchfull sted,
Nor leave his stand, untill his Captaine bed.
Who life did limit by almightie doome
(Quoth he) knowes best the termes established;

And he, that points the Centonell his roome,
Doth license him depart at sound of morning droome.

XLII

Is not his deed, what ever thing is donne
In heaven and earth? did not he all create
To die again? all ends that was begonne.
Their times in his eternall book of fate
Are written sure, and have their certaine date.
Who then can strive with strong necessitie,
That holds the world in his still chaunging state,
Or shunne the death ordaynd by destinie?
When houre of death is come, let none aske whence, nor why.

XLIII

The lenger life, I wote the greater sin,
The greater sin, the greater punishment:
All those great battels, which thou boasts to win,
Through strife, and blood-shed, and avengement,
Now praysd, hereafter deare thou shalt repent:
For life must life, and blood must blood repay.
Is not enough thy evill life forespent?
For he that once hath missed the right way,
The further he doth goe, the further he doth stray.

XLIV

Then do no further goe, no further stray,
But here lie downe, and to thy rest betake,
Th' ill to prevent, that life ensewen may.
For what hath life, that may it loved make,
And gives not rather cause it to forsake?
Feare, sicknesse, age, losse, labour, sorrow, strife,
Paine, hunger, cold, that makes the hart to quake;
And ever fickle fortune rageth rife,
All which, and thousands mo do make a loathsome life.

XLV

Thou wretched man, of death hast greatest need,
If in true ballance thou wilt weigh thy state:

For never knight, that dared warlike deede,
More lucklesse disaventures did amate:
Witnesse the dungeon deepe, wherein of late
Thy life shut up, for death so oft did call;
And though good lucke prolonged hath thy date,
Yet death then would the like mishaps forestall,
Into the which hereafter thou maiest happen fall.

XLVI

Why then doest thou, O man of sin, desire
To draw thy dayes forth to their last degree?
Is not the measure of thy sinfull hire
High heaped up with huge iniquitie,
Against the day of wrath, to burden thee?
Is not enough, that to this Ladie milde
Thou falsed hast thy faith with perjurie,
And sold thy selfe to serve Duessa vilde,
With whom in all abuse thou hast thy selfe defilde?

XLVII

Is not he just, that all this doth behold
From highest heaven, and beares an equall eye?
Shall he thy sins up in his knowledge fold,
And guilty be of thine impietie?
Is not his law, Let every sinner die:
Die shall all flesh? what then must needs be donne,
Is it not better to doe willinglie,
Then linger, till the glasse be all out ronne?
Death is the end of woes: die soone, O faeries son.

XLVIII

The knight was much enmoved with his speach,
That as a swords point through his hart did perse,
And in his conscience made a secret breach,
Well knowing true all that he did reherse,
And to his fresh remembraunce did reverse
The ugly vew of his deformed crimes,

That all his manly powres it did disperse,
As he were charmed with inchaunted rimes,
That oftentimes he quakt, and fainted oftentimes.

XLIX

In which amazement, when the Miscreant
Perceived him to waver weake and fraile,
Whiles trembling horror did his conscience dant,
And hellish anguish did his soul assaile,
To drive him to despaire, and quite to quaile,
He shew'd him painted in a table plaine,
The damned ghosts, that doe in torments waile,
And thousand feends that doe them endlesse paine
With fire and brimstone, which for ever shall remaine.

L

The sight whereof so throughly him dismaid,
That nought but death before his eyes he saw,
And ever burning wrath before him laid,
By righteous sentence of th' Almighties law.
Then gan the villein him to overcraw,
And brought unto him swords, ropes, poison, fire,
And all that might him to perdition draw;
And bad him choose, what death he would desire:
For death was due to him, that had provokt Gods ire.

LI

But when as none of them he saw him take,
He to him raught a dagger sharpe and keene,
And gave it him in hand: his hand did quake,
And tremble like a leafe of Aspin greene,
And troubled bloud through his pale face was seene
To come, and goe with tidings from the heart,
As it a running messenger had beene.
At last resolv'd to worke his finall smart,
He lifted up his hand, that backe again did start.

LII

Which whenas Una saw, through every vaine
The crudled cold ran to her well of life,
As in a swowne: but soone reliv'd again,
Out of his hand she snatcht the cursed knife,
And threw it to the ground, enraged rife,
And to him said, Fie, fie, faint harted knight,
What meanest thou by this reprochfull strife?
Is this the battell, which thou vauntst to fight
With that fire-mouthed Dragon, horrible and bright?

LIII

Come, come away, fraile, seely, fleshly wight,
Ne let vaine words bewitch thy manly hart,
Ne divelish thoughts dismay thy constant spright.
In heavenly mercies hast thou not a part?
Why shouldst thou then despeire, that chosen art?
Where justice growes, there grows eke greater grace,
The which doth quench the brond of hellish smart,
And that accurst hand-writing doth deface.
Arise, Sir knight, arise, and leave this cursed place.

LIV

So up he rose, and thence amounted streight.
Which when the carle beheld, and saw his guest
Would safe depart for all his subtill sleight,
He chose an halter from among the rest,
And with it hung himself, unbid unblest.
But death he could not worke himself thereby;
For thousand times he so himself had drest,
Yet nathelesse it could not doe him die,
Till he should die his last, that is, eternally.

MUTABILITIE CANTOS

Canto VI

Proud Change (not pleasd, in mortall things,
beneath the Moone, to raigne)
Pretends, as well of Gods, as Men,
to be the Soveraine.

I

What man that sees the ever-whirling wheele
Of Change, the which all mortall things doth sway,
But that therby doth find, & plainly feele,
How MUTABILITY in them doth play
Her cruell sports, to many mens decay?
Which that to all may better yet appeare,
I will rehearse that whylome I heard say,
How she at first her selfe began to reare,
Gainst all the Gods, and th'empire sought from them to beare.

II

But first, here falleth fittest to unfold
Her antique race and linage ancient,
As I have found it registred of old,
In Faery Land mongst records permanent:
She was, to weet, a daughter by descent
Of those old Titans, that did whylome strive
With Saturnes son for heavens regiment.
Whom, though high Jove of kingdome did deprive,
Yet many of their stemme long after did survive.

III

And many of them, afterwards obtain'd
Great power of Jove, and high authority;
As Hecaté, in whose almighty hand,
He plac't all rule and principality,
To be by her disposed diversly,
To Gods, and men, as she them list divide:
And drad Bellona, that doth sound on hie

Warres and allarums unto Nations wide,
That makes both heaven & earth to tremble at her pride.

IV
So likewise did this Titanesse aspire,
Rule and dominion to her selfe to gaine;
That as a Goddesse, men might her admire,
And heavenly honours yield, as to them twaine.
At first, on earth she sought it to obtaine;
Where she such proofe and sad examples shewed
Of her great power, to many ones great paine,
That not men only (whom she soone subdewed)
But eke all other creatures, her bad dooings rewed.

V
For, she the face of earthly things so changed,
That all which Nature had establisht first
In good estate, and in meet order ranged,
She did pervert, and all their statutes burst:
And all the worlds faire frame (which none yet durst
Of Gods or men to alter or misguide)
She alter'd quite, and made them all accurst
That God had blest; and did at first provide
In that still happy state for ever to abide.

VI
Ne shee the laws of Nature only brake,
But eke of Justice, and of Policie;
And wrong of right, and bad of good did make,
And death for life exchanged foolishlie:
Since which, all living wights have learn'd to die,
And all this world is woxen daily worse.
Of pittious worke of MUTABILITIE!
By which, we all are subject to that curse,
And death in stead of life have sucked from our Nurse.

VII
And now, when all the earth she thus had brought 7
To her behest, and thralled to her might,

She gan to cast in her ambitious thought,
T'attempt the empire of the heavens hight,
And Jove himself to shoulder from his right.
And first, she past the region of the ayre,
And of the fire, whose substance thin and slight,
Made no resistance, ne could her contraire,
But ready passage to her pleasure did prepaire.

VIII

Thence, to the Circle of the Moone she clambe,
Where Cynthia raignes in everlasting glory,
To whose bright shining palace straight she came,
All fairely deckt with heavens goodly story:
Whose silver gates (by which there sate an hory
Old aged Sire, with hower-glasse in hand,
Hight Time) she entred, were he liefe or sory:
Ne staide till she the highest stage had scand,
Where Cynthia did sit, that never still did stand.

IX

Her sitting on an Ivory throne shee found,
Drawne of two steeds, th'one black, the other white,
Environd with tenne thousand starres around,
That duly her attended day and night;
And by her side, there ran her Page, that hight
Vesper, whom we the Evening-starre intend:
That with his Torche, still twinkling like twylight,
Her lightened all the way where she should wend,
And joy to weary wandring travailers did lend:

X

That when the hardy Titanesse beheld
The goodly building of her Palace bright,
Made of the heavens substance, and up-held
With thousand Crystall pillors of huge hight,
Shee gan to burne in her ambitious spright,
And t'envie her that in such glorie raigned.

Eftsoones she cast by force and tortious might,
Her to displace; and to her selfe to have gained
The kingdome of the Night, and waters by her wained.

XI

Boldly she bid the Goddesse downe descend,
And let her selfe into that Ivory throne;
For, shee her selfe more worthy thereof wend,
And better able it to guide alone:
Whether to men, whose fall she did bemone,
Or unto Gods, whose state she did maligne,
Or to th'infernall Powers, her need give lone
Of her faire light, and bounty most benigne,
Her selfe of all that rule shee deemed most condigne.

XII

But shee that had to her that soveraigne seat
By highest Jove assign'd, therein to beare
Nights burning lamp, regarded not her threat,
Ne yielded ought for favour or for feare;
But with sterne countenance and disdainfull cheare,
Bending her horned browes, did put her back:
And boldly blaming her for comming there,
Bade her attonce from heavens coast to pack,
Or at her perill bide the wrathfull Thunders wrack.

XIII

Yet nathemore the Giantesse forbare:
But boldly preacing-on, raught forth her hand
To pluck her downe perforce from off her chaire;
And there-with lifting up her golden wand,
Threatned to strike her if she did with-stand.
Where-at the starres, which round about her blazed,
And eke the Moones bright wagon, still did stand,
All beeing with so bold attempt amazed,
And on her uncouth habit and sterne looke still gazed.

XIV

Meane-while, the lower World, which nothing knew
Of all that chaunced here, was darkned quite;
And eke the heavens, and all the heavenly crew
Of happy wights, now unpurvaide of light,
Were much afraid, and wondred at that sight;
Fearing least Chaos broken had his chaine,
And brought again on them eternall night:
But chiefely Mercury, that next doth raigne,
Ran forth in haste, unto the king of Gods to plaine.

XV

All ran together with a great out-cry,
To Joves faire Palace, fixt in heavens hight;
And beating at his gates full earnestly,
Gan call to him aloud with all their might,
To know what meant that suddaine lack of light.
The father of the Gods when this he heard,
Was troubled much at their so strange affright,
Doubting least Typhon were again uprear'd,
Or other his old foes, that once him sorely fear'd.

XVI

Eftsoones the son of Maia forth he sent
Downe to the Circle of the Moone, to knowe
The cause of this so strange astonishment,
And why shee did her wonted course forslowe;
And if that any were on earth belowe
That did with charmes or Magick her molest,
Him to attache, and downe to hell to throwe:
But, if from heaven it were, then to arrest
The Author, and him bring before his presence prest.

XVII

The wingd-foot God, so fast his plumes did beat,
That soone he came where-as the Titanesse
Was striving with faire Cynthia for her seat:

At whose strange sight, and haughty hardinesse,
He wondred much, and feared her no lesse.
Yet laying feare aside to doe his charge,
At last, he bade her (with bold stedfastnesse)
Ceasse to molest the Moone to walk at large,
Or come before high Jove, her dooings to discharge.

XVIII

And there-with-all, he on her shoulder laid
His snaky-wreathed Mace, whose awfull power
Doth make both Gods and hellish fiends affraid:
Where-at the Titanesse did sternely lower,
And stoutly answer'd, that in evill hower
He from his Jove such message to her brought,
To bid her leave faire Cynthias silver bower;
Sith shee his Jove and him esteemed nought,
No more then Cynthia's selfe; but all their kingdoms sought.

XIX

The Heavens Herald staid not to reply,
But past away, his doings to relate
Unto his Lord; who now in th'highest sky,
Was placed in his principall Estate,
With all the Gods about him congregate:
To whom when Hermes had his message told,
It did them all exceedingly amate,
Save Jove; who, changing nought his count'nance bold,
Did unto them at length these speeches wise unfold;

XX

"Harken to mee awhile yee heavenly Powers;
Ye may remember since th'Earths cursed seed
Sought to assaile the heavens eternall towers,
And to us all exceeding feare did breed:
But how we then defeated all their deed,
Yee all doe knowe, and them destroied quite;
Yet not so quite, but that there did succeed

An off-spring of their bloud, which did alite
Upon the fruitfull earth, which doth us yet despite.

XXI

"Of that bad seed is this bold woman bred,
That now with bold presumption doth aspire
To thrust faire Phoebe from her silver bed,
And eke our selves from heavens high Empire,
If that her might were match to her desire:
Wherefore, it now behoves us to advise
What way is best to drive her to retire;
Whether by open force, or counsell wise,
Areed ye sonnes of God, as best ye can devise."

XXII

So having said, he ceast; and with his brow
(His black eye-brow, whose doomefull dreaded beck
Is wont to wield the world unto his vow,
And even the highest Powers of heaven to check)
Made signe to them in their degrees to speak:
Who straight gan cast their counsell grave and wise.
Meane-while, th'Earths daughter, thogh she nought did reck
Of Hermes message; yet gan now advise,
What course were best to take in this hot bold emprize.

XXIII

Eftsoones she thus resolv'd; that whil'st the Gods
(After returne of Hermes Embassie)
Were troubled, and amongst themselves at ods,
Before they could new counsels re-allie,
To set upon them in that extasie;
And take what fortune time and place would lend:
So, forth she rose, and through the purest sky
To Joves high Palace straight cast to ascend,
To prosecute her plot: Good on-set boads good end.

XXIV

Shee there arriving, boldly in did pass;
Where all the Gods she found in counsell close,

All quite unarm'd, as then their manner was.
At sight of her they suddaine all arose,
In great amaze, ne wist what way to chose.
But Jove, all fearelesse, forc't them to aby;
And in his soveraine throne, gan straight dispose
Himself more full of grace and Majestie,
That mote encheare his friends, & foes mote terrifie.

XXV

That, when the haughty Titanesse beheld,
All were she fraught with pride and impudence,
Yet with the sight thereof was almost queld;
And inly quaking, seem'd as reft of sense,
And voyd of speech in that drad audience;
Untill that Jove himself, her selfe bespake:
"Speak thou fraile woman, speak with confidence,
Whence art thou, and what doost thou here now make?
What idle errand hast thou, earths mansion to forsake?"

XXVI

Shee, halfe confused with his great commaund,
Yet gathering spirit of her natures pride,
Him boldly answer'd thus to his demaund:
"I am a daughter, by the mothers side,
Of her that is Grand-mother magnifide
Of all the Gods, great Earth, great Chaos child:
But by the fathers (be it not envide)
I greater am in bloud (whereon I build)
Then all the Gods, though wrongfully from heaven exil'd.

XXVII

"For, Titan (as ye all acknowledge must)
Was Saturnes elder brother by birth-right;
Both, sonnes of Uranus: but by unjust
And guilefull meanes, through Corybantes slight,
The younger thrust the elder from his right:
Since which, thou Jove, injuriously hast held

The Heavens rule from Titans sonnes by might;
And them to hellish dungeons downe hast feld:
Witnesse ye Heavens the truth of all that I have teld."

XXVII

Whil'st she thus spake, the Gods that gave good eare
To her bold words, and marked well her grace,
Beeing of stature tall as any there
Of all the Gods, and beautifull of face,
As any of the Goddesses in place,
Stood all astonied, like a sort of Steeres;
Mongst whom, some beast of strange & forraine race,
Unwares is chaunc't, far straying from his peeres:
So did their ghastly gaze bewray their hidden feares.

XXIX

Till having pauz'd awhile, Jove thus bespake;
"Will never mortall thoughts ceasse to aspire,
In this bold sort, to Heaven claime to make,
And touch celestiall seates with earthly mire?
I would have thought, that bold Procrustes hire,
Or Typhons fall, or proud Ixions paine,
Or great Prometheus, tasting of our ire,
Would have suffiz'd, the rest for to restraine;
And warn'd all men by their example to refraine:

XXX

"But now, this off-scum of that cursed fry,
Dare to renew the like bold enterprize,
And chalenge th'heritage of this our skie;
Whom what should hinder, but that we likewise
Should handle as the rest of her allies,
And thunder-drive to hell?" With that, he shooke
His Nectar-deawed locks, with which the skyes
And all the world beneath for terror quooke,
And eft his burning levin-brond in hand he tooke.

XXXI

But, when he looked on her lovely face,
In which, faire beames of beauty did appeare,
That could the greatest wrath soone turne to grace
(Such sway doth beauty even in Heaven beare)
He staide his hand: and having chang'd his cheare,
He thus again in milder wise began;
"But ah! if Gods should strive with flesh yfere,
Then shortly should the progeny of Man
Be rooted out, if Jove should doe still what he can:

XXXII

"But thee faire Titans child, I rather weene,
Through some vaine errour or inducement light,
To see that mortall eyes have never seene;
Or through ensample of thy sisters might,
Bellona; whose great glory thou doost spight,
Since thou hast seene her dreadfull power belowe,
Mongst wretched men (dismaide with her affright)
To bandie Crownes, and Kingdomes to bestowe:
And sure thy worth, no lesse then hers doth seem to showe.

XXXIII

"But wote thou this, thou hardy Titanesse,
That not the worth of any living wight
May challenge ought in Heavens interesse;
Much lesse the Title of old Titans Right:
For, we by Conquest of our soveraine might,
And by eternall doome of Fates decree,
Have wonne the Empire of the Heavens bright;
Which to our selves we hold, and to whom wee
Shall worthy deeme partakers of our blisse to bee.

XXXIV

"Then ceasse thy idle claime thou foolish gerle,
And seeke by grace and goodnesse to obtaine
That place from which by folly Titan fell;

There-to thou maist perhaps, if so thou faine
Have Jove thy gratious Lord and Soveraigne.
So, having said, she thus to him replide;
"Ceasse Saturnes son, to seeke by proffers vaine
Of idle hopes t'allure mee to thy side,
For to betray my Right, before I haue it tride.

XXXV

"But thee, O Jove, no equall Judge I deeme
Of my desert, or of my dewfull Right;
That in thine own behalfe maist partiall seeme:
But to the highest him, that is behight
Father of Gods and men by equall might;
To weet, the God of Nature, I appeale."
There-at Jove wexed wroth, and in his spright
Did inly grudge, yet did it well conceale;
And bade Dan Phoebus Scribe her Appellation seale.

XXXVI

Eftsoones the time and place appointed were,
Where all, both heavenly Powers, & earthly wights,
Before great Natures presence should appeare,
For triall of their Titles and best Rights:
That was, to weet, upon the highest hights
Of Arlo-hill (Who knowes not Arlo-hill?)
That is the highest head (in all mens sights)
Of my old father Mole, whom Shepheards quill
Renowmed hath with hymnes fit for a rurall skill.

XXXVII

And, were it not ill fitting for this file,
To sing of hilles & woods, mongst warres & Knights,
I would abate the sternenesse of my stile,
Mongst these sterne stounds to mingle soft delights;
And tell how Arlo through Dianaes spights
(Beeing of old the best and fairest Hill
That was in all this holy-Islands hights)

Was made the most unpleasant, and most ill.
Meane while, O Clio, lend Calliope thy quill.

XXXVIII

Whylome, when IRELAND florished in fame
Of wealths and goodnesse, far above the rest
Of all that beare the British Islands name,
The Gods then us'd (for pleasure and for rest)
Oft to resort there-to, when seem'd them best:
But none of all there-in more pleasure found,
Then Cynthia; that is soveraine Queene profest
Of woods and forrests, which therein abound,
Sprinkled with wholsom waters, more then most on ground.

XXXIX

But mongst them all, as fittest for her game,
Either for chace of beasts with hound or boawe,
Or for to shroude in shade from Phoebus flame,
Or bathe in fountaines that doe freshly flowe,
Or from high hilles, or from the dales belowe,
She chose this Arlo; where shee did resort
With all her Nymphes enranged on a rowe,
With whom the woody Gods did oft consort:
For, with the Nymphes, the Satyres love to play & sport.

XL

Amongst the which, there was a Nymph that hight
Molanna; daughter of old father Mole,
And sister unto Mulla, faire and bright:
Unto whose bed false Bregog whylome stole,
That Shepheard Colin dearely did condole,
And made her lucklesse loves well knowne to be.
But this Molanna, were she not so shole,
Were no lesse faire and beautifull then shee:
Yet as she is, a fairer flood may no man see.

XLI

For, first, she springs out of two marble Rocks,
On which, a grove of Oakes high mounted growes,

That as a girlond seemes to deck the locks
Of som faire Bride, brought forth with pompous showes
Out of her bowre, that many flowers strowes:
So, through the flowry Dales she tumbling downe,
Through many woods, and shady coverts flowes
(That on each side her silver channell crowne)
Till to the Plaine she come, whose Valleyes shee doth drowne.

XLII

In her sweet streames, Diana used oft
(After her sweatie chace and toilesome play)
To bathe her selfe; and after, on the soft
And downy grasse, her dainty limbes to lay
In covert shade, where none behold her may:
For, much she hated sight of living eye.
Foolish God Faunus, though full many a day
He saw her clad, yet longed foolishly
To see her naked mongst her Nymphes in privity.

XLIII

No way he found to compasse his desire,
But to corrupt Molanna, this her maid,
Her to discover for some secret hire:
So, her with flattering words he first assaid;
And after, pleasing gifts for her purvaid,
Queene-apples, and red Cherries from the tree,
With which he her allured and betraid,
To tell what time he might her Lady see
When she her selfe did bathe, that he might secret bee.

XLIV

There-to hee promist, if shee would him pleasure
With this small boone, to quit her with a better;
To weet, that where-as shee had out of measure
Long lov'd the Fanchin, who by nought did set her,
That he would undertake, for this to get her
To be his Love, and of him liked well:

Besides all which, he vow'd to be her debter
For many moe good turnes then he would tell;
The least of which, this little pleasure should excell.

XLV

The simple maid did yield to him anone;
And eft him placed where he close might view
That never any saw, save only one;
Who, for his hire to so foole-hardy dew,
Was of his hounds devour'd in Hunters hew.
Tho, as her manner was on sunny day,
Diana, with her Nymphes about her, drew
To this sweet spring; where, doffing her array,
She bath'd her lovely limbes, for Jove a likely pray.

XLVI

There Faunus saw that pleased much his eye,
And made his hart to tickle in his brest,
That for great ioy of some-what he did spy,
He could him not containe in silent rest;
But breaking forth in laughter, loud profest
His foolish thought. O foolish Faune indeed,
That couldst not hold thy selfe so hidden blest,
But wouldest needs thine own conceit areed.
Babblers unworthy been of so divine a meed.

XLVII

The Goddesse, all abashed with that noise,
In haste forth started from the guilty brooke;
And running straight where-as she heard his voice,
Enclos'd the bush about, and there him tooke,
Like darred Larke; not daring up to looke
On her whose sight before so much he sought.
Thence, forth they drew him by the hornes, & shooke
Nigh all to peeces, that they left him nought;
And then into the open light they forth him brought.

XLVIII

Like as an huswife, that with busie care
Thinks of her Dairie to make wondrous gaine,
Finding where-as some wicked beast unware
That breakes into her Dayr'house, there doth draine
Her creaming pannes, and frustrate all her paine;
Hath in some snare or gin set close behind,
Entrapped him, and caught into her traine,
Then thinkes what punishment were best assign'd,
And thousand deathes deviseth in her vengefull mind:

XLIX

So did Diana and her maydens all
Use silly Faunus, now within their baile:
They mocke and scorne him, and him foule miscall;
Some by the nose him pluckt, some by the taile,
And by his goatish beard some did him haile:
Yet he (poore soul) with patience all did beare;
For, nought against their wils might countervaile:
Ne ought he said what ever he did hear;
But hanging downe his head, did like a Mome appeare.

L

At length, when they had flouted him their fill,
They gan to cast what penaunce him to give.
Some would have gelt him, but that same would spill
The Wood-gods breed, which must for ever live:
Others would through the river him have drive,
And ducked deepe: but that seem'd penaunce light;
But most agreed and did this sentence give,
Him in Deares skin to clad; and in that plight,
To hunt him with their hounds, him selfe save how hee might.

LI

But Cynthia's selfe, more angry then the rest,
Thought not enough, to punish him in sport,
And of her shame to make a gamesome jest;

But gan examine him in straighter sort,
Which of her Nymphes, or other close consort,
Him thither brought, and her to him betraid?
He, much affeard, to her confessed short,
That ‹twas Molanna which her so bewraid.
Then all attonce their hands vpon Molanna laid.

LII

But him (according as they had decreed)
With a Deeres-skin they covered, and then chast
With all their hounds that after him did speed;
But he more speedy, from them fled more fast
Then any Deere: so sore him dread aghast.
They after follow'd all with shrill out-cry,
Shouting as they the heavens would have brast:
That all the woods and dales where he did flie,
Did ring again, and loud reeccho to the skie.

LIII

So they him follow'd till they weary were;
When, back returning to Molann' again,
They, by commaund'ment of Diana, there
Her whelm'd with stones. Yet Faunus (for her paine)
Of her beloved Fanchin did obtaine,
That her he would receive unto his bed.
So now her waves passe through a pleasant Plaine,
Till with the Fanchin she her selfe doe wed,
And (both combin'd) themselves in one faire river spred.

LIV

Nath'lesse, Diana, full of indignation,
Thence-forth abandond her delicious brooke;
In whose sweet streame, before that bad occasion,
So much delight to bathe her limbes she tooke:
Ne only her, but also quite forsooke
All those faire forrests about Arlo hid,
And all that Mountaine, which doth over-looke

The richest champian that may else be rid,
And the faire Shure, in which are thousand Salmons bred.

LV

Them all, and all that she so deare did way,
Thence-forth she left; and parting from the place,
There-on an heavy haplesse curse did lay,
To weet, that Wolves, where she was wont to space,
Should harbour'd be, and all those Woods deface,
And Thieves should rob and spoile that Coast around.
Since which, those Woods, and all that goodly Chase,
Doth to this day with Wolves and Thieves abound:
Which too-too true that lands in-dwellers since have found.

CANTO VII

Pealing, from Jove, to Natur's Bar,
bold Alteration pleades
Large Evidence: but Nature soone
her righteous Doome areades.

I

Ah! whither doost thou now thou greater Muse
Me from these woods & pleasing forrests bring?
And my fraile spirit (that dooth oft refuse
This too high flight, unfit for her weake wing)
Lift up aloft, to tell of heavens King
(Thy soveraine Sire) his fortunate successe,
And victory, in bigger noates to sing,
Which he obtain'd against that Titanesse,
That him of heavens Empire sought to dispossesse.

II

Yet sith I needs must follow thy behest,
Doe thou my weaker wit with skill inspire,
Fit for this turne; and in my sable brest
Kindle fresh sparks of that immortall fire,
Which learned minds inflameth with desire

Of heavenly things: for, who but thou alone,
That art yborne of heaven and heavenly Sire,
Can tell things doen in heaven so long ygone:
So farre past memory of man that may be knowne.

III

Now, at the time that was before agreed,
The Gods assembled all on Arlo hill;
As well those that are sprung of heavenly seed,
As those that all the other world doe fill,
And rule both sea and land unto their will:
Only th'infernall Powers might not appeare;
Aswell for horror of their count'naunce ill,
As for th'unruly fiends which they did feare;
Yet Pluto and Proserpina were present there.

IV

And thither also came all other creatures,
What-ever life or motion doe retaine,
According to their sundry kinds of features;
That Arlo scarsly could them all containe;
So full they filled every hill and Plaine:
And had not Natures Sergeant (that is Order)
Them well disposed by his busie paine,
And raunged farre abroad in every border,
They would have caused much confusion and disorder.

V

Then forth issewed (great goddesse) great dame Nature,
With goodly port and gracious Majesty;
Being far greater and more tall of stature
Then any of the gods or Powers on hie:
Yet certes by her face and physnomy,
Whether she man or woman inly were,
That could not any creature well descry:
For, with a veile that wimpled every where,
Her head and face was hid, that mote to none appeare.

VI

That some doe say was so by skill devized,
To hide the terror of her uncouth hew,
From mortall eyes that should be sore agrized;
For that her face did like a Lion shew,
That eye of wight could not indure to view:
But others tell that it so beautious was,
And round about such beames of splendor threw,
That it the Sunne a thousand times did pass,
Ne could be seene, but like an image in a glass.

VII

That well may seemen true: for, well I weene
That this same day, when she on Arlo sat,
Her garment was so bright and wondrous sheene,
That my fraile wit cannot devize to what
It to compare, nor finde like stuffe to that,
As those three sacred Saints, though else most wise,
Yet on mount Thabor quite their wits forgat,
When they their glorious Lord in strange disguise
Transfigur'd sawe; his garments so did daze their eyes.

VIII

In a fayre Plaine upon an equall Hill,
She placed was in a pavilion;
Not such as Craftes-men by their idle skill
Are wont for Princes states to fashion:
But th'earth her self of her own motion,
Out of her fruitfull bosome made to growe
Most dainty trees; that, shooting up anon,
Did seeme to bow their bloosming heads full lowe,
For homage unto her, and like a throne did shew.

IX

So hard it is for any living wight,
All her array and vestiments to tell,
That old Dan Geffrey (in whose gentle spright

The pure well head of Poesie did dwell)
In his Foules parley durst not with it mel,
But it transferd to Alane, who he thought
Had in his Plaint of kindes describ'd it well:
Which who will read set forth so as it ought,
Go seek he out that Alane where he may be sought.

X

And all the earth far underneath her feete
Was dight with flowres, that voluntary grew
Out of the ground, and sent forth odours sweet;
Tenne thousand mores of sundry sent and hew,
That might delight the smell, or please the view:
The which, the Nymphes, from all the brooks thereby
Had gathered, which they at her foot-stoole threw;
That richer seem'd then any tapestry,
That Princes bowres adorne with painted imagery.

XI

And Mole himself, to honour her the more,
Did deck himself in freshest faire attire,
And his high head, that seemeth alwaies hore
With hardned frosts of former winters ire,
He with an Oaken girlond now did tire,
As if the love of some new Nymph late seene,
Had in him kindled youthfull fresh desire,
And made him change his gray attire to greene;
Ah gentle Mole! such joyance hath thee well beseene.

XII

Was never so great joyance since the day,
That all the gods whylome assembled were,
On Hæmus hill in their divine array,
To celebrate the solemne bridall cheare,
Twixt Peleus, and dame Thetis pointed there;
Where Phoebus self, that god of Poets hight,
They say did sing the spousall hymne full cleere,

That all the gods were ravisht with delight
Of his celestiall song, & Musicks wondrous might.

XIII
This great Grandmother of all creatures bred
Great Nature, ever young yet full of eld,
Still mooving, yet unmoved from her sted;
Unseene of any, yet of all beheld;
Thus sitting in her throne as I have teld,
Before her came dame Mutabilitie;
And being lowe before her presence feld,
With meek obaysance and humilitie,
Thus gan her plaintif Plea, with words to amplifie;

XIV
"To thee O greatest goddesse, only great,
An humble suppliant loe, I lowely fly
Seeking for Right, which I of thee entreat;
Who Right to all dost deale indifferently,
Damning all Wrong and tortious Injurie,
Which any of thy creatures doe to other
(Oppressing them with power, unequally)
Sith of them all thou art the equall mother,
And knittest each to each, as brother unto brother.

XV
"To thee therefore of this same Jove I plaine,
And of his fellow gods that faine to be,
That challenge to themselves the whole worlds raign;
Of which, the greatest part is due to me,
And heaven it selfe by heritage in Fee:
For, heaven and earth I both alike do deeme,
Sith heaven and earth are both alike to thee;
And, gods no more then men thou doest esteeme:
For, even the gods to thee, as men to gods do seeme.

XVI
"Then weigh, O soveraigne goddesse, by what right
These gods do claime the worlds whole soverainty;

And that is only dew unto thy might
Arrogate to themselves ambitiously:
As for the gods own principality,
Which Jove usurpes unjustly; that to be
My heritage, Jove's self cannot deny,
From my great Grandsire Titan, unto mee,
Deriv'd by dew descent; as is well known to thee.

XVII

Yet mauger Jove, and all his gods beside,
I doe possesse the worlds most regiment;
As, if ye please it into parts divide,
And every parts inholders to convent,
Shall to your eyes appeare incontinent.
And first, the Earth (great mother of us all)
That only seems unmov'd and permanent,
And unto Mutability not thrall;
Yet is she chang'd in part, and eeke in generall.

XVIII

"For, all that from her springs, and is ybredde,
How-ever fayre it flourish for a time,
Yet see we soone decay; and, being dead
To turne again unto their earthly slime:
Yet, out of their decay and mortall crime,
We daily see new creatures to arize;
And of their Winter spring another Prime,
Unlike in forme, and chang'd by strange disguise:
So turne they still about, and change in restlesse wise.

XIX

"As for her tenants; that is, man and beasts,
The beasts we daily see massacred dy,
As thralls and vassalls unto mens beheasts:
And men themselves doe change continually,
From youth to eld, from wealth to poverty,
From good to bad, from bad to worst of all.

Ne doe their bodies only flit and fly:
But eeke their minds (which they immortall call)
Still change and vary thoughts, as new occasions fall.

XX

"Ne is the water in more constant case;
Whether those same on high, or these belowe.
For, th'Ocean moveth stil, from place to place;
And every River still doth ebbe and flowe:
Ne any Lake, that seems most still and slowe,
Ne Poole so small, that can his smoothnesse hold,
When any winde doth under heaven blowe;
With which, the clouds are also tost and roll'd;
Now like great Hills; &, streight, like sluces, them unfold.

XXI

"So likewise are all watry living wights
Still tost, and turned, with continuall change
Never abyding in their stedfast plights.
The fish, still floting, doe at randon range,
And never rest; but evermore exchange
Their dwelling places, as the streames them carrie:
Ne have the watry foules a certaine grange,
Wherein to rest, ne in one stead do tarry;
But flitting still doe flie, and still their places vary.

XXII

"Next is the Ayre: which who feeles not by sense
(For, of all sense it is the middle meane)
To flit still? and, with subtill influence
Of his thin spirit, all creatures to maintaine,
In state of life? O weake life! that does leane
On thing so tickle as th'unsteady ayre;
Which every howre is chang'd, and altred cleane
With every blast that bloweth fowle or faire:
The faire doth it prolong; the fowle doth it impaire.

XXIII

"Therein the changes infinite behold,
Which to her creatures every minute chaunce;
Now, boyling hot: streight, friezing deadly cold:
Now, faire sun-shine, that makes all skip and daunce:
Streight, bitter storms and balefull countenance,
That makes them all to shiver and to shake:
Rayne, hayle, and snowe do pay them sad penance,
And dreadfull thunder-claps (that make them quake)
With flames & flashing lights that thousand changes make.

XXIV

"Last is the fire: which, though it live for ever,
Ne can be quenched quite; yet, every day,
Wee see his parts, so soone as they do sever,
To lose their heat, and shortly to decay;
So, makes himself his own consuming pray.
Ne any living creatures doth he breed:
But all, that are of others bredd, doth slay;
And, with their death, his cruell life dooth feed;
Nought leaving, but their barren ashes, without seede.

XXV

"Thus, all these fower (the which the ground-work bee
Of all the world, and of all living wights)
To thousand sorts of Change we subject see:
Yet are they chang'd (by other wondrous slights)
Into themselves, and lose their native mights;
The Fire to Aire, and th'Ayre to Water sheere,
And Water into Earth: yet Water fights
With Fire, and Aire with Earth approaching neere:
Yet all are in one body, and as one appeare.

XXVI

"So, in them all raignes Mutabilitie;
How-ever these, that Gods themselves do call,
Of them doe claime the rule and soverainty:

As, Vesta, of the fire æthereall;
Vulcan, of this, with us so usuall;
Ops, of the earth; and Juno of the Ayre;
Neptune, of Seas; and Nymphes, of Rivers all.
For, all those Rivers to me subject are:
And all the rest, which they usurp, be all my share.

XXVII

"Which to approven true, as I have told,
Vouchsafe, O goddesse, to thy presence call
The rest which doe the world in being hold:
As, times and seasons of the yeare that fall:
Of all the which, demand in generall,
Or judge thy selfe, by verdit of thine eye,
Whether to me they are not subject all."
Nature did yeeld thereto; and by-and-by,
Bade Order call them all, before her Majesty.

XXVIII

So, forth issew'd the Seasons of the yeare;
First, lusty Spring, all dight in leaves of flowres
That freshly budded and new bloosmes did beare
(In which a thousand birds had built their bowres
That sweetly sung, to call forth Paramours):
And in his hand a javelin he did beare,
And on his head (as fit for warlike stoures)
A guilt engraven morion he did weare;
That as some did him loue, so others did him feare.

XXIX

Then came the jolly Sommer, being dight
In a thin silken cassock coloured greene,
That was unlyned all, to be more light:
And on his head a girlond well beseene
He wore, from which as he had chauffed been
The sweat did drop; and in his hand he bore
A boawe and shaftes, as he in forrest greene

Had hunted late the Libbard or the Bore,
And now would bathe his limbes, with labor heated sore.

XXX

Then came the Autumne all in yellow clad,
As though he joyed in his plentious store,
Laden with fruits that made him laugh, full glad
That he had banisht hunger, which to-fore
Had by the belly oft him pinched sore.
Upon his head a wreath that was enrold
With eares of corne, of every sort he bore:
And in his hand a sickle he did hold,
To reape the ripened fruits the which the earth had yold.

XXXI

Lastly, came Winter cloathed all in frize,
Chattering his teeth for cold that did him chill,
Whil'st on his hoary beard his breath did freese;
And the dull drops that from his purpled bill
As from a limbeck did adown distill.
In his right hand a tipped staffe he held,
With which his feeble steps he stayed still:
For, he was faint with cold, and weak with eld;
That scarse his loosed limbes he hable was to weld.

XXXII

These, marching softly, thus in order went,
And after them, the Monthes all riding came;
First, sturdy March with brows full sternly bent,
And armed strongly, rode upon a Ram,
The same which over Hellespontus swam:
Yet in his hand a spade he also hent,
And in a bag all sorts of seeds ysame,
Which on the earth he strowed as he went,
And fild her womb with fruitfull hope of nourishment.

XXXIII

Next came fresh Aprill full of lustyhed,
And wanton as a Kid whose horne new buds:

Upon a Bull he rode, the same which led
Europa floting through th'Argolick fluds:
His hornes were gilden all with golden studs
And garnished with garlonds goodly dight
Of all the fairest flowres and freshest buds
Which th'earth brings forth, and wet he seem'd in sight
With waves, through which he waded for his loves delight.

XXXIV

Then came faire May, the fayrest mayd on ground,
Deckt all with dainties of her seasons pryde,
And throwing flowres out of her lap around:
Upon two brethrens shoulders she did ride,
The twinnes of Leda; which on eyther side
Supported her like to their soveraine Queene.
Lord! how all creatures laught, when her they spide,
And leapt and daunc't as they had ravisht beene!
And Cupid selfe about her fluttred all in greene.

XXXV

And after her, came jolly June, arrayd
All in greene leaves, as he a Player were;
Yet in his time, he wrought as well as playd,
That by his plough-yrons mote right well appeare:
Upon a Crab he rode, that him did beare
With crooked crawling steps an uncouth pase,
And backward yode, as Bargemen wont to fare
Bending their force contrary to their face,
Like that ungracious crew which faines demurest grace.

XXXVI

Then came hot July boyling like to fire,
That all his garments he had cast away:
Upon a Lyon raging yet with ire
He boldly rode and made him to obay:
It was the beast that whylome did forray
The Nemaean forrest, till th'Amphytrionide

Him slew, and with his hide did him array;
Behinde his back a sithe, and by his side
Under his belt he bore a sickle circling wide.

XXXVII

The sixt was August, being rich arrayd
In garment all of gold downe to the ground:
Yet rode he not, but led a lovely Mayd
Forth by the lilly hand, the which was cround
With eares of corne, and full her hand was found;
That was the righteous Virgin, which of old
Liv'd here on earth, and plenty made abound;
But, after Wrong was lov'd and Justice solde,
She left th'unrighteous world and was to heaven extold.

XXXVIII

Next him, September marched eeke on foote;
Yet was he heavy laden with the spoyle
Of harvests riches, which he made his boot,
And him enricht with bounty of the soyle:
In his one hand, as fit for harvests toyle,
He held a knife-hook; and in th'other hand
A paire of waights, with which he did assoyle
Both more and lesse, where it in doubt did stand,
And equall gave to each as Justice duly scann'd.

XXXIX

Then came October full of merry glee:
For, yet his noule was totty of the must,
Which he was treading in the wine-fats see,
And of the joyous oyle, whose gentle gust
Made him so frollick and so full of lust:
Upon a dreadfull Scorpion he did ride,
The same which by Dianaes doom unjust
Slew great Orion: and eeke by his side
He had his ploughing share, and coulter ready tyde.

XL

Next was November, he full grosse and fat,
As fed with lard, and that right well might seeme;
For, he had been a fatting hogs of late,
That yet his browes with sweat, did reek and steem,
And yet the season was full sharp and breem;
In planting eeke he took no small delight:
Whereon he rode, not easie was to deeme;
For it a dreadfull Centaure was in sight,
The seed of Saturne, and faire Nais, Chiron hight.

XLI

And after him, came next the chill December:
Yet he through merry feasting which he made,
And great bonfires, did not the cold remember;
His Saviours birth his mind so much did glad:
Upon a shaggy-bearded Goat he rode,
The same wherewith Dan Jove in tender yeares,
They say, was nourisht by th'Idaean mayd;
And in his hand a broad deepe boawle he beares;
Of which, he freely drinks an health to all his peeres.

XLII

Then came old January, wrapped well
In many weeds to keep the cold away;
Yet did he quake and quiver like to quell,
And blowe his nayles to warme them if he may:
For, they were numbd with holding all the day
An hatchet keene, with which he felled wood,
And from the trees did lop the needlesse spray:
Upon an huge great Earth-pot steane he stood;
From whose wide mouth, there flowed forth the Romane floud.

XLIII

And lastly, came cold February, sitting
In an old wagon, for he could not ride;
Drawne of two fishes for the season fitting,

Which through the flood before did softly slyde
And swim away: yet had he by his side
His plough and harnesse fit to till the ground,
And tooles to prune the trees, before the pride
Of hasting Prime did make them burgein round:
So past the twelve Months forth, & their dew places found.

XLIV

And after these, there came the Day, and Night,
Riding together both with equall pace,
Th'one on a Palfrey blacke, the other white;
But Night had covered her uncomely face
With a blacke veile, and held in hand a mace,
On top whereof the moon and stars were pight,
And sleep and darknesse round about did trace:
But Day did beare, upon his scepters hight,
The goodly Sun, encompast all with beames bright.

XLV

Then came the Howres, faire daughters of high Jove,
And timely Night, the which were all endewed
With wondrous beauty fit to kindle love;
But they were Virgins all, and love eschewed,
That might forslack the charge to them fore-shewed
By mighty Jove; who did them Porters make
Of heavens gate (whence all the gods issued)
Which they did dayly watch, and nightly wake
By even turnes, ne ever did their charge forsake.

XLVI

And after all came Life, and lastly Death;
Death with most grim and griesly visage seene,
Yet is he nought but parting of the breath;
Ne ought to see, but like a shade to weene,
Unbodied, unsoul'd, unheard, unseene.
But Life was like a faire young lusty boy,

Such as they faine Dan Cupid to have beene,
Full of delightfull health and lively joy.
Deckt all with flowres, and wings of gold fit to employ.

XLVII

When these were past, thus gan the Titanesse;
"Lo, mighty mother, now be judge and say,
Whether in all thy creatures more or lesse
Change doth not raign & beare the greatest sway:
For, who sees not, that Time on all doth pray?
But Times do change and move continually.
So nothing here long standeth in one stay:
Wherefore, this lower world who can deny
But to be subject still to Mutabilitie?"

XLVIII

Then thus gan Jove; "Right true it is, that these
And all things else that under heaven dwell
Are chaung'd of Time, who doth them all disseise
Of being: But, who is it (to me tell)
That Time himself doth move and still compell
To keepe his course? Is not that namely wee
Which poure that vertue from our heavenly cell,
That moves them all, and makes them changed be?
So them we gods doe rule, and in them also thee."

XLIX

To whom, thus Mutability: "The things
Which we see not how they are mov'd and swayd,
Ye may attribute to your selves as Kings,
And say they by your secret powre are made:
But what we see not, who shall us perswade?
But were they so, as ye them faine to be,
Mov'd by your might, and ordred by your ayde;
Yet what if I can prove, that even yee
Your selves are likewise chang'd, and subject unto mee?

L

"And first, concerning her that is the first,
Even you faire Cynthia, whom so much ye make
Joves dearest darling, she was bred and nurst
On Cynthus hill, whence she her name did take:
Then is she mortall borne, how-so ye crake;
Besides, her face and countenance every day
We changed see, and sundry forms partake,
Now hornd, now round, now bright, now brown & gray:
So that as changefull as the Moone men use to say.

LI

"Next, Mercury, who though he lesse appeare
To change his hew, and alwayes seeme as one;
Yet, he his course doth altar every yeare,
And is of late far out of order gone:
So Venus eeke, that goodly Paragone,
Though faire all night, yet is she darke all day;
And Phoebus self, who lightsome is alone,
Yet is he oft eclipsed by the way,
And fills the darkned world with terror and dismay.

LII

"Now Mars that valiant man is changed most:
For, he some times so far runs out of square,
That he his way doth seem quite to have lost,
And cleane without his usuall sphere to fare;
That even these Star-gazers stonisht are
At sight thereof, and damne their lying bookes:
So likewise, grim Sir Saturne oft doth spare
His sterne aspect, and calme his crabbed lookes:
So many turning cranks these have, so many crookes.

LIII

"But you Dan Jove, that only constant are,
And King of all the rest, as ye do clame,

Are you not subject eeke to this misfare?
Then let me aske you this withouten blame,
Where were ye borne? some say in Crete by name,
Others in Thebes, and others other-where;
But wheresoever they comment the same,
They all consent that ye begotten were,
And borne here in this world, ne other can appeare.

LIV

"Then are ye mortall borne, and thrall to me,
Unlesse the kingdome of the sky yee make
Immortall, and unchangeable to bee;
Besides, that power and vertue which ye spake,
That ye here worke, doth many changes take,
And your own natures change: for, each of you
That vertue have, or this, or that to make,
Is checkt and changed from his nature trew,
By others opposition or obliquid view.

LV

"Besides, the sundry motions of your Spheares,
So sundry ways and fashions as clerkes faine,
Some in short space, and some in longer yeares;
What is the same but alteration plaine?
Only the starrie skie doth still remaine:
Yet do the Starres and Signes therein still move,
And euen it self is mov'd, as wizards saine.
But all that moveth, doth mutation love:
Therefore both you and them to me I subject prove.

LVI

"Then since within this wide great Universe
Nothing doth firme and permanent appeare,
But all things tost and turned by transverse:
What then should let, but I aloft should reare
My Trophee, and from all, the triumph beare?

Now judge then (O thou greatest goddesse trew!)
According as thy selfe doest see and hear,
And unto me addoom that is my dew;
That is the rule of all, all being rul'd by you."

LVII

So having ended, silence long ensewed,
Ne Nature to or fro spake for a space,
But with firme eyes affixt, the ground still viewed.
Meane while, all creatures, looking in her face,
Expecting th'end of this so doubtfull case,
Did hang in long suspence what would ensew,
To whether side should fall the soveraigne place:
At length, she looking up with chearefull view,
The silence brake, and gave her doome in speeches few.

LVIII

"I well consider all that ye have sayd,
And find that all things stedfastnes doe hate
And changed be: yet being rightly wayd
They are not changed from their first estate;
But by their change their being doe dilate:
And turning to themselves at length again,
Doe worke their own perfection so by fate:
Then over them Change doth not rule and raigne;
But they raigne over change, and doe their states maintaine.

LIX

"Cease therefore daughter further to aspire,
And thee content thus to be rul'd by me:
For thy decay thou seekst by thy desire;
But time shall come that all shall changed bee,
And from thenceforth, none no more change shall see."
So was the Titaness put downe and whist,
And Jove confirm'd in his imperiall see.
Then was that whole assembly quite dismist,
And Natur's selfe did vanish, whither no man wist.

CANTO VIII, UNPERFITE

I

When I bethinke me on that speech whyleare,
Of Mutability, and well it way:
Me seemes, that though she all unworthy were
Of the Heav'ns Rule; yet very sooth to say,
In all things else she beares the greatest sway.
Which makes me loath this state of life so tickle,
And love of things so vaine to cast away;
Whose flowring pride, so fading and so fickle,
Short Time shall soon cut down with his consuming sickle.

II

Then gin I thinke on that which Nature sayd,
Of that same time when no more Change shall be,
But stedfast rest of all things firmely stayd
Upon the pillours of Eternity,
That is contrayr to Mutabilitie:
For, all that moveth, doth in Change delight:
But thence-forth all shall rest eternally
With Him that is the God of Sabbaoth hight:
O thou great Sabbaoth God, grant me that Sabaoths sight.

AMORETTI

I

HAPPY ye leaves! when as those lilly hands,
Which hold my life in their dead doing might,
Shall handle you, and hold in loves soft bands,
Lyke captives trembling at the victors sight.
And happy lines! on which, with starry light,
Those lamping eyes will deigne sometimes to look,
And read the sorrowes of my dying spright,
Written with teares in harts close bleeding book.
And happy rymes! bath'd in the sacred brooke
Of Helicon, whence she derived is,
When ye behold that angels blessed looke,
My soules long lacked foode, my heavens blis.
Leaves, lines, and rymes, seeke her to please alone,
Whom if ye please, I care for other none.

XXX

My love is lyke to yse, and I to fyre;
How comes it then that this her cold so great
Is not dissolv'd through my so hot desyre,
But harder growes the more I her intreat?
Or how comes it that my exceeding heat
Is not delayd by her hart frosen cold,
But that I burne much more in boyling sweat,
And feele my flames augmented manifold?
What more miraculous thing may be told,
That fire, which all things melts, should harden yse,

And yse, which is congeald with sencelesse cold,
Should kindle fyre by wonderful devyse?
Such is the powre of love in gentle mind,
That it can alter all the course of kynd.

LXXV

One day I wrote her name upon the strand,
But came the waves and washed it away:
Agayne I wrote it with a second hand,
But came the tyde, and made my paynes his pray.
Vayne man, sayd she, that doest in vaine assay
A mortall thing so to immortalize!
For I my selve shall lyke to this decay,
And eek my name bee wyped out lykewize.
Not so (quod I) let baser things devize
To dy in dust, but you shall live by fame:
My verse your vertues rare shall eternize,
And in the hevens wryte your glorious name;
Where, whenas death shall all the world subdew,
Our love shall live, and later life renew.

EPITHALAMION

I

Ye learned sisters which have oftentimes
Beene to me ayding, others to adorne:
Whom ye thought worthy of your gracefull rymes,
That even the greatest did not greatly scorne
To hear theyr names sung in your simple layes,
But joyed in theyr prayse.
And when ye list your own mishaps to mourne,
Which death, or love, or fortunes wreck did rayse,
Your string could soone to sadder tenor turne,
And teach the woods and waters to lament
Your dolefull dreriment.
Now lay those sorrowfull complaints aside,
And having all your heads with girland crownd,
Helpe me mine own loves prayses to resound,
Ne let the same of any be envide:
So Orpheus did for his own bride,
So I unto my selfe alone will sing,
The woods shall to me answer and my Eccho ring.

II

Early before the worlds light giving lampe,
His golden beame upon the hils doth spred,
Having disperst the nights unchearefull dampe,
Doe ye awake, and with fresh lusty hed,
Go to the bowre of my beloved love,
My truest turtle dove,

Bid her awake; for Hymen is awake,
And long since ready forth his maske to move,
With his bright Tead that flames with many a flake,
And many a bachelor to waite on him,
In theyr fresh garments trim.
Bid her awake therefore and soone her dight,
For lo the wished day is come at last,
That shall for all the paynes and sorrowes past,
Pay to her usury of long delight:
And whylest she doth her dight,
Doe ye to her of joy and solace sing,
That all the woods may answer and your eccho ring.

III

Bring with you all the Nymphes that you can hear
Both of the rivers and the forrests greene:
And of the sea that neighbours to her neare,
All with gay girlands goodly wel beseene.
And let them also with them bring in hand
Another gay girland
For my fayre love of lillyes and of roses,
Bound truelove wize with a blew silke riband.
And let them make great store of bridale poses,
And let them eeke bring store of other flowers
To deck the bridale bowers.
And let the ground whereas her foot shall tread,
For feare the stones her tender foot should wrong
Be strewed with fragrant flowers all along,
And diapred lyke the discolored mead.
Which done, doe at her chamber dore awayt,
For she will waken strayt,
The whiles doe ye this song unto her sing,
The woods shall to you answer and your Eccho ring.

IV

Ye Nymphes of Mulla which with carefull heed,
The silver scaly trouts doe tend full well,

And greedy pikes which use therein to feed,
(Those trouts and pikes all others doo excell)
And ye likewise which keepe the rushy lake,
Where none doo fishes take,
Bynd up the locks the which hang scatterd light,
And in his waters which your mirror make,
Behold your faces as the christall bright,
That when you come whereas my love doth lie,
No blemish she may spie.
And eke ye lightfoot mayds which keepe the deere,
That on the hoary mountayne use to tower,
And the wylde wolves which seeke them to devoure,
With your steele darts doo chace from comming neer,
Be also present heere,
To helpe to decke her and to help to sing,
That all the woods may answer and your eccho ring.

V

Wake, now my love, awake; for it is time,
The Rosy Morne long since left Tithones bed,
All ready to her silver coche to clyme,
And Phoebus gins to shew his glorious hed.
Hark how the cheerefull birds do chaunt theyr laies
And carroll of loves praise.
The merry Larke hir mattins sings aloft,
The thrush replyes, the Mavis descant playes,
The Ouzell shrills, the Ruddock warbles soft,
So goodly all agree with sweet consent,
To this dayes merriment.
Ah my deere love why doe ye sleepe thus long,
When meeter were that ye should now awake,
T'awayt the comming of your joyous make,
And hearken to the birds lovelearned song,
The deawy leaves among.
For they of joy and pleasance to you sing,
That all the woods them answer and theyr eccho ring.

VI

My love is now awake out of her dreames,
And her fayre eyes like stars that dimmed were
With darksome cloud, now shew theyr goodly beames
More bright then Hesperus his head doth rere.
Come now ye damzels, daughters of delight,
Helpe quickly her to dight,
But first come ye fayre houres which were begot
In Joves sweet paradice, of Day and Night,
Which doe the seasons of the yeare allot,
And all that ever in this world is fayre
Doe make and still repayre.
And ye three handmayds of the Cyprian Queene,
The which doe still adorne her beauties pride,
Helpe to addorne my beautifullest bride:
And as ye her array, still throw betweene
Some graces to be seene,
And as ye use to Venus, to her sing,
The whiles the woods shall answer and your eccho ring.

VII

Now is my love all ready forth to come,
Let all the virgins therefore well awayt,
And ye fresh boyes that tend upon her groome
Prepare your selves; for he is comming strayt.
Set all your things in seemely good aray
Fit for so joyfull day,
The joyfulst day that ever sunne did see.
Faire Sun, shew forth thy favourable ray,
And let thy lifull heat not fervent be
For feare of burning her sunshyny face,
Her beauty to disgrace.
O fayrest Phoebus, father of the Muse,
If ever I did honour thee aright,
Or sing the thing, that mote thy mind delight,
Doe not thy servants simple boone refuse,

But let this day let this one day be myne,
Let all the rest be thine.
Then I thy soverayne prayses loud will sing,
That all the woods shall answer and theyr eccho ring.

VIII

Harke how the Minstrels gin to shrill aloud
Their merry Musick that resounds from far,
The pipe, the tabor, and the trembling Croud,
That well agree withouten breach or jar.
But most of all the Damzels doe delite,
When they their tymbrels smyte,
And thereunto doe daunce and carrol sweet,
That all the sences they doe ravish quite,
The whyles the boyes run up and downe the street,
Crying aloud with strong confused noyce,
As if it were one voyce.
Hymen io Hymen, Hymen they do shout,
That even to the heavens theyr shouting shrill
Doth reach, and all the firmament doth fill,
To which the people standing all about,
As in approvance doe thereto applaud
And loud advaunce her laud,
And evermore they Hymen Hymen sing,
That all the woods them answer and theyr eccho ring.

IX

Loe where she comes along with portly pace
Lyke Phoebe from her chamber of the East,
Arysing forth to run her mighty race,
Clad all in white, that seemes a virgin best.
So well it her beseemes that ye would weene
Some angell she had beene.
Her long loose yellow locks lyke golden wyre,
Sprinckled with perle, and perling flowres a tweene,
Doe lyke a golden mantle her attyre,
And being crowned with a girland greene,

Seeme lyke some mayden Queene.
Her modest eyes abashed to behold
So many gazers, as on her do stare,
Upon the lowly ground affixed are.
Ne dare lift up her countenance too bold,
But blush to hear her prayses sung so loud,
So farre from being proud.
Nathlesse doe ye still loud her prayses sing,
That all the woods may answer and your eccho ring.

X

Tell me ye merchants daughters did ye see
So fayre a creature in your towne before?
So sweet, so lovely, and so mild as she,
Adornd with beautyes grace and vertues store,
Her goodly eyes lyke Saphyres shining bright,
Her forehead yvory white,
Her cheekes lyke apples which the sun hath rudded,
Her lips lyke cherryes charming men to byte,
Her brest like to a bowle of creame uncrudded,
Her paps lyke lyllies budded,
Her snowie necke lyke to a marble tower,
And all her body like a pallace fayre,
Ascending uppe with many a stately stayre,
To honors seat and chastities sweet bowre.
Why stand ye still ye virgins in amaze,
Upon her so to gaze,
Whiles ye forget your former lay to sing,
To which the woods did answer and your eccho ring.

XI

But if ye saw that which no eyes can see,
The inward beauty of her lively spright,
Garnisht with heavenly guifts of high degree,
Much more then would ye wonder at that sight,
And stand astonisht lyke to those which red
Medusaes mazeful hed.

There dwels sweet love and constant chastity,
Unspotted fayth and comely womenhed,
Regard of honour and mild modesty,
There vertue raynes as Queene in royal throne,
And giveth laws alone.
The which the base affections doe obay,
And yeeld theyr services unto her will,
Ne thought of thing uncomely ever may
Thereto approch to tempt her mind to ill.
Had ye once seene these her celestial threasures,
And unrevealed pleasures,
Then would ye wonder and her prayses sing,
That all the woods should answer and your eccho ring.

XII

Open the temple gates unto my love,
Open them wide that she may enter in,
And all the postes adorne as doth behove,
And all the pillours deck with girlands trim,
For to recyve this Saynt with honour dew,
That commeth in to you.
With trembling steps and humble reverence,
She commeth in, before th'almighties vew:
Of her ye virgins learn obedience,
When so ye come into those holy places,
To humble your proud faces;
Bring her up to th'high altar that she may,
The sacred ceremonies there partake,
The which do endlesse matrimony make,
And let the roring Organs loudly play
The praises of the Lord in lively notes,
The whiles with hollow throates
The Choristers the joyous Antheme sing,
That all the woods may answere and their eccho ring.

XIII

Behold whiles she before the altar stands
Hearing the holy priest that to her speakes

And blesseth her with his two happy hands,
How the red roses flush up in her cheekes,
And the pure snow with goodly vermill stayne,
Like crimsin dyde in grayne,
That even th'Angels which continually,
About the sacred Altare doe remaine,
Forget their service and about her fly,
Ofte peeping in her face that seemes more fayre,
The more they on it stare.
But her sad eyes still fastened on the ground,
Are governed with goodly modesty,
That suffers not one looke to glaunce awry,
Which may let in a little thought unsownd.
Why blush ye love to give to me your hand,
The pledge of all our band?
Sing ye sweet Angels, Alleluya sing,
That all the woods may answere and your eccho ring.

XIV

Now all is done; bring home the bride again,
Bring home the triumph of our victory,
Bring home with you the glory of her gaine,
With joyance bring her and with jollity.
Never had man more joyfull day then this,
Whom heaven would heape with blis.
Make feast therefore now all this live long day,
This day for ever to me holy is,
Poure out the wine without restraint or stay,
Poure not by cups, but by the belly full,
Poure out to all that wull,
And sprinkle all the postes and wals with wine,
That they may sweat, and drunken be withall.
Crowne ye God Bacchus with a coronall,
And Hymen also crowne with wreathes of vine,
And let the Graces daunce unto the rest;
For they can doo it best:

The whiles the maydens doe theyr carroll sing,
To which the woods shall answer and theyr eccho ring.

XV

Ring ye the bels, ye yong men of the towne,
And leave your wonted labors for this day:
This day is holy; doe ye write it downe,
That ye for ever it remember may.
This day the sunne is in his chiefest hight,
With Barnaby the bright,
From whence declining daily by degrees,
He somewhat loseth of his heat and light,
When once the Crab behind his back he sees.
But for this time it ill ordained was,
To chose the longest day in all the yeare,
And shortest night, when longest fitter weare:
Yet never day so long, but late would passe.
Ring ye the bels, to make it weare away,
And bonefiers make all day,
And daunce about them, and about them sing:
That all the woods may answer, and your eccho ring.

XVI

Ah when will this long weary day have end,
And lende me leave to come unto my love?
How slowly do the houres theyr numbers spend?
How slowly does sad Time his feathers move?
Hast thee O fayrest Planet to thy home
Within the Westerne fome:
Thy tyred steedes long since have need of rest.
Long though it be, at last I see it gloome,
And the bright evening star with golden creast
Appeare out of the East.
Fayre childe of beauty, glorious lampe of love
That all the host of heaven in rankes doost lead,
And guydest lovers through the nightes dread,
How chearefully thou lookest from above,

And seemst to laugh atweene thy twinkling light
As joying in the sight
Of these glad many which for joy doe sing,
That all the woods them answer and their echo ring.

XVII

Now ceasse ye damsels your delights forepast;
Enough is it, that all the day was youres:
Now day is doen, and night is nighing fast:
Now bring the Bryde into the brydall boures.
Now night is come, now soone her disaray,
And in her bed her lay;
Lay her in lillies and in violets,
And silken courteins over her display,
And odourd sheetes, and Arras coverlets.
Behold how goodly my faire love does ly
In proud humility;
Like unto Maia, when as Jove her tooke,
In Tempe, lying on the flowry gras,
Twixt sleepe and wake, after she weary was,
With bathing in the Acidalian brooke.
Now it is night, ye damsels may be gon,
And leave my love alone,
And leave likewise your former lay to sing:
The woods no more shall answere, nor your echo ring.

XVIII

Now welcome night, thou night so long expected,
That long daies labour doest at last defray,
And all my cares, which cruell love collected,
Hast sumd in one, and cancelled for aye:
Spread thy broad wing over my love and me,
That no man may us see,
And in thy sable mantle us enwrap,
From feare of perrill and foule horror free.
Let no false treason seeke us to entrap,
Nor any dread disquiet once annoy

The safety of our joy:
But let the night be calme and quietsome,
Without tempestuous storms or sad afray:
Lyke as when Jove with fayre Alcmena lay,
When he begot the great Tirynthian groome:
Or lyke as when he with thy selfe did lie,
And begot Majesty.
And let the mayds and yongmen cease to sing:
Ne let the woods them answer, nor theyr eccho ring.

XIX

Let no lamenting cryes, nor dolefull teares,
Be heard all night within nor yet without:
Ne let false whispers, breeding hidden feares,
Breake gentle sleepe with misconceived dout.
Let no deluding dreames, nor dreadful sights
Make sudden sad affrights;
Ne let housefyres, nor lightnings helpelesse harmes,
Ne let the Pouke, nor other evill sprights,
Ne let mischivous witches with theyr charmes,
Ne let hob Goblins, names whose sence we see not,
Fray us with things that be not.
Let not the shriech Oule, nor the Storke be heard:
Nor the night Raven that still deadly yels,
Nor damned ghosts cald up with mighty spels,
Nor griesly vultures make us once affeard:
Ne let th'unpleasant Quyre of Frogs still croking
Make us to wish theyr choking.
Let none of these theyr drery accents sing;
Ne let the woods them answer, nor theyr eccho ring.

XX

But let stil Silence trew night watches keepe,
That sacred peace may in assurance rayne,
And tymely sleep, when it is time to sleepe,
May poure his limbs forth on your pleasant playne,
The whiles an hundred little winged loves,

Like divers fethered doves,
Shall fly and flutter round about your bed,
And in the secret darke, that none reproves,
Their prety stelthes shall worke, and snares shall spread
To filch away sweet snatches of delight,
Conceald through covert night.
Ye sonnes of Venus, play your sports at will,
For greedy pleasure, carelesse of your toyes,
Thinks more upon her paradise of joyes,
Then what ye do, albe it good or ill.
All night therefore attend your merry play,
For it will soone be day:
Now none doth hinder you, that say or sing,
Ne will the woods now answer, nor your Eccho ring.

XXI

Who is the same, which at my window peepes?
Or whose is that faire face, that shines so bright,
Is it not Cinthia, she that never sleepes,
But walkes about high heaven all the night?
O fayrest goddesse, do thou not envy
My love with me to spy:
For thou likewise didst love, though now unthought,
And for a fleece of woll, which privily,
The Latmian shephard once unto thee brought,
His pleasures with thee wrought.
Therefore to us be favorable now;
And sith of wemens labours thou hast charge,
And generation goodly dost enlarge,
Encline thy will t'effect our wishfull vow,
And the chast wombe informe with timely seed,
That may our comfort breed:
Till which we cease our hopefull hap to sing,
Ne let the woods us answere, nor our Eccho ring.

XXII

And thou great Juno, which with awful might
The laws of wedlock still dost patronize,

And the religion of the faith first plight
With sacred rites hast taught to solemnize:
And eeke for comfort often called art
Of women in their smart,
Eternally bind thou this lovely band,
And all thy blessings unto us impart.
And thou glad Genius, in whose gentle hand,
The bridale bowre and geniall bed remaine,
Without blemish or staine,
And the sweet pleasures of theyr loves delight
With secret ayde doest succour and supply,
Till they bring forth the fruitfull progeny,
Send us the timely fruit of this same night.
And thou fayre Hebe, and thou Hymen free,
Grant that it may so be.
Til which we cease your further prayse to sing,
Ne any woods shall answer, nor your Eccho ring.

XXIII

And ye high heavens, the temple of the gods,
In which a thousand torches flaming bright
Doe burne, that to us wretched earthly clods,
In dreadful darknesse lend desired light;
And all ye powers which in the same remayne,
More then we men can fayne,
Poure out your blessing on us plentiously,
And happy influence upon us raine,
That we may raise a large posterity,
Which from the earth, which they may long possesse,
With lasting happinesse,
Up to your haughty pallaces may mount,
And for the guerdon of theyr glorious merit
May heavenly tabernacles there inherit,
Of blessed Saints for to increase the count.
So let us rest, sweet love, in hope of this,
And cease till then our tymely joyes to sing,
The woods no more us answer, nor our eccho ring.

XXIV

Song made in lieu of many ornaments,
With which my love should duly have bene dect,
Which cutting off through hasty accidents,
Ye would not stay your dew time to expect,
But promist both to recompens,
Be unto her a goodly ornament,
And for short time an endlesse moniment.

www.ingramcontent.com/pod-product-compliance
Lightning Source LLC
Chambersburg PA
CBHW070332170726
48291CB00001B/24

9781944482237